Doing Business 2010

COMPARING REGULATION IN 183 ECONOMIES

A COPUBLICATION OF PALGRAVE MACMILLAN,
IFC AND THE WORLD BANK

© 2009 The International Bank for Reconstruction and Development / The World Bank
1818 H Street NW
Washington, DC 20433
Telephone 202-473-1000
Internet www.worldbank.org
E-mail feedback@worldbank.org

A copublication of The World Bank, IFC and Palgrave MacMillan.

PALGRAVE MACMILLAN

Palgrave MacMillan in the UK is an imprint of MacMillan Publishers Limited, registered in England, company number 785998, of Houndsmills, Basingstoke, Hampshire, RG21 6XS.

Palgrave MacMillan in the US is a division of St Martin's Press LLC, 175 Fifth Avenue, New York, NY, 10010.

Palgrave MacMillan is the global academic imprint of the above companies and has companies and representatives throughout the world.

Palgrave® and MacMillan® are registered trademarks in the United States, the United Kingdom, Europe and other countries.

This volume is a product of the staff of the World Bank Group. The findings, interpretations, and conclusions expressed in this volume do not necessarily reflect the views of the Executive Directors of the World Bank or the governments they represent. The World Bank does not guarantee the accuracy of the data included in this work.

Rights and Permissions

Additional copies of *Doing Business 2010: Reforming through Difficult Times, Doing Business 2009, Doing Business 2008, Doing Business 2007: How to Reform, Doing Business in 2006: Creating Jobs, Doing Business in 2005: Removing Obstacles to Growth* and *Doing Business in 2004: Understanding Regulations* may be purchased at www.doingbusiness.org.

ISBN: 978-0-8213-7961-5
E-ISBN: 978-0-8213-7965-3
DOI: 10.1596/978-0-8213-7961-5
ISSN: 1729-2638

Library of Congress Cataloging-in-Publication data has been applied for.
Printed in the United States

Contents

Doing Business 2010 is the seventh in a series of annual reports investigating the regulations that enhance business activity and those that constrain it. Doing Business presents quantitative indicators on business regulations and the protection of property rights that can be compared across 183 economies—from Afghanistan to Zimbabwe—and over time.

Regulations affecting 10 stages of the life of a business are measured: starting a business, dealing with construction permits, employing workers, registering property, getting credit, protecting investors, paying taxes, trading across borders, enforcing contracts and closing a business. Data in Doing Business 2010 are current as of June 1, 2009. The indicators are used to analyze economic outcomes and identify what reforms have worked, where and why.

The methodology for the employing workers indicators changed for Doing Business 2010. See Data notes for details. Research is ongoing in 2 new areas: getting electricity and worker protection. Initial results are presented in this report.

THE DOING BUSINESS WEBSITE

Current features
News on the Doing Business project
http://www.doingbusiness.org

Rankings
How economies rank—from 1 to 183
http://www.doingbusiness.org/economyrankings

Reformers
Short summaries of DB2010 reforms, lists of reformers since DB2004 and a ranking simulation tool
http://www.doingbusiness.org/reformers

Historical data
Customized data sets since DB2004
http://www.doingbusiness.org/customquery

Methodology and research
The methodology and research papers underlying Doing Business
http://www.doingbusiness.org/MethodologySurveys

Download reports
Access to Doing Business reports as well as subnational and regional reports, reform case studies and customized country and regional profiles
http://www.doingbusiness.org/downloads

Subnational and regional projects
Differences in business regulations at the subnational and regional level
http://www.doingbusiness.org/subnational

Law library
Online collection of laws and regulations relating to business and gender issues
http://www.doingbusiness.org/lawlibrary
http://www.doingbusiness.org/genderlawlibrary

Local partners
More than 8,000 specialists in 183 economies who participate in Doing Business
http://www.doingbusiness.org/LocalPartners

Reformers' Club
Celebrating the top 10 Doing Business reformers
http://www.reformersclub.org

Business Planet
Interactive map on the ease of doing business
http://www.doingbusiness.org/map

About Doing Business

In 1664 William Petty, an adviser to England's Charles II, compiled the first known national accounts. He made 4 entries. On the expense side, "food, housing, clothes and all other necessaries" were estimated at £40 million. National income was split among 3 sources: £8 million from land, £7 million from other personal estates and £25 million from labor income.

In later centuries estimates of country income, expenditure and material inputs and outputs became more abundant. But it was not until the 1940s that a systematic framework was developed for measuring national income and expenditure, under the direction of British economist John Maynard Keynes. As the methodology became an international standard, comparisons of countries' financial positions became possible. Today the macroeconomic indicators in national accounts are standard in every country.

Governments committed to the economic health of their country and opportunities for its citizens now focus on more than macroeconomic conditions. They also pay attention to the laws, regulations and institutional arrangements that shape daily economic activity.

The global financial crisis has renewed interest in good rules and regulation. In times of recession, effective business regulation and institutions can support economic adjustment. Easy entry and exit of firms, and flexibility in redeploying resources, make it easier to stop doing things for which demand has weakened and to start doing new things. Clarification of property rights and strengthening of market infrastructure (such as credit information and collateral systems) can contribute to confidence as investors and entrepreneurs look to rebuild.

Until very recently, however, there were no globally available indicator sets for monitoring such microeconomic factors and analyzing their relevance. The first efforts, in the 1980s, drew on perceptions data from expert or business surveys. Such surveys are useful gauges of economic and policy conditions. But their reliance on perceptions and their incomplete coverage of poor countries constrain their usefulness for analysis.

The *Doing Business* project, launched 8 years ago, goes one step further. It looks at domestic small and medium-size companies and measures the regulations applying to them through their life cycle. *Doing Business* and the standard cost model initially developed and applied in the Netherlands are, for the present, the only standard tools used across a broad range of jurisdictions to measure the impact of government rule-making on business activity.[1]

The first *Doing Business* report, published in 2003, covered 5 indicator sets in 133 economies. This year's report covers 10 indicator sets in 183 economies. The project has benefited from feedback from governments, academics, practitioners and reviewers.[2] The initial goal remains: to provide an objective basis for understanding and improving the regulatory environment for business.

WHAT DOING BUSINESS COVERS

Doing Business provides a quantitative measure of regulations for starting a business, dealing with construction permits, employing workers, registering property, getting credit, protecting investors, paying taxes, trading across borders, enforcing contracts and closing a business—as they apply to domestic small and medium-size enterprises.

A fundamental premise of *Doing Business* is that economic activity requires good rules. These include rules that establish and clarify property rights and reduce the costs of resolving disputes, rules that increase the predictability of economic interactions and rules that provide contractual partners with core protections against abuse. The objective: regulations designed to be efficient, to be accessible to all who need to use them and to be simple in their implementation. Accordingly, some *Doing Business* indicators give a higher score for more regulation, such as stricter disclosure requirements in related-party transactions. Some give a higher score for a simplified way of implementing existing regulation, such as completing business start-up formalities in a one-stop shop.

The *Doing Business* project encompasses 2 types of data. The first come from readings of laws and regulations. The second are time and motion indicators that measure the efficiency in achieving a regulatory goal (such as granting the legal identity of a business). Within the time and motion indicators, cost estimates are recorded from official fee schedules where applicable. Here, *Doing Business* builds on Hernando de Soto's pioneering work in applying the time and motion approach first used by Frederick Taylor to revolutionize the production of the Model T Ford. De Soto used the approach in the 1980s to show the obstacles to setting up a garment factory on the outskirts of Lima.[3]

WHAT DOING BUSINESS DOES NOT COVER

Just as important as knowing what *Doing Business* does is to know what it does not do—to understand what limitations must be kept in mind in interpreting the data.

LIMITED IN SCOPE

Doing Business focuses on 10 topics, with the specific aim of measuring the regulation and red tape relevant to the life cycle of a domestic small to medium-size firm. Accordingly:

- *Doing Business* does not measure all aspects of the business environment that matter to firms or investors—or all factors that affect competitiveness. It does not, for example, measure security, macroeconomic stability, corruption, the labor skills of the population, the underlying strength of institutions or the quality of infrastructure.[4] Nor does it focus on regulations specific to foreign investment.

- *Doing Business* does not assess the strength of the financial system or financial market regulations, both important factors in understanding some of the underlying causes of the global financial crisis.

- *Doing Business* does not cover all regulations, or all regulatory goals, in any economy. As economies and technology advance, more areas of economic activity are being regulated. For example, the European Union's body of laws *(acquis)* has now grown to no fewer than 14,500 rule sets. *Doing Business* measures just 10 phases of a company's life cycle, through 10 specific sets of indicators. The indicator sets also do not cover all aspects of regulation in a particular area. For example, the indicators on starting a business or protecting investors do not cover all aspects of commercial legislation. The employing workers indicators do not cover all aspects of labor regulation. Measures for regulations addressing safety at work or right of collective bargaining, for example, are not included in the current indicator set.

BASED ON STANDARDIZED CASE SCENARIOS

Doing Business indicators are built on the basis of standardized case scenarios with specific assumptions, such as the business being located in the largest business city of the economy. Economic indicators commonly make limiting assumptions of this kind. Inflation statistics, for example, are often based on prices of con-

sumer goods in a few urban areas.

Such assumptions allow global coverage and enhance comparability. But they come at the expense of generality. Business regulation and its enforcement, particularly in federal states and large economies, differ across the country. And of course the challenges and opportunities of the largest business city—whether Mumbai or São Paulo, Nuku'alofa or Nassau—vary greatly across countries. Recognizing governments' interest in such variation, *Doing Business* has complemented its global indicators with subnational studies in such countries as Brazil, China, Colombia, the Arab Republic of Egypt, India, Kenya, Mexico, Morocco, Nigeria and the Philippines.[5]

In areas where regulation is complex and highly differentiated, the standardized case used to construct the *Doing Business* indicator needs to be carefully defined. Where relevant, the standardized case assumes a limited liability company. This choice is in part empirical: private, limited liability companies are the most prevalent business form in most economies around the world. The choice also reflects one focus of *Doing Business*: expanding opportunities for entrepreneurship. Investors are encouraged to venture into business when potential losses are limited to their capital participation.

FOCUSED ON THE FORMAL SECTOR

In constructing the indicators, *Doing Business* assumes that entrepreneurs are knowledgeable about all regulations in place and comply with them. In practice, entrepreneurs may spend considerable time finding out where to go and what documents to submit. Or they may avoid legally required procedures altogether—by not registering for social security, for example.

Where regulation is particularly onerous, levels of informality are higher. Informality comes at a cost: firms in the informal sector typically grow more slowly, have poorer access to credit and employ fewer workers—and their workers remain outside the protections of

labor law.[6] *Doing Business* measures one set of factors that help explain the occurrence of informality and give policy makers insights into potential areas of reform. Gaining a fuller understanding of the broader business environment, and a broader perspective on policy challenges, requires combining insights from *Doing Business* with data from other sources, such as the World Bank Enterprise Surveys.[7]

WHY THIS FOCUS

Doing Business functions as a kind of cholesterol test for the regulatory environment for domestic businesses. A cholesterol test does not tell us everything about the state of our health. But it does measure something important for our health. And it puts us on watch to change behaviors in ways that will improve not only our cholesterol rating but also our overall health.

One way to test whether *Doing Business* serves as a proxy for the broader business environment and for competitiveness is to look at correlations between the *Doing Business* rankings and other major economic benchmarks. The indicator set closest to *Doing Business* in what it measures is the Organisation for Economic Co-operation and Development's indicators of product market regulation; the correlation here is 0.75. The World Economic Forum's Global Competitiveness Index and IMD's *World Competitiveness Yearbook* are broader in scope, but these too are strongly correlated with *Doing Business* (0.79 and 0.72, respectively). These correlations suggest that where peace and macroeconomic stability are present, domestic business regulation makes an important difference in economic competitiveness.

A bigger question is whether the issues on which *Doing Business* focuses matter for development and poverty reduction. The World Bank study *Voices of the Poor* asked 60,000 poor people around the world how they thought they might escape poverty.[8] The answers were unequivocal: women and men alike pin their hopes above all on income from their own business or wages earned in employment. Enabling growth—and ensuring that poor people can participate in its benefits—requires an environment where new entrants with drive and good ideas, regardless of their gender or ethnic origin, can get started in business and where good firms can invest and grow, generating more jobs.

Small and medium-size enterprises are key drivers of competition, growth and job creation, particularly in developing countries. But in these economies up to 80% of economic activity takes place in the informal sector. Firms may be prevented from entering the formal sector by excessive bureaucracy and regulation.

Where regulation is burdensome and competition limited, success tends to depend more on whom you know than on what you can do. But where regulation is transparent, efficient and implemented in a simple way, it becomes easier for any aspiring entrepreneurs, regardless of their connections, to operate within the rule of law and to benefit from the opportunities and protections that the law provides.

In this sense *Doing Business* values good rules as a key to social inclusion. It also provides a basis for studying effects of regulations and their application. For example, *Doing Business 2004* found that faster contract enforcement was associated with perceptions of greater judicial fairness—suggesting that justice delayed is justice denied.[9]

In the current global crisis policy makers face particular challenges. Both developed and developing economies are seeing the impact of the financial crisis flowing through to the real economy, with rising unemployment and income loss. The foremost challenge for many governments is to create new jobs and economic opportunities. But many have limited fiscal space for publicly funded activities such as infrastructure investment or for the provision of publicly funded safety nets and social services. Reforms aimed at creating a better investment climate, including reforms of

business regulation, can be beneficial for several reasons. Flexible regulation and effective institutions, including efficient processes for starting a business and efficient insolvency or bankruptcy systems, can facilitate reallocation of labor and capital. And regulatory institutions and processes that are streamlined and accessible can help ensure that, as businesses rebuild, barriers between the informal and formal sectors are lowered, creating more opportunities for the poor.

DOING BUSINESS AS A BENCHMARKING EXERCISE

Doing Business, in capturing some key dimensions of regulatory regimes, has been found useful for benchmarking. Any benchmarking—for individuals, firms or economies—is necessarily partial: it is valid and useful if it helps sharpen judgment, less so if it substitutes for judgment.

Doing Business provides 2 takes on the data it collects: it presents "absolute" indicators for each economy for each of the 10 regulatory topics it addresses, and it provides rankings of economies, both by indicator and in aggregate. Judgment is required in interpreting these measures for any economy and in determining a sensible and politically feasible path for reform.

Reviewing the *Doing Business* rankings in isolation may show unexpected results. Some economies may rank unexpectedly high on some indicators. And some economies that have had rapid growth or attracted a great deal of investment may rank lower than others that appear to be less dynamic.

But for reform-minded governments, how much their indicators improve matters more than their absolute ranking. As economies develop, they strengthen and add to regulations to protect investor and property rights. Meanwhile, they find more efficient ways to implement existing regulations and cut outdated ones. One finding of *Doing Business*: dynamic and growing economies continually reform and update their

regulations and their way of implementing them, while many poor economies still work with regulatory systems dating to the late 1800s.

DOING BUSINESS— A USER'S GUIDE

Quantitative data and benchmarking can be useful in stimulating debate about policy, both by exposing potential challenges and by identifying where policy makers might look for lessons and good practices. These data also provide a basis for analyzing how different policy approaches—and different policy reforms—contribute to desired outcomes such as competitiveness, growth and greater employment and incomes.

Seven years of *Doing Business* data have enabled a growing body of research on how performance on *Doing Business* indicators—and reforms relevant to those indicators—relate to desired social and economic outcomes. Some 405 articles have been published in peer-reviewed academic journals, and about 1,143 working papers are available through Google Scholar.[10] Among the findings:

- Lower barriers to start-up are associated with a smaller informal sector.[11]
- Lower costs of entry encourage entrepreneurship, enhance firm productivity and reduce corruption.[12]
- Simpler start-up translates into greater employment opportunities.[13]

How do governments use *Doing Business*? A common first reaction is to doubt the quality and relevance of the *Doing Business* data. Yet the debate typically proceeds to a deeper discussion exploring the relevance of the data to the economy and areas where reform might make sense.

Most reformers start out by seeking examples, and *Doing Business* helps in this. For example, Saudi Arabia used the company law of France as a model for revising its own. Many countries in Africa look to Mauritius—the region's strongest performer on *Doing Business* indicators—as a source of good practices for reform. In the words of Luis Guillermo Plata, the minister of commerce, industry and tourism of Colombia,

It's not like baking a cake where you follow the recipe. No. We are all different. But we can take certain things, certain key lessons, and apply those lessons and see how they work in our environment.

Over the past 7 years there has been much activity by governments in reforming the regulatory environment for domestic businesses. Most reforms relating to *Doing Business* topics were nested in broader programs of reform aimed at enhancing economic competitiveness. In structuring their reform programs, governments use multiple data sources and indicators. And reformers respond to many stakeholders and interest groups, all of whom bring important issues and concerns into the reform debate.

World Bank support to these reform processes is designed to encourage critical use of the data, sharpening judgment and avoiding a narrow focus on improving *Doing Business* rankings.

METHODOLOGY AND DATA

Doing Business covers 183 economies—including small economies and some of the poorest countries, for which little or no data are available in other data sets. The *Doing Business* data are based on domestic laws and regulations as well as administrative requirements. (For a detailed explanation of the *Doing Business* methodology, see Data notes.)

INFORMATION SOURCES FOR THE DATA

Most of the indicators are based on laws and regulations. In addition, most of the cost indicators are backed by official fee schedules. *Doing Business* respondents both fill out written surveys and provide references to the relevant laws, regulations and fee schedules, aiding data checking and quality assurance.

For some indicators part of the cost component (where fee schedules

are lacking) and the time component are based on actual practice rather than the law on the books. This introduces a degree of subjectivity. The *Doing Business* approach has therefore been to work with legal practitioners or professionals who regularly undertake the transactions involved. Following the standard methodological approach for time and motion studies, *Doing Business* breaks down each process or transaction, such as starting and legally operating a business, into separate steps to ensure a better estimate of time. The time estimate for each step is given by practitioners with significant and routine experience in the transaction.

Over the past 7 years more than 11,000 professionals in 183 economies have assisted in providing the data that inform the *Doing Business* indicators. This year's report draws on the inputs of more than 8,000 professionals. Table 14.1 lists the number of respondents per indicator set. The *Doing Business* website indicates the number of respondents per economy and per indicator. Respondents are professionals or government officials who routinely administer or advise on the legal and regulatory requirements covered in each *Doing Business* topic. Because of the focus on legal and regulatory arrangements, most of the respondents are lawyers. The credit information survey is answered by officials of the credit registry or bureau. Freight forwarders, accountants, architects and other professionals answer the surveys related to trading across borders, taxes and construction permits.

The *Doing Business* approach to data collection contrasts with that of enterprise or firm surveys, which capture often one-time perceptions and experiences of businesses. A corporate lawyer registering 100–150 businesses a year will be more familiar with the process than an entrepreneur, who will register a business only once or maybe twice. A bankruptcy judge deciding dozens of cases a year will have more insight into bankruptcy than a company that may undergo the process.

DEVELOPMENT OF THE METHODOLOGY

The methodology for calculating each indicator is transparent, objective and easily replicable. Leading academics collaborate in the development of the indicators, ensuring academic rigor. Seven of the background papers underlying the indicators have been published in leading economic journals. One is at an advanced stage of publication.

Doing Business uses a simple averaging approach for weighting subindicators and calculating rankings. Other approaches were explored, including using principal components and unobserved components. The principal components and unobserved components approaches turn out to yield results nearly identical to those of simple averaging. The tests show that each set of indicators provides new information. The simple averaging approach is therefore robust to such tests.

IMPROVEMENTS TO THE METHODOLOGY AND DATA REVISIONS

The methodology has undergone continual improvement over the years. Changes have been made mainly in response to country suggestions. For enforcing contracts, for example, the amount of the disputed claim in the case study was increased from 50% to 200% of income per capita after the first year of data collection, as it became clear that smaller claims were unlikely to go to court.

Another change relates to starting a business. The minimum capital requirement can be an obstacle for potential entrepreneurs. Initially, *Doing Business* measured the required minimum capital regardless of whether it had to be paid up front or not. In many economies only part of the minimum capital has to be paid up front. To reflect the actual potential barrier to entry, the paid-in minimum capital has been used since 2004.

This year's report includes changes in the core methodology for one set of indicators, those on employing workers. The assumption for the standardized case study was changed to refer to a small to medium-size company with 60 employees rather than 201. The scope of the question on night and weekly holiday work has been limited to manufacturing activities in which continuous operation is economically necessary. Legally mandated wage premiums for night and weekly holiday work up to a threshold are no longer considered a restriction. In addition, the calculation of the minimum wage ratio was modified to ensure that an economy would not benefit in the scoring from lowering the minimum wage to below $1.25 a day, adjusted for purchasing power parity. This level is consistent with recent adjustments to the absolute poverty line. Finally, the calculation of the redundancy cost was adjusted so that having severance payments or unemployment protections below a certain threshold does not mean a better score for an economy.

All changes in methodology are explained in the Data notes as well as on the *Doing Business* website. In addition, historical data for each indicator and economy are available on the website, beginning with the first year the indicator or economy was included in the report. To provide a comparable time series for research, the data set is back-calculated to adjust for changes in methodology and any revisions in data due to corrections. The website also makes available all original data sets used for background papers.

Information on data corrections is provided in the Data notes and on the website. A transparent complaint procedure allows anyone to challenge the data. If errors are confirmed after a data verification process, they are expeditiously corrected.

NEW THIS YEAR

This year's report presents initial findings in 2 new areas: the ease of obtaining an electricity connection and the level of adoption in national legislation of aspects of the International Labour Organization's (ILO) core labor standards on child labor. Neither of these pilot indicator sets is included in the *Doing Business* rankings.

PILOT INDICATORS ON GETTING ELECTRICITY

Where the quality and accessibility of infrastructure services are poor, companies' productivity and growth suffer. According to firm surveys in 89 economies, electricity was one of the biggest constraints to their business.[14] The *Doing Business* pilot data set on getting electricity is the first to compare distribution utilities around the world on how efficiently they respond to customer requests for connections.

The pilot indicators track the process a standardized local private business goes through in obtaining an electricity connection. By applying its methodology to electricity provision, *Doing Business* aims to illustrate some of the real implications of weak infrastructure services for entrepreneurs. The indicators complement existing data that focus on generation capacity, consumption prices and the reliability of electricity supply.[15] And they allow further investigation of the effects of the process of getting an electricity connection on economic outcomes.

WORKER PROTECTION

The ILO core labor standards consist of freedom of association and recognition of the right to collective bargaining, the elimination of all forms of forced or compulsory labor, the abolition of child labor and equitable treatment in employment practices. The *Doing Business* indicators on employing workers are consistent with these core labor standards but do not measure compliance with them. To complement these indicators, *Doing Business* has launched research on the adoption of core labor standards in national legislation.

The initial research focuses on the national implementation of minimum age provisions included in 2 ILO conventions on child labor: Convention 138, on the minimum age for admission to employment (1973), and Convention 182, on the worst forms of child labor (1999).

This year's report presents initial findings on 102 countries (see annex on worker protection). For each country *Doing Business* examined whether national laws follow the minimum age threshold for general access to employment (14 or 15 years, depending on the development of the country's economy and educational facilities), for hazardous work (18 years) and for light work (12 or 13 years, depending on the development of the country's economy and educational facilities).

In the future the research will expand to more economies and to more areas covered by the core labor standards. On the basis of this, *Doing Business* plans to develop a worker protection indicator, a process that will benefit from the advice of a consultative group with broad representation of stakeholders. The ILO, which has leadership on the core labor standards, will serve as an essential source of guidance in this process.

1. The standard cost model is a quantitative methodology for determining the administrative burdens that regulation imposes on businesses. The method can be used to measure the effect of a single law or of selected areas of legislation or to perform a baseline measurement of all legislation in a country.

2. This included a review by the World Bank Independent Evaluation Group (2008).

3. De Soto (2000).

4. The indicators related to trading across borders and dealing with construction permits and the pilot indicators on getting electricity take into account limited aspects of an economy's infrastructure, including the inland transport of goods and utility connections for businesses.

5. http://subnational.doingbusiness.org.

6. Schneider (2005).

7. http://www.enterprisesurveys.org.

8. Narayan and others (2000).

9. World Bank (2003).

10. http://scholar.google.com.

11. For example, Masatlioglu and Rigolini (2008), Kaplan, Piedra and Seira (2008), Ardagna and Lusagi (2009) and Djankov and others (forthcoming).

12. For example, Alesina and others (2005), Perotti and Volpin (2004), Klapper,

Laeven and Rajan (2006), Fisman and Sarria-Allende (2004), Antunes and Cavalcanti (2007), Barseghyan (2008), Djankov and others (forthcoming) and Klapper, Lewin and Quesada Delgado (2009).

13. For example, Freund and Bolaky (2008), Chang, Kaltani and Loayza (2009) and Helpman, Melitz and Rubinstein (2008).

14. According to World Bank Enterprise Survey data for the 89 economies, 15.6% of managers consider electricity the most serious constraint, while a similar share (15.7%) consider access to finance the most serious constraint (http://www.enterprisesurveys.org).

15. See, for example, data of the International Energy Agency or the World Bank Enterprise Surveys (http://www.enterprisesurveys.org).

Overview

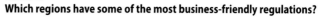

FIGURE 1.1

Which regions have some of the most business-friendly regulations?

DB2010 ranking on the ease of doing business (1–183)

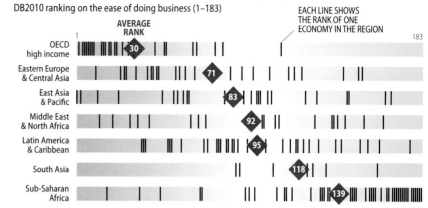

Source: Doing Business database.

The past year was a tough one for doing business. Firms around the world had to cope with the effects of a financial crisis that started in rich economies but led to a global economic downturn. Access to finance became more difficult. Demand for many products fell in domestic and international markets, and trade slowed globally. Policy makers and governments also faced big challenges—from stabilizing the financial sector and restoring confidence and trust to countering rising unemployment and providing necessary safety nets as an estimated 50 million people risked losing their jobs as a result of the crisis.[1] And all this in the face of rising public debt as fiscal stimulus packages collided with tightening fiscal revenues.

Despite the many challenges, in 2008/09 more governments implemented regulatory reforms aimed at making it easier to do business than in any year since 2004, when *Doing Business* started to track reforms through its indicators. *Doing Business* recorded 287 such reforms in 131 economies between June 2008 and May 2009, 20% more than in the year before. Reformers focused on making it easier to start and operate a business, strengthening property rights and improving the efficiency of commercial dispute resolution and bankruptcy procedures.

Reforming business regulation on its own is not a recipe for recovery from financial or economic distress. Many other factors come into play. The *Doing Business* indicators do not assess market regulation or the strength of the financial infrastructure, both important factors in understanding some of the underlying causes of the global financial crisis. Nor do they account for other factors important for business at any time, such as macroeconomic conditions, infrastructure, workforce skills or security.

But the regulatory environment for businesses can influence how well firms cope with the crisis and are able to seize opportunities when recovery begins. Where business regulation is transparent and efficient, it is easier for firms to reorient themselves and for new firms to start up. Efficient court and bankruptcy procedures help ensure that assets can be reallocated quickly. And strong property rights and investor protections can help establish the basis for trust when investors start investing again.

Recognizing the importance of firms—especially small and medium-size enterprises—for creating jobs and revenue, some governments, including those of China, the Republic of Korea, Malaysia and the Russian Federation, have included reforms of business regulation in their economic recovery plans. But most reforms recorded in 2008/09 were part of longer-term efforts to increase competitiveness and encourage firm and job creation by improving the regulatory environment for businesses. And most took place in developing economies (figure 1.2).

FIGURE 1.2

Reforms more likely in low- and lower-middle-income economies

Distribution by income group of reforms making it easier to do business (%)

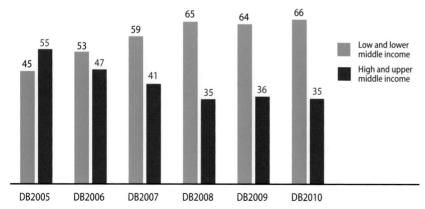

Source: Doing Business database.

TABLE 1.1
The top 10 reformers in 2008/09

Economy	Starting a business	Dealing with construction permits	Employing workers	Registering property	Getting credit	Protecting investors	Paying taxes	Trading across borders	Enforcing contracts	Closing a business
Rwanda	✔		✔	✔	✔	✔		✔		✔
Kyrgyz Republic	✔	✔	✔	✔	✔		✔	✔		
Macedonia, FYR	✔	✔	✔	✔	✔	✔	✔			
Belarus	✔	✔	✔	✔			✔	✔		
United Arab Emirates	✔	✔						✔		
Moldova	✔			✔			✔			
Colombia	✔	✔		✔	✔	✔	✔	✔		✔
Tajikistan	✔	✔			✔	✔				✔
Egypt, Arab Rep.	✔	✔			✔				✔	
Liberia	✔	✔						✔		

Note: Economies are ranked on the number and impact of reforms. First, *Doing Business* selects the economies that implemented reforms making it easier to do business in 3 or more of the *Doing Business* topics. Second, it ranks these economies on the increase in rank on the ease of doing business from the previous year. The larger the improvement, the higher the ranking as a reformer.

Source: Doing Business database.

DEVELOPING ECONOMIES SET A FAST PACE—WITH RWANDA IN THE LEAD

Low- and lower-middle-income economies accounted for two-thirds of reforms recorded by *Doing Business* in 2008/09, continuing a trend that started 3 years ago. Indeed, three-quarters of such economies covered by *Doing Business* reformed. And for the first time a Sub-Saharan African economy, Rwanda, led the world in *Doing Business* reforms (table 1.1).

Rwanda has steadily reformed its commercial laws and institutions since 2001. In the past year it introduced a new company law that simplified business start-up and strengthened minority shareholder protections (figure 1.3). Entrepreneurs can now start a business in 2 procedures and 3 days. Related-party transactions are subject to stricter approval and disclosure requirements. Legal provisions determining directors' liability in case of prejudicial transactions between interested parties were also tightened.

Rwanda improved regulations to ease access to credit through 2 new laws. Its new secured transactions act facilitates secured lending by allowing a wider range of assets to be used as collateral. The law also makes out-of-court enforcement of movable collateral available to secured creditors and gives them absolute priority within bankruptcy. Rwanda's new insolvency law streamlined reorganization procedures.

Reforms also included measures to speed up trade and property registration. Delays at the borders were reduced thanks to longer operating hours and simpler requirements for documents. Reforms removed bottlenecks at the property registry and the revenue authority, reducing the time required to register property by 255 days.

Five other low- or lower-middle-income economies—the Arab Republic of Egypt, Liberia, Moldova, the Kyrgyz Republic and Tajikistan—joined Rwanda on the list of global top reformers. These top 10 reformers are economies that, thanks to reforms in 3 or more of the 10 areas covered by *Doing Business*, improved the most on the ease of doing business. An economy's ranking on the ease of doing business does not tell the whole story about its business environment. And opportunities for reform remain—Liberia, for example, still ranks 149, and Tajikistan 152. Yet an improvement in this ranking does indicate that the government is taking action to make the local regulatory environment more conducive to doing business.

Such reforms are as timely as ever. Many firms in developing economies have been affected by lower demand for their exports and a drop in capital flows and remittances. At the same time businesses in low-income economies on average still face more than twice the regulatory burden that their counterparts in high-income economies do when starting a business, transferring property, filing taxes or resolving a commercial dispute through the courts. Only 2% of adults on average have a credit history in low-income economies, compared with 52% of adults in high-income economies. Developed economies have on average 10 times as many newly registered firms per adult as Africa and the Middle East—and a business density 4 times that in developing economies.[2]

Regulatory burdens can push firms—and employment—into the informal sector. There, firms are not registered, do not pay taxes and have limited access to formal credit and institutions—and workers do not benefit from the protections that the law provides. The global crisis is expected to further increase informal activity. Almost two-thirds of the world's workers are already estimated to be employed in the informal sector.[3] Most are in low- and lower-middle-income economies. And a disproportionate share are from already vulnerable groups, such as youth and women.[4]

Most *Doing Business* reforms in developing economies still focus on cutting red tape and simplifying bureaucratic

FIGURE 1.3
New company law in Rwanda simplifies starting a business and strengthens investor protections

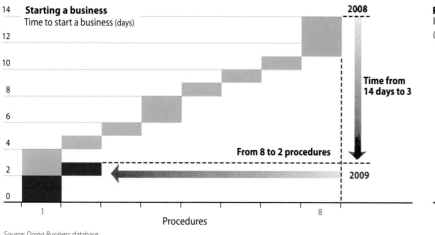

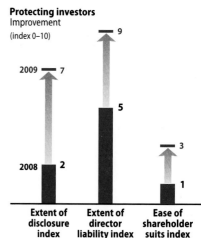

Source: Doing Business database.

formalities. Over the past 6 years 80% of reforms in low- and lower-middle-income economies were aimed at reducing the administrative burden for firms, mostly by easing business start-up and trade. This makes sense and addresses important needs. When informal firms were asked in 2008 about obstacles to formally registering their business, 67% in Côte d'Ivoire and 57% in Madagascar cited registration fees as a major or very severe obstacle.[5]

In easing business start-up and trade, much can be achieved through cost-effective administrative reforms. The one-stop shop for starting a business in Burkina Faso cost $200,000. Azerbaijan's cost $5 million. And the costs are far outweighed by the estimated savings for businesses—estimated at $1.7 million a year in Burkina Faso, $8.4 million in Azerbaijan. Efficient systems also facili-

TABLE 1.2
Top reformers in 2008/09 by indicator set

Starting a business	Samoa
Dealing with construction permits	United Kingdom
Employing workers	Rwanda
Registering property	Mauritius
Getting credit	Rwanda
Protecting investors	Rwanda
Paying taxes	Timor-Leste
Trading across borders	Georgia
Enforcing contracts	Botswana
Closing a business	Malawi

Source: Doing Business database.

tate enforcement, a particular challenge in many developing economies where resources are scarce. Risk-based inspection systems at customs or in the construction sector allow public officials to focus their resources and attention where they are most needed.

Some reforming governments have gone further, introducing new legislation to strengthen property rights and increase legal protections for investors. Several postconflict economies, including Afghanistan, Rwanda and Sierra Leone, introduced new company and collateral laws, laying the legal foundations for future markets (table 1.2).

Of course, many challenges remain. Banks in Afghanistan will not increase secured lending tomorrow just because of new legislation on the use of movable collateral. To be effective, new legislation must be well publicized and adopted by both the public and the private sector. Moreover, regulatory reform does not operate in a vacuum. New evidence suggests that an economy's governance structure and natural resources influence the motivation for reform.[6]

But even in difficult circumstances, creating a regulatory environment with efficient administrative processes and strong protection of property rights can set the stage for firms and investors to take opportunities as the economy develops. New research suggests that

given the right conditions, particularly in low-income economies, simple measures can make a difference. Analysis of 6 years of *Doing Business* reforms finds that in relatively poor but well-governed economies, a 10-day reduction in start-up time was associated with an increase of 0.4 percentage points in the growth rate and 0.27 percentage points in the investment rate.[7]

INSPIRED BY NEIGHBORS, REFORMERS PICK UP THE PACE

In 2008/09 *Doing Business* reforms picked up around the world, with at least 60% of economies reforming in every region (table 1.3). Reformers were particularly active in 2 regions, Eastern Europe and Central Asia and the Middle East and North Africa. In both, competition among neighbors played a part in motivating reforms.

Economies in Eastern Europe and Central Asia, the region most affected by the crisis, were the most active reformers for the sixth year in a row. Twenty-six of the region's 27 economies reformed business regulation in at least one area covered by *Doing Business*. In 2004/05 and 2005/06 the 10 European Union accession economies accounted for 84 reforms, 60% of the total in the region. Others followed, with some good results. Since 2004 private credit bureaus have

TABLE 1.3
Rankings on the ease of doing business

2010 RANK	2009 RANK	ECONOMY	2010 REFORMS	2010 RANK	2009 RANK	ECONOMY	2010 REFORMS	2010 RANK	2009 RANK	ECONOMY	2010 REFORMS
1	1	Singapore	3	62	51	Spain	1	123	123	Nepal	1
2	2	New Zealand	0	63	64	Kazakhstan	3	124	122	Paraguay	1
3	3	Hong Kong, China	3	64	53	Luxembourg	1	125	120	Nigeria	1
4	4	United States	0	65	60	Oman	2	126	124	Bhutan	1
5	6	United Kingdom	2	66	54	Namibia	0	127	125	Micronesia, Fed. Sts.	0
6	5	Denmark	0	67	143	Rwanda	7	128	130	Morocco	1
7	7	Ireland	1	68	59	Bahamas, The	0	129	127	Brazil	1
8	8	Canada	0	69	73	Tunisia	2	130	128	Lesotho	0
9	9	Australia	0	70	62	St. Vincent and the Grenadines	2	131	126	Tanzania	0
10	10	Norway	1	71	77	Montenegro	4	132	131	Malawi	2
11	16	Georgia	2	72	72	Poland	4	133	132	India	1
12	12	Thailand	1	73	63	Turkey	1	134	144	Madagascar	1
13	15	Saudi Arabia	2	74	66	Czech Republic	3	135	140	Mozambique	2
14	11	Iceland	1	75	67	Jamaica	1	136	134	Algeria	4
15	13	Japan	0	76	70	St. Kitts and Nevis	1	137	142	Iran, Islamic Rep.	4
16	14	Finland	1	77	83	Panama	2	138	133	Ecuador	0
17	24	Mauritius	6	78	74	Italy	0	139	137	West Bank and Gaza	2
18	17	Sweden	0	79	79	Kiribati	0	140	135	Gambia, The	0
19	23	Korea, Rep.	2	80	75	Belize	0	141	136	Honduras	3
20	18	Bahrain	1	81	78	Trinidad and Tobago	0	142	146	Ukraine	1
21	19	Switzerland	0	82	89	Albania	3	143	138	Syrian Arab Republic	1
22	20	Belgium	2	83	76	Dominica	0	144	141	Philippines	3
23	21	Malaysia	2	84	81	El Salvador	0	145	139	Cambodia	0
24	22	Estonia	2	85	85	Pakistan	1	146	147	Cape Verde	2
25	27	Germany	2	86	102	Dominican Republic	1	147	155	Burkina Faso	5
26	25	Lithuania	1	87	71	Maldives	0	148	156	Sierra Leone	5
27	30	Latvia	2	88	90	Serbia	2	149	159	Liberia	3
28	26	Austria	0	89	86	China	1	150	145	Uzbekistan	2
29	29	Israel	1	90	99	Zambia	1	151	154	Haiti	2
30	28	Netherlands	1	91	88	Grenada	2	152	164	Tajikistan	5
31	31	France	2	92	87	Ghana	1	153	150	Iraq	0
32	69	Macedonia, FYR	7	93	91	Vietnam	2	154	149	Sudan	2
33	47	United Arab Emirates	3	94	108	Moldova	3	155	148	Suriname	0
34	32	South Africa	1	95	84	Kenya	1	156	162	Mali	5
35	33	Puerto Rico	0	96	94	Brunei Darussalam	1	157	152	Senegal	1
36	34	St. Lucia	1	97	92	Palau	0	158	151	Gabon	0
37	49	Colombia	8	98	93	Marshall Islands	0	159	160	Zimbabwe	1
38	38	Azerbaijan	2	99	103	Yemen, Rep.	3	160	168	Afghanistan	3
39	37	Qatar	0	100	104	Jordan	6	161	158	Bolivia	0
40	36	Cyprus	0	101	98	Guyana	2	162	153	Comoros	0
41	80	Kyrgyz Republic	7	102	95	Papua New Guinea	1	163	157	Djibouti	1
42	35	Slovak Republic	1	103	110	Croatia	1	164	173	Timor-Leste	1
43	50	Armenia	3	104	96	Solomon Islands	0	165	166	Togo	2
44	42	Bulgaria	2	105	97	Sri Lanka	1	166	161	Mauritania	0
45	39	Botswana	2	106	116	Egypt, Arab Rep.	4	167	165	Lao PDR	1
46	61	Taiwan, China	2	107	111	Ethiopia	3	168	163	Côte d'Ivoire	0
47	41	Hungary	1	108	101	Lebanon	2	169	170	Angola	3
48	48	Portugal	4	109	100	Greece	1	170	169	Equatorial Guinea	0
49	40	Chile	0	110	117	Guatemala	4	171	167	Cameroon	3
50	44	Antigua and Barbuda	0	111	105	Seychelles	0	172	172	Benin	2
51	55	Mexico	2	112	106	Uganda	1	173	171	Guinea	0
52	46	Tonga	1	113	107	Kosovo	1	174	174	Niger	1
53	58	Slovenia	2	114	109	Uruguay	1	175	175	Eritrea	0
54	43	Fiji	1	115	114	Swaziland	0	176	177	Burundi	0
55	45	Romania	1	116	119	Bosnia and Herzegovina	1	177	178	Venezuela, R.B.	0
56	65	Peru	6	117	113	Nicaragua	0	178	176	Chad	0
57	68	Samoa	2	118	112	Argentina	1	179	179	Congo, Rep.	0
58	82	Belarus	6	119	115	Bangladesh	3	180	180	São Tomé and Principe	0
59	57	Vanuatu	1	120	118	Russian Federation	3	181	181	Guinea-Bissau	1
60	56	Mongolia	0	121	121	Costa Rica	1	182	182	Congo, Dem. Rep.	1
61	52	Kuwait	2	122	129	Indonesia	3	183	183	Central African Republic	1

Note: The rankings for all economies are benchmarked to June 2009 and reported in the country tables. Rankings on the ease of doing business are the average of the economy's rankings on the 10 topics covered in *Doing Business 2010*. Last year's rankings are presented in italics. These are adjusted for changes in the methodology, data corrections and the addition of 2 new economies. The number of reforms excludes reforms making it more difficult to do business.

Source: Doing Business database.

opened in 16 of the region's economies. Today 94% of adults in Serbia, 77% in Croatia and 30% in Kazakhstan and Romania have a credit history. Five years ago, none did. Enterprise surveys show that in 2008 fewer than 6% of firms expected to make informal payments to get things done in Estonia, Slovenia and the Slovak Republic—a far cry from the 18%, 14% and 33% in 2005.[8] In the past 3 years reforms have been moving eastward from the European Union. Albania, Belarus, the Kyrgyz Republic and the former Yugoslav Republic of Macedonia implemented reforms in several areas for the third year in row. Inspired by their neighbors, Kazakhstan, Montenegro and Tajikistan increased reform efforts this past year.

Governments in the Middle East and North Africa are now reforming at a rate similar to those in Eastern Europe and Central Asia (figure 1.4). Seventeen of 19 economies reformed in 2008/09. Egypt, Jordan and the United Arab Emirates were among the most active reformers. In recent years economies in the region have increasingly picked up reform practices from one another. Eight of the region's economies have reduced or eliminated their minimum capital requirement since 2005. Five of these 8 used to have among the highest requirements in the world—up to $120,000 in Saudi Arabia until 2007. Egypt, Jordan, Morocco, Saudi Arabia, Tunisia, the United Arab Emirates and the Republic of Yemen all operate one-stop shops for starting a business. In 2008/09 reforms also intensified in other areas, simplifying processes for getting construction permits, for trading across borders and for enforcing contracts through the courts.

Reforms in Latin America and the Caribbean also intensified, with 19 of 32 economies reforming. Colombia, Guatemala and Peru each reformed in at least 4 areas. And 3 Caribbean island states reformed for the first time—Grenada, St. Kitts and Nevis and St. Lucia.

In Sub-Saharan Africa 29 of 46 economies reformed in 2008/09, implementing 67 reforms. As in the previous year, nearly half the reforms in the re-

gion focused on making it easier to start a business or trade across borders. In South Asia 6 of 8 economies reformed. In East Asia and the Pacific 17 of 24 did.

Among OECD high-income economies 17 reformed, focusing mostly on easing the corporate tax burden and improving property registration systems. Germany created a new form of limited liability company, doing away with start-up requirements that were more than 100 years old. Germany is no stranger to regulatory competition. In recent years, taking advantage of the common EU market, German limited liability companies increasingly registered in the United Kingdom, where registration was easier and less costly, rather than in Germany. The new law may reverse this trend.

TIMES OF CRISIS— AN OPPORTUNITY FOR REFORM

Regulatory reform can be difficult and take time, particularly if legal changes are involved. Some reforms also require difficult political trade-offs. It is not surprising that most reforms recorded by *Doing Business* in 2008/09 were aimed at reducing administrative burdens. At least 30 economies improved processes for construction permitting, property registration or trading across borders, while 61 eased business start-up. By contrast, only 8 economies amended collateral or secured transactions laws—and only 11 amended labor regulations, 7 making them more flexible, 4 opting for more rigidity (figure 1.5). Outside pressures are often required to push through substantial legislative changes. In this sense the current crisis may represent an opportunity.

Historically, many reforms have been prompted by recession or financial crisis. The East Asian crisis motivated many economies to reengineer their bankruptcy systems. Some, such as Singapore and Thailand, reformed laws to strengthen investor protections. Postcrisis bankruptcy reforms were also carried out in Turkey in 2003/04

FIGURE 1.4

Eastern Europe & Central Asia and Middle East & North Africa— most active reformers in 2008/09

Share of economies with at least 1 reform making it easier to do business (%)
by *Doing Business* report year

Eastern Europe & Central Asia
(27 economies)

Middle East & North Africa
(19 economies)

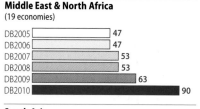

South Asia
(8 economies)

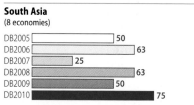

East Asia & Pacific
(24 economies)

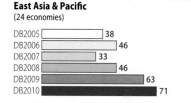

OECD high income
(27 economies)

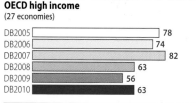

Sub-Saharan Africa
(46 economies)

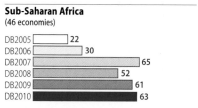

Latin America & Caribbean
(32 economies)

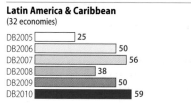

Note: The Czech Republic, Hungary and the Slovak Republic were reclassified from Eastern Europe and Central Asia to OECD high-income in 2008.

Source: Doing Business database.

FIGURE 1.5

287 reforms in 2008/09 made it easier to do business—27 made it more difficult

Reforms making it easier to do business

Starting a business (61)	Dealing with construction permits (31)	Employing workers (7)	Registering property (34)	Getting credit (27)
Afghanistan	Algeria	Belarus	Afghanistan	Afghanistan
Albania	Bahrain	Kyrgyz Republic	Algeria	Armenia
Argentina	Belarus	Macedonia, FYR	Angola	Azerbaijan
Armenia	Bosnia and Herzegovina	Mauritius	Belarus	Colombia
Bangladesh	Burkina Faso	Montenegro	Belgium	Egypt, Arab Rep.
Belarus	Colombia	Peru	Bulgaria	Greece
Botswana	Croatia	Rwanda	Burkina Faso	Guatemala
Brazil	Czech Republic		Colombia	Haiti
Bulgaria	Egypt, Arab Rep.		Czech Republic	Honduras
Burkina Faso	Georgia		Estonia	Kenya
Cameroon	Guatemala		Ethiopia	Kyrgyz Republic
Cape Verde	Honduras		France	Latvia
Central African Republic	Hong Kong, China		Guatemala	Macedonia, FYR
Colombia	Iran, Islamic Rep.		Hong Kong, China	Mauritius
Egypt, Arab Rep.	Jordan		Indonesia	Morocco
Ethiopia	Kazakhstan		Ireland	Nigeria
Germany	Kyrgyz Republic		Jamaica	Philippines
Ghana	Liberia		Jordan	Poland
Guinea-Bissau	Macedonia, FYR		Kyrgyz Republic	Rwanda
Guyana	Mali		Latvia	Serbia
Honduras	Montenegro		Macedonia, FYR	Sierra Leone
Hong Kong, China	Netherlands		Mauritius	Sri Lanka
Hungary	Panama		Moldova	Tajikistan
Indonesia	Portugal		Nepal	Turkey
Iran, Islamic Rep.	Saudi Arabia		Panama	Vanuatu
Jordan	Singapore		Peru	Yemen, Rep.
Kazakhstan	Slovenia		Portugal	Zambia
Korea, Rep.	Tajikistan		Romania	
Kyrgyz Republic	United Arab Emirates		Russian Federation	
Lebanon	United Kingdom		Rwanda	
Liberia	Uzbekistan		Singapore	
Luxembourg			United Kingdom	
Macedonia, FYR			West Bank and Gaza	
Madagascar			Zimbabwe	
Malaysia				
Mali				
Mexico				
Moldova				
Montenegro				
Mozambique				
Niger				
Oman				
Pakistan				
Peru				
Poland				
Rwanda				
Samoa				
Saudi Arabia				
Serbia				
Sierra Leone				
Singapore				
Slovenia				
St. Lucia				
St. Vincent and the Grenadines				
Syrian Arab Republic				
Taiwan, China				
Tajikistan				
Thailand				
Togo				
United Arab Emirates				
Yemen, Rep.				

Starting a business	Dealing with construction permits	Employing workers	Registering property	Getting credit

Reforms making it more difficult to do business

Starting a business	Dealing with construction permits	Employing workers	Registering property	Getting credit
West Bank and Gaza	Kenya	Honduras	Argentina	Cape Verde
	New Zealand	Luxembourg	Botswana	
	Romania	Maldives	Madagascar	
	Solomon Islands	Portugal	Sierra Leone	
	Sri Lanka		Suriname	
	Tanzania		Tajikistan	
			Uruguay	

Source: Doing Business database.

45

Algeria
Angola
Bangladesh
Belarus
Belgium
Benin
Brunei Darussalam
Cameroon
Cape Verde
Colombia
Czech Republic
Djibouti
Fiji
Finland
Guatemala
Iceland
Iran, Islamic Rep.
Israel
Jordan
Kazakhstan
Korea, Rep.
Kosovo
Kyrgyz Republic
Lao PDR
Lebanon
Macedonia, FYR
Mexico
Moldova
Montenegro
Oman
Peru
Philippines
Poland
Russian Federation
Sierra Leone
South Africa
Spain
St. Vincent and the Grenadines
Sudan
Taiwan, China
Timor-Leste
Togo
Tonga
Uzbekistan
Vietnam

38

Albania
Angola
Armenia
Azerbaijan
Bangladesh
Belarus
Benin
Burkina Faso
Cameroon
China
Colombia
Congo, Dem. Rep.
Georgia
Grenada
Guyana
Haiti
Iran, Islamic Rep.
Jordan
Kuwait
Kyrgyz Republic
Liberia
Malawi
Mali
Mauritius
Mozambique
Paraguay
Peru
Portugal
Rwanda
Senegal
Slovak Republic
St. Kitts and Nevis
Sudan
Tunisia
Uganda
United Arab Emirates
Vietnam
Yemen, Rep.

16

Algeria
Botswana
Burkina Faso
Costa Rica
Egypt, Arab Rep.
Ethiopia
Grenada
Jordan
Malaysia
Mali
Mauritius
Norway
Papua New Guinea
Peru
Portugal
West Bank and Gaza

18

Albania
Colombia
Estonia
France
Germany
India
Kuwait
Lithuania
Malawi
Mauritius
Philippines
Poland
Russian Federation
Rwanda
Samoa
Sierra Leone
Tajikistan
Uruguay

10

Colombia
Dominican Republic
Indonesia
Macedonia, FYR
Mali
Rwanda
Sierra Leone
Tajikistan
Tunisia
Ukraine

Protecting investors	Paying taxes	Trading across borders	Enforcing contracts	Closing a business

Cambodia
Congo, Dem. Rep.
Lithuania
Romania
Tunisia
Venezuela, R.B.

Sierra Leone

Romania

FIGURE 1.6

Three-quarters of economies have made it easier to start a business

Share of economies implementing reforms in each *Doing Business* topic (%)

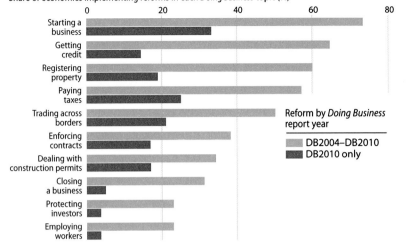

Reform by *Doing Business* report year

DB2004–DB2010

DB2010 only

Note: Not all indicators are covered for the full period. Registering property was introduced in *Doing Business 2005,* and paying taxes, trading across borders, dealing with construction permits and protecting investors in *Doing Business 2006.*
Source: Doing Business database.

and in Colombia in 1999. In the United States the Great Depression prompted the country's first comprehensive bankruptcy reform in 50 years. This past year 18 economies reformed their bankruptcy regimes, as measured by *Doing Business.* This number may increase in the future as economies face the need to deal with systemic distress. In times of recession, keeping viable companies operating as a going concern and preserving jobs becomes especially important. And the more quickly the assets of nonviable firms can be freed up, the easier it is to remobilize those assets.

France and Germany were among the first to reform bankruptcy systems in response to the current crisis. In Eastern Europe and Central Asia several economies have recently started to do so. Latvia's new insolvency law became effective in January 2008, Lithuania's in July 2008. And in December 2008 Estonia adopted a new reorganization act that establishes a legal procedure enabling distressed companies on the verge of insolvency to reorganize themselves, restructure their debt and take other measures to restore their financial health and profitability. Such efforts are timely. The region's average recovery rate following bankruptcy is 32%, far lower than the 69% in OECD high-income economies.

WHAT CONSISTENT REFORMERS DO

As *Doing Business* has tracked regulatory reforms over the past 6 years, some patterns have started to emerge. Regulatory reform tends to pick up when pressure rises. One reason can be increasing competition as economies join a common market or trade agreement, such as the European Union or the U.S.–Central American Free Trade Agreement. Financial crisis and economic downturn are another strong motivation for reform. So is the need to rebuild an economy following conflict, as in Liberia, Rwanda and Sierra Leone.

Whatever the motivation, governments that succeed in sustaining reform programs, as measured by *Doing Business,* tend to have common features. To begin with, they follow a longer-term agenda aimed at increasing the competitiveness of their firms and economy. Colombia, Egypt, Malaysia and Rwanda are all examples of economies incorporating business regulation reforms into a broader competitiveness agenda.

Such reformers continually push forward and stay proactive. Singapore and Hong Kong (China) rank among the top economies on the ease of doing business and are also some of the most

consistent reformers. This year Singapore once again tops the rankings on the ease of doing business—for the fourth year in a row. And in the past year it continued with reforms, implementing online and computer-based services to make it easier to start a business, deal with construction permits and transfer property.

But while successful reformers follow a clear direction in their policy agenda, they do not hesitate to respond to new economic realities. Mauritius, the top-ranked economy in Sub-Saharan Africa, just announced a new insolvency act "to maintain the viability of the commercial system in the country."[9]

Successful *Doing Business* reformers are comprehensive. Over the past 5 years Colombia, Egypt, Georgia, FYR Macedonia, Mauritius and Rwanda each implemented at least 19 reforms, covering 8 or more of the 10 areas measured by *Doing Business* (figure 1.7). This broad approach increases the chances of success and impact. Recent research suggests that reforms in different areas tend to be complementary. One study finds that after reforms reducing barriers to entry in India, states with more flexible employment regulations saw a 25% larger decrease in informal firms.[10] Other studies show that when economies open up their product markets to international competition, the benefits are greater if the cost of entry is lower. Lower barriers to entry allow firms to move more easily toward industries that most benefit from trade openness.[11]

Consistent reformers are inclusive. They involve all relevant public agencies and private sector representatives and institutionalize reform at the highest level. Colombia and Rwanda have formed regulatory reform committees reporting directly to the president or prime minister. More than 20 other economies, including Burkina Faso, India, Liberia, FYR Macedonia, the Syrian Arab Republic and Vietnam, have formed committees at the ministerial level. Reforms in Egypt involved 32 government agencies supported by the parliament.

Successful reformers stay focused

FIGURE 1.7

Consistent reformers continued reform efforts in 2008/09

Improvement in the ranking on the ease of doing business, DB2009–DB2010

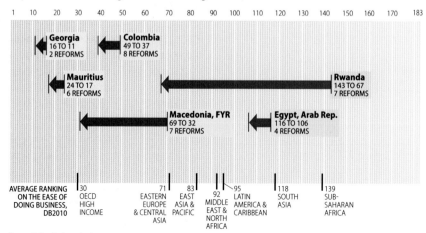

Source: Doing Business database.

thanks to a long-term vision supported by specific goals. Malaysia aims to be a fully developed economy by 2020. Colombian President Alvaro Uribe envisions a new Colombia in which, rather than 60% of the population living in poverty, most would be counted as middle class. Rwanda aims to become a technology and trade hub in the region. The Kyrgyz Republic wants to become the center for regional regulatory excellence in Central Asia, Azerbaijan the gateway to the region.

Setting long-term goals and keeping a steady course of reform might help economies recover from shocks, including the current global financial and economic crisis. In the words of Egyptian Minister of Investment Mahmoud Mohieldin,

It is not just a crisis of the economy. It is a crisis of economic thinking. It is a crisis that is confusing many reformers . . . [but] whatever crisis you are facing, you need to make life easier for those who are endeavoring and working hard to create opportunities for jobs, and this is the least that we can be doing.

1. Based on estimates by the International Labour Organization. This year *Doing Business* improved the methodology for the employing workers indicators to ensure that the existence of safety nets is taken into account in the current measures of flexibility. For further details, see About *Doing Business* and Data notes.

2. Klapper, Lewin and Quesada Delgado (2009). Business density is defined as the number of businesses as a percentage of the working-age population (ages 18–65).

3. OECD Development Centre (2009).

4. Ardagna and Lusagi (2009).

5. World Bank Enterprise Surveys (http://www.enterprisesurveys.org).

6. Amin and Djankov (2009a, 2009b).

7. Eifert (2008).

8. World Bank Enterprise Surveys (http://www.enterprisesurveys.org).

9. Mauritius, Corporate Affairs Division, http://www.gov.mu.

10. Sharma (2009).

11. Chang, Kaltani and Loayza (2009), Helpman, Melitz and Rubinstein (2008) and Freund and Bolaky (2008).

Starting a business

FIGURE 2.1

Top 10 reformers in starting a business

Average improvement (%)

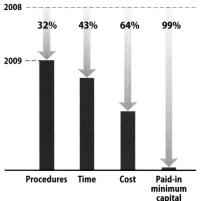

Rankings on the ease of starting a business		DB2010	DB2009
1.	**Samoa**	20	131
2.	**Belarus**	7	98
3.	**Taiwan, China**	29	119
4.	**Korea, Rep.**	53	133
5.	**United Arab Emirates**	44	118
6.	**Rwanda**	11	64
7.	**Madagascar**	12	60
8.	**Mozambique**	96	143
9.	**Armenia**	21	65
10.	**Serbia**	73	108

Source: Doing Business database.

In April 1973, in the midst of the oil crisis, Frederick W. Smith started a new package delivery company. On its first night of operations it delivered 186 packages to 25 cities. Today FedEx handles more than 7.5 million shipments a day worldwide. In the 1980s, during the economic downturn in the United States, a little-known television station struggled to get off the ground. Now 1.5 billion people in 212 economies watch CNN's 24-hour all-news channel.

Entrepreneurs launch new businesses even in times of economic crisis—though most do not become global players. Many start their business out of necessity rather than to be the next global star. In many low- and lower-middle-income economies poor people have seen starting a business or finding a job as the most effective way out of poverty.[1]

Faced with today's financial and economic crisis, policy makers continue to recognize the importance of private businesses and entrepreneurs in creating jobs and driving growth. Some economies even included specific measures aimed at encouraging formal entrepreneurship in their crisis response. Economies affected by earlier crises, such as Korea and Malaysia, were among the first to do so.[2] The European Union Recovery Act of November 2008 outlined measures to make it easier for new businesses to incorporate, especially small ones. This focus is not surprising. The 23 million small and medium-size enterprises in the European Union employ around 75 million people and account for half the new jobs created. In the United States small businesses have created 93.5% of net new jobs since 1989.[3]

Formal incorporation has several benefits. The legal identities of companies outlive their founders. Resources are often pooled as multiple shareholders join together to form a company. And companies have access to services and institutions ranging from courts to commercial banks. Among 388 informal firms interviewed in the World Bank Enterprise Surveys of 2008 in Côte d'Ivoire, Madagascar and Mauritius, 85% cited better access to finance and 68% better access to markets as main reasons for registration.[4]

Benefits go beyond the firm level. A growing body of empirical research relates easier start-up to greater entrepreneurship and higher productivity among existing firms, particularly in economies open to trade.[5] A recent study using data collected from company registries in 100 economies over 8 years found that simple business start-up is critical for fostering formal entrepreneurship. Economies with efficient business registration have a higher entry rate as well as greater business density.[6]

Another study found that in relatively poor but well-governed economies, a 10-day reduction in start-up time was associated with an increase of 0.4 percentage points in the growth rate and 0.27 percentage points in the invest-

TABLE 2.1

Where is business start-up easy—and where not?

Easiest	RANK	Most difficult	RANK
New Zealand	1	Cameroon	174
Canada	2	Iraq	175
Australia	3	West Bank and Gaza	176
Singapore	4	Djibouti	177
Georgia	5	Equatorial Guinea	178
Macedonia, FYR	6	Guinea	179
Belarus	7	Haiti	180
United States	8	Eritrea	181
Ireland	9	Chad	182
Mauritius	10	Guinea-Bissau	183

Note: Rankings are the average of the economy's rankings on the procedures, time, cost and paid-in minimum capital for starting a business. See Data notes for details.
Source: Doing Business database.

FIGURE 2.2

Starting a business: getting a local limited liability company up and running

Rankings are based on 4 subindicators

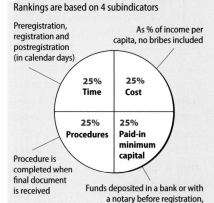

Note: See Data notes for details.

FIGURE 2.3

Regional averages in starting a business—big improvements since DB2005

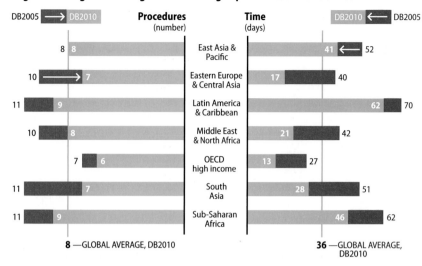

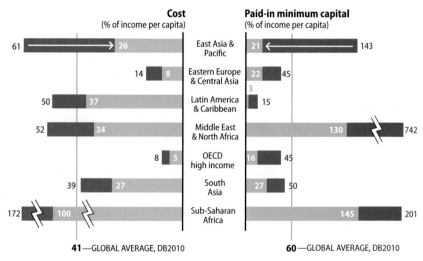

Note: Data refer to economies included in *Doing Business 2005*. Additional economies were added in subsequent years.
Source: Doing Business database.

ment rate.[7] Conversely, greater barriers to entry are correlated with higher perceived corruption and a larger informal sector. Vulnerable groups such as youth and women, because they mostly operate in the informal sector, are particularly affected by barriers to entry.[8]

Recognizing the potential gains from making start-up easier, 134 economies have done so since 2004, through 254 reforms recorded by *Doing Business*. Yet in many economies barriers to entry remain high. On average around the world, it still takes 8 procedures and 36 days to start a business (figure 2.3).

With so much evidence of the potential benefits of simple entry regula-tions, the question is why complicated procedures remain. One argument is that strict entry regulations provide more legal certainty and protection to the public. Yet global practice shows that legal certainty does not require costly and complex procedures. Look at the practice in New Zealand or Canada, both among the top 10 on the ease of starting a business. There, thanks to links between agencies, entrepreneurs can start a business by filing information once. They are free to decide on company capital and need no approval from a judge. Reformers focus on solutions to encourage formal registration by making services accessible, fast, low cost and predictable.

WHO REFORMED IN 2008/09?

Sixty-one economies made it easier to start a business in 2008/09 (table 2.2). Sub-Saharan Africa and Eastern Europe and Central Asia had the most reforms.

For the first time a small island state led the way. Samoa's new company act allows entrepreneurs to choose the amount of capital for their company. A flat fee replaced varying stamp duties. And thanks to standard forms, entre-preneurs can now opt not to use profes-sional legal services. The new act also eliminated the antiquated requirement for a company seal.

Belarus and Taiwan (China) were the runner-up reformers. Belarus simplified its registration formalities by merging 4 procedures, abolished the minimum capital requirement, made the use of a notary optional and removed the need for company seal approval. Start-up time was shortened by nearly 4 weeks. Taiwan (China), having cut the minimum capital requirement in half in 2008, this time abolished it altogether. It also did away with the business license, streamlined company and tax registrations and intro-duced time limits for incorporation and filings with labor authorities. Start-up time was shortened by about 3 weeks.

In addition to Samoa and Taiwan (China), 5 other economies in East Asia and the Pacific reformed. Almost all in-troduced standard documents and single registration forms. Hong Kong (China) streamlined registration procedures and introduced a new incorporation form, merging 3 procedures into 1. Indonesia introduced standard registration forms, cut the requirement to obtain a certificate of company domicile and made business and tax registration faster. Start-up time was cut by 16 days.

Malaysia set up a one-stop shop hosting the company registry, the In-land Revenue Board, customs, financial institutions and the pension and social security agencies. Singapore combined tax and company registration in a single online form. Thailand merged the ap-proval of the memorandum of association with business registration.

In Eastern Europe and Central Asia, besides Belarus, 12 other economies reformed. Six reduced or eliminated the minimum capital requirement: Albania, Armenia, Bulgaria, the Kyrgyz Republic, Poland and Tajikistan. Albania's electronic registry became operational, cutting the time by 3 days, and registration with chambers of commerce became voluntary. Armenia, the Kyrgyz Republic and Slovenia reformed outdated company seal requirements. The Kyrgyz Republic accelerated registration, reduced the documents required and abolished the fees for statistical and tax registration. Kazakhstan cut registration with the local tax office and simplified document requirements.

In FYR Macedonia starting a business now takes 4 days, because the central registry forwards relevant company information to other institutions. Several documents no longer have to be notarized. Moldova offers an expedited, 24-hour company registration service for an additional fee. Montenegro unified name verification and registration

with the company registry and expedited registrations with pension and health funds and social security and income tax authorities. Poland consolidated registrations with the company registry and statistics, tax and social security authorities. Serbia implemented a one-stop shop combining company and tax registration. Slovenia automated company registration, cutting the time by 13 days. Tajikistan made tax registration faster and now requires municipal licenses only for specific activities such as food and entertainment industries.

Four OECD high-income economies reformed. Germany created a new form of limited liability company, reducing one of the highest minimum capital requirements in Europe from €25,000 to €1. Hungary put company registration online, eliminating paper-based transactions. Korea eliminated its minimum capital requirement and dropped requirements for notarization. Luxembourg replaced a 0.5% capital duty with a fixed registration fee of €75.

In Latin America and the Caribbean 9 economies reformed, mostly

by simplifying administrative requirements. Argentina now offers expedited publication for an additional fee. As part of ongoing efforts to simplify municipal licensing across the country, Brazil no longer requires a fire brigade license and started implementing online services in a number of districts in São Paulo. Colombia established a new public-private health provider where employers and employees can be registered within a week. It also introduced online preenrollment with the social insurance system. Guyana replaced a 6% registration duty with a flat fee and accelerated tax registrations through a single tax identification number for corporate, value added and labor taxes.

Honduras accelerated its company and tax registration process. Mexico established an electronic platform for company registration, saving 2 weeks. It also dropped the requirement for companies to register with the statistical office. Peru implemented an electronic system allowing payroll books to be submitted online at no cost. St. Lucia implemented an electronic company registration system, and now name checks can be done online. St. Vincent and the Grenadines abolished the requirement for a company seal.

The Middle East and North Africa saw 9 reforms making start-up easier. Egypt and the United Arab Emirates eliminated the minimum capital requirement. Syria reduced the amount from more than 40 times income per capita to about 10 times—still the highest in the world. It also put registration forms online. But higher publication and incorporation fees almost doubled the total cost. The Islamic Republic of Iran streamlined and computerized internal procedures at the company registry, reducing the time by nearly 3 weeks.

Jordan replaced multiple counters at the one-stop shop with a single one for document filings. Lebanon abolished the requirement to have company books stamped at the commercial registry but reversed earlier reforms combining tax and company registration. Oman simplified name verification and fee payment

TABLE 2.2

Simplifying registration formalities—the most popular reform feature in 2008/09

Simplified other registration formalities (seal, publication, notarization, inspection, other requirements)	Albania, Argentina, Armenia, Belarus, Botswana, Bulgaria, Burkina Faso, Ethiopia, Ghana, Guinea-Bissau, Guyana, Honduras, Hong Kong (China), Indonesia, Islamic Republic of Iran, Jordan, Kazakhstan, Republic of Korea, Kyrgyz Republic, Madagascar, Moldova, Pakistan, Samoa, Slovenia, Taiwan (China), Thailand, Republic of Yemen
Cut or simplified postregistration procedures (tax registration, social security registration, licensing)	Albania, Argentina, Belarus, Botswana, Brazil, Cameroon, Colombia, Indonesia, Islamic Republic of Iran, Kazakhstan, Lebanon, Liberia, Mali, Montenegro, Niger, Samoa, Slovenia, St. Vincent and the Grenadines
Abolished or reduced minimum capital requirement	Albania, Armenia, Belarus, Bulgaria, Arab Republic of Egypt, Germany, Kyrgyz Republic, Madagascar, Mozambique, Poland, Samoa, Syrian Arab Republic, Taiwan (China), Tajikistan, United Arab Emirates
Introduced or improved online procedures	Bangladesh, Cape Verde, Hungary, Indonesia, Luxembourg, Mexico, Oman, Pakistan, Peru, Rwanda, Singapore, St. Lucia, Syrian Arab Republic
Created or improved one-stop shop	Afghanistan, Central African Republic, FYR Macedonia, Madagascar, Malaysia, Mali, Rwanda, Saudi Arabia, Serbia, Sierra Leone, Togo

Source: Doing Business database.

TABLE 2.3
Who makes business start-up easy—and who does not?

Procedures (number)

Fewest		Most	
Canada	1	Bolivia	15
New Zealand	1	Greece	15
Australia	2	Philippines	15
Madagascar	2	Brazil	16
Rwanda	2	Guinea-Bissau	16
Belgium	3	Venezuela, R.B.	16
Finland	3	Brunei Darussalam	18
Hong Kong, China	3	Uganda	18
Kyrgyz Republic	3	Chad	19
Singapore	3	Equatorial Guinea	20

Time (days)

Fastest		Slowest	
New Zealand	1	Lao PDR	100
Australia	2	Brunei Darussalam	116
Georgia	3	Brazil	120
Rwanda	3	Equatorial Guinea	136
Singapore	3	Venezuela, R.B.	141
Belgium	4	São Tomé and Principe	144
Hungary	4	Congo, Dem. Rep.	149
Macedonia, FYR	4	Haiti	195
Albania	5	Guinea-Bissau	213
Canada	5	Suriname	694

Cost (% of income per capita)

Least		Most	
Denmark	0.0	Chad	176.7
Slovenia	0.0	Comoros	182.1
Ireland	0.3	Djibouti	195.4
New Zealand	0.4	Togo	205.0
Canada	0.4	Gambia, The	215.1
Bahrain	0.5	Haiti	227.9
Sweden	0.6	Central African Republic	244.9
United States	0.7	Guinea-Bissau	323.0
Puerto Rico	0.7	Congo, Dem. Rep.	391.0
United Kingdom	0.7	Zimbabwe	499.5

Paid-in minimum capital

Most	% of income per capita	US$
Burkina Faso	428	2,049
Mauritania	450	4,082
Guinea	490	2,164
Ethiopia	492	1,387
Djibouti	501	5,655
Central African Republic	507	1,974
Togo	514	2,075
Niger	614	2,018
Guinea-Bissau	780	1,913
Syrian Arab Republic	1,013	70,660

Note: Eighty economies have no paid-in minimum capital requirement.
Source: Doing Business database.

at the company registry. Saudi Arabia combined all registration procedures for local limited liability companies. The Republic of Yemen removed the requirement to obtain a bank account certificate for company registration. West Bank and Gaza made it more difficult to start a business by increasing the minimum capital requirement 5-fold.

In South Asia, Afghanistan established a new one-stop shop and introduced a flat registration fee. Bangladesh implemented a modern electronic company registration system, cutting the time by almost a month. In Pakistan, thanks to an e-services project and the introduction of digital signatures, new companies can register and file tax returns online.

Sub-Saharan Africa had 16 reformers (figure 2.4). Botswana simplified business licensing and tax registration as part of an ongoing computerization effort. Burkina Faso allowed online publication at the time of registration. Cameroon waived the business tax for the first 2 years of a company's operations. Cape Verde implemented an online registration system. The Central African Republic established a one-stop shop with representatives from the entities involved in business registration, merging 4 procedures into 1. Ethiopia and Ghana simplified company registration as part of ongoing administrative reforms. Ghana aims for business registration in 1 day.

Guinea-Bissau made the company name search electronic and reduced registration fees. Liberia adopted a risk-based approach by removing the need for companies engaged in general business to obtain an environmental license. Madagascar and Mozambique abolished the minimum capital requirement. Madagascar also eliminated stamp duties and further streamlined filing requirements at its one-stop shop. Mali established a one-stop shop, merging 4 procedures into 1, and introduced a flat fee for registration. Niger eliminated registrations with the National Center for Transportation Users and the cham-

FIGURE 2.4
African countries made starting a business easier
Number of reforms in 2008/09

Sub-Saharan Africa (16)	Eastern Europe & Central Asia (13)	Latin America & Caribbean (9)	Middle East & North Africa (9)	East Asia & Pacific (7)	OECD high income (4)	South Asia (3)
Botswana						
Burkina Faso						
Cameroon						
Cape Verde	Albania					
Central African Republic	Armenia					
Ethiopia	Belarus	Argentina	Egypt, Arab Rep.			
Ghana	Bulgaria	Brazil	Iran, Islamic Rep.			
Guinea-Bissau	Kazakhstan	Colombia	Jordan	Hong Kong, China		
Liberia	Kyrgyz Republic	Guyana	Lebanon	Indonesia		
Madagascar	Macedonia, FYR	Honduras	Oman	Malaysia	Germany	
Mali	Moldova	Mexico	Saudi Arabia	Samoa	Hungary	
Mozambique	Montenegro	Peru	Syrian Arab Republic	Singapore	Korea, Rep.	Afghanistan
Niger	Poland	St. Lucia	United Arab Emirates	Taiwan, China	Luxembourg	Bangladesh
Rwanda	Serbia	St. Vincent and the Grenadines	Yemen, Rep.	Thailand		Pakistan
Sierra Leone	Slovenia					
Togo	Tajikistan					

Source: Doing Business database.

ber of commerce. Rwanda consolidated its name checking, payment, tax registration and company registration into a single procedure. It also made notarization optional. Sierra Leone's one-stop shop became operational. So did Togo's, eliminating 6 procedures.

TOWARD SMART REGULATION

Making business start-up easier has been the most popular of the *Doing Business* reforms since 2003. Starting a business need not be complicated. Two procedures—notification of a company's existence and tax registration—suffice. More economies are finding creative ways to ensure that good rules are implemented in the most efficient way, often learning from one another. Delegations from Botswana, China and Malaysia have visited New Zealand. Reformers in Central America have looked to Colombia and Panama for inspiration. Egypt took Ireland's registration system as a model.

Several reform features have emerged as the most popular and effective. Successful reformers often began by reviewing the need for existing requirements.

GETTING UP TO DATE

Creating or improving a one-stop shop has been the most popular reform feature since 2004. But combining or expediting procedures that are antiquated or do not fulfill their intended purpose makes little sense. One example is the company seal, still required in 70 economies. Developed in the Middle Ages, the seal is intended to avoid fraudulent use of company documents. But it can easily be forged. Most modern economies have abolished the requirement for a seal. Many allow electronic signatures instead.

Another outdated requirement is publication in legal journals of a notice of company establishment. Such notices can more easily be published electronically, as in Germany, FYR Macedonia and Mozambique, or at the registry, as in Burkina Faso.

CUTTING MINIMUM CAPITAL

Minimum capital requirements can be a big obstacle for entrepreneurs. They are often justified as a way to protect investors or prevent unscrupulous entrepreneurs from registering. But this makes little sense in practice. Fixed amounts of capital do not take into account dif-

ferences in commercial risks. And the capital is often withdrawn immediately after registration—hardly of value in insolvency. Better securities laws and more efficient courts might offer more protection for investors.

Thirty-five economies have reduced or eliminated their minimum capital requirement since 2004. Many of these reformers are in the Middle East and North Africa. Just 5 years ago, 5 of the region's reformers were among the 10 economies with the highest minimum capital requirements in the world. Many of the other reformers are in Eastern Europe and Central Asia.

High minimum capital requirements can discourage companies from registering. In Egypt in 2006, limited liability companies accounted for only 19% of registered firms. In 2008, after reforms, this share rose to 30%. Yet in many low- and lower-middle-income economies requirements remain high, up to 10 times income per capita. Among the 10 economies with the highest requirements today, 9 are in Sub-Saharan Africa.

Where formalities remain ingrained in old company laws, reform can take time and political coordination. Some

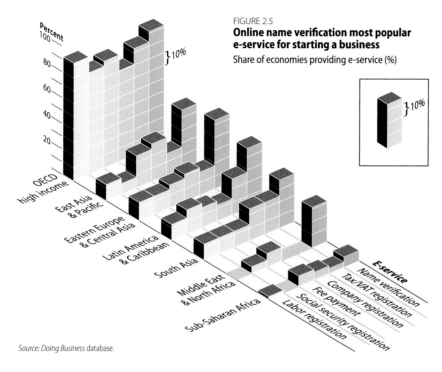

FIGURE 2.5
Online name verification most popular e-service for starting a business

Share of economies providing e-service (%)

Source: Doing Business database.

reformers found it easier to introduce a new company type. That is what Germany did. The update was needed. Within the European Union companies can register anywhere, regardless of where their main operations are. Before Germany's reform, several thousand of its companies chose to register in the United Kingdom, attracted by their cheaper and simpler start-up processes. In 2006 Japan created the *godo kaisha*, similar to the U.S. limited liability company and with no minimum capital requirement.

MAKING REGISTRATION ADMINISTRATIVE

Company registration is an administrative process. Yet in 17 economies courts are involved. This takes time and expertise away from resolving commercial disputes. In a few economies even higher-level approval is needed—in Suriname, the president's; in Equatorial Guinea, the prime minister's. As a result, the start-up process takes several months.

Most economies in Eastern Europe and Central Asia have moved registration out of court, including Serbia, the Slovak Republic and, most recently, Bulgaria. Before reform in 2002 Serbian judges spent almost 10% of their time on company registration. Reform freed up much-needed resources. Montenegro kept registration in the court, but made registrars and administrative officers responsible. In Latin America, Chile, Honduras and Nicaragua have already moved registration out of the court.

STANDARDIZING DOCUMENTS

A more efficient way to ensure that incorporation documents are legitimate is to standardize them. The United Kingdom did so in 1856. Standardizing incorporation documents can especially benefit small businesses, because it frees them from the need to consult a lawyer. And simpler documents mean fewer errors and omissions—saving hassle for registries and entrepreneurs alike. In Mauritius, which offers standard documents, the rejection rate is only about 8%. Applications can be processed in hours.

CENTRALIZING REGISTRATIONS

Legally, a company is formed once incorporated. In most economies the process ends with company registration. But entrepreneurs usually must also complete other procedures, involving multiple agencies. Centralizing registra-

tions can help. Such reforms often go hand-in-hand with introducing a unified registration form or single company identification (ID) number. Malaysia was the first to introduce a single company ID number for all government interactions, in 2001. Singapore just did so. India launched a single tax ID number, inspired by its success in using ID numbers for voters.

Since 2004, 44 economies have centralized registrations. In Ethiopia the company registry automatically forwards information to the license authority. In Zambia the one-stop shop has separate desks for representatives from different agencies. In Denmark, New Zealand and Norway entrepreneurs use a single electronic interface.

Physical one-stop shops can be implemented quickly and at relatively low cost—ranging from $200,000 in Burkina Faso to $5 million in Azerbaijan. The reform in Azerbaijan took less than a year—and is saving businesses an estimated $8.4 million annually. In Belarus the streamlining of registration is expected to yield cost savings for businesses of $21.5 million a year; in Burkina Faso, $1.7 million.

MAKING SERVICES ELECTRONIC

In 2006 Tonga's company registry burned down. Lesson learned: the registry computerized its records. Making registration records electronic not only improves safety but also aids transparency and information sharing. And it makes it easier to introduce new online services. Online name verification is now common not only among OECD high-income economies but also increasingly so in Eastern Europe and Central Asia and Latin America and the Caribbean (figure 2.5). Better service attracts more customers. In Bangladesh the online registration system increased name clearances by 80% and registrations by 90%.

As a last step, registration itself is made electronic. Around 40 economies offer electronic registration services. Implementation varies. In India, Norway and Singapore registration is fully electronic. In Sweden applications for company, tax and labor registrations can be made online, but most forms must still be printed and signed by hand. In Belgium and Hungary electronic registration is possible only through a notary or lawyer.

Electronic systems in many economies have reduced administrative costs. Malaysia's company registry invested $12.7 million in a sophisticated registration system over 5 years. The investment was fully covered by fees generated by the registry. In the 3 years after the reform, the number of registered businesses increased by 19%—and the compliance rate for filing annual tax returns rose from 28% to 91%. In the 6 weeks after Slovenia introduced its e-Vem automated system, 5,439 applications were recorded online. Moreover, the new system reduced administrative costs by 71.3%, saving €10.2 million a year.

Some reformers offer incentives to use e-systems. Malaysia and Pakistan offer electronic services free or at a lower cost. Croatia set a 24-hour deadline for responding to online applications, compared with 14 days for paper-based applications. Estonia requires no notarization for documents filed electronically.

New Zealand has one of the most innovative systems to ensure timeliness: any application not processed within a set time (10 minutes for a name application, for example) triggers an alarm for the team leader or senior manager. No wonder New Zealand ranks number 1 on the ease of starting a business.

1. Narayan and others (2000).
2. Suruhanjaya Syarikat Malaysia (Companies Commission of Malaysia), press release, March 31, 2009. Malaysia reduced company registration fees as part of the government's economic stimulus package, with the expected benefit being the registration of 320,000 new businesses in 2009.
3. National Small Business Association (http://www.nsba.biz).
4. World Bank Enterprise Surveys (http://www.enterprisesurveys.org).
5. For an overview and summary of the literature, see Djankov (2008).
6. Klapper, Lewin and Quesada Delgado (2009). *Entry rate* refers to newly registered firms as a percentage of total registered firms. *Business density* is defined as the number of businesses as a percentage of the working-age population (ages 18–65).
7. Eifert (2008).
8. Ardagna and Lusagi (2009).

Overview

Starting a business

Dealing with construction permits

Employing workers

Registering property

Getting credit

Protecting investors

Paying taxes

Trading across borders

Enforcing contracts

Closing a business

FIGURE 3.1

Top 10 reformers in dealing with construction permits

Average improvement (%)

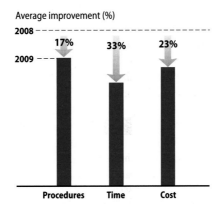

Rankings on the ease of construction permits		DB2010	DB2009
1.	**United Kingdom**	16	61
2.	**Liberia**	135	180
3.	**Burkina Faso**	80	122
4.	**Kazakhstan**	143	178
5.	**Croatia**	144	172
6.	**United Arab Emirates**	27	54
7.	**Iran, Islamic Rep.**	141	163
8.	**Hong Kong, China**	1	20
9.	**Belarus**	44	63
10.	**Kyrgyz Republic**	40	59

Source: Doing Business database.

For the construction business, 2008 was a difficult year. Demand for new projects fell as project finance and bank mortgage lending became scarce. All this put the brakes on construction projects around the world. Cities once humming with construction activity fell silent as small companies shut down and large ones downsized operations.

The construction industry accounts for 5–7% of GDP in most economies and for almost a third of gross capital formation globally.[1] This could in part explain why governments are eager to boost spending in the construction sector during economic crises. But resources spent for crisis mitigation may not be efficiently allocated when much of the industry operates informally.

TABLE 3.1

Where is dealing with construction permits easy—and where not?

Easiest	RANK	Most difficult	RANK
Hong Kong, China	1	Serbia	174
Singapore	2	India	175
St. Vincent and the Grenadines	3	Kosovo	176
		Tajikistan	177
Belize	4	Tanzania	178
Marshall Islands	5	Zimbabwe	179
New Zealand	6	China	180
Georgia	7	Ukraine	181
St. Kitts and Nevis	8	Russian Federation	182
Maldives	9	Eritrea[a]	183
Denmark	10		

Note: Rankings are the average of the economy's rankings on the procedures, time and cost to comply with formalities to build a warehouse. See Data notes for details.
a. No practice.
Source: Doing Business database.

Building authorities from Lisbon to Guatemala City saw fewer businesses apply for construction permits between the second half of 2008 and the first quarter of 2009. In some cases the slowdown turned out to be a blessing in disguise. With less demand for permits, building authorities could focus resources on completing reform programs launched in previous years. Less demand for permits meant more time for training staff and testing new systems. In Hong Kong (China) the Building Department put the final touches on its full-service one-stop center, the culmination of a 2-year reform program. The result? Hong Kong (China) now tops the rankings on the ease of dealing with construction permits (table 3.1).

Doing Business measures the procedures, time and cost for a small to medium-size enterprise to obtain all the necessary approvals to build a commercial structure and connect it to electricity, water, sewerage and telecommunications services (figure 3.2).

By some estimates about 60–80% of construction projects in developing economies are undertaken without a building permit because the approval process is too complex or oversight too lax.[2] World Bank Enterprise Surveys found that companies face more issues related to corruption in countries where it is more difficult to deal with construction permits (figure 3.3). In a recent survey of 218 companies in 19 Asia-Pacific

Economic Cooperation member economies, respondents identified the time and procedures for dealing with construction permits as the biggest "regulatory impediment" to doing business.[3]

Reforms that make regulation of construction more efficient and transparent can help reduce corruption and informality in the sector. By encouraging construction companies to go through formal channels, governments can reap the returns on investments made in reforming the sector. Good regulations ensure safety standards that protect the public while making the permitting process efficient, transparent and affordable for both building authorities and the private professionals who use it.

The ultimate beneficiaries of reforms in construction permitting are the

FIGURE 3.2

Dealing with construction permits: building a warehouse

Rankings are based on 3 subindicators

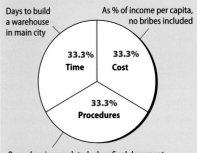

Procedure is completed when final document is received; construction permits, inspections and utility connections included

Note: See Data notes for details.

FIGURE 3.3
Difficulty in dealing with construction permits is associated with corruption

Share of firms that expect to give gifts
in exchange for construction permits (%)

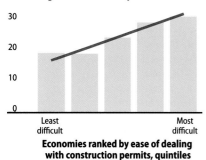

Economies ranked by ease of dealing
with construction permits, quintiles

Note: Relationships are significant at the 1% level and remain significant when controlling for income per capita.
Source: Doing Business database; World Bank Enterprise Survey database.

same businesses hit hard by the recent crisis. "Financing construction projects has become harder and we're under pressure to meet project deadlines. It helps to have a more efficient building authority to work with," says a builder in Dubai. This positive outlook is due in no small part to reforms undertaken by the Dubai Municipality to speed up the process with better electronic application and payment systems.

WHO REFORMED IN 2008/09?

Reforms to simplify construction permitting have been on the rise for the past 3 years. In 2008/09 *Doing Business* registered a record 31 reforms making it easier to deal with construction permits (table 3.2). Eleven economies, including 5 of the top 10 reformers, continued the reforms they had started the previous year.

The United Kingdom was the top reformer, the first time for an OECD high-income economy. Wider use of approved inspectors over several years has cut 8 procedures and 49 days from the process of dealing with construction approvals. Approved inspectors now have a 64% share of the commercial market, leaving local authorities to focus on residential projects.[4]

Liberia was the runner-up reformer, implementing a series of reforms to continue a program launched the previous

year. Before, the City Corporation of Monrovia levied a hefty fee on new construction projects—3% of the value of the proposed construction—in addition to the building permit fee charged by the Ministry of Public Works. That fee was cut to just 4 cents per square foot of construction. Tax waivers from the Ministry of Finance, once a requirement for obtaining a building permit, are no longer needed. Access to utilities also improved. Liberia Telecommunications Corporation started providing fixed telephone service for the first time since the country's conflict ended, and power generators became less expensive.

Among regions, Eastern Europe and Central Asia had the most reforms for the third year running. Reforms were recorded in Belarus, Bosnia and Herzegovina, Croatia, Georgia, Kazakhstan, the Kyrgyz Republic, FYR Macedonia, Montenegro, Slovenia, Tajikistan and Uzbekistan. The reforms cut procedures by 7%, time by 15% and cost by 26.5% on average.

Kazakhstan reduced the cost to connect new buildings to utilities. Before, builders in Almaty paid the equivalent of $65,452—almost 13 times income per capita—to connect to electricity. This unusually high fee—the second highest

in the world—was considered a contribution to the development of Almaty's infrastructure. Amendments to the electricity law eliminated the fee altogether. Neighboring Uzbekistan, in an attempt to mitigate the effects of the crisis, reduced the fees for building permit approval procedures by 25%.

Other reformers in the region continued efforts to streamline procedures and introduce more sophisticated permitting processes. The Kyrgyz Republic and Montenegro both introduced risk-based approvals for construction permits. Simpler construction projects now undergo a less cumbersome approval process, and building authorities can focus more on reviewing projects with potential environmental or public safety impacts. Meanwhile, Belarus, Bosnia and Herzegovina, Croatia, Georgia, FYR Macedonia and Slovenia all continued to improve the efficiency of the permitting process by streamlining procedures and cutting approval times.

The Middle East and North Africa saw its first big surge in reforms, with 7 economies making it easier to deal with construction permits—Algeria, Bahrain, Egypt, the Islamic Republic of Iran, Jordan, Saudi Arabia and the United Arab Emirates.

TABLE 3.2
Faster processing for permit applications—the most popular reform feature in 2008/09

Reduced time for processing permit applications	Belarus, Bosnia and Herzegovina, Colombia, Czech Republic, Georgia, Guatemala, Honduras, Hong Kong (China), Islamic Republic of Iran, Kazakhstan, Kyrgyz Republic, Liberia, FYR Macedonia, Mali, Montenegro, Panama, Portugal, Saudi Arabia, Slovenia, Tajikistan, United Arab Emirates
Reduced fees	Burkina Faso, Arab Republic of Egypt, Islamic Republic of Iran, Kazakhstan, Kyrgyz Republic, Liberia, Montenegro, Slovenia, Uzbekistan
Introduced or improved one-stop shop	Bahrain, Burkina Faso, Croatia, Arab Republic of Egypt, Hong Kong (China), Jordan, Kyrgyz Republic, Saudi Arabia, United Arab Emirates
Introduced risk-based approvals	Colombia, Georgia, Guatemala, Kyrgyz Republic, Montenegro, Portugal, Singapore, United Kingdom
Adopted new building regulations	Algeria, Arab Republic of Egypt, Guatemala, Montenegro, Netherlands
Improved electronic platforms or online services	Bahrain, Colombia, Islamic Republic of Iran, Saudi Arabia, United Arab Emirates
Improved building control process	Georgia, Kyrgyz Republic, United Kingdom

Source: Doing Business database.

Algeria and Egypt both introduced more comprehensive building codes. The new law in Algeria addresses illegal construction in Algiers and strengthens enforcement mechanisms. In the first few months after the new law entered into force in July 2008, the Algerian authorities recorded 12,607 infractions related to unlawful construction.[5] The new building code introduced in Egypt also took effect. The new regulations eliminated 3 preapproval procedures and reduced the time to obtain a building permit by almost 1 month.

Jordan and Saudi Arabia both centralized approvals in one-stop shops. The one-stop shop at the Greater Amman Municipality began accepting building permit applications for mid size and smaller commercial construction projects. The one-stop shop cut 3 procedures and 20 days. Plans are under way to introduce more one-stop shops in other districts of Amman. The Riyadh Municipality made it easier for builders by merging the location permit with the building permit process. Applicants wanting to build simple structures such as residential villas, workshops or warehouses can obtain a building permit from the Riyadh Municipality in 1 day. Building authorities allow them to begin building immediately and issue a final building permit within a week.

Bahrain, the Islamic Republic of Iran and the United Arab Emirates turned to electronic services to reduce processing times and streamline the approval process. Bahrain incorporated the preliminary approval from the electricity authority into the one-stop shop, eliminating 1 procedure. Bahrain also made it faster to obtain building permits. Rather than having to fill out 9 different forms and provide 15 pieces of supporting documentation, applicants complete a single application form online and upload all their documents and plans through a completely digitized process.

In Tehran builders no longer have to visit multiple government offices to seek approvals or follow up on applications. They can obtain location approvals,

building permits and building completion certificates through any of the 70 e-service offices throughout the city. The e-service offices accept applications and payments and track documents sent to the municipality to ensure timely processing. As a result, the time to obtain a construction permit in Tehran fell from 90 days to 30.

The United Arab Emirates also invested in e-services. Builders in Dubai can now apply for "no objection" certificates, building permits and completion certificates online. The continual

streamlining has cut 4 procedures and 33 days from the process of dealing with construction-related approvals.

In Latin America and the Caribbean 4 economies introduced major reforms: Colombia, Guatemala and Honduras—which have been reforming consistently for several years—as well as Panama. In 2008/09 all 4 reformers focused on speeding up the delivery of construction approvals by introducing risk-based approval processes. On average, they trimmed 35 days from the time required to deal with construction permits.

TABLE 3.3

Who makes dealing with construction permits easy—and who does not?

Procedures (number)

Fewest		Most	
Denmark	6	Azerbaijan	31
Hong Kong, China	7	Brunei Darussalam	32
New Zealand	7	Guinea	32
Vanuatu	7	Tajikistan	32
Sweden	8	El Salvador	34
Chad	9	Czech Republic	36
Maldives	9	China	37
St. Lucia	9	India	37
Georgia	10	Kazakhstan	37
Grenada	10	Russian Federation	54

Time (days)

Fastest		Slowest	
Singapore	25	Cameroon	426
Korea, Rep.	34	Suriname	431
Finland	38	Ukraine	476
United States	40	Lesotho	601
Bahrain	43	Côte d'Ivoire	629
Colombia	51	Cyprus	677
Vanuatu	51	Russian Federation	704
Marshall Islands	55	Cambodia	709
Solomon Islands	62	Haiti	1,179
United Arab Emirates	64	Zimbabwe	1,426

Cost (% of income per capita)

Least		Most	
Qatar	0.6	Serbia	1,907
Trinidad and Tobago	4.6	Guinea-Bissau	2,020
St. Kitts and Nevis	4.8	Russian Federation	2,141
Brunei Darussalam	4.9	Niger	2,355
Palau	5.4	India	2,395
St. Vincent and the Grenadines	6.9	Tanzania	3,281
Malaysia	7.1	Burundi	7,968
Hungary	9.8	Afghanistan	12,878
Dominica	11.3	Zimbabwe	24,468
Thailand	12.1	Liberia	28,296

Source: Doing Business database.

Colombia's new risk-based system shortened the approval time for building permits for buildings between 500 and 2,000 square meters to 25 calendar days. In Guatemala City a new land management plan introduced simpler approval processes for some categories of buildings, reducing the total time to deal with construction permits by 37 days. In Honduras further digitization of zoning maps and the introduction of risk-based mechanisms in the zoning regulations cut the time to obtain a location permit from 2 weeks to just 2 days. Stricter adherence to statutory time limits for approvals of environmental, design and construction permits cut 19 more days from the time required for complying with construction-related formalities. Panama made registration of newly completed buildings easier, saving builders 2 weeks.

Two economies in East Asia and the Pacific introduced significant reforms. Hong Kong (China) completed its "Be the Smart Regulator" reform program. A new one-stop center merged 8 procedures involving 6 local departments and 2 private utility companies, saving 52 days. Singapore introduced new workplace safety and health regulations that allow low-risk industries to submit documents online. Dealing with construction permits now takes less time in Singapore than in any other economy.

Besides the United Kingdom, 3 other OECD high-income economies simplified construction permitting. Portugal introduced a risk-based fire safety approval process, cutting 2 procedures and 41 days. The Netherlands passed a new spatial planning law—the first major overhaul of its planning regulation since 1965. The Czech Republic cut the time to register new buildings from 60 days to 30.

In Sub-Saharan Africa 2 economies besides Liberia reformed in 2008/09. Burkina Faso implemented a one-stop shop, reducing the time to obtain a construction permit by 2 months. Permit fees were reduced by more than half. Efforts by the National Water and Sanitation Office in Ouagadougou cut the time

to obtain a new water connection by 35 days. Mali also improved access to utilities. Obtaining a new water connection now takes 1 month less than before.

Six economies made it more difficult to deal with construction permits in 2008/09. Kenya made it obligatory for certain projects, such as warehouses, to obtain an environmental clearance from the National Environment Management Authority and increased the fees to obtain a building permit by almost 4 times. These changes overshadowed the improvements made by the Rapid Results Initiative reform program, which reduced the time to obtain building permits by 20 days. Following the security threats in 2008 in Colombo, Sri Lanka now requires clearance from the Defense Ministry for all new buildings erected within the city limits. Tanzania made it mandatory for new projects to obtain a geological survey before construction. While the procedure was intended to enhance building safety, there are too few inspectors to match the demand. As a result, dealing with construction permits takes 20 days longer on average. New Zealand, Romania and the Solomon Islands all increased the fees for construction-related approvals.

TOWARD SMART REGULATION

Construction regulation should provide incentives for compliance, even when times are hard. Good regulation ensures that safety standards are met while encouraging businesses to operate formally. Honduras is one example. In 2007 the municipality of Tegucigalpa streamlined the process for obtaining a building permit. The next year the revenue from construction permits was up by 167% and the area approved for construction by 72%. Impressive results, especially since the growth rate for construction in Honduras was only 3.5% at the time.[6]

Builders are more likely to comply with regulations when time limits are respected, clear guidelines exist and authorities are held accountable. When regulation is predictable, companies spend

fewer resources on chasing applications and paying bribes and more on meeting project deadlines and obtaining financing. In Mumbai construction companies regularly employ a design architect to work on the building plans and drawings and either a "consultancy architect" or facilitator whose sole purpose is to keep up with the bureaucracy. This practice is hardly surprising in a city where dealing with construction-related formalities takes 37 procedures and 195 days and costs 2,395% of income per capita.

In the past 5 years *Doing Business* has recorded 91 reforms in 62 economies aimed at making construction permitting more efficient and easier to comply with. Governments that regulate construction efficiently often take a systematic approach in their reforms. They identify areas of overlap among agencies, consult widely with stakeholders, opt for risk-based approval systems and introduce internal monitoring systems in their agencies.

IDENTIFYING AREAS OF OVERLAP AMONG AGENCIES

Dealing with construction permits involves multiple agencies and levels of approval—more than in any other area of regulation studied by *Doing Business*. To obtain all construction-related approvals and connect to utilities, builders around the world deal with 9 different agencies on average. Understanding how these agencies interact with one another and identifying areas of overlap is often the first step toward speeding up approvals while maintaining quality control.

In the Kyrgyz Republic, for example, the Union of Builders in 2007 mapped the approval processes of relevant agencies, identified bottlenecks and proposed pragmatic solutions. Its detailed analysis helped persuade the central government to reform in 2008 even in the face of strong opposition from powerful players such as the Bishkek mayor's office. In Hong Kong (China) 29 government agencies worked with focus groups to develop a comprehensive scheme identifying which procedures could be merged. The

FIGURE 3.4

The "Be the Smart Regulator" program speeds up permitting in Hong Kong, China

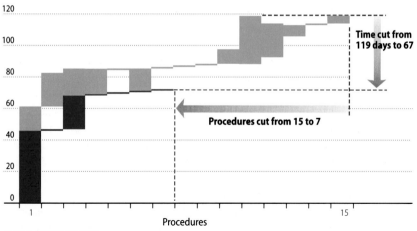

Source: *Doing Business* database.

authorities now conduct joint inspections once construction is completed. Before, the Building Department and Fire Services Department conducted separate checks. Through this exercise Hong Kong (China) managed to cut the number of procedures from 15 to 7—one of the most successful reforms in construction permitting (figure 3.4).

COMMUNICATING WITH STAKEHOLDERS

Successful reformers involve all relevant actors from the beginning. In Colombia, for example, the central government, the municipality of Bogotá and the private urban curators in charge of issuing the construction permits all needed to be on board before a new risk-based approval scheme could be approved in May 2009. Once the new system is implemented, all parties—from the implementing officials to the users of the system—have to be kept informed of changes or improvements. Building authorities in Liberia, Rwanda, Saudi Arabia and Sierra Leone publicized reforms through large-scale campaigns in the press and on their websites. Building authorities in Singapore and the United Kingdom organize periodic consultations with private professionals. "We treat them like equals, and rely a great deal on their professionalism," says an official from Singapore's Building and Construction Authority.

PILOTING REFORMS

Governments that make construction permitting easy are increasingly adopting risk-based approval mechanisms. Many start by piloting reforms to assess their effectiveness before full-scale implementation.

Some economies pilot reforms in specific zones to isolate any potential damage. Building authorities in Bosnia and Herzegovina and Honduras tested the functionality of new regulations by implementing them initially in a few districts. Egypt began piloting one-stop shops in 3 districts of Cairo in 2007. The early trial of the one-stop shops helped pave the way for the new building code passed the following year and the streamlining of procedures in 2009.

Germany and Portugal piloted new building approval processes by focusing only on certain types of projects. In Jordan the Greater Amman Municipality began by processing larger, more complex applications, reasoning that larger companies that had suffered the most from burdensome regulations could provide the best input for improving the system. Conversely, Saudi Arabia adopted the 1-day permitting procedure first for low-risk residential villas before extending the system to riskier projects such as warehouses and workshops.

USING INTERNAL MONITORING TO MATCH DEMAND

Implementing reforms requires flexibility and continual monitoring of new systems. Authorities in Jakarta have an internal real-time system for monitoring every step of the building permit approval process—from the moment the application is submitted to the time the permit is issued. The system includes the prescribed time limits for each internal procedure and notifies administrators of delays. So, for example, if the officer in charge of verifying the zoning takes more than the 5 days stipulated, the system will warn the supervisor about the delay. When this happens, the officer in charge must enter an explanation into the system.

Monitoring the entire process allows building authorities to identify bottlenecks, ensure better quality and allocate resources more efficiently. In Bahrain the municipal one-stop shop's technical support team prepares daily monitoring reports and posts them on the internal server for review by top management. If a permit is delayed because there are too few structural engineers, for example, managers can assign more to the task. Diligent monitoring of reforms gives policy makers the information they need to match their capacity to the demands of applicants. And it insures that their reform efforts continue to have impact for years to come.

1. Kenny (2007).
2. Moullier (2009).
3. Singapore Business Federation (2009).
4. Building Control Alliance (2008).
5. Idir (2008).
6. World Bank, World Development Indicators database.

Employing workers

FIGURE 4.1
Low-income economies have less flexible labor regulations

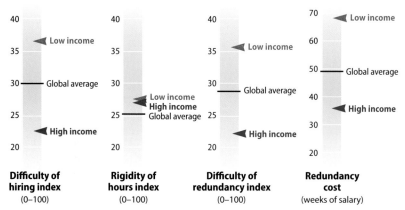

Note: Higher values indicate more rigid regulation.
Source: Doing Business database.

In Britain during the Industrial Revolution, two-thirds of those working in the newly powered textile factories were children. Working conditions were often perilous. Large steam engines made the heat almost unbearable. Machines were tightly packed, and their moving parts often exposed. Passing between them was difficult—the reason children were preferred. It was also dangerous.

These conditions gave rise to the Health and Morals of Apprentices Act of 1802, a first attempt to prevent such abuse and the first law regulating labor relations in Britain. Its regulations included this: "The master and mistress of the factory must observe the law... every apprentice is to be supplied with two complete suits of clothing with suitable linen, stockings, hats and shoes...

male and female apprentices are to be provided with separate sleeping apartments, and not more than two to sleep in one bed." A series of labor regulation acts followed.

Employment laws are needed to protect workers from arbitrary or unfair treatment and to ensure efficient contracting between employers and workers. *Doing Business*, in its indicators on employing workers, measures flexibility in the regulation of hiring, working hours and redundancy in a manner consistent with the conventions of the International Labour Organization (ILO). An economy can have the most flexible labor regulations as measured by *Doing Business* while ratifying and complying with all conventions directly relevant to the areas that *Doing Business* measures.

The ILO core labor standards—covering the right to collective bargaining, the elimination of forced labor, the abolition of child labor and equitable treatment in employment practices—are fundamental principles. The *Doing Business* employing workers indicators are fully consistent with the core labor standards but do not measure compliance with them. To complement these indicators, *Doing Business* has launched research on the adoption of core labor standards in national legislation as the basis for a future indicator on worker protection. Preliminary results on the implementation of minimum working age provisions are presented for a sample

of 102 countries (see annex on worker protection).

Governments all over the world face the challenge of finding the right balance between worker protection and labor market flexibility. The ILO, European Union and Organisation for Economic Co-operation and Development (OECD) have embraced the concept of "flexicurity," combining flexible regulation, safety nets (such as unemployment insurance) and active social policies. With the global financial and economic crisis, unemployment has risen sharply around the world. This makes the need for governments to adopt policies that stimulate job creation even more pressing. At the same time, adequate safety nets have to be in place to protect workers from sudden job loss, help them transition between jobs and

TABLE 4.1
Where is it easy to employ workers—and where not?

Easiest	RANK	Most difficult	RANK
Australia	1	Congo, Dem. Rep.	174
United States	2	Guinea-Bissau	175
Singapore	3	Morocco	176
Brunei Darussalam	4	Panama	177
Marshall Islands	5	Angola	178
Hong Kong, China	6	Paraguay	179
Uganda	7	São Tomé and Principe	180
Palau	8		
Denmark	9	Venezuela, R.B.	181
Georgia	10	Equatorial Guinea	182
		Bolivia	183

Note: Rankings are the average of the economy's rankings on the difficulty of hiring, rigidity of hours, difficulty of redundancy and redundancy cost indices. See Data notes for details.
Source: Doing Business database.

FIGURE 4.2
Employing workers: rules on hiring, work schedules and redundancy
Rankings are based on 4 subindicators

Note: See Data notes for details.

FIGURE 4.3

Rigid labor regulations are associated with a larger informal sector

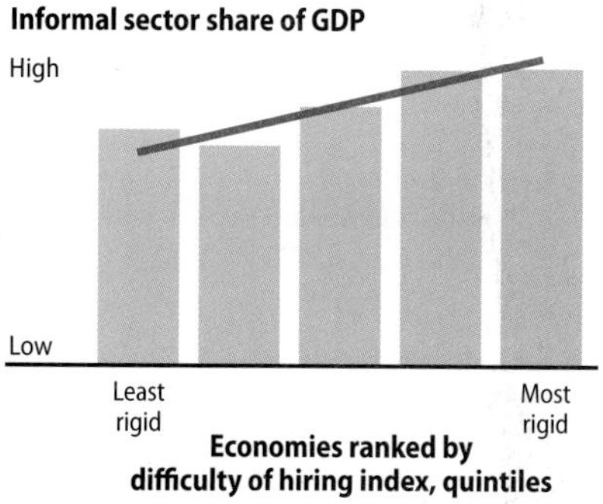

Informal sector share of GDP

Note: Relationships are significant at the 5% level and remain significant when controlling for income per capita.
Source: Doing Business database; Schneider (2007).

prevent more people from slipping into poverty. Both are critical for an economy's competitiveness.

In response to the crisis, many economies reformed unemployment protection schemes in recent months by expanding benefits or lowering eligibility thresholds. Brazil, Canada and the United States extended the period over which unemployment benefits are paid. Italy expanded coverage to those who previously did not qualify. Korea provided aid to vulnerable workers put on temporary unpaid leave. Chile, China, Germany, Japan, Mexico, the Philippines, Thailand and Vietnam similarly extended unemployment benefits.

In economies that cannot afford expensive social security systems, severance pay can serve as a substitute for unemployment benefits. This year *Doing Business* has introduced changes to the employing workers indicators to take account of the existence of safety nets—whether in the form of unemployment benefits or severance pay—for both permanent and temporary workers in cases of redundancy for economic reasons (see Data notes for details).

In many developing economies employers and employees continue to face overly rigid regulations. Faced with excessive restrictions, many firms simply choose to opt out of the regulated formal sector and operate or hire workers in the informal sector (figure 4.3). There, with less access to formal finance, institutions

and markets, firms tend to stay small and create fewer jobs.[1] Workers in the informal sector receive no benefits or social security, lack formal protection from arbitrary or discriminatory treatment and may receive lower wages.[2] According to a recent OECD study, 1.8 billion people are employed in the informal economy worldwide—far more than the 1.2 billion in the formal economy.[3]

Finding that burdensome regulation makes it difficult for workers to move between firms and industries, another study concludes that this probably leads to higher job losses due to external economic shocks.[4] Stringent employment regulation also reduces a firm's ability to respond adequately to demand or productivity shocks, according to a study of weekly labor choices in an international fast food chain covering 2,500 outlets in 43 economies.[5] And excessively rigid restrictions on hiring and redundancy tend to raise labor costs, reducing opportunities for firms to spend on innovation and adapt to new technologies.[6]

Labor reform is challenging. Most major developments in labor law have taken place in the context of big political or economic shifts. In Western economies the industrial revolutions of the 19th century brought about regulation to protect workers against abuses incidental to new forms of large-scale mining and manufacturing. Fundamental labor laws were adopted in Latin America following the Mexican Revolution ending in 1917 and in Russia following the October Revolution the same year.

In more recent times the collapse of the Soviet Union and the EU accession movement triggered a new wave of reforms. Since *Doing Business* started tracking reforms in 2004, close to two-thirds of Eastern European and Central Asian economies and half of OECD high-income economies have made labor regulation more flexible. Estonia, Hungary and Slovenia introduced new labor laws following the end of the cold war. The prospect of EU accession led several economies to introduce EU labor standards in domestic law, including Latvia,

FYR Macedonia, Poland, and the Slovak Republic.[7]

In contrast, developing economies have made few reforms in aspects of labor regulation covered by *Doing Business*. Take the 2 regions with the most rigid employment regulation: in Sub-Saharan Africa only 6 of 46 economies made labor regulations more flexible in the past 5 years (Burkina Faso, Mauritius, Mozambique, Namibia, Rwanda and Uganda); in Latin America only 3 did (Argentina, Colombia and Peru). In South Asia only Bhutan and Pakistan increased flexibility. In East Asia and the Pacific, Vietnam was the only developing economy to do so. Some of the economies with the most rigid regulation in the first place made it even more rigid—including Cape Verde, Djibouti, Fiji, The Gambia, Honduras, Maldives, Moldova, Togo and Zimbabwe.

Reform is challenging, but getting the level of employment regulation right is worth the effort. And it matters for the impact of other reforms. Following reforms to reduce barriers to entry in India, a recent study found that states with more flexible employment regulation saw a 25% larger reduction in the number of informal firms.[8] The most vulnerable groups, women and youth, could benefit the most from reforms. While employment protection laws may increase the likelihood that employed workers will stay in their job, for those without a job they reduce the chances of finding employment or reentering the labor market.[9] This particularly affects women, who tend to exit from and reenter the labor market more frequently during their career.

WHO REFORMED IN 2008/09?

Eleven economies reformed their labor laws in 2008/09 (table 4.2). Seven increased flexibility in employing workers; 4 reduced it. Eastern Europe and Central Asia had the most reforms, with 4 economies introducing more flexible regulation, followed by Sub-Saharan Africa.

Rwanda was the top reformer.

TABLE 4.2

Eliminating requirements relating to redundancy—a popular reform feature in 2008/09

Eliminated requirements relating to redundancy	Belarus, Kyrgyz Republic, FYR Macedonia, Mauritius, Montenegro, Rwanda
Made working hours more flexible	Kyrgyz Republic, FYR Macedonia, Rwanda, Peru
Eased restrictions on fixed-term contracts	FYR Macedonia, Montenegro, Rwanda
Reduced dismissal costs	Mauritius, Peru

Source: Doing Business database.

Amendments to the labor code increased flexibility in the use of fixed-term contracts by removing limits on their duration and renewal. Employers and employees now have greater flexibility in choosing the weekly rest day, and workers are entitled to statutory paid annual leave of 21 working days. When faced with the need to downsize and make one or more workers redundant for economic reasons, employers are no longer required to consult beforehand with the employees' representatives or notify the labor inspector. Instead, they inform the labor inspector in writing after the redundancy. The aim is to allow possible abuses to be detected while ensuring that employers are not deterred from hiring workers in the first place.

In Eastern Europe and Central Asia, FYR Macedonia, Montenegro, the Kyrgyz Republic and Belarus reformed. Amendments to their labor codes introduced greater flexibility in the scheduling of working hours and use of employment contracts and streamlined redundancy procedures. In FYR Macedonia fixed-term contracts may now be used for permanent tasks for up to 60 months. When arranging for night shifts, employers can choose the duration for scheduling and frequency of shift rotation. Employer and employees are free to agree on the weekly rest day and on the number of days of paid annual leave beyond the legal minimum of 20 working days. Requirements to retrain or reassign redundant workers and priority rules for reemployment no longer apply.

Montenegro also made the use of fixed-term contracts more flexible, allowing them for permanent tasks and with no limits on their cumulative dura-

tion. When having to make a worker redundant, employers are required to give notice of 15 calendar days and are no longer obliged to give prior notification to a third party.

In the Kyrgyz Republic amendments to the labor code increased flexibility in working hours and simplified procedures for redundancies for economic reasons. Employers and employees are now free to decide on the weekly rest day. Redundancy procedures for one or more workers were eased: notification requirements, priority rules and obligations to retrain or reassign redundant workers no longer apply. Belarus also simplified procedures for individual and collective redundancies.

In Sub-Saharan Africa, besides Rwanda, Mauritius reformed. Its new Employment Rights Act and Employment Relations Act entered into force, making redundancy procedures more flexible. Redundancies of one or more workers for economic reasons no longer require authorization, the notice period for redundancy is now 30 calendar days, and severance pay is mandatory only if the grounds for redundancy are found to be invalid. The new laws also increased mandatory annual leave to 22 working days.

In Latin America, Peru introduced a law easing labor regulations for small businesses. Redundancy pay was reduced to 17 weeks, and mandatory annual leave was set at 13 working days.

A few economies made employment regulation more rigid. Two raised the cost of redundancy—Honduras by 22 weeks and Luxembourg by 13 weeks. Portugal increased the notice period by 2 weeks. Maldives made hiring workers

more difficult by increasing the restrictions on the use of fixed-term contracts. It also tightened restrictions on weekly holiday work and increased mandatory annual leave.

TOWARD SMART REGULATION

Since 2004 Doing Business has recorded 88 reforms affecting the employing workers indicators. Of these, 54 made regulation more flexible, 34 more rigid. In searching for the right balance between flexibility and protection, reformers can look to the experience of economies around the world. The following measures are examples of reforms aimed at increasing flexibility without compromising protection.

ALLOWING FLEXIBLE SCHEDULING OF WORKING HOURS

Laws restricting working hours were created to protect employees. But they also limit the ability of firms to adjust for fluctuations in seasonal demand—and can take work away from willing workers. To mitigate this risk, most economies permit greater flexibility in activities in which continuous operation is economically necessary. More than half the economies in the Doing Business sample allow the averaging of hours. The Czech Republic and Finland allow the distribution of hours over 52 weeks; Angola, 6 months; and Australia, a year. Allowing pay premiums for overtime or work on the weekly rest day is another way economies deal with these needs.

PROMOTING YOUTH EMPLOYMENT

Young people are disproportionately affected by rigid employment regulation. Lack of training and experience is already an obstacle to finding a first job; burdensome regulation and high redundancy costs can further deter potential employers. One measure used to encourage the hiring of young people is to introduce apprentice wages. These allow businesses to hire first-time employees for a portion—typically 75%—of the mandatory minimum wage for a

FIGURE 4.4
Economies with unemployment protection schemes

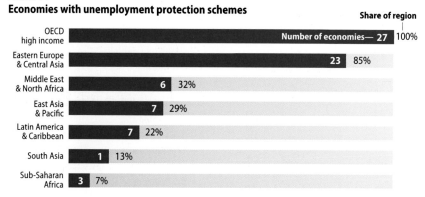

Source: Doing Business database.

FIGURE 4.5
Where is the cost of redundancy highest?
Average cost to terminate redundant workers
(weeks of salary)

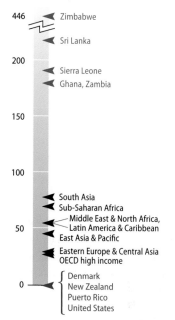

Note: Bolivia and República Bolivariana de Venezuela are excluded because redundancy for economic reasons is not possible.
Source: Doing Business database.

short period. Germany and the Netherlands have established apprentice wages through law or collective bargaining agreement. So have India and Lesotho. Such countries as Australia and Chile exempt young people and apprentices from the national minimum wage.

Apprentice contracts and trial periods are also used to promote the hiring of young people. First-time workers without experience get an opportunity to receive training while earning an income. Having invested in training these workers, employers have a greater incentive to hire them. Allowing the use of fixed-term contracts for permanent tasks can provide another point of entry and an incentive for employers to create jobs. But if strict regulations on permanent contracts are left in place, a dual system can be created, as in France and Spain, for example. This makes it difficult for fixed-term workers to transition to permanent employment. The low-skilled, the young and immigrants are the most affected. They are also the ones already bearing most of the burden of adjustment in times of crisis.[10]

SHIFTING FROM SEVERANCE PAY TO UNEMPLOYMENT INSURANCE

Italy, Norway and Singapore have no statutory minimum for severance payments and aid workers in transition between jobs with well-established unemployment assistance programs. Denmark and New Zealand combine flexible labor regulations with unemployment protection schemes.

Things can be different in developing economies. Many lack the financial resources and administrative capacity to provide comprehensive unemployment insurance (figure 4.4). Not surprisingly, mandatory severance payments remain the prevalent form of insurance against unemployment.[11] But many developing economies may err on the side of excessive rigidity. Severance pay in cases of redundancy sometimes even exceeds the typical unemployment benefits in rich economies (figure 4.5). In addition, many impose strict procedural requirements for redundancy of one or more workers for economic reasons—such as prior approval by the labor authority, as in the Republic of Congo, Gabon and Nepal.

Such requirements are created with good intentions—to protect workers from abuse or to provide a safety net in case of sudden job loss. But when it comes to making employment decisions for economic reasons, these requirements can give the authorities—not employers—the discretion. And excessive costs can deter employers from hiring workers in the first place. Reducing the complexity and costs of dismissals for economic reasons is a first step toward encouraging formal job creation.

Over time, a shift to less rigid employment regulation and greater social protection can also make sense in developing economies.[12] Evidence suggests that unemployment benefits can help reduce poverty.[13] Where social insurance mechanisms are inadequate or lacking

altogether, dismissed workers may be forced to accept the first job opportunity, even if it is not formal or productive. One study estimates that lack of access to insurance among poor rural households forces workers to engage in low-risk activities with lower returns. This reduces their potential earnings by 25% in rural Tanzania and by 50% in a sample of rural villages in India.[14]

Some low- and middle-income economies have unemployment schemes, including Algeria, Ecuador, the Kyrgyz Republic, Moldova, Thailand, Uzbekistan and Vietnam. But some of these also still maintain high redundancy costs. Employers in Ecuador face redundancy costs equal to 2.5 years of salary; in Vietnam, 1.5 years. On the other hand, Mauritius, with an unemployment protection scheme in place, has just eliminated severance pay for cases of retrenchment.

Introducing unemployment protection schemes is not straightforward. Such schemes risk prolonging unemployment if incentives for job search are distorted. One promising approach is the use of un-

TABLE 4.3

Who makes employing workers easy—and who does not?

Rigidity of employment index (0–100)			
Least		**Most**	
Australia	0	São Tomé and Principe	59
Hong Kong, China	0	Morocco	60
United States	0	Congo, Rep.	63
Singapore	0	Congo, Dem. Rep.	63
Brunei Darussalam	0	Angola	66
Marshall Islands	0	Equatorial Guinea	66
Uganda	0	Panama	66
St. Lucia	0	Niger	68
Kuwait	0	Venezuela, R.B.	69
Canada	4	Bolivia	77

Redundancy cost (weeks of salary)			
Least		**Most**	
Denmark	0	Mozambique	134
New Zealand	0	Ecuador	135
United States	0	Lao PDR	162
Puerto Rico	0	Zambia	178
Iraq	0	Ghana	178
Marshall Islands	0	Sierra Leone	189
Micronesia, Fed. Sts.	0	Sri Lanka	217
Palau	0	Zimbabwe	446
Tonga	0	Venezuela, R.B.	NOT POSSIBLE
Austria	2	Bolivia	NOT POSSIBLE

Note: Not possible indicates a full ban on dismissing low-paid workers for economic reasons. The rigidity of employment index is the average of the difficulty of hiring index, rigidity of hours index and difficulty of redundancy index. See Data notes for details.
Source: Doing Business database.

employment insurance savings accounts. Workers save a fraction of their earnings in their account and draw unemployment benefits from it. Economies such as Algeria, Belgium and Chile have developed such accounts in conjunction with a solidarity fund, to ensure increased benefits for unemployed workers.

1. For a review of research on employment regulation and effects, see Djankov and Ramalho (2009).

2. Duryea and others (2006).

3. OECD Development Centre (2009).

4. Ciccone and Papaioannou (2008).

5. Lafontaine and Sivadasan (2007).

6. Pierre and Scarpetta (2007) and Kuddo (2009).

7. Kuddo (forthcoming) and Doing Business database.

8. Sharma (2009).

9. Montenegro and Pagés (2004).

10. Pierre and Scarpetta (2007) and "When Jobs Disappear," The Economist, March 14–20, 2009, pp. 71–73.

11. Only 9 economies have neither mandatory redundancy payments nor unemployment protection: Brunei Darussalam, Iraq, Jordan, Kiribati, the Marshall Islands, the Federated States of Micronesia, Oman, Palau and Tonga.

12. Boeri, Helppie and Macis (2008).

13. Vodopivec (2009).

14. Pierre and Scarpetta (2007).

Registering property

FIGURE 5.1

Top 10 reformers in registering property

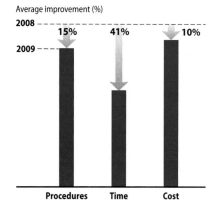

Average improvement (%)

Rankings on the ease of registering property	DB2010	DB2009
1. *Mauritius*	66	131
2. *Burkina Faso*	114	163
3. *Kyrgyz Republic*	19	52
4. *Portugal*	52	82
5. *Macedonia, FYR*	63	88
6. *Colombia*	51	78
7. *Latvia*	58	79
8. *Peru*	28	40
9. *Afghanistan*	164	176
10. *Estonia*	13	24

Source: Doing Business database.

When Abdulayeh decided to sell his business property in Ouagadougou this year, he checked the encumbrances on the property, had the sale agreement notarized, obtained a property valuation and applied for the property transfer at the newly created one-stop shop. The process took 4 steps and 59 days. Just 2 years ago it would have taken 8 steps and 182 days. Transfer taxes also fell, from 15% of the property value to 8%. The results speak for themselves: over the past 2 years the number of new title registrations in Ouagadougou boomed. And the easier it is to transfer property, the more likely the newly registered titles will stay formal.

Land is a fundamental economic asset in every society. Where property systems are poorly administered or property rights poorly defined, this can prevent land from being turned into produc-

tive capital. Hernando de Soto describes such land as "dead capital," assets whose use is limited or that cannot be used as collateral.[1] Formal titles can ease access to credit. A recent study in Peru suggests that property titles are associated with a 10% increase in approval rates on public sector loans for construction materials.[2]

Women and children can particularly benefit from easier access to land. A study in Nepal finds that women who own land are more empowered and their children are healthier.[3] But some countries, such as Cameroon, Chile and the Democratic Republic of Congo, still limit the ability of married women to buy, sell or mortgage land without the authorization of their husband.[4] In others, such as Tanzania, customary inheritance law can restrict landownership by women.[5]

Making property registration simple, fast and cheap allows entrepreneurs to focus on their business. Property owners with formal title invest up to 47% more in their property, a study in Argentina finds.[6] A study in Peru showed that property titles allowed people to work away from the home more—because they had less need to stay home keeping squatters at bay.[7] Another recent study looked at the impact of a program issuing nearly 11 million land titles to rural households in Vietnam. It found a small increase in investment in crops and more time spent in nonfarm activities.[8]

Doing Business records the full sequence of procedures necessary for a busi-

ness to purchase a property from another business and to transfer the property title to the buyer's name so that the purchasing business can securely use it to expand, use it as collateral in taking new loans or, if needed, sell it to another business (figure 5.2).

Streamlining property registration has become a popular reform. Economies keep finding ways to make the process easier and less costly. Reforms include practices common in the 10 economies where property registration is easiest, such as centralizing procedures at the registry, digitizing records, lowering transfer taxes and introducing standard forms (table 5.1). In fact, 9 of the top 10 economies on the ease of registering property reformed over the past 5 years. Some, such as Belarus and Georgia,

TABLE 5.1

Where is registering property easy—and where not?

Easiest	RANK	Most difficult	RANK
Saudi Arabia	1	Liberia	174
Georgia	2	Sierra Leone	175
New Zealand	3	Bangladesh	176
Lithuania	4	Guinea-Bissau	177
Armenia	5	Nigeria	178
Thailand	6	Brunei Darussalam	179
United Arab Emirates	7	Maldives	180
Norway	8	Marshall Islands	181
Azerbaijan	9	Micronesia, Fed. Sts.	182
Belarus	10	Timor-Leste	183

Note: Rankings are the average of the economy's rankings on the procedures, time and cost to register property. See Data notes for details.
Source: Doing Business database.

FIGURE 5.2

Registering property: transfer of property between 2 local companies

Rankings are based on 3 subindicators

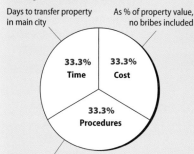

Days to transfer property in main city

As % of property value, no bribes included

Steps to check encumbrances, obtain clearance certificates, prepare deed and transfer title so that the property can be occupied, sold or used as collateral

Note: See Data notes for details.

TABLE 5.2

Putting procedures online—the most popular reform feature in 2008/09

Computerized procedures or put procedures online	Angola, Bulgaria, Colombia, Czech Republic, Estonia, France, Hong Kong (China), Indonesia, Panama, Rwanda, Singapore, United Kingdom, West Bank and Gaza
Introduced time limits	Belgium, Burkina Faso, Indonesia, FYR Macedonia, Mauritius, Romania, Russian Federation, Rwanda
Combined and reduced procedures	Algeria, Ethiopia, Guatemala, Kyrgyz Republic, Latvia, Moldova, Peru, Russian Federation
Reduced taxes or fees	Afghanistan, Ireland, Jamaica, Jordan, Nepal, Zimbabwe
Added new branches at land registry	Angola, Czech Republic, Ethiopia, Rwanda
Made the involvement of notaries optional	Belarus, Kyrgyz Republic, Portugal
Introduced fast-track procedures	Romania

Source: Doing Business database.

replaced complicated and costly registration systems. On average among the top 10, it now takes fewer than 3 procedures and, in most cases, 1–4 days and less than 1% of the property value to complete a property transfer. All countries, no matter their size, income level or geography, can make it easier to transfer property. And the benefits can show quickly. Armenia, Burkina Faso, Egypt and Ghana are among those that have seen increases in formal title transfers following reforms that eased property registration.

In the past year *Doing Business* recorded reforms easing property transfer in all regions.

WHO REFORMED IN 2008/09?

Thirty-four economies made it easier to register property in 2008/09. The most popular reform feature was to introduce online procedures, done in 11 economies (table 5.2). The second most popular, done in 8 economies, was to speed up procedures at the registry.

Mauritius was the top reformer, moving up 63 places in the rankings on the ease of registering property. The property registry was made fully electronic, and strict statutory time limits now apply to property registration. Six months were cut from the process. Burkina Faso was

the runner-up reformer, climbing 50 places in the rankings.

In Eastern Europe and Central Asia 9 economies eased property registration. Continuing past reform efforts, Belarus, the Kyrgyz Republic and Moldova simplified the process by cutting procedures. Moldova eliminated the requirement to obtain a cadastral sketch, speeding up the process by 43 days. Now property registration takes only 5 days. The Kyrgyz Republic simplified documentation and notarization requirements, cutting the time required to register a title almost in half—from 8 days to 5. Belarus removed the notarization requirement, reducing the number of steps to register property from 4 to 3. FYR Macedonia and Romania introduced time limits at the registry. This helped reduce the time to register property by 8 days in FYR Macedonia and by 35 in Romania. Estonia completed the computerization of its registry.

Six OECD high-income economies reformed property registration. Ireland lowered the maximum chargeable stamp duty for property transactions from 9% of the property value to 6%. Portugal amended the registry code to allow lawyers to perform notary functions. And computerization of the Portuguese registry reached Lisbon, reducing registration time from 42 days to 12 (figure 5.3). The Czech Republic reorganized its registry, increasing the number of staff and introducing administrative measures aimed at cutting bureaucracy. In the United Kingdom tax returns for land transactions are now processed automatically and electronically by the tax authority, reducing the time to register property from 21 days to 8. In Belgium a new 30-day statutory time limit to make property transfers opposable to third parties cut delays. In France, after publication of sales contracts, the registry now returns them in digital form to the notaries, with the registrar's electronic signature.

In Latin America and the Caribbean, Colombia, Guatemala, Jamaica, Panama and Peru were among the reformers. Jamaica reduced the property transfer tax from 6.5% of the property

FIGURE 5.3

Computerizing the property registry—a big time-saver

Time to register property (days)

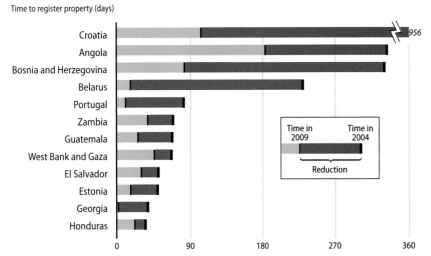

Source: Doing Business database.

value to 5%. Panama made the certificate of good standing from the tax agency available online, cutting the time for property registration from 44 days to 32. New online procedures also made it easier to transfer property in Uruguay. But a new law granted preemption rights to the municipality of Montevideo, adding 1 procedure to property transfers. Guatemala centralized procedures at the land registry, reorganized it and introduced greater use of electronic services. This cut 1 procedure and 3 days from property registration. Guatemala remains the region's best performer, with a ranking of 24 on the ease of registering property.

In the Middle East and North Africa, Algeria, Jordan and West Bank and Gaza had reforms. Algeria eliminated 3 procedures with the removal of the capital gains tax. It also made it less costly to register property by reducing notary fees by 0.4% of the property value. In West Bank and Gaza a project computerizing records at the land registry sped property registration by 15 days, cutting the total time to 47 days.

In Sub-Saharan Africa, besides Mauritius, 5 other economies made it easier to register property. Zimbabwe reduced the total cost from 25% of the property value to about 10%. In Burkina Faso new regulations reorganized the land registry and established statutory time limits. Inspections for property valuations were systematized with preestablished tables of values. And transfer taxes can now be paid at the land registry, at a special desk of the tax agency. Ethiopia decentralized administrative tasks to 10 neighborhoods in Addis Ababa and merged procedures at the land registry and municipality. Rwanda reorganized the land registry by establishing statutory time limits, dividing registration into 5 districts and making it possible to obtain the tax clearance certificate online from the revenue authority. Angola digitized the land registry and split it into 2 units, each covering half the land in Luanda, accelerating property transfers.

In East Asia and the Pacific, Indonesia introduced time limits for issuing the ownership certificate and for registration at the land registry. This cut the time to complete a property transfer by 17 days, from 39 to 22. Singapore continued improving its Computerized Systems of Government Agencies. Responses now come faster when conducting due diligence, and the time to register property has dropped from 9 days to 5.

Seven economies made property registration more difficult in 2008/09. To combat tax evasion and property undervaluation, Argentina and Botswana now require entrepreneurs to inform the tax agency before completing registration. Suriname implemented new valuation requirements to ensure proper tax payments at the land registry, adding to the procedures, cost and time to register property. Madagascar increased the cost of transferring property by 2.7% of the property value by making the use of notaries mandatory. Before, signatures could be legalized at the municipality. In Tajikistan the state duty for property transfer increased 3-fold, raising the cost to register property by 4.5% of the property value. And Sierra Leone reinstated a moratorium on the authorization of property transfers, delaying them by 6 months.

TABLE 5.3
Who makes property registration easy—and who does not?

Procedures (number)			
Fewest		**Most**	
Norway	1	Liberia	10
United Arab Emirates	1	Qatar	10
Bahrain	2	Algeria	11
Georgia	2	Greece	11
Netherlands	2	Swaziland	11
New Zealand	2	Eritrea	12
Oman	2	Uzbekistan	12
Saudi Arabia	2	Nigeria	13
Sweden	2	Uganda	13
Thailand	2	Brazil	14

Time (days)			
Fastest		**Slowest**	
New Zealand	2	Guinea-Bissau	211
Saudi Arabia	2	Sierra Leone	236
Thailand	2	Bangladesh	245
United Arab Emirates	2	Afghanistan	250
Georgia	3	Togo	295
Lithuania	3	Solomon Islands	297
Norway	3	Gambia, The	371
Armenia	4	Slovenia	391
Iceland	4	Haiti	405
Australia	5	Kiribati	513

Cost (% of property value)			
Least		**Most**	
Saudi Arabia	0.00	Côte d'Ivoire	13.9
Bhutan	0.01	Guinea	13.9
Belarus	0.02	Cameroon	17.8
Georgia	0.02	Central African Republic	18.6
Kiribati	0.03	Mali	20.0
Slovak Republic	0.05	Senegal	20.6
Kazakhstan	0.06	Comoros	20.8
New Zealand	0.09	Nigeria	20.9
Russian Federation	0.13	Chad	22.7
Azerbaijan	0.22	Syrian Arab Republic	28.0

Source: Doing Business database.

FIGURE 5.4
Big improvements, but still harder to register property in Sub-Saharan Africa

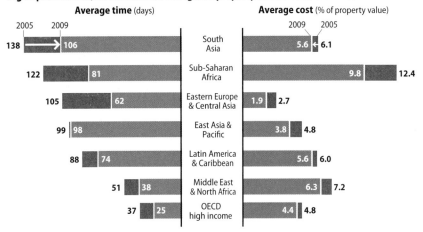

Note: Data refer to economies included in *Doing Business 2005*. Additional economies were added in subsequent years.
Source: *Doing Business* database.

TOWARD SMART REGULATION

In the past 5 years *Doing Business* has recorded 125 reforms in property registration in 93 economies, more than half of them in Africa and Eastern Europe and Central Asia. The largest share, 49 reforms, focused on reducing taxes and fees.

SIMPLIFYING AND LOWERING FEES

To register a property transfer, an entrepreneur in Uganda first has to arrange for a government official to inspect the property and assess its value. Then the entrepreneur has to complete an assessment form to pay the stamp duty at a bank and another assessment to pay property registration fees.

Nearly 30 of the 183 economies in the *Doing Business* sample require physical inspections to assess the value of the transferred property. Others impose multiple taxes and fees for property registration. In these economies not only are costs higher; the process is generally more cumbersome. More steps are required because payments must be made to different agencies and tax assessments may have to be obtained. Higher costs encourage informal transactions and underreporting of property values. And cumbersome processes can create incentives for the payment of bribes.

An alternative approach is to charge fixed fees, independent of the property value. Seventeen economies do so, including Armenia, Azerbaijan, Belarus, Bhutan, Egypt, Estonia, Georgia, Kazakhstan, Kosovo, the Kyrgyz Republic, New Zealand, Russia, Rwanda, Saudi Arabia and the Slovak Republic. "Fixed fees have reduced corruption at the registry," says a representative of the Real Estate Association of Georgia, where reforms introduced a fixed fee of $30.[9]

Another alternative is to lower fees charged as a percentage of the property value. Six economies, including Ireland and Nepal, did so in 2008/09, reducing taxes by 2.5% of the property value on average. And 49 economies have reduced percentage-based transfer fees since 2005. In the past 5 years Sub-Saharan Africa reduced taxes by 2.6% of the property value on average (figure 5.4). But more than 40 economies still have transfer taxes of more than 6% of the property value. In Chad, the Comoros, Mali, Nigeria, Senegal and Syria taxes and fees exceed 20% of the property value.

Reducing taxes and fees removes some of the incentives to underreport property values and promotes formal registration of transactions. It can also ease the burden on governments trying to detect cheaters. In 31 economies—including 13 in Africa, 8 in Latin America and 5 in the Middle East and North Africa—the government inspects property for valuation purposes during transfers. This procedure is costly and time consuming and can foster bribes. Switching to lower or fixed fees makes it faster and easier to transfer property while reducing underreporting of property values. It also means that the capital gains and property taxes collected later will be based on more realistic property values. And reducing taxes does not necessarily mean reducing revenues. Burkina Faso, Egypt, the Indian state of Maharashtra, Mozambique, Pakistan and the Slovak Republic all reduced fees yet saw total revenues stay almost steady or even rise, thanks to an increase in transactions.[10]

SIMPLIFYING AND COMBINING PROCEDURES

Simple measures such as reducing the number of documents can save entrepreneurs and officials valuable time and resources. More than 20 economies require cadastral certificates, and almost 70 require a proof of tax clearance from different levels of government. Eight economies, including Ethiopia, Gabon and República Bolivariana de Venezuela, go even further: they require certificates of payment from utility companies. Brazil and Greece require certificates of payment of social security or legal fees. And in 15 economies registration at the land registry is not enough: the new owner must register with multiple other institutions—such as the municipality, the tax agency and utility companies. To avoid the extra burden on entrepreneurs, governments can establish one-stop shops to deal with multiple payments and registrations all in one place.

After simplifying and combining procedures, government agencies can go a step further by linking their systems to exchange information. Guatemala is linking the land registry to municipalities to automatically update property values and ownership. Belarus introduced a successful one-stop shop 3 years ago. Entrepreneurs can get their tax payment verified and obtain clearance from the cadastral office at the one-stop shop. They don't even need to worry about the notariza-

FIGURE 5.5
Not all electronic land registries offer online access
Economies with electronic land registries, by type of access

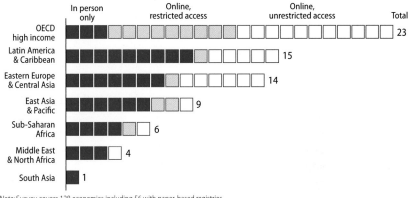

Note: Survey covers 128 economies including 56 with paper-based registries.
Source: Doing Business database.

tion requirement; representatives of the land registry have the same legal powers as notaries. Thanks in part to these reforms, Belarus has cut the steps for property registration from 7 in 2007 to 3, and the time from 231 days to 18.

EASING ACCESS TO THE REGISTRY

Easy access to information in the property registry helps reduce the time spent on lengthy and costly due diligence to verify ownership, encumbrances and other required documentation.

Where the internet is widely available, allowing online access to information is an effective way to reduce the time and cost to obtain documents. Among the 11 economies establishing online procedures in 2008/09, Bulgaria reduced the total time for property transfer by 4 days and Estonia by up to 33. Such reform has the biggest impact on the due diligence procedures typically carried out at the beginning of the transfer process, such as obtaining certificates of ownership, encumbrances, good standing of firms or transfer tax payment. Among a sample of 72 economies having electronic records for encumbrances, 14 of them, including France, make the records available online only to authorized parties such as notaries or lawyers. Thirty-three, including Antigua and Barbuda, Tunisia and Zambia, still require a visit to the land registry, because certificates can be obtained only in person; in some cases comput-

ers are available for searches. Only 25, including Australia, Canada and Latvia, make certificates available over the internet without restrictions (figure 5.5).

Where a personal visit to the registry is still necessary, decentralizing offices of the land registry or adding new ones can reduce backlogs and facilitate access to the registry. Angola, the Czech Republic, Ethiopia and Rwanda all decentralized their registry in 2008/09. Increasing administrative efficiency at the registry is another way to reduce delays for entrepreneurs. Belgium, Burkina Faso, Indonesia and 5 other economies did so in 2008/09 by introducing time limits—a necessary benchmark to measure registries' performance. Two more reduced backlogs by hiring more staff. Establishing fast-track procedures at a higher cost helps people who need speedier registration and are willing to pay for it—and allows the registry to prioritize its work. The fast-track option can save 21 days in Argentina, 16 in Azerbaijan, 7 in Armenia and 3 in Romania. Spain has an innovative system: if the delay exceeds 15 days, the registry's fees are cut by 30%.

COMPUTERIZING THE REGISTRY

Transferring property records from paper to a digital system speeds up processing. The 14 economies that have done so in the past 5 years have cut the time to transfer property in half, by about 4 months on average. This year, Angola

is the most striking example: a 5-year computerization effort at the registry reduced the total time to transfer property in Luanda from 334 days to 184.

In economies with computerized registries it takes only half as long to transfer property as it does in those with paper-based systems. Electronic processing can also improve title security, by making it easier to identify errors and overlapping titles. And digital records can be backed up and maintained more easily than paper ones. In Liberia many land books were lost or destroyed during the civil war, making it difficult to identify the rightful owners.[11] This can later lead to land disputes that have to be settled in court.

Going electronic can also increase registrations. Belarus has increased the number of transferred titles 3-fold since it began computerizing its system in 2005. Bosnia and Herzegovina has seen 33% growth in transferred titles since all municipal cadastres started working on computerization a few years ago. Angola, Portugal and West Bank and Gaza are other examples of economies that have started to reap the benefits of years of computerization efforts at their registries.

Switching from a paper-based property registry to an electronic one can take time—from 2 to 5 years—and can cost as much as $2 million. Reform in Georgia in 2005 cost $1.2 million. The cost is even higher when surveying and cadastre work is involved. In Croatia work at the land registry and cadastre is expected to cost $38 million. Technology is not always the ultimate solution. In low-income economies particularly, if paper records are inaccurate, making them electronic will not help. The focus should be first on improving the efficiency of current services and the accuracy of the registry.

1. De Soto (2000).
2. Field and Torero (2006).
3. Allendorf (2007).
4. *Doing Business* Gender Law Library,

http://www.doingbusiness.org/
genderlawlibrary.

5. World Bank (2008b).

6. Galiani and Schargrodsky (2005).

7. Field (2007).

8. Quy-Toan and Iyer (2008).

9. Fidas and McNicholas (2007).

10. On the experience in Egypt, see Haidar (2008).

11. World Bank (2008d).

Getting credit

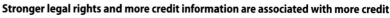

FIGURE 6.1

Stronger legal rights and more credit information are associated with more credit

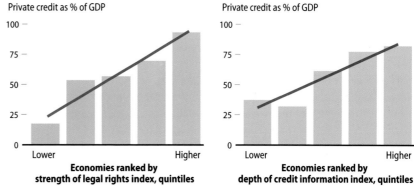

Note: Relationships are significant at the 5% level and remain significant when controlling for income per capita.
Source: Doing Business database; World Bank, World Development Indicators database (2008).

Tara grew a weaving hobby into a small textile business in the Federated States of Micronesia. Business picked up quickly, and within a year she was already starting to make a profit. With plans to expand, Tara approached Sangozi, a loan officer at her bank, for a line of credit. To find out whether Tara qualified for a low-interest loan program for female-owned businesses, Sangozi needed to check her credit record. But there was no database that shared information on credit histories.

With no credit report to show Tara's creditworthiness, Sangozi looked at which assets Tara could use as collateral. While Tara rents the premises for her business, she owns all the machinery. To raise the funds for start-up, Tara had created a nonpossessory pledge over these movable assets and registered it with the electronic collateral registry created 2 years before. Her inventory, machinery and other movable assets, together with the record of her assets from the collateral registry, proved to be enough: Sangozi gave Tara a line of credit. As long as Tara makes her loan payments, she continues to use the machinery securing her loan.

Access to information on credit and on registered assets used as collateral helps creditors assess the creditworthiness of potential future clients. Although a credit history is not a substitute for risk analysis, when banks share credit information, loan officers can assess borrowers' creditworthiness using objective measures. And if lenders are also reassured by strong creditors' rights, it allows them to take greater, well-informed risks.[1] This in turn can make access to finance easier, particularly for small and medium-size entrepreneurs. Where collateral laws are effective and credit registries are present, banks are more likely to extend loans (figure 6.1).[2]

Doing Business measures the legal rights of borrowers and lenders and the scope and quality of credit information systems. The first set of indicators describes how well collateral and bankruptcy laws facilitate lending. The second set measures the scope, quality and accessibility of credit information available through public credit registries and private credit bureaus and provides information on coverage (figure 6.2).

Many women are not as lucky as Tara. Female entrepreneurs are less likely to have the collateral needed for business loans.[3] This hinders their potential. Recent research in India shows that "given the difficulty that poor women in the rural sector have historically had in gaining access to the formal financial system, it is not surprising that when they are able to secure a loan, their probability of engaging in entrepreneurial activity shows a strong increase."[4]

Women tend to borrow from microfinance institutions, but in small amounts that often fall short of the minimum thresholds required by credit registries to build a credit history. Only 22% of public credit registries and 52% of private credit bureaus around the world

TABLE 6.1

Where is getting credit easy—and where not?

Easiest	RANK	Most difficult	RANK
Malaysia	1	Iraq	174
South Africa	2	Madagascar	175
United Kingdom	3	Tajikistan	176
Australia	4	Bhutan	177
Bulgaria	5	Djibouti	178
Hong Kong, China	6	Eritrea	179
Israel	7	Venezuela, R.B.	180
New Zealand	8	Syrian Arab Republic	181
Singapore	9		
United States	10	Timor-Leste	182
		Palau	183

Note: Rankings on the ease of getting credit are based on the sum of the strength of legal rights index and the depth of credit information index. See Data notes for details.
Source: Doing Business database.

FIGURE 6.2

Getting credit: collateral rules and credit information

Rankings are based on 2 subindicators

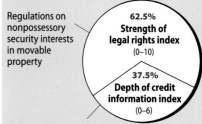

Regulations on nonpossessory security interests in movable property

62.5%
Strength of legal rights index
(0–10)

37.5%
Depth of credit information index
(0–6)

Scope, quality and accessibility of credit information through public and private credit registries

Note: Private bureau coverage and public registry coverage are measured but do not count for the rankings. See Data notes for details.

collect and distribute information from microfinance institutions, according to the *Doing Business* database. And 20% of bureaus and registries surveyed do not capture small loans. But credit bureaus and credit registries are not the only way to do so. Small loans that require collateral can also be recorded in a collateral registry. Yet only 40% of the economies covered by *Doing Business* have an operational collateral registry.

Particularly in developing economies, many small and medium-size companies do not have access to formal credit and have to rely on personal funds and operating profits. Many were hit hard by the financial and economic crisis as demand for their products fell. This makes it even more important to strengthen the regulatory environment to improve access to credit. One way is to encourage the sharing of information through credit registries or bureaus and strengthen the legal framework related to collateral.

Economies that rank high on the ease of getting credit typically have credit bureaus that share information on individuals and firms and include both positive and negative credit information obtained from banks, credit unions, mi-

crofinance institutions, retailers and utility providers. They tend to have bureaus that do not limit coverage to large loans and that provide historical information on borrowers. And they generally guarantee the right of borrowers to inspect their data. In addition, these economies have a legal framework that encourages lending by financial institutions to the private sector. Their laws ensure secured creditors' rights through a registration mechanism for secured interests, allow out-of-court enforcement of security rights and protect secured creditors during insolvency processes.

WHO REFORMED IN 2008/09?

Twenty-seven economies made it easier to get credit in 2008/09 (table 6.2). Rwanda was the top reformer. The country's new secured transactions law raised its score on the strength of legal rights index from 2 to 8. The new law makes it easier for small and medium-size enterprises to obtain loans. Before, banks would demand that borrowers give up possession of their secured property—or, if they were allowed to keep possession, the law required a specific description of the assets, and any change to the assets

would render the security agreement void. Now any individual or business can offer movable property as security for loans while maintaining possession. The law permits future assets to be used as collateral. It also established a collateral registry, protecting secured creditors against third parties.

Rwanda was not the only economy to reform in Sub-Saharan Africa. Zambia now requires banks and other financial institutions to provide data to the credit bureau and use credit reference reports. Mauritius adopted or amended several laws to allow the creation of a licensed private credit bureau and expanded the bureau's coverage to all credit facilities. Nigeria also adopted regulations to allow the creation of a private credit bureau. Sierra Leone passed a new company act in May 2009 that broadens the range of assets that can be used as collateral. The reform also clarified the legal framework for secured transactions. In Cape Verde the central bank introduced online access to the loan database for financial institutions. The minimum threshold for the loans included, however, was raised from 1,000 escudos to 5,000 ($61).

Eastern Europe and Central Asia saw the most reforms in getting credit in 2008/09. Seven economies reformed their credit information system. Armenia passed a new law establishing a legal framework for private credit bureaus and regulating credit information collection and credit reports. Latvia's new public credit registry started sharing data on loans from banks and bank subsidiaries on a quarterly basis, increasing its coverage to 47%. FYR Macedonia introduced new software allowing the public credit bureau to receive data on a monthly basis and lowered the threshold for the loans included. Serbia now guarantees borrowers the right to inspect their own data. Turkey's private credit bureau added firms to its database of borrowers and started generating credit ratings. Azerbaijan's public credit registry made it possible for banks to get credit reports for new borrowers online. Tajikistan adopted a new law allowing the creation

TABLE 6.2
Most popular reform features in getting credit in 2008/09

Introduced regulations guaranteeing that borrowers can inspect data in credit registry	Colombia, Guatemala, Serbia, Republic of Yemen
Expanded set of information collected in credit registry	Arab Republic of Egypt, Greece, Latvia, Turkey, Zambia
Improved regulatory framework related to sharing credit information	Armenia, Honduras, Kenya, Mauritius, Nigeria, Philippines, Tajikistan
Provided online access to or improved software at credit registry	Azerbaijan, Cape Verde, FYR Macedonia, Sri Lanka
Expanded range of revolving movable assets that can be used as collateral	Haiti, Kyrgyz Republic, Rwanda, Sierra Leone
Allowed maximum rather than specific amounts in debt agreements	Afghanistan, Kyrgyz Republic, Rwanda
Created a unified registry for movable property	Guatemala, Vanuatu
Established new credit bureau	Morocco
Gave priority to secured creditors' claims in bankruptcy procedures	Rwanda
Eliminated restrictions on who can hold or grant a security interest over movable property	Poland

Source: Doing Business database.

of a credit bureau. The law paves the way for exchanging positive and negative historical information on firms and individuals, making it mandatory for all financial companies and voluntary for utility firms and other creditors. The law also guarantees that all borrowers can check their information once a year free of charge and sets no minimum threshold for loans included in the database.

Two other economies in the region strengthened the legal rights of borrowers and lenders. The Kyrgyz Republic amended its civil code and pledge law to make secured lending more flexible by allowing general descriptions of encumbered assets and of debts and obligations. Poland amended its 1996 Act on Registered Pledges to broaden the category of persons who may hold or grant security interests.

In the Middle East and North Africa 3 economies improved their credit information system. Egypt's private credit bureau expanded the scope of information

collected and now also includes retailers. Morocco introduced a private credit bureau, replacing the public registry and increasing coverage. The Republic of Yemen issued circulars removing the minimum threshold for loans included in the database and guaranteeing the right of borrowers to view their credit reports. The country's central bank now has a credit information system—a gift from the central bank of the United Arab Emirates.

In Latin America and the Caribbean 4 economies reformed. Colombia passed a new law regulating data protection, with a special section on credit bureaus and on commercial and credit information. The law guarantees the right of citizens to inspect their information and establishes mechanisms for complaints in case of errors. But the law and subsequent decisions also limit the historical information available. In Guatemala a collateral registry became operational in Guatemala City in February 2009. The registry allows secured creditors to

make their security rights in all types of movable assets opposable to third parties. Guatemala also passed a new law guaranteeing borrowers' right to access their data in any public registry.

Haiti passed a law allowing small and medium-size businesses to create security interests in future assets while ensuring that the creditors' rights will extend to products and proceeds of the secured assets. Plans to create a collateral registry are under way. Honduras helped banks to better manage risks by categorizing borrowers in the public credit bureau. It also plans to adopt a new secured transactions law in the second half of 2009.

Among OECD high-income economies, only Greece reformed. Its private credit bureau now distributes positive as well as negative information in credit reports.

Two economies reformed in South Asia. Sri Lanka was the only reformer in credit information. The country strengthened its private credit bureau by consolidating all data from shareholder lending institutions, with no minimum threshold. Registry data have grown 10-fold since 2007. Afghanistan enacted a modern secured transactions law. The law improves the mechanisms available for businesses to secure a loan. Now companies can use a broad range of movable assets as security. The law also provides for the future implementation of a collateral registry.

In East Asia and the Pacific 2 economies reformed. The Philippines passed a new law establishing a credit information sharing system, and Vanuatu implemented a new collateral registry. Other reforms are on the way in the region. The Solomon Islands enacted a new secured transactions law, which will become effective once the collateral registry becomes operational in the second half of 2009. Tonga is drafting a new law on secured transactions that is expected to establish an electronic collateral registry. The Lao People's Democratic Republic plans to implement a new collateral registry by the end of 2009.

TABLE 6.3
Who has the most credit information and the most legal rights for borrowers and lenders—and who the least?

Legal rights for borrowers and lenders (strength of legal rights index, 0–10)			
Most		**Least**	
Hong Kong, China	10	Belarus	2
Kenya	10	Burundi	2
Kyrgyz Republic	10	Eritrea	2
Malaysia	10	Madagascar	2
Singapore	10	Bolivia	1
Australia	9	Djibouti	1
Denmark	9	Syrian Arab Republic	1
Israel	9	Timor-Leste	1
New Zealand	9	Palau	0
United Kingdom	9	West Bank and Gaza	0

Borrowers covered by credit registries (% of adults)			
Most		**Least**	
Argentina	100	Liberia	0.27
Australia	100	Nepal	0.27
Canada	100	Algeria	0.22
Iceland	100	Yemen, Rep.	0.22
Ireland	100	Djibouti	0.21
New Zealand	100	Chad	0.21
Norway	100	Burundi	0.19
Sweden	100	Mauritania	0.16
United Kingdom	100	Ethiopia	0.13
United States	100	Madagascar	0.07

Note: The rankings on borrower coverage reflected in the table include only economies with public or private credit registries (132 in total). Another 50 economies have no credit registry and therefore no coverage. See Data notes for details.
Source: Doing Business database.

TOWARD SMART REGULATION

In the past 5 years *Doing Business* has recorded 42 reforms strengthening the legal rights of borrowers and lenders in 32 economies around the world—and 108 reforms improving credit information systems in 70 economies. This count includes 27 new credit bureaus and 11 new collateral registries since 2005. Close to two-thirds of the new credit bureaus were created by economies in Eastern Europe and Central Asia. And the share of the adult population with a credit history in these economies has increased dramatically (figure 6.3).

CREATING A CREDIT BUREAU

Establishing a credit bureau need not be expensive. Costs range from $500,000 to $3 million, depending on the systems already in place and the readiness of the banking sector. Most of the costs can be recovered within a couple of years. But getting started can often take time. According to experts, it takes 12–24 months for a credit bureau to begin operations—from developing a business plan to issuing the first reports.[5]

The Armenian credit bureau, ACRA, cost $1 million to start up and took 3 years to begin operations. Coverage initially rose from 1.5% of adults to 13.5% and has almost doubled each year since. Efforts to improve the functioning of the bureau continue. In the past year Armenia strengthened the legal framework regulating the activities of credit bureaus and clarified the rules on sharing credit information. Coverage has risen to 35% of adults.

Setting up the credit bureau is only a part of any reform. Reformers need to create the regulatory framework that will allow the sharing of data and foster trust in the system by both banks and borrowers. This often requires adopting a new credit bureau law or amendments to existing banking and data protection laws. Six economies took this step in 2008/09.

In many economies credit bureaus have the capacity to collect more information but lack the legal backing to

FIGURE 6.3

Credit information coverage grew quickly in economies with new credit bureaus

Borrowers covered by credit registries (% of adults)

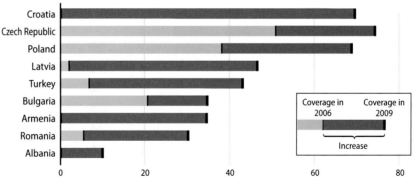

Source: *Doing Business* database.

do so. Take the Kyrgyz Republic, where there is no law governing the operations of credit bureaus. Only 6% of adults are covered, because banks are reluctant to share information. Economies in the Middle East and North Africa and those in Latin America and the Caribbean share the same amount of credit information on average, but they have very different coverage rates (figure 6.4). One reason for the difference could be the legal structure affecting the credit bureaus and the information that credit bureaus are allowed to collect and distribute. In Latin America and the Caribbean 59% of economies have credit bureaus that share information from utilities and retailers, for example, while in the Middle East and North Africa only 21% of economies do.

Including credit information from retailers and utility companies such as electricity providers and mobile phone

companies is an effective way to increase coverage. But this is among the harder aspects to reform because these companies often are regulated by different institutions than financial companies are. Only 40% of bureaus include information from such sources. Yet positive information on payment of electricity and phone bills can help establish a good credit history for those who need it the most—women and youth, many of whom have had no contact with the banking sector.

REFORMING SECURED TRANSACTIONS LAWS

Sound secured transactions laws allow businesses to use their assets—including movable assets such as machinery or accounts receivable—as security to generate capital for expansion. The ability to use such assets is particularly important for small and medium-size enterprises,

FIGURE 6.4

Coverage of borrowers varies widely across regions

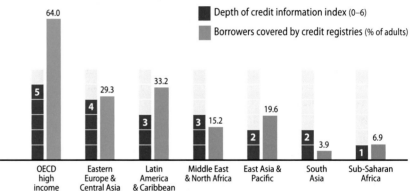

Source: *Doing Business* database.

which may not own land or buildings. Female entrepreneurs can benefit the most in countries such as Tanzania, where customary inheritance law means that few women have land to use as collateral for business loans.[6]

Economies as diverse as Cambodia, Guatemala, the Federated States of Micronesia and Rwanda have implemented new legal frameworks in recent years. Such legal changes often do not require large investments. The Dominican Republic, for example, estimates that it will spend about $68,500 on evaluating its existing secured transactions system and developing a new regulatory framework. Rwanda invested $55,320 in validation and translation of its new law as well as in the legislative process, excluding technical assistance from donors.

The experience of earlier reformers shows that such reform is well worth the effort. Where the law allows movable goods to be used as collateral, companies take advantage of this possibility. In Eastern Europe and Central Asia, the region with the most reforms in getting credit in the past 5 years, the share of companies using movable assets as collateral has increased significantly since 2005.[7] The use of machinery and other tangible movable property as collateral has risen the most (figure 6.5). Revolving movable assets such as inventory and accounts receivable are also used, though to a lesser extent. Financial institutions may still feel more comfortable using assets not susceptible to change over time. Moreover, trust in the use of a collateral registry, rather than possession of the collateral, can take time to develop.

SETTING UP A COLLATERAL REGISTRY

Where the necessary legal framework is in place, well-functioning collateral registries are needed so that companies can take advantage of the law and get access to credit. Results can show quickly. In Serbia, for example, the Register of Pledges over Movable Property and Rights began operating by mid-2005. It recorded 11,799 registered security interests in 2007, 16,974 in 2008

FIGURE 6.5
More borrowers are using movable collateral
Share of companies using machinery and equipment as collateral (%)

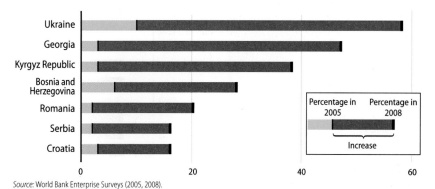

Source: World Bank Enterprise Surveys (2005, 2008).

and 7,583 between January a nd May 2009. The value of registered pledges is about $17 billion. In China, 20 months after the Credit Reference Center of the People's Bank of China had created an online registry for receivables in 2007, a total of 74,453 lending transactions using receivables as security had been recorded, for an estimated cumulative amount of more than 5 trillion yuan. More than 52% of these transactions involved small and medium-size enterprises. By now most mid size and large lenders in China have developed accounts receivable financing.[8]

With the legal framework in place, creating a new collateral registry need not be costly. Some small island states have established one in recent years, including the Federated States of Micronesia. Guatemala recently established a paper-based registry that also functions online. The reform process, which included the adoption of a new secured transactions law, took several years.[9] The initial budget to operate the new registry was $86,500. The total cost of establishing a new legal framework with an online collateral registry—including diagnostic and legal review, software, hardware, hosting and maintenance, along with international consulting during the entire process—can amount to about $350,000 or more. Reformers in the Dominican Republic expect a cost of $354,500 for such a comprehensive reform. Many economies have well-functioning paper-based collateral registries. According to

a recent survey of 25 economies with established registries, only 6 had registries allowing online registration.[10]

Reformers seeking to economize might consider combining reforms of collateral and credit information systems by focusing on what these systems have in common. Data collected by collateral registries are often similar to those used in credit reports. When implementing both reforms simultaneously, the biggest savings can be made on software. The software license and customization for a new credit registry, accounting for about half the total cost, can also be used to start a collateral registry.

1. Houston and others (2008).
2. Djankov, McLiesh and Shleifer (2007).
3. Deininger, Ali and Alemu (2009) and Joireman (2008).
4. Menon and van der Meulen Rodgers (2009, p. 14).
5. Based on World Bank project experience in Armenia, Bulgaria, Egypt, Nigeria, Romania, Russia, Rwanda, Sri Lanka, Uganda and the United Arab Emirates.
6. World Bank (2008b).
7. World Bank Enterprise Surveys (http://www.enterprisesurveys.org).
8. Marechal, Tekin and Guliyeva (forthcoming).
9. Croci Downes (forthcoming).
10. World Bank Group, Investment Climate Advisory Services, Movable Collateral Registry Survey, 2008.

Protecting investors

FIGURE 7.1

More investor protections associated with greater access for firms to equity markets and faster stock turnover

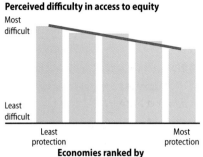

Perceived difficulty in access to equity

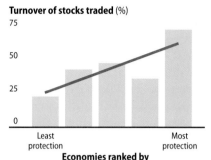

Turnover of stocks traded (%)

Note: Relationships are significant at the 1% and 5% level respectively and remain significant when controlling for income per capita. Economies are ranked on the perceived difficulty in financing through local equity market, with 134 being the most difficult.

Source: Doing Business database; WEF (2008); World Bank, World Development Indicators database.

Serghei, a minority shareholder in the Kyrgyz Republic, made good use of his country's new company law last year. A company in which he had invested was about to enter into a transaction that required pledging a big mortgage to a Kazakhstan financial group. The terms suggested that interests other than the company's were at play. Aided by the new law, Serghei and other minority shareholders forced the board to submit the transaction to an extraordinary shareholders meeting for approval. The new law gave the minority investors the power to block the transaction. This saved the company $150 million. And it reassured minority investors that their rights were protected.

Companies need capital to be able to grow and expand. For companies seeking to access finance through equity mar-

kets, the strength of investor protections is particularly important (figure 7.1). The current crisis has made access to equity markets more challenging. In times of uncertainty, investors become even more concerned about corporate governance risks and look for legal protections. Previous financial crises, such as the East Asian crisis of 1997, and corporate scandals such as those involving Enron and WorldCom have also brought attention to areas where stronger protections are needed. The lessons learned from them have proved to be a source of innovation and reform in investor protections.

Rules governing self-dealing, the use of corporate assets by company insiders for personal gain, are just one area of corporate governance. But they are among the most important, particularly in developing economies, where corporate ownership tends to be highly concentrated.[1] The most common examples of self-dealing are related-party transactions—those between company insiders and other companies they control. These include sales of goods or services to the company at inflated prices or purchases from it at excessively low prices.

Investors typically look for transparency in such corporate dealings, accountability from company directors for improper corporate practices and ability to take part in the major decisions of the company. If a country's laws do not provide these, investors may be reluctant to invest, except to become the controlling shareholder.

Doing Business measures the transparency of related-party transactions, the liability of company directors for self-dealing and the ability of shareholders to sue directors for misconduct (figure 7.2). A high ranking on the strength of investor protection index shows that an economy's regulations offer strong investor protections against self-dealing (table 7.1). The indicator is not a measure of the dynamism of capital markets or of protections for foreign investors.

WHO REFORMED IN 2008/09?

Ten economies strengthened investor protections in 2008/09 (table 7.2). Increasing disclosure requirements was once again the most popular reform feature, followed by regulating the approval

TABLE 7.1

Where are investors protected—and where not?

Most protected	RANK	Least protected	RANK
New Zealand	1	Gambia, The	174
Singapore	2	Micronesia, Fed. Sts.	175
Hong Kong, China	3	Palau	176
Malaysia	4	Vietnam	177
Canada	5	Venezuela, R.B.	178
Colombia	6	Djibouti	179
Ireland	7	Suriname	180
Israel	8	Swaziland	181
United States	9	Lao PDR	182
South Africa	10	Afghanistan	183

Note: Rankings are on the strength of investor protection index. See Data notes for details.
Source: Doing Business database.

FIGURE 7.2

Protecting investors: minority shareholder rights in related-party transactions

Rankings are based on 3 subindicators

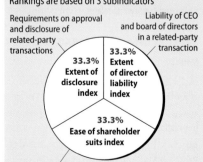

Requirements on approval and disclosure of related-party transactions

33.3% Extent of disclosure index

Liability of CEO and board of directors in a related-party transaction

33.3% Extent of director liability index

33.3% Ease of shareholder suits index

Type of evidence that can be collected before and during the trial

Note: See Data notes for details.

process for related-party transactions.

Rwanda was the top reformer. In April 2009 its parliament adopted a new company law. The new law regulates conflicts of interest by requiring shareholder approval of related-party transactions involving more than 5% of company assets. The law also introduces extensive requirements for disclosure of related-party transactions to the board of directors and in the company's annual report. And for the first time in Rwanda's legal history, the law sets out a clear catalogue of directors' duties.

Rwanda's new law also makes it easier to sue directors for prejudicial related-party transactions. If directors are found liable, they must compensate the company for the damage caused and repay all profits made from the transaction. And minority shareholders can now gain access to internal corporate documents either directly or through a government inspector.

Two other countries in Sub-Saharan Africa made important efforts to strengthen minority shareholders' rights. Sierra Leone adopted a new company law addressing both disclosure requirements for related-party transactions and the liability of directors in case such a transaction harms the company. Related-party transactions must now be approved by a shareholders meeting, and the interested party is not allowed to vote. Moreover,

judges now have the power to rescind harmful related-party transactions.

Mali amended its civil procedure code in May 2009. The new rules strengthen investor protections by increasing shareholders' ability to access internal corporate information during a trial to establish directors' liability.

The runner-up reformer was the Dominican Republic. One of the top 10 reformers in the previous year, the country targeted investor protections as a priority in 2008/09. The parliament adopted a new company law in December 2008, replacing the outdated commercial code of 1882. The new law requires board approval for related-party transactions representing less than 15% of the company's assets and shareholder approval for those representing more than 15%. The law makes directors liable for all damages caused to the company by transactions involving a conflict of interest. And to increase transparency, the law allows minority investors access to all internal corporate documents.

Colombia, another reformer in Latin America and the Caribbean, amended its company law through Decree 1925. The decree clarifies provisions regulating the liability of directors for prejudicial related-party transactions, making it easier to sue directors in such cases. If directors are found liable, they must pay damages caused to the company

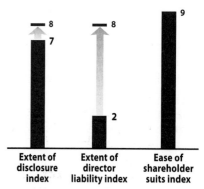

FIGURE 7.3
Colombia—the road to the top 10 in protecting investors
Total improvement, 2007–2009 (index 0–10)

Source: Doing Business database.

and disgorge the profit made from the transaction. Colombia has now reformed investor protections for 3 years running. This past year's reform brought Colombia into the top 10 on the strength of investor protection index—among the economies that protect minority investors the most from self-dealing (figure 7.3).

Eastern Europe and Central Asia had 3 reforms. In April 2009, after 9 years of parliamentary debate, Ukraine adopted the Law on Joint Stock Companies. The new law considerably strengthens the legal protections for minority shareholders. It requires the supervisory board to approve transactions between interested parties and prohibits those parties from participating in the process. The new law introduces detailed requirements for disclosing conflicts of interest to the supervisory board, increasing the transparency of the company's activities. It also spells out the duties of supervisory board members and their liability in the event that their actions or inactions cause harm to the company.

FYR Macedonia also reformed. In July 2008 the parliament approved amendments to the Trade Enterprise Law of 2004. The amendments increased disclosure obligations and modified the approval process for related-party transactions. Now directors must publish comprehensive information on such transactions in the annual report. Directors who are interested parties in

TABLE 7.2
Greater disclosure—the most popular reform feature in 2008/09

Increased disclosure requirements	Dominican Republic, Indonesia, FYR Macedonia, Rwanda, Sierra Leone, Tajikistan, Tunisia, Ukraine
Regulated approval of related-party transactions	Dominican Republic, FYR Macedonia, Rwanda, Sierra Leone, Tunisia, Ukraine
Passed a new company law	Dominican Republic, Rwanda, Sierra Leone, Ukraine
Made it easier to sue directors	Colombia, Dominican Republic, FYR Macedonia, Rwanda, Tajikistan
Allowed access to internal corporate information	Dominican Republic, Rwanda
Allowed rescission of prejudicial related-party transactions	Colombia, Rwanda, Sierra Leone, Tajikistan
Required an external body to review related-party transactions before they take place	Tajikistan, Tunisia
Allowed direct oral questioning of defendants and witnesses	Mali

Source: Doing Business database.

transactions that harm the company face special liability. In addition, the Macedonian Securities Commission adopted resolutions strengthening the requirements for periodic disclosures by listed companies.

Tajikistan reformed for the second year in a row. Amendments to the Joint Stock Companies Law increased the disclosure requirements for transactions involving a conflict of interest. The new law also makes it easier to sue directors who cause damage to the company and allows shareholders to request the rescission of harmful related-party transactions.

Indonesia was a repeat reformer and the only one in East Asia and the Pacific in 2008/09. The Indonesian Securities Commission, aiming to strengthen its already strong disclosure requirements for related-party transactions, issued a regulation setting out extensive new requirements for internal disclosure. Now a wider range of information must be disclosed to the board of directors and to shareholders meetings.

In Tunisia, increasing the transparency of companies' activities was the main goal of reformers. The parliament amended the Code des Sociétés Commerciales in March 2009. The new provisions require approval of related-party transactions by both the board of directors and a shareholders meeting. Interested parties are no longer allowed to participate in the approval process. In addition, the law requires review of the terms of such transactions by an independent auditor.

TOWARD SMART REGULATION

Doing Business has recorded 68 reforms to strengthen investor protections in 50 economies over the past 5 years. Economies that rank high on the strength of investor protection index protect minority investors from self-dealing through more disclosure, clear duties for directors and easy access to corporate information (table 7.3).

Examples are New Zealand, Singapore and the United Kingdom. These economies also have efficient, responsive judicial systems—without which good laws would have little impact on investor protections. In Singapore, for example, it takes 150 days on average to enforce a commercial contract in court, the fastest time in the world.

But many economies still offer minority investors only partial protections through the laws or the judicial system. While economies such as Bulgaria have extensive disclosure and approval requirements, for example, they lack clear rules regulating the liability of directors.

And while economies like the United Arab Emirates have clear, rigorous rules regulating the liability of directors, they lack such rules for regulating the disclosure of related-party transactions and access to internal corporate information.

How do economies fill the gaps? Reforms over the past 5 years show some common patterns. Reformers in Eastern Europe and Central Asia, the most active globally, focused on increasing disclosure requirements and determining clear duties for directors (figure 7.4). In recent years several low-income economies

TABLE 7.3

Who provides strong minority investor protections—and who does not?

Extent of disclosure index (0–10)			
Most		**Least**	
Bulgaria	10	Bolivia	1
China	10	Afghanistan	0
France	10	Honduras	0
Hong Kong, China	10	Lao PDR	0
Indonesia	10	Maldives	0
Ireland	10	Micronesia, Fed. Sts.	0
Malaysia	10	Palau	0
New Zealand	10	Sudan	0
Singapore	10	Swaziland	0
Thailand	10	Switzerland	0
Extent of director liability index (0–10)			
Most		**Least**	
Albania	9	Belarus	1
Cambodia	9	Bulgaria	1
Canada	9	Togo	1
Israel	9	Zimbabwe	1
Malaysia	9	Afghanistan	0
New Zealand	9	Marshall Islands	0
Rwanda	9	Micronesia, Fed. Sts.	0
Singapore	9	Palau	0
Slovenia	9	Suriname	0
Trinidad and Tobago	9	Vietnam	0
Ease of shareholder suits index (0–10)			
Easiest		**Most difficult**	
Kenya	10	Lao PDR	2
New Zealand	10	Senegal	2
Colombia	9	Syrian Arab Republic	2
Hong Kong, China	9	United Arab Emirates	2
Ireland	9	Venezuela, R.B.	2
Israel	9	Yemen, Rep.	2
Mauritius	9	Guinea	1
Poland	9	Morocco	1
Singapore	9	Djibouti	0
United States	9	Iran, Islamic Rep.	0

Source: Doing Business database.

took similar measures. Two examples are Rwanda and Sierra Leone, whose new company laws strengthened disclosure requirements and increased directors' liability (figure 7.5). Such reforms put into place much-needed legal protections without costing very much. Rwanda's adoption of its new company law cost $250,000, including translation services and costs associated with the legislative process. Sierra Leone spent $150,000 on technical assistance, communications and basic logistics when introducing its new company law.

BROADENING DISCLOSURE REQUIREMENTS

Reforms aimed at increasing market transparency have focused on both internal and external disclosure requirements. Requirements for internal disclosure of related-party transactions call for notifying the company's board of directors (or supervisory board) and its shareholders. Those for external disclosure include disclosure of the transaction to the stock exchange or market regulator within 24–72 hours after the transaction and disclosure in the company's annual report.

Reforming governments have both broadened the scope and improved the quality of the information that must be disclosed. In Indonesia and the Kyrgyz Republic, for example, directors must disclose the nature and amount of the

FIGURE 7.4
Increased disclosure and directors' liability in Eastern Europe and Central Asia

Average improvement (index 0–10)

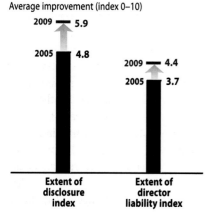

Source: Doing Business database.

FIGURE 7.5
Increased investor protections in Africa as a result of new company laws
Strength of investor protection index (0–10), 2006–09

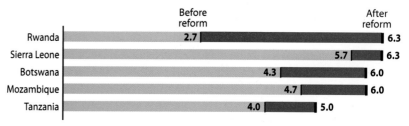

Source: Doing Business database.

transaction, explain the potential conflict of interest in detail and provide any other relevant information that could help the board or shareholders come to an informed decision.

But reformers need to watch out for potential legal loopholes allowing parties to bypass disclosure requirements. One signal: references in laws to the "ordinary course of business." Economies such as Switzerland require extensive disclosure of related-party transactions. But if a transaction is conducted as part of the company's "day-to-day activities," the disclosure provisions do not apply. Neither legislation nor case law adequately defines the "ordinary course of business." Often, any transaction could fit the exception, so disclosure requirements are of little use.

SPELLING OUT APPROVAL PROCESSES

Reformers that want to require approval of related-party transactions have 2 options: approval by the board of directors (or supervisory board) or by the shareholders. Either way, interested directors should not be allowed to participate in the process—or should not have their votes counted.

In economies with large corporations, modern legal systems and good communications infrastructure, such as France and Singapore, shareholder approval is the preferred route. But in economies with smaller companies and fewer shareholders, the tendency is to create thresholds for approval of transactions. In Albania and Rwanda, if a related-party transaction—or a group of such transactions—represents less than 5% of the

company's assets, it must be approved by the board of directors. If it represents more than 5% of the assets, it must be approved at a shareholders meeting. This model allows the company flexibility in conducting its day-to-day activities while ensuring that minority investors are involved in major decisions.

Many reforms have focused on the time at which approval of related-party transactions is required. Under Rwanda's new company law, related-party transactions representing more than 5% of the company's assets must be approved by an extraordinary shareholders meeting. In contrast, laws in Cameroon and Senegal require that disinterested investors approve every transaction between a company and its directors. This sounds sufficient. But the laws do not specify when disinterested investors must approve such transactions. In practice, the board of directors authorizes all related-party transactions during the fiscal year and waits for the annual shareholders meeting for the approval. So shareholders may not vote on a transaction until months after it has taken place—and possibly caused serious harm to the company.

BEING CLEAR ABOUT LIABILITY

Company directors are subject to strict rules and duties because they are fiduciaries. If they manage the business properly, they are rewarded. If they fail to do so, they are responsible for the consequences.

When regulating directors' duties, governments generally follow 1 of 2 paths. Either they set out in the law a detailed catalogue of rights and duties for company directors—the case in Mexico.[2] Or they create a special regime of liability for directors in case of prejudicial related-party transactions—the case in Georgia and FYR Macedonia. In both approaches directors found liable must compensate the company for damages and repay profits made from the transaction.

Many laws have only transparency provisions without making directors liable for prejudicial related-party transactions. This is the case in Kazakhstan and Moldova: as long as interested parties comply with the requirements for approval and disclosure of a related-party transaction, they are not liable for any damages caused. This deprives minority investors of an important tool for protecting their own interests and those of the company they invest in.

EASING ACCESS TO EVIDENCE

Minority investors are protected when they can bring a case before the court and expect the court to rule in a reasonable time. But to make their case, they need access to evidence before and during the trial.

Reformers have made it easier for minority investors to gain access to internal corporate information before the trial—either directly or through a government inspector. Indonesia and Japan offer both options. Mozambique and Rwanda allow shareholders access to any internal corporate documents except corporate secrets. And if the management fails to provide sufficient information, shareholders can ask the court to appoint a government inspector with full powers to access all corporate documents. But some economies, such as the Plurinational State of Bolivia and the Democratic Republic of Congo, lack laws allowing shareholders access to corporate information.

Others have facilitated access to evidence during the trial. Mali did so by amending its procedural rules. Now lawyers representing investors can question defendants and witnesses directly, without needing approval from the judge.

1. Djankov, La Porta, López-de-Silanes and Shleifer (2008).
2. Johns and Lobet (2007).

Paying taxes

FIGURE 8.1

104 economies reformed in paying taxes in 2004–08

Average percentage change, 2004–08

	Payments	Time to comply	Total tax rate
2004	1.7	–4.3 –5.9 –9.3 –4.6	–7.7
2008	–10.3 –12.8 –17.8		–11.7 –15.9 –10.6

Income group

H   High
UM Upper middle
LM Lower middle
L   Low

H   UM   LM   L   H   UM   LM   L   H   UM   LM   L

Payments   *Time to comply*   *Total tax rate*

Note: The percentage increase in payments in low-income economies is driven by 1 major reform in 1 economy that increased payments by 60% in 2006. Without this outlier, the average percentage decrease would be 1.09%.
Source: Doing Business database.

In Egypt during the 18th dynasty the pharaoh sent tax collectors 3 times a year. They were accompanied by a scribe who kept records. The scribe wrote down the names of the peasants and measured the fields. On the second visit the scribe and the tax collectors inspected the new crops. From this they calculated the taxes owed. The tax collectors made the third visit during the harvest to collect the pharaoh's share. The taxes were paid in sacks of grain.[1]

Governments need revenues to provide public services to society. For businesses, these services offer infrastructure, education and other amenities key to achieving a common goal of prosperous, functional and orderly societies. Many services directly affect businesses—from company and land registries to courts.

TABLE 8.1

Where is it easy to pay taxes—and where not?

Easiest	RANK	Most difficult	RANK
Maldives	1	Jamaica	174
Qatar	2	Mauritania	175
Hong Kong, China	3	Gambia, The	176
United Arab Emirates	4	Bolivia	177
Singapore	5	Uzbekistan	178
Ireland	6	Central African Republic	179
Saudi Arabia	7	Congo, Rep.	180
Oman	8	Ukraine	181
New Zealand	9	Venezuela, R.B.	182
Kiribati	10	Belarus	183

Note: Rankings are the average of the economy's rankings on the number of payments, time and total tax rate. See Data notes for details.
Source: Doing Business database.

To finance these services, the vast majority of governments must levy taxes. The challenge for governments is to find a way to do so that ensures public revenues while encouraging compliance.

Businesses from around the world have identified taxation as an area in which they would most like to see their governments improve.[2] How governments raise revenues can make an important difference to business and growth. And what can be a challenge in good times becomes even more complicated when things become difficult. The global financial and economic crisis has led to rising government debt and unemployment around the world. The question for many governments is how to ensure public revenues while supporting economic recovery by encouraging firm growth and investment.

Doing Business measures the total tax burden borne by a standard small to medium-size business as well as the number of payments and total time spent complying with tax laws in a given year (figure 8.2). Thus it compares tax systems and tracks reforms around the world from the perspective of local small to medium-size businesses. It does not measure the fiscal health of economies, the macroeconomic conditions under which governments collect revenues or the provision of public services supported by taxation.

Over the past year, as the financial and economic crisis affected economies

around the world, governments stayed on course with reform programs to lower the tax burden for businesses, broaden the tax base and make compliance easier. More economies reformed than in any previous year. A few economies, such as Russia and Korea, reduced corporate income tax rates or accelerated previously planned reform programs as part of economic stimulus packages. In several economies small and medium-size businesses benefited from other crisis response measures. Australia, for example, sought to encourage investments in assets by increasing capital allowance rates.[3] Twelve other economies introduced similar measures, including the Czech Republic, Korea and Lebanon. Five economies reduced property tax rates: Denmark, the Netherlands, Niger,

FIGURE 8.2

Paying taxes: tax compliance for a local manufacturing company

Rankings are based on 3 subindicators

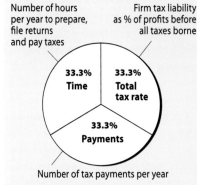

Number of hours per year to prepare, file returns and pay taxes

Firm tax liability as % of profits before all taxes borne

33.3% Time

33.3% Total tax rate

33.3% Payments

Number of tax payments per year

Note: See Data notes for details.

Portugal and Singapore.

In the past, tax reforms were often part of government responses to financial or economic crises. During the Asian financial crisis of the late 1990s Singapore was one economy that undertook elaborate tax reforms to combat the economic downturn. It lowered business costs through a series of tax cuts, rebates and exemptions introduced over the course of the crisis. It also reduced the number of payments by removing the stamp duty on almost all documents.[4] Today Singapore is still one of the easiest places in which to pay taxes as measured by *Doing Business*.

The size of the tax burden on businesses matters for investment and growth. Where taxes are high and corresponding gains seem low, the incentive for businesses to opt out of the formal sector increases. A recent study shows that higher tax rates are associated with lower private investment and fewer formal businesses. A 10 percentage point increase in the effective corporate tax rate is associated with a reduction in the ratio of investment to GDP of up to 2 percentage points and a decrease in the business entry rate of about 1 percentage point.[5] Other research suggests that a 1 percentage point increase in the statutory corporate tax rate would reduce the local profits of existing investments by 1.31 percentage points on average[6] and lead to an 18 percentage point increase in average debt-to-asset ratios (part of the reason for the lower reported profits).[7] A 1 percentage point increase in effective corporate tax rates reduces the likelihood of establishing a subsidiary in an economy by 2.9 percentage points.[8]

Besides the taxes paid, there are costs of complying with tax laws and of running the revenue authority. Worldwide on average, a standard small to medium-size business still spends 3 working days a month complying with tax obligations as measured by *Doing Business*. Where tax compliance imposes heavy burdens of cost and time, it can create a disincentive to investment and encourage informality.[9] Particularly in

TABLE 8.2

Reducing tax rates—the most popular reform feature in 2008/09

Reduced profit tax rates	Algeria, Bangladesh, Benin, Brunei Darussalam, Cape Verde, Fiji, Iceland, Israel, Kazakhstan, Republic of Korea, Kosovo, Montenegro, Philippines, Russian Federation, Spain, St. Vincent and the Grenadines, Sudan, Timor-Leste, Togo, Vietnam
Simplified process of paying taxes	Angola, Belarus, Belgium, Colombia, Czech Republic, Finland, Guatemala, Jordan, Kyrgyz Republic, Lao PDR, Lebanon, FYR Macedonia, Mexico, Peru, Poland, Sierra Leone, Taiwan (China), Tunisia
Revised tax code	Djibouti, Islamic Republic of Iran, Kazakhstan, Kyrgyz Republic, FYR Macedonia, Oman, Sierra Leone, Sudan, Timor-Leste, Tonga, Uzbekistan, Vietnam
Reduced labor tax or mandatory contribution rates	Belgium, Benin, Czech Republic, Kazakhstan, Kyrgyz Republic, FYR Macedonia, Moldova, Montenegro, Poland
Eliminated one or more taxes	Cameroon, Djibouti, Kyrgyz Republic, South Africa, Sudan, Timor-Leste, Vietnam

Source: *Doing Business* database.

developing economies, large informal sectors contribute to the creation of an uneven playing field for formal small and medium-size enterprises, squeezed between smaller informal competitors and larger competitors whose greater resources can help win a more effective audience with government and thus greater tax concessions.

Worldwide, economies that make paying taxes easy tend to focus on lower tax rates accompanied by wider tax bases, simpler and more efficient tax administration and one tax per tax base. They also tend to provide electronic filing and payment systems, which reduce the tax burden for firms while lightening their administrative requirements.

WHO REFORMED IN 2008/09?

Between June 2, 2008, and June 1, 2009, 45 economies made it easier for businesses to pay taxes—almost 20 more than in the previous year.[10] Reforms over this period both lowered the tax burden on businesses and simplified tax compliance processes. Twenty economies reduced corporate income tax rates, while 9 reduced labor tax rates (table 8.2). A second category of reforms focused on making it easier to file tax returns and pay taxes. Fourteen economies, more than in any previous year, introduced electronic filing and payment systems. Seven reduced the number of taxes paid

by consolidating or eliminating taxes. Twelve adopted new tax laws or substantially revised existing ones to simplify procedures and modernize tax regimes: Djibouti, the Islamic Republic of Iran, Kazakhstan, the Kyrgyz Republic, FYR Macedonia, Oman, Sierra Leone, Sudan, Timor-Leste, Tonga, Uzbekistan and Vietnam.

Timor-Leste was the top reformer in 2008/09. A new tax law came into force in July 2008, transforming the tax regime for businesses. It cut the profit tax rate from 30% to 10%, allowed all depreciable assets to be fully written off in the year of purchase and abolished the alternative minimum tax and the withholding tax on interest (table 8.3). Corporate income tax is now paid in quarterly rather than monthly installments when turnover is less than $1 million, with simple rules for its calculation. The time required for paying taxes fell by 364 hours a year.

Mexico was the runner-up reformer thanks to its introduction of electronic filing systems for payroll taxes, property taxes and social security. This reduced the number of payments in a year by 21, to 6.

For the third year in a row Eastern Europe and Central Asia had the largest number of reforms, with 10 economies reforming. Kazakhstan cut its corporate income tax rate by 10 percentage points. Kosovo, Montenegro and Russia also reduced their corporate income tax rates. Kazakhstan, the Kyrgyz Republic,

FYR Macedonia, Moldova, Montenegro and Poland reduced the rates for labor taxes and mandatory contributions paid by employers. Regionwide shifts have become evident. Traditionally, employers have borne a significant share of the tax burden through labor taxes. This is gradually reversing, with the region accounting for 55% of labor tax rate reforms in the past 2 years.

Electronic systems are increasingly used in the region. In Belarus the online tax portal has become fully operational for use by all taxpayers, and in FYR Macedonia electronic filing is now mandatory for all taxes. In the past 4 years changes such as these have reduced the average number of tax payments in the region by 4 and the time for tax compliance by almost 6 days. Other reforms also simplified tax compliance. Kazakhstan, FYR Macedonia and Uzbekistan introduced new tax codes. So did the Kyrgyz Republic, and it eliminated some taxes as well.

Sub-Saharan Africa accounted for almost a fifth of the total number of reforms last year. This is timely in a region where businesses still face the highest average tax burden in the world (figure 8.3). On average, African firms must pay 67% of profits in taxes and mandatory contributions and spend 38 days a year complying with 38 tax payments and filings.

Benin, Cape Verde, Sudan and Togo reduced the corporate income tax rate by 8.75 percentage points on average. Benin also reduced its payroll tax, by 4 percentage points. Sudan enacted a new tax code, reduced the capital gains tax by 5 percentage points and abolished an additional tax on labor. South Africa abolished the stamp duty, and Cameroon exempted new companies from the business license tax for 2 years. Electronic filing became more popular across the region. Angola and Kenya introduced electronic systems, making it easier to pay taxes. Sierra Leone eased tax compliance and increased transparency through administrative reforms at the tax authority and publication of a consolidated income tax act, now available online.

TABLE 8.3

Major cuts in corporate income tax rates in 2008/09

Region	Reduction in corporate income tax rate (%)
East Asia & Pacific	Brunei Darussalam from 25.5 to 23.5 Fiji from 31 to 29 Philippines from 35 to 30 Timor-Leste from 30 to 10 Vietnam from 28 to 25
Eastern Europe & Central Asia	Kazakhstan from 30 to 20 Kosovo from 20 to 10 Montenegro from 15 to 9 Russian Federation from 24 to 20
Sub-Saharan Africa	Benin from 38 to 30 Cape Verde from 30 to 25 Sudan from 30 to 15 Togo from 37 to 30
OECD high income	Iceland from 18 to 15 Republic of Korea from 25 to 22 Spain from 32.5 to 30
Middle East & North Africa	Algeria from 25 to 19 Israel from 29 to 27, and further to 26[a]
Latin America & Caribbean	St. Vincent and the Grenadines from 37.5 to 35, and further to 32.5[a]
South Asia	Bangladesh from 40 to 37.5

a. The statutory rate changed twice over the period 2008 to 2009.
Source: Doing Business database.

In East Asia and the Pacific, Brunei Darussalam, Fiji, the Philippines and Vietnam joined Timor-Leste in reducing corporate income tax rates. Vietnam cut the rate to 25% and also abolished the surtax on income from the transfer of land. Lao PDR consolidated the filing for 3 taxes in a single tax return and improved the lodgment process and staffing at the tax offices. Taiwan (China) extended electronic filing and payment to the value added tax. In Timor-Leste, Tonga and Vietnam new income tax laws came into effect.

In the Middle East and North Africa the trend of lowering corporate income tax rates and implementing online systems continued. Jordan simplified tax forms and introduced an online filing and payment system. Lebanon also introduced electronic payment. In Tunisia as of 2009, all companies with a turnover equivalent to at least $1.5 million must use the *télédeclaration* online tax system. Algeria and Israel reduced corporate income tax rates. Oman introduced a new

FIGURE 8.3

Overall tax burden still highest in Sub-Saharan Africa

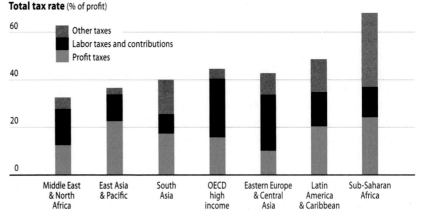

Total tax rate (% of profit)

Source: Doing Business database.

income tax law. Djibouti replaced its sales tax with a new value added tax, as did the Islamic Republic of Iran.

Among OECD high-income economies, Belgium, Finland and Spain made it even easier to file and pay taxes electronically. Iceland, Korea and Spain reduced corporate income tax rates. The Czech Republic mandated electronic filing for all taxes, reducing compliance time by 317 hours, and lowered the rate for social security contributions from 8% to 6.5%.

In Latin America and the Caribbean most major reforms enhanced electronic systems. This is a welcome development, since the region's businesses spend the greatest average time on tax payment and filings (figure 8.4). Aside from Mexico's reforms, Peru made it easier to pay value added tax by providing taxpayers with free software. Colombia's tax authority upgraded its electronic payment system (MUISCA) to allow electronic filing and payment of corporate income tax and value added tax. Guatemala introduced regulations mandating use of electronic systems for tax payments and filings, reducing the number of payments by 14. St. Vincent and the Grenadines lowered the corporate income tax rate from 37.5% to 35% in 2008 and to 32.5% in 2009.

In South Asia, only Bangladesh reformed, reducing the corporate income tax rate from 40% to 37.5%.

Only one economy increased the corporate income tax rate: Lithuania, from 15% to 20% in 2009. The Democratic Republic of Congo increased the sales tax from 13% to 15%. Two economies increased the labor tax and mandatory contribution rates: St. Vincent and the Grenadines by 1 percentage point and Tunisia by 1.07 percentage points. Romania increased the rates of 3 labor taxes.

Three economies introduced new taxes. Brunei Darussalam introduced a 12% building tax on commercial buildings. República Bolivariana de Venezuela had a new antidrug tax come into effect in 2008. Cambodia introduced a new social security contribution.

FIGURE 8.4

Most time consuming in Latin America & Caribbean

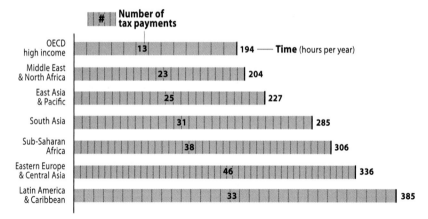

Source: Doing Business database.

TABLE 8.4

Who makes paying taxes easy and who does not—and where is the total tax rate highest and lowest?

Payments (number per year)			
Fewest		**Most**	
Maldives	1	Côte d'Ivoire	66
Qatar	1	Serbia	66
Sweden	2	Venezuela, R.B.	71
Hong Kong, China	4	Jamaica	72
Norway	4	Kyrgyz Republic	75
Singapore	5	Montenegro	89
Mexico	6	Uzbekistan	106
Timor-Leste	6	Belarus	107
Kiribati	7	Romania	113
Mauritius	7	Ukraine	147
Time (hours per year)			
Fastest		**Slowest**	
Maldives	0	Mauritania	696
United Arab Emirates	12	Ukraine	736
Bahrain	36	Venezuela, R.B.	864
Qatar	36	Belarus	900
Bahamas, The	58	Nigeria	938
Luxembourg	59	Armenia	958
Oman	62	Vietnam	1,050
Switzerland	63	Bolivia	1,080
New Zealand	70	Cameroon	1,400
Macedonia, FYR	75	Brazil	2,600
Total tax rate (% of profit)			
Lowest		**Highest**	
Timor-Leste	0.2	Tajikistan	85.9
Vanuatu	8.4	Mauritania	86.1
Maldives	9.1	Uzbekistan	94.9
Namibia	9.6	Belarus	99.7
Qatar	11.3	Argentina	108.1
United Arab Emirates	14.1	Central African Republic	203.8
Saudi Arabia	14.5	Sierra Leone	235.6
Bahrain	15.0	Burundi	278.6
Georgia	15.3	Gambia, The	292.4
Kuwait	15.5	Congo, Dem. Rep.	322.0

Source: Doing Business database.

TOWARD SMART REGULATION

In the past 5 years *Doing Business* has recorded 171 reforms in paying taxes in 105 economies around the world—reforms aimed at making tax compliance easier and the tax burden lighter for small and medium-size businesses. Reformers in economies as diverse as Egypt, Mauritius and Turkey have underscored the importance of tax reform in enhancing economic growth and investment, increasing competitiveness, combating unemployment and achieving good governance. In reforming their tax systems they have sought to eliminate various exemptions, broaden the tax base and modernize their tax systems.

EASING COMPLIANCE THROUGH BROAD-BASED REFORMS

Many tax reforms are aimed at simplifying the tax law and making it easier for firms to comply with regulations. A bold step in this direction involves eliminating tax exemptions, tax holidays and other special treatment for different types of businesses, to achieve equal treatment for all businesses. Eliminating tax exemptions can be difficult, because they are often used as tax incentives with specific objectives. Reform experiences in such economies as Egypt, Georgia, Mauritius and Turkey show that it takes political will and buy-in from stakeholders to succeed.

Jamaica also has a lesson to share: during its 1986 flat tax reform it used arguments of fairness to overcome opposition to reform—and eliminated 17 types of credits and 44 allowances.[11] In 2005 Egypt eliminated all tax exemptions and introduced a flat tax of 20% on corporate income, down from 32% or 40%, as well as electronic filing and self-assessment.[12] Sales tax revenue rose by 46%, and corporate tax collections by 24.7%. Mauritius shifted from a tiered rate to a single rate with a broader tax base. It also streamlined tax administration and made it electronic. The following year corporate tax collection exceeded projections by 13.5%.[13]

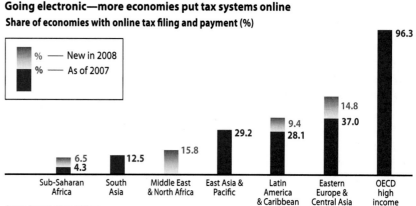

FIGURE 8.5

Going electronic—more economies put tax systems online
Share of economies with online tax filing and payment (%)

Source: *Doing Business* database.

Georgia's tax reform of 2008 was multifaceted, targeting different taxes simultaneously. It lowered the corporate tax rate, abolished the social tax and introduced online filing, reducing the number of tax payments and the tax burden. Easier compliance also made enforcement less burdensome. Surveys of businesses showed that the average number of visits or required meetings with tax officials fell from 8 in 2005 to only 0.4 in 2008.[14]

MAKING SYSTEMS ELECTRONIC

Almost 70 of the 183 economies covered by *Doing Business* offer electronic tax filing and payment options to businesses (figure 8.5). In 56 economies the electronic systems are used by a significant share of businesses. Not surprisingly, among OECD high-income economies all but one permit firms to file and pay taxes electronically. But the trend is also picking up among developing economies. In the past 5 years 31 have introduced fairly comprehensive electronic systems. Another 14 are introducing electronic filing or payment or have just done so and are encouraging wider use by taxpayers.

Many economies are eager to make use of technology to ease the paying of taxes—and with good reason. If properly implemented, and adopted by businesses, electronic tax systems speed up processing, improve data collection and reduce error rates. In the United States in 2009, the error rate was less than 1% for electronically prepared and filed returns

but about 20% for paper returns.[15] But taxpayers can be slow to take up the new technology. In many developing economies access to the internet remains an obstacle. But adoption of new systems can be slow for reasons that cut across economies at all levels of development.

Most critically, taxpayers need to trust the payment system. This requires high-quality security systems to protect data. Also required are laws addressing data protection and privacy concerns and allowing electronic signatures. Electronic payment can be implemented in several ways, including through the internet. Another way is through automatic bank transfer, popular across all regions and income levels, mainly because taxpayers perceive it as less prone to security risks.

In Lebanon taxpayers can make electronic payments at any post office. In Tunisia the government initially introduced an intermediate option allowing online filers to print a receipt number and make their payment in any tax office. The past year's reform consolidated electronic payment and filing through the *télédeclaration* online system.

Another issue is access to the system. To encourage use of new technology, Peru and South Africa provide free software that makes the filing process automatic.[16] France eased access while maintaining security by scrapping its electronic verification software. Taxpayers can now verify their identity with the numbers on their annual declaration and their notice of assessment. In Chile taxpayers can use their universal identification number and a password.

Faster refunds and processing times for online transactions are key incentives to encourage use of new technology. Australia, Ireland, Taiwan (China), the United Kingdom and the United States offer inducements such as these. South Africa waived late penalties for online filers in 2007. France introduced tax credits for individual taxpayers filing their returns electronically, though in the future this will apply only to first-time electronic filers. Sharing gains from administrative efficiency is a way to encourage taxpayers to use the system.

1. Oracle Education Foundation, Think-Quest, "Daily Life of the Egyptians," http://thinkquest.org/ library.

2. PricewaterhouseCoopers (2008).

3. Commonwealth of Australia (2009).

4. Chew (2009).

5. Djankov and others (forthcoming).

6. Huizinga and Laeven (2008).

7. Huizinga, Laeven and Nicodème (2008).

8. Nicodème (2008).

9. Everest-Phillips and Sandall (2009) and de Mooij and Nicodème (2008).

10. This year's report records all reforms with an impact on the paying taxes indicators between June 2008 and May 2009. Because the case study underlying the paying taxes indicators refers to the financial year ending December 31, 2008, reforms implemented between January 2009 and May 2009 are recorded in this year's report, but the impact will be reflected in the data in next year's report.

11. Hadler, Moloi and Wallace (2006).

12. World Bank (2006).

13. Cuttaree and Trumbic (forthcoming).

14. World Bank Enterprise Surveys (http://www.enterprisesurveys.org).

15. Kim Dixon, "Electronic Tax Filing Jumps 19 Percent—IRS," Reuters, April 30, 2009, http://uk.reuters.com/article/idUKN3032076020090430.

16. Wongtrakool (1998).

Trading across borders

FIGURE 9.1

Speeding up trade—especially in low-income economies
Reduction in the time to export (days)

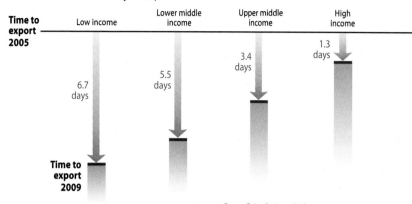

Source: Doing Business database.

Janet has been running a successful company in Rwanda producing and selling baskets and other traditional crafts. Business was going so well that a few years ago she started exporting her products to markets in the United States and Europe. But times have become more difficult. With the global financial and economic crisis, demand fell and new orders stopped coming in.

Janet is not the only one. The World Trade Organization estimates that trade volumes will drop by 10% in 2009, the first fall after 27 years of uninterrupted expansion. In response to political pressures to preserve jobs, import barriers have been rising around the world. But one lesson from the experience of the 1930s is that raising trade barriers can merely compound recessionary forces

and risks pushing economies into a prolonged contraction. Indeed, as Australian Minister for Trade Simon Crean notes, "international trade is one of the most important arenas in which we must combat the real effects of the crisis. Trade is itself a stimulus."[1]

Where the trade environment is more favorable, businesses are better positioned to take advantage of new opportunities, to grow and to create jobs when the global economy picks up again. Rather than resorting to protectionism, policy makers can help struggling traders by cutting red tape and burdensome procedural requirements to export and import (figure 9.1). Rwanda is one country that did so in the past year—and thanks to its reform, Janet's business can benefit from simpler documentation requirements and speedier border processing.

But in many economies cumbersome trade procedures, long delays and high trading costs continue to stifle trade potential. In Eritrea, for example, an exporter must spend 50 days and $1,431 to complete all export formalities from the time the sales contract is concluded until the goods are on the vessel. In Cambodia an exporter faces only half that time and cost.

Doing Business measures the procedural requirements, including the number of necessary documents and the associated time and cost (excluding tariffs), for exporting and importing by

ocean transport (figure 9.2). The indicators cover documentation requirements and procedures at customs and the port as well as inland transport to the largest business city. The more time consuming and costly it is to export or import, the more difficult it is for traders to be competitive and to reach international markets.

Traders in low-income economies face particular constraints. Recent studies show that manufacturing enterprises in Africa have difficulty exporting because of poor customs administration and restrictive trade and customs regulations.[2] Much attention is paid to tariff cuts. But better customs processes and trade logistics would also benefit African exporters. Take Ethiopia. One recent study shows that if it improved its logis-

TABLE 9.1

Where is trading easy—and where not?

Easiest	RANK	Most difficult	RANK
Singapore	1	Uzbekistan	174
Hong Kong, China	2	Burundi	175
Estonia	3	Burkina Faso	176
Finland	4	Azerbaijan	177
United Arab Emirates	5	Congo, Rep.	178
		Tajikistan	179
Denmark	6	Iraq	180
Sweden	7	Central African Republic	181
Korea, Rep.	8		
Norway	9	Kazakhstan	182
Panama	10	Afghanistan	183

Note: Rankings are the average of the economy's rankings on the documents, time and cost required to export and import. See Data notes for details.
Source: Doing Business database.

FIGURE 9.2

Trading across borders: exporting and importing by ocean transport
Rankings are based on 3 subindicators

All documents required by customs and other agencies

Document preparation, customs clearance and technical control, port and terminal handling, inland transport and handling

33.3% Documents to export and import

33.3% Time to export and import

33.3% Cost to export and import

US$ per 20-foot container, no bribes or tariffs included

Note: See Data notes for details.

tics to half the quality of South Africa's, the benefit would be equivalent to a 7.5% tariff cut.[3] An OECD study finds that reducing delays at borders by 6.3%, or the number of documents required for trading by 11%, could increase trade flows in Africa by 10%.[4]

Another recent study shows that high trade transactions costs constrain the trade performance of African, Caribbean and Pacific economies negotiating Economic Partnership Agreements with the European Union. The study estimates that reducing border delays in these economies by 1 day could increase exports by 1%.[5] And a study using data from 167 countries finds that every $1 reduction in trade costs could increase exports by more than $1,000.[6]

The potential benefits from reforms to facilitate trade are not limited to higher exports. The public treasury could be a big winner. Ask Peter Malinga, commissioner of customs in Uganda. The country's reforms to improve customs administration and reduce corruption helped increase customs revenue by 24% between 2007 and 2008. Trade facilitation reforms yield the greatest benefits when matched by reforms to improve the regulatory environment for businesses in other areas—such as start-up or contract enforcement.[7]

Economies that rank high on the ease of trading across borders have found ways to make exporting and importing as efficient as possible. They require fewer documents, so traders spend less time on bureaucratic approvals. They allow traders to submit those documents electronically, often even before the goods arrive at the port. They limit physical inspections to the riskiest cargo. And many have fast-track clearance procedures for selected companies, auditing their shipments only after clearance.

More than 90 economies have adopted such practices over the past 5 years. Korea is one that has continually reformed its trade logistics environment over the past decade. No wonder it is a key player in global supply chains, exporting automobiles, cell phones and

semiconductors around the world. In many low-income economies inefficient practices continue to constrain trade. But many are also reforming.

WHO REFORMED IN 2008/09?

Thirty-eight economies made it easier to trade in 2008/09 (table 9.2). Reformers in Sub-Saharan Africa were once again the most active: 14 of the region's economies reformed, thanks in part to greater donor support for aid-for-trade initiatives.[8] Motivated by plans to foster greater regional integration, 7 economies reformed in Latin America and the Caribbean and 6 in Eastern Europe and Central Asia. Economies in the OECD high-income group and East Asia and the Pacific had the fewest reforms, but many of them have already adopted global good practices.

Georgia, one of the most consistent reformers over the past 5 years, was the top reformer in trade in 2008/09. Responding to business complaints about slow processing of paperwork, the government issued new regulations reducing the number of documents required for trading to 4. New job performance measures for customs officers require them to examine customs declarations within 2 hours of receipt. Promotions

depend on it. Before, says Mr. Megrelishvili, a freight forwarder in Georgia, "you could never say which terminal was better or worse. All were the same: a long physical inspection process, poor professionalism, flourishing bribery and a permanent wasting of time and nerves. Today the process is quicker."

Elsewhere in Eastern Europe and Central Asia, Albania, Azerbaijan, Belarus and the Kyrgyz Republic reformed. They made it easier for traders to submit documents to customs electronically or implemented risk-based inspection systems. Albania upgraded its electronic data interchange system, allowing traders to access the system by the internet. Armenia, another top reformer in trade, improved the transparency and efficiency of customs by increasing the number of licensed customs brokers, clarifying valuation rules and inspection requirements and reducing the number of documents required to clear goods.

As part of the East African Customs Union harmonization program, Kenya, Rwanda and Uganda are strengthening their border cooperation with the aim of improving data sharing. Angola, Benin, Mali, Mauritius, Senegal and Sudan are seeing the results of several years of continual efforts to improve customs clearance through better use of electronic

TABLE 9.2

Electronic data interchange—the most popular reform feature in 2008/09

Introduced or improved electronic data interchange system	Albania, Angola, Bangladesh, Benin, Colombia, Guyana, Haiti, Jordan, Kuwait, Mali, Mauritius, Paraguay, Senegal, Slovak Republic, St. Kitts and Nevis, Sudan, Tunisia, Uganda, Republic of Yemen
Introduced or improved risk-based inspections	Albania, Azerbaijan, Belarus, Cameroon, Georgia, Islamic Republic of Iran, Jordan, Kyrgyz Republic, Liberia, Malawi, Mali, Mozambique, Paraguay, Sudan, Republic of Yemen
Improved customs administration	Angola, Armenia, Belarus, Benin, Georgia, Grenada, Islamic Republic of Iran, Kuwait, Mozambique, Portugal, Rwanda, Uganda, Vietnam
Reduced number of trade documents	Angola, Armenia, China, Georgia, Kyrgyz Republic, Mali, Rwanda, United Arab Emirates
Improved procedures at ports	Democratic Republic of Congo, Haiti, Kuwait, Peru, Senegal, United Arab Emirates
Introduced or improved single window	Azerbaijan, Burkina Faso, Cameroon, Liberia
Implemented border cooperation agreements	Rwanda, Uganda

Source: Doing Business database.

data interchange systems. Madagascar and Senegal are benefiting from having privatized the management of their container terminals. In Liberia some inspections are now being carried out jointly by customs and border security authorities, and a single window has opened at the port.

In Latin America and the Caribbean, Colombia, Guyana, Haiti, Paraguay and St. Kitts and Nevis implemented electronic data interchange systems—and traders can now submit their documents electronically. Grenada is improving customs administration by providing ad-ditional training to officers and streamlining interdepartmental coordination. Paraguay improved its risk-based inspection system by upgrading to a green, yellow, and red lane system, reducing the share of goods inspected. Peru installed additional cranes at its port, reducing port and terminal handling times.

In the Middle East and North Africa, the Republic of Yemen introduced an electronic data interchange system that has helped reduce the time to clear customs. Jordan and Tunisia made clearance faster by allowing 24-hour online access to the e-trade portal. In Kuwait manifests can now be submitted electronically to customs. This change, along with better coordination between customs and the port authority, has reduced the time to export and import. The Islamic Republic of Iran reduced inspection delays at the port of Shahid Rajae by installing 2 scanners, and the United Arab Emirates continued to improve its customs and port infrastructure.

In East Asia, China relaxed restrictions on foreign exchange prepayments for exporters and deferred payments for importers, making it easier for smaller companies to carry out international

TABLE 9.3

Who makes exporting easy—and who does not?

Documents (number)			
Fewest		**Most**	
France	2	Cambodia	11
Estonia	3	Namibia	11
Korea, Rep.	3	Mauritania	11
Panama	3	Angola	11
Canada	3	Malawi	11
Micronesia, Fed. Sts.	3	Burkina Faso	11
Singapore	4	Congo, Rep.	11
Hong Kong, China	4	Kazakhstan	11
Finland	4	Afghanistan	12
United Arab Emirates	4	Fiji	13

Time (days)			
Fastest		**Slowest**	
Singapore	5	Central African Republic	54
Estonia	5	Niger	59
Denmark	5	Kyrgyz Republic	63
Hong Kong, China	6	Angola	65
Netherlands	6	Uzbekistan	71
United States	6	Afghanistan	74
Luxembourg	6	Chad	75
Norway	7	Tajikistan	82
Germany	7	Kazakhstan	89
Cyprus	7	Iraq	102

Cost (US$ per container)			
Least		**Most**	
Malaysia	450	Uzbekistan	3,100
Singapore	456	Tajikistan	3,150
China	500	Uganda	3,190
Finland	540	Rwanda	3,275
United Arab Emirates	593	Zimbabwe	3,280
Latvia	600	Afghanistan	3,350
Pakistan	611	Niger	3,545
Hong Kong, China	625	Iraq	3,900
Thailand	625	Central African Republic	5,491
Brunei Darussalam	630	Chad	5,497

Who makes importing easy—and who does not?

Documents (number)			
Fewest		**Most**	
France	2	Uzbekistan	11
Denmark	3	Burkina Faso	11
Sweden	3	Afghanistan	11
Korea, Rep.	3	Congo, Rep.	12
Thailand	3	Fiji	13
Singapore	4	Russian Federation	13
Hong Kong, China	4	Eritrea	13
Estonia	4	Kazakhstan	13
Norway	4	Azerbaijan	14
Panama	4	Central African Republic	17

Time (days)			
Fastest		**Slowest**	
Singapore	3	Venezuela, R.B.	71
Hong Kong, China	5	Burundi	71
Estonia	5	Kyrgyz Republic	72
Denmark	5	Zimbabwe	73
Cyprus	5	Kazakhstan	76
United States	5	Afghanistan	77
Sweden	6	Tajikistan	83
Netherlands	6	Uzbekistan	92
Luxembourg	6	Chad	100
Norway	7	Iraq	101

Cost (US$ per container)			
Least		**Most**	
Singapore	439	Niger	3,545
Malaysia	450	Burkina Faso	3,830
China	545	Iraq	3,900
São Tomé and Principe	577	Burundi	4,285
United Arab Emirates	579	Tajikistan	4,550
Hong Kong, China	583	Uzbekistan	4,600
Israel	605	Rwanda	5,070
Finland	620	Zimbabwe	5,101
Fiji	630	Central African Republic	5,554
Qatar	657	Chad	6,150

Source: Doing Business database.

trade transactions. Vietnam improved the efficiency of its customs clearance by introducing postcustoms clearance audits and installing software that allows traders to determine the duties applicable to goods being cleared. Finally, in South Asia traders in Bangladesh benefited from the introduction of an automated import and export customs clearance system at Chittagong port.

TOWARD SMART REGULATION

In the past 5 years *Doing Business* has recorded 140 trade facilitation reforms in 92 economies. The most active reformers have been Mauritius, Rwanda and Uganda, in Sub-Saharan Africa; India, in South Asia; Egypt and Morocco, in the Middle East and North Africa; and Brazil and Colombia, in Latin America and the Caribbean. Here are some of the most effective reform features that have been implemented over the years.

GOING ELECTRONIC
Across economies, regardless of income level, installing electronic data interchange systems for submitting and processing documents remains a popular and effective way to reduce delays in the trading process. In 2008/09, 19 economies implemented or improved such a system, 7 of them in Africa. Thanks in part to systems recently put into place in Benin, Guyana, Haiti, Jordan, Mali and Uganda, traders in those economies saw the time to clear goods cut by at least 2 days.

Such reforms can also boost government revenues. Take Afghanistan. As part of a $31.2 million World Bank project to modernize customs and facilitate trade, Afghanistan computerized its customs processes at 4 major border crossings. More trade is now passing through official channels. Customs revenues soared from $50 million in 2004 to more than $399 million in 2008, a 700% increase. Truckers also gained: the waiting time at the Kabul Inland Clearance Depot is a quarter of what it was before. Challenges remain, with other border crossings yet to be tackled. But the project is increas-

ing government revenues and supporting legitimate trade.

Electronic data interchange systems are an investment. The cost of implementation varies, depending in part on the system's complexity. Off-the-shelf systems tend to be less expensive than customized ones—though customized systems may be better tailored to addressing the specificities of an economy's trade procedures. In Afghanistan the cost was estimated to be $1.6 million. But in Jamaica it was $5.5 million—and in Turkey, $32 million.

Technology is no magic wand. The benefits of electronic data interchange systems can be undercut by many factors. Traders in several African economies that have developed automated customs systems—such as Ghana, Kenya and Tanzania—complain about lack of access to uninterrupted power supply and high-speed internet connections. In Bangladesh technical glitches initially hampered the operation of the electronic system at the Chittagong Customs House. But the problems were overcome, and now most of the traders prefer to use the new system because they believe it provides faster service and limits the scope for bribes.

Lack of legislation on electronic signatures and transactions can also cause problems and lead to duplications in the clearance system. In Tunisia, for ex-

ample, traders still have to file paper documents even though an electronic system is in place.

For electronic data interchange reforms to succeed, all these concerns need to be addressed.

CREATING A SINGLE WINDOW
Implementing a single window for trade transactions is another way to make it faster and easier to trade. By 2003 Korea Customs Service already had in place an electronic data interchange system that cut firms' costs from trade-related paperwork by 80%. Yet it set its sights higher, embarking on a comprehensive single-window project aimed at making Korea the logistics hub of North Asia. Completed in July 2008, the system allows traders, government agencies and private sector participants—including traders, banks, customs brokers, insurance companies and freight forwarders—to exchange information in real time, speeding up approvals. Firms' savings in labor, printing, paper delivery, storage and inventory costs are estimated at more than 2,582 billion won, or about $2 billion, a year (figure 9.3).[9] And the reform efforts are not over. Korea Customs Service is now working with the customs services of other economies to link their systems as well.

Reforms do not always go smoothly. Because a single window brings together

FIGURE 9.3

The Republic of Korea cuts firms' costs by reforming trade facilitation

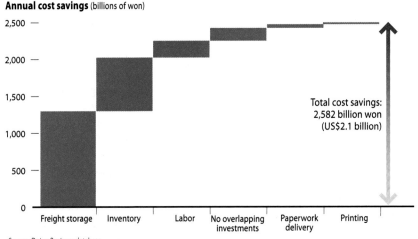

Annual cost savings (billions of won)

Total cost savings: 2,582 billion won (US$2.1 billion)

Source: Doing Business database.

several parties, some of which may have to cede some control, it requires strong political support to succeed. Reformers in Colombia and Senegal, for example, first had to overcome resistance from opposing parties. In Korea the single window succeeded thanks to the priority accorded to trade facilitation reforms at high levels of government. The National e-Trade Committee was chaired by the prime minister and included 10 ministers, the commissioner of customs and the chairs and presidents of leading private industry associations, including those for small and medium-size businesses.

EASING PRIVATE SECTOR PARTICIPATION IN TRADE SERVICES

Customs formalities are not the only factor affecting the time and cost for trading across borders. Private providers of trade services—such as customs brokers, trucking companies and port service providers—all play an important role. The quality of their services and the fees they charge inevitably affect trade competitiveness. By removing overly burdensome restrictions on their operations, governments can help increase competition and thus improve the quality and lower the cost of service.

In several developing economies, despite lower wage levels, traders must pay higher fees to customs brokers than their counterparts in developed econo-

mies. In Uganda customs brokers charge clients $150 on average to clear a 20-foot container. In Germany, where income per capita is more than 100 times as high, customs brokers charge clients $50 on average for the same service. Traders in Uganda are not alone (figure 9.4). Customs brokers are often regulated by government agencies. But caps on the number of brokers, high license fees, onerous eligibility requirements and infrequent training opportunities restrict entry, limit competition and contribute to higher brokerage fees.

Greater competition makes a difference. After Algeria accelerated the approval of license applications for brokers, customs clearance fees dropped by 40–50%. Armenia saw costs fall after improving training opportunities and licensing new customs brokers. Yet in some economies the high service fees reflect the facilitation payments brokers must pay to navigate the maze of trade procedures. These should be tackled first.

Competition is just as critical in trucking. Transporting a container load from Lusaka (Zambia) to the seaport in Durban (South Africa) costs $2,100; from Ndjamena (Chad) to the seaport in Yaoundé (Cameroon), it costs $4,000. What's surprising? Durban is much farther away from Lusaka (1,630 kilometers) than Yaoundé is from Ndjamena (996 kilometers). A recent study concludes that "traders in landlocked developing countries may be confronted with bad infrastructure or long distances, but the main sources of higher cost have to do with rent-seeking, inefficient markets for services such as trucking and inadequate transit procedures."[10]

This does not have to be the case. The Zambian trucking market can offer relatively competitive rates because several foreign trucking companies, most from South Africa, operate along Zambian trade corridors.[11] In Rwanda greater border cooperation has allowed more trucks from neighboring countries such as Kenya and Uganda to augment the domestic fleet. "Before these reforms many foreign truckers were de-

terred from coming to Rwanda because of some of the difficulties in passing through borders," says Eric, a Rwandese freight forwarder. Trade can be boosted by reforms that ease entry restrictions in trucking services within economies and streamline cumbersome transport procedures at borders, allowing trucks to pass through neighboring economies with fewer restrictions.

Maritime transport accounts for some 80% of trade. So access to competitive, efficient ports can provide a big boost to an economy's trade prospects. Low-income economies generally face higher port costs, in part because of poorer infrastructure (figure 9.5). And port infrastructure is costly. The development of an economy's port competitiveness can be hindered by many issues, one of which is unfavorable regulations.

Based on a sample of container terminals around the world, one study finds that private sector participation can improve the efficiency of port operation, which in turn increases port competitiveness.[12] But in many economies regulations restrict or discourage private participation in the provision of port services. And without the right regulatory regime and incentive structure, an inefficient public service provider could simply be replaced by an inefficient private monopoly service provider. Good contractual and regulatory design and oversight—embodied in

FIGURE 9.4
Higher customs-related charges in low-income economies

Average customs-related charges
(US$ per container)

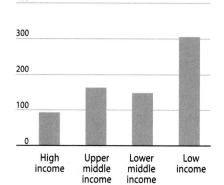

Source: Doing Business database.

FIGURE 9.5
Higher port and terminal charges in low-income economies

Average port and terminal handling charges (US$ per container)

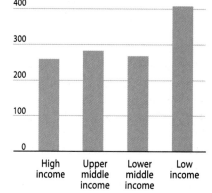

Source: Doing Business database.

favorable pricing policies, labor regulations and contract duration—can help translate private participation into competitive port services.[13]

Take the port of Dakar. Until recently it lacked critical infrastructure investments even though private companies provided container terminal services. The problem was that the contracts signed with the private participants had such short durations that no one was interested in committing to costly investments that would yield returns only in the long run.

This has changed. The winner of the bid to manage the container terminal was awarded a long-term contract. The company has since invested heavily in gantry cranes and a world-class container management system. With cargo now moving through more quickly, the port of Dakar remains the only one on the west coast of Africa that faces no congestion surcharges. Recent years have seen a similar turnaround in performance at the ports of Djibouti; Aqaba, Jordan; and Toamasina, Madagascar, thanks in part to favorable contractual and regulatory design encouraging investments by some of the world's leading private container terminal operators.

1. Crean (2009, p. 13).
2. Iwanow and Kirkpatrick (2009) and Clarke (2005).
3. Portugal-Perez and Wilson (2008).
4. Wilson (2009).
5. Person (2008).
6. Martinez-Zarzosa and Márquez-Ramos (2008).
7. Iwanow and Kirkpatrick (2007) and Ranjan and Lee (2007).
8. World Bank (2009a).
9. Yang (2009).
10. World Bank (2008c, p. 13).
11. Raballand, Kunuka and Giersing (2008).
12. Tongzon and Heng (2005).
13. For comprehensive coverage of issues related to port reform, see World Bank (2007).

Enforcing contracts

FIGURE 10.1

Reformers reduce the time to enforce a contract in 2008/09

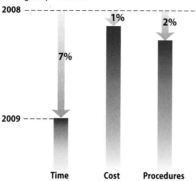

Note: Based on average improvement of the 16 reforming economies.
Source: Doing Business database.

These are busy times for courts. The financial and economic crisis has brought more litigation to courts all over the world. Businesses are collecting debt more actively, because they need the money to keep operating. Debtors are more likely to become insolvent, especially where court proceedings drag on for years. Countries such as Iceland, New Zealand, Ukraine and the United Kingdom have reported greater caseloads due to crisis-related litigation. In Iceland commercial cases rose by 33%, from fewer than 15,000 in 2007 to 20,000 in 2008.[1]

Courts must deliver despite growing caseloads and looming budget problems. Recent research shows that a country's ability to enforce contracts is an important determinant of its comparative advantage in the global economy: among comparable economies, those with good contract enforcement tend to produce and export more customized products than those with poor contract enforcement.[2]

The efficiency of courts varies greatly around the world. Enforcing a contract can take less than a year in Norway or Korea, both among the top 10 on the ease of enforcing contracts, but more than 4 years in Bangladesh or Angola (table 10.1). Worldwide on average, exchanging written and oral arguments, including expert testimony during trial, takes almost two-thirds of the total time. Enforcing the judgment takes about a third of the time. It accounts for 17% of the total cost, and court and expert fees for about the same share. Attorney fees are the biggest driver of cost.

Doing Business measures the time, cost and procedural complexity of resolving a commercial lawsuit between 2 domestic businesses. The dispute involves the breach of a sales contract worth twice the income per capita of the economy. The case study assumes that the court hears an expert on the quality of the goods in dispute. This distinguishes the case from simple debt enforcement.

TABLE 10.1

Where is enforcing contracts easy—and where not?

Easiest	RANK	Most difficult	RANK
Luxembourg	1	Cameroon	174
Iceland	2	Honduras	175
Hong Kong, China	3	Syrian Arab Republic	176
Norway	4		
Korea, Rep.	5	Benin	177
France	6	Suriname	178
Germany	7	São Tomé and Principe	179
Finland	8		
United States	9	Bangladesh	180
New Zealand	10	Angola	181
		India	182
		Timor-Leste	183

Note: Rankings are the average of the economy's rankings on the procedures, time and cost to resolve a commercial dispute through the courts. See Data notes for details.

Source: Doing Business database.

Sixteen economies made it faster, cheaper or less cumbersome to enforce a contract through the courts in 2008/09 (figure 10.1). The reforms included comprehensive reviews of civil procedure rules, programs to reduce case backlogs, redistribution of caseloads and the introduction or expansion of computerized case management systems (table 10.2). Introducing specialized commercial courts and making enforcement of judgment more efficient continued to be popular. Sub-Saharan Africa and the Middle East and North Africa saw the most significant reforms in commercial litigation. Eastern European and Central Asian economies continued to build on previous reforms. In South Asia no reforms were recorded.

FIGURE 10.2

Enforcing contracts: resolving a commercial dispute through the courts

Rankings are based on 3 subindicators

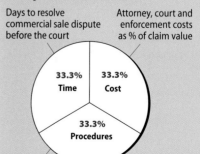

Note: See Data notes for details.

TABLE 10.2
Computerizing case management—the most popular reform feature in 2008/09

Introduced or expanded computerized case management system	Algeria, Botswana, Ethiopia, Jordan, Norway, West Bank and Gaza
Undertook review of civil procedure rules	Algeria, Botswana, Mali, Norway, Peru
Implemented program to reduce case backlog or redistribute caseload	Ethiopia, Grenada, Jordan, Malaysia, West Bank and Gaza
Introduced or expanded specialized commercial court	Arab Republic of Egypt, Jordan, Mauritius, Papua New Guinea
Made enforcement of judgment more efficient	Ethiopia, Jordan, Portugal, West Bank and Gaza
Reviewed rules on modes of service and notification	Costa Rica, Peru
Changed cost regime	Burkina Faso

Source: Doing Business database.

Botswana was the top reformer in 2008/09. New rules for its high court, in force since mid-2008, have reduced the average time to resolve a commercial dispute by 30%, from 987 days to 687. The rules introduced pretrial conferences, leading to faster resolution. Judges no longer merely hear cases but actively manage them, setting a timetable and ensuring compliance. A sophisticated new computerized case management system makes it easy to keep close tabs on whether court personnel and litigants are complying with deadlines. The system also allows court officers to dismiss "aged matters"—cases in which litigants have remained inactive for long periods.

Ethiopia was the runner-up reformer. It reduced the average time to resolve a commercial dispute by 10%—and rose 13 places in the rankings on the ease of enforcing contracts. The Ethiopian courts are implementing a backlog reduction program with a new twist: summer recess is being devoted to disposing of backlogged cases. Two-thirds of judges volunteered to hear cases during special summer sessions.

Like Botswana, Ethiopia now has a computerized case management system that helps to sustain the improvements. Addis Ababa's automated system allows users to search for cases more easily. Anyone can access the court schedule—online, over the telephone or from a touch screen at the court building. The system produces real-time data on the number of cases assigned to each court chamber, making it possible to measure the performance of judges, chambers and courts across the country. Over time these data will help determine which

courts have heavier caseloads and guide the allocation of resources.

Three other Sub-Saharan African countries reformed. Mali amended its procedural rules. Now litigants can file suit without applying and waiting for a judge's order authorizing service—less procedural steps and 7 fewer days to file and serve process. The new rules go beyond contract enforcement. Counsel can now interrogate witnesses directly, without prior approval by the judge, improving Mali's score on the strength of investor protection index. Recruitment of additional judges for Bamako's commercial court reduced the average trial time from 315 days to 240. Between January and June 2009 the court disposed of 344 cases, as against 359 new cases lodged.

Mauritius set up its first specialized commercial court in January 2009, as a division of the supreme court. Two of the 16 supreme court judges are now assigned exclusively to commercial cases. By May 2009, after just 5 months of operation, the commercial division had disposed of 593 cases. That's a big share of its total of 959, of which 657 were old cases transferred to the new division.

Burkina Faso reduced official court costs by replacing a percentage-based filing fee with a nominal fixed fee of 6,000 CFA francs (about $12). It also abolished the stamp duty that creditors previously had to pay to register a judgment before enforcement.

In the Middle East and North Africa 4 economies reformed. Egypt and Jordan both introduced specialized courts. Egypt established a separate commercial court to deal with commercial matters. Jordan set up commercial divisions within the existing courts.

Jordan is trying to better distribute caseload by raising the threshold for cases heard by its lowest first-instance civil court, the "conciliation court," from 3,000 Jordanian dinars to 7,000 (about $10,000). It also introduced a computerized case management system, Mizan II, an improved version of the original used in neighboring West Bank and Gaza. The system adds features such as text mes-

FIGURE 10.3
Enforcement of the judgment takes about a third of the time to enforce a contract

Global distribution of time and cost to enforce a contract

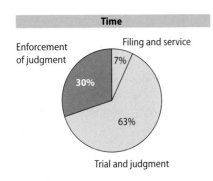

Time

Enforcement of judgment
Filing and service 7%
30%
63%
Trial and judgment

Cost

Enforcement of judgment
Attorney fees
17%
Court costs and expert fees 18%
65%

Source: Doing Business database.

TABLE 10.3
Who makes enforcing contracts easy—and who does not?

Procedures (number of steps)

Fewest		Most	
Ireland	20	Guinea	50
Singapore	21	Kuwait	50
Hong Kong, China	24	Belize	51
Rwanda	24	Iraq	51
Austria	25	Oman	51
Belgium	25	Timor-Leste	51
Netherlands	25	Kosovo	53
Iceland	26	Sudan	53
Luxembourg	26	Syrian Arab Republic	55
Czech Republic	27	Brunei Darussalam	58

Time (days)

Fastest		Slowest	
Singapore	150	Slovenia	1,290
Uzbekistan	195	Sri Lanka	1,318
New Zealand	216	Trinidad and Tobago	1,340
Belarus	225	Colombia	1,346
Bhutan	225	India	1,420
Korea, Rep.	230	Timor-Leste	1,435
Azerbaijan	237	Bangladesh	1,442
Kyrgyz Republic	260	Guatemala	1,459
Rwanda	260	Afghanistan	1,642
Namibia	270	Suriname	1,715

Cost (% of claim)

Least		Most	
Bhutan	0.1	Burkina Faso	83.0
Iceland	6.2	Comoros	89.4
Luxembourg	9.7	Cambodia	102.7
Norway	9.9	Papua New Guinea	110.3
Korea, Rep.	10.3	Indonesia	122.7
Finland	10.4	Malawi	142.4
China	11.1	Mozambique	142.5
Poland	12.0	Sierra Leone	149.5
Thailand	12.3	Congo, Dem. Rep.	151.8
Slovenia	12.7	Timor-Leste	163.2

Source: Doing Business database.

sage notification of attorneys, online access to court records for authorized users and the possibility to consult electronic copies of each case file.

West Bank and Gaza is piloting Mizan II. It is also implementing wide-ranging court reforms. New judges have been recruited and trained. Courts with a substantial caseload, such as the Ramallah magistrates' court, have been assigned an enforcement judge responsible solely for handling issues arising from the execution of judgments. The reforms reduced the average time to resolve a commercial dispute from 700 days to 600.

In Algeria a new civil procedure code came into force in April 2009. The code introduces nonmandatory arbitration and mediation. It also reinforces procedural time limits, setting caps not only on delays but also on the number of hearings (5) to dispose of a case.

In Latin America and the Caribbean, Costa Rica, Grenada and Peru reformed. All 3 reviewed their procedural rules. Costa Rica now allows the use of ordinary mail and e-mail for serving process on defendants. To make this easier, it is setting up a national registry recording the home and business ad-

dresses of all citizens. Those who move must update the register. Costa Rica also allows the first announcement of a public auction of seized assets to include a second and third date, in case the assets are not sold in the initial sale. Eliminating the need to publish second and third announcements saves judgment creditors time and costs.

Peru requires attempts at conciliation even before litigation is initiated. New procedural laws have introduced deadlines to file evidence and dispose of inactive cases. Peru is also moving toward greater use of e-services. The law recognizes notification by electronic means. The justices of the peace, Peru's lowest civil courts, are piloting a system in which judgments are uploaded on their websites as soon as they are delivered. Grenada issued practice notes to bolster its civil procedure code and hired a second judge, doubling the size of the small island state's judiciary.

In East Asia and the Pacific, Malaysia and Papua New Guinea reformed. Malaysia cut filing and service time by 15 days by adding administrative staff to deal with incoming cases and setting stricter deadlines. It also improved caseload allocation by creating a fast track in the commercial division of the Kuala Lumpur high court, to deal exclusively with interlocutory matters. In Papua New Guinea a specialized commercial division of the national court is now fully operational.

Among OECD high-income economies, Norway and Portugal were reformers. Already among the top 10 on enforcing contracts, Norway is enforcing procedural deadlines more strictly. The computer system that tracks incoming cases now requires judges to justify delays in any case not resolved within the prescribed 6 months. This has reduced the time to enforce a contract by 10%. Portugal carried out an extensive review of its law on the execution of judgments. The result: streamlined procedures with less intervention by judges and broader powers for bailiffs. And lawyers fulfilling certain requirements can now apply to be licensed as bailiffs.

TOWARD SMART REGULATION

In the past 6 years *Doing Business* has recorded 97 reforms in enforcing contracts. Policy makers often assume that judicial reform takes years and costs millions of dollars. Saudi Arabia, for example, plans to spend almost $2 billion to upgrade its court system over the coming years. But improving court efficiency can often be achieved through simple, targeted measures. An initial analysis of the entire process of taking a commercial case through the court system, along with collection of court statistics, helps focus reform efforts. Related consultancy fees range from $80,000 to $500,000, depending on the size of the judicial system and the quality of the data.

Depending on the caseload of the courts, it can make sense to establish new commercial courts. Uganda did so and invested $1.5 million. Nigeria and Tanzania each spent $10 million on setting up new courts. Where a limited number of commercial cases needs to be handled, specialized commercial sections provide a less expensive alternative. In Cairo a one-step filing procedure was introduced in the busiest first-instance court to increase efficiency and reduce opportunities for bribes. The initiative, including relocation and training of staff, the creation of new forms and even building renovations, cost less than $1 million.

UPDATING CLAIM THRESHOLDS

Most economies redistribute the responsibilities of first-instance courts to ensure more efficient processing of cases. Of the 183 economies covered by *Doing Business*, 128 operate a 2-tiered civil court system. Depending on the litigation value of the claim and, in some cases, the subject matter, first-instance cases go either to a lower court—often the magistrate's court, city court or justice of the peace—or to the higher court. Some economies further divide lower and higher jurisdictions. Kenya's magistrate's court has 5 different levels.

Where economies draw the line between their lower and higher courts dif-

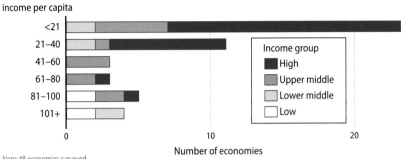

FIGURE 10.4
Most economies limit small claims filings to equivalent of 20% or less of income per capita

Claim limit as % of income per capita

Number of economies

Note: 48 economies surveyed.
Source: Doing Business database.

fers starkly. The thresholds range from $240 in Guyana to $45,000 in Australia—and from one-eighth of income per capita in the Dominican Republic, Germany and the Netherlands to 4 times income per capita in Papua New Guinea. Globally, higher courts deal with cases above 126% of income per capita on average.

Regardless of the level, monetary thresholds have to be updated regularly to ensure that the workload is distributed as initially intended. With economic growth and inflation, thresholds can quickly become outdated, and higher jurisdictions overburdened. Some economies have recently adjusted thresholds. In 2007 Tonga quintupled the threshold for cases assigned to magistrates. In 2009 Jordan more than doubled the threshold for its lower court. The United Kingdom raised the minimum threshold for its high court from £15,000 to £25,000.

RELYING ON SMALL CLAIMS COURTS

Simple commercial disputes can often be resolved in small claims courts, lessening the burden on higher-instance courts. Simplified procedural rules help speed up trial and judgment. These include the use of standard forms to file claims, oral proceedings and limits on types of evidence and on cross-examination. Small claims courts also oblige judges to issue a decision shortly after concluding a hearing.

Small claims courts exist in 48 of the 183 economies covered by *Doing Business*. They deal with claims ranging from as little as $200 in India to as much as

$21,000 in Korea. Most economies with small claims courts fix the threshold at 20% or less of income per capita (figure 10.4). In Korea more than 70% of civil suits are decided under the small claims procedure.[3] The process of resolving a commercial dispute in Seoul is one of the fastest in the world, taking 230 days on average.

Small and medium-size businesses can especially benefit from small claims courts. Recognizing this, in January 2009 the European Union issued a new regulation to create a small claims procedure for cross-border cases of less than €2,000. The measure is aimed at tackling inefficient debt enforcement, one of the "major reasons threatening the survival of businesses, particularly small and medium-sized enterprises, and resulting in numerous job losses."[4]

USING BENCHMARKS AS A GUIDE

Global comparisons can help determine time limits and assess resource needs. Take the appeals process. In 71% of the economies in the *Doing Business* sample, a judgment creditor knows within a month after the first judgment whether the debtor is appealing. In 31 economies, mainly in Sub-Saharan Africa and Latin America, the law allows debtors more than a month to appeal. Judgment creditors have their patience particularly tested in Cameroon, The Gambia and Nigeria, where the debtor has 3 months to lodge an appeal. Policy makers in these countries might consider reducing the time to appeal to the global average: 1 month.

A global comparison of the number of judges involved in the standardized case used by *Doing Business* is equally informative. In most economies just 1 judge would be assigned to this simple commercial case. But in roughly 10% of economies, mainly in the Middle East and North Africa, the law requires 3 judges to hear the case. While additional judges can add value to the decision-making process, many commercial cases, particularly routine ones, can be handled by a single judge.

MAKING LEGAL INFORMATION PUBLIC

Making information readily available on the law, and on the courts' interpretation of the law, benefits both the general public and the courts. Public information makes the law more predictable. It also helps potential parties to a lawsuit more easily find an out-of-court solution—and that helps reduce the workload of the courts.

Today, 104 economies make legal texts and recent court judgments available to the general public. But more than 30 economies, most of them low-income ones in Sub-Saharan Africa, still do not provide access to such information.

1. Courts of Iceland, http://www.domstolar.is/.
2. Nunn (2007).
3. Supreme Court of Korea, "Proceedings," http://eng.scourt.go.kr/.
4. Directive 2000/35/EC of the European Parliament and of the Council of 29 June 2000 on Combating Late Payment in Commercial Transactions, http://eur-lex.europa.eu/.

Closing a business

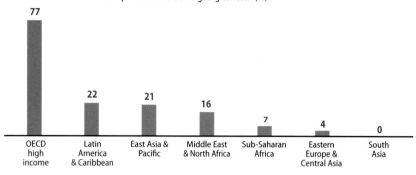

FIGURE 11.1

In OECD high-income economies viable businesses are more likely to keep running after bankruptcy

Share of economies where companies are sold as a going concern (%)

Note: Sale as a going concern is considered an efficient outcome in the *Doing Business* case study.
Source: Doing Business database.

Perhaps no business regulations have been more tested by the global financial and economic crisis than those relating to insolvency. Bankruptcies have increased sharply, and policy makers around the world are debating whether existing insolvency laws and regulations can adequately respond or whether more needs to be done.

The global financial crisis has had unequal effects across regions. Some numbers for OECD high-income economies are daunting. In Spain 2,902 orders of *concurso* (a type of reorganization procedure) were issued in 2008, 183% more than in the previous year. Spanish courts registered 1,558 insolvency proceedings in the first quarter of 2009 alone, 366% more than in the same period of 2008.[1] In Ireland company insolvencies rose by 113% from 2007 to 2008.[2] In the United Kingdom insolvency proceedings increased by 92% in 2008.[3] Canada's bankruptcies increased by 33% between April 2008 and April 2009. In Norway corporate bankruptcies are expected to at least double in 2009. Other regions, such as Latin America and the Caribbean, so far have not experienced a remarkable increase in the number of bankruptcies.

History shows that financial crises provide good opportunities for bankruptcy reforms.[4] In times of recession, keeping viable companies operating as a going concern and preserving jobs becomes especially important. The Great Depression prompted the first comprehensive reform of U.S. bankruptcy law in 50 years. Under the Chandler Act of 1938, the predecessor of today's Chapter 11, bankruptcy was no longer synonymous with liquidation. Instead, troubled firms had a chance to reorganize and to survive difficult times. The 1938 reform also established the authority of bankruptcy administrators, vesting them with powers to help effect reorganizations.

The Asian financial crisis spurred efforts across East Asia to restructure national bankruptcy procedures. Before 1998 Korea and Thailand had outdated and inadequate procedures that were rarely used. So the laws were never tested under normal economic circumstances. When illiquidity spread across the region in 1997–98, the entire financial sector was dragged down and liquidations became widespread. To forestall this trend, Korea and Thailand modified their laws to favor rehabilitation of distressed firms.[5]

Ineffective procedures for dealing with insolvency can deepen and prolong a crisis. Effective procedures can speed recovery: viable businesses are restructured and nonviable ones are quickly liquidated (figure 11.3). Resources can be reallocated and remobilized. Chile's bankruptcy reform was one reason for its relatively quick emergence from a deep recession in the early 1980s.[6] Colombia streamlined reorganization procedures in 1999 with positive effect, in the midst of the financial crisis spreading across Latin America in the late 1990s.[7]

If history is any guide, we might

TABLE 11.1

Where is it easy to close a business—and where not?

Easiest	RECOVERY RATE	Most difficult	RECOVERY RATE
Japan	92.5	Liberia	8.3
Singapore	91.3	Suriname	8.1
Norway	89.0	Mauritania	6.7
Canada	88.7	Venezuela, R.B.	6.0
Finland	87.3	Congo, Dem. Rep.	5.4
Ireland	86.6	Philippines	4.4
Denmark	86.5	Micronesia, Fed. Sts.	3.5
Belgium	86.3	Haiti	2.7
United Kingdom	84.2	Zimbabwe	0.0
Netherlands	82.7	Central African Republic	0.0

Note: Rankings are based on the recovery rate: how many cents on the dollar claimants (creditors, tax authorities and employees) recover from the insolvent firm. See Data notes for details.

Source: Doing Business database.

FIGURE 11.2

Closing a business: time, cost and outcome of bankruptcy of a local company

Rankings are based on 1 subindicator

Recovery rate is a function of time, cost and other factors such as lending rate and the likelihood of the company continuing to operate

100%
Recovery rate

Note: Time and cost do not count separately for the ranking. See Data notes for details.

FIGURE 11.3
Higher recovery rates associated with greater business density

Business density (%)

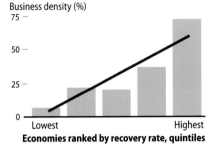

Economies ranked by recovery rate, quintiles

Note: Business density is the number of registered corporations divided by the working-age population. Relationships are significant at the 1% level and remain significant when controlling for income per capita. The data include 76 economies.
Source: Doing Business database; World Bank Group Entrepreneurship Survey, 2008.

expect to see more insolvency reforms in the next few years. *Doing Business* recorded few insolvency reforms in 2008/09 that were directly related to the global crisis. The demand for reform may increase if the effects of the crisis on the real economy intensify and as governments see the effectiveness of their insolvency regimes tested under difficult conditions.

Some economies took early action to respond to the crisis. One of them is Germany, which no longer obliges potentially viable companies to file for bankruptcy in case of overindebtedness. Instead, they can continue to operate. This change, intended as temporary relief during the financial crisis, will be effective only until December 31, 2010. France relaxed the entry requirements for its "safeguard procedure," an in-court preinsolvency restructuring introduced in 2006. Kuwait made it possible for firms to reorganize while on the verge of insolvency.

Other economies are working on future reform programs. In March 2009 the Czech Republic approved a plan to amend its insolvency act as part of a crisis recovery plan. The aim is to help businesses stay alive by making it easier for debtors to obtain funds after filing for bankruptcy. In May 2009, 10 governments in the Middle East and North Africa signed a joint declaration on intended reforms. Meeting in Abu Dhabi, representatives from Egypt, Jordan, Lebanon, Libya, Oman, Qatar, Saudi Arabia, Sudan, the United Arab Emirates

and West Bank and Gaza agreed to set up public-private partnerships to strengthen their outdated insolvency regimes.[8]

Doing Business studies the time, cost and outcomes of bankruptcy proceedings involving domestic entities. Speed, low cost and continuation of viable business operations characterize the top-performing economies. In these economies viable businesses are more likely to be sold or reorganized as a going concern rather than liquidated through piecemeal sales. Economies with efficient insolvency regimes achieve higher recovery rates than those without such systems. *Doing Business* does not measure bankruptcy proceedings of financial institutions, which normally are not subject to bankruptcy laws.[9]

WHO REFORMED IN 2008/09?

Malawi was the top reformer in closing a business in 2008/09. Its Companies Regulation 2009 took effect on June 1, 2009. The new regulation sets a cap on the liquidator's fees: 5% of the value of the estate. Before, liquidators had the discretion to set their own fees, usually at around 10% of the value of the estate. The overall cost of the insolvency procedure in Malawi fell from 30% of the value of the estate to 25%, and the mechanism for payment of liquidators has become more transparent.

In Eastern Europe and Central Asia, among the regions hit hard by the global crisis, 6 economies had reforms making it easier to close a business. Lithuania

amended its Enterprise Bankruptcy Law to eliminate the 3-month wait for creditors wishing to initiate bankruptcy proceedings. Now a creditor in Vilnius can simply notify the debtor of its intention to file a bankruptcy petition and allow a 30-day grace period to repay the debt.

Poland amended its bankruptcy law, expanding the grounds for filing for reorganization. Companies facing financial difficulties can apply for legal protection earlier than before. Like Poland, Estonia made it possible for distressed companies on the verge of insolvency to restructure their debt and take other measures to restore profitability.

Russia amended its insolvency law to introduce professional qualification standards for administrators and regulate their compensation. Albania amended its bankruptcy law to establish the Agency of Insolvency Supervision, to supervise and issue licenses to insolvency administrators. The new law also introduced professional qualification standards for administrators. Tajikistan amended its bankruptcy law to streamline timetables for its rehabilitation and winding-up procedures (table 11.2).

Two economies in Latin America and the Caribbean joined the list of reformers in 2008/09. Uruguay enacted a new insolvency law, consolidating its many existing mechanisms into one reorganization procedure. Colombia issued decrees in 2008/09 to more strictly regulate the profession of insolvency administrators.

Among OECD high-income economies, France and Germany reformed.

TABLE 11.2
Establishing or promoting reorganization procedures— the most popular reform feature in 2008/09

Established or promoted reorganization procedures or prepackaged reorganizations	Estonia, France, Kuwait, Mauritius, Philippines, Poland, Rwanda, Sierra Leone, Uruguay
Regulated the profession of insolvency administrators	Albania, Colombia, Malawi, Philippines, Russian Federation
Introduced or tightened time limits	Albania, Lithuania, Russian Federation, Tajikistan
Established receivership	Samoa
Promoted specialized courts	India
Temporarily eased obligation for management to file for bankruptcy	Germany

Source: Doing Business database.

TABLE 11.3
Who makes it easy to close a business—and who does not?

Time *(years)*			
Fastest		**Slowest**	
Ireland	0.4	Ecuador	5.3
Japan	0.6	Indonesia	5.5
Canada	0.8	Haiti	5.7
Singapore	0.8	Philippines	5.7
Belgium	0.9	Belarus	5.8
Finland	0.9	Angola	6.2
Norway	0.9	Czech Republic	6.5
Australia	1.0	Maldives	6.7
Belize	1.0	India	7.0
Iceland	1.0	Mauritania	8.0

Cost *(% of estate)*			
Least		**Most**	
Colombia	1.0	Micronesia, Fed. Sts.	38.0
Kuwait	1.0	Philippines	38.0
Norway	1.0	Samoa	38.0
Singapore	1.0	Solomon Islands	38.0
Bahamas, The	3.5	Vanuatu	38.0
Belgium	3.5	Venezuela, R.B.	38.0
Brunei Darussalam	3.5	Sierra Leone	42.0
Canada	3.5	Ukraine	42.0
Finland	3.5	Liberia	42.5
Georgia	3.5	Central African Republic	76.0

Source: Doing Business database.

France amended its legislation to make it easier for firms to qualify for its safeguard procedure. The aim is to encourage firms to apply for court protection early on, before they become insolvent. Germany, as a temporary relief during the financial crisis, eliminated management's obligation to file for bankruptcy in the case of overindebtedness, where business survival is more likely than in the case of illiquidity.

Three economies besides Malawi reformed in Sub-Saharan Africa. Mauritius passed a new insolvency law, establishing a rehabilitation procedure for companies as an alternative to winding up. The law sets clear time limits, defines the rights and obligations of creditors and debtors and outlines sanctions for those who abuse the system. Rwanda adopted a new law promoting reorganization procedures as a viable option for distressed firms and setting clear time limits during the insolvency process. Sierra Leone passed a new company act that makes a reorganization procedure available to companies.

In East Asia and the Pacific, Samoa and the Philippines reformed. Samoa passed 2 new laws: the Companies Amendment Act 2006, which regulates 3 stages in insolvency—administration, compromise and liquidation—and the Receivership Act 2006, which provides for the appointment of receivers of companies. The Philippines adopted the Rules of Procedure on Corporate Rehabilitation, introducing the concept of prenegotiated reorganizations and requiring receivers to have certain qualifications.

In South Asia, India reformed. More judges were assigned to the specialized debt recovery tribunals, enabling them to pick up the pace of resolving foreclosures. And the Securitization and Reconstruction of Financial Assets and Enforcement of Security Interest Act 2002—has made it easier for courts to handle foreclosure procedures.

Kuwait was the only reformer in the Middle East and North Africa. A new procedure allows the reorganization of companies that face financial difficulties but are not yet insolvent.

Romania made it more difficult to go through insolvency procedures by increasing the cost. A November 2008 amendment to its insolvency law requires 1.5% of the amount recovered from each insolvency procedure to go to a fund for reimbursing the expenses of insolvency administrators. The aim is to ensure that insolvency administrators are paid even when debtors have no assets. This reform reduces the amount creditors recover in cases where the company has assets and increases inefficiency in cases where few or no assets are available. Other economies seek to handle this problem by limiting professional intervention where the possibilities of recovery are slim.

TOWARD SMART REGULATION

In times of crisis, overburdened courts, unqualified liquidators and rigid laws become even bigger obstacles to the orderly exit of nonviable businesses. And reorganizing viable firms to preserve jobs becomes more important than ever. Governments can help by encouraging firms to seek preinsolvency solutions, improving the efficiency of courts and training receivers and liquidators to do a good job in administering distressed companies and selling their assets efficiently. *Doing Business* has recorded 76 reforms making it easier to close a business in the past 6 years. OECD high-income economies reformed the most (figure 11.4).

FACING REALITY EARLY ON

Debtors should not wait until it is too late to save the company. In economies where reorganization functions well, such as Finland and Norway, companies typically file for bankruptcy a couple of weeks after default. Many economies, particularly those with old bankruptcy regimes, could save more companies by getting debtors to face reality early on.

One way policy makers can encourage businesses to seek timely solutions is to expand the grounds on which compa-

FIGURE 11.4

OECD high-income economies reformed the most since 2004

Share of economies in region making it easier to close a business (%)

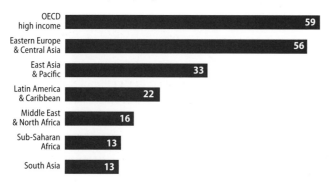

OECD high income	59
Eastern Europe & Central Asia	56
East Asia & Pacific	33
Latin America & Caribbean	22
Middle East & North Africa	16
Sub-Saharan Africa	13
South Asia	13

Source: *Doing Business* database.

nies suffering financial problems can file for reorganization. The law should allow debtors to file for reorganization when facing financial distress rather than requiring that they wait for the much worse situation of insolvency. Of the 18 economies that reformed in 2008/09, 5 implemented rescue statutes introducing or promoting the use of preinsolvency procedures: Estonia, France, Kuwait, the Philippines and Poland. The Slovak Republic did so in its Bankruptcy and Restructuring Act that went into effect in 2006.

Requiring debtors to file for insolvency as soon as they default or as soon as default is imminent is another way to encourage companies to face reality before it is too late. In Poland and Spain, filing for bankruptcy too late can subject a company's management to penalties. In 2008 Uruguay's new bankruptcy law introduced an obligation for management to file within 30 days of learning of the company's insolvency. If implemented well, this provision will reduce delays.

Creating a framework for prepackaged reorganizations can help keep companies operating as a going concern. Italy and Korea introduced prepackaged reorganizations in 2006/07. Now a firm can negotiate a reorganization plan with its creditors before filing for bankruptcy. Once it reaches an agreement with the required majority of creditors, the firm files for bankruptcy and asks the court to approve its reorganization plan. Once the court approves, it imposes the agree-

ment on the creditors still holding out. The advance negotiations with creditors clear the way for quickly scheduling a court hearing, allowing a rapid exit from bankruptcy.[10]

SPEEDING UP COURT PROCEDURES

Once an insolvency case is brought before the court, a timely resolution becomes essential, especially if the aim is to save the company. Proceedings that end with an efficient outcome—the firm continuing to operate or being sold as a going concern—go through the insolvency process in less than 2 years. In the OECD high-income group 77% of economies achieve such an outcome. Japan's rehabilitation procedure is one example of a well-functioning system of in-court restructuring.

Economies in South Asia have the longest insolvency proceedings, averaging 4.5 years. They also have the longest average time to enforce a contract through the courts: 1,053 days. The length of these procedures reduces the value of firms, making it unlikely that they will continue as a going concern after insolvency proceedings.

The court systems in many economies lack the infrastructure, training and technical expertise to resolve commercial disputes in a timely way.[11] In the coming years growth in the number of bankruptcy filings could further strain the capacity of courts, increasing their risk of becoming overwhelmed. But some economies in recent years have in-

troduced specialized bankruptcy courts to deal more efficiently with insolvency procedures.

One country that has increased court efficiency is the United States. Thanks to an online case management system, anyone can consult any document in a bankruptcy case. Bankruptcy judges can work from anywhere, signing orders with the click of a mouse. Developed at the end of the 1990s and rolled out in all states by 2005, the system provides one level of information to the general public, another to lawyers with an account and a third level to bankruptcy judges.

TRAINING ADMINISTRATORS

Receivers and liquidators play essential roles in insolvency procedures. Receivers take part in managing debtor companies—either replacing management or coadministering with it. Liquidators are in charge of selling the assets of nonviable companies. Many economies have launched reforms to ensure that both professions have adequate business and educational qualifications and are being well supervised. In recent years such economies as Bulgaria, Canada, Chile, China, Poland, Romania, the United Kingdom and the United States have introduced qualification standards (figure 11.5).

In 2008/09 Albania, Colombia and Russia adopted regulations imposing licensing requirements for receivers. In June 2006 FYR Macedonia created a chamber of bankruptcy trustees and implemented a licensing regime. In 2005

FIGURE 11.5

Economies with specialized bankruptcy courts have higher recovery rates

Recovery rate (cents on the dollar)

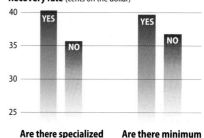

Are there specialized bankruptcy courts?

Are there minimum qualifications for trustees?

Source: *Doing Business* database.

Chile established a system to ensure rigorous surveillance by the bankruptcy commissioner and to link receivers' fees to the proceeds realized from asset sales. The aim is to encourage trustees to sell distressed assets quickly, maximizing returns.

1. Spain, National Statistics Institute, http://www.ine.es/jaxi/tabla.do.

2. Euler Hermes, "A Remarkable Acceleration in Business Insolvencies," press release, June 4, 2009, http://www.eulerhermes.com/.

3. Insolvency Service, "Insolvencies in the Fourth Quarter 2008," statistics release, February 6, 2009, http://www.insolvency.gov.uk/.

4. Gine and Love (2008).

5. Carruthers and Halliday (2007).

6. Bergoeing and others (2007).

7. Gine and Love (2008).

8. The symposium was organized by Hawkamah, the Institute for Corporate Governance, in association with the Organisation for Economic Co-operation and Development, the World Bank, INSOL International, the Abu Dhabi Chamber of Commerce and Industry and the Abu Dhabi Centre for Corporate Governance, and supported by Latham & Watkins.

9. Djankov (2009a).

10. Djankov (2009b).

11. Djankov (2009b).

Annex: pilot indicators on getting electricity

Infrastructure services such as roads, water, electricity and telecommunications matter for private businesses. Where access and quality are poor, they can slow a company's growth. Managers responding to World Bank Enterprise Surveys in 89 economies between 2006 and 2009 estimated that their spending on such items as fuel, electricity, telecommunications and water amounted to 9% of annual sales, more than for machinery. They reported losses due to electricity outages amounting to 3.2 percent of sales. And when asked about the biggest constraint to the operation and growth of their business, more managers identified weak electricity services and access to finance than any other issue.[1]

To move into higher-value-added activities that rely on electricity-based technologies, small and medium-size enterprises depend on a reliable and affordable supply of electricity. But because of capacity constraints in power utilities, especially in low-income economies, this important input often cannot be guaranteed. Whether electricity is reliably available or not, the first step for a customer is always to gain access by obtaining a connection. It is this first and key step that *Doing Business* aims to measure through a new set of pilot indicators on the process a private business must go through to do so.

By applying its methodology to the question of electricity provision, *Doing Business* aims to illustrate the implications for entrepreneurs of weak commercial services by distribution companies and to complement existing data sets. Consistent, objective data on connection services can inform utilities, regulators and governments seeking to strengthen sector performance and serve as an input for research on links to economic outcomes.

The data differ in important ways from other electricity data sets. The new indicators do not reflect the costs associated with electricity consumption or measure the percentage of households and businesses connected to electricity in each economy. Nor do the indicators measure problems of quality, such as the frequency of service interruptions, energy losses and voltage drops, which represent a significant burden on businesses. But analysis using data on the new indicators as well as from the World Economic Forum's *Global Competitiveness Report* suggests a positive correlation between the efficiency of the connection process and entrepreneurs' perceptions of the overall quality of infrastructure services (figure 12.1).

CONSTRUCTING THE INDICATORS

Doing Business tracks all procedures required for a business to obtain an electricity connection for a newly constructed building, including an extension or expansion of the existing infrastruc-

ture.[2] To ensure that the data are comparable across economies, respondents in the 140 economies covered were presented with a standard case study:

An entrepreneur would like to connect his newly built warehouse for cold meat storage to electricity. The internal wiring up to the metering point has already been completed by the electrician employed by the construction firm, and the entrepreneur would now like to obtain the final electricity connection from the local distribution utility. The electrician working for the entrepreneur estimates that the warehouse will need a 140-kilovolt-ampere (kVA) connection.[3]

FIGURE 12.1

Easier connection—better perception of overall infrastructure quality

Perceived quality of infrastructure services overall

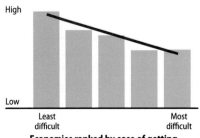

Note: Relationships are significant at the 1% level and remain significant when controlling for income per capita.
Source: Doing Business database; WEF (2008).

Based on the case study, distribution utilities in the main business city of each economy were asked to describe the procedures for obtaining an electricity connection along with the time and cost of completing them. From their responses, a list of procedures was drawn up and verified through e-mail and telephone interviews with independent professionals such as electricians, electrical engineers, electrical contractors and construction companies. For details on methodology see data notes on page 95.

WHO MAKES IT EASY TO GET ELECTRICITY?

An entrepreneur in Ukraine seeking to get his cold-storage business connected to electricity has to go through 9 different procedures to obtain design approvals, technical certificates for the required power lines and multiple inspections of the connection works, including an inspection from the State Inspectorate for Protection of Labor. The process takes 306 days and costs $8,419, or 262% of income per capita.

Economies such as Denmark, Germany and Japan make it much easier for businesses to connect to electricity (table 12.1). In Germany, which has the fastest process, it takes only 3 interactions with the utility and 17 days. An entrepreneur simply needs to sign a supply contract with an electricity retailer and have his licensed master electrician take care of the electricity application. The utility then completes the external connection works. The entrepreneur's warehouse is hooked up to electricity in less than 3 weeks, with a total connection cost of $2,151 (5% of income per capita).

Procedures are few in economies where utilities:

- *Coordinate with other agencies*, such as the municipality or the building department, freeing customers from having to contact the same agencies several times. In Romania the private contractor hired to complete the connection works must get a separate construction license for the

TABLE 12.1

Who makes it easy to get electricity—and who does not?

Procedures (number)			
Fewest		**Most**	
Denmark	3	Angola	8
Germany	3	Armenia	8
Japan	3	Azerbaijan	8
Mauritius	3	Guinea-Bissau	8
Qatar	3	Honduras	8
Saudi Arabia	3	Nigeria	8
St. Vincent and the Grenadines	3	Russian Federation	8
Sweden	3	Tajikistan	8
Switzerland	3	Ukraine	9
Antigua and Barbuda	4	Bosnia and Herzegovina	10

Time (days)			
Least		**Most**	
Germany	17	Russian Federation	272
St. Kitts and Nevis	18	Czech Republic	279
Iceland	22	Cyprus	306
Austria	23	Ukraine	306
St. Lucia	25	Kyrgyz Republic	325
Grenada	30	Tanzania	382
Chile	31	Madagascar	419
Puerto Rico	32	Afghanistan	424
Honduras	33	Guinea-Bissau	437
Panama	35	Sierra Leone	441

Cost (% of income per capita)			
Least		**Most**	
Japan	0	Ethiopia	6,967
Hong Kong, China	2	Gambia, The	6,975
Qatar	4	Senegal	7,007
Germany	5	Madagascar	8,466
Iceland	9	Malawi	11,655
Panama	11	Central African Republic	14,378
Israel	13	Burkina Faso	15,443
Cyprus	14	Benin	15,817
Norway	14	Congo, Dem. Rep.	28,304
Australia	15	Burundi	43,020

Source: Doing Business database.

distribution transformer needed for the connection. In both Serbia and Montenegro the same construction license can be obtained from the municipality together with the main construction permit.

- *Transfer responsibility for safety compliance* of the building's internal wiring to private electricians. This is done in Denmark, Germany, Japan and Mauritius. But in economies such as Ukraine contractors have to obtain multiple approvals from different

agencies to comply with safety standards.

- *Ensure efficient procurement planning*, freeing customers from having to obtain the materials needed. In economies like Bangladesh, Tanzania and the Central African Republic customers may be asked to provide such materials as poles, meter boxes or transformers because the utility does not have them in stock.

The number of interactions customers have with the utility and other agencies is the biggest determinant of connection delays. In economies where businesses have to go through 6–10 procedures to get connected, the process takes 144 days on average. In economies with 3–5 procedures, it takes 104 days on average. It takes 56 days to get connected in the 10 economies with the fewest procedures, and 215 days in the 10 economies with the most.

Differences in the voltage level to which customers need to connect are the biggest driver of differences in connection costs across economies. High-income economies often have electricity distribution systems that can connect a customer requesting a 140-kVA connection simply by extending an overhead line or underground cable. The cost in these cases is a quarter to a half of the cost in cases where the customer's premises must be connected to the next higher voltage level.

But connection costs vary significantly among economies within income groups, suggesting room to reduce costs regardless of existing infrastructure. In the 10 lowest-cost economies (all high-income economies except Panama) the average cost for a connection is no more than 9% of income per capita, an eighth of the average for all high-income economies (75% of income per capita). In the 10 highest-cost economies (all low-income economies) the average is 15,803% of income per capita, more than twice the average for the low-income group (7,384% of income per capita).

Connection costs can be divided into 2 main categories: a fixed connection fee that should reflect a cost model on how to spread the fixed costs of operating a distribution grid over all customers,[4] and the variable costs for each connection, accounting for the labor, material and inspections required.[5] In many economies the bill also includes the costs of a security deposit and payments to other agencies for permits, inspections and approvals.[6]

Where the connection process is more complex, the variable costs a customer must pay account for a larger share of the total. While fixed costs represent an average 59% of the total cost in the 10 lowest-cost economies, they amount to only 8% of the total in the 10 highest-cost economies. This reduces the transparency of connection costs and utilities' accountability to customers, possibly leaving more room for corruption.

WHAT IS TO COME?

Data have been collected for 140 economies (table 12.2). More detailed data for each economy can be found on the *Doing Business* website. In the coming year the sample of economies will be expanded, with the aim of covering the same sample as the main *Doing Business* indicators. As more data become available, the data set on the *Doing Business* website will be updated. A report with a more detailed analysis of findings is under preparation, as is a background paper on the methodology. Feedback from governments and utilities is welcome and will be used as input in further refining the methodology.

TABLE 12.2
Getting electricity data

Economy	Procedures (number)	Time (days)	Cost (% of income per capita)	Economy	Procedures (number)	Time (days)	Cost (% of income per capita)
Afghanistan	4	424	618.2	Gambia, The	4	178	6,975.1
Albania	5	162	614.5	Georgia	4	71	666.3
Angola	8	41	1,102.3	Germany	3	17	5.1
Antigua and Barbuda	4	42	140.0	Ghana	4	78	2,240.5
Argentina	6	74	25.2	Greece	6	77	35.6
Armenia	8	242	673.0	Grenada	4	30	244.6
Australia	5	46	15.4	Guatemala	4	39	677.4
Austria	5	23	110.7	Guinea-Bissau	8	437	4,125.8
Azerbaijan	8	225	624.4	Honduras	8	33	963.4
Bahamas, The	7	61	45.0	Hong Kong, China	4	101	1.8
Bahrain	5	72	47.8	Hungary	6	252	98.3
Bangladesh	7	109	3,171.4	Iceland	4	22	8.7
Belarus	6	218	1,291.4	India	7	67	504.9
Belgium	4	50	44.2	Iran, Islamic Rep.	6	143	1,050.3
Belize	5	106	341.9	Ireland	4	106	21.3
Benin	5	172	15,816.9	Israel	6	113	12.7
Bhutan	5	241	1,675.4	Jamaica	6	48	80.1
Bolivia	7	51	1,484.4	Japan	3	105	0
Bosnia and Herzegovina	10	127	276.7	Jordan	5	43	525.2
Botswana	5	117	465.4	Kazakhstan	5	103	300.5
Brazil	6	36	163.2	Kenya	5	162	1,405.3
Bulgaria	6	102	295.1	Kyrgyz Republic	6	325	2,478.4
Burkina Faso	4	158	15,443	Lao PDR	5	127	3,245.2
Burundi	4	158	43,020.5	Latvia	5	193	335.1
Cambodia	4	169	3,854.1	Lebanon	5	75	29.9
Cameroon	4	67	1,735.3	Lesotho	5	86	2,675.7
Canada	8	133	164.4	Lithuania	4	98	62.3
Cape Verde	4	46	1,112.9	Luxembourg	5	120	51.5
Central African Republic	6	210	14,377.7	Macedonia, FYR	5	90	924.9
Chile	6	31	88.4	Madagascar	5	419	8,466.2
China	4	118	835.7	Malawi	5	179	11,654.8
Colombia	5	150	1,243.6	Malaysia	6	51	42.6
Congo, Dem. Rep.	6	73	28,304.0	Maldives	6	101	823.1
Costa Rica	5	62	329.0	Mauritius	3	44	262.8
Côte d'Ivoire	5	43	4,303.7	Mexico	7	169	577.1
Croatia	5	70	319.8	Moldova	7	126	650.7
Cyprus	4	306	13.9	Montenegro	4	67	409.3
Czech Republic	6	279	184.9	Morocco	5	71	2,295
Denmark	3	43	106.2	Namibia	7	40	403.9
Djibouti	4	180	6,473.4	Nepal	6	73	2,890.0
Dominica	5	73	1,188.1	Netherlands	5	125	38.9
Ecuador	5	89	973.5	New Zealand	5	47	73.3
Egypt, Arab Rep.	7	50	453.5	Nicaragua	6	70	1,695.3
El Salvador	7	74	467.3	Niger	4	165	4,295.9
Estonia	4	99	206.1	Nigeria	8	260	1,146.8
Ethiopia	4	75	6,967.3	Norway	4	59	14.1
Fiji	6	46	794.8	Oman	5	66	70.8
Finland	5	53	20.9	Pakistan	5	233	2,334.7
France	5	123	27.9	Panama	5	35	10.7
Gabon	5	160	256.9	Paraguay	4	53	409.8

Economy	Procedures (number)	Time (days)	Cost (% of income per capita)
Peru	5	118	521.8
Philippines	5	63	466.5
Poland	4	143	233.2
Puerto Rico	5	32	433.8
Qatar	3	90	3.8
Romania	7	207	312.8
Russian Federation	8	272	4,521.6
Saudi Arabia	3	71	78.0
Senegal	6	125	7,007.0
Serbia	4	81	513.4
Seychelles	5	132	479.5
Sierra Leone	8	441	1,279.1
Singapore	5	76	34.2
Slovenia	5	38	115.4
South Africa	5	171	443.2
Spain	4	85	169.6
Sri Lanka	4	132	1,548.5
St. Kitts and Nevis	4	18	377.3
St. Lucia	4	25	469.9
St. Vincent and the Grenadines	3	52	459.6
Suriname	5	128	745.7
Sweden	3	52	21.1
Switzerland	3	39	68.8
Syrian Arab Republic	5	71	994.2
Tajikistan	8	211	1,456.8
Tanzania	4	382	251.4
Tonga	5	50	128.8
Trinidad and Tobago	5	56	53.6
Tunisia	4	58	1,136.1
Turkey	4	62	812.6
Uganda	5	151	5,209.9
Ukraine	9	306	262.0
United Arab Emirates	4	55	15.9
United Kingdom	5	111	42.2
United States	5	48	16.8
Uzbekistan	7	123	2,532.8
Vietnam	4	127	1,685.1
West Bank and Gaza	6	70	1,567.1
Yemen, Rep.	4	35	6,926.1
Zambia	4	103	1,042.7

1. According to World Bank Enterprise Surveys for 89 economies, 15.6% of managers consider electricity the most serious constraint, and a similar share (15.7%) consider access to finance the most serious constraint (http://www.enterprisesurveys.org).

2. An *extension* involves extending the network by laying low-voltage underground cables or installing low-voltage overhead wires from the metering point to the closest substation. An *expansion* involves installing a pole- or pad-mounted distribution transformer and connecting it between the customer's metering point and the utility's medium-voltage network.

3. The load of 140 kVA was chosen to reflect the energy needs of a relatively electricity-intensive small or medium-size enterprise. By comparison, a residential customer would need 20–40 kVA. A 140-kVA load is also significant enough to assume that the entrepreneur cannot opt to steal electricity instead.

4. Where connection fees are fixed, they are usually calculated as a function of the peak electricity demand of the facility to be connected. These fixed fees can often be found on the website of the utility or the regulator.

5. Detailed information on different cost components for each economy can be found on the *Doing Business* website (http://www.doingbusiness.org).

6. Security deposits represent a significant financial burden. In Ethiopia a medium-size company requesting an electricity connection will lose an amount equivalent to 148% of income per capita because of the security deposit, required as a guarantee that it will pay future electricity bills. Because the utility holds the deposit until the end of the contract and repays it without interest, the company cannot put that money to a more productive use. Security deposits are charged by utilities in both the top 10 economies on the cost of a new electricity connection and the bottom 10. But in the better-performing economies they are significantly lower and utilities offer arrangements reducing the financial burden. In Australia, Hong Kong (China) and Panama customers can opt in part for a guarantee from a bank, at a lower cost than the interest that would be lost on the deposit.

Annex: worker protection

Last year's report included a table showing ratification of the International Labour Organization's core labor standards by the 181 economies covered by that report and indicated that *Doing Business* would be conducting further analysis on those standards.[1] These standards are included in the 8 ILO conventions covering the freedom of association and right to collective bargaining, the elimination of forced labor, equitable treatment in employment practices and the abolition of child labor.

Building on the initial analysis on the core labor standards, *Doing Business* plans to develop a new worker protection indicator, a process that will benefit from the advice of a working group with broad stakeholder representation. The ILO, which has leadership on the core labor standards, will serve as an essential source of guidance in this process.

In accordance with the standard

methodology, *Doing Business* intends to measure implementation of core labor standards, that is, the adoption of the core labor standards in national legislation. Data are collected from readings of laws and regulations. Child labor was selected as the first area of research. Estimates reported in a 2006 ILO study of child labor are high: worldwide, more than 190 million children between the ages of 5 and 14 are economically active.[2]

In 2008 *Doing Business* initiated research on the national implementation of the minimum age provisions included in 2 ILO conventions on child labor: Convention 138, on the minimum age for admission to employment, ratified by 154 countries, and Convention 182, on the worst forms of child labor, ratified by 171 countries.[3] These conventions establish clear minimum age thresholds that ratifying countries must implement in their national legislation. The results of the research are not included in the indicators on employing workers.

In a sample of 102 countries selected to represent different regions and income groups, the research looked at whether national laws are in line with the ILO conventions on child labor (table 13.1). Labor law experts completed survey questions on national child labor provisions. Answers were verified using the text of the laws. The survey did not cover enforcement of child labor laws.

ILO CONVENTIONS ON CHILD LABOR

When the ILO was formed in 1919, child labor was the subject of its first conventions. In 1973 Convention 138 revised 10 conventions that had covered minimum age for admission to employment or work in specific sectors since 1919. Convention 138 sets the minimum age of admission to the labor force at "not less than the age of completion of compulsory schooling, and, in any case, not less than 15 years."[4] For countries "whose economy or educational facilities are insufficiently developed," the minimum age may be set at 14.[5]

The convention establishes a minimum age of 18 for hazardous work, de-

fined as "work which by its nature or the circumstances . . . is likely to jeopardize the health, safety or morals of young persons."[6] In 1999 Convention 182 was adopted to eliminate the worst forms of child labor. Convention 182 classifies hazardous work as among the 4 worst forms of child labor, with the other 3 being child slavery and practices similar to slavery, child prostitution and child pornography and illicit activities such as drug trafficking.[7] According to the 2006 ILO study, of the 190.7 million children between 5 and 14 involved in economic activity, 70.9 million were engaged in some form of hazardous work.[8]

Specific minimum age thresholds exist for "light work." Convention 138 allows national laws to permit children ages 13–15 to engage in light work "which is not likely to harm their health or development or prejudice their school attendance."[9] Countries "whose economy or educational facilities are insufficiently developed" may allow children ages 12–14 to do light work. As a proxy for countries "whose economy and educational facilities are insufficiently developed," *Doing Business* used the World Bank country classifications *low income* and *lower middle income*.[10]

RATIFICATION OF ILO CONVENTION 138

Among the 102 countries covered by the research, 20 have not ratified Convention 138 (table 13.2). While ratifying the relevant ILO conventions is important, not ratifying the conventions does not necessarily mean that standards are not implemented

TABLE 13.1
Countries in the sample

Region	Countries
East Asia & Pacific	16
Eastern Europe & Central Asia	13
Latin America & Caribbean	16
Middle East & North Africa	18
OECD high income	14
South Asia	5
Sub-Saharan Africa	20
Total	102

Source: Doing Business database.

TABLE 13.2
Implementation of minimum working age by nonratifying sample countries

Minimum age limit	Countries
Higher	8
Same	3
Lower	5
None	4
Total	20

Note: Table shows sample countries that have not ratified Convention 138 by minimum working age relative to that set in the convention (14 years for low- and lower-middle-income countries, 15 for high- and upper-middle-income countries).

Source: Doing Business database.

TABLE 13.3
Implementation of minimum working age by all sample countries

Region	Higher limit	Same limit	Lower limit	No limit
East Asia & Pacific	9	3	2	2
Eastern Europe & Central Asia	9	4	0	0
Latin America & Caribbean	6	6	4	0
Middle East & North Africa	10	5	3	0
OECD high income	4	7	2	1
South Asia	2	2	0	1
Sub-Saharan Africa	7	11	2	0
Total	47	38	13	4

Note: Table shows sample countries by minimum working age relative to that set in Convention 138 (14 years for low- and lower-middle-income countries, 15 for high- and upper-middle-income countries).

Source: Doing Business database.

TABLE 13.4
Implementation of minimum age for hazardous work by all sample countries

Minimum age limit	Countries
Same	73
Lower	13
None	16
Total	102

Note: Table shows sample countries by minimum age for hazardous work relative to that set in Convention 138 (18 years).
Source: Doing Business database.

MINIMUM AGE FOR HAZARDOUS WORK

National provisions specifying a minimum age for hazardous work exist in 86% of low- and lower-middle-income, 83% of upper-middle-income and 81% of high-income countries in the sample of 102 countries. Of the 102 countries, 86 have laws prohibiting hazardous work below a certain age (table 13.4). Among these 86 countries, 73 set the standard minimum age of 18 for hazardous work. Thirteen have lower age thresholds, including the United Arab Emirates (17), Namibia (16) and Samoa (15).

Sixteen countries, including Antigua and Barbuda, the Netherlands and Palau, have no age limit applying specifically to hazardous work.

MINIMUM AGE FOR LIGHT WORK

Of the 102 countries surveyed, only 44 (or 43%) have established an age limit specifically for light work (table 13.5). Three countries allow light work but do not specify an age limit. The 47 coun-

in national legislation. For example, while Ghana and Saudi Arabia have not ratified Convention 138, their laws establish a minimum working age of 15.

Half the 20 countries that have not ratified the convention are low- and lower-middle-income countries. These 10 countries all meet or exceed the minimum age of 14 established by the convention for countries "whose economy or educational facilities are insufficiently developed." Afghanistan and Bhutan are examples. Each has legislation establishing a minimum working age of 18, exceeding the minimum age required by the convention by 4 years.

Five of the 20 countries that have not ratified the convention have not implemented the convention's standards: Bahrain, Brunei Darussalam, Canada, Mexico and the United States. These 5 high- and upper- middle-income countries have established 14 as the minimum age, 1 year below the minimum age prescribed by the convention.

MINIMUM AGE FOR ADMISSION TO THE LABOR FORCE

Of the 102 countries in the sample, 85 have a minimum age for admission to the labor force that complies with the minimum age prescribed by Convention 138 (table 13.3).

In Sub-Saharan Africa 18 of 20 countries have a minimum age that meets or exceeds the age limit set by the convention. In the Middle East and North Africa 15 of 18 countries do. And

reforms are under way. Kuwait is changing its labor law to raise the minimum age from 14 years to 15. In South Asia 2 countries that did not ratify the convention, Afghanistan and Bhutan, set a minimum working age of 18, exceeding the requirement of the ILO convention and raising the average in the region. In Eastern Europe and Central Asia all countries have adopted the minimum age threshold of 15.

In East Asia and the Pacific some countries, such as China, Mongolia and Papua New Guinea, exceed the requirement by setting 16 as the minimum age. In the Middle East and North Africa, Algeria, Jordan and Tunisia have done the same.

Only 17 of the 102 countries have an age limit below the minimum specified in the convention or have set no minimum age at all. This is the case for 4 countries in East Asia and the Pacific and 4 in Latin America and the Caribbean. The law in Belize is unclear, mentioning 2 different minimum working ages, 12 and 14, in different provisions of the text.[11] The Federated States of Micronesia's law does not set a minimum age.

In East Asia and the Pacific 9 of 11 low- and lower-middle-income countries, including Cambodia, Fiji and Timor-Leste, have not used the exception for "countries whose economy or educational facilities are insufficiently developed," which would allow them to set a minimum age of 14. Instead, they set their minimum working age at 15.

TABLE 13.5
Implementation of minimum age for light work by all sample countries

Minimum age limit	Countries
Higher	24
Same	20
No minimum age in provision for light work	3
No provision for light work	55
Total	102

Note: Table shows sample countries by minimum age for light work relative to that set in Convention 138 (12 years for low- and lower-middle-income countries, 13 for high- and upper-middle-income countries).

Source: Doing Business database.

tries that allow light work include such examples as seasonal agricultural work, helping out in the family business and vocational training. In The Bahamas the law specifically allows children to sell newspapers or nuts after school hours.

The 44 countries that have established a specific minimum age for light work include countries that have not ratified Convention 138, including the United States (14), Saudi Arabia (13) and Bangladesh (12).

1. World Bank (2008a, p.147).
2. ILO (2006).
3. http://www.ilo.org/ilolex/english/docs/declworld.htm.
4. Convention 138, Article 2.3.
5. Convention 138, Article 2.4.
6. Convention 138, Article 3.
7. Convention 182, Article 3.
8. ILO (2006).
9. Convention 138, Article 7.
10. World Bank country income group classifications are available at http://www.worldbank.org/data/countryclass.
11. Belize Labor Act (Chapter 297), Revised Edition 2000, Section 164 and Section 169 (a).

References

Alesina, Alberto, Silvia Ardagna, Giuseppe Nicoletti and Fabio Schiantarelli. 2005. "Regulation and Investment." *Journal of the European Economic Association* 3 (4): 791–825.

Allendorf, Keera. 2007. "Do Women's Land Rights Promote Empowerment and Child Health in Nepal?" *World Development* 35 (11): 1975–88.

Amin, Mohammad, and Simeon Djankov. 2009a. "Democracy and Reforms." Policy Research Working Paper 4835, World Bank, Washington, DC.

____. 2009b. "Natural Resources and Reforms." Policy Research Working Paper 4882, World Bank, Washington, DC.

Antunes, Antonio, and Tiago Cavalcanti. 2007. "Start Up Costs, Limited Enforcement, and the Hidden Economy." *European Economic Review* 51 (1): 203–24.

Ardagna, Silvia, and Annamaria Lusagi. 2009. *Where Does Regulation Hurt? Evidence from New Businesses across Countries.* NBER Working Paper 14747. Cambridge, MA: National Bureau of Economic Research.

Barseghyan, Levon. 2008. "Entry Costs and Cross-Country Differences in Productivity and Output." *Journal of Economic Growth* 13 (2): 145–67.

Bergoeing, Raphael, Patrick Kehoe, Timothy Kehoe and Raimundo Soto. 2007. "A Decade Lost and Found: Mexico and Chile in the 1980s." http://www.econ.umn.edu/~tkehoe/papers/mexico-chile.pdf.

Boeri, Tito, Brooke Helppie and Mario Macis. 2008. "Labor Regulations in Developing Countries: A Review of the Evidence and Directions for Future Research." Social Protection Discussion Paper 0833, Human Development Network, World Bank, Washington, DC.

Botero, Juan C., Simeon Djankov, Rafael La Porta, Florencio López-de-Silanes and Andrei Shleifer. 2004. "The Regulation of Labor." *Quarterly Journal of Economics* 119 (4): 1339–82.

Building Control Alliance. 2008. *Survey of Building Control Bodies.* Report commissioned by U.K. Department for Communities and Local Government. London: Her Majesty's Stationery Office. http://www.communities.gov.uk/.

Carruthers, Bruce, and Terence Halliday. 2007. "Institutionalizing Creative Destruction: Predictable and Transparent Bankruptcy Law in the Wake of the East Asian Financial Crisis." In Meredith Woo-Cummings, ed., *Neoliberalism and Institutional Reform in East Asia: A Comparative Study.* New York: Palgrave Macmillan.

Chang, Roberto, Linda Kaltani and Norman Loayza. 2009. "Openness Can Be Good for Growth: The Role of Policy Complementarities." *Journal of Development Economics* 90: 33–49.

Chew, Valerie. 2009. "Financial Crisis: 1997–1998." National Library Board Singapore. http://infopedia.nl.sg/articles/SIP_1530_2009-06-09.html.

Ciccone, Antonio, and Elias Papaioannou. 2008. "Entry Regulation and Intersectoral Reallocation." Working paper. http://www.crei.cat/files/filesPublication/16/090402112944_erandreallocpaper321[1].pdf.

Clarke, George R. G. 2005. "Beyond Tariffs and Quotas: Why Don't African Manufacturing Enterprises Export More?" Policy Research Working Paper 3617, World Bank, Washington, DC.

Commonwealth of Australia. 2009. *Tax Laws Amendment (Small Business and General Business Tax Break) Bill 2009, Explanatory Memorandum (enacted as no. 31, 2009).* Canberra.

Crean, Simon. 2009. "Protectionism and the Global Economic Crisis: The Role of Trade in the Response." In Richard Baldwin and Simon Evenett, eds., *The Collapse of Global Trade, Murky Protectionism, and the Crisis: Recommendations to the G20.* London: Centre for Economic Policy Research and VoxEU.

Croci Downes, Santiago. Forthcoming. "Going Forward with Secured Lending: The Guatemalan Experience." World Bank, Washington, DC. http://www.reformersclub.org/.

Cuttaree, Sarah and Tea Trumbic. Forthcoming. "The Importance of Being Easiest: Simplifying Taxes in Mauritius." World Bank, Washington, DC. http://www.reformersclub.org/.

Deininger, Klaus, Daniel Ayalew Ali and Tekie Alemu. 2009. *Impacts of Land Certification on Tenure Security, Investment, and Land Markets: Evidence from Ethiopia.* Washington, DC: World Bank Group.

de Mooij, Ruud A., and Gaëtan Nicodème. 2008. "Corporate Tax Policy and Incorporation in the EU." EC Taxation Paper 11, Directorate-General for Taxation and Customs Union, European Commission, Luxembourg.

de Soto, Hernando. 2000. *The Mystery of Capital: Why Capitalism Triumphs in the West and Fails Everywhere Else.* New York: Basic Books.

Djankov, Simeon. 2008. "The Regulation of Entry: A Survey." Discussion Paper DP7080, Centre for Economic Policy Research, London.

____. 2009a. "Bankruptcy Regimes during Financial Distress." World Bank, Washington, DC.

____. 2009b. "Briefing Note on Corporate Debt Burden, Insolvency, and World Bank Group Response." World Bank, Washington, DC.

Djankov, Simeon, and Rita Ramalho. 2009. "Employment Laws in Developing Countries." *Journal of Comparative Economics* 37 (1): 3–13.

Djankov, Simeon, Caroline Freund and Cong Pham. Forthcoming. "Trading on Time." *Review of Economics and Statistics.*

Djankov, Simeon, Caralee McLiesh and Andrei Shleifer. 2007. "Private Credit in 129 Countries." *Journal of Financial Economics* 84 (2): 299–329.

Djankov, Simeon, Oliver Hart, Caralee McLiesh and Andrei Shleifer. 2008. "Enforcement around the World." *Journal of Political Economy* 116 (6): 1105–49.

Djankov, Simeon, Rafael La Porta, Florencio López-de-Silanes and Andrei Shleifer. 2002. "The Regulation of Entry." *Quarterly Journal of Economics* 117 (1): 1–37.

____. 2003. "Courts." *Quarterly Journal of Economics* 118 (2): 453–517.

____. 2008. "The Law and Economics of Self-Dealing." *Journal of Financial Economics* 88 (3): 430–65.

Djankov, Simeon, Darshini Manraj, Caralee McLiesh and Rita Ramalho. 2005. "Doing Business Indicators: Why Aggregate, and How to Do It." World Bank, Washington, DC.

Djankov, Simeon, Tim Ganser, Caralee McLiesh, Rita Ramalho and Andrei Shleifer. Forthcoming. "The Effect of Corporate Taxes on Investment and Entrepreneurship." *American Economic Journal: Macroeconomics.*

Duryea, Suzanne, Gustavo Marquéz, Carmen Pagés and Stefano Scarpetta. 2006. "For Better or for Worse? Job and Earnings Mobility in Nine Middle- and Low-Income Countries." In *Brookings Trade Forum 2006: Global Labor Markets.* Washington, DC: Brookings Institution Press.

Eifert, Benjamin P. 2008. "Do Regulatory Reforms Stimulate Investment and Growth? Evidence from the Doing Business Data, 2003–07." Department of Economics, University of California at Berkeley.

Everest-Phillips, Max, and Richard Sandall. 2009. "Linking Business Tax Reform with Governance: How to Measure Success." In Practice note series, Investment Climate Department, World Bank Group, Washington, DC.

Fidas, Penelope, and Jim McNicholas. 2007. "Need Land Administration Reform? Start a Revolution." In World Bank, *Celebrating Reform 2007.* Washington, DC: World Bank Group and U.S. Agency for International Development.

Field, Erica. 2007. "Entitled to Work: Urban Property Rights and Labor Supply in Peru." *Quarterly Journal of Economics* 122 (4): 1561–602.

Field, Erica, and Maximo Torero. 2006. "Do Property Titles Increase Credit Access among the Urban Poor? Evidence from a Nationwide Titling Program." Working paper, Department of Economics, Harvard University, Cambridge, MA.

Fisman, Raymond, and Virginia Sarria-Allende. 2004. *Regulation of Entry and the Distortion of Industrial Organization.* NBER Working Paper 10929. Cambridge, MA: National Bureau of Economic Research.

Freund, Caroline, and Bineswaree Bolaky. 2008. "Trade, Regulation and Income." *Journal of Development Economics* 87: 309–21.

Galiani, Sebastian, and Ernesto Schargrodsky. 2005. "Property Rights for the Poor: Effects of Land Titling." Business School Working Paper 06/2005, Universidad Torcuato Di Tella, Buenos Aires.

Gine, Xavier, and Inessa Love. 2008. "Do Reorganization Costs Matter for Efficiency? Evidence from a Bankruptcy Reform in Colombia." Policy Research Working Paper 3970, World Bank, Washington, DC.

Hadler, Sandra, Christine Moloi and Sally Wallace. 2006. "Flat or Flattened? A Review of International Trends in Tax Simplification and Reform." Report prepared for U.S. Agency for International Development. http://www.fiscalreform.net/.

Haidar, Jamal. 2008. "Egypt: How to Raise Revenues by Lowering Fees." In World Bank, *Celebrating Reform 2008.* Washington, DC: World Bank Group and U.S. Agency for International Development.

Helpman, Elhanan, Marc Melitz and Yona Rubinstein. 2008. "Estimating Trade Flows: Trading Partners and Trading Volumes." *Quarterly Journal of Economics* 123 (2): 441–87.

Houston, Joel F., Chen Lin, Ping Lin and Yue Ma. 2008. "Creditor Rights, Information Sharing, and Bank Risk Taking." Available at SSRN: http://ssrn.com/abstract=1318458.

Huizinga, Harry, and Luc Laeven. 2008. "International Profit Shifting within Multinationals: A Multi-Country Perspective." *Journal of Public Economics* 92: 1164–82.

Huizinga, Harry, Luc Laeven and Gaëtan Nicodème. 2008. "Capital Structure and International Debt Shifting." *Journal of Financial Economics* 88: 80–118.

Idir, Ali. 2008. "Algérie: une nouvelle loi durcit les conditions d'obtention et d'exécution d'un permis de construire." *Tout sur l'Algérie,* August 24. http://www.tsa-algerie.com/.

ILO (International Labour Organization). 2006. *The End of Child Labour: Within Reach.* Geneva: International Labour Office.

Iwanow, Tomasz, and Colin Kirkpatrick. 2007. "Trade Facilitation, Regulatory Quality and Export Performance." *Journal of International Development* 19 (6): 735–53.

———. 2009. "Facilitation and Manufactured Exports: Is Africa Different?" *World Development* 37 (6): 1039–50.

Johns, Melissa, and Jean Michel Lobet. 2007. "Protecting Investors from Self-Dealing." In World Bank, *Celebrating Reform 2007.* Washington, DC: World Bank Group and U.S. Agency for International Development.

Joireman, S. F. 2008. "The Mystery of Capital Formation in Sub-Saharan Africa: Women, Property Rights, and Customary Law." *World Development* 36 (7): 1233–46.

Kaplan, David, Eduardo Piedra and Enrique Seira. 2008. "Entry Regulation and Business Start-Ups: Evidence from Mexico." Working Paper, Enterprise Analysis Unit, World Bank, Washington, DC.

Kenny, Charles. 2007. "Construction, Corruption, and Developing Countries." Policy Research Working Paper 4271, World Bank, Washington, DC.

Klapper, Leora, Luc Laeven and Raghuram Rajan. 2006. "Entry Regulation as a Barrier to Entrepreneurship." *Journal of Financial Economics* 82 (3): 591–629.

Klapper, Leora, Anat Lewin and Juan Manuel Quesada Delgado. 2009. "The Impact of the Business Environment on the Business Creation Process." Policy Research Working Paper 4937, World Bank, Washington, DC.

Kuddo, Arvo. 2009. "Impact of Labor Regulations on Labor Market Outcomes in Eastern European and Central Asian Countries." Human Development Sector Unit, Europe and Central Asia Region, World Bank, Washington, DC.

———. Forthcoming. "Labor Laws in Eastern European and Central Asian Countries: Minimum Norms and Practices." Social Protection Discussion Paper, Human Development Network, World Bank, Washington, DC.

Lafontaine, Francine, and Jagadeesh Sivadasan. 2007. "The Microeconomic Implications of Input Market Regulations: Cross-Country Evidence from within the Firm." IPC Working Paper 22, International Policy Center, Gerald R. Ford School of Public Policy, University of Michigan, Ann Arbor.

Marechal, Valerie, Pelin Tekin and Humay Guliyeva. Forthcoming. "China's New Property Rights Law: An Important Step towards Improving Access to Credit for Small and Medium Enterprises." World Bank, Washington, DC. http://www.reformersclub.org/.

Martinez-Zarzosa, Imma, and Laura Márquez-Ramos. 2008. "The Effect of Trade Facilitation on Sectoral Trade." *B.E. Journal of Economic Analysis & Policy* 8 (1), article 42.

Masatlioglu, Yusufcan, and Jamele Rigolini. 2008. "Informality Traps." Department of Economics, University of Michigan, Ann Arbor.

Menon, Nidhiya, and Yana van der Meulen Rodgers. 2009. "Self-Employment in Household Enterprises and Access to Credit: Gender Differences during India's Rural Banking Reform." Presentation at World Bank conference "Female Entrepreneurship: Constraints and Opportunities," Washington, DC, June 3.

Montenegro, Claudio E., and Carmen Pagés. 2004. "Who Benefits from Labor Market Regulations? Chile, 1960–1998." In James J. Heckman and Carmen Pagés, eds., *Law and Employment: Lessons from Latin America and the Caribbean.* Chicago and London: University of Chicago Press.

Moullier, Thomas. 2009. "Reforming Building Permits: Why Is It Important and What Can IFC Really Do?" International Finance Corporation, Washington, DC.

Narayan, Deepa, Robert Chambers, Meera Kaul Shah and Patti Petesh. 2000. *Voices of the Poor: Crying Out for Change.* Washington, DC: World Bank.

Nicodème, Gaëtan. 2008. "Corporate Income Tax and Economic Distortions." CESifo Working Paper 2477, CESifo Group, Munich.

Nunn, Nathan. 2007. "Relationship-Specificity, Incomplete Contracts, and the Pattern of Trade." *Quarterly Journal of Economics* 122 (2): 569–600.

OECD Development Centre. 2009. *Is Informal Normal? Towards More and Better Jobs in Developing Countries.* Paris: OECD.

Perotti, Enrico, and Paolo Volpin. 2004. "Lobbying on Entry." CEPR Discussion Paper 4519, Centre for Economic Policy Research, London.

Person, Maria. 2008. "Trade Facilitation and the EU-ACP Economic Partnership Agreements." *Journal of Economic Integration* 23 (3): 518–46.

Pierre, Gaëlle, and Stefano Scarpetta. 2007. "How Labor Market Policies Can Combine Workers' Protection with Job Creation: A Partial Review of Some Key Issues and Policy Options." Social Protection Discussion Paper 0716, Human Development Network, World Bank, Washington, DC.

Portugal-Perez, Alberto, and John Wilson. 2008. "Trade Costs in Africa: Barriers and Opportunities to Reform." Policy Research Working Paper 4619, World Bank, Washington, DC.

PricewaterhouseCoopers. 2008. *Compete and Collaborate: What Is Success in a Connected World?* 11th Annual Global CEO Survey. London.

Quy-Toan, Do, and Lakshmi Iyer. 2008. "Land Titling and Rural Transition in Vietnam." *Economic Development and Cultural Change* 56: 531–79.

Raballand, Gael, Charles Kunuka and Bo Giersing. 2008. "The Impact of Regional Liberalization and Harmonization in Road Transport Services: A Focus on Zambia and Lessons for Landlocked Countries." Policy Research Working Paper 4482, World Bank, Washington, DC.

Ranjan, Priya, and Jae Young Lee. 2007. "Contract Enforcement and International Trade." *Economics and Politics* 19: 191–218.

Schneider, Friedrich. 2005. "The Informal Sector in 145 Countries." Department of Economics, University Linz.

____. 2007. "Shadow Economies and Corruption All Over the World: New Estimates for 145 Countries." *Economics: The Open-Access, Open-Assessment E-Journal* 1 (9). http://www.economics-ejournal.org/.

Sharma, Siddharth. 2009. "Entry Regulation, Labor Laws and Informality." Working paper, Enterprise Analysis Unit, World Bank, Washington, DC.

Singapore Business Federation. 2009. "Key Findings from ABAC 'Ease of Doing Business' (EoDB) Survey." Presentation at Singapore Business Federation dialogue session "Removing Barriers for Business Growth in APEC," Singapore, July 9.

Tongzon, Jose, and Wu Heng. 2005. "Port Privatization, Efficiency and Competitiveness: Some Empirical Evidence from Container Ports (Terminals)." *Transportation Research Part A: Policy and Practice* 39 (5): 405–24.

Vodopivec, Milan. 2009. "Introducing Unemployment Insurance to Developing Countries." Social Protection Discussion Paper 0907, Human Development Network, World Bank, Washington, DC.

WEF (World Economic Forum). 2007. *The Global Competitiveness Report 2007–2008.* New York: Palgrave Macmillan.

____. 2008. *The Global Competitiveness Report 2008–2009.* New York: Palgrave Macmillan.

Wilson, Norbert. 2009. "Examining the Effect of Certain Customs and Administrative Procedures on Trade." In Organisation for Economic Co-operation and Development (OECD), *Overcoming Border Bottlenecks: The Costs and Benefits of Trade Facilitation.* Paris: OECD.

Wongtrakool, Bonnie. 1998. "Does Paperless Mean Painless?" Final paper submitted for course on Internet and Society, Harvard University. http://cyber.law.harvard.edu/fallsem98/final_papers/Wongtrakool.html.

World Bank. 2003. *Doing Business in 2004: Understanding Regulation.* Washington, DC: World Bank Group.

____. 2006. *Doing Business 2007: How to Reform.* Washington, DC: World Bank Group.

____. 2007. *Port Reform Toolkit.* Washington, DC: World Bank Group.

____. 2008a. *Doing Business 2009: Comparing Regulation in 181 Economies.* Washington, DC: World Bank Group.

____. 2008b. *Doing Business: Women in Africa.* Washington, DC: World Bank Group.

____. 2008c. *Improving Trade and Transport for Landlocked Developing Countries.* Washington, DC: World Bank Group.

____. 2008d. "Insecurity of Land Tenure, Land Law and Land Registration in Liberia." Report 46134-LR, Environment and Natural Resource Management Unit, Africa Region, World Bank, Washington, DC.

____. 2009a. *Unlocking Global Opportunities: The Aid for Trade Program of the World Bank Group.* Washington, DC: World Bank Group.

____. 2009b. *World Development Indicators 2009.* Washington, DC: World Bank Group.

World Bank Independent Evaluation Group. 2008. *Doing Business: An Independent Evaluation—Taking the Measure of the World Bank–IFC Doing Business Indicators.* Washington, DC: World Bank Group.

Yang, Junsok. 2009. "Small and Medium Enterprises (SME) Adjustments to Information Technology (IT) in Trade Facilitation: The South Korean Experience." ARTNeT Working Paper Series, no. 61, Asia-Pacific Research and Training Network on Trade, Bangkok.

Data notes

The indicators presented and analyzed in *Doing Business* measure business regulation and the protection of property rights—and their effect on businesses, especially small and medium-size domestic firms. First, the indicators document the degree of regulation, such as the number of procedures to start a business or to register and transfer commercial property. Second, they gauge regulatory outcomes, such as the time and cost to enforce a contract, go through bankruptcy or trade across borders. Third, they measure the extent of legal protections of property, for example, the protections of investors against looting by company directors or the range of assets that can be used as collateral according to secured transactions laws. Fourth, they measure the flexibility of employment regulation. Finally, a set of indicators documents the tax burden on businesses. For details on how the rankings on these indicators are constructed, see Ease of doing business, page 97.

The data for all sets of indicators in *Doing Business 2010* are for June 2009.[1] Two new economies—Cyprus and Kosovo—were added to the sample, now comprising 183 economies.

METHODOLOGY

The *Doing Business* data are collected in a standardized way. To start, the *Doing Business* team, with academic advisers, designs a survey. The survey uses a simple business case to ensure comparability across economies and over time—with assumptions about the legal form of the business, its size, its location and the nature of its operations. Surveys are administered through more than 8,000 local experts, including lawyers, business consultants, accountants, freight forwarders, government officials and other professionals routinely administering or advising on legal and regulatory requirements (table 14.1). These experts have several (typically 4) rounds of interaction with the *Doing Business* team, involving conference calls, written correspondence and visits by the team. For *Doing Business 2010* team members visited 43 economies to verify data and recruit respondents. The data from surveys are subjected to numerous tests for robustness, which lead to revisions or expansions of the information collected.

The *Doing Business* methodology offers several advantages. It is transparent, using factual information about what laws and regulations say and allowing multiple interactions with local respondents to clarify potential misinterpretations of questions. Having representative samples of respondents is not an issue, as the texts of the relevant laws and regulations are collected and answers checked for accuracy. The methodology is inexpensive and easily replicable, so data can be collected in a large sample of economies. Because standard assumptions are used in the data collection, comparisons and benchmarks are valid across economies. Finally, the data not only highlight the extent of specific regulatory obstacles to business but also identify their source and point to what might be reformed.

LIMITS TO WHAT IS MEASURED

The *Doing Business* methodology has 5 limitations that should be considered when interpreting the data. First, the collected data refer to businesses in the economy's largest business city and may not be representative of regulation in other parts of the economy. To address this limitation, subnational *Doing Business* indicators were created for 17 economies in 2008/09: Albania, Bosnia and Herzegovina, China, Colombia, Croatia, Egypt, India, Italy (Veneto region), Kosovo, FYR Macedonia, Mexico, Montenegro, Morocco, Nigeria, the Philippines, Serbia and the United Arab Emirates (Abu Dhabi).[2] Five other subnational studies are under way, in Central Asia, Indonesia, Kenya, the Russian Federation and Ukraine. Some existing subnational studies are updated annually to measure progress over time or to expand geographic coverage. This is the case in Colombia, India, Mexico, Nigeria, Pakistan and the Philippines. These subnational studies point to significant differences in the speed of reform and the ease of doing business across cities in the same economy.

Second, the data often focus on a specific business form—generally a limited liability company (or its legal equivalent) of a specified size—and may not be representative of the regulation on other businesses, for example, sole proprietorships. Third, transactions described in a standardized case scenario refer to a specific set of issues and may not represent the full set of issues a business encounters. Fourth, the measures of

TABLE 14.1

How many experts does *Doing Business* consult?

Indicator set	Number of contributors
Starting a business	1,403
Dealing with construction permits	639
Employing workers	997
Registering property	1,010
Getting credit	1,173
Protecting investors	877
Paying taxes	926
Trading across borders	1,455
Enforcing contracts	1,029
Closing a business	863

time involve an element of judgment by the expert respondents. When sources indicate different estimates, the time indicators reported in *Doing Business* represent the median values of several responses given under the assumptions of the standardized case.

Finally, the methodology assumes that a business has full information on what is required and does not waste time when completing procedures. In practice, completing a procedure may take longer if the business lacks information or is unable to follow up promptly. Alternatively, the business may choose to disregard some burdensome procedures. For both reasons the time delays reported in *Doing Business 2010* would differ from the recollection of entrepreneurs reported in the World Bank Enterprise Surveys or other perception surveys.

CHANGES IN WHAT IS MEASURED

The methodology for one of the *Doing Business* topics—employing workers—was updated this year.[3] The assumptions for the standardized case study were changed to refer to a small- to medium-size company with 60 employees rather than 201. The scope of the question on night and weekly holiday work has been limited to manufacturing activities in which continuous operation is economically necessary. Legally mandated wage premiums for night and weekly holiday work up to a threshold are no longer considered a restriction. In addition, the calculation of the minimum wage ratio was modified to ensure that an economy would not benefit in the scoring from lowering the minimum wage to below $1.25 a day, adjusted for purchasing power parity. This level is consistent with recent adjustments to the absolute poverty line. Finally, the calculation of the redundancy cost was adjusted so that having severance payments or unemployment protections below a certain threshold does not mean a better score for an economy.

Economy characteristics

GROSS NATIONAL INCOME (GNI) PER CAPITA

Doing Business 2010 reports 2008 income per capita as published in the World Bank's *World Development Indicators 2009*. Income is calculated using the Atlas method (current US$). For cost indicators expressed as a percentage of income per capita, 2008 GNI in local currency units is used as the denominator. GNI data were not available from the World Bank for Afghanistan, The Bahamas, Bahrain, Brunei Darussalam, Cyprus, Guinea, the Islamic Republic of Iran, Iraq, Kosovo, Kuwait, Mauritania, Oman, Puerto Rico, Qatar, Saudi Arabia, Taiwan (China), the United Arab Emirates and Zimbabwe. In these cases GDP or GNP per capita data and growth rates from the International Monetary Fund's World Economic Outlook database and the Economist Intelligence Unit were used.

REGION AND INCOME GROUP

Doing Business uses the World Bank regional and income group classifications, available at http://www.worldbank.org/data/countryclass.

POPULATION

Doing Business 2010 reports midyear 2008 population statistics as published in *World Development Indicators 2009*.

DATA CHALLENGES AND REVISIONS

Most laws and regulations underlying the *Doing Business* data are available on the *Doing Business* website at http://www.doingbusiness.org. All the sample surveys and the details underlying the indicators are also published on the website. Questions on the methodology and challenges to data can be submitted through the website's "Ask a Question" function at http://www.doingbusiness.org.

Doing Business publishes 8,967 indicators each year. To create these indicators, the team measures more than 52,000 data points, each of which is made available on the *Doing Busines* website. Historical data for each indicator and economy are available on the website, beginning with the first year the indicator or economy was included in the report. To provide a comparable time series for research, the data set is back-calculated to adjust for changes in methodology and any revisions in data due to corrections. The website also makes available all original data sets used for background papers. The correction rate between *Doing Business 2009* and *Doing Business 2010* was 5.5%.

STARTING A BUSINESS

Doing Business records all procedures that are officially required for an entrepreneur to start up and formally operate an industrial or commercial business. These include obtaining all necessary licenses and permits and completing any required notifications, verifications or inscriptions for the company and employees with relevant authorities.

After a study of laws, regulations and publicly available information on business entry, a detailed list of procedures is developed, along with the time and cost of complying with each procedure under normal circumstances and the paid-in minimum capital requirements. Subsequently, local incorporation lawyers and government officials complete and verify the data.

Information is also collected on the sequence in which procedures are to be completed and whether procedures may be carried out simultaneously. It is assumed that any required information is readily available and that all agencies involved in the start-up process function without corruption. If answers by local experts differ, inquiries continue until the data are reconciled.

To make the data comparable across economies, several assumptions about the business and the procedures are used.

ASSUMPTIONS ABOUT THE BUSINESS

The business:

- Is a limited liability company. If there is more than one type of limited liability company in the economy, the limited liability form most popular among domestic firms is chosen. Information on the most popular form is obtained from incorporation lawyers or the statistical office.
- Operates in the economy's largest business city.
- Is 100% domestically owned and has 5 owners, none of whom is a legal entity.
- Has start-up capital of 10 times income per capita at the end of 2008, paid in cash.
- Performs general industrial or commercial activities, such as the production or sale to the public of products or services. The business does not perform foreign trade activities and does not handle products subject to a special tax regime, for example, liquor or tobacco. It is not using heavily polluting production processes.
- Leases the commercial plant and offices and is not a proprietor of real estate.
- Does not qualify for investment incentives or any special benefits.
- Has at least 10 and up to 50 employees 1 month after the commencement of operations, all of them nationals.
- Has a turnover of at least 100 times income per capita.
- Has a company deed 10 pages long.

PROCEDURES

A procedure is defined as any interaction of the company founders with external parties (for example, government agencies, lawyers, auditors or notaries). Interactions between company founders or company officers and employees are not counted as procedures. Procedures that

TABLE 14.2

What does starting a business measure?

Procedures to legally start and operate a company (number)
- Preregistration (for example, name verification or reservation, notarization)
- Registration in the economy's largest business city
- Postregistration (for example, social security registration, company seal)

Time required to complete each procedure (calendar days)
- Does not include time spent gathering information
- Each procedure starts on a separate day
- Procedure completed once final document is received
- No prior contact with officials

Cost required to complete each procedure (% of income per capita)
- Official costs only, no bribes
- No professional fees unless services required by law

Paid-in minimum capital (% of income per capita)
- Deposited in a bank or with a notary before registration begins

Source: Doing Business database.

must be completed in the same building but in different offices are counted as separate procedures. If founders have to visit the same office several times for different sequential procedures, each is counted separately. The founders are assumed to complete all procedures themselves, without middlemen, facilitators, accountants or lawyers, unless the use of such a third party is mandated by law. If the services of professionals are required, procedures conducted by such professionals on behalf of the company are counted separately. Each electronic procedure is counted separately. If 2 procedures can be completed through the same website but require separate filings, they are counted as 2 procedures.

Both pre- and postincorporation procedures that are officially required for an entrepreneur to formally operate a business are recorded (table 14.2).

Procedures required for official correspondence or transactions with public agencies are also included. For example, if a company seal or stamp is required on official documents, such as tax declarations, obtaining the seal or stamp is counted. Similarly, if a company must open a bank account before registering for sales tax or value added tax, this transaction is included as a procedure. Shortcuts are counted only if they fulfill 4 criteria: they are legal, they are available to the general public, they are used by

the majority of companies, and avoiding them causes substantial delays.

Only procedures required of all businesses are covered. Industry-specific procedures are excluded. For example, procedures to comply with environmental regulations are included only when they apply to all businesses conducting general commercial or industrial activities. Procedures that the company undergoes to connect to electricity, water, gas and waste disposal services are not included.

TIME

Time is recorded in calendar days. The measure captures the median duration that incorporation lawyers indicate is necessary to complete a procedure with minimum follow-up with government agencies and no extra payments. It is assumed that the minimum time required for each procedure is 1 day. Although procedures may take place simultaneously, they cannot start on the same day (that is, simultaneous procedures start on consecutive days). A procedure is considered completed once the company has received the final document, such as the company registration certificate or tax number. If a procedure can be accelerated for an additional cost, the fastest procedure is chosen. It is assumed that the entrepreneur does not waste time and commits to completing each remaining procedure without delay. The time that the entrepreneur spends on gathering information is ignored. It is assumed that the entrepreneur is aware of all entry regulations and their sequence from the beginning but has had no prior contact with any of the officials.

COST

Cost is recorded as a percentage of the economy's income per capita. It includes all official fees and fees for legal or professional services if such services are required by law. Fees for purchasing and legalizing company books are included if these transactions are required by law. The company law, the commercial code and specific regulations and fee schedules are used as sources for calculating costs. In the absence of fee schedules, a government officer's estimate is taken as an official source. In the absence of a government officer's estimate, estimates of incorporation lawyers are used. If several incorporation lawyers provide different estimates, the median reported value is applied. In all cases the cost excludes bribes.

PAID-IN MINIMUM CAPITAL

The paid-in minimum capital requirement reflects the amount that the entrepreneur needs to deposit in a bank or with a notary before registration and up to 3 months following incorporation and is recorded as a percentage of the economy's income per capita. The amount is typically specified in the commercial code or the company law. Many economies have a minimum capital requirement but allow businesses to pay only a part of it before registration, with the rest to be paid after the first year of operation. In Italy in June 2009, the minimum capital requirement for limited liability companies was €10,000, of which at least €2,500 was payable before registration. The paid-in minimum capital recorded for Italy is therefore €2,500, or 9.7% of income per capita. In Mexico the minimum capital requirement was 50,000 pesos, of which one-fifth needed to be paid before registration. The paid-in minimum capital

recorded for Mexico is therefore 10,000 pesos, or 8.9% of income per capita.

The data details on starting a business can be found for each economy at http://www.doingbusiness.org by selecting the economy in the drop-down list. This methodology was developed in Djankov and others (2002) and is adopted here with minor changes.

DEALING WITH CONSTRUCTION PERMITS

Doing Business records all procedures required for a business in the construction industry to build a standardized warehouse. These procedures include submitting all relevant project-specific documents (for example, building plans and site maps) to the authorities; obtaining all necessary clearances, licenses, permits and certificates; completing all required notifications; and receiving all necessary inspections. *Doing Business* also records procedures for obtaining connections for electricity, water, sewerage and a fixed land line. Procedures necessary to register the property so that it can be used as collateral or transferred to another entity are also counted. The survey divides the process of building a warehouse into distinct procedures and calculates the time and cost of completing each procedure in practice under normal circumstances.

Information is collected from experts in construction licensing, including architects, construction lawyers, construction firms, utility service providers and public officials who deal with building regulations, including approvals and inspections. To make the data comparable across economies, several assumptions about the business, the warehouse project and the utility connections are used.

ASSUMPTIONS ABOUT THE CONSTRUCTION COMPANY

The business (BuildCo):
- Is a limited liability company.
- Operates in the economy's largest business city.

- Is 100% domestically and privately owned.
- Has 5 owners, none of whom is a legal entity.
- Is fully licensed and insured to carry out construction projects, such as building warehouses.
- Has 60 builders and other employees, all of them nationals with the technical expertise and professional experience necessary to obtain construction permits and approvals.
- Has at least 1 employee who is a licensed architect and registered with the local association of architects.
- Has paid all taxes and taken out all necessary insurance applicable to its general business activity (for example, accidental insurance for construction workers and third-person liability).
- Owns the land on which the warehouse is built.

ASSUMPTIONS ABOUT THE WAREHOUSE

The warehouse:
- Will be used for general storage activities, such as storage of books or stationery. The warehouse will not be used for any goods requiring special conditions, such as food, chemicals or pharmaceuticals.
- Has 2 stories, both above ground, with a total surface of approximately 1,300.6 square meters (14,000 square feet). Each floor is 3 meters (9 feet, 10 inches) high.
- Has road access and is located in the periurban area of the economy's largest business city (that is, on the fringes of the city but still within its official limits).
- Is not located in a special economic or industrial zone. The zoning requirements for warehouses are met by building in an area where similar warehouses can be found.
- Is located on a land plot of 929 square meters (10,000 square feet) that is 100% owned by BuildCo and is accurately registered in the cadastre and land registry.
- Is a new construction (there was no previous construction on the land).

TABLE 14.3
What does dealing with construction permits measure?

Procedures to legally build a warehouse *(number)*

- Submitting all relevant documents and obtaining all necessary clearances, licenses, permits and certificates
- Completing all required notifications and receiving all necessary inspections
- Obtaining utility connections for electricity, water, sewerage and a land telephone line
- Registering the warehouse after its completion (if required for use as collateral or for transfer of warehouse)

Time required to complete each procedure *(calendar days)*

- Does not include time spent gathering information
- Each procedure starts on a separate day
- Procedure completed once final document is received
- No prior contact with officials

Cost required to complete each procedure *(% of income per capita)*

- Official costs only, no bribes

Source: Doing Business database.

- Has complete architectural and technical plans prepared by a licensed architect.
- Will include all technical equipment required to make the warehouse fully operational.
- Will take 30 weeks to construct (excluding all delays due to administrative and regulatory requirements).

ASSUMPTIONS ABOUT THE UTILITY CONNECTIONS

The electricity connection:

- Is 10 meters (32 feet, 10 inches) from the main electricity network.
- Is a medium-tension, 3-phase, 4-wire Y, 140-kVA connection. Three-phase service is available in the construction area.
- Will be delivered by an overhead service, unless overhead service is not available in the periurban area.
- Consists of a simple hookup unless installation of a private substation (transformer) or extension of network is required.
- Requires the installation of only one electricity meter.

BuildCo is assumed to have a licensed electrician on its team to complete the internal wiring for the warehouse.

The water and sewerage connection:

- Is 10 meters (32 feet, 10 inches) from the existing water source and sewer tap.
- Does not require water for fire protection reasons; a fire extinguishing system (dry system) will be used instead. If a wet fire protection system is required by law, it is assumed that the water demand specified below also covers the water needed for fire protection.
- Has an average water use of 662 liters (175 gallons) a day and an average wastewater flow of 568 liters (150 gallons) a day.
- Has a peak water use of 1,325 liters (350 gallons) a day and a peak wastewater flow of 1,136 liters (300 gallons) a day.
- Will have a constant level of water demand and wastewater flow throughout the year.

The telephone connection:

- Is 10 meters (32 feet, 10 inches) from the main telephone network.
- Is a fixed land line.

PROCEDURES

A procedure is any interaction of the company's employees or managers with external parties, including government agencies, notaries, the land registry, the cadastre, utility companies, public and private inspectors and technical experts apart from in-house architects and engineers. Interactions between company employees, such as development of the warehouse plans and inspections conducted by employees, are not counted as procedures. Procedures that the company undergoes to connect to electricity, water, sewerage and telephone services are included. All procedures that are legally or in practice required for building a warehouse are counted, even if they may be avoided in exceptional cases (table 14.3).

TIME

Time is recorded in calendar days. The measure captures the median duration that local experts indicate is necessary to complete a procedure in practice. It is assumed that the minimum time required for each procedure is 1 day. Although procedures may take place simultaneously, they cannot start on the same day (that is, simultaneous procedures start on consecutive days). If a procedure can be accelerated legally for an additional cost, the fastest procedure is chosen. It is assumed that BuildCo does not waste time and commits to completing each remaining procedure without delay. The time that BuildCo spends on gathering information is ignored. It is assumed that BuildCo is aware of all building requirements and their sequence from the beginning.

COST

Cost is recorded as a percentage of the economy's income per capita. Only official costs are recorded. All the fees associated with completing the procedures to legally build a warehouse are recorded, including those associated with obtaining land use approvals and preconstruction design clearances; receiving inspections before, during and after construction; getting utility connections; and registering the warehouse property. Nonrecurring taxes required for the completion of the warehouse project also are recorded. The building code, information from local experts and specific regulations and fee schedules are used as sources for costs. If several local partners provide different estimates, the median reported value is used.

The data details on dealing with construction permits can be found for each economy at http://www.doingbusiness.org by selecting the economy in the drop-down list.

EMPLOYING WORKERS

Doing Business measures the regulation of employment, specifically as it affects the hiring and redundancy of workers and the rigidity of working hours. In 2007 improvements were made to align the methodology for the employing workers indicators with the International Labour Organization (ILO) conventions.

This year further changes were made to the methodology for the employing workers indicators. First, the standardized case study was changed to refer to a small to medium-size company with 60 employees rather than 201. Second, restrictions on night and weekly holiday work are taken into account if they apply to manufacturing activities in which continuous operation is economically necessary. Third, legally mandated wage premiums for work performed on the designated weekly holiday or for night work are scored on the basis of a 4-tiered scale. Fourth, economies that mandate 8 or fewer weeks of severance pay and do not offer unemployment protection do not receive a better score. Finally, the calculation of the minimum wage ratio was modified to ensure that an economy would not benefit in the scoring from lowering the minimum wage to below $1.25 a day, adjusted for purchasing power parity. This level is consistent with recent adjustments to the absolute poverty line.

Only 4 of the 188 ILO conventions cover areas measured by *Doing Business*: employee termination, weekend work, holiday with pay and night work. The *Doing Business* methodology is fully consistent with these 4 conventions. It is possible for an economy to receive the best score on the ease of employing workers and comply with all relevant ILO conventions (specifically, the 4 related to *Doing Business*)—and no economy can achieve a better score by failing to comply with these conventions.

The ILO conventions covering areas related to the employing workers indicators do not include the ILO core labor standards—8 conventions covering the right to collective bargaining, the elimination of forced labor, the abolition of child labor and equitable treatment in employment practices.

In the past year *Doing Business* conducted research on implementation (by adoption in national law) of 2 ILO conventions on child labor. This year's report includes preliminary findings for 102 countries (see annex on worker protection). *Doing Business* does not measure or rank ratification or compliance with ILO conventions.

The data on employing workers are based on a detailed survey of employment regulations that is completed by local lawyers and public officials. Employment laws and regulations as well as secondary sources are reviewed to ensure accuracy. To make the data comparable across economies, several assumptions about the worker and the business are used.

ASSUMPTIONS ABOUT THE WORKER
The worker:
- Is a 42-year-old, nonexecutive, full-time, male employee.
- Has worked at the same company for 20 years.
- Earns a salary plus benefits equal to the economy's average wage during the entire period of his employment.
- Is a lawful citizen who belongs to the same race and religion as the majority of the economy's population.
- Resides in the economy's largest business city.
- Is not a member of a labor union, unless membership is mandatory.

ASSUMPTIONS ABOUT THE BUSINESS
The business:
- Is a limited liability company.
- Operates in the economy's largest business city.
- Is 100% domestically owned.
- Operates in the manufacturing sector.
- Has 60 employees.
- Is subject to collective bargaining agreements in economies where such agreements cover more than half the manufacturing sector and apply even to firms not party to them.
- Abides by every law and regulation but does not grant workers more benefits than mandated by law, regulation or (if applicable) collective bargaining agreement.

RIGIDITY OF EMPLOYMENT INDEX
The rigidity of employment index is the average of 3 subindices: a difficulty of hiring index, a rigidity of hours index and a difficulty of redundancy index (table 14.4). All the subindices have several components. And all take values between 0 and 100, with higher values indicating more rigid regulation.

The difficulty of hiring index measures (i) whether fixed-term contracts are prohibited for permanent tasks; (ii) the maximum cumulative duration of fixed-term contracts; and (iii) the ratio of the minimum wage for a trainee or first-time employee to the average value added per worker.[4] An economy is assigned a score of 1 if fixed-term contracts are prohibited for permanent tasks and a score of 0 if they can be used for any task. A score of 1 is assigned if the maximum cumulative duration of fixed-term contracts is less than 3 years; 0.5 if it is 3 years or more but less than 5 years; and 0 if fixed-term contracts can last 5 years or more. Finally, a score of 1 is assigned if the ratio of the minimum wage to the average value added per worker is 0.75 or more; 0.67 for a ratio of 0.50 or more but less than 0.75; 0.33 for a ratio of 0.25 or more but less than 0.50; and 0 for a ratio of less than 0.25. In Benin, for example, fixed-term contracts are not prohibited for permanent tasks (a score of 0), and they can be used for a maximum of 4 years (a score of 0.5). The ratio of the mandated minimum wage to the value added per worker is 0.59 (a score of 0.67). Averaging the 3 values and scaling the index to 100 gives Benin a score of 39.

What does employing workers measure?

Difficulty of hiring index *(0–100)*

- Applicability and maximum duration of fixed-term contracts
- Minimum wage for trainee or first-time employee

Rigidity of hours index *(0–100)*

- Restrictions on night work and weekend work
- Allowed maximum length of the workweek in days and hours, including overtime
- Paid annual vacation days

Difficulty of redundancy index *(0–100)*

- Notification and approval requirements for termination of a redundant worker or group of redundant workers
- Obligation to reassign or retrain and priority rules for redundancy and reemployment

Rigidity of employment index *(0–100)*

- Simple average of the difficulty of hiring, rigidity of hours and difficulty of redundancy indices

Redundancy cost *(weeks of salary)*

- Notice requirements, severance payments and penalties due when terminating a redundant worker, expressed in weeks of salary

Source: Doing Business database.

The rigidity of hours index has 5 components: (i) whether there are restrictions on night work; (ii) whether there are restrictions on weekly holiday work; (iii) whether the workweek can consist of 5.5 days; (iv) whether the workweek can extend to 50 hours or more (including overtime) for 2 months a year to respond to a seasonal increase in production; and (v) whether paid annual vacation is 21 working days or fewer. For questions (i) and (ii), when restrictions other than premiums apply, a score of 1 is given. If the only restriction is a premium for night work and weekly holiday work, a score of 0, 0.33, 0.66 or 1 is given according to the quartile in which the economy's premium falls. If there are no restrictions, the economy receives a score of 0. For questions (iii), (iv) and (v), when the answer is no, a score of 1 is assigned; otherwise a score of 0 is assigned.

For example, Honduras imposes restrictions on night work (a score of 1) but not on weekly holiday work (a score of 0), allows 6-day workweeks (a score of 0), permits 50-hour workweeks for 2 months (a score of 0) and requires paid annual vacation of 20 working days (a score of 0). Averaging the scores and scaling the result to 100 gives a final index of 20 for Honduras.

The difficulty of redundancy index has 8 components: (i) whether redundancy is disallowed as a basis for terminating workers; (ii) whether the employer needs to notify a third party (such as a government agency) to terminate 1 redundant worker; (iii) whether the employer needs to notify a third party to terminate a group of 9 redundant workers; (iv) whether the employer needs approval from a third party to terminate 1 redundant worker; (v) whether the employer needs approval from a third party to terminate a group of 9 redundant workers; (vi) whether the law requires the employer to reassign or retrain a worker before making the worker redundant; (vii) whether priority rules apply for redundancies; and (viii) whether priority rules apply for reemployment. For the first question an answer of yes for workers of any income level gives a score of 10 and means that the rest of the questions do not apply. An answer of yes to question (iv) gives a score of 2. For every other question, if the answer is yes, a score of 1 is assigned; otherwise a score of 0 is given. Questions (i) and (iv), as the most restrictive regulations, have greater weight in the construction of the index.

In Tunisia, for example, redundancy is allowed as grounds for termination (a score of 0). An employer has to both no-

tify a third party (a score of 1) and obtain its approval (a score of 2) to terminate a single redundant worker, and has to both notify a third party (a score of 1) and obtain its approval (a score of 1) to terminate a group of 9 redundant workers. The law mandates retraining or alternative placement before termination (a score of 1). There are priority rules for termination (a score of 1) and reemployment (a score of 1). Adding the scores and scaling to 100 gives a final index of 80.

REDUNDANCY COST

The redundancy cost indicator measures the cost of advance notice requirements, severance payments and penalties due when terminating a redundant worker, expressed in weeks of salary. If the redundancy cost adds up to 8 or fewer weeks of salary and the worker can benefit from unemployment protection, a score of 0 is assigned for the purposes of calculating the aggregate ease of doing business ranking. If the redundancy cost adds up to 8 or fewer weeks of salary and the worker cannot benefit from any type of unemployment protection, a score of 8.1 weeks is assigned for the purpose of calculating the aggregate ease of doing business. If the cost adds up to more than 8 weeks of salary, the score is the number of weeks. One month is recorded as 4 and 1/3 weeks.

In Mauritania, for example, an employer is required to give 1 month's notice before a redundancy termination, and the severance pay for a worker with 20 years of service equals 6.25 months of wages. No penalty is levied. Altogether, the employer pays the equivalent of 31.4 weeks of salary to dismiss the worker.

The data details on employing workers can be found for each economy at http://www.doingbusiness.org by selecting the economy in the drop-down list. The Doing Business *website provides historical data sets adjusted for changes in methodology to allow comparison of data across years. This methodology was developed in Botero and others (2004) and is adopted here with minor changes.*

REGISTERING PROPERTY

Doing Business records the full sequence of procedures necessary for a business (buyer) to purchase a property from another business (seller) and to transfer the property title to the buyer's name so that the buyer can use the property for expanding its business, use the property as collateral in taking new loans or, if necessary, sell the property to another business. The process starts with obtaining the necessary documents, such as a copy of the seller's title if necessary, and conducting due diligence if required. The transaction is considered complete when it is opposable to third parties and when the buyer can use the property, use it as collateral for a bank loan or resell it.

Every procedure required by law or necessary in practice is included, whether it is the responsibility of the seller or the buyer or must be completed by a third party on their behalf. Local property lawyers, notaries and property registries provide information on procedures as well as the time and cost to complete each of them.

To make the data comparable across economies, several assumptions about the parties to the transaction, the property and the procedures are used.

ASSUMPTIONS ABOUT THE PARTIES

The parties (buyer and seller):
- Are limited liability companies.
- Are located in the periurban area of the economy's largest business city.
- Are 100% domestically and privately owned.
- Have 50 employees each, all of whom are nationals.
- Perform general commercial activities.

ASSUMPTIONS ABOUT THE PROPERTY

The property:
- Has a value of 50 times income per capita. The sale price equals the value.
- Is fully owned by the seller.
- Has no mortgages attached and has been under the same ownership for the past 10 years.

TABLE 14.5

What does registering property measure?

Procedures to legally transfer title on immovable property *(number)*
· Preregistration (for example, checking for liens, notarizing sales agreement, paying property transfer taxes)
· Registration in the economy's largest business city
· Postregistration (for example, filing title with municipality)

Time required to complete each procedure *(calendar days)*
· Does not include time spent gathering information
· Each procedure starts on a separate day
· Procedure completed once final document is received
· No prior contact with officials

Cost required to complete each procedure *(% of property value)*
· Official costs only, no bribes
· No value added or capital gains taxes included

Source: Doing Business database.

- Is registered in the land registry or cadastre, or both, and is free of title disputes.
- Is located in a periurban commercial zone, and no rezoning is required.
- Consists of land and a building. The land area is 557.4 square meters (6,000 square feet). A 2-story warehouse of 929 square meters (10,000 square feet) is located on the land. The warehouse is 10 years old, is in good condition and complies with all safety standards, building codes and other legal requirements. The property of land and building will be transferred in its entirety.
- Will not be subject to renovations or additional building following the purchase.
- Has no trees, natural water sources, natural reserves or historical monuments of any kind.
- Will not be used for special purposes, and no special permits, such as for residential use, industrial plants, waste storage or certain types of agricultural activities, are required.
- Has no occupants (legal or illegal), and no other party holds a legal interest in it.

PROCEDURES

A procedure is defined as any interaction of the buyer or the seller, their agents (if an agent is legally or in practice required) or the property with external parties, including government agencies, inspec-tors, notaries and lawyers. Interactions between company officers and employ-ees are not considered. All procedures that are legally or in practice required for registering property are recorded, even if they may be avoided in exceptional cases (table 14.5). It is assumed that the buyer follows the fastest legal option available and used by the majority of property owners. Although the buyer may use lawyers or other professionals where necessary in the registration process, it is assumed that it does not employ an outside facilitator in the registration pro-cess unless legally or in practice required to do so.

TIME

Time is recorded in calendar days. The measure captures the median duration that property lawyers, notaries or reg-istry officials indicate is necessary to complete a procedure. It is assumed that the minimum time required for each procedure is 1 day. Although procedures may take place simultaneously, they can-not start on the same day. It is assumed that the buyer does not waste time and commits to completing each remaining procedure without delay. If a procedure can be accelerated for an additional cost, the fastest legal procedure available and used by the majority of property owners is chosen. If procedures can be under-taken simultaneously, it is assumed that they are. It is assumed that the parties involved are aware of all regulations and their sequence from the beginning. Time spent on gathering information is not considered.

COST

Cost is recorded as a percentage of the property value, assumed to be equivalent to 50 times income per capita. Only official costs required by law are recorded, including fees, transfer taxes, stamp duties and any other payment to the property registry, notaries, public agencies or lawyers. Other taxes, such as capital gains tax or value added tax, are excluded from the cost measure. Both costs borne by the buyer and those borne by the seller are included. If cost estimates differ among sources, the median reported value is used.

The data details on registering property can be found for each economy at http:// www.doingbusiness.org by selecting the economy in the drop-down list.

GETTING CREDIT

Doing Business constructs measures of the legal rights of borrowers and lenders and the sharing of credit information. The first set of indicators describes how well collateral and bankruptcy laws facilitate lending. The second set measures the coverage, scope, quality and accessibility of credit information available through public and private credit registries.

The data on the legal rights of borrowers and lenders are gathered through a survey of financial lawyers and verified through analysis of laws and regulations as well as public sources of information on collateral and bankruptcy laws. The data on credit information sharing are built in 2 stages. First, banking supervision authorities and public information sources are surveyed to confirm the presence of public credit registries and private credit information bureaus. Second, when applicable, a detailed survey on the public or private credit registry's structure, law and associated rules is administered to the credit registry. Survey responses are verified through several rounds of follow-up communication with respondents as well as by contacting third parties and consulting public sources. The survey data are confirmed through teleconference calls or on-site visits in all economies.

STRENGTH OF LEGAL RIGHTS INDEX

The strength of legal rights index measures the degree to which collateral and bankruptcy laws protect the rights of borrowers and lenders and thus facilitate lending (table 14.6). Two case scenarios are used to determine the scope of the secured transactions system, involving a secured borrower, the company ABC, and a secured lender, BizBank.

Several assumptions about the secured borrower and lender are used:
- ABC is a domestic, limited liability company.
- ABC has its headquarters and only base of operations in the economy's largest business city.

- To fund its business expansion plans, ABC obtains a loan from BizBank for an amount up to 10 times income per capita in local currency.
- Both ABC and BizBank are 100% domestically owned.

The case scenarios also involve assumptions. In case A, as collateral for the loan, ABC grants BizBank a nonpossessory security interest in one category of revolving movable assets, for example, its accounts receivable or its inventory. ABC wants to keep both possession and ownership of the collateral. In economies in which the law does not allow nonpossessory security interests in movable property, ABC and BizBank use a fiduciary transfer-of-title arrangement (or a similar substitute for nonpossessory security interests).

In case B, ABC grants BizBank a business charge, enterprise charge, floating charge or any charge that gives BizBank a security interest over ABC's combined assets (or as much of ABC's assets as possible). ABC keeps ownership and possession of the assets.

The strength of legal rights index includes 8 aspects related to legal rights in collateral law and 2 aspects in bankruptcy law. A score of 1 is assigned for each of the following features of the laws:
- Any business may use movable assets as collateral while keeping possession of the assets, and any financial institution may accept such assets as collateral.
- The law allows a business to grant a nonpossessory security right in a single category of revolving movable assets (such as accounts receivable or inventory), without requiring a specific description of the secured assets.
- The law allows a business to grant a nonpossessory security right in substantially all of its assets, without requiring a specific description of the secured assets.

TABLE 14.6
What does getting credit measure?

Strength of legal rights index (0–10)
· Protection of rights of borrowers and lenders through collateral and bankruptcy laws
· Security interest is a nonpossessory one in movable assets

Depth of credit information index (0–6)
· Scope and accessibility of credit information distributed by public and private credit registries
· Quality of data distributed by public and private credit registries

Public credit registry coverage (% of adults)
· Number of individuals and firms listed in a public credit registry as percentage of adult population

Private credit bureau coverage (% of adults)
· Number of individuals and firms listed in a private credit bureau as percentage of adult population

Source: Doing Business database.

- A security right may extend to future or after-acquired assets and may extend automatically to the products, proceeds or replacements of the original assets.
- General description of debts and obligations is permitted in collateral agreements and in registration documents, so that all types of obligations and debts can be secured by stating a maximum rather than a specific amount between the parties.
- A collateral registry is in operation that is unified geographically and by asset type and that is indexed by the name of the grantor of a security right.
- Secured creditors are paid first (for example, before general tax claims and employee claims) when a debtor defaults outside an insolvency procedure.
- Secured creditors are paid first (for example, before general tax claims and employee claims) when a business is liquidated.
- Secured creditors are not subject to an automatic stay or moratorium on enforcement procedures when a debtor enters a court-supervised reorganization procedure.
- The law allows parties to agree in a collateral agreement that the lender may enforce its security right out of court.

The index ranges from 0 to 10, with higher scores indicating that collateral and bankruptcy laws are better designed to expand access to credit.

DEPTH OF CREDIT INFORMATION INDEX

The depth of credit information index measures rules affecting the scope, accessibility and quality of credit information available through either public or private credit registries. A score of 1 is assigned for each of the following 6 features of the public registry or the private credit bureau (or both):

- Both positive credit information (for example, loan amounts and pattern of on-time repayments) and negative information (for example, late payments, number and amount of defaults and bankruptcies) are distributed.
- Data on both firms and individuals are distributed.
- Data from retailers, utility companies as well as financial institutions are distributed.
- More than 2 years of historical data are distributed. Registries that erase data on defaults as soon as they are repaid obtain a score of 0 for this indicator.
- Data on loans below 1% of income per capita are distributed. A registry must have a minimum coverage of 1% of the adult population to score a 1 for this indicator.
- By law, borrowers have the right to access their data in the largest registry in the economy.

The index ranges from 0 to 6, with higher values indicating the availability of more credit information, from either a public registry or a private bureau, to facilitate lending decisions. If the registry is not operational or has coverage of less than 0.1% of the adult population, the score on the depth of credit information index is 0.

In Turkey, for example, both a public and a private registry operate. Both distribute positive and negative information (a score of 1). Both also distribute data on firms as well as individuals (a score of 1). The public and private registries share data among financial institutions only; no data are collected from retailers or utilities (a score of 0). The private bureau distributes more than 2 years of historical data (a score of 1). The public registry collects data on loans of $3,493 (44% of income per capita) or more, but the private bureau collects information on loans of any value (a score of 1). Borrowers have the right to access their data in both the private and the public registry (a score of 1). Summing across the indicators gives Turkey a total score of 5.

PUBLIC CREDIT REGISTRY COVERAGE

The public credit registry coverage indicator reports the number of individuals and firms listed in a public credit registry with information on repayment history, unpaid debts or credit outstanding from the past 5 years. The number is expressed as a percentage of the adult population (the population aged 15 and above in 2009 according to the World Bank's *World Development Indicators*). A public credit registry is defined as a database managed by the public sector, usually by the central bank or the superintendent of banks that collects information on the creditworthiness of borrowers (persons or businesses) in the financial system and makes it available to financial institutions. If no public registry operates, the coverage value is 0.

PRIVATE CREDIT BUREAU COVERAGE

The private credit bureau coverage indicator reports the number of individuals and firms listed by a private credit bureau with information on repayment history, unpaid debts or credit outstanding from the past 5 years. The number is expressed as a percentage of the adult population (the population aged 15 and above in 2009 according to the World Bank's *World Development Indicators*). A private credit bureau is defined as a private firm or nonprofit organization that maintains a database on the creditworthiness of borrowers (persons or businesses) in the financial system and facilitates the exchange of credit information among banks and financial institutions. Credit investigative bureaus and credit reporting firms that do not directly facilitate information exchange among banks and other financial institutions are not considered. If no private bureau operates, the coverage value is 0.

The data details on getting credit can be found for each economy at http://www.doingbusiness.org by selecting the economy in the drop-down list. This methodology was developed in Djankov, McLiesh and Shleifer (2007) and is adopted here with minor changes.

PROTECTING INVESTORS

Doing Business measures the strength of minority shareholder protections against directors' misuse of corporate assets for personal gain. The indicators distinguish 3 dimensions of investor protection: transparency of related-party transactions (extent of disclosure index), liability for self-dealing (extent of director liability index) and shareholders' ability to sue officers and directors for misconduct (ease of shareholder suits index). The data come from a survey of corporate lawyers and are based on securities regulations, company laws and court rules of evidence.

To make the data comparable across economies, several assumptions about the business and the transaction are used.

ASSUMPTIONS ABOUT THE BUSINESS

The business (Buyer):

- Is a publicly traded corporation listed on the economy's most important stock exchange. If the number of publicly traded companies listed on that exchange is less than 10, or if there is no stock exchange in the economy, it is assumed that Buyer is a large private company with multiple shareholders.
- Has a board of directors and a chief executive officer (CEO) who may legally act on behalf of Buyer where permitted, even if this is not specifically required by law.
- Is a food manufacturer.
- Has its own distribution network.

ASSUMPTIONS ABOUT THE TRANSACTION

- Mr. James is Buyer's controlling shareholder and a member of Buyer's board of directors. He owns 60% of Buyer and elected 2 directors to Buyer's 5-member board.
- Mr. James also owns 90% of Seller, a company that operates a chain of retail hardware stores. Seller recently closed a large number of its stores.
- Mr. James proposes that Buyer purchase Seller's unused fleet of trucks to expand Buyer's distribution of its food products, a proposal to which Buyer agrees. The price is equal to 10% of Buyer's assets and is higher than the market value.
- The proposed transaction is part of the company's ordinary course of business and is not outside the authority of the company.
- Buyer enters into the transaction. All required approvals are obtained, and all required disclosures made (that is, the transaction is not fraudulent).
- The transaction is unfair to Buyer. Shareholders sue Mr. James and the other parties that approved the transaction.

EXTENT OF DISCLOSURE INDEX

The extent of disclosure index has 5 components (table 14.7):

- What corporate body can provide legally sufficient approval for the transaction. A score of 0 is assigned if it is the CEO or the managing director alone; 1 if the board of directors or shareholders must vote and Mr. James is permitted to vote; 2 if the board of directors must vote and Mr. James is not permitted to vote; 3 if shareholders must vote and Mr. James is not permitted to vote.
- Whether immediate disclosure of the transaction to the public, the regulator or the shareholders is required. A score of 0 is assigned if no disclosure is required; 1 if disclosure on the terms of the transaction is required but not on Mr. James's conflict of interest; 2 if disclosure on both the terms and Mr. James's conflict of interest is required.
- Whether disclosure in the annual report is required. A score of 0 is assigned if no disclosure on the transaction is required; 1 if disclosure on the terms of the transaction is required but not on Mr. James's conflict of interest; 2 if disclosure on both the terms and Mr. James's conflict of interest is required.
- Whether disclosure by Mr. James to the board of directors is required. A score of 0 is assigned if no disclosure is required; 1 if a general disclosure of the existence of a conflict of interest is required without any specifics; 2 if full disclosure of all material facts relating to Mr. James's interest in the Buyer-Seller transaction is required.
- Whether it is required that an external body, for example, an external auditor, review the transaction before it takes place. A score of 0 is assigned if no; 1 if yes.

The index ranges from 0 to 10, with higher values indicating greater disclo-

---

TABLE 14.7

What does protecting investors measure?

Extent of disclosure index (0–10)

- Who can approve related-party transactions
- Disclosure requirements in case of related-party transactions

Extent of director liability index (0–10)

- Ability of the shareholders to hold the interested party and the approving body liable in case of related-party transactions
- Available legal remedies (damages, repayment of profits, fines and imprisonment)
- Ability of shareholders to sue directly or derivatively

Ease of shareholder suits index (0–10)

- Documents and information available during trial
- Direct access to internal documents of the company and use of a government inspector without filing a suit in court

Strength of investor protection index (0–10)

- Simple average of the extent of disclosure, extent of director liability and ease of shareholder suits indices

Source: Doing Business database.

sure. In Poland, for example, the board of directors must approve the transaction and Mr. James is not allowed to vote (a score of 2). Buyer is required to disclose immediately all information affecting the stock price, including the conflict of interest (a score of 2). In its annual report Buyer must also disclose the terms of the transaction and Mr. James's ownership in Buyer and Seller (a score of 2). Before the transaction Mr. James must disclose his conflict of interest to the other directors, but he is not required to provide specific information about it (a score of 1). Poland does not require an external body to review the transaction (a score of 0). Adding these numbers gives Poland a score of 7 on the extent of disclosure index.

EXTENT OF DIRECTOR LIABILITY INDEX

The extent of director liability index has 7 components:

- Whether a shareholder plaintiff is able to hold Mr. James liable for damage the Buyer-Seller transaction causes to the company. A score of 0 is assigned if Mr. James cannot be held liable or he can be held liable only for fraud or bad faith; 1 if Mr. James can be held liable only if he influenced the approval of the transaction or was negligent; 2 if Mr. James can be held liable when the transaction is unfair or prejudicial to the other shareholders.
- Whether a shareholder plaintiff is able to hold the approving body (the CEO or board of directors) liable for the damage the transaction causes to the company. A score of 0 is assigned if the approving body cannot be held liable or it can be held liable only for fraud or bad faith; 1 if the approving body can be held liable for negligence; 2 if the approving body can be held liable when the transaction is unfair or prejudicial to the other shareholders.
- Whether a court can void the transaction upon a successful claim by a shareholder plaintiff. A score of 0

is assigned if rescission is unavailable or it is available only in case of fraud or bad faith; 1 if rescission is available when the transaction is oppressive or prejudicial to the other shareholders; 2 if rescission is available when the transaction is unfair or entails a conflict of interest.
- Whether Mr. James pays damages for the harm caused to the company upon a successful claim by the shareholder plaintiff. A score of 0 is assigned if no; 1 if yes.
- Whether Mr. James repays profits made from the transaction upon a successful claim by the shareholder plaintiff. A score of 0 is assigned if no; 1 if yes.
- Whether fines and imprisonment can be applied against Mr. James. A score of 0 is assigned if no; 1 if yes.
- Whether shareholder plaintiffs are able to sue directly or derivatively for the damage the transaction causes to the company. A score of 0 is assigned if suits are unavailable or are available only for shareholders holding more than 10% of the company's share capital; 1 if direct or derivative suits are available for shareholders holding 10% or less of share capital.

The index ranges from 0 to 10, with higher values indicating greater liability of directors. To hold Mr. James liable in Panama, for example, a plaintiff must prove that Mr. James influenced the approving body or acted negligently (a score of 1). To hold the other directors liable, a plaintiff must prove that they acted negligently (a score of 1). The unfair transaction cannot be voided (a score of 0). If Mr. James is found liable, he must pay damages (a score of 1) but he is not required to disgorge his profits (a score of 0). Mr. James cannot be fined or imprisoned (a score of 0). Direct suits are available for shareholders holding 10% or less of share capital (a score of 1). Adding these numbers gives Panama a score of 4 on the extent of director liability index.

EASE OF SHAREHOLDER SUITS INDEX

The ease of shareholder suits index has 6 components:

- What range of documents is available to the shareholder plaintiff from the defendant and witnesses during trial. A score of 1 is assigned for each of the following types of documents available: information that the defendant has indicated he intends to rely on for his defense; information that directly proves specific facts in the plaintiff's claim; any information relevant to the subject matter of the claim; and any information that may lead to the discovery of relevant information.
- Whether the plaintiff can directly examine the defendant and witnesses during trial. A score of 0 is assigned if no; 1 if yes, with prior approval of the questions by the judge; 2 if yes, without prior approval.
- Whether the plaintiff can obtain categories of relevant documents from the defendant without identifying each document specifically. A score of 0 is assigned if no; 1 if yes.
- Whether shareholders owning 10% or less of the company's share capital can request that a government inspector investigate the Buyer-Seller transaction without filing suit in court. A score of 0 is assigned if no; 1 if yes.
- Whether shareholders owning 10% or less of the company's share capital have the right to inspect the transaction documents before filing suit. A score of 0 is assigned if no; 1 if yes.
- Whether the standard of proof for civil suits is lower than that for a criminal case. A score of 0 is assigned if no; 1 if yes.

The index ranges from 0 to 10, with higher values indicating greater powers of shareholders to challenge the transaction. In Greece, for example, the plaintiff can access documents that the defendant intends to rely on for his defense and that directly prove facts in the plaintiff's claim (a score of 2). The plaintiff can examine the defendant and witnesses during trial, though only with prior approval of the questions by the court (a score of 1). The plaintiff must specifically identify the documents being sought (for example, the Buyer-Seller purchase agreement of July 15, 2006) and cannot just request categories (for example, all documents related to the transaction) (a score of 0). A shareholder holding 5% of Buyer's shares can request that a government inspector review suspected mismanagement by Mr. James and the CEO without filing suit in court (a score of 1). Any shareholder can inspect the transaction documents before deciding whether to sue (a score of 1). The standard of proof for civil suits is the same as that for a criminal case (a score of 0). Adding these numbers gives Greece a score of 5 on the ease of shareholder suits index.

STRENGTH OF INVESTOR PROTECTION INDEX

The strength of investor protection index is the average of the extent of disclosure index, the extent of director liability index and the ease of shareholder suits index. The index ranges from 0 to 10, with higher values indicating more investor protection.

The data details on protecting investors can be found for each economy at http:// www.doingbusiness.org by selecting the economy in the drop-down list. This methodology was developed in Djankov, La Porta, López-de-Silanes and Shleifer (2008).

PAYING TAXES

Doing Business records the taxes and mandatory contributions that a medium-size company must pay in a given year, as well as measures of the administrative burden of paying taxes and contributions. Taxes and contributions measured include the profit or corporate income tax, social contributions and labor taxes paid by the employer, property taxes, property transfer taxes, dividend tax, capital gains tax, financial transactions tax, waste collection taxes and vehicle and road taxes.

Doing Business measures all taxes and contributions that are government mandated (at any level—federal, state or local), apply to the standardized business and have an impact in its income statements. In doing so, *Doing Business* goes beyond the traditional definition of a tax: as defined for the purposes of government national accounts, taxes include only compulsory, unrequited payments to general government. *Doing Business* departs from this definition because it measures imposed charges that affect business accounts, not government accounts. The main differences relate to labor contributions and value added tax. The *Doing Business* measure includes government-mandated contributions paid by the employer to a requited private pension fund or workers' insurance fund. The indicator includes, for example, Australia's compulsory superannuation guarantee and workers' compensation insurance. It excludes value added taxes because they do not affect the accounting profits of the business—that is, they are not reflected in the income statement.

Doing Business uses a case scenario to measure the taxes and contributions paid by a standardized business and the complexity of an economy's tax compliance system. This case scenario uses a set of financial statements and assumptions about transactions made over the year. Tax experts in each economy compute the taxes and mandatory contributions due in their jurisdiction based on the standardized case study facts. Informa-

tion is also compiled on the frequency of filing and payments as well as time taken to comply with tax laws in an economy. The project was developed and implemented in cooperation with PricewaterhouseCoopers.

To make the data comparable across economies, several assumptions about the business and the taxes and contributions are used.

ASSUMPTIONS ABOUT THE BUSINESS
The business:

- Is a limited liability, taxable company. If there is more than one type of limited liability company in the economy, the limited liability form most popular among domestic firms is chosen. The most popular form is reported by incorporation lawyers or the statistical office.
- Started operations on January 1, 2007. At that time the company purchased all the assets shown in its balance sheet and hired all its workers.
- Operates in the economy's largest business city.
- Is 100% domestically owned and has 5 owners, all of whom are natural persons.
- Has a start-up capital of 102 times income per capita at the end of 2007.
- Performs general industrial or commercial activities. Specifically, it produces ceramic flowerpots and sells them at retail. It does not participate in foreign trade (no import or export) and does not handle products subject to a special tax regime, for example, liquor or tobacco.
- At the beginning of 2007, owns 2 plots of land, 1 building, machinery, office equipment, computers and 1 truck and leases 1 truck.
- Does not qualify for investment incentives or any benefits apart from those related to the age or size of the company.
- Has 60 employees—4 managers, 8 assistants and 48 workers. All are nationals, and 1 manager is also an owner.

- Has a turnover of 1,050 times income per capita.
- Makes a loss in the first year of operation.
- Has a gross margin (pretax) of 20% (that is, sales are 120% of the cost of goods sold).
- Distributes 50% of its net profits as dividends to the owners at the end of the second year.
- Sells one of its plots of land at a profit at the beginning of the second year.
- Has annual fuel costs for its trucks equal to twice income per capita.
- Is subject to a series of detailed assumptions on expenses and transactions to further standardize the case. All financial statement variables are proportional to 2006 income per capita. For example, the owner who is also a manager spends 10% of income per capita on traveling for the company (20% of this owner's expenses are purely private, 20% are for entertaining customers and 60% for business travel).

ASSUMPTIONS ABOUT THE TAXES AND CONTRIBUTIONS

- All the taxes and contributions paid in the second year of operation (fiscal 2008) are recorded. A tax or contribution is considered distinct if it has a different name or is collected by a different agency. Taxes and contributions with the same name and agency, but charged at different rates depending on the business, are counted as the same tax or contribution.
- The number of times the company pays taxes and contributions in a year is the number of different taxes or contributions multiplied by the frequency of payment (or withholding) for each one. The frequency of payment includes advance payments (or withholding) as well as regular payments (or withholding).

TAX PAYMENTS

The tax payments indicator reflects the total number of taxes and contributions paid, the method of payment, the frequency of payment, the frequency of filing and the number of agencies involved for this standardized case during the second year of operation (table 14.8). It includes consumption taxes paid by the company, such as sales tax or value added tax. These taxes are traditionally collected from the consumer on behalf of the tax agencies. Although they do not affect the income statements of the company, they add to the administrative burden of complying with the tax system and so are included in the tax payments measure.

The number of payments takes into account electronic filing. Where full electronic filing and payment is allowed and it is used by the majority of medium-size businesses, the tax is counted as paid once a year even if filings and payments are more frequent.

Where 2 or more taxes or contributions are filed for and paid jointly using the same form, each of these joint payments is counted once. For example, if mandatory health insurance contributions and mandatory pension contributions are filed for and paid together, only one of these contributions would be included in the number of payments.

TIME

Time is recorded in hours per year. The indicator measures the time taken to prepare, file and pay 3 major types of taxes and contributions: the corporate income tax, value added or sales tax and labor taxes, including payroll taxes and social contributions. Preparation time includes the time to collect all information necessary to compute the tax payable and to calculate the amount payable. If separate accounting books must be kept for tax purposes—or separate calculations made—the time associated with these processes is included. This extra time is included only if the regular accounting work is not enough to fulfill the tax accounting requirements. Filing time includes the time to complete all necessary tax return forms and file the relevant returns at the tax authority. Payment time considers the hours needed to make the payment online or at the tax authorities. Where taxes and contributions are paid in person, the time includes delays while waiting.

TOTAL TAX RATE

The total tax rate measures the amount of taxes and mandatory contributions borne by the business in the second year of operation, expressed as a share of commercial profit. *Doing Business 2010*

TABLE 14.8
What does paying taxes measure?

Tax payments for a manufacturing company in 2008 (number per year)
· Total number of taxes and contributions paid, including consumption taxes (value added tax, sales tax or goods and service tax)
· Method and frequency of filing and payment

Time required to comply with 3 major taxes (hours per year)
· Collecting information and computing the tax payable
· Completing tax return forms, filing with proper agencies
· Arranging payment or withholding
· Preparing separate tax accounting books, if required

Total tax rate (% of profit)
· Profit or corporate income tax
· Social contributions and labor taxes paid by the employer
· Property and property transfer taxes
· Dividend, capital gains and financial transactions taxes
· Waste collection, vehicle, road and other taxes

Source: Doing Business database.

TABLE 14.9

Computing the total tax rate for Sweden

Type of tax (tax base)	Statutory rate (r)	Statutory tax base (b)	Actual tax payable (a) $a = r \times b$	Commercial profit[1] (c)	Total tax rate (t) $t = a/c$
		SKr	SKr	SKr	
Corporate income tax (taxable income)	28%	10,330,966	2,892,670	17,619,223	16.4%
Real estate tax (land and buildings)	0.375%	26,103,545	97,888	17,619,223	0.6%
Payroll tax (taxable wages)	32.42%	19,880,222	6,445,168	17,619,223	36.6%
Fuel tax (fuel price)	SKr 4.16 per liter	45,565 liters	189,550	17,619,223	1.1%
TOTAL			**9,625,726**		**54.56%**

1. Profit before all taxes borne.
Note: SKr is Swedish kronor. Commercial profit is assumed to be 59.4 times income per capita.
Source: Doing Business database.

reports the total tax rate for fiscal 2008. The total amount of taxes borne is the sum of all the different taxes and contributions payable after accounting for allowable deductions and exemptions. The taxes withheld (such as personal income tax) or collected by the company and remitted to the tax authorities (such as value added tax, sales tax or goods and service tax) but not borne by the company are excluded. The taxes included can be divided into 5 categories: profit or corporate income tax, social contributions and labor taxes paid by the employer (in respect of which all mandatory contributions are included, even if paid to a private entity such as a requited pension fund), property taxes, turnover taxes and other taxes (such as municipal fees and vehicle and fuel taxes).

The total tax rate is designed to provide a comprehensive measure of the cost of all the taxes a business bears. It differs from the statutory tax rate, which merely provides the factor to be applied to the tax base. In computing the total tax rate, the actual tax payable is divided by commercial profit. Data for Sweden illustrate (table 14.9).

Commercial profit is essentially net profit before all taxes borne. It differs from the conventional profit before tax, reported in financial statements. In computing profit before tax, many of the taxes borne by a firm are deductible. In computing commercial profit, these taxes are not deductible. Commercial profit therefore presents a clear picture of the actual profit of a business before

any of the taxes it bears in the course of the fiscal year.

Commercial profit is computed as sales minus cost of goods sold, minus gross salaries, minus administrative expenses, minus other expenses, minus provisions, plus capital gains (from the property sale) minus interest expense, plus interest income and minus commercial depreciation. To compute the commercial depreciation, a straight-line depreciation method is applied, with the following rates: 0% for the land, 5% for the building, 10% for the machinery, 33% for the computers, 20% for the office equipment, 20% for the truck and 10% for business development expenses. Commercial profit amounts to 59.4 times income per capita.

This methodology is consistent with the Total Tax Contribution framework developed by PricewaterhouseCoopers. This framework measures taxes that are borne by companies and affect their income statements, as does *Doing Business.* But while PricewaterhouseCoopers bases its calculation on data from the largest companies in the economy, *Doing Business* focuses on a standardized medium-size company.

The data details on paying taxes can be found for each economy at http://www .doingbusiness.org by selecting the economy in the drop-down list. This methodology was developed in Djankov and others (forthcoming).

TRADING ACROSS BORDERS

Doing Business compiles procedural requirements for exporting and importing a standardized cargo of goods by ocean transport. Every official procedure for exporting and importing the goods is recorded—from the contractual agreement between the 2 parties to the delivery of goods—along with the time and cost necessary for completion. All documents needed by the trader to export or import the goods across the border are also recorded. For exporting goods, procedures range from packing the goods at the warehouse to their departure from the port of exit. For importing goods, procedures range from the vessel's arrival at the port of entry to the cargo's delivery at the warehouse. The time and cost for ocean transport are not included. Payment is made by letter of credit, and the time, cost and documents required for the issuance or advising of a letter of credit are taken into account.

Local freight forwarders, shipping lines, customs brokers, port officials and banks provide information on required documents and cost as well as the time to complete each procedure. To make the data comparable across economies, several assumptions about the business and the traded goods are used.

ASSUMPTIONS ABOUT THE BUSINESS

The business:
- Has 60 employees.
- Is located in the economy's largest business city.

- Is a private, limited liability company. It does not operate in an export processing zone or an industrial estate with special export or import privileges.
- Is domestically owned with no foreign ownership.
- Exports more than 10% of its sales.

ASSUMPTIONS ABOUT THE TRADED GOODS

The traded product travels in a dry-cargo, 20-foot, full container load. It weighs 10 tons and is valued at $20,000. The product:

- Is not hazardous nor does it include military items.
- Does not require refrigeration or any other special environment.
- Does not require any special phytosanitary or environmental safety standards other than accepted international standards.

DOCUMENTS

All documents required per shipment to export and import the goods are recorded (table 14.10). It is assumed that the contract has already been agreed upon and signed by both parties. Documents required for clearance by gov-

TABLE 14.10
What does trading across borders measure?

Documents required to export and import *(number)*
· Bank documents
· Customs clearance documents
· Port and terminal handling documents
· Transport documents
Time required to export and import *(days)*
· Obtaining all the documents
· Inland transport and handling
· Customs clearance and inspections
· Port and terminal handling
· Does not include ocean transport time
Cost required to export and import *(US$ per container)*
· All documentation
· Inland transport and handling
· Customs clearance and inspections
· Port and terminal handling
· Official costs only, no bribes

Source: Doing Business database.

ernment ministries, customs authorities, port and container terminal authorities, health and technical control agencies and banks are taken into account. Since payment is by letter of credit, all documents required by banks for the issuance or securing of a letter of credit are also taken into account. Documents that are renewed annually and that do not require renewal per shipment (for example, an annual tax clearance certificate) are not included.

TIME

The time for exporting and importing is recorded in calendar days. The time calculation for a procedure starts from the moment it is initiated and runs until it is completed. If a procedure can be accelerated for an additional cost and is available to all trading companies, the fastest legal procedure is chosen. Fast-track procedures applying to firms located in an export processing zone are not taken into account because they are not available to all trading companies. Ocean transport time is not included. It is assumed that neither the exporter nor the importer wastes time and that each commits to completing each remaining procedure without delay. Procedures that can be completed in parallel are measured as simultaneous. The waiting time between procedures—for example, during unloading of the cargo—is included in the measure.

COST

Cost measures the fees levied on a 20-foot container in U.S. dollars. All the fees associated with completing the procedures to export or import the goods are included. These include costs for documents, administrative fees for customs clearance and technical control, customs broker fees, terminal handling charges and inland transport. The cost does not include customs tariffs and duties or costs related to ocean transport. Only official costs are recorded.

The data details on trading across borders can be found for each economy at http://www.doingbusiness.org *by selecting the economy in the drop-down list. This methodology was developed in Djankov, Freund and Pham (forthcoming) and is adopted here with minor changes.*

ENFORCING CONTRACTS

Indicators on enforcing contracts measure the efficiency of the judicial system in resolving a commercial dispute. The data are built by following the step-by-step evolution of a commercial sale dispute before local courts. The data are collected through study of the codes of civil procedure and other court regulations as well as surveys completed by local litigation lawyers (and, in a quarter of the economies, by judges as well).

The name of the relevant court in each economy—the court in the largest business city with jurisdiction over commercial cases worth 200% of income per capita—is published at http://www.doingbusiness.org/ExploreTopics/EnforcingContracts/.

ASSUMPTIONS ABOUT THE CASE

- The value of the claim equals 200% of the economy's income per capita.
- The dispute concerns a lawful transaction between 2 businesses (Seller and Buyer), located in the economy's largest business city. Seller sells goods worth 200% of the economy's income per capita to Buyer. After Seller delivers the goods to Buyer, Buyer refuses to pay for the goods on the grounds that the delivered goods were not of adequate quality.
- Seller (the plaintiff) sues Buyer (the defendant) to recover the amount under the sales agreement (that is, 200% of the economy's income per capita). Buyer opposes Seller's claim, saying that the quality of the goods is not adequate. The claim is disputed on the merits.
- A court in the economy's largest business city with jurisdiction over commercial cases worth 200% of income per capita decides the dispute.

- Seller attaches Buyer's movable assets (for example, office equipment, vehicles) prior to obtaining a judgment because Seller fears that Buyer may become insolvent.
- Expert opinions are given on the quality of the delivered goods. If it is standard practice in the economy for each party to call its own expert witness, the parties each call one expert witness. If it is standard practice for the judge to appoint an independent expert, the judge does so. In this case the judge does not allow opposing expert testimony.
- The judgment is 100% in favor of Seller: the judge decides that the goods are of adequate quality and that Buyer must pay the agreed price.
- Buyer does not appeal the judgment. The judgment becomes final.
- Seller takes all required steps for prompt enforcement of the judgment. The money is successfully collected through a public sale of Buyer's movable assets (for example, office equipment, vehicles).

PROCEDURES

The list of procedural steps compiled for each economy traces the chronology of a commercial dispute before the relevant

TABLE 14.11

What does enforcing contracts measure?

Procedures to enforce a contract *(number)*
· Any interaction between the parties in a commercial dispute, or between them and the judge or court officer
· Steps to file the case
· Steps for trial and judgment
· Steps to enforce the judgment
Time required to complete each procedure *(calendar days)*
· Measured in calendar days
· Time to file the case
· Time for trial and obtaining judgment
· Time to enforce the judgment
Cost required to complete each procedure *(% of claim)*
· No bribes
· Average attorney fees
· Court costs, including expert fees
· Enforcement costs

Source: Doing Business database.

court. A procedure is defined as any interaction between the parties, or between them and the judge or court officer. This includes steps to file the case, steps for trial and judgment and steps necessary to enforce the judgment (table 14.11).

The survey allows respondents to record procedures that exist in civil law but not common law jurisdictions, and vice versa. For example, in civil law countries the judge can appoint an independent expert, while in common law countries each party submits a list of expert witnesses to the court. To indicate overall efficiency, 1 procedure is subtracted from the total number for economies that have specialized commercial courts, and 1 procedure for economies that allow electronic filing of court cases. Some procedural steps that take place simultaneously with or are included in other procedural steps are not counted in the total number of procedures.

TIME

Time is recorded in calendar days, counted from the moment the plaintiff files the lawsuit in court until payment. This includes both the days when actions take place and the waiting periods between. The average duration of different stages of dispute resolution is recorded: the completion of service of process (time to file the case), the issuance of judgment (time for the trial and obtaining the judgment) and the moment of payment (time for enforcement of judgment).

COST

Cost is recorded as a percentage of the claim, assumed to be equivalent to 200% of income per capita. No bribes are recorded. Three types of costs are recorded: court costs, enforcement costs and average attorney fees.

Court costs include all court costs and expert fees. Seller (plaintiff) must advance to the court regardless of the final cost to Seller. Expert fees, if required by law or necessary in practice, are included in court costs. Enforcement costs are all costs Seller (plaintiff)

must advance to enforce the judgment through a public sale of Buyer's movable assets, regardless of the final cost to Seller. Average attorneys fees are the fees Seller (plaintiff) must advance to a local attorney to represent Seller in the standardized case.

The data details on enforcing contracts can be found for each economy at http://www.doingbusiness.org by selecting the economy in the drop-down list. This methodology was developed in Djankov and others (2003) and is adopted here with minor changes.

CLOSING A BUSINESS

Doing Business studies the time, cost and outcomes of bankruptcy proceedings involving domestic entities. The data are derived from survey responses by local insolvency practitioners and verified through a study of laws and regulations as well as public information on bankruptcy systems.

To make the data comparable across economies, several assumptions about the business and the case are used.

ASSUMPTIONS ABOUT THE BUSINESS

The business:
- Is a limited liability company.
- Operates in the economy's largest business city.
- Is 100% domestically owned, with the founder, who is also the chairman of the supervisory board, owning 51% (no other shareholder holds more than 5% of shares).
- Has downtown real estate, where it runs a hotel, as its major asset. The hotel is valued at 100 times income per capita or $200,000, whichever is larger.
- Has a professional general manager.
- Has 201 employees and 50 suppliers, each of which is owed money for the last delivery.
- Borrowed from a domestic bank 5 years ago (the loan has 10 years to full repayment) and bought real

estate (the hotel building), using it as security for the bank loan.

- Has observed the payment schedule and all other conditions of the loan up to now.
- Has a mortgage, with the value of the mortgage principal being exactly equal to the market value of the hotel.

ASSUMPTIONS ABOUT THE CASE

The business is experiencing liquidity problems. The company's loss in 2008 reduced its net worth to a negative figure. There is no cash to pay the bank interest or principal in full, due tomorrow. The business therefore defaults on its loan. Management believes that losses will be incurred in 2009 and 2010 as well.

The bank holds a floating charge against the hotel in economies where floating charges are possible. If the law does not permit a floating charge but contracts commonly use some other provision to that effect, this provision is specified in the lending contract.

The business has too many creditors to negotiate an informal out-of-court workout. It has the following options: a judicial procedure aimed at the rehabilitation or reorganization of the business to permit its continued operation; a judicial procedure aimed at the liquidation

TABLE 14.12

What does closing a business measure?

Time required to recover debt (years)

- Measured in calendar years
- Appeals and requests for extension are included

Cost required to recover debt (% of estate)

- Measured as percentage of estate value
- Court fees
- Lawyers' fees
- Independent assessors' fees
- Accountants' fees

Recovery rate for creditors (cents on the dollar)

- Measures the cents on the dollar recovered by creditors
- Present value of debt recovered
- Official costs of the insolvency proceedings are deducted
- Depreciation of assets is taken into account
- Outcome for the business affects the maximum value that can be recovered

Source: Doing Business database.

or winding-up of the company; or a debt enforcement or foreclosure procedure aimed at selling the hotel either piecemeal or as a going concern, enforced either in court (or through a government authority like a debt collection agency) or out of court (for example, by appointing a receiver).

If an economy has had fewer than 5 cases a year over the past 5 years involving a judicial reorganization, judicial liquidation or debt enforcement procedure, the economy receives a "no practice" mark. This means that creditors are unlikely to recover their debt through the legal process (in or out of court).

TIME

Time for creditors to recover their debt is recorded in calendar years. Information is collected on the sequence of procedures and on whether any procedures can be carried out simultaneously. Potential delay tactics by the parties, such as the filing of dilatory appeals or requests for extension, are taken into consideration (table 14.12).

COST

The cost of the proceedings is recorded as a percentage of the estate's value. The cost is calculated on the basis of survey responses by insolvency practitioners and includes court fees as well as fees of insolvency practitioners, independent assessors, lawyers and accountants. Respondents provide cost estimates from among the following options: less than 2%, 2–5%, 5–8%, 8–11%, 11–18%, 18–25%, 25–33%, 33–50%, 50–75% and more than 75% of the value of the business estate.

RECOVERY RATE

The recovery rate is recorded as cents on the dollar recouped by creditors through the bankruptcy, insolvency or debt enforcement proceedings. The calculation takes into account whether the business emerges from the proceedings as a going concern as well as costs and the loss in value due to the time spent closing down. If the business keeps operating, no value

is lost on the initial claim, set at 100 cents on the dollar. If it does not, the initial 100 cents on the dollar are reduced to 70 cents on the dollar. Then the official costs of the insolvency procedure are deducted (1 cent for each percentage of the initial value). Finally, the value lost as a result of the time the money remains tied up in insolvency proceedings is taken into account, including the loss of value due to depreciation of the hotel furniture. Consistent with international accounting practice, the depreciation rate for furniture is taken to be 20%. The furniture is assumed to account for a quarter of the total value of assets. The recovery rate is the present value of the remaining proceeds, based on end-2007 lending rates from the International Monetary Fund's *International Financial Statistics,* supplemented with data from central banks. The recovery rate for economies with "no practice" is zero. For *Doing Business 2010,* 2007 lending rates are used to avoid effects of the global financial and economic crisis on data comparability over time.

This methodology was developed in Djankov, Hart, McLiesh and Shleifer (2008).

1. The data for paying taxes refer to January–December 2008.

2. These are available at http:// subnational.doingbusiness.org.

3. The *Doing Business* website (http://www .doingbusiness.org) provides a comparable time series of historical data for research, with a data set back-calculated to adjust for changes in methodology and data revisions due to corrections.

4. The average value added per worker is the ratio of an economy's GNI per capita to the working-age population as a percentage of the total population.

PILOT INDICATORS ON GETTING ELECTRICITY

Pilot indicators on getting electricity are not included in the ease of doing business index. *Doing Business* records all procedures required for a business to obtain a permanent electricity connection and supply for a standardized warehouse. These procedures include applications and contracts with electricity utilities, all necessary clearances from other agencies and the external and final connection works.

Data are collected from the electricity distribution utility, then completed and verified by independent professionals such as electricians, electrical engineers, electrical contractors and construction companies. In some cases regulatory agencies are also contacted. The electricity distribution utility surveyed is the one serving the area (or areas) in which warehouses are located. If there is a choice of distribution utilities, the one serving the largest number of customers is selected. The data in this year's report were contributed by 573 respondents in 140 economies.

To make the data comparable across economies, several assumptions about the warehouse and the electricity connection are used.

ASSUMPTIONS ABOUT THE WAREHOUSE

The warehouse:
- Is located in the economy's largest business city.
- Is located within the official limits of the city and in an area in which other warehouses are located (a nonresidential area).
- Is not located in a special economic or investment zone; that is, the electricity connection is not eligible for subsidization or faster service under a special investment promotion regime. If several options for location are available, the warehouse is located where electricity is most easily available.

- Is used for storage of refrigerated goods.
- Is a new construction (that is, there was no previous construction on the land where it is located). It is being connected to electricity for the first time.

ASSUMPTIONS ABOUT THE ELECTRICITY CONNECTION

The electricity connection:
- Is a permanent one.
- Is a 3-phase, 4-wire Y, 140-kilovolt-ampere (kVA) connection.
- Is the length considered to be the most likely. The connection is overhead or underground, whichever is more common in the economy and in the area in which the warehouse is located.
- Involves the installation of only one electricity meter. The monthly electricity consumption will be 0.07 gigawatt hour (GWh).

The internal electrical wiring has already been completed.

PROCEDURES

A procedure is defined as any interaction of the company employees or the company's main electrician (that is, the one who did the internal wiring) with external parties, such as the electricity distribution utility, electricity supply utilities, government agencies, other electricians and electrical firms. Interactions between company employees and steps related to the internal electrical wiring, such as the design and execution of the internal electrical installation plans, are not counted as procedures. Procedures that must be completed with the same utility but with different departments are counted as separate procedures.

The company employees are assumed to complete all procedures themselves unless the use of a third party is mandated (for example, only an electrician registered with the utility is allowed to submit an application). If the company can, but is not required to, request the services of professionals (such as a pri-

vate firm rather than the utility for the external works), these procedures are recorded if they are commonly done. For all procedures, only the most likely cases (for example, more than 50% of the time the utility has the material) and those often followed in practice for connecting a warehouse to electricity are counted.

TIME

Time is recorded in calendar days. The measure captures the median duration that the electricity utility and experts indicate is necessary in practice, rather than required by law, to complete a procedure with minimum follow-up and no extra payments. It is also assumed that the minimum time required for each procedure is 1 day. Although procedures may take place simultaneously, they cannot start on the same day (that is, simultaneous procedures start on consecutive days). It is assumed that the company does not waste time and commits to completing each remaining procedure without delay. The time that the company spends on gathering information is ignored. It is assumed that the company is aware of all electricity connection requirements and their sequence from the beginning.

COST

Cost is recorded as a percentage of the economy's income per capita. Costs are recorded exclusive of value added tax. All the fees associated with completing the procedures to connect a warehouse to electricity are recorded, including those related to obtaining clearances from government agencies, applying for the connection, receiving inspections of both the site and the internal wiring, purchasing material, getting the actual connection works and paying a security deposit. Information from local experts and specific regulations and fee schedules are used as sources for costs. If several local partners provide different estimates, the median reported value is used. In all cases the cost excludes bribes.

SECURITY DEPOSIT

Utilities require security deposits as a guarantee against the possible failure of customers to pay their consumption bills. For this reason security deposits are most often calculated as a function of the estimated consumption of the new customer.

Doing Business does not record the full amount of the security deposit. Instead, it records the present value of the losses in interest earnings experienced by the customer because the utility holds the security deposit over a prolonged period, in most cases until the end of the contract (assumed to be after 5 years). In cases in which the security deposit is used to cover the first monthly consumption bills, it is not recorded. To calculate the present value of the lost interest earnings, the end-2008 lending rates from the International Monetary Fund's *International Financial Statistics* are used. In cases in which the security deposit is returned with interest, the difference between the lending rate and the interest paid by the utility is used to calculate the present value.

In some economies the security deposit can be put up in the form of a bond: the company can obtain from a bank or an insurance company a guarantee issued on the assets it holds with that financial institution. In contrast to the scenario in which the customer pays the deposit in cash to the utility, in this scenario the company does not lose ownership control over the full amount and can continue using it. In return the company will pay the bank a commission for obtaining the bond. The commission charged may vary depending on the credit standing of the company. The best possible credit standing and thus the lowest possible commission are assumed. Where a bond can be used, the value recorded for the deposit is the annual commission times the 5 years assumed to be the length of the contract. If both options exist, the cheaper alternative is recorded.

In Belize in June 2009, a customer requesting a 140-kVA electricity connection would have had to put up a security deposit of 22,662 Belize dollars in cash or check, and the deposit would be returned only at the end of the contract. The customer could instead have invested this money at the prevailing lending rate of 14.1%. Over the 5 years of the contract this would imply a present value of lost interest earnings of BZ$10,923. In contrast, if the customer had been allowed to settle the deposit with a bank guarantee at an annual rate of 1.75%, the amount lost over the 5 years would have been just BZ$1,983.

LIMITS TO WHAT IS MEASURED

The methodology has limitations that should be considered when interpreting the data. First, the collected data refer to businesses in the economy's largest business city and may not be representative of regulation in other parts of the economy. Second, the measures of time involve an element of judgment by the expert respondents. When sources indicate different time estimates, the time indicators reported represent the median values of several responses given under the assumptions of the standardized case. Finally, the methodology assumes that the business has full information on what is required and does not waste time when completing procedures. In practice, a procedure may take longer if the business lacks information or is unable to follow up promptly. Alternatively, the business may choose to disregard some burdensome procedures. For both reasons the time delays reported could differ from the responses of entrepreneurs reported in the World Bank Enterprise Surveys.

Feedback from governments and utilities on methodology is welcome and will be used as input in further refining the methodology.

The data details on getting electricity can be found for each economy at http://www .doingbusiness.org.

Ease of doing business

The ease of doing business index ranks economies from 1 to 183. For each economy the index is calculated as the ranking on the simple average of its percentile rankings on each of the 10 topics covered in *Doing Business 2010,* i.e. exclusive of the electricity pilot data. The ranking on each topic is the simple average of the percentile rankings on its component indicators (table 15.1).

If an economy has no laws or regulations covering a specific area—for example, bankruptcy—it receives a "no practice" mark. Similarly, an economy receives a "no practice" or "not possible" mark if regulation exists but is never used in practice or if a competing regulation prohibits such practice. Either way, a "no practice" mark puts the economy at the bottom of the ranking on the relevant indicator.

Here is one example of how the ranking is constructed. In Iceland it takes 5 procedures, 5 days and 3% of annual income per capita in fees to open a business. The minimum capital required amounts to 15.8% of income per capita. On these 4 indicators Iceland ranks in the 14th, 4th, 19th and 67th percentiles. So on average Iceland ranks in the 26th percentile on the ease of starting a business. It ranks in the 50th percentile on protecting investors, 38th percentile on trading across borders, 8th percentile on enforcing contracts, 8th percentile on closing a business and so on. Higher rankings indicate simpler regulation and

stronger protection of property rights. The simple average of Iceland's percentile rankings on all topics is 25%. When all economies are ordered by their average percentile rank, Iceland is in 14th place.

More complex aggregation methods—such as principal components and unobserved components—yield a nearly identical ranking.[1] The choice of aggregation method has little influence on the rankings because the 10 sets of indicators in *Doing Business* provide sufficiently broad coverage across topics. So *Doing Business* uses the simplest method.

The ease of doing business index is limited in scope. It does not account for a economy's proximity to large markets, the quality of its infrastructure services (other than services related to trading across borders), the strength of the financial system, the security of property from theft and looting, macroeconomic conditions or the strength of underlying institutions. There remains a large unfinished agenda for research into what regulation constitutes binding constraints, what package of reforms is most effective and how these issues are shaped by the context on an economy. The *Doing Business* indicators provide a new empirical data set that may improve understanding of these issues.

Doing Business also uses a simple method to calculate the top reformers. First, it selects the economies that re-

formed in 3 or more of the 10 *Doing Business* topics. This year 38 economies met this criterion: Afghanistan, Albania, Algeria, Angola, Armenia, Bangladesh, Belarus, Burkina Faso, Cameroon, Colombia, the Czech Republic, Egypt, Ethiopia, Guatemala, Honduras, Hong Kong (China), Indonesia, the Islamic Republic of Iran, Jordan, Kazakhstan, the Kyrgyz Republic, Liberia, FYR Macedonia, Mali, Mauritius, Moldova, Montenegro, Peru, the Philippines, Poland, Portugal, Russia, Rwanda, Sierra Leone, Singapore, Tajikistan, the United Arab Emirates and the Republic of Yemen (table 15.2). Second, *Doing Business* ranks these economies on the increase in their ranking on the ease of doing business from the previous year using comparable rankings.

1. See Djankov and others (2005).

TABLE 15.1
Which indicators make up the ranking?

Starting a business	*Protecting investors*
Procedures, time, cost and paid-in minimum capital to open a new business	Strength of investor protection index: extent of disclosure index, extent of director liability index and ease of shareholder suits index
Dealing with construction permits	*Paying taxes*
Procedures, time and cost to obtain construction permits, inspections and utility connections	Number of tax payments, time to prepare and file tax returns and to pay taxes, total taxes as a share of profit before all taxes borne
Employing workers	*Trading across borders*
Difficulty of hiring index, rigidity of hours index, difficulty of redundancy index, redundancy cost	Documents, time and cost to export and import
Registering property	*Enforcing contracts*
Procedures, time and cost to transfer commercial real estate	Procedures, time and cost to resolve a commercial dispute
Getting credit	*Closing a business*
Strength of legal rights index, depth of credit information index	Recovery rate in bankruptcy

TABLE 15.2

Economy	Starting a business	Dealing with construction permits	Employing workers	Registering property	Getting credit	Protecting investors	Paying taxes	Trading across borders	Enforcing contracts	Closing a business
Afghanistan	✔			✔	✔					
Albania	✔							✔		✔
Algeria		✔		✔			✔		✔	
Angola				✔			✔	✔		
Antigua and Barbuda										
Argentina	✔			✗						
Armenia	✔				✔			✔		
Australia										
Austria										
Azerbaijan					✔			✔		
Bahamas, The										
Bahrain		✔								
Bangladesh	✔						✔	✔		
Belarus	✔	✔	✔	✔			✔	✔		
Belgium				✔			✔			
Belize										
Benin							✔	✔		
Bhutan										
Bolivia										
Bosnia and Herzegovina		✔								
Botswana	✔			✗					✔	
Brazil	✔									
Brunei Darussalam							✔			
Bulgaria	✔			✔						
Burkina Faso	✔	✔		✔				✔	✔	
Burundi										
Cambodia							✗			
Cameroon	✔						✔	✔		
Canada										
Cape Verde	✔				✗		✔			
Central African Republic	✔									
Chad										
Chile										
China								✔		
Colombia	✔	✔		✔	✔	✔	✔	✔		✔
Comoros										
Congo, Dem. Rep.							✗	✔		
Congo, Rep.										
Costa Rica									✔	
Côte d'Ivoire										
Croatia		✔								
Cyprus										
Czech Republic		✔		✔			✔			
Denmark										
Djibouti							✔			
Dominica										
Dominican Republic						✔				
Ecuador										
Egypt, Arab Rep.	✔	✔			✔				✔	

✔ Reforms making it easier to do business   ✗ Reforms making it more difficult to do business

Economy	Starting a business	Dealing with construction permits	Employing workers	Registering property	Getting credit	Protecting investors	Paying taxes	Trading across borders	Enforcing contracts	Closing a business
El Salvador										
Equatorial Guinea										
Eritrea										
Estonia				✔						✔
Ethiopia	✔			✔					✔	
Fiji							✔			
Finland							✔			
France				✔						✔
Gabon										
Gambia, The										
Georgia		✔						✔		
Germany	✔									✔
Ghana	✔									
Greece					✔					
Grenada								✔	✔	
Guatemala		✔		✔	✔		✔			
Guinea										
Guinea-Bissau	✔									
Guyana	✔							✔		
Haiti					✔			✔		
Honduras	✔	✔	✗		✔					
Hong Kong, China	✔	✔		✔						
Hungary	✔									
Iceland							✔			
India										✔
Indonesia	✔			✔		✔				
Iran, Islamic Rep.	✔	✔					✔	✔		
Iraq										
Ireland				✔						
Israel							✔			
Italy										
Jamaica				✔						
Japan										
Jordan	✔	✔		✔			✔	✔	✔	
Kazakhstan	✔	✔					✔			
Kenya		✗			✔					
Kiribati										
Korea, Rep.	✔						✔			
Kosovo							✔			
Kuwait								✔		✔
Kyrgyz Republic	✔	✔	✔	✔	✔		✔	✔		
Lao PDR							✔			
Latvia				✔	✔					
Lebanon	✔						✔			
Lesotho										
Liberia	✔	✔						✔		
Lithuania							✗			✔
Luxembourg	✔		✗							
Macedonia, FYR	✔	✔	✔	✔	✔	✔	✔			

✔ Reforms making it easier to do business   ✗ Reforms making it more difficult to do business

Economy	Starting a business	Dealing with construction permits	Employing workers	Registering property	Getting credit	Protecting investors	Paying taxes	Trading across borders	Enforcing contracts	Closing a business
Madagascar	✔			✗						
Malawi								✔		✔
Malaysia	✔								✔	
Maldives			✗							
Mali	✔	✔				✔		✔	✔	
Marshall Islands										
Mauritania										
Mauritius			✔	✔	✔			✔	✔	✔
Mexico	✔						✔			
Micronesia, Fed. Sts.										
Moldova	✔			✔			✔			
Mongolia										
Montenegro	✔	✔	✔				✔			
Morocco					✔					
Mozambique	✔							✔		
Namibia										
Nepal				✔						
Netherlands		✔								
New Zealand		✗								
Nicaragua										
Niger	✔									
Nigeria					✔					
Norway									✔	
Oman	✔						✔			
Pakistan	✔									
Palau										
Panama		✔		✔						
Papua New Guinea									✔	
Paraguay								✔		
Peru	✔		✔	✔			✔	✔	✔	
Philippines					✔		✔			✔
Poland	✔			✔			✔			✔
Portugal		✔	✗	✔				✔	✔	
Puerto Rico										
Qatar										
Romania		✗		✔			✗			✗
Russian Federation				✔			✔			✔
Rwanda	✔		✔	✔	✔	✔		✔		✔
Samoa	✔									✔
São Tomé and Principe										
Saudi Arabia	✔	✔								
Senegal								✔		
Serbia	✔				✔					
Seychelles										
Sierra Leone	✔			✗	✔	✔	✔	✗		✔
Singapore	✔	✔		✔						
Slovak Republic								✔		
Slovenia	✔	✔								
Solomon Islands		✗								
South Africa							✔			

✔ Reforms making it easier to do business ✗ Reforms making it more difficult to do business

Economy	Starting a business	Dealing with construction permits	Employing workers	Registering property	Getting credit	Protecting investors	Paying taxes	Trading across borders	Enforcing contracts	Closing a business
Reforms in 2008/09										
Spain							✔			
Sri Lanka		✗			✔					
St. Kitts and Nevis								✔		
St. Lucia	✔									
St. Vincent and the Grenadines	✔						✔			
Sudan							✔	✔		
Suriname				✗						
Swaziland										
Sweden										
Switzerland										
Syrian Arab Republic	✔									
Taiwan, China	✔						✔			
Tajikistan	✔	✔		✗	✔	✔				✔
Tanzania		✗								
Thailand	✔									
Timor-Leste							✔			
Togo	✔						✔			
Tonga							✔			
Trinidad and Tobago										
Tunisia						✔	✗	✔		
Turkey					✔					
Uganda								✔		
Ukraine						✔				
United Arab Emirates	✔	✔						✔		
United Kingdom		✔		✔						
United States										
Uruguay				✗						✔
Uzbekistan		✔					✔			
Vanuatu					✔					
Venezuela, R.B.							✗			
Vietnam							✔	✔		
West Bank and Gaza	✗			✔					✔	
Yemen, Rep.	✔				✔			✔		
Zambia					✔					
Zimbabwe				✔						

✔ Reforms making it easier to do business ✗ Reforms making it more difficult to do business

Country
tables

AFGHANISTAN

		South Asia	GNI per capita (US$)	429
Ease of doing business (rank)	160	Low income	Population (m)	27.2
✔ **Starting a business** (rank)	23	✔ **Registering property** (rank)	164	**Trading across borders** (rank)	183

✔ **Starting a business** (rank)	23	✔ **Registering property** (rank)	164	**Trading across borders** (rank)	183
Procedures (number)	4	Procedures (number)	9	Documents to export (number)	12
Time (days)	7	Time (days)	250	Time to export (days)	74
Cost (% of income per capita)	30.2	Cost (% of property value)	4.0	Cost to export (US$ per container)	3,350
Minimum capital (% of income per capita)	0.0			Documents to import (number)	11
		✔ **Getting credit** (rank)	127	Time to import (days)	77
Dealing with construction permits (rank)	149	Strength of legal rights index (0-10)	6	Cost to import (US$ per container)	3,000
Procedures (number)	13	Depth of credit information index (0-6)	0		
Time (days)	340	Public registry coverage (% of adults)	0.0	**Enforcing contracts** (rank)	164
Cost (% of income per capita)	12,877.6	Private bureau coverage (% of adults)	0.0	Procedures (number)	47
				Time (days)	1,642
Employing workers (rank)	69	**Protecting investors** (rank)	183	Cost (% of claim)	25.0
Difficulty of hiring index (0-100)	0	Extent of disclosure index (0-10)	0		
Rigidity of hours index (0-100)	20	Extent of director liability index (0-10)	0	**Closing a business** (rank)	183
Difficulty of redundancy index (0-100)	40	Ease of shareholder suits index (0-10)	2	Time (years)	NO PRACTICE
Rigidity of employment index (0-100)	20	Strength of investor protection index (0-10)	0.7	Cost (% of estate)	NO PRACTICE
Redundancy cost (weeks of salary)	30			Recovery rate (cents on the dollar)	0.0
		Paying taxes (rank)	55		
		Payments (number per year)	8		
		Time (hours per year)	275		
		Total tax rate (% of profit)	36.4		

ALBANIA

		Eastern Europe & Central Asia		GNI per capita (US$)	3,836
Ease of doing business (rank)	82	Lower middle income		Population (m)	3.1
✔ **Starting a business** (rank)	46	**Registering property** (rank)	70	✔ **Trading across borders** (rank)	66
Procedures (number)	5	Procedures (number)	6	Documents to export (number)	7
Time (days)	5	Time (days)	42	Time to export (days)	19
Cost (% of income per capita)	17.0	Cost (% of property value)	3.4	Cost to export (US$ per container)	725
Minimum capital (% of income per capita)	0.0			Documents to import (number)	9
		Getting credit (rank)	15	Time to import (days)	18
Dealing with construction permits (rank)	173	Strength of legal rights index (0-10)	9	Cost to import (US$ per container)	710
Procedures (number)	24	Depth of credit information index (0-6)	4		
Time (days)	331	Public registry coverage (% of adults)	9.9	**Enforcing contracts** (rank)	91
Cost (% of income per capita)	386.1	Private bureau coverage (% of adults)	0.0	Procedures (number)	39
				Time (days)	390
Employing workers (rank)	105	**Protecting investors** (rank)	15	Cost (% of claim)	38.7
Difficulty of hiring index (0-100)	44	Extent of disclosure index (0-10)	8		
Rigidity of hours index (0-100)	20	Extent of director liability index (0-10)	9	✔ **Closing a business** (rank)	183
Difficulty of redundancy index (0-100)	10	Ease of shareholder suits index (0-10)	5	Time (years)	NO PRACTICE
Rigidity of employment index (0-100)	25	Strength of investor protection index (0-10)	7.3	Cost (% of estate)	NO PRACTICE
Redundancy cost (weeks of salary)	56			Recovery rate (cents on the dollar)	0.0
		Paying taxes (rank)	138		
		Payments (number per year)	44		
		Time (hours per year)	244		
		Total tax rate (% of profit)	44.9		

ALGERIA

		Middle East & North Africa		GNI per capita (US$)	4,260
Ease of doing business (rank)	136	Upper middle income		Population (m)	34.4
Starting a business (rank)	148	✔ **Registering property** (rank)	160	**Trading across borders** (rank)	122
Procedures (number)	14	Procedures (number)	11	Documents to export (number)	8
Time (days)	24	Time (days)	47	Time to export (days)	17
Cost (% of income per capita)	12.1	Cost (% of property value)	7.1	Cost to export (US$ per container)	1,248
Minimum capital (% of income per capita)	31.0			Documents to import (number)	9
		Getting credit (rank)	135	Time to import (days)	23
✔ **Dealing with construction permits** (rank)	110	Strength of legal rights index (0-10)	3	Cost to import (US$ per container)	1,428
Procedures (number)	22	Depth of credit information index (0-6)	2		
Time (days)	240	Public registry coverage (% of adults)	0.2	✔ **Enforcing contracts** (rank)	123
Cost (% of income per capita)	39.6	Private bureau coverage (% of adults)	0.0	Procedures (number)	46
				Time (days)	630
Employing workers (rank)	122	**Protecting investors** (rank)	73	Cost (% of claim)	21.9
Difficulty of hiring index (0-100)	44	Extent of disclosure index (0-10)	6		
Rigidity of hours index (0-100)	40	Extent of director liability index (0-10)	6	**Closing a business** (rank)	51
Difficulty of redundancy index (0-100)	40	Ease of shareholder suits index (0-10)	4	Time (years)	2.5
Rigidity of employment index (0-100)	41	Strength of investor protection index (0-10)	5.3	Cost (% of estate)	7.0
Redundancy cost (weeks of salary)	17			Recovery rate (cents on the dollar)	41.7
		✔ **Paying taxes** (rank)	168		
		Payments (number per year)	34		
		Time (hours per year)	451		
		Total tax rate (% of profit)	72.0		

✔ Reforms making it easier to do business   ✘ Reforms making it more difficult to do business

ANGOLA

		Sub-Saharan Africa			GNI per capita (US$)	3,447
Ease of doing business (rank)	169	Lower middle income			Population (m)	18.0
Starting a business (rank)	165	✔ **Registering property** (rank)	173		✔ **Trading across borders** (rank)	171
Procedures (number)	8	Procedures (number)	7		Documents to export (number)	11
Time (days)	68	Time (days)	184		Time to export (days)	65
Cost (% of income per capita)	151.1	Cost (% of property value)	11.4		Cost to export (US$ per container)	2,250
Minimum capital (% of income per capita)	29.0				Documents to import (number)	8
		Getting credit (rank)	87		Time to import (days)	59
Dealing with construction permits (rank)	123	Strength of legal rights index (0-10)	4		Cost to import (US$ per container)	3,240
Procedures (number)	12	Depth of credit information index (0-6)	4			
Time (days)	328	Public registry coverage (% of adults)	2.5		**Enforcing contracts** (rank)	181
Cost (% of income per capita)	597.7	Private bureau coverage (% of adults)	0.0		Procedures (number)	46
					Time (days)	1,011
Employing workers (rank)	178	**Protecting investors** (rank)	57		Cost (% of claim)	44.4
Difficulty of hiring index (0-100)	67	Extent of disclosure index (0-10)	5			
Rigidity of hours index (0-100)	60	Extent of director liability index (0-10)	6		**Closing a business** (rank)	144
Difficulty of redundancy index (0-100)	70	Ease of shareholder suits index (0-10)	6		Time (years)	6.2
Rigidity of employment index (0-100)	66	Strength of investor protection index (0-10)	5.7		Cost (% of estate)	22.0
Redundancy cost (weeks of salary)	58				Recovery rate (cents on the dollar)	10.0
		✔ **Paying taxes** (rank)	139			
		Payments (number per year)	31			
		Time (hours per year)	272			
		Total tax rate (% of profit)	53.2			

ANTIGUA AND BARBUDA

		Latin America & Caribbean			GNI per capita (US$)	13,617
Ease of doing business (rank)	50	High income			Population (m)	0.1
Starting a business (rank)	59	**Registering property** (rank)	103		**Trading across borders** (rank)	53
Procedures (number)	8	Procedures (number)	6		Documents to export (number)	5
Time (days)	21	Time (days)	26		Time to export (days)	15
Cost (% of income per capita)	9.6	Cost (% of property value)	10.8		Cost to export (US$ per container)	1,133
Minimum capital (% of income per capita)	0.0				Documents to import (number)	5
		Getting credit (rank)	113		Time to import (days)	15
Dealing with construction permits (rank)	21	Strength of legal rights index (0-10)	7		Cost to import (US$ per container)	1,633
Procedures (number)	13	Depth of credit information index (0-6)	0			
Time (days)	156	Public registry coverage (% of adults)	0.0		**Enforcing contracts** (rank)	71
Cost (% of income per capita)	21.3	Private bureau coverage (% of adults)	0.0		Procedures (number)	45
					Time (days)	351
Employing workers (rank)	54	**Protecting investors** (rank)	27		Cost (% of claim)	22.7
Difficulty of hiring index (0-100)	11	Extent of disclosure index (0-10)	4			
Rigidity of hours index (0-100)	0	Extent of director liability index (0-10)	8		**Closing a business** (rank)	64
Difficulty of redundancy index (0-100)	20	Ease of shareholder suits index (0-10)	7		Time (years)	3.0
Rigidity of employment index (0-100)	10	Strength of investor protection index (0-10)	6.3		Cost (% of estate)	7.0
Redundancy cost (weeks of salary)	52				Recovery rate (cents on the dollar)	35.5
		Paying taxes (rank)	127			
		Payments (number per year)	56			
		Time (hours per year)	207			
		Total tax rate (% of profit)	41.5			

ARGENTINA

		Latin America & Caribbean			GNI per capita (US$)	7,201
Ease of doing business (rank)	118	Upper middle income			Population (m)	39.9
✔ **Starting a business** (rank)	138	✘ **Registering property** (rank)	115		**Trading across borders** (rank)	110
Procedures (number)	15	Procedures (number)	6		Documents to export (number)	9
Time (days)	27	Time (days)	52		Time to export (days)	13
Cost (% of income per capita)	11.0	Cost (% of property value)	7.0		Cost to export (US$ per container)	1,480
Minimum capital (% of income per capita)	2.9				Documents to import (number)	7
		Getting credit (rank)	61		Time to import (days)	16
Dealing with construction permits (rank)	169	Strength of legal rights index (0-10)	4		Cost to import (US$ per container)	1,810
Procedures (number)	28	Depth of credit information index (0-6)	6			
Time (days)	338	Public registry coverage (% of adults)	34.3		**Enforcing contracts** (rank)	46
Cost (% of income per capita)	145.1	Private bureau coverage (% of adults)	100.0		Procedures (number)	36
					Time (days)	590
Employing workers (rank)	101	**Protecting investors** (rank)	109		Cost (% of claim)	16.5
Difficulty of hiring index (0-100)	44	Extent of disclosure index (0-10)	6			
Rigidity of hours index (0-100)	20	Extent of director liability index (0-10)	2		**Closing a business** (rank)	86
Difficulty of redundancy index (0-100)	0	Ease of shareholder suits index (0-10)	6		Time (years)	12.0
Rigidity of employment index (0-100)	21	Strength of investor protection index (0-10)	4.7		Cost (% of estate)	2.8
Redundancy cost (weeks of salary)	95				Recovery rate (cents on the dollar)	29.8
		Paying taxes (rank)	142			
		Payments (number per year)	9			
		Time (hours per year)	453			
		Total tax rate (% of profit)	108.1			

ARMENIA

		Eastern Europe & Central Asia		GNI per capita (US$)		3,354
Ease of doing business (rank)	43	Lower middle income		Population (m)		3.1
✔ **Starting a business** (rank)	21	**Registering property** (rank)	5	✔ **Trading across borders** (rank)		102
Procedures (number)	6	Procedures (number)	3	Documents to export (number)		5
Time (days)	15	Time (days)	4	Time to export (days)		17
Cost (% of income per capita)	2.6	Cost (% of property value)	0.3	Cost to export (US$ per container)		1,731
Minimum capital (% of income per capita)	0.0			Documents to import (number)		7
		✔ **Getting credit** (rank)	43	Time to import (days)		20
Dealing with construction permits (rank)	72	Strength of legal rights index (0-10)	6	Cost to import (US$ per container)		2,096
Procedures (number)	20	Depth of credit information index (0-6)	5			
Time (days)	137	Public registry coverage (% of adults)	4.4	**Enforcing contracts** (rank)		62
Cost (% of income per capita)	104.9	Private bureau coverage (% of adults)	34.5	Procedures (number)		48
				Time (days)		285
Employing workers (rank)	62	**Protecting investors** (rank)	93	Cost (% of claim)		19.0
Difficulty of hiring index (0-100)	33	Extent of disclosure index (0-10)	5			
Rigidity of hours index (0-100)	20	Extent of director liability index (0-10)	2	**Closing a business** (rank)		49
Difficulty of redundancy index (0-100)	10	Ease of shareholder suits index (0-10)	8	Time (years)		1.9
Rigidity of employment index (0-100)	21	Strength of investor protection index (0-10)	5.0	Cost (% of estate)		4
Redundancy cost (weeks of salary)	13			Recovery rate (cents on the dollar)		41.8
		Paying taxes (rank)	153			
		Payments (number per year)	50			
		Time (hours per year)	958			
		Total tax rate (% of profit)	36.2			

AUSTRALIA

		OECD high income		GNI per capita (US$)		40,351
Ease of doing business (rank)	9	High income		Population (m)		21.4
Starting a business (rank)	3	**Registering property** (rank)	34	**Trading across borders** (rank)		27
Procedures (number)	2	Procedures (number)	5	Documents to export (number)		6
Time (days)	2	Time (days)	5	Time to export (days)		9
Cost (% of income per capita)	0.8	Cost (% of property value)	4.9	Cost to export (US$ per container)		1,060
Minimum capital (% of income per capita)	0.0			Documents to import (number)		5
		Getting credit (rank)	4	Time to import (days)		8
Dealing with construction permits (rank)	62	Strength of legal rights index (0-10)	9	Cost to import (US$ per container)		1,119
Procedures (number)	16	Depth of credit information index (0-6)	5			
Time (days)	221	Public registry coverage (% of adults)	0.0	**Enforcing contracts** (rank)		16
Cost (% of income per capita)	12.9	Private bureau coverage (% of adults)	100.0	Procedures (number)		28
				Time (days)		395
Employing workers (rank)	1	**Protecting investors** (rank)	57	Cost (% of claim)		20.7
Difficulty of hiring index (0-100)	0	Extent of disclosure index (0-10)	8			
Rigidity of hours index (0-100)	0	Extent of director liability index (0-10)	2	**Closing a business** (rank)		14
Difficulty of redundancy index (0-100)	0	Ease of shareholder suits index (0-10)	7	Time (years)		1.0
Rigidity of employment index (0-100)	0	Strength of investor protection index (0-10)	5.7	Cost (% of estate)		8
Redundancy cost (weeks of salary)	4			Recovery rate (cents on the dollar)		78.8
		Paying taxes (rank)	47			
		Payments (number per year)	12			
		Time (hours per year)	107			
		Total tax rate (% of profit)	48.0			

AUSTRIA

		OECD high income		GNI per capita (US$)		46,264
Ease of doing business (rank)	28	High income		Population (m)		8.3
Starting a business (rank)	122	**Registering property** (rank)	39	**Trading across borders** (rank)		24
Procedures (number)	8	Procedures (number)	3	Documents to export (number)		4
Time (days)	28	Time (days)	32	Time to export (days)		7
Cost (% of income per capita)	5.1	Cost (% of property value)	4.5	Cost to export (US$ per container)		1,180
Minimum capital (% of income per capita)	52.0			Documents to import (number)		5
		Getting credit (rank)	15	Time to import (days)		8
Dealing with construction permits (rank)	54	Strength of legal rights index (0-10)	7	Cost to import (US$ per container)		1,195
Procedures (number)	14	Depth of credit information index (0-6)	6			
Time (days)	194	Public registry coverage (% of adults)	1.4	**Enforcing contracts** (rank)		11
Cost (% of income per capita)	71.4	Private bureau coverage (% of adults)	39.2	Procedures (number)		25
				Time (days)		397
Employing workers (rank)	60	**Protecting investors** (rank)	132	Cost (% of claim)		18.0
Difficulty of hiring index (0-100)	0	Extent of disclosure index (0-10)	3			
Rigidity of hours index (0-100)	33	Extent of director liability index (0-10)	5	**Closing a business** (rank)		20
Difficulty of redundancy index (0-100)	40	Ease of shareholder suits index (0-10)	4	Time (years)		1.1
Rigidity of employment index (0-100)	24	Strength of investor protection index (0-10)	4.0	Cost (% of estate)		18
Redundancy cost (weeks of salary)	2			Recovery rate (cents on the dollar)		71.5
		Paying taxes (rank)	102			
		Payments (number per year)	22			
		Time (hours per year)	170			
		Total tax rate (% of profit)	55.5			

✔ Reforms making it easier to do business   ✘ Reforms making it more difficult to do business

AZERBAIJAN

		Eastern Europe & Central Asia		GNI per capita (US$)	3,829
Ease of doing business (rank)	38	Lower middle income		Population (m)	8.7
Starting a business (rank)	17	**Registering property** (rank)	9	✔ **Trading across borders** (rank)	177
Procedures (number)	6	Procedures (number)	4	Documents to export (number)	9
Time (days)	10	Time (days)	11	Time to export (days)	46
Cost (% of income per capita)	2.9	Cost (% of property value)	0.2	Cost to export (US$ per container)	2,980
Minimum capital (% of income per capita)	0.0			Documents to import (number)	14
		✔ **Getting credit** (rank)	15	Time to import (days)	50
Dealing with construction permits (rank)	158	Strength of legal rights index (0-10)	8	Cost to import (US$ per container)	3,480
Procedures (number)	31	Depth of credit information index (0-6)	5		
Time (days)	207	Public registry coverage (% of adults)	6.9	**Enforcing contracts** (rank)	26
Cost (% of income per capita)	369.6	Private bureau coverage (% of adults)	0.0	Procedures (number)	39
				Time (days)	237
Employing workers (rank)	33	**Protecting investors** (rank)	20	Cost (% of claim)	18.5
Difficulty of hiring index (0-100)	0	Extent of disclosure index (0-10)	7		
Rigidity of hours index (0-100)	20	Extent of director liability index (0-10)	5	**Closing a business** (rank)	84
Difficulty of redundancy index (0-100)	10	Ease of shareholder suits index (0-10)	8	Time (years)	2.7
Rigidity of employment index (0-100)	10	Strength of investor protection index (0-10)	6.7	Cost (% of estate)	8
Redundancy cost (weeks of salary)	22			Recovery rate (cents on the dollar)	30.1
		Paying taxes (rank)	108		
		Payments (number per year)	22		
		Time (hours per year)	376		
		Total tax rate (% of profit)	40.9		

BAHAMAS, THE

		Latin America & Caribbean		GNI per capita (US$)	22,907
Ease of doing business (rank)	68	High income		Population (m)	0.3
Starting a business (rank)	61	**Registering property** (rank)	149	**Trading across borders** (rank)	37
Procedures (number)	7	Procedures (number)	7	Documents to export (number)	5
Time (days)	31	Time (days)	48	Time to export (days)	16
Cost (% of income per capita)	8.5	Cost (% of property value)	12.5	Cost to export (US$ per container)	930
Minimum capital (% of income per capita)	0.0			Documents to import (number)	5
		Getting credit (rank)	71	Time to import (days)	13
Dealing with construction permits (rank)	100	Strength of legal rights index (0-10)	9	Cost to import (US$ per container)	1,380
Procedures (number)	18	Depth of credit information index (0-6)	0		
Time (days)	197	Public registry coverage (% of adults)	0.0	**Enforcing contracts** (rank)	120
Cost (% of income per capita)	208.6	Private bureau coverage (% of adults)	0.0	Procedures (number)	49
				Time (days)	427
Employing workers (rank)	42	**Protecting investors** (rank)	109	Cost (% of claim)	28.9
Difficulty of hiring index (0-100)	0	Extent of disclosure index (0-10)	2		
Rigidity of hours index (0-100)	0	Extent of director liability index (0-10)	5	**Closing a business** (rank)	31
Difficulty of redundancy index (0-100)	40	Ease of shareholder suits index (0-10)	7	Time (years)	5.0
Rigidity of employment index (0-100)	13	Strength of investor protection index (0-10)	4.7	Cost (% of estate)	4
Redundancy cost (weeks of salary)	26			Recovery rate (cents on the dollar)	54.7
		Paying taxes (rank)	43		
		Payments (number per year)	17		
		Time (hours per year)	58		
		Total tax rate (% of profit)	47.0		

BAHRAIN

		Middle East & North Africa		GNI per capita (US$)	27,248
Ease of doing business (rank)	20	High income		Population (m)	0.8
Starting a business (rank)	63	**Registering property** (rank)	22	**Trading across borders** (rank)	32
Procedures (number)	7	Procedures (number)	2	Documents to export (number)	5
Time (days)	9	Time (days)	31	Time to export (days)	14
Cost (% of income per capita)	0.5	Cost (% of property value)	0.9	Cost to export (US$ per container)	955
Minimum capital (% of income per capita)	195.2			Documents to import (number)	6
		Getting credit (rank)	87	Time to import (days)	15
✔ **Dealing with construction permits** (rank)	14	Strength of legal rights index (0-10)	4	Cost to import (US$ per container)	995
Procedures (number)	13	Depth of credit information index (0-6)	4		
Time (days)	43	Public registry coverage (% of adults)	0.0	**Enforcing contracts** (rank)	117
Cost (% of income per capita)	54.6	Private bureau coverage (% of adults)	34.9	Procedures (number)	48
				Time (days)	635
Employing workers (rank)	13	**Protecting investors** (rank)	57	Cost (% of claim)	14.7
Difficulty of hiring index (0-100)	0	Extent of disclosure index (0-10)	8		
Rigidity of hours index (0-100)	0	Extent of director liability index (0-10)	4	**Closing a business** (rank)	26
Difficulty of redundancy index (0-100)	30	Ease of shareholder suits index (0-10)	5	Time (years)	2.5
Rigidity of employment index (0-100)	10	Strength of investor protection index (0-10)	5.7	Cost (% of estate)	10
Redundancy cost (weeks of salary)	4			Recovery rate (cents on the dollar)	63.2
		Paying taxes (rank)	13		
		Payments (number per year)	25		
		Time (hours per year)	36		
		Total tax rate (% of profit)	15.0		

BANGLADESH

		South Asia		GNI per capita (US$)	516
Ease of doing business (rank)	119	Low income		Population (m)	160.0

✔ **Starting a business** (rank)	98	**Registering property** (rank)	176	✔ **Trading across borders** (rank)	107
Procedures (number)	7	Procedures (number)	8	Documents to export (number)	6
Time (days)	44	Time (days)	245	Time to export (days)	25
Cost (% of income per capita)	36.2	Cost (% of property value)	10.2	Cost to export (US$ per container)	970
Minimum capital (% of income per capita)	0.0			Documents to import (number)	8
		Getting credit (rank)	71	Time to import (days)	29
Dealing with construction permits (rank)	118	Strength of legal rights index (0-10)	7	Cost to import (US$ per container)	1,375
Procedures (number)	14	Depth of credit information index (0-6)	2		
Time (days)	231	Public registry coverage (% of adults)	0.9	**Enforcing contracts** (rank)	180
Cost (% of income per capita)	645.1	Private bureau coverage (% of adults)	0.0	Procedures (number)	41
				Time (days)	1,442
Employing workers (rank)	124	**Protecting investors** (rank)	20	Cost (% of claim)	63.3
Difficulty of hiring index (0-100)	44	Extent of disclosure index (0-10)	6		
Rigidity of hours index (0-100)	0	Extent of director liability index (0-10)	7	**Closing a business** (rank)	108
Difficulty of redundancy index (0-100)	40	Ease of shareholder suits index (0-10)	7	Time (years)	4.0
Rigidity of employment index (0-100)	28	Strength of investor protection index (0-10)	6.7	Cost (% of estate)	8
Redundancy cost (weeks of salary)	104			Recovery rate (cents on the dollar)	23.2
		✔ **Paying taxes** (rank)	89		
		Payments (number per year)	21		
		Time (hours per year)	302		
		Total tax rate (% of profit)	35.0		

BELARUS

		Eastern Europe & Central Asia		GNI per capita (US$)	5,384
Ease of doing business (rank)	58	Upper middle income		Population (m)	9.7

✔ **Starting a business** (rank)	7	✔ **Registering property** (rank)	10	✔ **Trading across borders** (rank)	129
Procedures (number)	5	Procedures (number)	3	Documents to export (number)	8
Time (days)	6	Time (days)	18	Time to export (days)	16
Cost (% of income per capita)	1.7	Cost (% of property value)	0.0	Cost to export (US$ per container)	1,772
Minimum capital (% of income per capita)	0.0			Documents to import (number)	8
		Getting credit (rank)	113	Time to import (days)	21
✔ **Dealing with construction permits** (rank)	44	Strength of legal rights index (0-10)	2	Cost to import (US$ per container)	1,770
Procedures (number)	15	Depth of credit information index (0-6)	5		
Time (days)	161	Public registry coverage (% of adults)	23.4	**Enforcing contracts** (rank)	12
Cost (% of income per capita)	35.1	Private bureau coverage (% of adults)	0.0	Procedures (number)	28
				Time (days)	225
✔ **Employing workers** (rank)	32	**Protecting investors** (rank)	109	Cost (% of claim)	23.4
Difficulty of hiring index (0-100)	0	Extent of disclosure index (0-10)	5		
Rigidity of hours index (0-100)	13	Extent of director liability index (0-10)	1	**Closing a business** (rank)	74
Difficulty of redundancy index (0-100)	20	Ease of shareholder suits index (0-10)	8	Time (years)	5.8
Rigidity of employment index (0-100)	11	Strength of investor protection index (0-10)	4.7	Cost (% of estate)	22
Redundancy cost (weeks of salary)	22			Recovery rate (cents on the dollar)	33.4
		✔ **Paying taxes** (rank)	183		
		Payments (number per year)	107		
		Time (hours per year)	900		
		Total tax rate (% of profit)	99.7		

BELGIUM

		OECD high income		GNI per capita (US$)	44,326
Ease of doing business (rank)	22	High income		Population (m)	10.7

Starting a business (rank)	31	✔ **Registering property** (rank)	167	**Trading across borders** (rank)	43
Procedures (number)	3	Procedures (number)	7	Documents to export (number)	4
Time (days)	4	Time (days)	79	Time to export (days)	8
Cost (% of income per capita)	5.3	Cost (% of property value)	12.7	Cost to export (US$ per container)	1,619
Minimum capital (% of income per capita)	19.4			Documents to import (number)	5
		Getting credit (rank)	43	Time to import (days)	9
Dealing with construction permits (rank)	46	Strength of legal rights index (0-10)	7	Cost to import (US$ per container)	1,600
Procedures (number)	14	Depth of credit information index (0-6)	4		
Time (days)	169	Public registry coverage (% of adults)	56.5	**Enforcing contracts** (rank)	21
Cost (% of income per capita)	63.5	Private bureau coverage (% of adults)	0.0	Procedures (number)	25
				Time (days)	505
Employing workers (rank)	48	**Protecting investors** (rank)	16	Cost (% of claim)	16.6
Difficulty of hiring index (0-100)	11	Extent of disclosure index (0-10)	8		
Rigidity of hours index (0-100)	40	Extent of director liability index (0-10)	6	**Closing a business** (rank)	8
Difficulty of redundancy index (0-100)	0	Ease of shareholder suits index (0-10)	7	Time (years)	0.9
Rigidity of employment index (0-100)	17	Strength of investor protection index (0-10)	7.0	Cost (% of estate)	4
Redundancy cost (weeks of salary)	16			Recovery rate (cents on the dollar)	86.3
		✔ **Paying taxes** (rank)	73		
		Payments (number per year)	11		
		Time (hours per year)	156		
		Total tax rate (% of profit)	57.3		

✔ Reforms making it easier to do business   ✘ Reforms making it more difficult to do business

BELIZE

		Latin America & Caribbean		GNI per capita (US$)		3,819
Ease of doing business (rank)	80	Lower middle income		Population (m)		0.3
Starting a business (rank)	147	**Registering property** (rank)	128	**Trading across borders** (rank)		117
Procedures (number)	9	Procedures (number)	8	Documents to export (number)		7
Time (days)	44	Time (days)	60	Time to export (days)		21
Cost (% of income per capita)	50.6	Cost (% of property value)	4.7	Cost to export (US$ per container)		1,710
Minimum capital (% of income per capita)	0.0			Documents to import (number)		6
		Getting credit (rank)	87	Time to import (days)		21
Dealing with construction permits (rank)	4	Strength of legal rights index (0-10)	8	Cost to import (US$ per container)		1,870
Procedures (number)	11	Depth of credit information index (0-6)	0			
Time (days)	66	Public registry coverage (% of adults)	0.0	**Enforcing contracts** (rank)		168
Cost (% of income per capita)	17.6	Private bureau coverage (% of adults)	0.0	Procedures (number)		51
				Time (days)		892
Employing workers (rank)	23	**Protecting investors** (rank)	119	Cost (% of claim)		27.5
Difficulty of hiring index (0-100)	22	Extent of disclosure index (0-10)	3			
Rigidity of hours index (0-100)	0	Extent of director liability index (0-10)	4	**Closing a business** (rank)		25
Difficulty of redundancy index (0-100)	0	Ease of shareholder suits index (0-10)	6	Time (years)		1.0
Rigidity of employment index (0-100)	7	Strength of investor protection index (0-10)	4.3	Cost (% of estate)		23
Redundancy cost (weeks of salary)	24			Recovery rate (cents on the dollar)		63.4
		Paying taxes (rank)	57			
		Payments (number per year)	40			
		Time (hours per year)	147			
		Total tax rate (% of profit)	28.9			

BENIN

		Sub-Saharan Africa		GNI per capita (US$)		687
Ease of doing business (rank)	172	Low income		Population (m)		8.7
Starting a business (rank)	155	**Registering property** (rank)	126	✔ **Trading across borders** (rank)		128
Procedures (number)	7	Procedures (number)	4	Documents to export (number)		7
Time (days)	31	Time (days)	120	Time to export (days)		30
Cost (% of income per capita)	155.5	Cost (% of property value)	11.8	Cost to export (US$ per container)		1,251
Minimum capital (% of income per capita)	290.8			Documents to import (number)		7
		Getting credit (rank)	150	Time to import (days)		32
Dealing with construction permits (rank)	134	Strength of legal rights index (0-10)	3	Cost to import (US$ per container)		1,400
Procedures (number)	15	Depth of credit information index (0-6)	1			
Time (days)	410	Public registry coverage (% of adults)	10.9	**Enforcing contracts** (rank)		177
Cost (% of income per capita)	254.4	Private bureau coverage (% of adults)	0.0	Procedures (number)		42
				Time (days)		825
Employing workers (rank)	139	**Protecting investors** (rank)	154	Cost (% of claim)		64.7
Difficulty of hiring index (0-100)	39	Extent of disclosure index (0-10)	6			
Rigidity of hours index (0-100)	40	Extent of director liability index (0-10)	1	**Closing a business** (rank)		133
Difficulty of redundancy index (0-100)	40	Ease of shareholder suits index (0-10)	3	Time (years)		4.0
Rigidity of employment index (0-100)	40	Strength of investor protection index (0-10)	3.3	Cost (% of estate)		22
Redundancy cost (weeks of salary)	36			Recovery rate (cents on the dollar)		16.7
		✔ **Paying taxes** (rank)	167			
		Payments (number per year)	55			
		Time (hours per year)	270			
		Total tax rate (% of profit)	73.3			

BHUTAN

		South Asia		GNI per capita (US$)		1,896
Ease of doing business (rank)	126	Lower middle income		Population (m)		0.7
Starting a business (rank)	80	**Registering property** (rank)	41	**Trading across borders** (rank)		153
Procedures (number)	8	Procedures (number)	5	Documents to export (number)		8
Time (days)	46	Time (days)	64	Time to export (days)		38
Cost (% of income per capita)	8.0	Cost (% of property value)	0.0	Cost to export (US$ per container)		1,210
Minimum capital (% of income per capita)	0.0			Documents to import (number)		11
		Getting credit (rank)	177	Time to import (days)		38
Dealing with construction permits (rank)	127	Strength of legal rights index (0-10)	2	Cost to import (US$ per container)		2,140
Procedures (number)	25	Depth of credit information index (0-6)	0			
Time (days)	183	Public registry coverage (% of adults)	0.0	**Enforcing contracts** (rank)		33
Cost (% of income per capita)	149.0	Private bureau coverage (% of adults)	0.0	Procedures (number)		47
				Time (days)		225
Employing workers (rank)	12	**Protecting investors** (rank)	132	Cost (% of claim)		0.1
Difficulty of hiring index (0-100)	0	Extent of disclosure index (0-10)	5			
Rigidity of hours index (0-100)	0	Extent of director liability index (0-10)	3	**Closing a business** (rank)		183
Difficulty of redundancy index (0-100)	20	Ease of shareholder suits index (0-10)	4	Time (years)		NO PRACTICE
Rigidity of employment index (0-100)	7	Strength of investor protection index (0-10)	4.0	Cost (% of estate)		NO PRACTICE
Redundancy cost (weeks of salary)	10			Recovery rate (cents on the dollar)		0.0
		Paying taxes (rank)	90			
		Payments (number per year)	18			
		Time (hours per year)	274			
		Total tax rate (% of profit)	40.6			

BOLIVIA

		Latin America & Caribbean		GNI per capita (US$)	1,457
Ease of doing business (rank)	161	Lower middle income		Population (m)	9.7
Starting a business (rank)	167	**Registering property** (rank)	135	**Trading across borders** (rank)	121
Procedures (number)	15	Procedures (number)	7	Documents to export (number)	8
Time (days)	50	Time (days)	92	Time to export (days)	19
Cost (% of income per capita)	99.2	Cost (% of property value)	4.8	Cost to export (US$ per container)	1,425
Minimum capital (% of income per capita)	2.5			Documents to import (number)	7
		Getting credit (rank)	113	Time to import (days)	23
Dealing with construction permits (rank)	101	Strength of legal rights index (0-10)	1	Cost to import (US$ per container)	1,747
Procedures (number)	17	Depth of credit information index (0-6)	6		
Time (days)	249	Public registry coverage (% of adults)	11.6	**Enforcing contracts** (rank)	136
Cost (% of income per capita)	107.4	Private bureau coverage (% of adults)	33.9	Procedures (number)	40
				Time (days)	591
Employing workers (rank)	183	**Protecting investors** (rank)	132	Cost (% of claim)	33.2
Difficulty of hiring index (0-100)	78	Extent of disclosure index (0-10)	1		
Rigidity of hours index (0-100)	53	Extent of director liability index (0-10)	5	**Closing a business** (rank)	62
Difficulty of redundancy index (0-100)	100	Ease of shareholder suits index (0-10)	6	Time (years)	1.8
Rigidity of employment index (0-100)	77	Strength of investor protection index (0-10)	4.0	Cost (% of estate)	15
Redundancy cost (weeks of salary)	NOT POSSIBLE			Recovery rate (cents on the dollar)	37.3
		Paying taxes (rank)	177		
		Payments (number per year)	42		
		Time (hours per year)	1,080		
		Total tax rate (% of profit)	80.0		

BOSNIA AND HERZEGOVINA

		Eastern Europe & Central Asia		GNI per capita (US$)	4,506
Ease of doing business (rank)	116	Upper middle income		Population (m)	3.8
Starting a business (rank)	160	**Registering property** (rank)	139	**Trading across borders** (rank)	63
Procedures (number)	12	Procedures (number)	7	Documents to export (number)	6
Time (days)	60	Time (days)	84	Time to export (days)	16
Cost (% of income per capita)	15.8	Cost (% of property value)	5.2	Cost to export (US$ per container)	1,125
Minimum capital (% of income per capita)	29.8			Documents to import (number)	7
		Getting credit (rank)	61	Time to import (days)	16
✔ **Dealing with construction permits** (rank)	136	Strength of legal rights index (0-10)	5	Cost to import (US$ per container)	1,090
Procedures (number)	16	Depth of credit information index (0-6)	5		
Time (days)	255	Public registry coverage (% of adults)	23.2	**Enforcing contracts** (rank)	124
Cost (% of income per capita)	564.7	Private bureau coverage (% of adults)	64.3	Procedures (number)	38
				Time (days)	595
Employing workers (rank)	111	**Protecting investors** (rank)	93	Cost (% of claim)	38.4
Difficulty of hiring index (0-100)	56	Extent of disclosure index (0-10)	3		
Rigidity of hours index (0-100)	13	Extent of director liability index (0-10)	6	**Closing a business** (rank)	63
Difficulty of redundancy index (0-100)	30	Ease of shareholder suits index (0-10)	6	Time (years)	3.3
Rigidity of employment index (0-100)	33	Strength of investor protection index (0-10)	5.0	Cost (% of estate)	9
Redundancy cost (weeks of salary)	31			Recovery rate (cents on the dollar)	35.9
		Paying taxes (rank)	128		
		Payments (number per year)	51		
		Time (hours per year)	422		
		Total tax rate (% of profit)	27.1		

BOTSWANA

		Sub-Saharan Africa		GNI per capita (US$)	6,471
Ease of doing business (rank)	45	Upper middle income		Population (m)	1.9
✔ **Starting a business** (rank)	83	✗ **Registering property** (rank)	44	**Trading across borders** (rank)	150
Procedures (number)	10	Procedures (number)	5	Documents to export (number)	6
Time (days)	61	Time (days)	16	Time to export (days)	30
Cost (% of income per capita)	2.1	Cost (% of property value)	5.0	Cost to export (US$ per container)	2,810
Minimum capital (% of income per capita)	0.0			Documents to import (number)	9
		Getting credit (rank)	43	Time to import (days)	41
Dealing with construction permits (rank)	122	Strength of legal rights index (0-10)	7	Cost to import (US$ per container)	3,264
Procedures (number)	24	Depth of credit information index (0-6)	4		
Time (days)	167	Public registry coverage (% of adults)	0.0	✔ **Enforcing contracts** (rank)	79
Cost (% of income per capita)	246.2	Private bureau coverage (% of adults)	51.9	Procedures (number)	29
				Time (days)	687
Employing workers (rank)	71	**Protecting investors** (rank)	41	Cost (% of claim)	28.0
Difficulty of hiring index (0-100)	0	Extent of disclosure index (0-10)	7		
Rigidity of hours index (0-100)	0	Extent of director liability index (0-10)	8	**Closing a business** (rank)	27
Difficulty of redundancy index (0-100)	40	Ease of shareholder suits index (0-10)	3	Time (years)	1.7
Rigidity of employment index (0-100)	13	Strength of investor protection index (0-10)	6.0	Cost (% of estate)	15
Redundancy cost (weeks of salary)	90			Recovery rate (cents on the dollar)	60.3
		Paying taxes (rank)	18		
		Payments (number per year)	19		
		Time (hours per year)	140		
		Total tax rate (% of profit)	17.1		

✔ Reforms making it easier to do business   ✘ Reforms making it more difficult to do business

BRAZIL

		Latin America & Caribbean		GNI per capita (US$)		7,351
Ease of doing business (rank)	129	Upper middle income		Population (m)		192.0
✔ **Starting a business** (rank)	126	**Registering property** (rank)	120	**Trading across borders** (rank)		100
Procedures (number)	16	Procedures (number)	14	Documents to export (number)		8
Time (days)	120	Time (days)	42	Time to export (days)		12
Cost (% of income per capita)	6.9	Cost (% of property value)	2.7	Cost to export (US$ per container)		1,540
Minimum capital (% of income per capita)	0.0			Documents to import (number)		7
		Getting credit (rank)	87	Time to import (days)		16
Dealing with construction permits (rank)	113	Strength of legal rights index (0-10)	3	Cost to import (US$ per container)		1,440
Procedures (number)	18	Depth of credit information index (0-6)	5			
Time (days)	411	Public registry coverage (% of adults)	23.7	**Enforcing contracts** (rank)		100
Cost (% of income per capita)	50.6	Private bureau coverage (% of adults)	59.2	Procedures (number)		45
				Time (days)		616
Employing workers (rank)	138	**Protecting investors** (rank)	73	Cost (% of claim)		16.5
Difficulty of hiring index (0-100)	78	Extent of disclosure index (0-10)	6			
Rigidity of hours index (0-100)	60	Extent of director liability index (0-10)	7	**Closing a business** (rank)		131
Difficulty of redundancy index (0-100)	0	Ease of shareholder suits index (0-10)	3	Time (years)		4.0
Rigidity of employment index (0-100)	46	Strength of investor protection index (0-10)	5.3	Cost (% of estate)		12
Redundancy cost (weeks of salary)	46			Recovery rate (cents on the dollar)		17.1
		Paying taxes (rank)	150			
		Payments (number per year)	10			
		Time (hours per year)	2,600			
		Total tax rate (% of profit)	69.2			

BRUNEI DARUSSALAM

		East Asia & Pacific		GNI per capita (US$)		37,053
Ease of doing business (rank)	96	High income		Population (m)		0.4
Starting a business (rank)	153	**Registering property** (rank)	183	**Trading across borders** (rank)		48
Procedures (number)	18	Procedures (number)	NO PRACTICE	Documents to export (number)		6
Time (days)	116	Time (days)	NO PRACTICE	Time to export (days)		28
Cost (% of income per capita)	9.8	Cost (% of property value)	NO PRACTICE	Cost to export (US$ per container)		630
Minimum capital (% of income per capita)	0.0			Documents to import (number)		6
		Getting credit (rank)	113	Time to import (days)		19
Dealing with construction permits (rank)	75	Strength of legal rights index (0-10)	7	Cost to import (US$ per container)		708
Procedures (number)	32	Depth of credit information index (0-6)	0			
Time (days)	163	Public registry coverage (% of adults)	0.0	**Enforcing contracts** (rank)		160
Cost (% of income per capita)	4.9	Private bureau coverage (% of adults)	0.0	Procedures (number)		58
				Time (days)		540
Employing workers (rank)	4	**Protecting investors** (rank)	119	Cost (% of claim)		36.6
Difficulty of hiring index (0-100)	0	Extent of disclosure index (0-10)	3			
Rigidity of hours index (0-100)	0	Extent of director liability index (0-10)	2	**Closing a business** (rank)		37
Difficulty of redundancy index (0-100)	0	Ease of shareholder suits index (0-10)	8	Time (years)		2.5
Rigidity of employment index (0-100)	0	Strength of investor protection index (0-10)	4.3	Cost (% of estate)		4
Redundancy cost (weeks of salary)	4			Recovery rate (cents on the dollar)		47.2
		✔ **Paying taxes** (rank)	22			
		Payments (number per year)	15			
		Time (hours per year)	144			
		Total tax rate (% of profit)	30.3			

BULGARIA

		Eastern Europe & Central Asia		GNI per capita (US$)		5,487
Ease of doing business (rank)	44	Upper middle income		Population (m)		7.6
✔ **Starting a business** (rank)	50	✔ **Registering property** (rank)	56	**Trading across borders** (rank)		106
Procedures (number)	4	Procedures (number)	8	Documents to export (number)		5
Time (days)	18	Time (days)	15	Time to export (days)		23
Cost (% of income per capita)	1.7	Cost (% of property value)	2.3	Cost to export (US$ per container)		1,551
Minimum capital (% of income per capita)	20.7			Documents to import (number)		7
		Getting credit (rank)	4	Time to import (days)		21
Dealing with construction permits (rank)	119	Strength of legal rights index (0-10)	8	Cost to import (US$ per container)		1,666
Procedures (number)	24	Depth of credit information index (0-6)	6			
Time (days)	139	Public registry coverage (% of adults)	34.8	**Enforcing contracts** (rank)		87
Cost (% of income per capita)	436.5	Private bureau coverage (% of adults)	6.2	Procedures (number)		39
				Time (days)		564
Employing workers (rank)	53	**Protecting investors** (rank)	41	Cost (% of claim)		23.8
Difficulty of hiring index (0-100)	17	Extent of disclosure index (0-10)	10			
Rigidity of hours index (0-100)	40	Extent of director liability index (0-10)	1	**Closing a business** (rank)		78
Difficulty of redundancy index (0-100)	0	Ease of shareholder suits index (0-10)	7	Time (years)		3.3
Rigidity of employment index (0-100)	19	Strength of investor protection index (0-10)	6.0	Cost (% of estate)		9
Redundancy cost (weeks of salary)	9			Recovery rate (cents on the dollar)		32.1
		Paying taxes (rank)	95			
		Payments (number per year)	17			
		Time (hours per year)	616			
		Total tax rate (% of profit)	31.4			

BURKINA FASO

		Sub-Saharan Africa		GNI per capita (US$)	479
Ease of doing business (rank)	147	Low income		Population (m)	15.2
✔ **Starting a business** (rank)	115	✔ **Registering property** (rank)	114	✔ **Trading across borders** (rank)	176
Procedures (number)	4	Procedures (number)	4	Documents to export (number)	11
Time (days)	14	Time (days)	59	Time to export (days)	41
Cost (% of income per capita)	50.3	Cost (% of property value)	13.2	Cost to export (US$ per container)	2,262
Minimum capital (% of income per capita)	428.2			Documents to import (number)	11
		Getting credit (rank)	150	Time to import (days)	49
✔ **Dealing with construction permits** (rank)	80	Strength of legal rights index (0-10)	3	Cost to import (US$ per container)	3,830
Procedures (number)	15	Depth of credit information index (0-6)	1		
Time (days)	132	Public registry coverage (% of adults)	1.9	✔ **Enforcing contracts** (rank)	110
Cost (% of income per capita)	721.2	Private bureau coverage (% of adults)	0.0	Procedures (number)	37
				Time (days)	446
Employing workers (rank)	82	**Protecting investors** (rank)	147	Cost (% of claim)	83.0
Difficulty of hiring index (0-100)	33	Extent of disclosure index (0-10)	6		
Rigidity of hours index (0-100)	20	Extent of director liability index (0-10)	1	**Closing a business** (rank)	112
Difficulty of redundancy index (0-100)	10	Ease of shareholder suits index (0-10)	4	Time (years)	4.0
Rigidity of employment index (0-100)	21	Strength of investor protection index (0-10)	3.7	Cost (% of estate)	9
Redundancy cost (weeks of salary)	34			Recovery rate (cents on the dollar)	21.7
		Paying taxes (rank)	144		
		Payments (number per year)	46		
		Time (hours per year)	270		
		Total tax rate (% of profit)	44.9		

BURUNDI

		Sub-Saharan Africa		GNI per capita (US$)	135
Ease of doing business (rank)	176	Low income		Population (m)	8.1
Starting a business (rank)	130	**Registering property** (rank)	118	**Trading across borders** (rank)	175
Procedures (number)	11	Procedures (number)	5	Documents to export (number)	9
Time (days)	32	Time (days)	94	Time to export (days)	47
Cost (% of income per capita)	151.6	Cost (% of property value)	6.3	Cost to export (US$ per container)	2,747
Minimum capital (% of income per capita)	0.0			Documents to import (number)	10
		Getting credit (rank)	167	Time to import (days)	71
Dealing with construction permits (rank)	172	Strength of legal rights index (0-10)	2	Cost to import (US$ per container)	4,285
Procedures (number)	22	Depth of credit information index (0-6)	1		
Time (days)	212	Public registry coverage (% of adults)	0.2	**Enforcing contracts** (rank)	172
Cost (% of income per capita)	7,968.2	Private bureau coverage (% of adults)	0.0	Procedures (number)	44
				Time (days)	832
Employing workers (rank)	88	**Protecting investors** (rank)	154	Cost (% of claim)	38.6
Difficulty of hiring index (0-100)	0	Extent of disclosure index (0-10)	4		
Rigidity of hours index (0-100)	53	Extent of director liability index (0-10)	1	**Closing a business** (rank)	183
Difficulty of redundancy index (0-100)	30	Ease of shareholder suits index (0-10)	5	Time (years)	NO PRACTICE
Rigidity of employment index (0-100)	28	Strength of investor protection index (0-10)	3.3	Cost (% of estate)	NO PRACTICE
Redundancy cost (weeks of salary)	26			Recovery rate (cents on the dollar)	0.0
		Paying taxes (rank)	116		
		Payments (number per year)	32		
		Time (hours per year)	140		
		Total tax rate (% of profit)	278.6		

CAMBODIA

		East Asia & Pacific		GNI per capita (US$)	603
Ease of doing business (rank)	145	Low income		Population (m)	14.7
Starting a business (rank)	173	**Registering property** (rank)	116	**Trading across borders** (rank)	127
Procedures (number)	9	Procedures (number)	7	Documents to export (number)	11
Time (days)	85	Time (days)	56	Time to export (days)	22
Cost (% of income per capita)	138.4	Cost (% of property value)	4.4	Cost to export (US$ per container)	732
Minimum capital (% of income per capita)	36.6			Documents to import (number)	11
		Getting credit (rank)	87	Time to import (days)	30
Dealing with construction permits (rank)	145	Strength of legal rights index (0-10)	8	Cost to import (US$ per container)	872
Procedures (number)	23	Depth of credit information index (0-6)	0		
Time (days)	709	Public registry coverage (% of adults)	0.0	**Enforcing contracts** (rank)	141
Cost (% of income per capita)	53.6	Private bureau coverage (% of adults)	0.0	Procedures (number)	44
				Time (days)	401
Employing workers (rank)	134	**Protecting investors** (rank)	73	Cost (% of claim)	102.7
Difficulty of hiring index (0-100)	44	Extent of disclosure index (0-10)	5		
Rigidity of hours index (0-100)	33	Extent of director liability index (0-10)	9	**Closing a business** (rank)	183
Difficulty of redundancy index (0-100)	30	Ease of shareholder suits index (0-10)	2	Time (years)	NO PRACTICE
Rigidity of employment index (0-100)	36	Strength of investor protection index (0-10)	5.3	Cost (% of estate)	NO PRACTICE
Redundancy cost (weeks of salary)	39			Recovery rate (cents on the dollar)	0.0
		✗ **Paying taxes** (rank)	58		
		Payments (number per year)	39		
		Time (hours per year)	173		
		Total tax rate (% of profit)	22.7		

✔ Reforms making it easier to do business ✘ Reforms making it more difficult to do business

CAMEROON

		Sub-Saharan Africa		GNI per capita (US$)		1,153
Ease of doing business (rank)	171	Lower middle income		Population (m)		18.9
✔ **Starting a business** (rank)	174	**Registering property** (rank)	143	✔ **Trading across borders** (rank)		149
Procedures (number)	12	Procedures (number)	5	Documents to export (number)		10
Time (days)	34	Time (days)	93	Time to export (days)		23
Cost (% of income per capita)	121.1	Cost (% of property value)	17.8	Cost to export (US$ per container)		1,250
Minimum capital (% of income per capita)	182.9			Documents to import (number)		11
		Getting credit (rank)	135	Time to import (days)		26
Dealing with construction permits (rank)	164	Strength of legal rights index (0-10)	3	Cost to import (US$ per container)		2,002
Procedures (number)	15	Depth of credit information index (0-6)	2			
Time (days)	426	Public registry coverage (% of adults)	1.8	**Enforcing contracts** (rank)		174
Cost (% of income per capita)	1,242.5	Private bureau coverage (% of adults)	0.0	Procedures (number)		43
				Time (days)		800
Employing workers (rank)	126	**Protecting investors** (rank)	119	Cost (% of claim)		46.6
Difficulty of hiring index (0-100)	28	Extent of disclosure index (0-10)	6			
Rigidity of hours index (0-100)	20	Extent of director liability index (0-10)	1	**Closing a business** (rank)		98
Difficulty of redundancy index (0-100)	70	Ease of shareholder suits index (0-10)	6	Time (years)		3.2
Rigidity of employment index (0-100)	39	Strength of investor protection index (0-10)	4.3	Cost (% of estate)		15
Redundancy cost (weeks of salary)	33			Recovery rate (cents on the dollar)		25.5
		✔ **Paying taxes** (rank)	170			
		Payments (number per year)	41			
		Time (hours per year)	1,400			
		Total tax rate (% of profit)	50.5			

CANADA

		OECD high income		GNI per capita (US$)		41,729
Ease of doing business (rank)	8	High income		Population (m)		33.3
Starting a business (rank)	2	**Registering property** (rank)	35	**Trading across borders** (rank)		38
Procedures (number)	1	Procedures (number)	6	Documents to export (number)		3
Time (days)	5	Time (days)	17	Time to export (days)		7
Cost (% of income per capita)	0.4	Cost (% of property value)	1.8	Cost to export (US$ per container)		1,610
Minimum capital (% of income per capita)	0.0			Documents to import (number)		4
		Getting credit (rank)	30	Time to import (days)		11
Dealing with construction permits (rank)	29	Strength of legal rights index (0-10)	6	Cost to import (US$ per container)		1,660
Procedures (number)	14	Depth of credit information index (0-6)	6			
Time (days)	75	Public registry coverage (% of adults)	0.0	**Enforcing contracts** (rank)		58
Cost (% of income per capita)	100.7	Private bureau coverage (% of adults)	100.0	Procedures (number)		36
				Time (days)		570
Employing workers (rank)	17	**Protecting investors** (rank)	5	Cost (% of claim)		22.3
Difficulty of hiring index (0-100)	11	Extent of disclosure index (0-10)	8			
Rigidity of hours index (0-100)	0	Extent of director liability index (0-10)	9	**Closing a business** (rank)		4
Difficulty of redundancy index (0-100)	0	Ease of shareholder suits index (0-10)	8	Time (years)		0.8
Rigidity of employment index (0-100)	4	Strength of investor protection index (0-10)	8.3	Cost (% of estate)		4
Redundancy cost (weeks of salary)	28			Recovery rate (cents on the dollar)		88.7
		Paying taxes (rank)	28			
		Payments (number per year)	9			
		Time (hours per year)	119			
		Total tax rate (% of profit)	43.6			

CAPE VERDE

		Sub-Saharan Africa		GNI per capita (US$)		3,131
Ease of doing business (rank)	146	Lower middle income		Population (m)		0.5
✔ **Starting a business** (rank)	136	**Registering property** (rank)	126	**Trading across borders** (rank)		58
Procedures (number)	9	Procedures (number)	6	Documents to export (number)		5
Time (days)	24	Time (days)	73	Time to export (days)		19
Cost (% of income per capita)	17.0	Cost (% of property value)	7.6	Cost to export (US$ per container)		1,325
Minimum capital (% of income per capita)	38.9			Documents to import (number)		5
		✘ **Getting credit** (rank)	150	Time to import (days)		18
Dealing with construction permits (rank)	83	Strength of legal rights index (0-10)	2	Cost to import (US$ per container)		1,129
Procedures (number)	18	Depth of credit information index (0-6)	2			
Time (days)	120	Public registry coverage (% of adults)	23.0	**Enforcing contracts** (rank)		38
Cost (% of income per capita)	523.3	Private bureau coverage (% of adults)	0.0	Procedures (number)		37
				Time (days)		425
Employing workers (rank)	167	**Protecting investors** (rank)	132	Cost (% of claim)		21.8
Difficulty of hiring index (0-100)	33	Extent of disclosure index (0-10)	1			
Rigidity of hours index (0-100)	33	Extent of director liability index (0-10)	5	**Closing a business** (rank)		183
Difficulty of redundancy index (0-100)	70	Ease of shareholder suits index (0-10)	6	Time (years)		NO PRACTICE
Rigidity of employment index (0-100)	46	Strength of investor protection index (0-10)	4.0	Cost (% of estate)		NO PRACTICE
Redundancy cost (weeks of salary)	93			Recovery rate (cents on the dollar)		0.0
		✔ **Paying taxes** (rank)	112			
		Payments (number per year)	56			
		Time (hours per year)	100			
		Total tax rate (% of profit)	49.7			

CENTRAL AFRICAN REPUBLIC

		Sub-Saharan Africa		GNI per capita (US$)	408
Ease of doing business (rank)	183	Low income		Population (m)	4.4
✔ **Starting a business** (rank)	159	**Registering property** (rank)	138	**Trading across borders** (rank)	181
Procedures (number)	8	Procedures (number)	5	Documents to export (number)	9
Time (days)	22	Time (days)	75	Time to export (days)	54
Cost (% of income per capita)	244.9	Cost (% of property value)	18.6	Cost to export (US$ per container)	5,491
Minimum capital (% of income per capita)	507.1			Documents to import (number)	17
		Getting credit (rank)	135	Time to import (days)	62
Dealing with construction permits (rank)	147	Strength of legal rights index (0-10)	3	Cost to import (US$ per container)	5,554
Procedures (number)	21	Depth of credit information index (0-6)	2		
Time (days)	239	Public registry coverage (% of adults)	2.1	**Enforcing contracts** (rank)	171
Cost (% of income per capita)	275.2	Private bureau coverage (% of adults)	0.0	Procedures (number)	43
				Time (days)	660
Employing workers (rank)	144	**Protecting investors** (rank)	132	Cost (% of claim)	82.0
Difficulty of hiring index (0-100)	61	Extent of disclosure index (0-10)	6		
Rigidity of hours index (0-100)	40	Extent of director liability index (0-10)	1	**Closing a business** (rank)	183
Difficulty of redundancy index (0-100)	50	Ease of shareholder suits index (0-10)	5	Time (years)	4.8
Rigidity of employment index (0-100)	50	Strength of investor protection index (0-10)	4.0	Cost (% of estate)	76
Redundancy cost (weeks of salary)	22			Recovery rate (cents on the dollar)	0.0
		Paying taxes (rank)	179		
		Payments (number per year)	54		
		Time (hours per year)	504		
		Total tax rate (% of profit)	203.8		

CHAD

		Sub-Saharan Africa		GNI per capita (US$)	535
Ease of doing business (rank)	178	Low income		Population (m)	11.1
Starting a business (rank)	182	**Registering property** (rank)	136	**Trading across borders** (rank)	169
Procedures (number)	19	Procedures (number)	6	Documents to export (number)	6
Time (days)	75	Time (days)	44	Time to export (days)	75
Cost (% of income per capita)	176.7	Cost (% of property value)	22.7	Cost to export (US$ per container)	5,497
Minimum capital (% of income per capita)	369.3			Documents to import (number)	10
		Getting credit (rank)	150	Time to import (days)	100
Dealing with construction permits (rank)	73	Strength of legal rights index (0-10)	3	Cost to import (US$ per container)	6,150
Procedures (number)	9	Depth of credit information index (0-6)	1		
Time (days)	181	Public registry coverage (% of adults)	0.2	**Enforcing contracts** (rank)	170
Cost (% of income per capita)	985.9	Private bureau coverage (% of adults)	0.0	Procedures (number)	41
				Time (days)	743
Employing workers (rank)	118	**Protecting investors** (rank)	132	Cost (% of claim)	77.4
Difficulty of hiring index (0-100)	39	Extent of disclosure index (0-10)	6		
Rigidity of hours index (0-100)	20	Extent of director liability index (0-10)	1	**Closing a business** (rank)	183
Difficulty of redundancy index (0-100)	40	Ease of shareholder suits index (0-10)	5	Time (years)	NO PRACTICE
Rigidity of employment index (0-100)	33	Strength of investor protection index (0-10)	4.0	Cost (% of estate)	NO PRACTICE
Redundancy cost (weeks of salary)	36			Recovery rate (cents on the dollar)	0.0
		Paying taxes (rank)	133		
		Payments (number per year)	54		
		Time (hours per year)	122		
		Total tax rate (% of profit)	60.9		

CHILE

		Latin America & Caribbean		GNI per capita (US$)	9,396
Ease of doing business (rank)	49	Upper middle income		Population (m)	16.8
Starting a business (rank)	69	**Registering property** (rank)	42	**Trading across borders** (rank)	56
Procedures (number)	9	Procedures (number)	6	Documents to export (number)	6
Time (days)	27	Time (days)	31	Time to export (days)	21
Cost (% of income per capita)	6.9	Cost (% of property value)	1.3	Cost to export (US$ per container)	745
Minimum capital (% of income per capita)	0.0			Documents to import (number)	7
		Getting credit (rank)	71	Time to import (days)	21
Dealing with construction permits (rank)	66	Strength of legal rights index (0-10)	4	Cost to import (US$ per container)	795
Procedures (number)	18	Depth of credit information index (0-6)	5		
Time (days)	155	Public registry coverage (% of adults)	32.9	**Enforcing contracts** (rank)	69
Cost (% of income per capita)	97.8	Private bureau coverage (% of adults)	33.9	Procedures (number)	36
				Time (days)	480
Employing workers (rank)	72	**Protecting investors** (rank)	41	Cost (% of claim)	28.6
Difficulty of hiring index (0-100)	33	Extent of disclosure index (0-10)	7		
Rigidity of hours index (0-100)	0	Extent of director liability index (0-10)	6	**Closing a business** (rank)	114
Difficulty of redundancy index (0-100)	20	Ease of shareholder suits index (0-10)	5	Time (years)	4.5
Rigidity of employment index (0-100)	18	Strength of investor protection index (0-10)	6.0	Cost (% of estate)	15
Redundancy cost (weeks of salary)	52			Recovery rate (cents on the dollar)	21.3
		Paying taxes (rank)	45		
		Payments (number per year)	10		
		Time (hours per year)	316		
		Total tax rate (% of profit)	25.3		

✔ Reforms making it easier to do business   ✘ Reforms making it more difficult to do business

CHINA

	East Asia & Pacific		GNI per capita (US$)	2,775
Ease of doing business (rank)	89	Lower middle income	Population (m)	1,325.6
Starting a business (rank)	151	**Registering property** (rank)	32	✔ **Trading across borders** (rank)	44
Procedures (number)	14	Procedures (number)	4	Documents to export (number)	7
Time (days)	37	Time (days)	29	Time to export (days)	21
Cost (% of income per capita)	4.9	Cost (% of property value)	3.1	Cost to export (US$ per container)	500
Minimum capital (% of income per capita)	130.9			Documents to import (number)	5
		Getting credit (rank)	61	Time to import (days)	24
Dealing with construction permits (rank)	180	Strength of legal rights index (0-10)	6	Cost to import (US$ per container)	545
Procedures (number)	37	Depth of credit information index (0-6)	4		
Time (days)	336	Public registry coverage (% of adults)	62.1	**Enforcing contracts** (rank)	18
Cost (% of income per capita)	579.2	Private bureau coverage (% of adults)	0.0	Procedures (number)	34
				Time (days)	406
Employing workers (rank)	140	**Protecting investors** (rank)	93	Cost (% of claim)	11.1
Difficulty of hiring index (0-100)	11	Extent of disclosure index (0-10)	10		
Rigidity of hours index (0-100)	33	Extent of director liability index (0-10)	1	**Closing a business** (rank)	65
Difficulty of redundancy index (0-100)	50	Ease of shareholder suits index (0-10)	4	Time (years)	1.7
Rigidity of employment index (0-100)	31	Strength of investor protection index (0-10)	5.0	Cost (% of estate)	22
Redundancy cost (weeks of salary)	91			Recovery rate (cents on the dollar)	35.3
		Paying taxes (rank)	130		
		Payments (number per year)	7		
		Time (hours per year)	504		
		Total tax rate (% of profit)	78.5		

COLOMBIA

	Latin America & Caribbean		GNI per capita (US$)	4,658
Ease of doing business (rank)	37	Upper middle income	Population (m)	44.5
✔ **Starting a business** (rank)	74	✔ **Registering property** (rank)	51	✔ **Trading across borders** (rank)	97
Procedures (number)	9	Procedures (number)	7	Documents to export (number)	6
Time (days)	20	Time (days)	20	Time to export (days)	14
Cost (% of income per capita)	12.8	Cost (% of property value)	2.0	Cost to export (US$ per container)	1,770
Minimum capital (% of income per capita)	0.0			Documents to import (number)	8
		✔ **Getting credit** (rank)	61	Time to import (days)	14
✔ **Dealing with construction permits** (rank)	32	Strength of legal rights index (0-10)	5	Cost to import (US$ per container)	1,750
Procedures (number)	11	Depth of credit information index (0-6)	5		
Time (days)	51	Public registry coverage (% of adults)	0.0	**Enforcing contracts** (rank)	152
Cost (% of income per capita)	402.8	Private bureau coverage (% of adults)	60.5	Procedures (number)	34
				Time (days)	1,346
Employing workers (rank)	63	✔ **Protecting investors** (rank)	5	Cost (% of claim)	52.6
Difficulty of hiring index (0-100)	11	Extent of disclosure index (0-10)	8		
Rigidity of hours index (0-100)	20	Extent of director liability index (0-10)	8	✔ **Closing a business** (rank)	32
Difficulty of redundancy index (0-100)	0	Ease of shareholder suits index (0-10)	9	Time (years)	3.0
Rigidity of employment index (0-100)	10	Strength of investor protection index (0-10)	8.3	Cost (% of estate)	1
Redundancy cost (weeks of salary)	59			Recovery rate (cents on the dollar)	52.8
		✔ **Paying taxes** (rank)	115		
		Payments (number per year)	20		
		Time (hours per year)	208		
		Total tax rate (% of profit)	78.7		

COMOROS

	Sub-Saharan Africa		GNI per capita (US$)	751
Ease of doing business (rank)	162	Low income	Population (m)	0.6
Starting a business (rank)	168	**Registering property** (rank)	96	**Trading across borders** (rank)	133
Procedures (number)	11	Procedures (number)	5	Documents to export (number)	10
Time (days)	24	Time (days)	24	Time to export (days)	30
Cost (% of income per capita)	182.1	Cost (% of property value)	20.8	Cost to export (US$ per container)	1,073
Minimum capital (% of income per capita)	261.8			Documents to import (number)	10
		Getting credit (rank)	167	Time to import (days)	21
Dealing with construction permits (rank)	66	Strength of legal rights index (0-10)	3	Cost to import (US$ per container)	1,057
Procedures (number)	18	Depth of credit information index (0-6)	0		
Time (days)	164	Public registry coverage (% of adults)	0.0	**Enforcing contracts** (rank)	153
Cost (% of income per capita)	72.6	Private bureau coverage (% of adults)	0.0	Procedures (number)	43
				Time (days)	506
Employing workers (rank)	164	**Protecting investors** (rank)	132	Cost (% of claim)	89.4
Difficulty of hiring index (0-100)	39	Extent of disclosure index (0-10)	6		
Rigidity of hours index (0-100)	40	Extent of director liability index (0-10)	1	**Closing a business** (rank)	183
Difficulty of redundancy index (0-100)	40	Ease of shareholder suits index (0-10)	5	Time (years)	NO PRACTICE
Rigidity of employment index (0-100)	40	Strength of investor protection index (0-10)	4.0	Cost (% of estate)	NO PRACTICE
Redundancy cost (weeks of salary)	100			Recovery rate (cents on the dollar)	0.0
		Paying taxes (rank)	41		
		Payments (number per year)	20		
		Time (hours per year)	100		
		Total tax rate (% of profit)	41.1		

CONGO, DEM. REP.

		Sub-Saharan Africa		GNI per capita (US$)	153
Ease of doing business (rank)	182	Low income		Population (m)	64.2
Starting a business (rank)	154	**Registering property** (rank)	157	✔ **Trading across borders** (rank)	165
Procedures (number)	13	Procedures (number)	8	Documents to export (number)	8
Time (days)	149	Time (days)	57	Time to export (days)	44
Cost (% of income per capita)	391.0	Cost (% of property value)	9.8	Cost to export (US$ per container)	2,607
Minimum capital (% of income per capita)	0.0			Documents to import (number)	9
		Getting credit (rank)	167	Time to import (days)	63
Dealing with construction permits (rank)	146	Strength of legal rights index (0-10)	3	Cost to import (US$ per container)	2,483
Procedures (number)	14	Depth of credit information index (0-6)	0		
Time (days)	322	Public registry coverage (% of adults)	0.0	**Enforcing contracts** (rank)	172
Cost (% of income per capita)	1,485.1	Private bureau coverage (% of adults)	0.0	Procedures (number)	43
				Time (days)	625
Employing workers (rank)	174	**Protecting investors** (rank)	154	Cost (% of claim)	151.8
Difficulty of hiring index (0-100)	72	Extent of disclosure index (0-10)	3		
Rigidity of hours index (0-100)	47	Extent of director liability index (0-10)	3	**Closing a business** (rank)	152
Difficulty of redundancy index (0-100)	70	Ease of shareholder suits index (0-10)	4	Time (years)	5.2
Rigidity of employment index (0-100)	63	Strength of investor protection index (0-10)	3.3	Cost (% of estate)	29
Redundancy cost (weeks of salary)	31			Recovery rate (cents on the dollar)	5.4
		✘ **Paying taxes** (rank)	157		
		Payments (number per year)	32		
		Time (hours per year)	308		
		Total tax rate (% of profit)	322.0		

CONGO, REP.

		Sub-Saharan Africa		GNI per capita (US$)	1,973
Ease of doing business (rank)	179	Lower middle income		Population (m)	3.6
Starting a business (rank)	166	**Registering property** (rank)	169	**Trading across borders** (rank)	178
Procedures (number)	10	Procedures (number)	7	Documents to export (number)	11
Time (days)	37	Time (days)	116	Time to export (days)	50
Cost (% of income per capita)	86.5	Cost (% of property value)	10.3	Cost to export (US$ per container)	2,490
Minimum capital (% of income per capita)	96.5			Documents to import (number)	12
		Getting credit (rank)	135	Time to import (days)	62
Dealing with construction permits (rank)	69	Strength of legal rights index (0-10)	3	Cost to import (US$ per container)	2,959
Procedures (number)	14	Depth of credit information index (0-6)	2		
Time (days)	169	Public registry coverage (% of adults)	3.0	**Enforcing contracts** (rank)	159
Cost (% of income per capita)	265.6	Private bureau coverage (% of adults)	0.0	Procedures (number)	44
				Time (days)	560
Employing workers (rank)	169	**Protecting investors** (rank)	154	Cost (% of claim)	53.2
Difficulty of hiring index (0-100)	78	Extent of disclosure index (0-10)	6		
Rigidity of hours index (0-100)	40	Extent of director liability index (0-10)	1	**Closing a business** (rank)	120
Difficulty of redundancy index (0-100)	70	Ease of shareholder suits index (0-10)	3	Time (years)	3.0
Rigidity of employment index (0-100)	63	Strength of investor protection index (0-10)	3.3	Cost (% of estate)	24
Redundancy cost (weeks of salary)	33			Recovery rate (cents on the dollar)	20.4
		Paying taxes (rank)	180		
		Payments (number per year)	61		
		Time (hours per year)	606		
		Total tax rate (% of profit)	65.5		

COSTA RICA

		Latin America & Caribbean		GNI per capita (US$)	6,063
Ease of doing business (rank)	121	Upper middle income		Population (m)	4.5
Starting a business (rank)	127	**Registering property** (rank)	49	**Trading across borders** (rank)	60
Procedures (number)	12	Procedures (number)	6	Documents to export (number)	6
Time (days)	60	Time (days)	21	Time to export (days)	13
Cost (% of income per capita)	20.0	Cost (% of property value)	3.4	Cost to export (US$ per container)	1,190
Minimum capital (% of income per capita)	0.0			Documents to import (number)	7
		Getting credit (rank)	61	Time to import (days)	15
Dealing with construction permits (rank)	129	Strength of legal rights index (0-10)	5	Cost to import (US$ per container)	1,190
Procedures (number)	23	Depth of credit information index (0-6)	5		
Time (days)	191	Public registry coverage (% of adults)	24.3	✔ **Enforcing contracts** (rank)	132
Cost (% of income per capita)	183.6	Private bureau coverage (% of adults)	56.0	Procedures (number)	40
				Time (days)	852
Employing workers (rank)	110	**Protecting investors** (rank)	165	Cost (% of claim)	24.3
Difficulty of hiring index (0-100)	78	Extent of disclosure index (0-10)	2		
Rigidity of hours index (0-100)	40	Extent of director liability index (0-10)	5	**Closing a business** (rank)	101
Difficulty of redundancy index (0-100)	0	Ease of shareholder suits index (0-10)	2	Time (years)	3.5
Rigidity of employment index (0-100)	39	Strength of investor protection index (0-10)	3.0	Cost (% of estate)	15
Redundancy cost (weeks of salary)	29			Recovery rate (cents on the dollar)	25.4
		Paying taxes (rank)	154		
		Payments (number per year)	42		
		Time (hours per year)	282		
		Total tax rate (% of profit)	54.8		

✔ Reforms making it easier to do business   ✘ Reforms making it more difficult to do business

CÔTE D'IVOIRE

Ease of doing business (rank)	168	Sub-Saharan Africa		GNI per capita (US$)	984	
		Lower middle income		Population (m)	20.6	
Starting a business (rank)	172	**Registering property** (rank)	145	**Trading across borders** (rank)	160	
Procedures (number)	10	Procedures (number)	6	Documents to export (number)	10	
Time (days)	40	Time (days)	62	Time to export (days)	25	
Cost (% of income per capita)	133.3	Cost (% of property value)	13.9	Cost to export (US$ per container)	1,969	
Minimum capital (% of income per capita)	204.9			Documents to import (number)	9	
		Getting credit (rank)	150	Time to import (days)	36	
Dealing with construction permits (rank)	167	Strength of legal rights index (0-10)	3	Cost to import (US$ per container)	2,577	
Procedures (number)	22	Depth of credit information index (0-6)	1			
Time (days)	629	Public registry coverage (% of adults)	2.7	**Enforcing contracts** (rank)	127	
Cost (% of income per capita)	230.9	Private bureau coverage (% of adults)	0.0	Procedures (number)	33	
				Time (days)	770	
Employing workers (rank)	129	**Protecting investors** (rank)	154	Cost (% of claim)	41.7	
Difficulty of hiring index (0-100)	33	Extent of disclosure index (0-10)	6			
Rigidity of hours index (0-100)	47	Extent of director liability index (0-10)	1	**Closing a business** (rank)	71	
Difficulty of redundancy index (0-100)	20	Ease of shareholder suits index (0-10)	3	Time (years)	2.2	
Rigidity of employment index (0-100)	33	Strength of investor protection index (0-10)	3.3	Cost (% of estate)	18	
Redundancy cost (weeks of salary)	49			Recovery rate (cents on the dollar)	34.0	
		Paying taxes (rank)	152			
		Payments (number per year)	66			
		Time (hours per year)	270			
		Total tax rate (% of profit)	44.7			

CROATIA

Ease of doing business (rank)	103	Eastern Europe & Central Asia		GNI per capita (US$)	13,574	
		High income		Population (m)	4.4	
Starting a business (rank)	101	**Registering property** (rank)	109	**Trading across borders** (rank)	96	
Procedures (number)	7	Procedures (number)	5	Documents to export (number)	7	
Time (days)	22	Time (days)	104	Time to export (days)	20	
Cost (% of income per capita)	8.4	Cost (% of property value)	5.0	Cost to export (US$ per container)	1,281	
Minimum capital (% of income per capita)	13.4			Documents to import (number)	8	
		Getting credit (rank)	61	Time to import (days)	16	
✔ **Dealing with construction permits** (rank)	144	Strength of legal rights index (0-10)	6	Cost to import (US$ per container)	1,141	
Procedures (number)	14	Depth of credit information index (0-6)	4			
Time (days)	420	Public registry coverage (% of adults)	0.0	**Enforcing contracts** (rank)	45	
Cost (% of income per capita)	895.2	Private bureau coverage (% of adults)	77.0	Procedures (number)	38	
				Time (days)	561	
Employing workers (rank)	163	**Protecting investors** (rank)	132	Cost (% of claim)	13.8	
Difficulty of hiring index (0-100)	61	Extent of disclosure index (0-10)	1			
Rigidity of hours index (0-100)	40	Extent of director liability index (0-10)	5	**Closing a business** (rank)	82	
Difficulty of redundancy index (0-100)	50	Ease of shareholder suits index (0-10)	6	Time (years)	3.1	
Rigidity of employment index (0-100)	50	Strength of investor protection index (0-10)	4.0	Cost (% of estate)	15	
Redundancy cost (weeks of salary)	39			Recovery rate (cents on the dollar)	30.5	
		Paying taxes (rank)	39			
		Payments (number per year)	17			
		Time (hours per year)	196			
		Total tax rate (% of profit)	32.5			

CYPRUS

Ease of doing business (rank)	40	Eastern Europe & Central Asia		GNI per capita (US$)	24,940	
		High income		Population (m)	0.9	
Starting a business (rank)	25	**Registering property** (rank)	64	**Trading across borders** (rank)	15	
Procedures (number)	6	Procedures (number)	3	Documents to export (number)	5	
Time (days)	8	Time (days)	34	Time to export (days)	7	
Cost (% of income per capita)	13.3	Cost (% of property value)	10.0	Cost to export (US$ per container)	820	
Minimum capital (% of income per capita)	0.0			Documents to import (number)	6	
		Getting credit (rank)	71	Time to import (days)	5	
Dealing with construction permits (rank)	77	Strength of legal rights index (0-10)	9	Cost to import (US$ per container)	1,030	
Procedures (number)	13	Depth of credit information index (0-6)	0			
Time (days)	677	Public registry coverage (% of adults)	0.0	**Enforcing contracts** (rank)	107	
Cost (% of income per capita)	50.2	Private bureau coverage (% of adults)	0.0	Procedures (number)	43	
				Time (days)	735	
Employing workers (rank)	93	**Protecting investors** (rank)	93	Cost (% of claim)	16.4	
Difficulty of hiring index (0-100)	33	Extent of disclosure index (0-10)	4			
Rigidity of hours index (0-100)	0	Extent of director liability index (0-10)	4	**Closing a business** (rank)	21	
Difficulty of redundancy index (0-100)	40	Ease of shareholder suits index (0-10)	7	Time (years)	1.5	
Rigidity of employment index (0-100)	24	Strength of investor protection index (0-10)	5.0	Cost (% of estate)	15	
Redundancy cost (weeks of salary)	64			Recovery rate (cents on the dollar)	70.7	
		Paying taxes (rank)	37			
		Payments (number per year)	27			
		Time (hours per year)	149			
		Total tax rate (% of profit)	28.8			

CZECH REPUBLIC

		OECD high income		GNI per capita (US$)		16,605
Ease of doing business (rank)	74	High income		Population (m)		10.4
Starting a business (rank)	113	✔ **Registering property** (rank)	62	**Trading across borders** (rank)		53
Procedures (number)	8	Procedures (number)	4	Documents to export (number)		4
Time (days)	15	Time (days)	78	Time to export (days)		17
Cost (% of income per capita)	9.2	Cost (% of property value)	3.0	Cost to export (US$ per container)		1,060
Minimum capital (% of income per capita)	30.5			Documents to import (number)		7
		Getting credit (rank)	43	Time to import (days)		20
✔ **Dealing with construction permits** (rank)	76	Strength of legal rights index (0-10)	6	Cost to import (US$ per container)		1,165
Procedures (number)	36	Depth of credit information index (0-6)	5			
Time (days)	150	Public registry coverage (% of adults)	4.9	**Enforcing contracts** (rank)		82
Cost (% of income per capita)	16.2	Private bureau coverage (% of adults)	73.1	Procedures (number)		27
				Time (days)		611
Employing workers (rank)	25	**Protecting investors** (rank)	93	Cost (% of claim)		33.0
Difficulty of hiring index (0-100)	33	Extent of disclosure index (0-10)	2			
Rigidity of hours index (0-100)	0	Extent of director liability index (0-10)	5	**Closing a business** (rank)		116
Difficulty of redundancy index (0-100)	0	Ease of shareholder suits index (0-10)	8	Time (years)		6.5
Rigidity of employment index (0-100)	11	Strength of investor protection index (0-10)	5.0	Cost (% of estate)		15
Redundancy cost (weeks of salary)	22			Recovery rate (cents on the dollar)		20.9
		✔ **Paying taxes** (rank)	121			
		Payments (number per year)	12			
		Time (hours per year)	613			
		Total tax rate (% of profit)	47.2			

DENMARK

		OECD high income		GNI per capita (US$)		59,128
Ease of doing business (rank)	6	High income		Population (m)		5.5
Starting a business (rank)	28	**Registering property** (rank)	47	**Trading across borders** (rank)		6
Procedures (number)	4	Procedures (number)	6	Documents to export (number)		4
Time (days)	6	Time (days)	42	Time to export (days)		5
Cost (% of income per capita)	0.0	Cost (% of property value)	0.6	Cost to export (US$ per container)		744
Minimum capital (% of income per capita)	38.6			Documents to import (number)		3
		Getting credit (rank)	15	Time to import (days)		5
Dealing with construction permits (rank)	10	Strength of legal rights index (0-10)	9	Cost to import (US$ per container)		744
Procedures (number)	6	Depth of credit information index (0-6)	4			
Time (days)	69	Public registry coverage (% of adults)	0.0	**Enforcing contracts** (rank)		28
Cost (% of income per capita)	58.7	Private bureau coverage (% of adults)	5.2	Procedures (number)		34
				Time (days)		380
Employing workers (rank)	9	**Protecting investors** (rank)	27	Cost (% of claim)		23.3
Difficulty of hiring index (0-100)	0	Extent of disclosure index (0-10)	7			
Rigidity of hours index (0-100)	20	Extent of director liability index (0-10)	5	**Closing a business** (rank)		7
Difficulty of redundancy index (0-100)	0	Ease of shareholder suits index (0-10)	7	Time (years)		1.1
Rigidity of employment index (0-100)	7	Strength of investor protection index (0-10)	6.3	Cost (% of estate)		4
Redundancy cost (weeks of salary)	0			Recovery rate (cents on the dollar)		86.5
		Paying taxes (rank)	13			
		Payments (number per year)	9			
		Time (hours per year)	135			
		Total tax rate (% of profit)	29.2			

DJIBOUTI

		Middle East & North Africa		GNI per capita (US$)		1,130
Ease of doing business (rank)	163	Lower middle income		Population (m)		0.8
Starting a business (rank)	177	**Registering property** (rank)	140	**Trading across borders** (rank)		34
Procedures (number)	11	Procedures (number)	7	Documents to export (number)		5
Time (days)	37	Time (days)	40	Time to export (days)		19
Cost (% of income per capita)	195.1	Cost (% of property value)	13.2	Cost to export (US$ per container)		836
Minimum capital (% of income per capita)	500.5			Documents to import (number)		5
		Getting credit (rank)	177	Time to import (days)		18
Dealing with construction permits (rank)	102	Strength of legal rights index (0-10)	1	Cost to import (US$ per container)		911
Procedures (number)	14	Depth of credit information index (0-6)	1			
Time (days)	195	Public registry coverage (% of adults)	0.2	**Enforcing contracts** (rank)		161
Cost (% of income per capita)	948.3	Private bureau coverage (% of adults)	0.0	Procedures (number)		40
				Time (days)		1,225
Employing workers (rank)	151	**Protecting investors** (rank)	178	Cost (% of claim)		34.0
Difficulty of hiring index (0-100)	67	Extent of disclosure index (0-10)	5			
Rigidity of hours index (0-100)	40	Extent of director liability index (0-10)	2	**Closing a business** (rank)		135
Difficulty of redundancy index (0-100)	30	Ease of shareholder suits index (0-10)	0	Time (years)		5.0
Rigidity of employment index (0-100)	46	Strength of investor protection index (0-10)	2.3	Cost (% of estate)		18
Redundancy cost (weeks of salary)	56			Recovery rate (cents on the dollar)		15.9
		✔ **Paying taxes** (rank)	65			
		Payments (number per year)	35			
		Time (hours per year)	114			
		Total tax rate (% of profit)	38.7			

✔ Reforms making it easier to do business   ✘ Reforms making it more difficult to do business

DOMINICA

		Latin America & Caribbean		GNI per capita (US$)	4,767
Ease of doing business (rank)	83	Upper middle income		Population (m)	0.1
Starting a business (rank)	38	**Registering property** (rank)	113	**Trading across borders** (rank)	86
Procedures (number)	5	Procedures (number)	5	Documents to export (number)	7
Time (days)	14	Time (days)	42	Time to export (days)	13
Cost (% of income per capita)	22.6	Cost (% of property value)	13.7	Cost to export (US$ per container)	1,297
Minimum capital (% of income per capita)	0.0			Documents to import (number)	8
		Getting credit (rank)	71	Time to import (days)	15
Dealing with construction permits (rank)	25	Strength of legal rights index (0-10)	9	Cost to import (US$ per container)	1,310
Procedures (number)	13	Depth of credit information index (0-6)	0		
Time (days)	182	Public registry coverage (% of adults)	0.0	**Enforcing contracts** (rank)	167
Cost (% of income per capita)	11.3	Private bureau coverage (% of adults)	0.0	Procedures (number)	47
				Time (days)	681
Employing workers (rank)	80	**Protecting investors** (rank)	27	Cost (% of claim)	36.0
Difficulty of hiring index (0-100)	11	Extent of disclosure index (0-10)	4		
Rigidity of hours index (0-100)	13	Extent of director liability index (0-10)	8	**Closing a business** (rank)	183
Difficulty of redundancy index (0-100)	20	Ease of shareholder suits index (0-10)	7	Time (years)	NO PRACTICE
Rigidity of employment index (0-100)	15	Strength of investor protection index (0-10)	6.3	Cost (% of estate)	NO PRACTICE
Redundancy cost (weeks of salary)	58			Recovery rate (cents on the dollar)	0.0
		Paying taxes (rank)	68		
		Payments (number per year)	38		
		Time (hours per year)	120		
		Total tax rate (% of profit)	37.0		

DOMINICAN REPUBLIC

		Latin America & Caribbean		GNI per capita (US$)	4,392
Ease of doing business (rank)	86	Upper middle income		Population (m)	9.8
Starting a business (rank)	107	**Registering property** (rank)	112	**Trading across borders** (rank)	36
Procedures (number)	8	Procedures (number)	7	Documents to export (number)	6
Time (days)	19	Time (days)	60	Time to export (days)	9
Cost (% of income per capita)	17.3	Cost (% of property value)	3.7	Cost to export (US$ per container)	916
Minimum capital (% of income per capita)	0.0			Documents to import (number)	7
		Getting credit (rank)	71	Time to import (days)	10
Dealing with construction permits (rank)	92	Strength of legal rights index (0-10)	3	Cost to import (US$ per container)	1,150
Procedures (number)	17	Depth of credit information index (0-6)	6		
Time (days)	214	Public registry coverage (% of adults)	29.7	**Enforcing contracts** (rank)	86
Cost (% of income per capita)	131.6	Private bureau coverage (% of adults)	46.1	Procedures (number)	34
				Time (days)	460
Employing workers (rank)	97	✔ **Protecting investors** (rank)	57	Cost (% of claim)	40.9
Difficulty of hiring index (0-100)	44	Extent of disclosure index (0-10)	5		
Rigidity of hours index (0-100)	20	Extent of director liability index (0-10)	4	**Closing a business** (rank)	146
Difficulty of redundancy index (0-100)	0	Ease of shareholder suits index (0-10)	8	Time (years)	3.5
Rigidity of employment index (0-100)	21	Strength of investor protection index (0-10)	5.7	Cost (% of estate)	38
Redundancy cost (weeks of salary)	88			Recovery rate (cents on the dollar)	8.9
		Paying taxes (rank)	70		
		Payments (number per year)	9		
		Time (hours per year)	324		
		Total tax rate (% of profit)	39.0		

ECUADOR

		Latin America & Caribbean		GNI per capita (US$)	3,643
Ease of doing business (rank)	138	Lower middle income		Population (m)	13.5
Starting a business (rank)	163	**Registering property** (rank)	69	**Trading across borders** (rank)	125
Procedures (number)	13	Procedures (number)	9	Documents to export (number)	9
Time (days)	64	Time (days)	16	Time to export (days)	20
Cost (% of income per capita)	37.7	Cost (% of property value)	2.1	Cost to export (US$ per container)	1,345
Minimum capital (% of income per capita)	10.6			Documents to import (number)	7
		Getting credit (rank)	87	Time to import (days)	29
Dealing with construction permits (rank)	86	Strength of legal rights index (0-10)	3	Cost to import (US$ per container)	1,332
Procedures (number)	19	Depth of credit information index (0-6)	5		
Time (days)	155	Public registry coverage (% of adults)	37.2	**Enforcing contracts** (rank)	101
Cost (% of income per capita)	230.6	Private bureau coverage (% of adults)	46.0	Procedures (number)	39
				Time (days)	588
Employing workers (rank)	160	**Protecting investors** (rank)	132	Cost (% of claim)	27.2
Difficulty of hiring index (0-100)	44	Extent of disclosure index (0-10)	1		
Rigidity of hours index (0-100)	40	Extent of director liability index (0-10)	5	**Closing a business** (rank)	134
Difficulty of redundancy index (0-100)	30	Ease of shareholder suits index (0-10)	6	Time (years)	5.3
Rigidity of employment index (0-100)	38	Strength of investor protection index (0-10)	4.0	Cost (% of estate)	18
Redundancy cost (weeks of salary)	135			Recovery rate (cents on the dollar)	16.1
		Paying taxes (rank)	77		
		Payments (number per year)	8		
		Time (hours per year)	600		
		Total tax rate (% of profit)	34.9		

EGYPT, ARAB REP.

Ease of doing business (rank)	106	Middle East & North Africa		GNI per capita (US$)		1,801
		Lower middle income		Population (m)		81.5

✔ **Starting a business** (rank)	24	**Registering property** (rank)	87	**Trading across borders** (rank)	29
Procedures (number)	6	Procedures (number)	7	Documents to export (number)	6
Time (days)	7	Time (days)	72	Time to export (days)	14
Cost (% of income per capita)	16.1	Cost (% of property value)	0.9	Cost to export (US$ per container)	737
Minimum capital (% of income per capita)	0.0			Documents to import (number)	6
		✔ **Getting credit** (rank)	71	Time to import (days)	15
✔ **Dealing with construction permits** (rank)	156	Strength of legal rights index (0-10)	3	Cost to import (US$ per container)	823
Procedures (number)	25	Depth of credit information index (0-6)	6		
Time (days)	218	Public registry coverage (% of adults)	2.5	✔ **Enforcing contracts** (rank)	148
Cost (% of income per capita)	331.6	Private bureau coverage (% of adults)	8.2	Procedures (number)	41
				Time (days)	1,010
Employing workers (rank)	120	**Protecting investors** (rank)	73	Cost (% of claim)	26.2
Difficulty of hiring index (0-100)	0	Extent of disclosure index (0-10)	8		
Rigidity of hours index (0-100)	20	Extent of director liability index (0-10)	3	**Closing a business** (rank)	132
Difficulty of redundancy index (0-100)	60	Ease of shareholder suits index (0-10)	5	Time (years)	4.2
Rigidity of employment index (0-100)	27	Strength of investor protection index (0-10)	5.3	Cost (% of estate)	22
Redundancy cost (weeks of salary)	132			Recovery rate (cents on the dollar)	16.8
		Paying taxes (rank)	140		
		Payments (number per year)	29		
		Time (hours per year)	480		
		Total tax rate (% of profit)	43.0		

EL SALVADOR

Ease of doing business (rank)	84	Latin America & Caribbean		GNI per capita (US$)		3,482
		Lower middle income		Population (m)		6.1

Starting a business (rank)	121	**Registering property** (rank)	46	**Trading across borders** (rank)	61
Procedures (number)	8	Procedures (number)	5	Documents to export (number)	8
Time (days)	17	Time (days)	31	Time to export (days)	14
Cost (% of income per capita)	38.7	Cost (% of property value)	3.8	Cost to export (US$ per container)	880
Minimum capital (% of income per capita)	2.9			Documents to import (number)	8
		Getting credit (rank)	43	Time to import (days)	10
Dealing with construction permits (rank)	128	Strength of legal rights index (0-10)	5	Cost to import (US$ per container)	820
Procedures (number)	34	Depth of credit information index (0-6)	6		
Time (days)	155	Public registry coverage (% of adults)	21.0	**Enforcing contracts** (rank)	50
Cost (% of income per capita)	166.2	Private bureau coverage (% of adults)	94.6	Procedures (number)	30
				Time (days)	786
Employing workers (rank)	106	**Protecting investors** (rank)	119	Cost (% of claim)	19.2
Difficulty of hiring index (0-100)	33	Extent of disclosure index (0-10)	5		
Rigidity of hours index (0-100)	40	Extent of director liability index (0-10)	2	**Closing a business** (rank)	81
Difficulty of redundancy index (0-100)	0	Ease of shareholder suits index (0-10)	6	Time (years)	4.0
Rigidity of employment index (0-100)	24	Strength of investor protection index (0-10)	4.3	Cost (% of estate)	9
Redundancy cost (weeks of salary)	86			Recovery rate (cents on the dollar)	30.8
		Paying taxes (rank)	134		
		Payments (number per year)	53		
		Time (hours per year)	320		
		Total tax rate (% of profit)	35.0		

EQUATORIAL GUINEA

Ease of doing business (rank)	170	Sub-Saharan Africa		GNI per capita (US$)		14,980
		High income		Population (m)		0.7

Starting a business (rank)	178	**Registering property** (rank)	76	**Trading across borders** (rank)	138
Procedures (number)	20	Procedures (number)	6	Documents to export (number)	7
Time (days)	136	Time (days)	23	Time to export (days)	30
Cost (% of income per capita)	100.4	Cost (% of property value)	6.2	Cost to export (US$ per container)	1,411
Minimum capital (% of income per capita)	12.4			Documents to import (number)	7
		Getting credit (rank)	135	Time to import (days)	49
Dealing with construction permits (rank)	90	Strength of legal rights index (0-10)	3	Cost to import (US$ per container)	1,411
Procedures (number)	18	Depth of credit information index (0-6)	2		
Time (days)	201	Public registry coverage (% of adults)	3.0	**Enforcing contracts** (rank)	72
Cost (% of income per capita)	128.4	Private bureau coverage (% of adults)	0.0	Procedures (number)	40
				Time (days)	553
Employing workers (rank)	182	**Protecting investors** (rank)	147	Cost (% of claim)	18.5
Difficulty of hiring index (0-100)	67	Extent of disclosure index (0-10)	6		
Rigidity of hours index (0-100)	60	Extent of director liability index (0-10)	1	**Closing a business** (rank)	183
Difficulty of redundancy index (0-100)	70	Ease of shareholder suits index (0-10)	4	Time (years)	NO PRACTICE
Rigidity of employment index (0-100)	66	Strength of investor protection index (0-10)	3.7	Cost (% of estate)	NO PRACTICE
Redundancy cost (weeks of salary)	133			Recovery rate (cents on the dollar)	0.0
		Paying taxes (rank)	163		
		Payments (number per year)	46		
		Time (hours per year)	296		
		Total tax rate (% of profit)	59.5		

✔ Reforms making it easier to do business   ✘ Reforms making it more difficult to do business

ERITREA

		Sub-Saharan Africa		GNI per capita (US$)	299
Ease of doing business (rank)	175	Low income		Population (m)	5.0

Starting a business (rank)	181	**Registering property** (rank)	171	**Trading across borders** (rank)	164
Procedures (number)	13	Procedures (number)	12	Documents to export (number)	9
Time (days)	84	Time (days)	101	Time to export (days)	50
Cost (% of income per capita)	76.5	Cost (% of property value)	5.2	Cost to export (US$ per container)	1,431
Minimum capital (% of income per capita)	297.0			Documents to import (number)	13
		Getting credit (rank)	177	Time to import (days)	60
Dealing with construction permits (rank)	183	Strength of legal rights index (0-10)	2	Cost to import (US$ per container)	1,581
Procedures (number)	NO PRACTICE	Depth of credit information index (0-6)	0		
Time (days)	NO PRACTICE	Public registry coverage (% of adults)	0.0	**Enforcing contracts** (rank)	48
Cost (% of income per capita)	NO PRACTICE	Private bureau coverage (% of adults)	0.0	Procedures (number)	39
				Time (days)	405
Employing workers (rank)	86	**Protecting investors** (rank)	109	Cost (% of claim)	22.6
Difficulty of hiring index (0-100)	0	Extent of disclosure index (0-10)	4		
Rigidity of hours index (0-100)	40	Extent of director liability index (0-10)	5	**Closing a business** (rank)	183
Difficulty of redundancy index (0-100)	20	Ease of shareholder suits index (0-10)	5	Time (years)	NO PRACTICE
Rigidity of employment index (0-100)	20	Strength of investor protection index (0-10)	4.7	Cost (% of estate)	NO PRACTICE
Redundancy cost (weeks of salary)	69			Recovery rate (cents on the dollar)	0.0
		Paying taxes (rank)	110		
		Payments (number per year)	18		
		Time (hours per year)	216		
		Total tax rate (% of profit)	84.5		

ESTONIA

		Eastern Europe & Central Asia		GNI per capita (US$)	14,270
Ease of doing business (rank)	24	High income		Population (m)	1.3

Starting a business (rank)	37	✔ **Registering property** (rank)	13	**Trading across borders** (rank)	3
Procedures (number)	5	Procedures (number)	3	Documents to export (number)	3
Time (days)	7	Time (days)	18	Time to export (days)	5
Cost (% of income per capita)	1.7	Cost (% of property value)	0.5	Cost to export (US$ per container)	730
Minimum capital (% of income per capita)	23.2			Documents to import (number)	4
		Getting credit (rank)	43	Time to import (days)	5
Dealing with construction permits (rank)	20	Strength of legal rights index (0-10)	6	Cost to import (US$ per container)	740
Procedures (number)	14	Depth of credit information index (0-6)	5		
Time (days)	118	Public registry coverage (% of adults)	0.0	**Enforcing contracts** (rank)	49
Cost (% of income per capita)	26.9	Private bureau coverage (% of adults)	20.6	Procedures (number)	36
				Time (days)	425
Employing workers (rank)	161	**Protecting investors** (rank)	57	Cost (% of claim)	26.3
Difficulty of hiring index (0-100)	33	Extent of disclosure index (0-10)	8		
Rigidity of hours index (0-100)	60	Extent of director liability index (0-10)	3	✔ **Closing a business** (rank)	61
Difficulty of redundancy index (0-100)	60	Ease of shareholder suits index (0-10)	6	Time (years)	3.0
Rigidity of employment index (0-100)	51	Strength of investor protection index (0-10)	5.7	Cost (% of estate)	9
Redundancy cost (weeks of salary)	35			Recovery rate (cents on the dollar)	37.5
		Paying taxes (rank)	38		
		Payments (number per year)	10		
		Time (hours per year)	81		
		Total tax rate (% of profit)	49.1		

ETHIOPIA

		Sub-Saharan Africa		GNI per capita (US$)	282
Ease of doing business (rank)	107	Low income		Population (m)	80.7

Starting a business (rank)	93	✔ **Registering property** (rank)	110	**Trading across borders** (rank)	159
Procedures (number)	5	Procedures (number)	10	Documents to export (number)	8
Time (days)	9	Time (days)	41	Time to export (days)	49
Cost (% of income per capita)	18.9	Cost (% of property value)	2.2	Cost to export (US$ per container)	1,940
Minimum capital (% of income per capita)	492.4			Documents to import (number)	8
		Getting credit (rank)	127	Time to import (days)	45
Dealing with construction permits (rank)	60	Strength of legal rights index (0-10)	4	Cost to import (US$ per container)	2,993
Procedures (number)	12	Depth of credit information index (0-6)	2		
Time (days)	128	Public registry coverage (% of adults)	0.1	✔ **Enforcing contracts** (rank)	57
Cost (% of income per capita)	561.3	Private bureau coverage (% of adults)	0.0	Procedures (number)	37
				Time (days)	620
Employing workers (rank)	98	**Protecting investors** (rank)	119	Cost (% of claim)	15.2
Difficulty of hiring index (0-100)	33	Extent of disclosure index (0-10)	4		
Rigidity of hours index (0-100)	20	Extent of director liability index (0-10)	4	**Closing a business** (rank)	77
Difficulty of redundancy index (0-100)	30	Ease of shareholder suits index (0-10)	5	Time (years)	3.0
Rigidity of employment index (0-100)	28	Strength of investor protection index (0-10)	4.3	Cost (% of estate)	15
Redundancy cost (weeks of salary)	40			Recovery rate (cents on the dollar)	32.2
		Paying taxes (rank)	43		
		Payments (number per year)	19		
		Time (hours per year)	198		
		Total tax rate (% of profit)	31.1		

FIJI

		East Asia & Pacific		GNI per capita (US$)	3,934
Ease of doing business (rank)	54	Upper middle income		Population (m)	0.8
Starting a business (rank)	104	**Registering property** (rank)	43	**Trading across borders** (rank)	116
Procedures (number)	8	Procedures (number)	3	Documents to export (number)	13
Time (days)	46	Time (days)	68	Time to export (days)	24
Cost (% of income per capita)	25.3	Cost (% of property value)	2.0	Cost to export (US$ per container)	654
Minimum capital (% of income per capita)	0.0			Documents to import (number)	13
		Getting credit (rank)	43	Time to import (days)	24
Dealing with construction permits (rank)	58	Strength of legal rights index (0-10)	7	Cost to import (US$ per container)	630
Procedures (number)	19	Depth of credit information index (0-6)	4		
Time (days)	135	Public registry coverage (% of adults)	0.0	**Enforcing contracts** (rank)	65
Cost (% of income per capita)	50.4	Private bureau coverage (% of adults)	48.6	Procedures (number)	34
				Time (days)	397
Employing workers (rank)	31	**Protecting investors** (rank)	41	Cost (% of claim)	38.9
Difficulty of hiring index (0-100)	11	Extent of disclosure index (0-10)	3		
Rigidity of hours index (0-100)	0	Extent of director liability index (0-10)	8	**Closing a business** (rank)	122
Difficulty of redundancy index (0-100)	20	Ease of shareholder suits index (0-10)	7	Time (years)	1.8
Rigidity of employment index (0-100)	10	Strength of investor protection index (0-10)	6.0	Cost (% of estate)	38
Redundancy cost (weeks of salary)	22			Recovery rate (cents on the dollar)	20.1
		✔ **Paying taxes** (rank)	81		
		Payments (number per year)	33		
		Time (hours per year)	150		
		Total tax rate (% of profit)	41.2		

FINLAND

		OECD high income		GNI per capita (US$)	48,125
Ease of doing business (rank)	16	High income		Population (m)	5.3
Starting a business (rank)	30	**Registering property** (rank)	27	**Trading across borders** (rank)	4
Procedures (number)	3	Procedures (number)	3	Documents to export (number)	4
Time (days)	14	Time (days)	14	Time to export (days)	8
Cost (% of income per capita)	0.9	Cost (% of property value)	4.1	Cost to export (US$ per container)	540
Minimum capital (% of income per capita)	7.2			Documents to import (number)	5
		Getting credit (rank)	30	Time to import (days)	8
Dealing with construction permits (rank)	47	Strength of legal rights index (0-10)	7	Cost to import (US$ per container)	620
Procedures (number)	18	Depth of credit information index (0-6)	5		
Time (days)	38	Public registry coverage (% of adults)	0.0	**Enforcing contracts** (rank)	8
Cost (% of income per capita)	119.7	Private bureau coverage (% of adults)	14.7	Procedures (number)	32
				Time (days)	375
Employing workers (rank)	132	**Protecting investors** (rank)	57	Cost (% of claim)	10.4
Difficulty of hiring index (0-100)	44	Extent of disclosure index (0-10)	6		
Rigidity of hours index (0-100)	40	Extent of director liability index (0-10)	4	**Closing a business** (rank)	5
Difficulty of redundancy index (0-100)	40	Ease of shareholder suits index (0-10)	7	Time (years)	0.9
Rigidity of employment index (0-100)	41	Strength of investor protection index (0-10)	5.7	Cost (% of estate)	4
Redundancy cost (weeks of salary)	26			Recovery rate (cents on the dollar)	87.3
		✔ **Paying taxes** (rank)	71		
		Payments (number per year)	8		
		Time (hours per year)	243		
		Total tax rate (% of profit)	47.7		

FRANCE

		OECD high income		GNI per capita (US$)	43,550
Ease of doing business (rank)	31	High income		Population (m)	62.0
Starting a business (rank)	22	✔ **Registering property** (rank)	159	**Trading across borders** (rank)	25
Procedures (number)	5	Procedures (number)	8	Documents to export (number)	2
Time (days)	7	Time (days)	98	Time to export (days)	9
Cost (% of income per capita)	0.9	Cost (% of property value)	6.1	Cost to export (US$ per container)	1,078
Minimum capital (% of income per capita)	0.0			Documents to import (number)	2
		Getting credit (rank)	43	Time to import (days)	11
Dealing with construction permits (rank)	17	Strength of legal rights index (0-10)	7	Cost to import (US$ per container)	1,248
Procedures (number)	13	Depth of credit information index (0-6)	4		
Time (days)	137	Public registry coverage (% of adults)	32.5	**Enforcing contracts** (rank)	6
Cost (% of income per capita)	22.9	Private bureau coverage (% of adults)	0.0	Procedures (number)	29
				Time (days)	331
Employing workers (rank)	155	**Protecting investors** (rank)	73	Cost (% of claim)	17.4
Difficulty of hiring index (0-100)	67	Extent of disclosure index (0-10)	10		
Rigidity of hours index (0-100)	60	Extent of director liability index (0-10)	1	✔ **Closing a business** (rank)	42
Difficulty of redundancy index (0-100)	30	Ease of shareholder suits index (0-10)	5	Time (years)	1.9
Rigidity of employment index (0-100)	52	Strength of investor protection index (0-10)	5.3	Cost (% of estate)	9
Redundancy cost (weeks of salary)	32			Recovery rate (cents on the dollar)	44.7
		Paying taxes (rank)	59		
		Payments (number per year)	7		
		Time (hours per year)	132		
		Total tax rate (% of profit)	65.8		

✔ Reforms making it easier to do business ✘ Reforms making it more difficult to do business

GABON

		Sub-Saharan Africa			GNI per capita (US$)		7,243
Ease of doing business (rank)	158	Upper middle income			Population (m)		1.4
Starting a business (rank)	152	**Registering property** (rank)	130		**Trading across borders** (rank)		135
Procedures (number)	9	Procedures (number)	7		Documents to export (number)		7
Time (days)	58	Time (days)	39		Time to export (days)		20
Cost (% of income per capita)	17.8	Cost (% of property value)	10.5		Cost to export (US$ per container)		1,945
Minimum capital (% of income per capita)	26.5				Documents to import (number)		8
		Getting credit (rank)	135		Time to import (days)		22
Dealing with construction permits (rank)	63	Strength of legal rights index (0-10)	3		Cost to import (US$ per container)		1,955
Procedures (number)	16	Depth of credit information index (0-6)	2				
Time (days)	210	Public registry coverage (% of adults)	3.9		**Enforcing contracts** (rank)		150
Cost (% of income per capita)	34.5	Private bureau coverage (% of adults)	0.0		Procedures (number)		38
					Time (days)		1,070
Employing workers (rank)	165	**Protecting investors** (rank)	154		Cost (% of claim)		34.3
Difficulty of hiring index (0-100)	17	Extent of disclosure index (0-10)	6				
Rigidity of hours index (0-100)	60	Extent of director liability index (0-10)	1		**Closing a business** (rank)		137
Difficulty of redundancy index (0-100)	80	Ease of shareholder suits index (0-10)	3		Time (years)		5.0
Rigidity of employment index (0-100)	52	Strength of investor protection index (0-10)	3.3		Cost (% of estate)		15
Redundancy cost (weeks of salary)	43				Recovery rate (cents on the dollar)		15.2
		Paying taxes (rank)	107				
		Payments (number per year)	26				
		Time (hours per year)	272				
		Total tax rate (% of profit)	44.7				

GAMBIA, THE

		Sub-Saharan Africa			GNI per capita (US$)		393
Ease of doing business (rank)	140	Low income			Population (m)		1.7
Starting a business (rank)	114	**Registering property** (rank)	117		**Trading across borders** (rank)		81
Procedures (number)	8	Procedures (number)	5		Documents to export (number)		6
Time (days)	27	Time (days)	371		Time to export (days)		24
Cost (% of income per capita)	215.1	Cost (% of property value)	4.6		Cost to export (US$ per container)		831
Minimum capital (% of income per capita)	0.0				Documents to import (number)		8
		Getting credit (rank)	135		Time to import (days)		23
Dealing with construction permits (rank)	79	Strength of legal rights index (0-10)	5		Cost to import (US$ per container)		922
Procedures (number)	17	Depth of credit information index (0-6)	0				
Time (days)	146	Public registry coverage (% of adults)	0.0		**Enforcing contracts** (rank)		67
Cost (% of income per capita)	336.4	Private bureau coverage (% of adults)	0.0		Procedures (number)		32
					Time (days)		434
Employing workers (rank)	85	**Protecting investors** (rank)	172		Cost (% of claim)		37.9
Difficulty of hiring index (0-100)	0	Extent of disclosure index (0-10)	2				
Rigidity of hours index (0-100)	40	Extent of director liability index (0-10)	1		**Closing a business** (rank)		123
Difficulty of redundancy index (0-100)	40	Ease of shareholder suits index (0-10)	5		Time (years)		3.0
Rigidity of employment index (0-100)	27	Strength of investor protection index (0-10)	2.7		Cost (% of estate)		15
Redundancy cost (weeks of salary)	26				Recovery rate (cents on the dollar)		19.5
		Paying taxes (rank)	176				
		Payments (number per year)	50				
		Time (hours per year)	376				
		Total tax rate (% of profit)	292.4				

GEORGIA

		Eastern Europe & Central Asia			GNI per capita (US$)		2,472
Ease of doing business (rank)	11	Lower middle income			Population (m)		4.4
Starting a business (rank)	5	**Registering property** (rank)	2		✔ **Trading across borders** (rank)		30
Procedures (number)	3	Procedures (number)	2		Documents to export (number)		4
Time (days)	3	Time (days)	3		Time to export (days)		10
Cost (% of income per capita)	3.7	Cost (% of property value)	0.0		Cost to export (US$ per container)		1,270
Minimum capital (% of income per capita)	0.0				Documents to import (number)		4
		Getting credit (rank)	30		Time to import (days)		13
✔ **Dealing with construction permits** (rank)	7	Strength of legal rights index (0-10)	6		Cost to import (US$ per container)		1,250
Procedures (number)	10	Depth of credit information index (0-6)	6				
Time (days)	98	Public registry coverage (% of adults)	0.0		**Enforcing contracts** (rank)		41
Cost (% of income per capita)	21.6	Private bureau coverage (% of adults)	12.2		Procedures (number)		36
					Time (days)		285
Employing workers (rank)	9	**Protecting investors** (rank)	41		Cost (% of claim)		29.9
Difficulty of hiring index (0-100)	0	Extent of disclosure index (0-10)	8				
Rigidity of hours index (0-100)	20	Extent of director liability index (0-10)	6		**Closing a business** (rank)		95
Difficulty of redundancy index (0-100)	0	Ease of shareholder suits index (0-10)	4		Time (years)		3.3
Rigidity of employment index (0-100)	7	Strength of investor protection index (0-10)	6.0		Cost (% of estate)		4
Redundancy cost (weeks of salary)	4				Recovery rate (cents on the dollar)		27.9
		Paying taxes (rank)	64				
		Payments (number per year)	18				
		Time (hours per year)	387				
		Total tax rate (% of profit)	15.3				

GERMANY

		OECD high income		GNI per capita (US$)	42,436
Ease of doing business (rank)	25	High income		Population (m)	82.1
✔ **Starting a business** (rank)	84	**Registering property** (rank)	57	**Trading across borders** (rank)	14
Procedures (number)	9	Procedures (number)	4	Documents to export (number)	4
Time (days)	18	Time (days)	40	Time to export (days)	7
Cost (% of income per capita)	4.7	Cost (% of property value)	5.2	Cost to export (US$ per container)	872
Minimum capital (% of income per capita)	0.0			Documents to import (number)	5
		Getting credit (rank)	15	Time to import (days)	7
		Strength of legal rights index (0-10)	7	Cost to import (US$ per container)	937
Dealing with construction permits (rank)	18	Depth of credit information index (0-6)	6		
Procedures (number)	12	Public registry coverage (% of adults)	0.8	**Enforcing contracts** (rank)	7
Time (days)	100	Private bureau coverage (% of adults)	98.3	Procedures (number)	30
Cost (% of income per capita)	60.2			Time (days)	394
		Protecting investors (rank)	93	Cost (% of claim)	14.4
Employing workers (rank)	158	Extent of disclosure index (0-10)	5		
Difficulty of hiring index (0-100)	33	Extent of director liability index (0-10)	5	✔ **Closing a business** (rank)	35
Rigidity of hours index (0-100)	53	Ease of shareholder suits index (0-10)	5	Time (years)	1.2
Difficulty of redundancy index (0-100)	40	Strength of investor protection index (0-10)	5.0	Cost (% of estate)	8
Rigidity of employment index (0-100)	42			Recovery rate (cents on the dollar)	52.2
Redundancy cost (weeks of salary)	69				
		Paying taxes (rank)	71		
		Payments (number per year)	16		
		Time (hours per year)	196		
		Total tax rate (% of profit)	44.9		

GHANA

		Sub-Saharan Africa		GNI per capita (US$)	674
Ease of doing business (rank)	92	Low income		Population (m)	23.4
✔ **Starting a business** (rank)	135	**Registering property** (rank)	33	**Trading across borders** (rank)	83
Procedures (number)	8	Procedures (number)	5	Documents to export (number)	6
Time (days)	33	Time (days)	34	Time to export (days)	19
Cost (% of income per capita)	26.4	Cost (% of property value)	1.1	Cost to export (US$ per container)	1,013
Minimum capital (% of income per capita)	13.4			Documents to import (number)	7
		Getting credit (rank)	113	Time to import (days)	29
		Strength of legal rights index (0-10)	7	Cost to import (US$ per container)	1,203
Dealing with construction permits (rank)	153	Depth of credit information index (0-6)	0		
Procedures (number)	18	Public registry coverage (% of adults)	0.0	**Enforcing contracts** (rank)	47
Time (days)	220	Private bureau coverage (% of adults)	0.0	Procedures (number)	36
Cost (% of income per capita)	1,099.0			Time (days)	487
		Protecting investors (rank)	41	Cost (% of claim)	23.0
Employing workers (rank)	133	Extent of disclosure index (0-10)	7		
Difficulty of hiring index (0-100)	11	Extent of director liability index (0-10)	5	**Closing a business** (rank)	106
Rigidity of hours index (0-100)	20	Ease of shareholder suits index (0-10)	6	Time (years)	1.9
Difficulty of redundancy index (0-100)	50	Strength of investor protection index (0-10)	6.0	Cost (% of estate)	22
Rigidity of employment index (0-100)	27			Recovery rate (cents on the dollar)	24.0
Redundancy cost (weeks of salary)	178				
		Paying taxes (rank)	79		
		Payments (number per year)	33		
		Time (hours per year)	224		
		Total tax rate (% of profit)	32.7		

GREECE

		OECD high income		GNI per capita (US$)	28,650
Ease of doing business (rank)	109	High income		Population (m)	11.2
Starting a business (rank)	140	**Registering property** (rank)	107	**Trading across borders** (rank)	80
Procedures (number)	15	Procedures (number)	11	Documents to export (number)	5
Time (days)	19	Time (days)	22	Time to export (days)	20
Cost (% of income per capita)	10.9	Cost (% of property value)	4.0	Cost to export (US$ per container)	1,153
Minimum capital (% of income per capita)	21.4			Documents to import (number)	6
		✔ **Getting credit** (rank)	87	Time to import (days)	25
		Strength of legal rights index (0-10)	3	Cost to import (US$ per container)	1,265
Dealing with construction permits (rank)	50	Depth of credit information index (0-6)	5		
Procedures (number)	15	Public registry coverage (% of adults)	0.0	**Enforcing contracts** (rank)	89
Time (days)	169	Private bureau coverage (% of adults)	46.9	Procedures (number)	39
Cost (% of income per capita)	50.7			Time (days)	819
		Protecting investors (rank)	154	Cost (% of claim)	14.4
Employing workers (rank)	147	Extent of disclosure index (0-10)	1		
Difficulty of hiring index (0-100)	44	Extent of director liability index (0-10)	4	**Closing a business** (rank)	43
Rigidity of hours index (0-100)	67	Ease of shareholder suits index (0-10)	5	Time (years)	2.0
Difficulty of redundancy index (0-100)	40	Strength of investor protection index (0-10)	3.3	Cost (% of estate)	9
Rigidity of employment index (0-100)	50			Recovery rate (cents on the dollar)	44.2
Redundancy cost (weeks of salary)	24				
		Paying taxes (rank)	76		
		Payments (number per year)	10		
		Time (hours per year)	224		
		Total tax rate (% of profit)	47.4		

✔ Reforms making it easier to do business   ✘ Reforms making it more difficult to do business

GRENADA

		Latin America & Caribbean		GNI per capita (US$)		5,709
Ease of doing business (rank)	91	Upper middle income		Population (m)		0.1
Starting a business (rank)	52	**Registering property** (rank)	162	✔ **Trading across borders** (rank)		79
Procedures (number)	6	Procedures (number)	8	Documents to export (number)		6
Time (days)	20	Time (days)	77	Time to export (days)		14
Cost (% of income per capita)	24.6	Cost (% of property value)	7.4	Cost to export (US$ per container)		1,226
Minimum capital (% of income per capita)	0.0			Documents to import (number)		5
		Getting credit (rank)	87	Time to import (days)		19
Dealing with construction permits (rank)	15	Strength of legal rights index (0-10)	8	Cost to import (US$ per container)		2,479
Procedures (number)	10	Depth of credit information index (0-6)	0			
Time (days)	149	Public registry coverage (% of adults)	0.0	✔ **Enforcing contracts** (rank)		162
Cost (% of income per capita)	25.3	Private bureau coverage (% of adults)	0.0	Procedures (number)		47
				Time (days)		688
Employing workers (rank)	49	**Protecting investors** (rank)	27	Cost (% of claim)		32.6
Difficulty of hiring index (0-100)	44	Extent of disclosure index (0-10)	4			
Rigidity of hours index (0-100)	0	Extent of director liability index (0-10)	8	**Closing a business** (rank)		183
Difficulty of redundancy index (0-100)	0	Ease of shareholder suits index (0-10)	7	Time (years)		NO PRACTICE
Rigidity of employment index (0-100)	15	Strength of investor protection index (0-10)	6.3	Cost (% of estate)		NO PRACTICE
Redundancy cost (weeks of salary)	29			Recovery rate (cents on the dollar)		0.0
		Paying taxes (rank)	82			
		Payments (number per year)	30			
		Time (hours per year)	140			
		Total tax rate (% of profit)	45.3			

GUATEMALA

		Latin America & Caribbean		GNI per capita (US$)		2,679
Ease of doing business (rank)	110	Lower middle income		Population (m)		13.7
Starting a business (rank)	156	✔ **Registering property** (rank)	24	**Trading across borders** (rank)		119
Procedures (number)	11	Procedures (number)	4	Documents to export (number)		10
Time (days)	29	Time (days)	27	Time to export (days)		17
Cost (% of income per capita)	45.4	Cost (% of property value)	1.0	Cost to export (US$ per container)		1,182
Minimum capital (% of income per capita)	23.5			Documents to import (number)		10
		✔ **Getting credit** (rank)	4	Time to import (days)		17
✔ **Dealing with construction permits** (rank)	150	Strength of legal rights index (0-10)	8	Cost to import (US$ per container)		1,302
Procedures (number)	22	Depth of credit information index (0-6)	6			
Time (days)	178	Public registry coverage (% of adults)	16.9	**Enforcing contracts** (rank)		103
Cost (% of income per capita)	1,079.3	Private bureau coverage (% of adults)	28.4	Procedures (number)		31
				Time (days)		1,459
Employing workers (rank)	127	**Protecting investors** (rank)	132	Cost (% of claim)		26.5
Difficulty of hiring index (0-100)	44	Extent of disclosure index (0-10)	3			
Rigidity of hours index (0-100)	40	Extent of director liability index (0-10)	3	**Closing a business** (rank)		93
Difficulty of redundancy index (0-100)	0	Ease of shareholder suits index (0-10)	6	Time (years)		3.0
Rigidity of employment index (0-100)	28	Strength of investor protection index (0-10)	4.0	Cost (% of estate)		15
Redundancy cost (weeks of salary)	101			Recovery rate (cents on the dollar)		28.2
		✔ **Paying taxes** (rank)	109			
		Payments (number per year)	24			
		Time (hours per year)	344			
		Total tax rate (% of profit)	40.9			

GUINEA

		Sub-Saharan Africa		GNI per capita (US$)		442
Ease of doing business (rank)	173	Low income		Population (m)		9.8
Starting a business (rank)	179	**Registering property** (rank)	163	**Trading across borders** (rank)		130
Procedures (number)	13	Procedures (number)	6	Documents to export (number)		7
Time (days)	41	Time (days)	104	Time to export (days)		33
Cost (% of income per capita)	139.2	Cost (% of property value)	13.9	Cost to export (US$ per container)		855
Minimum capital (% of income per capita)	489.7			Documents to import (number)		9
		Getting credit (rank)	167	Time to import (days)		32
Dealing with construction permits (rank)	170	Strength of legal rights index (0-10)	3	Cost to import (US$ per container)		1,391
Procedures (number)	32	Depth of credit information index (0-6)	0			
Time (days)	255	Public registry coverage (% of adults)	0.0	**Enforcing contracts** (rank)		131
Cost (% of income per capita)	249.6	Private bureau coverage (% of adults)	0.0	Procedures (number)		50
				Time (days)		276
Employing workers (rank)	79	**Protecting investors** (rank)	172	Cost (% of claim)		45.0
Difficulty of hiring index (0-100)	33	Extent of disclosure index (0-10)	6			
Rigidity of hours index (0-100)	20	Extent of director liability index (0-10)	1	**Closing a business** (rank)		111
Difficulty of redundancy index (0-100)	20	Ease of shareholder suits index (0-10)	1	Time (years)		3.8
Rigidity of employment index (0-100)	24	Strength of investor protection index (0-10)	2.7	Cost (% of estate)		8
Redundancy cost (weeks of salary)	26			Recovery rate (cents on the dollar)		22.0
		Paying taxes (rank)	171			
		Payments (number per year)	56			
		Time (hours per year)	416			
		Total tax rate (% of profit)	49.9			

GUINEA-BISSAU

		Sub-Saharan Africa			GNI per capita (US$)	245
Ease of doing business (rank)	181	Low income			Population (m)	1.6
✔ **Starting a business** (rank)	183	**Registering property** (rank)	177		**Trading across borders** (rank)	115
Procedures (number)	16	Procedures (number)	9		Documents to export (number)	6
Time (days)	213	Time (days)	211		Time to export (days)	23
Cost (% of income per capita)	323.0	Cost (% of property value)	7.6		Cost to export (US$ per container)	1,545
Minimum capital (% of income per capita)	779.9				Documents to import (number)	6
		Getting credit (rank)	150		Time to import (days)	22
Dealing with construction permits (rank)	114	Strength of legal rights index (0-10)	3		Cost to import (US$ per container)	2,349
Procedures (number)	15	Depth of credit information index (0-6)	1			
Time (days)	167	Public registry coverage (% of adults)	1.1		**Enforcing contracts** (rank)	143
Cost (% of income per capita)	2,020.0	Private bureau coverage (% of adults)	0.0		Procedures (number)	41
					Time (days)	1,140
Employing workers (rank)	175	**Protecting investors** (rank)	132		Cost (% of claim)	25.0
Difficulty of hiring index (0-100)	67	Extent of disclosure index (0-10)	6			
Rigidity of hours index (0-100)	27	Extent of director liability index (0-10)	1		**Closing a business** (rank)	183
Difficulty of redundancy index (0-100)	70	Ease of shareholder suits index (0-10)	5		Time (years)	NO PRACTICE
Rigidity of employment index (0-100)	54	Strength of investor protection index (0-10)	4.0		Cost (% of estate)	NO PRACTICE
Redundancy cost (weeks of salary)	87				Recovery rate (cents on the dollar)	0.0
		Paying taxes (rank)	129			
		Payments (number per year)	46			
		Time (hours per year)	208			
		Total tax rate (% of profit)	45.9			

GUYANA

		Latin America & Caribbean			GNI per capita (US$)	1,416
Ease of doing business (rank)	101	Lower middle income			Population (m)	0.8
✔ **Starting a business** (rank)	97	**Registering property** (rank)	72		✔ **Trading across borders** (rank)	76
Procedures (number)	8	Procedures (number)	6		Documents to export (number)	7
Time (days)	34	Time (days)	34		Time to export (days)	20
Cost (% of income per capita)	32.8	Cost (% of property value)	4.5		Cost to export (US$ per container)	730
Minimum capital (% of income per capita)	0.0				Documents to import (number)	8
		Getting credit (rank)	150		Time to import (days)	24
Dealing with construction permits (rank)	39	Strength of legal rights index (0-10)	4		Cost to import (US$ per container)	730
Procedures (number)	11	Depth of credit information index (0-6)	0			
Time (days)	133	Public registry coverage (% of adults)	0.0		**Enforcing contracts** (rank)	75
Cost (% of income per capita)	229.3	Private bureau coverage (% of adults)	0.0		Procedures (number)	36
					Time (days)	581
Employing workers (rank)	87	**Protecting investors** (rank)	73		Cost (% of claim)	25.2
Difficulty of hiring index (0-100)	22	Extent of disclosure index (0-10)	5			
Rigidity of hours index (0-100)	13	Extent of director liability index (0-10)	5		**Closing a business** (rank)	129
Difficulty of redundancy index (0-100)	20	Ease of shareholder suits index (0-10)	6		Time (years)	3.0
Rigidity of employment index (0-100)	19	Strength of investor protection index (0-10)	5.3		Cost (% of estate)	29
Redundancy cost (weeks of salary)	56				Recovery rate (cents on the dollar)	17.6
		Paying taxes (rank)	113			
		Payments (number per year)	34			
		Time (hours per year)	288			
		Total tax rate (% of profit)	38.9			

HAITI

		Latin America & Caribbean			GNI per capita (US$)	661
Ease of doing business (rank)	151	Low income			Population (m)	9.8
Starting a business (rank)	180	**Registering property** (rank)	129		✔ **Trading across borders** (rank)	144
Procedures (number)	13	Procedures (number)	5		Documents to export (number)	8
Time (days)	195	Time (days)	405		Time to export (days)	35
Cost (% of income per capita)	227.9	Cost (% of property value)	6.4		Cost to export (US$ per container)	1,005
Minimum capital (% of income per capita)	22.4				Documents to import (number)	10
		✔ **Getting credit** (rank)	135		Time to import (days)	33
Dealing with construction permits (rank)	126	Strength of legal rights index (0-10)	3		Cost to import (US$ per container)	1,545
Procedures (number)	11	Depth of credit information index (0-6)	2			
Time (days)	1,179	Public registry coverage (% of adults)	0.7		**Enforcing contracts** (rank)	92
Cost (% of income per capita)	569.5	Private bureau coverage (% of adults)	0.0		Procedures (number)	35
					Time (days)	508
Employing workers (rank)	28	**Protecting investors** (rank)	165		Cost (% of claim)	42.6
Difficulty of hiring index (0-100)	11	Extent of disclosure index (0-10)	2			
Rigidity of hours index (0-100)	20	Extent of director liability index (0-10)	3		**Closing a business** (rank)	155
Difficulty of redundancy index (0-100)	0	Ease of shareholder suits index (0-10)	4		Time (years)	5.7
Rigidity of employment index (0-100)	10	Strength of investor protection index (0-10)	3.0		Cost (% of estate)	30
Redundancy cost (weeks of salary)	17				Recovery rate (cents on the dollar)	2.7
		Paying taxes (rank)	99			
		Payments (number per year)	42			
		Time (hours per year)	160			
		Total tax rate (% of profit)	40.1			

HONDURAS

		Latin America & Caribbean		GNI per capita (US$)	1,799
Ease of doing business (rank)	141	Lower middle income		Population (m)	7.2
✔ **Starting a business** (rank)	144	**Registering property** (rank)	91	**Trading across borders** (rank)	114
Procedures (number)	13	Procedures (number)	7	Documents to export (number)	7
Time (days)	14	Time (days)	23	Time to export (days)	20
Cost (% of income per capita)	47.3	Cost (% of property value)	5.5	Cost to export (US$ per container)	1,163
Minimum capital (% of income per capita)	17.3			Documents to import (number)	10
		✔ **Getting credit** (rank)	30	Time to import (days)	23
✔ **Dealing with construction permits** (rank)	74	Strength of legal rights index (0-10)	6	Cost to import (US$ per container)	1,190
Procedures (number)	17	Depth of credit information index (0-6)	6		
Time (days)	106	Public registry coverage (% of adults)	21.7	**Enforcing contracts** (rank)	175
Cost (% of income per capita)	465.1	Private bureau coverage (% of adults)	58.7	Procedures (number)	45
				Time (days)	900
✘ **Employing workers** (rank)	168	**Protecting investors** (rank)	165	Cost (% of claim)	35.2
Difficulty of hiring index (0-100)	100	Extent of disclosure index (0-10)	0		
Rigidity of hours index (0-100)	20	Extent of director liability index (0-10)	5	**Closing a business** (rank)	118
Difficulty of redundancy index (0-100)	50	Ease of shareholder suits index (0-10)	4	Time (years)	3.8
Rigidity of employment index (0-100)	57	Strength of investor protection index (0-10)	3.0	Cost (% of estate)	15
Redundancy cost (weeks of salary)	95			Recovery rate (cents on the dollar)	20.8
		Paying taxes (rank)	146		
		Payments (number per year)	47		
		Time (hours per year)	224		
		Total tax rate (% of profit)	48.3		

HONG KONG, CHINA

		East Asia & Pacific		GNI per capita (US$)	31,422
Ease of doing business (rank)	3	High income		Population (m)	7.0
✔ **Starting a business** (rank)	18	✔ **Registering property** (rank)	75	**Trading across borders** (rank)	2
Procedures (number)	3	Procedures (number)	5	Documents to export (number)	4
Time (days)	6	Time (days)	45	Time to export (days)	6
Cost (% of income per capita)	1.8	Cost (% of property value)	5.0	Cost to export (US$ per container)	625
Minimum capital (% of income per capita)	0.0			Documents to import (number)	4
		Getting credit (rank)	4	Time to import (days)	5
✔ **Dealing with construction permits** (rank)	1	Strength of legal rights index (0-10)	10	Cost to import (US$ per container)	583
Procedures (number)	7	Depth of credit information index (0-6)	4		
Time (days)	67	Public registry coverage (% of adults)	0.0	**Enforcing contracts** (rank)	3
Cost (% of income per capita)	18.7	Private bureau coverage (% of adults)	71.9	Procedures (number)	24
				Time (days)	280
Employing workers (rank)	6	**Protecting investors** (rank)	3	Cost (% of claim)	19.5
Difficulty of hiring index (0-100)	0	Extent of disclosure index (0-10)	10		
Rigidity of hours index (0-100)	0	Extent of director liability index (0-10)	8	**Closing a business** (rank)	13
Difficulty of redundancy index (0-100)	0	Ease of shareholder suits index (0-10)	9	Time (years)	1.1
Rigidity of employment index (0-100)	0	Strength of investor protection index (0-10)	9.0	Cost (% of estate)	9
Redundancy cost (weeks of salary)	10			Recovery rate (cents on the dollar)	79.8
		Paying taxes (rank)	3		
		Payments (number per year)	4		
		Time (hours per year)	80		
		Total tax rate (% of profit)	24.2		

HUNGARY

		OECD high income		GNI per capita (US$)	12,810
Ease of doing business (rank)	47	High income		Population (m)	10.0
✔ **Starting a business** (rank)	39	**Registering property** (rank)	61	**Trading across borders** (rank)	70
Procedures (number)	4	Procedures (number)	4	Documents to export (number)	5
Time (days)	4	Time (days)	17	Time to export (days)	18
Cost (% of income per capita)	8.0	Cost (% of property value)	11.0	Cost to export (US$ per container)	1,225
Minimum capital (% of income per capita)	10.2			Documents to import (number)	7
		Getting credit (rank)	30	Time to import (days)	17
Dealing with construction permits (rank)	88	Strength of legal rights index (0-10)	7	Cost to import (US$ per container)	1,215
Procedures (number)	31	Depth of credit information index (0-6)	5		
Time (days)	204	Public registry coverage (% of adults)	0.0	**Enforcing contracts** (rank)	14
Cost (% of income per capita)	9.8	Private bureau coverage (% of adults)	10.3	Procedures (number)	33
				Time (days)	395
Employing workers (rank)	77	**Protecting investors** (rank)	119	Cost (% of claim)	13.0
Difficulty of hiring index (0-100)	0	Extent of disclosure index (0-10)	2		
Rigidity of hours index (0-100)	67	Extent of director liability index (0-10)	4	**Closing a business** (rank)	58
Difficulty of redundancy index (0-100)	0	Ease of shareholder suits index (0-10)	7	Time (years)	2.0
Rigidity of employment index (0-100)	22	Strength of investor protection index (0-10)	4.3	Cost (% of estate)	15
Redundancy cost (weeks of salary)	35			Recovery rate (cents on the dollar)	38.4
		Paying taxes (rank)	122		
		Payments (number per year)	14		
		Time (hours per year)	330		
		Total tax rate (% of profit)	57.5		

ICELAND

		OECD high income		GNI per capita (US$)	40,074
Ease of doing business (rank)	14	High income		Population (m)	0.3
Starting a business (rank)	33	**Registering property** (rank)	13	**Trading across borders** (rank)	73
Procedures (number)	5	Procedures (number)	3	Documents to export (number)	5
Time (days)	5	Time (days)	4	Time to export (days)	19
Cost (% of income per capita)	3.0	Cost (% of property value)	2.4	Cost to export (US$ per container)	1,532
Minimum capital (% of income per capita)	15.8			Documents to import (number)	5
		Getting credit (rank)	30	Time to import (days)	14
		Strength of legal rights index (0-10)	7	Cost to import (US$ per container)	1,674
Dealing with construction permits (rank)	31	Depth of credit information index (0-6)	5		
Procedures (number)	18	Public registry coverage (% of adults)	0.0	**Enforcing contracts** (rank)	2
Time (days)	75	Private bureau coverage (% of adults)	100.0	Procedures (number)	26
Cost (% of income per capita)	22.2			Time (days)	417
		Protecting investors (rank)	73	Cost (% of claim)	6.2
Employing workers (rank)	56	Extent of disclosure index (0-10)	5		
Difficulty of hiring index (0-100)	44	Extent of director liability index (0-10)	5	**Closing a business** (rank)	16
Rigidity of hours index (0-100)	20	Ease of shareholder suits index (0-10)	6	Time (years)	1.0
Difficulty of redundancy index (0-100)	0	Strength of investor protection index (0-10)	5.3	Cost (% of estate)	4
Rigidity of employment index (0-100)	21			Recovery rate (cents on the dollar)	76.6
Redundancy cost (weeks of salary)	13	**✔ Paying taxes** (rank)	31		
		Payments (number per year)	31		
		Time (hours per year)	140		
		Total tax rate (% of profit)	25.0		

INDIA

		South Asia		GNI per capita (US$)	1,066
Ease of doing business (rank)	133	Lower middle income		Population (m)	1,140.0
Starting a business (rank)	169	**Registering property** (rank)	93	**Trading across borders** (rank)	94
Procedures (number)	13	Procedures (number)	5	Documents to export (number)	8
Time (days)	30	Time (days)	44	Time to export (days)	17
Cost (% of income per capita)	66.1	Cost (% of property value)	7.4	Cost to export (US$ per container)	945
Minimum capital (% of income per capita)	210.9			Documents to import (number)	9
		Getting credit (rank)	30	Time to import (days)	20
		Strength of legal rights index (0-10)	8	Cost to import (US$ per container)	960
Dealing with construction permits (rank)	175	Depth of credit information index (0-6)	4		
Procedures (number)	37	Public registry coverage (% of adults)	0.0	**Enforcing contracts** (rank)	182
Time (days)	195	Private bureau coverage (% of adults)	10.2	Procedures (number)	46
Cost (% of income per capita)	2,394.9			Time (days)	1,420
		Protecting investors (rank)	41	Cost (% of claim)	39.6
Employing workers (rank)	104	Extent of disclosure index (0-10)	7		
Difficulty of hiring index (0-100)	0	Extent of director liability index (0-10)	4	**✔ Closing a business** (rank)	138
Rigidity of hours index (0-100)	20	Ease of shareholder suits index (0-10)	7	Time (years)	7.0
Difficulty of redundancy index (0-100)	70	Strength of investor protection index (0-10)	6.0	Cost (% of estate)	9
Rigidity of employment index (0-100)	30			Recovery rate (cents on the dollar)	15.1
Redundancy cost (weeks of salary)	56	**Paying taxes** (rank)	169		
		Payments (number per year)	59		
		Time (hours per year)	271		
		Total tax rate (% of profit)	64.7		

INDONESIA

		East Asia & Pacific		GNI per capita (US$)	2,007
Ease of doing business (rank)	122	Lower middle income		Population (m)	228.2
✔ Starting a business (rank)	161	**✔ Registering property** (rank)	95	**Trading across borders** (rank)	45
Procedures (number)	9	Procedures (number)	6	Documents to export (number)	5
Time (days)	60	Time (days)	22	Time to export (days)	21
Cost (% of income per capita)	26.0	Cost (% of property value)	10.7	Cost to export (US$ per container)	704
Minimum capital (% of income per capita)	59.7			Documents to import (number)	6
		Getting credit (rank)	113	Time to import (days)	27
		Strength of legal rights index (0-10)	3	Cost to import (US$ per container)	660
Dealing with construction permits (rank)	61	Depth of credit information index (0-6)	4		
Procedures (number)	14	Public registry coverage (% of adults)	22.0	**Enforcing contracts** (rank)	146
Time (days)	160	Private bureau coverage (% of adults)	0.0	Procedures (number)	39
Cost (% of income per capita)	194.8			Time (days)	570
		✔ Protecting investors (rank)	41	Cost (% of claim)	122.7
Employing workers (rank)	149	Extent of disclosure index (0-10)	10		
Difficulty of hiring index (0-100)	61	Extent of director liability index (0-10)	5	**Closing a business** (rank)	142
Rigidity of hours index (0-100)	0	Ease of shareholder suits index (0-10)	3	Time (years)	5.5
Difficulty of redundancy index (0-100)	60	Strength of investor protection index (0-10)	6.0	Cost (% of estate)	18
Rigidity of employment index (0-100)	40			Recovery rate (cents on the dollar)	13.7
Redundancy cost (weeks of salary)	108	**Paying taxes** (rank)	126		
		Payments (number per year)	51		
		Time (hours per year)	266		
		Total tax rate (% of profit)	37.6		

✔ Reforms making it easier to do business ✘ Reforms making it more difficult to do business

IRAN, ISLAMIC REP.

		Middle East & North Africa		GNI per capita (US$)	4,732
Ease of doing business (rank)	137	Lower middle income		Population (m)	72.0
✔ **Starting a business** (rank)	48	**Registering property** (rank)	153	✔ **Trading across borders** (rank)	134
Procedures (number)	7	Procedures (number)	9	Documents to export (number)	7
Time (days)	9	Time (days)	36	Time to export (days)	25
Cost (% of income per capita)	3.9	Cost (% of property value)	10.5	Cost to export (US$ per container)	1,061
Minimum capital (% of income per capita)	0.8			Documents to import (number)	8
		Getting credit (rank)	113	Time to import (days)	38
✔ **Dealing with construction permits** (rank)	141	Strength of legal rights index (0-10)	4	Cost to import (US$ per container)	1,706
Procedures (number)	17	Depth of credit information index (0-6)	3		
Time (days)	322	Public registry coverage (% of adults)	31.3	**Enforcing contracts** (rank)	53
Cost (% of income per capita)	365.9	Private bureau coverage (% of adults)	0.0	Procedures (number)	39
				Time (days)	520
Employing workers (rank)	137	**Protecting investors** (rank)	165	Cost (% of claim)	17.0
Difficulty of hiring index (0-100)	11	Extent of disclosure index (0-10)	5		
Rigidity of hours index (0-100)	27	Extent of director liability index (0-10)	4	**Closing a business** (rank)	109
Difficulty of redundancy index (0-100)	50	Ease of shareholder suits index (0-10)	0	Time (years)	4.5
Rigidity of employment index (0-100)	29	Strength of investor protection index (0-10)	3.0	Cost (% of estate)	9
Redundancy cost (weeks of salary)	87			Recovery rate (cents on the dollar)	23.1
		✔ **Paying taxes** (rank)	117		
		Payments (number per year)	22		
		Time (hours per year)	344		
		Total tax rate (% of profit)	44.2		

IRAQ

		Middle East & North Africa		GNI per capita (US$)	2,815
Ease of doing business (rank)	153	Lower middle income		Population (m)	30.1
Starting a business (rank)	175	**Registering property** (rank)	53	**Trading across borders** (rank)	180
Procedures (number)	11	Procedures (number)	5	Documents to export (number)	10
Time (days)	77	Time (days)	8	Time to export (days)	102
Cost (% of income per capita)	75.9	Cost (% of property value)	7.7	Cost to export (US$ per container)	3,900
Minimum capital (% of income per capita)	30.3			Documents to import (number)	10
		Getting credit (rank)	167	Time to import (days)	101
Dealing with construction permits (rank)	94	Strength of legal rights index (0-10)	3	Cost to import (US$ per container)	3,900
Procedures (number)	14	Depth of credit information index (0-6)	0		
Time (days)	215	Public registry coverage (% of adults)	0.0	**Enforcing contracts** (rank)	139
Cost (% of income per capita)	397.9	Private bureau coverage (% of adults)	0.0	Procedures (number)	51
				Time (days)	520
Employing workers (rank)	59	**Protecting investors** (rank)	119	Cost (% of claim)	27.3
Difficulty of hiring index (0-100)	33	Extent of disclosure index (0-10)	4		
Rigidity of hours index (0-100)	20	Extent of director liability index (0-10)	5	**Closing a business** (rank)	183
Difficulty of redundancy index (0-100)	20	Ease of shareholder suits index (0-10)	4	Time (years)	NO PRACTICE
Rigidity of employment index (0-100)	24	Strength of investor protection index (0-10)	4.3	Cost (% of estate)	NO PRACTICE
Redundancy cost (weeks of salary)	0			Recovery rate (cents on the dollar)	0.0
		Paying taxes (rank)	53		
		Payments (number per year)	13		
		Time (hours per year)	312		
		Total tax rate (% of profit)	28.4		

IRELAND

		OECD high income		GNI per capita (US$)	49,592
Ease of doing business (rank)	7	High income		Population (m)	4.5
Starting a business (rank)	9	✔ **Registering property** (rank)	79	**Trading across borders** (rank)	21
Procedures (number)	4	Procedures (number)	5	Documents to export (number)	4
Time (days)	13	Time (days)	38	Time to export (days)	7
Cost (% of income per capita)	0.3	Cost (% of property value)	6.7	Cost to export (US$ per container)	1,109
Minimum capital (% of income per capita)	0.0			Documents to import (number)	4
		Getting credit (rank)	15	Time to import (days)	12
Dealing with construction permits (rank)	30	Strength of legal rights index (0-10)	8	Cost to import (US$ per container)	1,121
Procedures (number)	11	Depth of credit information index (0-6)	5		
Time (days)	185	Public registry coverage (% of adults)	0.0	**Enforcing contracts** (rank)	37
Cost (% of income per capita)	44.8	Private bureau coverage (% of adults)	100.0	Procedures (number)	20
				Time (days)	515
Employing workers (rank)	27	**Protecting investors** (rank)	5	Cost (% of claim)	26.9
Difficulty of hiring index (0-100)	11	Extent of disclosure index (0-10)	10		
Rigidity of hours index (0-100)	0	Extent of director liability index (0-10)	6	**Closing a business** (rank)	6
Difficulty of redundancy index (0-100)	20	Ease of shareholder suits index (0-10)	9	Time (years)	0.4
Rigidity of employment index (0-100)	10	Strength of investor protection index (0-10)	8.3	Cost (% of estate)	9
Redundancy cost (weeks of salary)	18			Recovery rate (cents on the dollar)	86.6
		Paying taxes (rank)	6		
		Payments (number per year)	9		
		Time (hours per year)	76		
		Total tax rate (% of profit)	26.5		

ISRAEL

		Middle East & North Africa		GNI per capita (US$)	24,698
Ease of doing business (rank)	29	High income		Population (m)	7.3

Starting a business (rank)	34	**Registering property** (rank)	147	**Trading across borders** (rank)	11
Procedures (number)	5	Procedures (number)	7	Documents to export (number)	5
Time (days)	34	Time (days)	144	Time to export (days)	12
Cost (% of income per capita)	4.2	Cost (% of property value)	5.0	Cost to export (US$ per container)	665
Minimum capital (% of income per capita)	0.0			Documents to import (number)	4
		Getting credit (rank)	4	Time to import (days)	12
Dealing with construction permits (rank)	120	Strength of legal rights index (0-10)	9	Cost to import (US$ per container)	605
Procedures (number)	20	Depth of credit information index (0-6)	5		
Time (days)	235	Public registry coverage (% of adults)	0.0	**Enforcing contracts** (rank)	99
Cost (% of income per capita)	107.2	Private bureau coverage (% of adults)	89.8	Procedures (number)	35
				Time (days)	890
Employing workers (rank)	90	**Protecting investors** (rank)	5	Cost (% of claim)	25.3
Difficulty of hiring index (0-100)	11	Extent of disclosure index (0-10)	7		
Rigidity of hours index (0-100)	40	Extent of director liability index (0-10)	9	**Closing a business** (rank)	41
Difficulty of redundancy index (0-100)	0	Ease of shareholder suits index (0-10)	9	Time (years)	4.0
Rigidity of employment index (0-100)	17	Strength of investor protection index (0-10)	8.3	Cost (% of estate)	23
Redundancy cost (weeks of salary)	91			Recovery rate (cents on the dollar)	44.9
		✔ **Paying taxes** (rank)	83		
		Payments (number per year)	33		
		Time (hours per year)	230		
		Total tax rate (% of profit)	32.6		

ITALY

		OECD high income		GNI per capita (US$)	35,236
Ease of doing business (rank)	78	High income		Population (m)	59.9

Starting a business (rank)	75	**Registering property** (rank)	98	**Trading across borders** (rank)	50
Procedures (number)	6	Procedures (number)	8	Documents to export (number)	4
Time (days)	10	Time (days)	27	Time to export (days)	20
Cost (% of income per capita)	17.9	Cost (% of property value)	4.6	Cost to export (US$ per container)	1,231
Minimum capital (% of income per capita)	9.7			Documents to import (number)	4
		Getting credit (rank)	87	Time to import (days)	18
Dealing with construction permits (rank)	85	Strength of legal rights index (0-10)	3	Cost to import (US$ per container)	1,231
Procedures (number)	14	Depth of credit information index (0-6)	5		
Time (days)	257	Public registry coverage (% of adults)	12.2	**Enforcing contracts** (rank)	156
Cost (% of income per capita)	137.2	Private bureau coverage (% of adults)	77.5	Procedures (number)	40
				Time (days)	1,210
Employing workers (rank)	99	**Protecting investors** (rank)	57	Cost (% of claim)	29.9
Difficulty of hiring index (0-100)	33	Extent of disclosure index (0-10)	7		
Rigidity of hours index (0-100)	40	Extent of director liability index (0-10)	4	**Closing a business** (rank)	29
Difficulty of redundancy index (0-100)	40	Ease of shareholder suits index (0-10)	6	Time (years)	1.8
Rigidity of employment index (0-100)	38	Strength of investor protection index (0-10)	5.7	Cost (% of estate)	22
Redundancy cost (weeks of salary)	11			Recovery rate (cents on the dollar)	56.6
		Paying taxes (rank)	135		
		Payments (number per year)	15		
		Time (hours per year)	334		
		Total tax rate (% of profit)	68.4		

JAMAICA

		Latin America & Caribbean		GNI per capita (US$)	4,871
Ease of doing business (rank)	75	Upper middle income		Population (m)	2.7

Starting a business (rank)	19	✔ **Registering property** (rank)	122	**Trading across borders** (rank)	104
Procedures (number)	6	Procedures (number)	6	Documents to export (number)	6
Time (days)	8	Time (days)	55	Time to export (days)	21
Cost (% of income per capita)	5.3	Cost (% of property value)	9.5	Cost to export (US$ per container)	1,750
Minimum capital (% of income per capita)	0.0			Documents to import (number)	6
		Getting credit (rank)	87	Time to import (days)	22
Dealing with construction permits (rank)	49	Strength of legal rights index (0-10)	8	Cost to import (US$ per container)	1,420
Procedures (number)	10	Depth of credit information index (0-6)	0		
Time (days)	156	Public registry coverage (% of adults)	0.0	**Enforcing contracts** (rank)	128
Cost (% of income per capita)	265.7	Private bureau coverage (% of adults)	0.0	Procedures (number)	35
				Time (days)	655
Employing workers (rank)	39	**Protecting investors** (rank)	73	Cost (% of claim)	45.6
Difficulty of hiring index (0-100)	11	Extent of disclosure index (0-10)	4		
Rigidity of hours index (0-100)	0	Extent of director liability index (0-10)	8	**Closing a business** (rank)	23
Difficulty of redundancy index (0-100)	0	Ease of shareholder suits index (0-10)	4	Time (years)	1.1
Rigidity of employment index (0-100)	4	Strength of investor protection index (0-10)	5.3	Cost (% of estate)	18
Redundancy cost (weeks of salary)	62			Recovery rate (cents on the dollar)	64.5
		Paying taxes (rank)	174		
		Payments (number per year)	72		
		Time (hours per year)	414		
		Total tax rate (% of profit)	51.3		

✔ Reforms making it easier to do business   ✗ Reforms making it more difficult to do business

JAPAN

		OECD high income		GNI per capita (US$)	38,207
Ease of doing business (rank)	15	High income		Population (m)	127.7
Starting a business (rank)	91	**Registering property** (rank)	54	**Trading across borders** (rank)	17
Procedures (number)	8	Procedures (number)	6	Documents to export (number)	4
Time (days)	23	Time (days)	14	Time to export (days)	10
Cost (% of income per capita)	7.5	Cost (% of property value)	5.0	Cost to export (US$ per container)	989
Minimum capital (% of income per capita)	0.0			Documents to import (number)	5
		Getting credit (rank)	15	Time to import (days)	11
Dealing with construction permits (rank)	45	Strength of legal rights index (0-10)	7	Cost to import (US$ per container)	1,047
Procedures (number)	15	Depth of credit information index (0-6)	6		
Time (days)	187	Public registry coverage (% of adults)	0.0	**Enforcing contracts** (rank)	20
Cost (% of income per capita)	19.3	Private bureau coverage (% of adults)	76.2	Procedures (number)	30
				Time (days)	360
Employing workers (rank)	40	**Protecting investors** (rank)	16	Cost (% of claim)	22.7
Difficulty of hiring index (0-100)	11	Extent of disclosure index (0-10)	7		
Rigidity of hours index (0-100)	7	Extent of director liability index (0-10)	6	**Closing a business** (rank)	1
Difficulty of redundancy index (0-100)	30	Ease of shareholder suits index (0-10)	8	Time (years)	0.6
Rigidity of employment index (0-100)	16	Strength of investor protection index (0-10)	7.0	Cost (% of estate)	4
Redundancy cost (weeks of salary)	4			Recovery rate (cents on the dollar)	92.5
		Paying taxes (rank)	123		
		Payments (number per year)	13		
		Time (hours per year)	355		
		Total tax rate (% of profit)	55.7		

JORDAN

		Middle East & North Africa		GNI per capita (US$)	3,306
Ease of doing business (rank)	100	Lower middle income		Population (m)	5.9
✔ **Starting a business** (rank)	125	✔ **Registering property** (rank)	106	✔ **Trading across borders** (rank)	71
Procedures (number)	8	Procedures (number)	7	Documents to export (number)	7
Time (days)	13	Time (days)	21	Time to export (days)	17
Cost (% of income per capita)	49.5	Cost (% of property value)	7.5	Cost to export (US$ per container)	730
Minimum capital (% of income per capita)	19.9			Documents to import (number)	7
		Getting credit (rank)	127	Time to import (days)	19
✔ **Dealing with construction permits** (rank)	92	Strength of legal rights index (0-10)	4	Cost to import (US$ per container)	1,290
Procedures (number)	19	Depth of credit information index (0-6)	2		
Time (days)	87	Public registry coverage (% of adults)	1.0	✔ **Enforcing contracts** (rank)	124
Cost (% of income per capita)	697.1	Private bureau coverage (% of adults)	0.0	Procedures (number)	38
				Time (days)	689
Employing workers (rank)	51	**Protecting investors** (rank)	119	Cost (% of claim)	31.2
Difficulty of hiring index (0-100)	11	Extent of disclosure index (0-10)	5		
Rigidity of hours index (0-100)	0	Extent of director liability index (0-10)	4	**Closing a business** (rank)	96
Difficulty of redundancy index (0-100)	60	Ease of shareholder suits index (0-10)	4	Time (years)	4.3
Rigidity of employment index (0-100)	24	Strength of investor protection index (0-10)	4.3	Cost (% of estate)	9
Redundancy cost (weeks of salary)	4			Recovery rate (cents on the dollar)	27.3
		✔ **Paying taxes** (rank)	26		
		Payments (number per year)	26		
		Time (hours per year)	101		
		Total tax rate (% of profit)	31.1		

KAZAKHSTAN

		Eastern Europe & Central Asia		GNI per capita (US$)	6,140
Ease of doing business (rank)	63	Upper middle income		Population (m)	15.7
✔ **Starting a business** (rank)	82	**Registering property** (rank)	31	**Trading across borders** (rank)	182
Procedures (number)	7	Procedures (number)	5	Documents to export (number)	11
Time (days)	20	Time (days)	40	Time to export (days)	89
Cost (% of income per capita)	4.8	Cost (% of property value)	0.1	Cost to export (US$ per container)	3,005
Minimum capital (% of income per capita)	13.4			Documents to import (number)	13
		Getting credit (rank)	43	Time to import (days)	76
✔ **Dealing with construction permits** (rank)	143	Strength of legal rights index (0-10)	5	Cost to import (US$ per container)	3,055
Procedures (number)	37	Depth of credit information index (0-6)	6		
Time (days)	211	Public registry coverage (% of adults)	0.0	**Enforcing contracts** (rank)	34
Cost (% of income per capita)	119.7	Private bureau coverage (% of adults)	29.5	Procedures (number)	38
				Time (days)	390
Employing workers (rank)	38	**Protecting investors** (rank)	57	Cost (% of claim)	22.0
Difficulty of hiring index (0-100)	0	Extent of disclosure index (0-10)	7		
Rigidity of hours index (0-100)	20	Extent of director liability index (0-10)	1	**Closing a business** (rank)	54
Difficulty of redundancy index (0-100)	30	Ease of shareholder suits index (0-10)	9	Time (years)	1.5
Rigidity of employment index (0-100)	17	Strength of investor protection index (0-10)	5.7	Cost (% of estate)	15
Redundancy cost (weeks of salary)	9			Recovery rate (cents on the dollar)	40.6
		✔ **Paying taxes** (rank)	52		
		Payments (number per year)	9		
		Time (hours per year)	271		
		Total tax rate (% of profit)	35.9		

KENYA

		Sub-Saharan Africa		GNI per capita (US$)	767
Ease of doing business (rank)	95	Low income		Population (m)	38.5
Starting a business (rank)	124	**Registering property** (rank)	125	**Trading across borders** (rank)	147
Procedures (number)	12	Procedures (number)	8	Documents to export (number)	9
Time (days)	34	Time (days)	64	Time to export (days)	27
Cost (% of income per capita)	36.5	Cost (% of property value)	4.2	Cost to export (US$ per container)	2,055
Minimum capital (% of income per capita)	0.0			Documents to import (number)	8
		✔ **Getting credit** (rank)	4	Time to import (days)	25
✗ **Dealing with construction permits** (rank)	34	Strength of legal rights index (0-10)	10	Cost to import (US$ per container)	2,190
Procedures (number)	11	Depth of credit information index (0-6)	4		
Time (days)	120	Public registry coverage (% of adults)	0.0	**Enforcing contracts** (rank)	126
Cost (% of income per capita)	161.7	Private bureau coverage (% of adults)	2.3	Procedures (number)	40
				Time (days)	465
Employing workers (rank)	78	**Protecting investors** (rank)	93	Cost (% of claim)	47.2
Difficulty of hiring index (0-100)	22	Extent of disclosure index (0-10)	3		
Rigidity of hours index (0-100)	0	Extent of director liability index (0-10)	2	**Closing a business** (rank)	79
Difficulty of redundancy index (0-100)	30	Ease of shareholder suits index (0-10)	10	Time (years)	4.5
Rigidity of employment index (0-100)	17	Strength of investor protection index (0-10)	5.0	Cost (% of estate)	22
Redundancy cost (weeks of salary)	47			Recovery rate (cents on the dollar)	31.6
		Paying taxes (rank)	164		
		Payments (number per year)	41		
		Time (hours per year)	417		
		Total tax rate (% of profit)	49.7		

KIRIBATI

		East Asia & Pacific		GNI per capita (US$)	1,995
Ease of doing business (rank)	79	Lower middle income		Population (m)	0.1
Starting a business (rank)	119	**Registering property** (rank)	66	**Trading across borders** (rank)	77
Procedures (number)	6	Procedures (number)	5	Documents to export (number)	6
Time (days)	21	Time (days)	513	Time to export (days)	21
Cost (% of income per capita)	38.0	Cost (% of property value)	0.0	Cost to export (US$ per container)	1,070
Minimum capital (% of income per capita)	20.5			Documents to import (number)	7
		Getting credit (rank)	135	Time to import (days)	21
Dealing with construction permits (rank)	71	Strength of legal rights index (0-10)	5	Cost to import (US$ per container)	1,070
Procedures (number)	14	Depth of credit information index (0-6)	0		
Time (days)	160	Public registry coverage (% of adults)	0.0	**Enforcing contracts** (rank)	80
Cost (% of income per capita)	422.1	Private bureau coverage (% of adults)	0.0	Procedures (number)	32
				Time (days)	660
Employing workers (rank)	29	**Protecting investors** (rank)	41	Cost (% of claim)	25.8
Difficulty of hiring index (0-100)	0	Extent of disclosure index (0-10)	6		
Rigidity of hours index (0-100)	0	Extent of director liability index (0-10)	5	**Closing a business** (rank)	183
Difficulty of redundancy index (0-100)	50	Ease of shareholder suits index (0-10)	7	Time (years)	NO PRACTICE
Rigidity of employment index (0-100)	17	Strength of investor protection index (0-10)	6.0	Cost (% of estate)	NO PRACTICE
Redundancy cost (weeks of salary)	4			Recovery rate (cents on the dollar)	0.0
		Paying taxes (rank)	10		
		Payments (number per year)	7		
		Time (hours per year)	120		
		Total tax rate (% of profit)	31.8		

KOREA, REP.

		OECD high income		GNI per capita (US$)	21,525
Ease of doing business (rank)	19	High income		Population (m)	48.6
✔ **Starting a business** (rank)	53	**Registering property** (rank)	71	**Trading across borders** (rank)	8
Procedures (number)	8	Procedures (number)	7	Documents to export (number)	3
Time (days)	14	Time (days)	11	Time to export (days)	8
Cost (% of income per capita)	14.7	Cost (% of property value)	5.1	Cost to export (US$ per container)	742
Minimum capital (% of income per capita)	0.0			Documents to import (number)	3
		Getting credit (rank)	15	Time to import (days)	8
Dealing with construction permits (rank)	23	Strength of legal rights index (0-10)	7	Cost to import (US$ per container)	742
Procedures (number)	13	Depth of credit information index (0-6)	6		
Time (days)	34	Public registry coverage (% of adults)	0.0	**Enforcing contracts** (rank)	5
Cost (% of income per capita)	135.6	Private bureau coverage (% of adults)	93.8	Procedures (number)	35
				Time (days)	230
Employing workers (rank)	150	**Protecting investors** (rank)	73	Cost (% of claim)	10.3
Difficulty of hiring index (0-100)	44	Extent of disclosure index (0-10)	7		
Rigidity of hours index (0-100)	40	Extent of director liability index (0-10)	2	**Closing a business** (rank)	12
Difficulty of redundancy index (0-100)	30	Ease of shareholder suits index (0-10)	7	Time (years)	1.5
Rigidity of employment index (0-100)	38	Strength of investor protection index (0-10)	5.3	Cost (% of estate)	4
Redundancy cost (weeks of salary)	91			Recovery rate (cents on the dollar)	80.5
		✔ **Paying taxes** (rank)	49		
		Payments (number per year)	14		
		Time (hours per year)	250		
		Total tax rate (% of profit)	31.9		

✔ Reforms making it easier to do business   ✘ Reforms making it more difficult to do business

KOSOVO

Ease of doing business (rank)	113	Eastern Europe & Central Asia			GNI per capita (US$)		1,800
		Lower middle income			Population (m)		2.1
Starting a business (rank)	164	**Registering property** (rank)	68		**Trading across borders** (rank)		132
Procedures (number)	9	Procedures (number)	8		Documents to export (number)		8
Time (days)	52	Time (days)	33		Time to export (days)		17
Cost (% of income per capita)	43.3	Cost (% of property value)	1.0		Cost to export (US$ per container)		2,270
Minimum capital (% of income per capita)	169.5				Documents to import (number)		8
		Getting credit (rank)	43		Time to import (days)		16
Dealing with construction permits (rank)	176	Strength of legal rights index (0-10)	8		Cost to import (US$ per container)		2,330
Procedures (number)	21	Depth of credit information index (0-6)	3				
Time (days)	320	Public registry coverage (% of adults)	18.9		**Enforcing contracts** (rank)		157
Cost (% of income per capita)	1291.0	Private bureau coverage (% of adults)	0.0		Procedures (number)		53
					Time (days)		420
Employing workers (rank)	34	**Protecting investors** (rank)	172		Cost (% of claim)		61.2
Difficulty of hiring index (0-100)	0	Extent of disclosure index (0-10)	3				
Rigidity of hours index (0-100)	0	Extent of director liability index (0-10)	2		**Closing a business** (rank)		28
Difficulty of redundancy index (0-100)	30	Ease of shareholder suits index (0-10)	3		Time (years)		2
Rigidity of employment index (0-100)	10	Strength of investor protection index (0-10)	2.7		Cost (% of estate)		15
Redundancy cost (weeks of salary)	30				Recovery rate (cents on the dollar)		56.8
		✔ **Paying taxes** (rank)	50				
		Payments (number per year)	33				
		Time (hours per year)	163				
		Total tax rate (% of profit)	28.3				

KUWAIT

Ease of doing business (rank)	61	Middle East & North Africa			GNI per capita (US$)		45,920
		High income			Population (m)		2.7
Starting a business (rank)	137	**Registering property** (rank)	89		✔ **Trading across borders** (rank)		109
Procedures (number)	13	Procedures (number)	8		Documents to export (number)		8
Time (days)	35	Time (days)	55		Time to export (days)		17
Cost (% of income per capita)	1.0	Cost (% of property value)	0.5		Cost to export (US$ per container)		1,060
Minimum capital (% of income per capita)	59.2				Documents to import (number)		10
		Getting credit (rank)	87		Time to import (days)		19
Dealing with construction permits (rank)	81	Strength of legal rights index (0-10)	4		Cost to import (US$ per container)		1,217
Procedures (number)	25	Depth of credit information index (0-6)	4				
Time (days)	104	Public registry coverage (% of adults)	0.0		**Enforcing contracts** (rank)		113
Cost (% of income per capita)	124.1	Private bureau coverage (% of adults)	30.4		Procedures (number)		50
					Time (days)		566
Employing workers (rank)	24	**Protecting investors** (rank)	27		Cost (% of claim)		18.8
Difficulty of hiring index (0-100)	0	Extent of disclosure index (0-10)	7				
Rigidity of hours index (0-100)	0	Extent of director liability index (0-10)	7		✔ **Closing a business** (rank)		69
Difficulty of redundancy index (0-100)	0	Ease of shareholder suits index (0-10)	5		Time (years)		4.2
Rigidity of employment index (0-100)	0	Strength of investor protection index (0-10)	6.3		Cost (% of estate)		1
Redundancy cost (weeks of salary)	78				Recovery rate (cents on the dollar)		34.5
		Paying taxes (rank)	11				
		Payments (number per year)	15				
		Time (hours per year)	118				
		Total tax rate (% of profit)	15.5				

KYRGYZ REPUBLIC

Ease of doing business (rank)	41	Eastern Europe & Central Asia			GNI per capita (US$)		741
		Low income			Population (m)		5.3
✔ **Starting a business** (rank)	14	✔ **Registering property** (rank)	19		✔ **Trading across borders** (rank)		154
Procedures (number)	3	Procedures (number)	4		Documents to export (number)		7
Time (days)	11	Time (days)	5		Time to export (days)		63
Cost (% of income per capita)	5.2	Cost (% of property value)	2.8		Cost to export (US$ per container)		3,000
Minimum capital (% of income per capita)	0.0				Documents to import (number)		7
		✔ **Getting credit** (rank)	15		Time to import (days)		72
✔ **Dealing with construction permits** (rank)	40	Strength of legal rights index (0-10)	10		Cost to import (US$ per container)		3,250
Procedures (number)	12	Depth of credit information index (0-6)	3				
Time (days)	137	Public registry coverage (% of adults)	0.0		**Enforcing contracts** (rank)		54
Cost (% of income per capita)	165.2	Private bureau coverage (% of adults)	5.9		Procedures (number)		39
					Time (days)		260
✔ **Employing workers** (rank)	47	**Protecting investors** (rank)	12		Cost (% of claim)		29.0
Difficulty of hiring index (0-100)	33	Extent of disclosure index (0-10)	8				
Rigidity of hours index (0-100)	20	Extent of director liability index (0-10)	7		**Closing a business** (rank)		140
Difficulty of redundancy index (0-100)	0	Ease of shareholder suits index (0-10)	8		Time (years)		4.0
Rigidity of employment index (0-100)	18	Strength of investor protection index (0-10)	7.7		Cost (% of estate)		15
Redundancy cost (weeks of salary)	17				Recovery rate (cents on the dollar)		14.2
		✔ **Paying taxes** (rank)	156				
		Payments (number per year)	75				
		Time (hours per year)	202				
		Total tax rate (% of profit)	59.4				

LAO PDR

		East Asia & Pacific		GNI per capita (US$)	740
Ease of doing business (rank)	167	Low income		Population (m)	6.2

Starting a business (rank)	89	**Registering property** (rank)	161	**Trading across borders** (rank)	168
Procedures (number)	7	Procedures (number)	9	Documents to export (number)	9
Time (days)	100	Time (days)	135	Time to export (days)	50
Cost (% of income per capita)	12.3	Cost (% of property value)	4.1	Cost to export (US$ per container)	1,860
Minimum capital (% of income per capita)	0.0			Documents to import (number)	10
		Getting credit (rank)	150	Time to import (days)	50
Dealing with construction permits (rank)	115	Strength of legal rights index (0-10)	4	Cost to import (US$ per container)	2,040
Procedures (number)	24	Depth of credit information index (0-6)	0		
Time (days)	172	Public registry coverage (% of adults)	0.0	**Enforcing contracts** (rank)	111
Cost (% of income per capita)	144.0	Private bureau coverage (% of adults)	0.0	Procedures (number)	42
				Time (days)	443
Employing workers (rank)	107	**Protecting investors** (rank)	182	Cost (% of claim)	31.6
Difficulty of hiring index (0-100)	11	Extent of disclosure index (0-10)	0		
Rigidity of hours index (0-100)	0	Extent of director liability index (0-10)	3	**Closing a business** (rank)	183
Difficulty of redundancy index (0-100)	50	Ease of shareholder suits index (0-10)	2	Time (years)	NO PRACTICE
Rigidity of employment index (0-100)	20	Strength of investor protection index (0-10)	1.7	Cost (% of estate)	NO PRACTICE
Redundancy cost (weeks of salary)	162			Recovery rate (cents on the dollar)	0.0
		✔ **Paying taxes** (rank)	113		
		Payments (number per year)	34		
		Time (hours per year)	362		
		Total tax rate (% of profit)	33.7		

LATVIA

		Eastern Europe & Central Asia		GNI per capita (US$)	11,864
Ease of doing business (rank)	27	Upper middle income		Population (m)	2.3

Starting a business (rank)	51	✔ **Registering property** (rank)	58	**Trading across borders** (rank)	22
Procedures (number)	5	Procedures (number)	6	Documents to export (number)	6
Time (days)	16	Time (days)	45	Time to export (days)	13
Cost (% of income per capita)	2.1	Cost (% of property value)	2.0	Cost to export (US$ per container)	600
Minimum capital (% of income per capita)	14.2			Documents to import (number)	6
		✔ **Getting credit** (rank)	4	Time to import (days)	12
Dealing with construction permits (rank)	78	Strength of legal rights index (0-10)	9	Cost to import (US$ per container)	801
Procedures (number)	25	Depth of credit information index (0-6)	5		
Time (days)	187	Public registry coverage (% of adults)	46.5	**Enforcing contracts** (rank)	15
Cost (% of income per capita)	17.3	Private bureau coverage (% of adults)	0.0	Procedures (number)	27
				Time (days)	309
Employing workers (rank)	128	**Protecting investors** (rank)	57	Cost (% of claim)	23.1
Difficulty of hiring index (0-100)	50	Extent of disclosure index (0-10)	5		
Rigidity of hours index (0-100)	40	Extent of director liability index (0-10)	4	**Closing a business** (rank)	88
Difficulty of redundancy index (0-100)	40	Ease of shareholder suits index (0-10)	8	Time (years)	3.0
Rigidity of employment index (0-100)	43	Strength of investor protection index (0-10)	5.7	Cost (% of estate)	13
Redundancy cost (weeks of salary)	17			Recovery rate (cents on the dollar)	29.0
		Paying taxes (rank)	45		
		Payments (number per year)	7		
		Time (hours per year)	279		
		Total tax rate (% of profit)	33.0		

LEBANON

		Middle East & North Africa		GNI per capita (US$)	6,353
Ease of doing business (rank)	108	Upper middle income		Population (m)	4.1

✔ **Starting a business** (rank)	108	**Registering property** (rank)	111	**Trading across borders** (rank)	95
Procedures (number)	5	Procedures (number)	8	Documents to export (number)	5
Time (days)	9	Time (days)	25	Time to export (days)	26
Cost (% of income per capita)	78.2	Cost (% of property value)	5.8	Cost to export (US$ per container)	1,002
Minimum capital (% of income per capita)	51.0			Documents to import (number)	7
		Getting credit (rank)	87	Time to import (days)	35
Dealing with construction permits (rank)	125	Strength of legal rights index (0-10)	3	Cost to import (US$ per container)	1,203
Procedures (number)	20	Depth of credit information index (0-6)	5		
Time (days)	211	Public registry coverage (% of adults)	8.3	**Enforcing contracts** (rank)	121
Cost (% of income per capita)	194.8	Private bureau coverage (% of adults)	0.0	Procedures (number)	37
				Time (days)	721
Employing workers (rank)	66	**Protecting investors** (rank)	93	Cost (% of claim)	30.8
Difficulty of hiring index (0-100)	44	Extent of disclosure index (0-10)	9		
Rigidity of hours index (0-100)	0	Extent of director liability index (0-10)	1	**Closing a business** (rank)	124
Difficulty of redundancy index (0-100)	30	Ease of shareholder suits index (0-10)	5	Time (years)	4.0
Rigidity of employment index (0-100)	25	Strength of investor protection index (0-10)	5.0	Cost (% of estate)	22
Redundancy cost (weeks of salary)	17			Recovery rate (cents on the dollar)	19.0
		✔ **Paying taxes** (rank)	34		
		Payments (number per year)	19		
		Time (hours per year)	180		
		Total tax rate (% of profit)	30.2		

✔ Reforms making it easier to do business ✘ Reforms making it more difficult to do business

LESOTHO

		Sub-Saharan Africa		GNI per capita (US$)	1,080
Ease of doing business (rank)	130	Lower middle income		Population (m)	2.0

Starting a business (rank)	131	**Registering property** (rank)	142	**Trading across borders** (rank)	143
Procedures (number)	7	Procedures (number)	6	Documents to export (number)	6
Time (days)	40	Time (days)	101	Time to export (days)	44
Cost (% of income per capita)	27.0	Cost (% of property value)	8.0	Cost to export (US$ per container)	1,549
Minimum capital (% of income per capita)	11.9			Documents to import (number)	8
		Getting credit (rank)	113	Time to import (days)	49
Dealing with construction permits (rank)	155	Strength of legal rights index (0-10)	7	Cost to import (US$ per container)	1,715
Procedures (number)	15	Depth of credit information index (0-6)	0		
Time (days)	601	Public registry coverage (% of adults)	0.0	**Enforcing contracts** (rank)	105
Cost (% of income per capita)	670.4	Private bureau coverage (% of adults)	0.0	Procedures (number)	41
				Time (days)	695
Employing workers (rank)	67	**Protecting investors** (rank)	147	Cost (% of claim)	19.5
Difficulty of hiring index (0-100)	22	Extent of disclosure index (0-10)	2		
Rigidity of hours index (0-100)	20	Extent of director liability index (0-10)	1	**Closing a business** (rank)	72
Difficulty of redundancy index (0-100)	0	Ease of shareholder suits index (0-10)	8	Time (years)	2.6
Rigidity of employment index (0-100)	14	Strength of investor protection index (0-10)	3.7	Cost (% of estate)	8
Redundancy cost (weeks of salary)	44			Recovery rate (cents on the dollar)	33.9
		Paying taxes (rank)	63		
		Payments (number per year)	21		
		Time (hours per year)	324		
		Total tax rate (% of profit)	18.5		

LIBERIA

		Sub-Saharan Africa		GNI per capita (US$)	167
Ease of doing business (rank)	149	Low income		Population (m)	3.8

✔ **Starting a business** (rank)	57	**Registering property** (rank)	174	✔ **Trading across borders** (rank)	112
Procedures (number)	5	Procedures (number)	10	Documents to export (number)	10
Time (days)	20	Time (days)	50	Time to export (days)	17
Cost (% of income per capita)	52.9	Cost (% of property value)	13.2	Cost to export (US$ per container)	1,232
Minimum capital (% of income per capita)	0.0			Documents to import (number)	9
		Getting credit (rank)	135	Time to import (days)	15
✔ **Dealing with construction permits** (rank)	135	Strength of legal rights index (0-10)	4	Cost to import (US$ per container)	1,212
Procedures (number)	24	Depth of credit information index (0-6)	1		
Time (days)	77	Public registry coverage (% of adults)	0.3	**Enforcing contracts** (rank)	166
Cost (% of income per capita)	28,295.9	Private bureau coverage (% of adults)	0.0	Procedures (number)	41
				Time (days)	1,280
Employing workers (rank)	121	**Protecting investors** (rank)	147	Cost (% of claim)	35.0
Difficulty of hiring index (0-100)	22	Extent of disclosure index (0-10)	4		
Rigidity of hours index (0-100)	20	Extent of director liability index (0-10)	1	**Closing a business** (rank)	148
Difficulty of redundancy index (0-100)	40	Ease of shareholder suits index (0-10)	6	Time (years)	3.0
Rigidity of employment index (0-100)	27	Strength of investor protection index (0-10)	3.7	Cost (% of estate)	43
Redundancy cost (weeks of salary)	84			Recovery rate (cents on the dollar)	8.3
		Paying taxes (rank)	85		
		Payments (number per year)	32		
		Time (hours per year)	158		
		Total tax rate (% of profit)	43.7		

LITHUANIA

		Eastern Europe & Central Asia		GNI per capita (US$)	11,871
Ease of doing business (rank)	26	Upper middle income		Population (m)	3.4

Starting a business (rank)	99	**Registering property** (rank)	4	**Trading across borders** (rank)	28
Procedures (number)	7	Procedures (number)	2	Documents to export (number)	6
Time (days)	26	Time (days)	3	Time to export (days)	10
Cost (% of income per capita)	2.4	Cost (% of property value)	0.5	Cost to export (US$ per container)	870
Minimum capital (% of income per capita)	31.1			Documents to import (number)	6
		Getting credit (rank)	43	Time to import (days)	11
Dealing with construction permits (rank)	64	Strength of legal rights index (0-10)	5	Cost to import (US$ per container)	980
Procedures (number)	17	Depth of credit information index (0-6)	6		
Time (days)	162	Public registry coverage (% of adults)	12.1	**Enforcing contracts** (rank)	17
Cost (% of income per capita)	95.7	Private bureau coverage (% of adults)	18.4	Procedures (number)	30
				Time (days)	275
Employing workers (rank)	119	**Protecting investors** (rank)	93	Cost (% of claim)	23.6
Difficulty of hiring index (0-100)	33	Extent of disclosure index (0-10)	5		
Rigidity of hours index (0-100)	60	Extent of director liability index (0-10)	4	✔ **Closing a business** (rank)	36
Difficulty of redundancy index (0-100)	20	Ease of shareholder suits index (0-10)	6	Time (years)	1.5
Rigidity of employment index (0-100)	38	Strength of investor protection index (0-10)	5.0	Cost (% of estate)	7
Redundancy cost (weeks of salary)	30			Recovery rate (cents on the dollar)	49.4
		✘ **Paying taxes** (rank)	51		
		Payments (number per year)	12		
		Time (hours per year)	166		
		Total tax rate (% of profit)	42.7		

LUXEMBOURG

Ease of doing business (rank)	64

OECD high income
High income

GNI per capita (US$)	84,892
Population (m)	0.5

✔ **Starting a business** (rank)	72
Procedures (number)	6
Time (days)	24
Cost (% of income per capita)	1.8
Minimum capital (% of income per capita)	19.9

Registering property (rank)	131
Procedures (number)	8
Time (days)	29
Cost (% of property value)	10.3

Trading across borders (rank)	31
Documents to export (number)	5
Time to export (days)	6
Cost to export (US$ per container)	1,420
Documents to import (number)	4
Time to import (days)	6
Cost to import (US$ per container)	1,420

Dealing with construction permits (rank)	43
Procedures (number)	13
Time (days)	217
Cost (% of income per capita)	19.9

Getting credit (rank)	113
Strength of legal rights index (0-10)	7
Depth of credit information index (0-6)	0
Public registry coverage (% of adults)	0.0
Private bureau coverage (% of adults)	0.0

Enforcing contracts (rank)	1
Procedures (number)	26
Time (days)	321
Cost (% of claim)	9.7

✘ **Employing workers** (rank)	170
Difficulty of hiring index (0-100)	67
Rigidity of hours index (0-100)	60
Difficulty of redundancy index (0-100)	40
Rigidity of employment index (0-100)	56
Redundancy cost (weeks of salary)	52

Protecting investors (rank)	119
Extent of disclosure index (0-10)	6
Extent of director liability index (0-10)	4
Ease of shareholder suits index (0-10)	3
Strength of investor protection index (0-10)	4.3

Closing a business (rank)	50
Time (years)	2.0
Cost (% of estate)	15
Recovery rate (cents on the dollar)	41.7

Paying taxes (rank)	15
Payments (number per year)	22
Time (hours per year)	59
Total tax rate (% of profit)	20.9

MACEDONIA, FYR

Ease of doing business (rank)	32

Eastern Europe & Central Asia
Upper middle income

GNI per capita (US$)	4,138
Population (m)	2.0

✔ **Starting a business** (rank)	6
Procedures (number)	4
Time (days)	4
Cost (% of income per capita)	2.5
Minimum capital (% of income per capita)	0.0

✔ **Registering property** (rank)	63
Procedures (number)	5
Time (days)	58
Cost (% of property value)	3.2

Trading across borders (rank)	62
Documents to export (number)	6
Time to export (days)	12
Cost to export (US$ per container)	1,436
Documents to import (number)	6
Time to import (days)	11
Cost to import (US$ per container)	1,420

✔ **Dealing with construction permits** (rank)	137
Procedures (number)	21
Time (days)	146
Cost (% of income per capita)	1,604.8

✔ **Getting credit** (rank)	43
Strength of legal rights index (0-10)	7
Depth of credit information index (0-6)	4
Public registry coverage (% of adults)	28.1
Private bureau coverage (% of adults)	0.0

Enforcing contracts (rank)	64
Procedures (number)	37
Time (days)	370
Cost (% of claim)	33.1

✔ **Employing workers** (rank)	58
Difficulty of hiring index (0-100)	11
Rigidity of hours index (0-100)	20
Difficulty of redundancy index (0-100)	10
Rigidity of employment index (0-100)	14
Redundancy cost (weeks of salary)	26

✔ **Protecting investors** (rank)	20
Extent of disclosure index (0-10)	9
Extent of director liability index (0-10)	7
Ease of shareholder suits index (0-10)	4
Strength of investor protection index (0-10)	6.7

Closing a business (rank)	115
Time (years)	2.9
Cost (% of estate)	28
Recovery rate (cents on the dollar)	20.9

✔ **Paying taxes** (rank)	26
Payments (number per year)	40
Time (hours per year)	75
Total tax rate (% of profit)	16.4

MADAGASCAR

Ease of doing business (rank)	134

Sub-Saharan Africa
Low income

GNI per capita (US$)	406
Population (m)	19.1

✔ **Starting a business** (rank)	12
Procedures (number)	2
Time (days)	7
Cost (% of income per capita)	7.1
Minimum capital (% of income per capita)	0.0

✘ **Registering property** (rank)	152
Procedures (number)	7
Time (days)	74
Cost (% of property value)	9.7

Trading across borders (rank)	111
Documents to export (number)	4
Time to export (days)	21
Cost to export (US$ per container)	1,279
Documents to import (number)	9
Time to import (days)	26
Cost to import (US$ per container)	1,660

Dealing with construction permits (rank)	108
Procedures (number)	16
Time (days)	178
Cost (% of income per capita)	630.7

Getting credit (rank)	167
Strength of legal rights index (0-10)	2
Depth of credit information index (0-6)	1
Public registry coverage (% of adults)	0.1
Private bureau coverage (% of adults)	0.0

Enforcing contracts (rank)	155
Procedures (number)	38
Time (days)	871
Cost (% of claim)	42.4

Employing workers (rank)	152
Difficulty of hiring index (0-100)	89
Rigidity of hours index (0-100)	40
Difficulty of redundancy index (0-100)	40
Rigidity of employment index (0-100)	56
Redundancy cost (weeks of salary)	30

Protecting investors (rank)	57
Extent of disclosure index (0-10)	5
Extent of director liability index (0-10)	6
Ease of shareholder suits index (0-10)	6
Strength of investor protection index (0-10)	5.7

✔ **Closing a business** (rank)	183
Time (years)	NO PRACTICE
Cost (% of estate)	NO PRACTICE
Recovery rate (cents on the dollar)	0.0

Paying taxes (rank)	74
Payments (number per year)	23
Time (hours per year)	201
Total tax rate (% of profit)	39.2

MALAWI

		Sub-Saharan Africa		GNI per capita (US$)		288
Ease of doing business (rank)	132	Low income		Population (m)		14.3
Starting a business (rank)	128	**Registering property** (rank)	101	✔ **Trading across borders** (rank)		172
Procedures (number)	10	Procedures (number)	6	Documents to export (number)		11
Time (days)	39	Time (days)	88	Time to export (days)		41
Cost (% of income per capita)	108.0	Cost (% of property value)	3.2	Cost to export (US$ per container)		1,713
Minimum capital (% of income per capita)	0.0			Documents to import (number)		10
		Getting credit (rank)	87	Time to import (days)		51
Dealing with construction permits (rank)	163	Strength of legal rights index (0-10)	8	Cost to import (US$ per container)		2,570
Procedures (number)	21	Depth of credit information index (0-6)	0			
Time (days)	213	Public registry coverage (% of adults)	0.0	**Enforcing contracts** (rank)		142
Cost (% of income per capita)	1,094.8	Private bureau coverage (% of adults)	0.0	Procedures (number)		42
				Time (days)		432
Employing workers (rank)	92	**Protecting investors** (rank)	73	Cost (% of claim)		142.4
Difficulty of hiring index (0-100)	44	Extent of disclosure index (0-10)	4			
Rigidity of hours index (0-100)	0	Extent of director liability index (0-10)	7	✔ **Closing a business** (rank)		130
Difficulty of redundancy index (0-100)	20	Ease of shareholder suits index (0-10)	5	Time (years)		2.6
Rigidity of employment index (0-100)	21	Strength of investor protection index (0-10)	5.3	Cost (% of estate)		25
Redundancy cost (weeks of salary)	84			Recovery rate (cents on the dollar)		17.5
		Paying taxes (rank)	24			
		Payments (number per year)	19			
		Time (hours per year)	157			
		Total tax rate (% of profit)	25.8			

MALAYSIA

		East Asia & Pacific		GNI per capita (US$)	6,967
Ease of doing business (rank)	23	Upper middle income		Population (m)	27.0
✔ **Starting a business** (rank)	88	**Registering property** (rank)	86	**Trading across borders** (rank)	35
Procedures (number)	9	Procedures (number)	5	Documents to export (number)	7
Time (days)	11	Time (days)	144	Time to export (days)	18
Cost (% of income per capita)	11.9	Cost (% of property value)	2.6	Cost to export (US$ per container)	450
Minimum capital (% of income per capita)	0.0			Documents to import (number)	7
		Getting credit (rank)	1	Time to import (days)	14
Dealing with construction permits (rank)	109	Strength of legal rights index (0-10)	10	Cost to import (US$ per container)	450
Procedures (number)	25	Depth of credit information index (0-6)	6		
Time (days)	261	Public registry coverage (% of adults)	48.5	✔ **Enforcing contracts** (rank)	59
Cost (% of income per capita)	7.1	Private bureau coverage (% of adults)	82.0	Procedures (number)	30
				Time (days)	585
Employing workers (rank)	61	**Protecting investors** (rank)	4	Cost (% of claim)	27.5
Difficulty of hiring index (0-100)	0	Extent of disclosure index (0-10)	10		
Rigidity of hours index (0-100)	0	Extent of director liability index (0-10)	9	**Closing a business** (rank)	57
Difficulty of redundancy index (0-100)	30	Ease of shareholder suits index (0-10)	7	Time (years)	2.3
Rigidity of employment index (0-100)	10	Strength of investor protection index (0-10)	8.7	Cost (% of estate)	15
Redundancy cost (weeks of salary)	75			Recovery rate (cents on the dollar)	38.6
		Paying taxes (rank)	24		
		Payments (number per year)	12		
		Time (hours per year)	145		
		Total tax rate (% of profit)	34.2		

MALDIVES

		South Asia		GNI per capita (US$)	3,626
Ease of doing business (rank)	87	Lower middle income		Population (m)	0.3
Starting a business (rank)	49	**Registering property** (rank)	183	**Trading across borders** (rank)	126
Procedures (number)	5	Procedures (number)	NO PRACTICE	Documents to export (number)	8
Time (days)	9	Time (days)	NO PRACTICE	Time to export (days)	21
Cost (% of income per capita)	10.0	Cost (% of property value)	NO PRACTICE	Cost to export (US$ per container)	1,348
Minimum capital (% of income per capita)	4.0			Documents to import (number)	9
		Getting credit (rank)	150	Time to import (days)	20
Dealing with construction permits (rank)	9	Strength of legal rights index (0-10)	4	Cost to import (US$ per container)	1,348
Procedures (number)	9	Depth of credit information index (0-6)	0		
Time (days)	118	Public registry coverage (% of adults)	0.0	**Enforcing contracts** (rank)	92
Cost (% of income per capita)	21.9	Private bureau coverage (% of adults)	0.0	Procedures (number)	41
				Time (days)	665
✘ **Employing workers** (rank)	41	**Protecting investors** (rank)	73	Cost (% of claim)	16.5
Difficulty of hiring index (0-100)	33	Extent of disclosure index (0-10)	0		
Rigidity of hours index (0-100)	20	Extent of director liability index (0-10)	8	**Closing a business** (rank)	126
Difficulty of redundancy index (0-100)	0	Ease of shareholder suits index (0-10)	8	Time (years)	6.7
Rigidity of employment index (0-100)	18	Strength of investor protection index (0-10)	5.3	Cost (% of estate)	4
Redundancy cost (weeks of salary)	9			Recovery rate (cents on the dollar)	18.2
		Paying taxes (rank)	1		
		Payments (number per year)	1		
		Time (hours per year)	-		
		Total tax rate (% of profit)	9.1		

MALI

		Sub-Saharan Africa		GNI per capita (US$)	579
Ease of doing business (rank)	156	Low income		Population (m)	12.7

✔ **Starting a business** (rank)	139	**Registering property** (rank)	99	✔ **Trading across borders** (rank)	156
Procedures (number)	7	Procedures (number)	5	Documents to export (number)	7
Time (days)	15	Time (days)	29	Time to export (days)	32
Cost (% of income per capita)	89.2	Cost (% of property value)	20.0	Cost to export (US$ per container)	2,075
Minimum capital (% of income per capita)	334.6			Documents to import (number)	10
		Getting credit (rank)	150	Time to import (days)	37
✔ **Dealing with construction permits** (rank)	94	Strength of legal rights index (0-10)	3	Cost to import (US$ per container)	2,955
Procedures (number)	14	Depth of credit information index (0-6)	1		
Time (days)	185	Public registry coverage (% of adults)	4.0	✔ **Enforcing contracts** (rank)	135
Cost (% of income per capita)	818.5	Private bureau coverage (% of adults)	0.0	Procedures (number)	36
				Time (days)	626
Employing workers (rank)	100	✔ **Protecting investors** (rank)	147	Cost (% of claim)	52.0
Difficulty of hiring index (0-100)	33	Extent of disclosure index (0-10)	6		
Rigidity of hours index (0-100)	20	Extent of director liability index (0-10)	1	**Closing a business** (rank)	117
Difficulty of redundancy index (0-100)	40	Ease of shareholder suits index (0-10)	4	Time (years)	3.6
Rigidity of employment index (0-100)	31	Strength of investor protection index (0-10)	3.7	Cost (% of estate)	18
Redundancy cost (weeks of salary)	31			Recovery rate (cents on the dollar)	20.9
		Paying taxes (rank)	158		
		Payments (number per year)	58		
		Time (hours per year)	270		
		Total tax rate (% of profit)	52.1		

MARSHALL ISLANDS

		East Asia & Pacific		GNI per capita (US$)	3,273
Ease of doing business (rank)	98	Lower middle income		Population (m)	0.1

Starting a business (rank)	39	**Registering property** (rank)	183	**Trading across borders** (rank)	64
Procedures (number)	5	Procedures (number)	NO PRACTICE	Documents to export (number)	5
Time (days)	17	Time (days)	NO PRACTICE	Time to export (days)	21
Cost (% of income per capita)	16.2	Cost (% of property value)	NO PRACTICE	Cost to export (US$ per container)	945
Minimum capital (% of income per capita)	0.0			Documents to import (number)	5
		Getting credit (rank)	150	Time to import (days)	33
Dealing with construction permits (rank)	5	Strength of legal rights index (0-10)	4	Cost to import (US$ per container)	945
Procedures (number)	10	Depth of credit information index (0-6)	0		
Time (days)	55	Public registry coverage (% of adults)	0.0	**Enforcing contracts** (rank)	63
Cost (% of income per capita)	33.7	Private bureau coverage (% of adults)	0.0	Procedures (number)	36
				Time (days)	476
Employing workers (rank)	4	**Protecting investors** (rank)	154	Cost (% of claim)	27.4
Difficulty of hiring index (0-100)	0	Extent of disclosure index (0-10)	2		
Rigidity of hours index (0-100)	0	Extent of director liability index (0-10)	0	**Closing a business** (rank)	128
Difficulty of redundancy index (0-100)	0	Ease of shareholder suits index (0-10)	8	Time (years)	2.0
Rigidity of employment index (0-100)	0	Strength of investor protection index (0-10)	3.3	Cost (% of estate)	38
Redundancy cost (weeks of salary)	0			Recovery rate (cents on the dollar)	17.9
		Paying taxes (rank)	93		
		Payments (number per year)	21		
		Time (hours per year)	128		
		Total tax rate (% of profit)	64.9		

MAURITANIA

		Sub-Saharan Africa		GNI per capita (US$)	906
Ease of doing business (rank)	166	Low income		Population (m)	3.2

Starting a business (rank)	149	**Registering property** (rank)	74	**Trading across borders** (rank)	163
Procedures (number)	9	Procedures (number)	4	Documents to export (number)	11
Time (days)	19	Time (days)	49	Time to export (days)	39
Cost (% of income per capita)	34.7	Cost (% of property value)	5.2	Cost to export (US$ per container)	1,520
Minimum capital (% of income per capita)	450.4			Documents to import (number)	11
		Getting credit (rank)	150	Time to import (days)	42
Dealing with construction permits (rank)	154	Strength of legal rights index (0-10)	3	Cost to import (US$ per container)	1,523
Procedures (number)	25	Depth of credit information index (0-6)	1		
Time (days)	201	Public registry coverage (% of adults)	0.2	**Enforcing contracts** (rank)	83
Cost (% of income per capita)	506.3	Private bureau coverage (% of adults)	0.0	Procedures (number)	46
				Time (days)	370
Employing workers (rank)	125	**Protecting investors** (rank)	147	Cost (% of claim)	23.2
Difficulty of hiring index (0-100)	56	Extent of disclosure index (0-10)	5		
Rigidity of hours index (0-100)	20	Extent of director liability index (0-10)	3	**Closing a business** (rank)	150
Difficulty of redundancy index (0-100)	40	Ease of shareholder suits index (0-10)	3	Time (years)	8.0
Rigidity of employment index (0-100)	39	Strength of investor protection index (0-10)	3.7	Cost (% of estate)	9
Redundancy cost (weeks of salary)	31			Recovery rate (cents on the dollar)	6.7
		Paying taxes (rank)	175		
		Payments (number per year)	38		
		Time (hours per year)	696		
		Total tax rate (% of profit)	86.1		

MAURITIUS

		Sub-Saharan Africa		GNI per capita (US$)	6,401
Ease of doing business (rank)	17	Upper middle income		Population (m)	1.3
Starting a business (rank)	10	✔ **Registering property** (rank)	66	✔ **Trading across borders** (rank)	19
Procedures (number)	5	Procedures (number)	4	Documents to export (number)	5
Time (days)	6	Time (days)	26	Time to export (days)	14
Cost (% of income per capita)	4.1	Cost (% of property value)	10.7	Cost to export (US$ per container)	737
Minimum capital (% of income per capita)	0.0			Documents to import (number)	6
		✔ **Getting credit** (rank)	87	Time to import (days)	14
Dealing with construction permits (rank)	42	Strength of legal rights index (0-10)	5	Cost to import (US$ per container)	689
Procedures (number)	18	Depth of credit information index (0-6)	3		
Time (days)	107	Public registry coverage (% of adults)	36.8	✔ **Enforcing contracts** (rank)	66
Cost (% of income per capita)	35.5	Private bureau coverage (% of adults)	0.0	Procedures (number)	36
				Time (days)	720
✔ **Employing workers** (rank)	36	**Protecting investors** (rank)	12	Cost (% of claim)	17.4
Difficulty of hiring index (0-100)	0	Extent of disclosure index (0-10)	6		
Rigidity of hours index (0-100)	33	Extent of director liability index (0-10)	8	✔ **Closing a business** (rank)	73
Difficulty of redundancy index (0-100)	20	Ease of shareholder suits index (0-10)	9	Time (years)	1.7
Rigidity of employment index (0-100)	18	Strength of investor protection index (0-10)	7.7	Cost (% of estate)	15
Redundancy cost (weeks of salary)	4			Recovery rate (cents on the dollar)	33.6
		Paying taxes (rank)	12		
		Payments (number per year)	7		
		Time (hours per year)	161		
		Total tax rate (% of profit)	22.9		

MEXICO

		Latin America & Caribbean		GNI per capita (US$)	9,981
Ease of doing business (rank)	51	Upper middle income		Population (m)	106.4
✔ **Starting a business** (rank)	90	**Registering property** (rank)	99	**Trading across borders** (rank)	74
Procedures (number)	8	Procedures (number)	5	Documents to export (number)	5
Time (days)	13	Time (days)	74	Time to export (days)	14
Cost (% of income per capita)	11.7	Cost (% of property value)	5.2	Cost to export (US$ per container)	1,472
Minimum capital (% of income per capita)	8.9			Documents to import (number)	5
		Getting credit (rank)	61	Time to import (days)	17
Dealing with construction permits (rank)	37	Strength of legal rights index (0-10)	4	Cost to import (US$ per container)	2,050
Procedures (number)	12	Depth of credit information index (0-6)	6		
Time (days)	138	Public registry coverage (% of adults)	0.0	**Enforcing contracts** (rank)	81
Cost (% of income per capita)	113.1	Private bureau coverage (% of adults)	77.5	Procedures (number)	38
				Time (days)	415
Employing workers (rank)	136	**Protecting investors** (rank)	41	Cost (% of claim)	32.0
Difficulty of hiring index (0-100)	33	Extent of disclosure index (0-10)	8		
Rigidity of hours index (0-100)	20	Extent of director liability index (0-10)	5	**Closing a business** (rank)	24
Difficulty of redundancy index (0-100)	70	Ease of shareholder suits index (0-10)	5	Time (years)	1.8
Rigidity of employment index (0-100)	41	Strength of investor protection index (0-10)	6.0	Cost (% of estate)	18
Redundancy cost (weeks of salary)	52			Recovery rate (cents on the dollar)	64.2
		✔ **Paying taxes** (rank)	106		
		Payments (number per year)	6		
		Time (hours per year)	517		
		Total tax rate (% of profit)	51.0		

MICRONESIA, FED. STS.

		East Asia & Pacific		GNI per capita (US$)	2,338
Ease of doing business (rank)	127	Lower middle income		Population (m)	0.1
Starting a business (rank)	79	**Registering property** (rank)	183	**Trading across borders** (rank)	98
Procedures (number)	7	Procedures (number)	NO PRACTICE	Documents to export (number)	3
Time (days)	16	Time (days)	NO PRACTICE	Time to export (days)	30
Cost (% of income per capita)	136.9	Cost (% of property value)	NO PRACTICE	Cost to export (US$ per container)	1,295
Minimum capital (% of income per capita)	0.0			Documents to import (number)	6
		Getting credit (rank)	113	Time to import (days)	30
Dealing with construction permits (rank)	11	Strength of legal rights index (0-10)	7	Cost to import (US$ per container)	1,295
Procedures (number)	14	Depth of credit information index (0-6)	0		
Time (days)	73	Public registry coverage (% of adults)	0.0	**Enforcing contracts** (rank)	149
Cost (% of income per capita)	19.9	Private bureau coverage (% of adults)	0.0	Procedures (number)	34
				Time (days)	965
Employing workers (rank)	14	**Protecting investors** (rank)	172	Cost (% of claim)	66.0
Difficulty of hiring index (0-100)	22	Extent of disclosure index (0-10)	0		
Rigidity of hours index (0-100)	0	Extent of director liability index (0-10)	0	**Closing a business** (rank)	154
Difficulty of redundancy index (0-100)	0	Ease of shareholder suits index (0-10)	8	Time (years)	5.3
Rigidity of employment index (0-100)	7	Strength of investor protection index (0-10)	2.7	Cost (% of estate)	38
Redundancy cost (weeks of salary)	0			Recovery rate (cents on the dollar)	3.5
		Paying taxes (rank)	86		
		Payments (number per year)	21		
		Time (hours per year)	128		
		Total tax rate (% of profit)	58.7		

MOLDOVA

		Eastern Europe & Central Asia		GNI per capita (US$)	1,469
Ease of doing business (rank)	94	Lower middle income		Population (m)	3.6
✔ **Starting a business** (rank)	77	✔ **Registering property** (rank)	17	**Trading across borders** (rank)	140
Procedures (number)	8	Procedures (number)	5	Documents to export (number)	6
Time (days)	10	Time (days)	5	Time to export (days)	32
Cost (% of income per capita)	7.0	Cost (% of property value)	0.9	Cost to export (US$ per container)	1,815
Minimum capital (% of income per capita)	11.4			Documents to import (number)	7
		Getting credit (rank)	87	Time to import (days)	35
Dealing with construction permits (rank)	161	Strength of legal rights index (0-10)	8	Cost to import (US$ per container)	1,945
Procedures (number)	30	Depth of credit information index (0-6)	0		
Time (days)	292	Public registry coverage (% of adults)	0.0	**Enforcing contracts** (rank)	22
Cost (% of income per capita)	120.5	Private bureau coverage (% of adults)	0.0	Procedures (number)	31
				Time (days)	365
Employing workers (rank)	141	**Protecting investors** (rank)	109	Cost (% of claim)	20.9
Difficulty of hiring index (0-100)	44	Extent of disclosure index (0-10)	7		
Rigidity of hours index (0-100)	40	Extent of director liability index (0-10)	1	**Closing a business** (rank)	90
Difficulty of redundancy index (0-100)	40	Ease of shareholder suits index (0-10)	6	Time (years)	2.8
Rigidity of employment index (0-100)	41	Strength of investor protection index (0-10)	4.7	Cost (% of estate)	9
Redundancy cost (weeks of salary)	37			Recovery rate (cents on the dollar)	28.6
		✔ **Paying taxes** (rank)	101		
		Payments (number per year)	48		
		Time (hours per year)	228		
		Total tax rate (% of profit)	31.1		

MONGOLIA

		East Asia & Pacific		GNI per capita (US$)	1,676
Ease of doing business (rank)	60	Lower middle income		Population (m)	2.6
Starting a business (rank)	78	**Registering property** (rank)	25	**Trading across borders** (rank)	155
Procedures (number)	7	Procedures (number)	5	Documents to export (number)	8
Time (days)	13	Time (days)	11	Time to export (days)	46
Cost (% of income per capita)	3.0	Cost (% of property value)	2.1	Cost to export (US$ per container)	2,131
Minimum capital (% of income per capita)	44.0			Documents to import (number)	8
		Getting credit (rank)	71	Time to import (days)	47
Dealing with construction permits (rank)	103	Strength of legal rights index (0-10)	6	Cost to import (US$ per container)	2,274
Procedures (number)	21	Depth of credit information index (0-6)	3		
Time (days)	215	Public registry coverage (% of adults)	22.2	**Enforcing contracts** (rank)	36
Cost (% of income per capita)	61.2	Private bureau coverage (% of adults)	0.0	Procedures (number)	32
				Time (days)	314
Employing workers (rank)	44	**Protecting investors** (rank)	27	Cost (% of claim)	30.6
Difficulty of hiring index (0-100)	11	Extent of disclosure index (0-10)	5		
Rigidity of hours index (0-100)	40	Extent of director liability index (0-10)	8	**Closing a business** (rank)	110
Difficulty of redundancy index (0-100)	0	Ease of shareholder suits index (0-10)	6	Time (years)	4.0
Rigidity of employment index (0-100)	17	Strength of investor protection index (0-10)	6.3	Cost (% of estate)	8
Redundancy cost (weeks of salary)	9			Recovery rate (cents on the dollar)	22.0
		Paying taxes (rank)	69		
		Payments (number per year)	43		
		Time (hours per year)	192		
		Total tax rate (% of profit)	22.8		

MONTENEGRO

		Eastern Europe & Central Asia		GNI per capita (US$)	6,440
Ease of doing business (rank)	71	Upper middle income		Population (m)	0.6
✔ **Starting a business** (rank)	85	**Registering property** (rank)	131	**Trading across borders** (rank)	47
Procedures (number)	12	Procedures (number)	8	Documents to export (number)	7
Time (days)	13	Time (days)	86	Time to export (days)	14
Cost (% of income per capita)	2.6	Cost (% of property value)	3.3	Cost to export (US$ per container)	775
Minimum capital (% of income per capita)	0.0			Documents to import (number)	7
		Getting credit (rank)	43	Time to import (days)	14
✔ **Dealing with construction permits** (rank)	160	Strength of legal rights index (0-10)	9	Cost to import (US$ per container)	890
Procedures (number)	19	Depth of credit information index (0-6)	2		
Time (days)	230	Public registry coverage (% of adults)	27.6	**Enforcing contracts** (rank)	133
Cost (% of income per capita)	1,086.0	Private bureau coverage (% of adults)	0.0	Procedures (number)	49
				Time (days)	545
✔ **Employing workers** (rank)	46	**Protecting investors** (rank)	27	Cost (% of claim)	25.7
Difficulty of hiring index (0-100)	0	Extent of disclosure index (0-10)	5		
Rigidity of hours index (0-100)	20	Extent of director liability index (0-10)	8	**Closing a business** (rank)	44
Difficulty of redundancy index (0-100)	20	Ease of shareholder suits index (0-10)	6	Time (years)	2.0
Rigidity of employment index (0-100)	13	Strength of investor protection index (0-10)	6.3	Cost (% of estate)	8
Redundancy cost (weeks of salary)	28			Recovery rate (cents on the dollar)	43.7
		✔ **Paying taxes** (rank)	145		
		Payments (number per year)	89		
		Time (hours per year)	372		
		Total tax rate (% of profit)	28.9		

MOROCCO

		Middle East & North Africa	GNI per capita (US$)	2,579
Ease of doing business (rank)	128	Lower middle income	Population (m)	31.2
Starting a business (rank)	76	**Registering property** (rank)	123	**Trading across borders** (rank)	72

Ease of doing business (rank) — 128 — Lower middle income — Population (m) — 31.2

Starting a business (rank) — 76
Procedures (number) — 6
Time (days) — 12
Cost (% of income per capita) — 16.1
Minimum capital (% of income per capita) — 11.8

Registering property (rank) — 123
Procedures (number) — 8
Time (days) — 47
Cost (% of property value) — 4.9

Trading across borders (rank) — 72
Documents to export (number) — 7
Time to export (days) — 14
Cost to export (US$ per container) — 700
Documents to import (number) — 10
Time to import (days) — 17
Cost to import (US$ per container) — 1,000

Dealing with construction permits (rank) — 99
Procedures (number) — 19
Time (days) — 163
Cost (% of income per capita) — 263.7

✔ **Getting credit** (rank) — 87
Strength of legal rights index (0-10) — 3
Depth of credit information index (0-6) — 5
Public registry coverage (% of adults) — 0.0
Private bureau coverage (% of adults) — 14.0

Enforcing contracts (rank) — 108
Procedures (number) — 40
Time (days) — 615
Cost (% of claim) — 25.2

Employing workers (rank) — 176
Difficulty of hiring index (0-100) — 89
Rigidity of hours index (0-100) — 40
Difficulty of redundancy index (0-100) — 50
Rigidity of employment index (0-100) — 60
Redundancy cost (weeks of salary) — 85

Protecting investors (rank) — 165
Extent of disclosure index (0-10) — 6
Extent of director liability index (0-10) — 2
Ease of shareholder suits index (0-10) — 1
Strength of investor protection index (0-10) — 3.0

Closing a business (rank) — 67
Time (years) — 1.8
Cost (% of estate) — 18
Recovery rate (cents on the dollar) — 35.1

Paying taxes (rank) — 125
Payments (number per year) — 28
Time (hours per year) — 358
Total tax rate (% of profit) — 41.7

MOZAMBIQUE

Ease of doing business (rank) — 135 — Sub-Saharan Africa — GNI per capita (US$) — 373
— Low income — Population (m) — 21.8

✔ **Starting a business** (rank) — 96
Procedures (number) — 10
Time (days) — 26
Cost (% of income per capita) — 19.3
Minimum capital (% of income per capita) — 0.0

Registering property (rank) — 151
Procedures (number) — 8
Time (days) — 42
Cost (% of property value) — 11.3

✔ **Trading across borders** (rank) — 136
Documents to export (number) — 7
Time to export (days) — 23
Cost to export (US$ per container) — 1,100
Documents to import (number) — 10
Time to import (days) — 30
Cost to import (US$ per container) — 1,475

Dealing with construction permits (rank) — 159
Procedures (number) — 17
Time (days) — 381
Cost (% of income per capita) — 632.0

Getting credit (rank) — 127
Strength of legal rights index (0-10) — 2
Depth of credit information index (0-6) — 4
Public registry coverage (% of adults) — 2.3
Private bureau coverage (% of adults) — 0.0

Enforcing contracts (rank) — 129
Procedures (number) — 30
Time (days) — 730
Cost (% of claim) — 142.5

Employing workers (rank) — 156
Difficulty of hiring index (0-100) — 67
Rigidity of hours index (0-100) — 33
Difficulty of redundancy index (0-100) — 20
Rigidity of employment index (0-100) — 40
Redundancy cost (weeks of salary) — 134

Protecting investors (rank) — 41
Extent of disclosure index (0-10) — 5
Extent of director liability index (0-10) — 4
Ease of shareholder suits index (0-10) — 9
Strength of investor protection index (0-10) — 6.0

Closing a business (rank) — 136
Time (years) — 5.0
Cost (% of estate) — 9
Recovery rate (cents on the dollar) — 15.2

Paying taxes (rank) — 97
Payments (number per year) — 37
Time (hours per year) — 230
Total tax rate (% of profit) — 34.3

NAMIBIA

Ease of doing business (rank) — 66 — Sub-Saharan Africa — GNI per capita (US$) — 4,200
— Upper middle income — Population (m) — 2.1

Starting a business (rank) — 123
Procedures (number) — 10
Time (days) — 66
Cost (% of income per capita) — 20.4
Minimum capital (% of income per capita) — 0.0

Registering property (rank) — 134
Procedures (number) — 9
Time (days) — 23
Cost (% of property value) — 9.6

Trading across borders (rank) — 151
Documents to export (number) — 11
Time to export (days) — 29
Cost to export (US$ per container) — 1,686
Documents to import (number) — 9
Time to import (days) — 24
Cost to import (US$ per container) — 1,813

Dealing with construction permits (rank) — 38
Procedures (number) — 12
Time (days) — 139
Cost (% of income per capita) — 124.7

Getting credit (rank) — 15
Strength of legal rights index (0-10) — 8
Depth of credit information index (0-6) — 5
Public registry coverage (% of adults) — 0.0
Private bureau coverage (% of adults) — 57.7

Enforcing contracts (rank) — 41
Procedures (number) — 33
Time (days) — 270
Cost (% of claim) — 35.8

Employing workers (rank) — 43
Difficulty of hiring index (0-100) — 0
Rigidity of hours index (0-100) — 20
Difficulty of redundancy index (0-100) — 20
Rigidity of employment index (0-100) — 13
Redundancy cost (weeks of salary) — 24

Protecting investors (rank) — 73
Extent of disclosure index (0-10) — 5
Extent of director liability index (0-10) — 5
Ease of shareholder suits index (0-10) — 6
Strength of investor protection index (0-10) — 5.3

Closing a business (rank) — 55
Time (years) — 1.5
Cost (% of estate) — 15
Recovery rate (cents on the dollar) — 39.5

Paying taxes (rank) — 97
Payments (number per year) — 37
Time (hours per year) — 375
Total tax rate (% of profit) — 9.6

NEPAL

		South Asia		GNI per capita (US$)		404
Ease of doing business (rank)	123	Low income		Population (m)		28.6
Starting a business (rank)	87	✔ **Registering property** (rank)	26	**Trading across borders** (rank)		161
Procedures (number)	7	Procedures (number)	3	Documents to export (number)		9
Time (days)	31	Time (days)	5	Time to export (days)		41
Cost (% of income per capita)	53.6	Cost (% of property value)	4.8	Cost to export (US$ per container)		1,764
Minimum capital (% of income per capita)	0.0			Documents to import (number)		10
				Time to import (days)		35
Dealing with construction permits (rank)	131	**Getting credit** (rank)	113	Cost to import (US$ per container)		1,825
Procedures (number)	15	Strength of legal rights index (0-10)	5			
Time (days)	424	Depth of credit information index (0-6)	2	**Enforcing contracts** (rank)		122
Cost (% of income per capita)	221.3	Public registry coverage (% of adults)	0.0	Procedures (number)		39
		Private bureau coverage (% of adults)	0.3	Time (days)		735
Employing workers (rank)	148			Cost (% of claim)		26.8
Difficulty of hiring index (0-100)	67	**Protecting investors** (rank)	73			
Rigidity of hours index (0-100)	0	Extent of disclosure index (0-10)	6	**Closing a business** (rank)		105
Difficulty of redundancy index (0-100)	70	Extent of director liability index (0-10)	1	Time (years)		5.0
Rigidity of employment index (0-100)	46	Ease of shareholder suits index (0-10)	9	Cost (% of estate)		9
Redundancy cost (weeks of salary)	90	Strength of investor protection index (0-10)	5.3	Recovery rate (cents on the dollar)		24.5
		Paying taxes (rank)	124			
		Payments (number per year)	34			
		Time (hours per year)	338			
		Total tax rate (% of profit)	38.8			

NETHERLANDS

		OECD high income		GNI per capita (US$)	50,150
Ease of doing business (rank)	30	High income		Population (m)	16.4
Starting a business (rank)	70	**Registering property** (rank)	29	**Trading across borders** (rank)	13
Procedures (number)	6	Procedures (number)	2	Documents to export (number)	4
Time (days)	10	Time (days)	5	Time to export (days)	6
Cost (% of income per capita)	5.6	Cost (% of property value)	6.2	Cost to export (US$ per container)	895
Minimum capital (% of income per capita)	49.4			Documents to import (number)	5
		Getting credit (rank)	43	Time to import (days)	6
✔ **Dealing with construction permits** (rank)	104	Strength of legal rights index (0-10)	6	Cost to import (US$ per container)	942
Procedures (number)	18	Depth of credit information index (0-6)	5		
Time (days)	230	Public registry coverage (% of adults)	0.0	**Enforcing contracts** (rank)	30
Cost (% of income per capita)	107.2	Private bureau coverage (% of adults)	83.5	Procedures (number)	25
				Time (days)	514
Employing workers (rank)	123	**Protecting investors** (rank)	109	Cost (% of claim)	24.4
Difficulty of hiring index (0-100)	17	Extent of disclosure index (0-10)	4		
Rigidity of hours index (0-100)	40	Extent of director liability index (0-10)	4	**Closing a business** (rank)	10
Difficulty of redundancy index (0-100)	70	Ease of shareholder suits index (0-10)	6	Time (years)	1.1
Rigidity of employment index (0-100)	42	Strength of investor protection index (0-10)	4.7	Cost (% of estate)	4
Redundancy cost (weeks of salary)	17			Recovery rate (cents on the dollar)	82.7
		Paying taxes (rank)	33		
		Payments (number per year)	9		
		Time (hours per year)	164		
		Total tax rate (% of profit)	39.3		

NEW ZEALAND

		OECD high income		GNI per capita (US$)	27,936
Ease of doing business (rank)	2	High income		Population (m)	4.3
Starting a business (rank)	1	**Registering property** (rank)	3	**Trading across borders** (rank)	26
Procedures (number)	1	Procedures (number)	2	Documents to export (number)	7
Time (days)	1	Time (days)	2	Time to export (days)	10
Cost (% of income per capita)	0.4	Cost (% of property value)	0.1	Cost to export (US$ per container)	868
Minimum capital (% of income per capita)	0.0			Documents to import (number)	5
		Getting credit (rank)	4	Time to import (days)	9
✘ **Dealing with construction permits** (rank)	5	Strength of legal rights index (0-10)	9	Cost to import (US$ per container)	850
Procedures (number)	7	Depth of credit information index (0-6)	5		
Time (days)	65	Public registry coverage (% of adults)	0.0	**Enforcing contracts** (rank)	10
Cost (% of income per capita)	37.3	Private bureau coverage (% of adults)	100.0	Procedures (number)	30
				Time (days)	216
Employing workers (rank)	15	**Protecting investors** (rank)	1	Cost (% of claim)	22.4
Difficulty of hiring index (0-100)	11	Extent of disclosure index (0-10)	10		
Rigidity of hours index (0-100)	0	Extent of director liability index (0-10)	9	**Closing a business** (rank)	17
Difficulty of redundancy index (0-100)	10	Ease of shareholder suits index (0-10)	10	Time (years)	1.3
Rigidity of employment index (0-100)	7	Strength of investor protection index (0-10)	9.7	Cost (% of estate)	4
Redundancy cost (weeks of salary)	0			Recovery rate (cents on the dollar)	76.2
		Paying taxes (rank)	9		
		Payments (number per year)	8		
		Time (hours per year)	70		
		Total tax rate (% of profit)	32.8		

NICARAGUA

Ease of doing business (rank)	117	Latin America & Caribbean		GNI per capita (US$)		1,079
		Lower middle income		Population (m)		5.7

Starting a business (rank)	95	**Registering property** (rank)	143	**Trading across borders** (rank)	99
Procedures (number)	6	Procedures (number)	8	Documents to export (number)	5
Time (days)	39	Time (days)	124	Time to export (days)	29
Cost (% of income per capita)	111.7	Cost (% of property value)	3.8	Cost to export (US$ per container)	1,340
Minimum capital (% of income per capita)	0.0			Documents to import (number)	5
		Getting credit (rank)	87	Time to import (days)	29
Dealing with construction permits (rank)	138	Strength of legal rights index (0-10)	3	Cost to import (US$ per container)	1,420
Procedures (number)	17	Depth of credit information index (0-6)	5		
Time (days)	219	Public registry coverage (% of adults)	16.0	**Enforcing contracts** (rank)	67
Cost (% of income per capita)	719.3	Private bureau coverage (% of adults)	28.4	Procedures (number)	35
				Time (days)	540
Employing workers (rank)	84	**Protecting investors** (rank)	93	Cost (% of claim)	26.8
Difficulty of hiring index (0-100)	22	Extent of disclosure index (0-10)	4		
Rigidity of hours index (0-100)	60	Extent of director liability index (0-10)	5	**Closing a business** (rank)	70
Difficulty of redundancy index (0-100)	0	Ease of shareholder suits index (0-10)	6	Time (years)	2.2
Rigidity of employment index (0-100)	27	Strength of investor protection index (0-10)	5.0	Cost (% of estate)	15
Redundancy cost (weeks of salary)	22			Recovery rate (cents on the dollar)	34.3
		Paying taxes (rank)	165		
		Payments (number per year)	64		
		Time (hours per year)	240		
		Total tax rate (% of profit)	63.2		

NIGER

Ease of doing business (rank)	174	Sub-Saharan Africa		GNI per capita (US$)	329
		Low income		Population (m)	14.7

✔ **Starting a business** (rank)	157	**Registering property** (rank)	85	**Trading across borders** (rank)	173
Procedures (number)	9	Procedures (number)	4	Documents to export (number)	8
Time (days)	17	Time (days)	35	Time to export (days)	59
Cost (% of income per capita)	118.7	Cost (% of property value)	11.0	Cost to export (US$ per container)	3,545
Minimum capital (% of income per capita)	613.7			Documents to import (number)	10
		Getting credit (rank)	150	Time to import (days)	64
Dealing with construction permits (rank)	166	Strength of legal rights index (0-10)	3	Cost to import (US$ per container)	3,545
Procedures (number)	17	Depth of credit information index (0-6)	1		
Time (days)	265	Public registry coverage (% of adults)	0.9	**Enforcing contracts** (rank)	138
Cost (% of income per capita)	2,355.0	Private bureau coverage (% of adults)	0.0	Procedures (number)	39
				Time (days)	545
Employing workers (rank)	173	**Protecting investors** (rank)	154	Cost (% of claim)	59.6
Difficulty of hiring index (0-100)	100	Extent of disclosure index (0-10)	6		
Rigidity of hours index (0-100)	53	Extent of director liability index (0-10)	1	**Closing a business** (rank)	141
Difficulty of redundancy index (0-100)	50	Ease of shareholder suits index (0-10)	3	Time (years)	5.0
Rigidity of employment index (0-100)	68	Strength of investor protection index (0-10)	3.3	Cost (% of estate)	18
Redundancy cost (weeks of salary)	35			Recovery rate (cents on the dollar)	14.0
		Paying taxes (rank)	141		
		Payments (number per year)	41		
		Time (hours per year)	270		
		Total tax rate (% of profit)	46.5		

NIGERIA

Ease of doing business (rank)	125	Sub-Saharan Africa		GNI per capita (US$)	1,161
		Lower middle income		Population (m)	151.3

Starting a business (rank)	108	**Registering property** (rank)	178	**Trading across borders** (rank)	146
Procedures (number)	8	Procedures (number)	13	Documents to export (number)	10
Time (days)	31	Time (days)	82	Time to export (days)	25
Cost (% of income per capita)	76.7	Cost (% of property value)	20.9	Cost to export (US$ per container)	1,263
Minimum capital (% of income per capita)	0.0			Documents to import (number)	9
		✔ **Getting credit** (rank)	87	Time to import (days)	41
Dealing with construction permits (rank)	162	Strength of legal rights index (0-10)	8	Cost to import (US$ per container)	1,440
Procedures (number)	18	Depth of credit information index (0-6)	0		
Time (days)	350	Public registry coverage (% of adults)	0.0	**Enforcing contracts** (rank)	94
Cost (% of income per capita)	573.4	Private bureau coverage (% of adults)	0.0	Procedures (number)	39
				Time (days)	457
Employing workers (rank)	37	**Protecting investors** (rank)	57	Cost (% of claim)	32.0
Difficulty of hiring index (0-100)	0	Extent of disclosure index (0-10)	5		
Rigidity of hours index (0-100)	0	Extent of director liability index (0-10)	7	**Closing a business** (rank)	94
Difficulty of redundancy index (0-100)	20	Ease of shareholder suits index (0-10)	5	Time (years)	2.0
Rigidity of employment index (0-100)	7	Strength of investor protection index (0-10)	5.7	Cost (% of estate)	22
Redundancy cost (weeks of salary)	50			Recovery rate (cents on the dollar)	28.0
		Paying taxes (rank)	132		
		Payments (number per year)	35		
		Time (hours per year)	938		
		Total tax rate (% of profit)	32.2		

NORWAY

		OECD high income		GNI per capita (US$)	87,067
Ease of doing business (rank)	10	High income		Population (m)	4.8

Starting a business (rank)	35	**Registering property** (rank)	8	**Trading across borders** (rank)	9
Procedures (number)	5	Procedures (number)	1	Documents to export (number)	4
Time (days)	7	Time (days)	3	Time to export (days)	7
Cost (% of income per capita)	1.9	Cost (% of property value)	2.5	Cost to export (US$ per container)	830
Minimum capital (% of income per capita)	18.7			Documents to import (number)	4
		Getting credit (rank)	43	Time to import (days)	7
Dealing with construction permits (rank)	65	Strength of legal rights index (0-10)	7	Cost to import (US$ per container)	729
Procedures (number)	14	Depth of credit information index (0-6)	4		
Time (days)	252	Public registry coverage (% of adults)	0.0	✔ **Enforcing contracts** (rank)	4
Cost (% of income per capita)	41.4	Private bureau coverage (% of adults)	100.0	Procedures (number)	33
				Time (days)	280
Employing workers (rank)	114	**Protecting investors** (rank)	20	Cost (% of claim)	9.9
Difficulty of hiring index (0-100)	61	Extent of disclosure index (0-10)	7		
Rigidity of hours index (0-100)	40	Extent of director liability index (0-10)	6	**Closing a business** (rank)	3
Difficulty of redundancy index (0-100)	30	Ease of shareholder suits index (0-10)	7	Time (years)	0.9
Rigidity of employment index (0-100)	44	Strength of investor protection index (0-10)	6.7	Cost (% of estate)	1
Redundancy cost (weeks of salary)	13			Recovery rate (cents on the dollar)	89.0
		Paying taxes (rank)	17		
		Payments (number per year)	4		
		Time (hours per year)	87		
		Total tax rate (% of profit)	41.6		

OMAN

		Middle East & North Africa		GNI per capita (US$)	18,988
Ease of doing business (rank)	65	High income		Population (m)	2.8

✔ **Starting a business** (rank)	62	**Registering property** (rank)	20	**Trading across borders** (rank)	123
Procedures (number)	5	Procedures (number)	2	Documents to export (number)	10
Time (days)	12	Time (days)	16	Time to export (days)	22
Cost (% of income per capita)	2.2	Cost (% of property value)	3.0	Cost to export (US$ per container)	821
Minimum capital (% of income per capita)	273.6			Documents to import (number)	10
		Getting credit (rank)	127	Time to import (days)	26
Dealing with construction permits (rank)	130	Strength of legal rights index (0-10)	4	Cost to import (US$ per container)	1,037
Procedures (number)	16	Depth of credit information index (0-6)	2		
Time (days)	242	Public registry coverage (% of adults)	17.0	**Enforcing contracts** (rank)	106
Cost (% of income per capita)	427.9	Private bureau coverage (% of adults)	0.0	Procedures (number)	51
				Time (days)	598
Employing workers (rank)	21	**Protecting investors** (rank)	93	Cost (% of claim)	13.5
Difficulty of hiring index (0-100)	0	Extent of disclosure index (0-10)	8		
Rigidity of hours index (0-100)	40	Extent of director liability index (0-10)	5	**Closing a business** (rank)	66
Difficulty of redundancy index (0-100)	0	Ease of shareholder suits index (0-10)	2	Time (years)	4.0
Rigidity of employment index (0-100)	13	Strength of investor protection index (0-10)	5.0	Cost (% of estate)	4
Redundancy cost (weeks of salary)	4			Recovery rate (cents on the dollar)	35.1
		✔ **Paying taxes** (rank)	8		
		Payments (number per year)	14		
		Time (hours per year)	62		
		Total tax rate (% of profit)	21.6		

PAKISTAN

		South Asia		GNI per capita (US$)	981
Ease of doing business (rank)	85	Lower middle income		Population (m)	166.0

✔ **Starting a business** (rank)	63	**Registering property** (rank)	119	**Trading across borders** (rank)	78
Procedures (number)	10	Procedures (number)	6	Documents to export (number)	9
Time (days)	20	Time (days)	50	Time to export (days)	22
Cost (% of income per capita)	5.8	Cost (% of property value)	7.2	Cost to export (US$ per container)	611
Minimum capital (% of income per capita)	0.0			Documents to import (number)	8
		Getting credit (rank)	61	Time to import (days)	18
Dealing with construction permits (rank)	105	Strength of legal rights index (0-10)	6	Cost to import (US$ per container)	680
Procedures (number)	12	Depth of credit information index (0-6)	4		
Time (days)	223	Public registry coverage (% of adults)	5.6	**Enforcing contracts** (rank)	158
Cost (% of income per capita)	716.3	Private bureau coverage (% of adults)	1.5	Procedures (number)	47
				Time (days)	976
Employing workers (rank)	146	**Protecting investors** (rank)	27	Cost (% of claim)	23.8
Difficulty of hiring index (0-100)	78	Extent of disclosure index (0-10)	6		
Rigidity of hours index (0-100)	20	Extent of director liability index (0-10)	6	**Closing a business** (rank)	56
Difficulty of redundancy index (0-100)	30	Ease of shareholder suits index (0-10)	7	Time (years)	2.8
Rigidity of employment index (0-100)	43	Strength of investor protection index (0-10)	6.3	Cost (% of estate)	4
Redundancy cost (weeks of salary)	90			Recovery rate (cents on the dollar)	39.2
		Paying taxes (rank)	143		
		Payments (number per year)	47		
		Time (hours per year)	560		
		Total tax rate (% of profit)	31.6		

✔ Reforms making it easier to do business   ✘ Reforms making it more difficult to do business

PALAU

		East Asia & Pacific		GNI per capita (US$)	8,646
Ease of doing business (rank)	97	Upper middle income		Population (m)	0.02
Starting a business (rank)	103	**Registering property** (rank)	18	**Trading across borders** (rank)	124
Procedures (number)	8	Procedures (number)	5	Documents to export (number)	6
Time (days)	28	Time (days)	14	Time to export (days)	29
Cost (% of income per capita)	4.3	Cost (% of property value)	0.3	Cost to export (US$ per container)	1,190
Minimum capital (% of income per capita)	11.6			Documents to import (number)	10
		Getting credit (rank)	183	Time to import (days)	33
		Strength of legal rights index (0-10)	0	Cost to import (US$ per container)	1,132
Dealing with construction permits (rank)	54	Depth of credit information index (0-6)	0		
Procedures (number)	25	Public registry coverage (% of adults)	0.0	**Enforcing contracts** (rank)	144
Time (days)	118	Private bureau coverage (% of adults)	0.0	Procedures (number)	38
Cost (% of income per capita)	5.4			Time (days)	885
		Protecting investors (rank)	172	Cost (% of claim)	35.3
Employing workers (rank)	8	Extent of disclosure index (0-10)	0		
Difficulty of hiring index (0-100)	11	Extent of director liability index (0-10)	0	**Closing a business** (rank)	59
Rigidity of hours index (0-100)	0	Ease of shareholder suits index (0-10)	8	Time (years)	1.0
Difficulty of redundancy index (0-100)	0	Strength of investor protection index (0-10)	2.7	Cost (% of estate)	23
Rigidity of employment index (0-100)	4			Recovery rate (cents on the dollar)	38.2
Redundancy cost (weeks of salary)	0				
		Paying taxes (rank)	91		
		Payments (number per year)	19		
		Time (hours per year)	128		
		Total tax rate (% of profit)	73.0		

PANAMA

		Latin America & Caribbean		GNI per capita (US$)	6,178
Ease of doing business (rank)	77	Upper middle income		Population (m)	3.4
Starting a business (rank)	27	✔ **Registering property** (rank)	65	**Trading across borders** (rank)	10
Procedures (number)	6	Procedures (number)	7	Documents to export (number)	3
Time (days)	12	Time (days)	32	Time to export (days)	9
Cost (% of income per capita)	10.3	Cost (% of property value)	2.4	Cost to export (US$ per container)	729
Minimum capital (% of income per capita)	0.0			Documents to import (number)	4
		Getting credit (rank)	30	Time to import (days)	9
		Strength of legal rights index (0-10)	6	Cost to import (US$ per container)	879
✔ **Dealing with construction permits** (rank)	68	Depth of credit information index (0-6)	6		
Procedures (number)	20	Public registry coverage (% of adults)	0.0	**Enforcing contracts** (rank)	119
Time (days)	116	Private bureau coverage (% of adults)	45.9	Procedures (number)	31
Cost (% of income per capita)	107.2			Time (days)	686
		Protecting investors (rank)	109	Cost (% of claim)	50.0
Employing workers (rank)	177	Extent of disclosure index (0-10)	1		
Difficulty of hiring index (0-100)	78	Extent of director liability index (0-10)	4	**Closing a business** (rank)	75
Rigidity of hours index (0-100)	60	Ease of shareholder suits index (0-10)	9	Time (years)	2.5
Difficulty of redundancy index (0-100)	60	Strength of investor protection index (0-10)	4.7	Cost (% of estate)	18
Rigidity of employment index (0-100)	66			Recovery rate (cents on the dollar)	32.4
Redundancy cost (weeks of salary)	44				
		Paying taxes (rank)	173		
		Payments (number per year)	59		
		Time (hours per year)	482		
		Total tax rate (% of profit)	50.1		

PAPUA NEW GUINEA

		East Asia & Pacific		GNI per capita (US$)	1,009
Ease of doing business (rank)	102	Lower middle income		Population (m)	6.4
Starting a business (rank)	104	**Registering property** (rank)	83	**Trading across borders** (rank)	89
Procedures (number)	8	Procedures (number)	4	Documents to export (number)	7
Time (days)	56	Time (days)	72	Time to export (days)	26
Cost (% of income per capita)	20.5	Cost (% of property value)	5.1	Cost to export (US$ per container)	664
Minimum capital (% of income per capita)	0.0			Documents to import (number)	9
		Getting credit (rank)	135	Time to import (days)	29
		Strength of legal rights index (0-10)	5	Cost to import (US$ per container)	722
Dealing with construction permits (rank)	121	Depth of credit information index (0-6)	0		
Procedures (number)	24	Public registry coverage (% of adults)	0.0	✔ **Enforcing contracts** (rank)	162
Time (days)	217	Private bureau coverage (% of adults)	0.0	Procedures (number)	42
Cost (% of income per capita)	82.8			Time (days)	591
		Protecting investors (rank)	41	Cost (% of claim)	110.3
Employing workers (rank)	26	Extent of disclosure index (0-10)	5		
Difficulty of hiring index (0-100)	11	Extent of director liability index (0-10)	5	**Closing a business** (rank)	104
Rigidity of hours index (0-100)	0	Ease of shareholder suits index (0-10)	8	Time (years)	3.0
Difficulty of redundancy index (0-100)	0	Strength of investor protection index (0-10)	6.0	Cost (% of estate)	23
Rigidity of employment index (0-100)	4			Recovery rate (cents on the dollar)	24.7
Redundancy cost (weeks of salary)	39				
		Paying taxes (rank)	96		
		Payments (number per year)	33		
		Time (hours per year)	194		
		Total tax rate (% of profit)	42.3		

PARAGUAY

Ease of doing business (rank)	124	Latin America & Caribbean		GNI per capita (US$)		2,180
		Lower middle income		Population (m)		6.2

Starting a business (rank)	100	**Registering property** (rank)	79	✔ **Trading across borders** (rank)	152
Procedures (number)	7	Procedures (number)	6	Documents to export (number)	8
Time (days)	35	Time (days)	46	Time to export (days)	33
Cost (% of income per capita)	56.7	Cost (% of property value)	3.5	Cost to export (US$ per container)	1,440
Minimum capital (% of income per capita)	0.0			Documents to import (number)	10
		Getting credit (rank)	71	Time to import (days)	33
Dealing with construction permits (rank)	106	Strength of legal rights index (0-10)	3	Cost to import (US$ per container)	1,750
Procedures (number)	13	Depth of credit information index (0-6)	6		
Time (days)	291	Public registry coverage (% of adults)	10.9	**Enforcing contracts** (rank)	104
Cost (% of income per capita)	298.3	Private bureau coverage (% of adults)	47.4	Procedures (number)	38
				Time (days)	591
Employing workers (rank)	179	**Protecting investors** (rank)	57	Cost (% of claim)	30.0
Difficulty of hiring index (0-100)	56	Extent of disclosure index (0-10)	6		
Rigidity of hours index (0-100)	53	Extent of director liability index (0-10)	5	**Closing a business** (rank)	119
Difficulty of redundancy index (0-100)	60	Ease of shareholder suits index (0-10)	6	Time (years)	3.9
Rigidity of employment index (0-100)	56	Strength of investor protection index (0-10)	5.7	Cost (% of estate)	9
Redundancy cost (weeks of salary)	99			Recovery rate (cents on the dollar)	20.7
		Paying taxes (rank)	110		
		Payments (number per year)	35		
		Time (hours per year)	328		
		Total tax rate (% of profit)	35.0		

PERU

Ease of doing business (rank)	56	Latin America & Caribbean		GNI per capita (US$)		3,987
		Upper middle income		Population (m)		28.8

✔ **Starting a business** (rank)	112	✔ **Registering property** (rank)	28	✔ **Trading across borders** (rank)	91
Procedures (number)	9	Procedures (number)	4	Documents to export (number)	7
Time (days)	41	Time (days)	14	Time to export (days)	23
Cost (% of income per capita)	24.5	Cost (% of property value)	3.3	Cost to export (US$ per container)	875
Minimum capital (% of income per capita)	0.0			Documents to import (number)	8
		Getting credit (rank)	15	Time to import (days)	24
Dealing with construction permits (rank)	116	Strength of legal rights index (0-10)	7	Cost to import (US$ per container)	895
Procedures (number)	21	Depth of credit information index (0-6)	6		
Time (days)	205	Public registry coverage (% of adults)	23.0	✔ **Enforcing contracts** (rank)	114
Cost (% of income per capita)	130.1	Private bureau coverage (% of adults)	31.8	Procedures (number)	41
				Time (days)	428
✔ **Employing workers** (rank)	112	**Protecting investors** (rank)	20	Cost (% of claim)	35.7
Difficulty of hiring index (0-100)	44	Extent of disclosure index (0-10)	8		
Rigidity of hours index (0-100)	13	Extent of director liability index (0-10)	5	**Closing a business** (rank)	99
Difficulty of redundancy index (0-100)	60	Ease of shareholder suits index (0-10)	7	Time (years)	3.1
Rigidity of employment index (0-100)	39	Strength of investor protection index (0-10)	6.7	Cost (% of estate)	7
Redundancy cost (weeks of salary)	17			Recovery rate (cents on the dollar)	25.4
		✔ **Paying taxes** (rank)	87		
		Payments (number per year)	9		
		Time (hours per year)	380		
		Total tax rate (% of profit)	40.3		

PHILIPPINES

Ease of doing business (rank)	144	East Asia & Pacific		GNI per capita (US$)		1,886
		Lower middle income		Population (m)		90.3

Starting a business (rank)	162	**Registering property** (rank)	102	**Trading across borders** (rank)	68
Procedures (number)	15	Procedures (number)	8	Documents to export (number)	8
Time (days)	52	Time (days)	33	Time to export (days)	16
Cost (% of income per capita)	28.2	Cost (% of property value)	4.3	Cost to export (US$ per container)	816
Minimum capital (% of income per capita)	5.5			Documents to import (number)	8
		✔ **Getting credit** (rank)	127	Time to import (days)	16
Dealing with construction permits (rank)	111	Strength of legal rights index (0-10)	3	Cost to import (US$ per container)	819
Procedures (number)	24	Depth of credit information index (0-6)	3		
Time (days)	203	Public registry coverage (% of adults)	0.0	**Enforcing contracts** (rank)	118
Cost (% of income per capita)	81.7	Private bureau coverage (% of adults)	6.1	Procedures (number)	37
				Time (days)	842
Employing workers (rank)	115	**Protecting investors** (rank)	132	Cost (% of claim)	26.0
Difficulty of hiring index (0-100)	56	Extent of disclosure index (0-10)	2		
Rigidity of hours index (0-100)	0	Extent of director liability index (0-10)	2	✔ **Closing a business** (rank)	153
Difficulty of redundancy index (0-100)	30	Ease of shareholder suits index (0-10)	8	Time (years)	5.7
Rigidity of employment index (0-100)	29	Strength of investor protection index (0-10)	4.0	Cost (% of estate)	38
Redundancy cost (weeks of salary)	91			Recovery rate (cents on the dollar)	4.4
		✔ **Paying taxes** (rank)	135		
		Payments (number per year)	47		
		Time (hours per year)	195		
		Total tax rate (% of profit)	49.4		

✔ Reforms making it easier to do business   ✘ Reforms making it more difficult to do business

POLAND

		Eastern Europe & Central Asia		GNI per capita (US$)		11,883
Ease of doing business (rank)	72	Upper middle income		Population (m)		38.1
✔ **Starting a business** (rank)	117	**Registering property** (rank)	88	**Trading across borders** (rank)		42
Procedures (number)	6	Procedures (number)	6	Documents to export (number)		5
Time (days)	32	Time (days)	197	Time to export (days)		17
Cost (% of income per capita)	17.9	Cost (% of property value)	0.5	Cost to export (US$ per container)		884
Minimum capital (% of income per capita)	15.3			Documents to import (number)		5
		✔ **Getting credit** (rank)	15	Time to import (days)		25
Dealing with construction permits (rank)	164	Strength of legal rights index (0-10)	9	Cost to import (US$ per container)		884
Procedures (number)	30	Depth of credit information index (0-6)	4			
Time (days)	308	Public registry coverage (% of adults)	0.0	**Enforcing contracts** (rank)		75
Cost (% of income per capita)	124.2	Private bureau coverage (% of adults)	68.3	Procedures (number)		38
				Time (days)		830
Employing workers (rank)	76	**Protecting investors** (rank)	41	Cost (% of claim)		12.0
Difficulty of hiring index (0-100)	11	Extent of disclosure index (0-10)	7			
Rigidity of hours index (0-100)	33	Extent of director liability index (0-10)	2	✔ **Closing a business** (rank)		85
Difficulty of redundancy index (0-100)	30	Ease of shareholder suits index (0-10)	9	Time (years)		3.0
Rigidity of employment index (0-100)	25	Strength of investor protection index (0-10)	6.0	Cost (% of estate)		20
Redundancy cost (weeks of salary)	13			Recovery rate (cents on the dollar)		29.8
		✔ **Paying taxes** (rank)	151			
		Payments (number per year)	40			
		Time (hours per year)	395			
		Total tax rate (% of profit)	42.5			

PORTUGAL

		OECD high income		GNI per capita (US$)		20,556
Ease of doing business (rank)	48	High income		Population (m)		10.6
Starting a business (rank)	60	✔ **Registering property** (rank)	52	✔ **Trading across borders** (rank)		19
Procedures (number)	6	Procedures (number)	5	Documents to export (number)		4
Time (days)	6	Time (days)	12	Time to export (days)		16
Cost (% of income per capita)	6.4	Cost (% of property value)	7.4	Cost to export (US$ per container)		685
Minimum capital (% of income per capita)	33.5			Documents to import (number)		5
		Getting credit (rank)	87	Time to import (days)		15
✔ **Dealing with construction permits** (rank)	111	Strength of legal rights index (0-10)	3	Cost to import (US$ per container)		999
Procedures (number)	19	Depth of credit information index (0-6)	5			
Time (days)	287	Public registry coverage (% of adults)	81.3	✔ **Enforcing contracts** (rank)		25
Cost (% of income per capita)	52.9	Private bureau coverage (% of adults)	16.4	Procedures (number)		31
				Time (days)		547
✘ **Employing workers** (rank)	171	**Protecting investors** (rank)	41	Cost (% of claim)		13.0
Difficulty of hiring index (0-100)	33	Extent of disclosure index (0-10)	6			
Rigidity of hours index (0-100)	47	Extent of director liability index (0-10)	5	**Closing a business** (rank)		22
Difficulty of redundancy index (0-100)	50	Ease of shareholder suits index (0-10)	7	Time (years)		2.0
Rigidity of employment index (0-100)	43	Strength of investor protection index (0-10)	6.0	Cost (% of estate)		9
Redundancy cost (weeks of salary)	97			Recovery rate (cents on the dollar)		69.4
		Paying taxes (rank)	80			
		Payments (number per year)	8			
		Time (hours per year)	328			
		Total tax rate (% of profit)	42.9			

PUERTO RICO

		Latin America & Caribbean		GNI per capita (US$)		15,630
Ease of doing business (rank)	35	High income		Population (m)		4.0
Starting a business (rank)	15	**Registering property** (rank)	124	**Trading across borders** (rank)		105
Procedures (number)	7	Procedures (number)	8	Documents to export (number)		7
Time (days)	7	Time (days)	194	Time to export (days)		15
Cost (% of income per capita)	0.7	Cost (% of property value)	1.4	Cost to export (US$ per container)		1,250
Minimum capital (% of income per capita)	0.0			Documents to import (number)		10
		Getting credit (rank)	30	Time to import (days)		16
Dealing with construction permits (rank)	148	Strength of legal rights index (0-10)	7	Cost to import (US$ per container)		1,250
Procedures (number)	22	Depth of credit information index (0-6)	5			
Time (days)	209	Public registry coverage (% of adults)	0.0	**Enforcing contracts** (rank)		97
Cost (% of income per capita)	506.5	Private bureau coverage (% of adults)	73.8	Procedures (number)		39
				Time (days)		620
Employing workers (rank)	22	**Protecting investors** (rank)	16	Cost (% of claim)		24.3
Difficulty of hiring index (0-100)	22	Extent of disclosure index (0-10)	7			
Rigidity of hours index (0-100)	0	Extent of director liability index (0-10)	6	**Closing a business** (rank)		30
Difficulty of redundancy index (0-100)	20	Ease of shareholder suits index (0-10)	8	Time (years)		3.8
Rigidity of employment index (0-100)	14	Strength of investor protection index (0-10)	7.0	Cost (% of estate)		8
Redundancy cost (weeks of salary)	0			Recovery rate (cents on the dollar)		55.2
		Paying taxes (rank)	104			
		Payments (number per year)	16			
		Time (hours per year)	218			
		Total tax rate (% of profit)	64.7			

QATAR

Ease of doing business (rank)	39

Starting a business (rank) 68
Procedures (number) 6
Time (days) 6
Cost (% of income per capita) 7.1
Minimum capital (% of income per capita) 59.0

Dealing with construction permits (rank) 28
Procedures (number) 19
Time (days) 76
Cost (% of income per capita) 0.6

Employing workers (rank) 68
Difficulty of hiring index (0-100) 0
Rigidity of hours index (0-100) 20
Difficulty of redundancy index (0-100) 20
Rigidity of employment index (0-100) 13
Redundancy cost (weeks of salary) 69

Middle East & North Africa
High income

Registering property (rank) 55
Procedures (number) 10
Time (days) 16
Cost (% of property value) 0.3

Getting credit (rank) 135
Strength of legal rights index (0-10) 3
Depth of credit information index (0-6) 2
Public registry coverage (% of adults) 0.0
Private bureau coverage (% of adults) 0.0

Protecting investors (rank) 93
Extent of disclosure index (0-10) 5
Extent of director liability index (0-10) 6
Ease of shareholder suits index (0-10) 4
Strength of investor protection index (0-10) 5.0

Paying taxes (rank) 2
Payments (number per year) 1
Time (hours per year) 36
Total tax rate (% of profit) 11.3

GNI per capita (US$)	93,204
Population (m)	1.3

Trading across borders (rank) 41
Documents to export (number) 5
Time to export (days) 21
Cost to export (US$ per container) 735
Documents to import (number) 7
Time to import (days) 20
Cost to import (US$ per container) 657

Enforcing contracts (rank) 95
Procedures (number) 43
Time (days) 570
Cost (% of claim) 21.6

Closing a business (rank) 33
Time (years) 2.8
Cost (% of estate) 22
Recovery rate (cents on the dollar) 52.7

ROMANIA

Ease of doing business (rank)	55

Starting a business (rank) 42
Procedures (number) 6
Time (days) 10
Cost (% of income per capita) 2.9
Minimum capital (% of income per capita) 0.9

✘ **Dealing with construction permits** (rank) 91
Procedures (number) 17
Time (days) 243
Cost (% of income per capita) 87.9

Employing workers (rank) 113
Difficulty of hiring index (0-100) 67
Rigidity of hours index (0-100) 40
Difficulty of redundancy index (0-100) 30
Rigidity of employment index (0-100) 46
Redundancy cost (weeks of salary) 8

Eastern Europe & Central Asia
Upper middle income

✔ **Registering property** (rank) 92
Procedures (number) 8
Time (days) 48
Cost (% of property value) 1.3

Getting credit (rank) 15
Strength of legal rights index (0-10) 8
Depth of credit information index (0-6) 5
Public registry coverage (% of adults) 5.7
Private bureau coverage (% of adults) 30.2

Protecting investors (rank) 41
Extent of disclosure index (0-10) 9
Extent of director liability index (0-10) 5
Ease of shareholder suits index (0-10) 4
Strength of investor protection index (0-10) 6.0

✘ **Paying taxes** (rank) 149
Payments (number per year) 113
Time (hours per year) 202
Total tax rate (% of profit) 44.6

GNI per capita (US$)	7,928
Population (m)	21.5

Trading across borders (rank) 46
Documents to export (number) 5
Time to export (days) 12
Cost to export (US$ per container) 1,275
Documents to import (number) 6
Time to import (days) 13
Cost to import (US$ per container) 1,175

Enforcing contracts (rank) 55
Procedures (number) 31
Time (days) 512
Cost (% of claim) 28.9

✘ **Closing a business** (rank) 91
Time (years) 3.3
Cost (% of estate) 11
Recovery rate (cents on the dollar) 28.5

RUSSIAN FEDERATION

Ease of doing business (rank)	120

Starting a business (rank) 106
Procedures (number) 9
Time (days) 30
Cost (% of income per capita) 2.7
Minimum capital (% of income per capita) 1.8

Dealing with construction permits (rank) 182
Procedures (number) 54
Time (days) 704
Cost (% of income per capita) 2,140.7

Employing workers (rank) 109
Difficulty of hiring index (0-100) 33
Rigidity of hours index (0-100) 40
Difficulty of redundancy index (0-100) 40
Rigidity of employment index (0-100) 38
Redundancy cost (weeks of salary) 17

Eastern Europe & Central Asia
Upper middle income

✔ **Registering property** (rank) 45
Procedures (number) 6
Time (days) 43
Cost (% of property value) 0.1

Getting credit (rank) 87
Strength of legal rights index (0-10) 3
Depth of credit information index (0-6) 5
Public registry coverage (% of adults) 0.0
Private bureau coverage (% of adults) 14.3

Protecting investors (rank) 93
Extent of disclosure index (0-10) 6
Extent of director liability index (0-10) 2
Ease of shareholder suits index (0-10) 7
Strength of investor protection index (0-10) 5.0

✔ **Paying taxes** (rank) 103
Payments (number per year) 11
Time (hours per year) 320
Total tax rate (% of profit) 48.3

GNI per capita (US$)	9,623
Population (m)	141.8

Trading across borders (rank) 162
Documents to export (number) 8
Time to export (days) 36
Cost to export (US$ per container) 1,850
Documents to import (number) 13
Time to import (days) 36
Cost to import (US$ per container) 1,850

Enforcing contracts (rank) 19
Procedures (number) 37
Time (days) 281
Cost (% of claim) 13.4

✔ **Closing a business** (rank) 92
Time (years) 3.8
Cost (% of estate) 9
Recovery rate (cents on the dollar) 28.2

RWANDA

		Sub-Saharan Africa		GNI per capita (US$)	407
Ease of doing business (rank)	67	Low income		Population (m)	9.7
✔ **Starting a business** (rank)	11	✔ **Registering property** (rank)	38	✔ **Trading across borders** (rank)	170
Procedures (number)	2	Procedures (number)	4	Documents to export (number)	9
Time (days)	3	Time (days)	60	Time to export (days)	38
Cost (% of income per capita)	10.1	Cost (% of property value)	0.5	Cost to export (US$ per container)	3,275
Minimum capital (% of income per capita)	0.0			Documents to import (number)	9
		✔ **Getting credit** (rank)	61	Time to import (days)	35
Dealing with construction permits (rank)	89	Strength of legal rights index (0-10)	8	Cost to import (US$ per container)	5,070
Procedures (number)	14	Depth of credit information index (0-6)	2		
Time (days)	210	Public registry coverage (% of adults)	0.4	**Enforcing contracts** (rank)	40
Cost (% of income per capita)	456.1	Private bureau coverage (% of adults)	0.0	Procedures (number)	24
				Time (days)	260
✔ **Employing workers** (rank)	30	✔ **Protecting investors** (rank)	27	Cost (% of claim)	78.7
Difficulty of hiring index (0-100)	11	Extent of disclosure index (0-10)	7		
Rigidity of hours index (0-100)	0	Extent of director liability index (0-10)	9	✔ **Closing a business** (rank)	183
Difficulty of redundancy index (0-100)	10	Ease of shareholder suits index (0-10)	3	Time (years)	NO PRACTICE
Rigidity of employment index (0-100)	7	Strength of investor protection index (0-10)	6.3	Cost (% of estate)	NO PRACTICE
Redundancy cost (weeks of salary)	26			Recovery rate (cents on the dollar)	0.0
		Paying taxes (rank)	60		
		Payments (number per year)	34		
		Time (hours per year)	160		
		Total tax rate (% of profit)	31.3		

SAMOA

		East Asia & Pacific		GNI per capita (US$)	2,778
Ease of doing business (rank)	57	Lower middle income		Population (m)	0.2
✔ **Starting a business** (rank)	20	**Registering property** (rank)	81	**Trading across borders** (rank)	88
Procedures (number)	5	Procedures (number)	5	Documents to export (number)	7
Time (days)	9	Time (days)	147	Time to export (days)	27
Cost (% of income per capita)	9.9	Cost (% of property value)	1.6	Cost to export (US$ per container)	820
Minimum capital (% of income per capita)	0.0			Documents to import (number)	7
		Getting credit (rank)	127	Time to import (days)	31
Dealing with construction permits (rank)	48	Strength of legal rights index (0-10)	6	Cost to import (US$ per container)	848
Procedures (number)	18	Depth of credit information index (0-6)	0		
Time (days)	88	Public registry coverage (% of adults)	0.0	**Enforcing contracts** (rank)	83
Cost (% of income per capita)	79.8	Private bureau coverage (% of adults)	0.0	Procedures (number)	44
				Time (days)	455
Employing workers (rank)	18	**Protecting investors** (rank)	27	Cost (% of claim)	19.7
Difficulty of hiring index (0-100)	11	Extent of disclosure index (0-10)	5		
Rigidity of hours index (0-100)	13	Extent of director liability index (0-10)	6	✔ **Closing a business** (rank)	139
Difficulty of redundancy index (0-100)	0	Ease of shareholder suits index (0-10)	8	Time (years)	2.5
Rigidity of employment index (0-100)	8	Strength of investor protection index (0-10)	6.3	Cost (% of estate)	38
Redundancy cost (weeks of salary)	9			Recovery rate (cents on the dollar)	14.3
		Paying taxes (rank)	67		
		Payments (number per year)	37		
		Time (hours per year)	224		
		Total tax rate (% of profit)	18.9		

SÃO TOMÉ AND PRINCIPE

		Sub-Saharan Africa		GNI per capita (US$)	1,020
Ease of doing business (rank)	180	Lower middle income		Population (m)	0.2
Starting a business (rank)	140	**Registering property** (rank)	156	**Trading across borders** (rank)	90
Procedures (number)	10	Procedures (number)	7	Documents to export (number)	8
Time (days)	144	Time (days)	62	Time to export (days)	27
Cost (% of income per capita)	81.7	Cost (% of property value)	10.9	Cost to export (US$ per container)	690
Minimum capital (% of income per capita)	0.0			Documents to import (number)	8
		Getting credit (rank)	167	Time to import (days)	29
Dealing with construction permits (rank)	116	Strength of legal rights index (0-10)	3	Cost to import (US$ per container)	577
Procedures (number)	13	Depth of credit information index (0-6)	0		
Time (days)	255	Public registry coverage (% of adults)	0.0	**Enforcing contracts** (rank)	179
Cost (% of income per capita)	631.4	Private bureau coverage (% of adults)	0.0	Procedures (number)	43
				Time (days)	1,185
Employing workers (rank)	180	**Protecting investors** (rank)	154	Cost (% of claim)	50.5
Difficulty of hiring index (0-100)	50	Extent of disclosure index (0-10)	3		
Rigidity of hours index (0-100)	67	Extent of director liability index (0-10)	1	**Closing a business** (rank)	183
Difficulty of redundancy index (0-100)	60	Ease of shareholder suits index (0-10)	6	Time (years)	NO PRACTICE
Rigidity of employment index (0-100)	59	Strength of investor protection index (0-10)	3.3	Cost (% of estate)	NO PRACTICE
Redundancy cost (weeks of salary)	91			Recovery rate (cents on the dollar)	0.0
		Paying taxes (rank)	160		
		Payments (number per year)	42		
		Time (hours per year)	424		
		Total tax rate (% of profit)	47.2		

SAUDI ARABIA

		Middle East & North Africa		GNI per capita (US$)	19,345
Ease of doing business (rank)	13	High income		Population (m)	24.6
✔ **Starting a business** (rank)	13	**Registering property** (rank)	1	**Trading across borders** (rank)	23
Procedures (number)	4	Procedures (number)	2	Documents to export (number)	5
Time (days)	5	Time (days)	2	Time to export (days)	17
Cost (% of income per capita)	7.7	Cost (% of property value)	0.0	Cost to export (US$ per container)	681
Minimum capital (% of income per capita)	0.0			Documents to import (number)	5
		Getting credit (rank)	61	Time to import (days)	18
✔ **Dealing with construction permits** (rank)	33	Strength of legal rights index (0-10)	4	Cost to import (US$ per container)	678
Procedures (number)	17	Depth of credit information index (0-6)	6		
Time (days)	94	Public registry coverage (% of adults)	0.0	**Enforcing contracts** (rank)	140
Cost (% of income per capita)	32.8	Private bureau coverage (% of adults)	17.9	Procedures (number)	43
				Time (days)	635
Employing workers (rank)	73	**Protecting investors** (rank)	16	Cost (% of claim)	27.5
Difficulty of hiring index (0-100)	0	Extent of disclosure index (0-10)	9		
Rigidity of hours index (0-100)	40	Extent of director liability index (0-10)	8	**Closing a business** (rank)	60
Difficulty of redundancy index (0-100)	0	Ease of shareholder suits index (0-10)	4	Time (years)	1.5
Rigidity of employment index (0-100)	13	Strength of investor protection index (0-10)	7.0	Cost (% of estate)	22
Redundancy cost (weeks of salary)	80			Recovery rate (cents on the dollar)	37.5
		Paying taxes (rank)	7		
		Payments (number per year)	14		
		Time (hours per year)	79		
		Total tax rate (% of profit)	14.5		

SENEGAL

		Sub-Saharan Africa		GNI per capita (US$)	968
Ease of doing business (rank)	157	Low income		Population (m)	12.2
Starting a business (rank)	102	**Registering property** (rank)	166	✔ **Trading across borders** (rank)	57
Procedures (number)	4	Procedures (number)	6	Documents to export (number)	6
Time (days)	8	Time (days)	124	Time to export (days)	11
Cost (% of income per capita)	63.7	Cost (% of property value)	20.6	Cost to export (US$ per container)	1,098
Minimum capital (% of income per capita)	206.9			Documents to import (number)	5
		Getting credit (rank)	150	Time to import (days)	14
Dealing with construction permits (rank)	124	Strength of legal rights index (0-10)	3	Cost to import (US$ per container)	1,940
Procedures (number)	16	Depth of credit information index (0-6)	1		
Time (days)	220	Public registry coverage (% of adults)	4.4	**Enforcing contracts** (rank)	151
Cost (% of income per capita)	463.1	Private bureau coverage (% of adults)	0.0	Procedures (number)	44
				Time (days)	780
Employing workers (rank)	172	**Protecting investors** (rank)	165	Cost (% of claim)	26.5
Difficulty of hiring index (0-100)	72	Extent of disclosure index (0-10)	6		
Rigidity of hours index (0-100)	53	Extent of director liability index (0-10)	1	**Closing a business** (rank)	80
Difficulty of redundancy index (0-100)	50	Ease of shareholder suits index (0-10)	2	Time (years)	3.0
Rigidity of employment index (0-100)	59	Strength of investor protection index (0-10)	3.0	Cost (% of estate)	7
Redundancy cost (weeks of salary)	38			Recovery rate (cents on the dollar)	31.6
		Paying taxes (rank)	172		
		Payments (number per year)	59		
		Time (hours per year)	666		
		Total tax rate (% of profit)	46.0		

SERBIA

		Eastern Europe & Central Asia		GNI per capita (US$)	5,705
Ease of doing business (rank)	88	Upper middle income		Population (m)	7.3
✔ **Starting a business** (rank)	73	**Registering property** (rank)	105	**Trading across borders** (rank)	69
Procedures (number)	7	Procedures (number)	6	Documents to export (number)	6
Time (days)	13	Time (days)	111	Time to export (days)	12
Cost (% of income per capita)	7.1	Cost (% of property value)	2.8	Cost to export (US$ per container)	1,398
Minimum capital (% of income per capita)	6.1			Documents to import (number)	6
		✔ **Getting credit** (rank)	4	Time to import (days)	14
Dealing with construction permits (rank)	174	Strength of legal rights index (0-10)	8	Cost to import (US$ per container)	1,559
Procedures (number)	20	Depth of credit information index (0-6)	6		
Time (days)	279	Public registry coverage (% of adults)	0.0	**Enforcing contracts** (rank)	97
Cost (% of income per capita)	1,907.5	Private bureau coverage (% of adults)	94.2	Procedures (number)	36
				Time (days)	635
Employing workers (rank)	94	**Protecting investors** (rank)	73	Cost (% of claim)	28.9
Difficulty of hiring index (0-100)	78	Extent of disclosure index (0-10)	7		
Rigidity of hours index (0-100)	7	Extent of director liability index (0-10)	6	**Closing a business** (rank)	102
Difficulty of redundancy index (0-100)	20	Ease of shareholder suits index (0-10)	3	Time (years)	2.7
Rigidity of employment index (0-100)	35	Strength of investor protection index (0-10)	5.3	Cost (% of estate)	23
Redundancy cost (weeks of salary)	25			Recovery rate (cents on the dollar)	25.4
		Paying taxes (rank)	137		
		Payments (number per year)	66		
		Time (hours per year)	279		
		Total tax rate (% of profit)	34.0		

SEYCHELLES

Ease of doing business (rank)	111	Sub-Saharan Africa		GNI per capita (US$)	10,292
		Upper middle income		Population (m)	0.1
Starting a business (rank)	81	**Registering property** (rank)	59	**Trading across borders** (rank)	93
Procedures (number)	9	Procedures (number)	4	Documents to export (number)	6
Time (days)	38	Time (days)	33	Time to export (days)	17
Cost (% of income per capita)	7.3	Cost (% of property value)	7.0	Cost to export (US$ per container)	1,839
Minimum capital (% of income per capita)	0.0			Documents to import (number)	5
		Getting credit (rank)	150	Time to import (days)	19
Dealing with construction permits (rank)	56	Strength of legal rights index (0-10)	4	Cost to import (US$ per container)	1,839
Procedures (number)	19	Depth of credit information index (0-6)	0		
Time (days)	144	Public registry coverage (% of adults)	0.0	**Enforcing contracts** (rank)	70
Cost (% of income per capita)	30.3	Private bureau coverage (% of adults)	0.0	Procedures (number)	38
				Time (days)	720
Employing workers (rank)	130	**Protecting investors** (rank)	57	Cost (% of claim)	14.3
Difficulty of hiring index (0-100)	44	Extent of disclosure index (0-10)	4		
Rigidity of hours index (0-100)	13	Extent of director liability index (0-10)	8	**Closing a business** (rank)	183
Difficulty of redundancy index (0-100)	50	Ease of shareholder suits index (0-10)	5	Time (years)	NO PRACTICE
Rigidity of employment index (0-100)	36	Strength of investor protection index (0-10)	5.7	Cost (% of estate)	NO PRACTICE
Redundancy cost (weeks of salary)	39			Recovery rate (cents on the dollar)	0.0
		Paying taxes (rank)	34		
		Payments (number per year)	16		
		Time (hours per year)	76		
		Total tax rate (% of profit)	44.1		

SIERRA LEONE

Ease of doing business (rank)	148	Sub-Saharan Africa		GNI per capita (US$)	321
		Low income		Population (m)	5.6
✔ **Starting a business** (rank)	58	✘ **Registering property** (rank)	175	✘ **Trading across borders** (rank)	137
Procedures (number)	6	Procedures (number)	7	Documents to export (number)	7
Time (days)	12	Time (days)	236	Time to export (days)	26
Cost (% of income per capita)	118.8	Cost (% of property value)	12.4	Cost to export (US$ per container)	1,573
Minimum capital (% of income per capita)	0.0			Documents to import (number)	7
		✔ **Getting credit** (rank)	127	Time to import (days)	31
Dealing with construction permits (rank)	171	Strength of legal rights index (0-10)	6	Cost to import (US$ per container)	1,639
Procedures (number)	25	Depth of credit information index (0-6)	0		
Time (days)	283	Public registry coverage (% of adults)	0.0	**Enforcing contracts** (rank)	144
Cost (% of income per capita)	368.5	Private bureau coverage (% of adults)	0.0	Procedures (number)	40
				Time (days)	515
Employing workers (rank)	166	✔ **Protecting investors** (rank)	27	Cost (% of claim)	149.5
Difficulty of hiring index (0-100)	33	Extent of disclosure index (0-10)	6		
Rigidity of hours index (0-100)	40	Extent of director liability index (0-10)	7	✔ **Closing a business** (rank)	147
Difficulty of redundancy index (0-100)	50	Ease of shareholder suits index (0-10)	6	Time (years)	2.6
Rigidity of employment index (0-100)	41	Strength of investor protection index (0-10)	6.3	Cost (% of estate)	42
Redundancy cost (weeks of salary)	189			Recovery rate (cents on the dollar)	8.5
		✔ **Paying taxes** (rank)	160		
		Payments (number per year)	29		
		Time (hours per year)	357		
		Total tax rate (% of profit)	235.6		

SINGAPORE

Ease of doing business (rank)	1	East Asia & Pacific		GNI per capita (US$)	34,762
		High income		Population (m)	4.8
✔ **Starting a business** (rank)	4	✔ **Registering property** (rank)	16	**Trading across borders** (rank)	1
Procedures (number)	3	Procedures (number)	3	Documents to export (number)	4
Time (days)	3	Time (days)	5	Time to export (days)	5
Cost (% of income per capita)	0.7	Cost (% of property value)	2.8	Cost to export (US$ per container)	456
Minimum capital (% of income per capita)	0.0			Documents to import (number)	4
		Getting credit (rank)	4	Time to import (days)	3
✔ **Dealing with construction permits** (rank)	2	Strength of legal rights index (0-10)	10	Cost to import (US$ per container)	439
Procedures (number)	11	Depth of credit information index (0-6)	4		
Time (days)	25	Public registry coverage (% of adults)	0.0	**Enforcing contracts** (rank)	13
Cost (% of income per capita)	19.9	Private bureau coverage (% of adults)	40.3	Procedures (number)	21
				Time (days)	150
Employing workers (rank)	1	**Protecting investors** (rank)	2	Cost (% of claim)	25.8
Difficulty of hiring index (0-100)	0	Extent of disclosure index (0-10)	10		
Rigidity of hours index (0-100)	0	Extent of director liability index (0-10)	9	**Closing a business** (rank)	2
Difficulty of redundancy index (0-100)	0	Ease of shareholder suits index (0-10)	9	Time (years)	0.8
Rigidity of employment index (0-100)	0	Strength of investor protection index (0-10)	9.3	Cost (% of estate)	1
Redundancy cost (weeks of salary)	4			Recovery rate (cents on the dollar)	91.3
		Paying taxes (rank)	5		
		Payments (number per year)	5		
		Time (hours per year)	84		
		Total tax rate (% of profit)	27.8		

SLOVAK REPUBLIC

		OECD high income		GNI per capita (US$)		14,541
Ease of doing business (rank)	42	High income		Population (m)		5.4
Starting a business (rank)	66	**Registering property** (rank)	11	✔ **Trading across borders** (rank)		113
Procedures (number)	6	Procedures (number)	3	Documents to export (number)		6
Time (days)	16	Time (days)	17	Time to export (days)		20
Cost (% of income per capita)	2.0	Cost (% of property value)	0.1	Cost to export (US$ per container)		1,445
Minimum capital (% of income per capita)	23.8			Documents to import (number)		8
		Getting credit (rank)	15	Time to import (days)		25
Dealing with construction permits (rank)	56	Strength of legal rights index (0-10)	9	Cost to import (US$ per container)		1,445
Procedures (number)	13	Depth of credit information index (0-6)	4			
Time (days)	287	Public registry coverage (% of adults)	1.4	**Enforcing contracts** (rank)		61
Cost (% of income per capita)	13.6	Private bureau coverage (% of adults)	44.0	Procedures (number)		30
				Time (days)		565
Employing workers (rank)	81	**Protecting investors** (rank)	109	Cost (% of claim)		30.0
Difficulty of hiring index (0-100)	17	Extent of disclosure index (0-10)	3			
Rigidity of hours index (0-100)	20	Extent of director liability index (0-10)	4	**Closing a business** (rank)		39
Difficulty of redundancy index (0-100)	30	Ease of shareholder suits index (0-10)	7	Time (years)		4.0
Rigidity of employment index (0-100)	22	Strength of investor protection index (0-10)	4.7	Cost (% of estate)		18
Redundancy cost (weeks of salary)	26			Recovery rate (cents on the dollar)		45.9
		Paying taxes (rank)	120			
		Payments (number per year)	31			
		Time (hours per year)	257			
		Total tax rate (% of profit)	48.6			

SLOVENIA

		Eastern Europe & Central Asia		GNI per capita (US$)		24,013
Ease of doing business (rank)	53	High income		Population (m)		2.0
✔ **Starting a business** (rank)	26	**Registering property** (rank)	108	**Trading across borders** (rank)		84
Procedures (number)	3	Procedures (number)	6	Documents to export (number)		6
Time (days)	6	Time (days)	391	Time to export (days)		20
Cost (% of income per capita)	0.0	Cost (% of property value)	2.0	Cost to export (US$ per container)		1,075
Minimum capital (% of income per capita)	43.3			Documents to import (number)		8
		Getting credit (rank)	87	Time to import (days)		21
✔ **Dealing with construction permits** (rank)	59	Strength of legal rights index (0-10)	6	Cost to import (US$ per container)		1,130
Procedures (number)	14	Depth of credit information index (0-6)	2			
Time (days)	197	Public registry coverage (% of adults)	2.7	**Enforcing contracts** (rank)		60
Cost (% of income per capita)	79.9	Private bureau coverage (% of adults)	0.0	Procedures (number)		32
				Time (days)		1,290
Employing workers (rank)	162	**Protecting investors** (rank)	20	Cost (% of claim)		12.7
Difficulty of hiring index (0-100)	78	Extent of disclosure index (0-10)	3			
Rigidity of hours index (0-100)	53	Extent of director liability index (0-10)	9	**Closing a business** (rank)		40
Difficulty of redundancy index (0-100)	30	Ease of shareholder suits index (0-10)	8	Time (years)		2.0
Rigidity of employment index (0-100)	54	Strength of investor protection index (0-10)	6.7	Cost (% of estate)		8
Redundancy cost (weeks of salary)	37			Recovery rate (cents on the dollar)		45.5
		Paying taxes (rank)	84			
		Payments (number per year)	22			
		Time (hours per year)	260			
		Total tax rate (% of profit)	37.5			

SOLOMON ISLANDS

		East Asia & Pacific		GNI per capita (US$)		1,180
Ease of doing business (rank)	104	Lower middle income		Population (m)		0.5
Starting a business (rank)	111	**Registering property** (rank)	172	**Trading across borders** (rank)		82
Procedures (number)	7	Procedures (number)	10	Documents to export (number)		7
Time (days)	57	Time (days)	297	Time to export (days)		24
Cost (% of income per capita)	52.7	Cost (% of property value)	4.8	Cost to export (US$ per container)		1,023
Minimum capital (% of income per capita)	0.0			Documents to import (number)		4
		Getting credit (rank)	167	Time to import (days)		21
✘ **Dealing with construction permits** (rank)	40	Strength of legal rights index (0-10)	3	Cost to import (US$ per container)		1,237
Procedures (number)	12	Depth of credit information index (0-6)	0			
Time (days)	62	Public registry coverage (% of adults)	0.0	**Enforcing contracts** (rank)		108
Cost (% of income per capita)	504.1	Private bureau coverage (% of adults)	0.0	Procedures (number)		37
				Time (days)		455
Employing workers (rank)	65	**Protecting investors** (rank)	57	Cost (% of claim)		78.9
Difficulty of hiring index (0-100)	22	Extent of disclosure index (0-10)	3			
Rigidity of hours index (0-100)	0	Extent of director liability index (0-10)	7	**Closing a business** (rank)		107
Difficulty of redundancy index (0-100)	20	Ease of shareholder suits index (0-10)	7	Time (years)		1.0
Rigidity of employment index (0-100)	14	Strength of investor protection index (0-10)	5.7	Cost (% of estate)		38
Redundancy cost (weeks of salary)	44			Recovery rate (cents on the dollar)		23.6
		Paying taxes (rank)	48			
		Payments (number per year)	33			
		Time (hours per year)	80			
		Total tax rate (% of profit)	36.3			

✔ Reforms making it easier to do business   ✗ Reforms making it more difficult to do business

SOUTH AFRICA

Ease of doing business (rank)	34	Sub-Saharan Africa		GNI per capita (US$)	5,819
		Upper middle income		Population (m)	48.7
Starting a business (rank)	67	**Registering property** (rank)	90	**Trading across borders** (rank)	148
Procedures (number)	6	Procedures (number)	6	Documents to export (number)	8
Time (days)	22	Time (days)	24	Time to export (days)	30
Cost (% of income per capita)	5.9	Cost (% of property value)	8.7	Cost to export (US$ per container)	1,531
Minimum capital (% of income per capita)	0.0			Documents to import (number)	9
		Getting credit (rank)	2	Time to import (days)	35
Dealing with construction permits (rank)	52	Strength of legal rights index (0-10)	9	Cost to import (US$ per container)	1,807
Procedures (number)	17	Depth of credit information index (0-6)	6		
Time (days)	174	Public registry coverage (% of adults)	0.0	**Enforcing contracts** (rank)	85
Cost (% of income per capita)	24.5	Private bureau coverage (% of adults)	54.7	Procedures (number)	30
				Time (days)	600
Employing workers (rank)	102	**Protecting investors** (rank)	10	Cost (% of claim)	33.2
Difficulty of hiring index (0-100)	56	Extent of disclosure index (0-10)	8		
Rigidity of hours index (0-100)	20	Extent of director liability index (0-10)	8	**Closing a business** (rank)	76
Difficulty of redundancy index (0-100)	30	Ease of shareholder suits index (0-10)	8	Time (years)	2.0
Rigidity of employment index (0-100)	35	Strength of investor protection index (0-10)	8.0	Cost (% of estate)	18
Redundancy cost (weeks of salary)	24			Recovery rate (cents on the dollar)	32.2
		✔ **Paying taxes** (rank)	23		
		Payments (number per year)	9		
		Time (hours per year)	200		
		Total tax rate (% of profit)	30.2		

SPAIN

Ease of doing business (rank)	62	OECD high income		GNI per capita (US$)	31,963
		High income		Population (m)	45.6
Starting a business (rank)	146	**Registering property** (rank)	48	**Trading across borders** (rank)	59
Procedures (number)	10	Procedures (number)	4	Documents to export (number)	6
Time (days)	47	Time (days)	18	Time to export (days)	9
Cost (% of income per capita)	15.0	Cost (% of property value)	7.2	Cost to export (US$ per container)	1,221
Minimum capital (% of income per capita)	12.8			Documents to import (number)	8
		Getting credit (rank)	43	Time to import (days)	10
Dealing with construction permits (rank)	53	Strength of legal rights index (0-10)	6	Cost to import (US$ per container)	1,221
Procedures (number)	11	Depth of credit information index (0-6)	5		
Time (days)	233	Public registry coverage (% of adults)	45.3	**Enforcing contracts** (rank)	52
Cost (% of income per capita)	60.9	Private bureau coverage (% of adults)	7.6	Procedures (number)	39
				Time (days)	515
Employing workers (rank)	157	**Protecting investors** (rank)	93	Cost (% of claim)	17.2
Difficulty of hiring index (0-100)	78	Extent of disclosure index (0-10)	5		
Rigidity of hours index (0-100)	40	Extent of director liability index (0-10)	6	**Closing a business** (rank)	19
Difficulty of redundancy index (0-100)	30	Ease of shareholder suits index (0-10)	4	Time (years)	1.0
Rigidity of employment index (0-100)	49	Strength of investor protection index (0-10)	5.0	Cost (% of estate)	15
Redundancy cost (weeks of salary)	56			Recovery rate (cents on the dollar)	73.2
		✔ **Paying taxes** (rank)	78		
		Payments (number per year)	8		
		Time (hours per year)	213		
		Total tax rate (% of profit)	56.9		

SRI LANKA

Ease of doing business (rank)	105	South Asia		GNI per capita (US$)	1,788
		Lower middle income		Population (m)	20.0
Starting a business (rank)	41	**Registering property** (rank)	148	**Trading across borders** (rank)	65
Procedures (number)	4	Procedures (number)	8	Documents to export (number)	8
Time (days)	38	Time (days)	83	Time to export (days)	21
Cost (% of income per capita)	5.9	Cost (% of property value)	5.1	Cost to export (US$ per container)	715
Minimum capital (% of income per capita)	0.0			Documents to import (number)	6
		✔ **Getting credit** (rank)	71	Time to import (days)	20
✗ **Dealing with construction permits** (rank)	168	Strength of legal rights index (0-10)	4	Cost to import (US$ per container)	745
Procedures (number)	22	Depth of credit information index (0-6)	5		
Time (days)	214	Public registry coverage (% of adults)	0.0	**Enforcing contracts** (rank)	137
Cost (% of income per capita)	1,458.8	Private bureau coverage (% of adults)	14.3	Procedures (number)	40
				Time (days)	1,318
Employing workers (rank)	96	**Protecting investors** (rank)	73	Cost (% of claim)	22.8
Difficulty of hiring index (0-100)	0	Extent of disclosure index (0-10)	4		
Rigidity of hours index (0-100)	0	Extent of director liability index (0-10)	5	**Closing a business** (rank)	45
Difficulty of redundancy index (0-100)	60	Ease of shareholder suits index (0-10)	7	Time (years)	1.7
Rigidity of employment index (0-100)	20	Strength of investor protection index (0-10)	5.3	Cost (% of estate)	5
Redundancy cost (weeks of salary)	217			Recovery rate (cents on the dollar)	43.4
		Paying taxes (rank)	166		
		Payments (number per year)	62		
		Time (hours per year)	256		
		Total tax rate (% of profit)	63.7		

ST. KITTS AND NEVIS

		Latin America & Caribbean		GNI per capita (US$)	10,961
Ease of doing business (rank)	76	Upper middle income		Population (m)	0.05
Starting a business (rank)	86	**Registering property** (rank)	153	✔ **Trading across borders** (rank)	53
Procedures (number)	8	Procedures (number)	6	Documents to export (number)	6
Time (days)	45	Time (days)	81	Time to export (days)	12
Cost (% of income per capita)	11.9	Cost (% of property value)	13.3	Cost to export (US$ per container)	850
Minimum capital (% of income per capita)	0.0			Documents to import (number)	6
		Getting credit (rank)	87	Time to import (days)	13
Dealing with construction permits (rank)	8	Strength of legal rights index (0-10)	8	Cost to import (US$ per container)	2,138
Procedures (number)	14	Depth of credit information index (0-6)	0		
Time (days)	67	Public registry coverage (% of adults)	0.0	**Enforcing contracts** (rank)	114
Cost (% of income per capita)	4.8	Private bureau coverage (% of adults)	0.0	Procedures (number)	47
				Time (days)	578
Employing workers (rank)	19	**Protecting investors** (rank)	27	Cost (% of claim)	20.5
Difficulty of hiring index (0-100)	11	Extent of disclosure index (0-10)	4		
Rigidity of hours index (0-100)	0	Extent of director liability index (0-10)	8	**Closing a business** (rank)	183
Difficulty of redundancy index (0-100)	10	Ease of shareholder suits index (0-10)	7	Time (years)	NO PRACTICE
Rigidity of employment index (0-100)	7	Strength of investor protection index (0-10)	6.3	Cost (% of estate)	NO PRACTICE
Redundancy cost (weeks of salary)	13			Recovery rate (cents on the dollar)	0.0
		Paying taxes (rank)	100		
		Payments (number per year)	24		
		Time (hours per year)	155		
		Total tax rate (% of profit)	52.7		

ST. LUCIA

		Latin America & Caribbean		GNI per capita (US$)	5,530
Ease of doing business (rank)	36	Upper middle income		Population (m)	0.2
✔ **Starting a business** (rank)	36	**Registering property** (rank)	76	**Trading across borders** (rank)	103
Procedures (number)	5	Procedures (number)	6	Documents to export (number)	5
Time (days)	14	Time (days)	16	Time to export (days)	14
Cost (% of income per capita)	21.8	Cost (% of property value)	7.4	Cost to export (US$ per container)	1,600
Minimum capital (% of income per capita)	0.0			Documents to import (number)	8
		Getting credit (rank)	87	Time to import (days)	18
Dealing with construction permits (rank)	12	Strength of legal rights index (0-10)	8	Cost to import (US$ per container)	2,645
Procedures (number)	9	Depth of credit information index (0-6)	0		
Time (days)	139	Public registry coverage (% of adults)	0.0	**Enforcing contracts** (rank)	165
Cost (% of income per capita)	29.5	Private bureau coverage (% of adults)	0.0	Procedures (number)	47
				Time (days)	635
Employing workers (rank)	20	**Protecting investors** (rank)	27	Cost (% of claim)	37.3
Difficulty of hiring index (0-100)	0	Extent of disclosure index (0-10)	4		
Rigidity of hours index (0-100)	0	Extent of director liability index (0-10)	8	**Closing a business** (rank)	47
Difficulty of redundancy index (0-100)	0	Ease of shareholder suits index (0-10)	7	Time (years)	2.0
Rigidity of employment index (0-100)	0	Strength of investor protection index (0-10)	6.3	Cost (% of estate)	9
Redundancy cost (weeks of salary)	56			Recovery rate (cents on the dollar)	42.9
		Paying taxes (rank)	40		
		Payments (number per year)	32		
		Time (hours per year)	92		
		Total tax rate (% of profit)	34.4		

ST. VINCENT AND THE GRENADINES

		Latin America & Caribbean		GNI per capita (US$)	5,141
Ease of doing business (rank)	70	Upper middle income		Population (m)	0.1
✔ **Starting a business** (rank)	45	**Registering property** (rank)	137	**Trading across borders** (rank)	52
Procedures (number)	7	Procedures (number)	7	Documents to export (number)	6
Time (days)	11	Time (days)	38	Time to export (days)	12
Cost (% of income per capita)	21.0	Cost (% of property value)	11.9	Cost to export (US$ per container)	1,290
Minimum capital (% of income per capita)	0.0			Documents to import (number)	6
		Getting credit (rank)	87	Time to import (days)	11
Dealing with construction permits (rank)	3	Strength of legal rights index (0-10)	8	Cost to import (US$ per container)	1,290
Procedures (number)	11	Depth of credit information index (0-6)	0		
Time (days)	74	Public registry coverage (% of adults)	0.0	**Enforcing contracts** (rank)	102
Cost (% of income per capita)	6.9	Private bureau coverage (% of adults)	0.0	Procedures (number)	45
				Time (days)	394
Employing workers (rank)	57	**Protecting investors** (rank)	27	Cost (% of claim)	30.3
Difficulty of hiring index (0-100)	11	Extent of disclosure index (0-10)	4		
Rigidity of hours index (0-100)	0	Extent of director liability index (0-10)	8	**Closing a business** (rank)	183
Difficulty of redundancy index (0-100)	20	Ease of shareholder suits index (0-10)	7	Time (years)	NO PRACTICE
Rigidity of employment index (0-100)	10	Strength of investor protection index (0-10)	6.3	Cost (% of estate)	NO PRACTICE
Redundancy cost (weeks of salary)	54			Recovery rate (cents on the dollar)	0.0
		✔ **Paying taxes** (rank)	62		
		Payments (number per year)	32		
		Time (hours per year)	117		
		Total tax rate (% of profit)	41.0		

✔ Reforms making it easier to do business   ✗ Reforms making it more difficult to do business

SUDAN

		Sub-Saharan Africa		GNI per capita (US$)		1,125
Ease of doing business (rank)	154	Lower middle income		Population (m)		41.3
Starting a business (rank)	118	**Registering property** (rank)	37	✔ **Trading across borders** (rank)		142
Procedures (number)	10	Procedures (number)	6	Documents to export (number)		6
Time (days)	36	Time (days)	9	Time to export (days)		32
Cost (% of income per capita)	36.0	Cost (% of property value)	3.0	Cost to export (US$ per container)		2,050
Minimum capital (% of income per capita)	0.0			Documents to import (number)		6
		Getting credit (rank)	135	Time to import (days)		46
Dealing with construction permits (rank)	139	Strength of legal rights index (0-10)	5	Cost to import (US$ per container)		2,900
Procedures (number)	19	Depth of credit information index (0-6)	0			
Time (days)	271	Public registry coverage (% of adults)	0.0	**Enforcing contracts** (rank)		146
Cost (% of income per capita)	206.4	Private bureau coverage (% of adults)	0.0	Procedures (number)		53
				Time (days)		810
Employing workers (rank)	153	**Protecting investors** (rank)	154	Cost (% of claim)		19.8
Difficulty of hiring index (0-100)	39	Extent of disclosure index (0-10)	0			
Rigidity of hours index (0-100)	20	Extent of director liability index (0-10)	6	**Closing a business** (rank)		183
Difficulty of redundancy index (0-100)	50	Ease of shareholder suits index (0-10)	4	Time (years)		NO PRACTICE
Rigidity of employment index (0-100)	36	Strength of investor protection index (0-10)	3.3	Cost (% of estate)		NO PRACTICE
Redundancy cost (weeks of salary)	118			Recovery rate (cents on the dollar)		0.0
		✔ **Paying taxes** (rank)	94			
		Payments (number per year)	42			
		Time (hours per year)	180			
		Total tax rate (% of profit)	36.1			

SURINAME

		Latin America & Caribbean		GNI per capita (US$)		4,990
Ease of doing business (rank)	155	Upper middle income		Population (m)		0.5
Starting a business (rank)	171	✗ **Registering property** (rank)	168	**Trading across borders** (rank)		101
Procedures (number)	13	Procedures (number)	6	Documents to export (number)		8
Time (days)	694	Time (days)	197	Time to export (days)		25
Cost (% of income per capita)	112.8	Cost (% of property value)	13.8	Cost to export (US$ per container)		975
Minimum capital (% of income per capita)	0.7			Documents to import (number)		7
		Getting credit (rank)	135	Time to import (days)		25
Dealing with construction permits (rank)	97	Strength of legal rights index (0-10)	5	Cost to import (US$ per container)		885
Procedures (number)	14	Depth of credit information index (0-6)	0			
Time (days)	431	Public registry coverage (% of adults)	0.0	**Enforcing contracts** (rank)		178
Cost (% of income per capita)	95.7	Private bureau coverage (% of adults)	0.0	Procedures (number)		44
				Time (days)		1,715
Employing workers (rank)	70	**Protecting investors** (rank)	180	Cost (% of claim)		37.1
Difficulty of hiring index (0-100)	0	Extent of disclosure index (0-10)	1			
Rigidity of hours index (0-100)	13	Extent of director liability index (0-10)	0	**Closing a business** (rank)		149
Difficulty of redundancy index (0-100)	50	Ease of shareholder suits index (0-10)	5	Time (years)		5.0
Rigidity of employment index (0-100)	21	Strength of investor protection index (0-10)	2.0	Cost (% of estate)		30
Redundancy cost (weeks of salary)	26			Recovery rate (cents on the dollar)		8.1
		Paying taxes (rank)	32			
		Payments (number per year)	17			
		Time (hours per year)	199			
		Total tax rate (% of profit)	27.9			

SWAZILAND

		Sub-Saharan Africa		GNI per capita (US$)		2,522
Ease of doing business (rank)	115	Lower middle income		Population (m)		1.2
Starting a business (rank)	158	**Registering property** (rank)	158	**Trading across borders** (rank)		158
Procedures (number)	13	Procedures (number)	11	Documents to export (number)		9
Time (days)	61	Time (days)	46	Time to export (days)		21
Cost (% of income per capita)	33.9	Cost (% of property value)	7.1	Cost to export (US$ per container)		2,184
Minimum capital (% of income per capita)	0.5			Documents to import (number)		11
		Getting credit (rank)	43	Time to import (days)		33
Dealing with construction permits (rank)	24	Strength of legal rights index (0-10)	6	Cost to import (US$ per container)		2,249
Procedures (number)	13	Depth of credit information index (0-6)	5			
Time (days)	93	Public registry coverage (% of adults)	0.0	**Enforcing contracts** (rank)		130
Cost (% of income per capita)	91.8	Private bureau coverage (% of adults)	42.3	Procedures (number)		40
				Time (days)		972
Employing workers (rank)	55	**Protecting investors** (rank)	180	Cost (% of claim)		23.1
Difficulty of hiring index (0-100)	11	Extent of disclosure index (0-10)	0			
Rigidity of hours index (0-100)	0	Extent of director liability index (0-10)	1	**Closing a business** (rank)		68
Difficulty of redundancy index (0-100)	20	Ease of shareholder suits index (0-10)	5	Time (years)		2.0
Rigidity of employment index (0-100)	10	Strength of investor protection index (0-10)	2.0	Cost (% of estate)		15
Redundancy cost (weeks of salary)	53			Recovery rate (cents on the dollar)		34.9
		Paying taxes (rank)	53			
		Payments (number per year)	33			
		Time (hours per year)	104			
		Total tax rate (% of profit)	36.6			

SWEDEN

		OECD high income		GNI per capita (US$)		50,943
Ease of doing business (rank)	18	High income		Population (m)		9.2
Starting a business (rank)	43	**Registering property** (rank)	20	**Trading across borders** (rank)		7
Procedures (number)	3	Procedures (number)	2	Documents to export (number)		4
Time (days)	15	Time (days)	15	Time to export (days)		8
Cost (% of income per capita)	0.6	Cost (% of property value)	3.0	Cost to export (US$ per container)		697
Minimum capital (% of income per capita)	28.5			Documents to import (number)		3
		Getting credit (rank)	71	Time to import (days)		6
Dealing with construction permits (rank)	19	Strength of legal rights index (0-10)	5	Cost to import (US$ per container)		735
Procedures (number)	8	Depth of credit information index (0-6)	4			
Time (days)	116	Public registry coverage (% of adults)	0.0	**Enforcing contracts** (rank)		51
Cost (% of income per capita)	103.3	Private bureau coverage (% of adults)	100.0	Procedures (number)		30
				Time (days)		508
Employing workers (rank)	117	**Protecting investors** (rank)	57	Cost (% of claim)		31.2
Difficulty of hiring index (0-100)	33	Extent of disclosure index (0-10)	6			
Rigidity of hours index (0-100)	40	Extent of director liability index (0-10)	4	**Closing a business** (rank)		18
Difficulty of redundancy index (0-100)	40	Ease of shareholder suits index (0-10)	7	Time (years)		2.0
Rigidity of employment index (0-100)	38	Strength of investor protection index (0-10)	5.7	Cost (% of estate)		9
Redundancy cost (weeks of salary)	26			Recovery rate (cents on the dollar)		75.1
		Paying taxes (rank)	42			
		Payments (number per year)	2			
		Time (hours per year)	122			
		Total tax rate (% of profit)	54.6			

SWITZERLAND

		OECD high income		GNI per capita (US$)		65,334
Ease of doing business (rank)	21	High income		Population (m)		7.6
Starting a business (rank)	71	**Registering property** (rank)	15	**Trading across borders** (rank)		39
Procedures (number)	6	Procedures (number)	4	Documents to export (number)		4
Time (days)	20	Time (days)	16	Time to export (days)		8
Cost (% of income per capita)	2.0	Cost (% of property value)	0.4	Cost to export (US$ per container)		1,537
Minimum capital (% of income per capita)	26.4			Documents to import (number)		5
		Getting credit (rank)	15	Time to import (days)		9
Dealing with construction permits (rank)	35	Strength of legal rights index (0-10)	8	Cost to import (US$ per container)		1,540
Procedures (number)	14	Depth of credit information index (0-6)	5			
Time (days)	154	Public registry coverage (% of adults)	0.0	**Enforcing contracts** (rank)		29
Cost (% of income per capita)	49.9	Private bureau coverage (% of adults)	22.5	Procedures (number)		31
				Time (days)		417
Employing workers (rank)	16	**Protecting investors** (rank)	165	Cost (% of claim)		24.0
Difficulty of hiring index (0-100)	0	Extent of disclosure index (0-10)	0			
Rigidity of hours index (0-100)	20	Extent of director liability index (0-10)	5	**Closing a business** (rank)		38
Difficulty of redundancy index (0-100)	0	Ease of shareholder suits index (0-10)	4	Time (years)		3.0
Rigidity of employment index (0-100)	7	Strength of investor protection index (0-10)	3.0	Cost (% of estate)		4
Redundancy cost (weeks of salary)	13			Recovery rate (cents on the dollar)		46.8
		Paying taxes (rank)	21			
		Payments (number per year)	24			
		Time (hours per year)	63			
		Total tax rate (% of profit)	29.7			

SYRIAN ARAB REPUBLIC

		Middle East & North Africa		GNI per capita (US$)		2,094
Ease of doing business (rank)	143	Lower middle income		Population (m)		21.2
✔ **Starting a business** (rank)	133	**Registering property** (rank)	82	**Trading across borders** (rank)		118
Procedures (number)	7	Procedures (number)	4	Documents to export (number)		8
Time (days)	17	Time (days)	19	Time to export (days)		15
Cost (% of income per capita)	27.8	Cost (% of property value)	28.0	Cost to export (US$ per container)		1,190
Minimum capital (% of income per capita)	1,012.5			Documents to import (number)		9
		Getting credit (rank)	181	Time to import (days)		21
Dealing with construction permits (rank)	132	Strength of legal rights index (0-10)	1	Cost to import (US$ per container)		1,625
Procedures (number)	26	Depth of credit information index (0-6)	0			
Time (days)	128	Public registry coverage (% of adults)	0.0	**Enforcing contracts** (rank)		176
Cost (% of income per capita)	540.3	Private bureau coverage (% of adults)	0.0	Procedures (number)		55
				Time (days)		872
Employing workers (rank)	91	**Protecting investors** (rank)	119	Cost (% of claim)		29.3
Difficulty of hiring index (0-100)	11	Extent of disclosure index (0-10)	6			
Rigidity of hours index (0-100)	0	Extent of director liability index (0-10)	5	**Closing a business** (rank)		87
Difficulty of redundancy index (0-100)	50	Ease of shareholder suits index (0-10)	2	Time (years)		4.1
Rigidity of employment index (0-100)	20	Strength of investor protection index (0-10)	4.3	Cost (% of estate)		9
Redundancy cost (weeks of salary)	80			Recovery rate (cents on the dollar)		29.5
		Paying taxes (rank)	105			
		Payments (number per year)	20			
		Time (hours per year)	336			
		Total tax rate (% of profit)	42.9			

TAIWAN, CHINA

		East Asia & Pacific		GNI per capita (US$)		17,273
Ease of doing business (rank)	46	High income		Population (m)		22.7
✔ **Starting a business** (rank)	29	**Registering property** (rank)	30	**Trading across borders** (rank)		33
Procedures (number)	6	Procedures (number)	3	Documents to export (number)		7
Time (days)	23	Time (days)	5	Time to export (days)		13
Cost (% of income per capita)	3.9	Cost (% of property value)	6.2	Cost to export (US$ per container)		720
Minimum capital (% of income per capita)	0.0			Documents to import (number)		7
		Getting credit (rank)	71	Time to import (days)		12
Dealing with construction permits (rank)	97	Strength of legal rights index (0-10)	4	Cost to import (US$ per container)		732
Procedures (number)	28	Depth of credit information index (0-6)	5			
Time (days)	142	Public registry coverage (% of adults)	0.0	**Enforcing contracts** (rank)		90
Cost (% of income per capita)	96.2	Private bureau coverage (% of adults)	63.2	Procedures (number)		47
				Time (days)		510
Employing workers (rank)	153	**Protecting investors** (rank)	73	Cost (% of claim)		17.7
Difficulty of hiring index (0-100)	78	Extent of disclosure index (0-10)	7			
Rigidity of hours index (0-100)	20	Extent of director liability index (0-10)	4	**Closing a business** (rank)		11
Difficulty of redundancy index (0-100)	40	Ease of shareholder suits index (0-10)	5	Time (years)		1.9
Rigidity of employment index (0-100)	46	Strength of investor protection index (0-10)	5.3	Cost (% of estate)		4
Redundancy cost (weeks of salary)	91			Recovery rate (cents on the dollar)		80.9
		✔ **Paying taxes** (rank)	92			
		Payments (number per year)	18			
		Time (hours per year)	281			
		Total tax rate (% of profit)	40.4			

TAJIKISTAN

		Eastern Europe & Central Asia		GNI per capita (US$)		596
Ease of doing business (rank)	152	Low income		Population (m)		6.8
✔ **Starting a business** (rank)	143	✘ **Registering property** (rank)	78	**Trading across borders** (rank)		179
Procedures (number)	12	Procedures (number)	6	Documents to export (number)		10
Time (days)	25	Time (days)	37	Time to export (days)		82
Cost (% of income per capita)	24.3	Cost (% of property value)	4.6	Cost to export (US$ per container)		3,150
Minimum capital (% of income per capita)	9.9			Documents to import (number)		10
		✔ **Getting credit** (rank)	167	Time to import (days)		83
✔ **Dealing with construction permits** (rank)	177	Strength of legal rights index (0-10)	3	Cost to import (US$ per container)		4,550
Procedures (number)	32	Depth of credit information index (0-6)	0			
Time (days)	250	Public registry coverage (% of adults)	0.0	**Enforcing contracts** (rank)		39
Cost (% of income per capita)	1,022.9	Private bureau coverage (% of adults)	0.0	Procedures (number)		34
				Time (days)		430
Employing workers (rank)	143	✔ **Protecting investors** (rank)	73	Cost (% of claim)		25.5
Difficulty of hiring index (0-100)	33	Extent of disclosure index (0-10)	6			
Rigidity of hours index (0-100)	73	Extent of director liability index (0-10)	5	✔ **Closing a business** (rank)		100
Difficulty of redundancy index (0-100)	40	Ease of shareholder suits index (0-10)	5	Time (years)		3.0
Rigidity of employment index (0-100)	49	Strength of investor protection index (0-10)	5.3	Cost (% of estate)		9
Redundancy cost (weeks of salary)	30			Recovery rate (cents on the dollar)		25.4
		Paying taxes (rank)	162			
		Payments (number per year)	54			
		Time (hours per year)	224			
		Total tax rate (% of profit)	85.9			

TANZANIA

		Sub-Saharan Africa		GNI per capita (US$)		432
Ease of doing business (rank)	131	Low income		Population (m)		42.5
Starting a business (rank)	120	**Registering property** (rank)	145	**Trading across borders** (rank)		108
Procedures (number)	12	Procedures (number)	9	Documents to export (number)		5
Time (days)	29	Time (days)	73	Time to export (days)		24
Cost (% of income per capita)	36.8	Cost (% of property value)	4.4	Cost to export (US$ per container)		1,262
Minimum capital (% of income per capita)	0.0			Documents to import (number)		7
		Getting credit (rank)	87	Time to import (days)		31
✘ **Dealing with construction permits** (rank)	178	Strength of legal rights index (0-10)	8	Cost to import (US$ per container)		1,475
Procedures (number)	22	Depth of credit information index (0-6)	0			
Time (days)	328	Public registry coverage (% of adults)	0.0	**Enforcing contracts** (rank)		31
Cost (% of income per capita)	3,281.3	Private bureau coverage (% of adults)	0.0	Procedures (number)		38
				Time (days)		462
Employing workers (rank)	131	**Protecting investors** (rank)	93	Cost (% of claim)		14.3
Difficulty of hiring index (0-100)	100	Extent of disclosure index (0-10)	3			
Rigidity of hours index (0-100)	13	Extent of director liability index (0-10)	4	**Closing a business** (rank)		113
Difficulty of redundancy index (0-100)	50	Ease of shareholder suits index (0-10)	8	Time (years)		3.0
Rigidity of employment index (0-100)	54	Strength of investor protection index (0-10)	5.0	Cost (% of estate)		22
Redundancy cost (weeks of salary)	18			Recovery rate (cents on the dollar)		21.3
		Paying taxes (rank)	119			
		Payments (number per year)	48			
		Time (hours per year)	172			
		Total tax rate (% of profit)	45.2			

THAILAND

Ease of doing business (rank)	12	East Asia & Pacific		GNI per capita (US$)	2,844
		Lower middle income		Population (m)	67.4
✔ **Starting a business** (rank)	55	**Registering property** (rank)	6	**Trading across borders** (rank)	12
Procedures (number)	7	Procedures (number)	2	Documents to export (number)	4
Time (days)	32	Time (days)	2	Time to export (days)	14
Cost (% of income per capita)	6.3	Cost (% of property value)	1.1	Cost to export (US$ per container)	625
Minimum capital (% of income per capita)	0.0			Documents to import (number)	3
				Time to import (days)	13
Dealing with construction permits (rank)	13	**Getting credit** (rank)	71	Cost to import (US$ per container)	795
Procedures (number)	11	Strength of legal rights index (0-10)	4		
Time (days)	156	Depth of credit information index (0-6)	5	**Enforcing contracts** (rank)	24
Cost (% of income per capita)	12.1	Public registry coverage (% of adults)	0.0	Procedures (number)	35
		Private bureau coverage (% of adults)	32.9	Time (days)	479
				Cost (% of claim)	12.3
Employing workers (rank)	52	**Protecting investors** (rank)	12		
Difficulty of hiring index (0-100)	33	Extent of disclosure index (0-10)	10	**Closing a business** (rank)	48
Rigidity of hours index (0-100)	0	Extent of director liability index (0-10)	7	Time (years)	2.7
Difficulty of redundancy index (0-100)	0	Ease of shareholder suits index (0-10)	6	Cost (% of estate)	36
Rigidity of employment index (0-100)	11	Strength of investor protection index (0-10)	7.7	Recovery rate (cents on the dollar)	42.4
Redundancy cost (weeks of salary)	54				
		Paying taxes (rank)	88		
		Payments (number per year)	23		
		Time (hours per year)	264		
		Total tax rate (% of profit)	37.2		

TIMOR-LESTE

Ease of doing business (rank)	164	East Asia & Pacific		GNI per capita (US$)	2,464
		Lower middle income		Population (m)	1.1
Starting a business (rank)	150	**Registering property** (rank)	183	**Trading across borders** (rank)	85
Procedures (number)	10	Procedures (number)	NO PRACTICE	Documents to export (number)	6
Time (days)	83	Time (days)	NO PRACTICE	Time to export (days)	25
Cost (% of income per capita)	4.1	Cost (% of property value)	NO PRACTICE	Cost to export (US$ per container)	1,010
Minimum capital (% of income per capita)	202.9			Documents to import (number)	7
		Getting credit (rank)	181	Time to import (days)	26
Dealing with construction permits (rank)	87	Strength of legal rights index (0-10)	1	Cost to import (US$ per container)	1,015
Procedures (number)	22	Depth of credit information index (0-6)	0		
Time (days)	208	Public registry coverage (% of adults)	0.0	**Enforcing contracts** (rank)	183
Cost (% of income per capita)	38.6	Private bureau coverage (% of adults)	0.0	Procedures (number)	51
				Time (days)	1,435
Employing workers (rank)	89	**Protecting investors** (rank)	132	Cost (% of claim)	163.2
Difficulty of hiring index (0-100)	33	Extent of disclosure index (0-10)	3		
Rigidity of hours index (0-100)	13	Extent of director liability index (0-10)	4	**Closing a business** (rank)	183
Difficulty of redundancy index (0-100)	50	Ease of shareholder suits index (0-10)	5	Time (years)	NO PRACTICE
Rigidity of employment index (0-100)	32	Strength of investor protection index (0-10)	4.0	Cost (% of estate)	NO PRACTICE
Redundancy cost (weeks of salary)	17			Recovery rate (cents on the dollar)	0.0
		✔ **Paying taxes** (rank)	19		
		Payments (number per year)	6		
		Time (hours per year)	276		
		Total tax rate (% of profit)	0.2		

TOGO

Ease of doing business (rank)	165	Sub-Saharan Africa		GNI per capita (US$)	404
		Low income		Population (m)	6.5
✔ **Starting a business** (rank)	170	**Registering property** (rank)	155	**Trading across borders** (rank)	87
Procedures (number)	7	Procedures (number)	5	Documents to export (number)	6
Time (days)	75	Time (days)	295	Time to export (days)	24
Cost (% of income per capita)	205.0	Cost (% of property value)	13.1	Cost to export (US$ per container)	940
Minimum capital (% of income per capita)	514.0			Documents to import (number)	8
		Getting credit (rank)	150	Time to import (days)	29
Dealing with construction permits (rank)	152	Strength of legal rights index (0-10)	3	Cost to import (US$ per container)	963
Procedures (number)	15	Depth of credit information index (0-6)	1		
Time (days)	277	Public registry coverage (% of adults)	2.7	**Enforcing contracts** (rank)	154
Cost (% of income per capita)	1,285.3	Private bureau coverage (% of adults)	0.0	Procedures (number)	41
				Time (days)	588
Employing workers (rank)	159	**Protecting investors** (rank)	147	Cost (% of claim)	47.5
Difficulty of hiring index (0-100)	83	Extent of disclosure index (0-10)	6		
Rigidity of hours index (0-100)	40	Extent of director liability index (0-10)	1	**Closing a business** (rank)	97
Difficulty of redundancy index (0-100)	40	Ease of shareholder suits index (0-10)	4	Time (years)	3.0
Rigidity of employment index (0-100)	54	Strength of investor protection index (0-10)	3.7	Cost (% of estate)	15
Redundancy cost (weeks of salary)	36			Recovery rate (cents on the dollar)	26.6
		✔ **Paying taxes** (rank)	155		
		Payments (number per year)	53		
		Time (hours per year)	270		
		Total tax rate (% of profit)	52.7		

✔ Reforms making it easier to do business   ✘ Reforms making it more difficult to do business

TONGA

Ease of doing business (rank)	52	East Asia & Pacific		GNI per capita (US$)		2,561
		Lower middle income		Population (m)		0.1
Starting a business (rank)	32	**Registering property** (rank)	121	**Trading across borders** (rank)		51
Procedures (number)	4	Procedures (number)	4	Documents to export (number)		7
Time (days)	25	Time (days)	108	Time to export (days)		19
Cost (% of income per capita)	8.2	Cost (% of property value)	10.2	Cost to export (US$ per container)		650
Minimum capital (% of income per capita)	0.0			Documents to import (number)		6
		Getting credit (rank)	113	Time to import (days)		24
Dealing with construction permits (rank)	35	Strength of legal rights index (0-10)	7	Cost to import (US$ per container)		725
Procedures (number)	11	Depth of credit information index (0-6)	0			
Time (days)	76	Public registry coverage (% of adults)	0.0	**Enforcing contracts** (rank)		55
Cost (% of income per capita)	317.7	Private bureau coverage (% of adults)	0.0	Procedures (number)		37
				Time (days)		350
Employing workers (rank)	11	**Protecting investors** (rank)	109	Cost (% of claim)		30.5
Difficulty of hiring index (0-100)	0	Extent of disclosure index (0-10)	3			
Rigidity of hours index (0-100)	20	Extent of director liability index (0-10)	3	**Closing a business** (rank)		103
Difficulty of redundancy index (0-100)	0	Ease of shareholder suits index (0-10)	8	Time (years)		2.7
Rigidity of employment index (0-100)	7	Strength of investor protection index (0-10)	4.7	Cost (% of estate)		22
Redundancy cost (weeks of salary)	0			Recovery rate (cents on the dollar)		25.2
		✔ **Paying taxes** (rank)	30			
		Payments (number per year)	20			
		Time (hours per year)	164			
		Total tax rate (% of profit)	27.5			

TRINIDAD AND TOBAGO

Ease of doing business (rank)	81	Latin America & Caribbean		GNI per capita (US$)		16,538
		High income		Population (m)		1.3
Starting a business (rank)	65	**Registering property** (rank)	170	**Trading across borders** (rank)		49
Procedures (number)	9	Procedures (number)	8	Documents to export (number)		5
Time (days)	43	Time (days)	162	Time to export (days)		14
Cost (% of income per capita)	0.7	Cost (% of property value)	7.0	Cost to export (US$ per container)		866
Minimum capital (% of income per capita)	0.0			Documents to import (number)		6
		Getting credit (rank)	30	Time to import (days)		26
Dealing with construction permits (rank)	82	Strength of legal rights index (0-10)	8	Cost to import (US$ per container)		1,100
Procedures (number)	20	Depth of credit information index (0-6)	4			
Time (days)	261	Public registry coverage (% of adults)	0.0	**Enforcing contracts** (rank)		169
Cost (% of income per capita)	4.6	Private bureau coverage (% of adults)	41.7	Procedures (number)		42
				Time (days)		1,340
Employing workers (rank)	45	**Protecting investors** (rank)	20	Cost (% of claim)		33.5
Difficulty of hiring index (0-100)	0	Extent of disclosure index (0-10)	4			
Rigidity of hours index (0-100)	0	Extent of director liability index (0-10)	9	**Closing a business** (rank)		183
Difficulty of redundancy index (0-100)	20	Ease of shareholder suits index (0-10)	7	Time (years)		NO PRACTICE
Rigidity of employment index (0-100)	7	Strength of investor protection index (0-10)	6.7	Cost (% of estate)		NO PRACTICE
Redundancy cost (weeks of salary)	67			Recovery rate (cents on the dollar)		0.0
		Paying taxes (rank)	56			
		Payments (number per year)	40			
		Time (hours per year)	114			
		Total tax rate (% of profit)	33.1			

TUNISIA

Ease of doing business (rank)	69	Middle East & North Africa		GNI per capita (US$)		3,292
		Lower middle income		Population (m)		10.3
Starting a business (rank)	47	**Registering property** (rank)	59	✔ **Trading across borders** (rank)		40
Procedures (number)	10	Procedures (number)	4	Documents to export (number)		5
Time (days)	11	Time (days)	39	Time to export (days)		15
Cost (% of income per capita)	5.7	Cost (% of property value)	6.1	Cost to export (US$ per container)		783
Minimum capital (% of income per capita)	0.0			Documents to import (number)		7
		Getting credit (rank)	87	Time to import (days)		21
Dealing with construction permits (rank)	107	Strength of legal rights index (0-10)	3	Cost to import (US$ per container)		858
Procedures (number)	20	Depth of credit information index (0-6)	5			
Time (days)	84	Public registry coverage (% of adults)	19.9	**Enforcing contracts** (rank)		77
Cost (% of income per capita)	998.3	Private bureau coverage (% of adults)	0.0	Procedures (number)		39
				Time (days)		565
Employing workers (rank)	108	✔ **Protecting investors** (rank)	73	Cost (% of claim)		21.8
Difficulty of hiring index (0-100)	28	Extent of disclosure index (0-10)	5			
Rigidity of hours index (0-100)	13	Extent of director liability index (0-10)	5	**Closing a business** (rank)		34
Difficulty of redundancy index (0-100)	80	Ease of shareholder suits index (0-10)	6	Time (years)		1.3
Rigidity of employment index (0-100)	40	Strength of investor protection index (0-10)	5.3	Cost (% of estate)		7
Redundancy cost (weeks of salary)	17			Recovery rate (cents on the dollar)		52.3
		✘ **Paying taxes** (rank)	118			
		Payments (number per year)	22			
		Time (hours per year)	228			
		Total tax rate (% of profit)	62.8			

TURKEY

		Eastern Europe & Central Asia		GNI per capita (US$)	9,345
Ease of doing business (rank)	73	Upper middle income		Population (m)	73.9
Starting a business (rank)	56	**Registering property** (rank)	36	**Trading across borders** (rank)	67
Procedures (number)	6	Procedures (number)	6	Documents to export (number)	7
Time (days)	6	Time (days)	6	Time to export (days)	14
Cost (% of income per capita)	14.2	Cost (% of property value)	3.0	Cost to export (US$ per container)	990
Minimum capital (% of income per capita)	9.5			Documents to import (number)	8
		✔ **Getting credit** (rank)	71	Time to import (days)	15
Dealing with construction permits (rank)	133	Strength of legal rights index (0-10)	4	Cost to import (US$ per container)	1,063
Procedures (number)	25	Depth of credit information index (0-6)	5		
Time (days)	188	Public registry coverage (% of adults)	15.9	**Enforcing contracts** (rank)	27
Cost (% of income per capita)	218.8	Private bureau coverage (% of adults)	42.9	Procedures (number)	35
				Time (days)	420
Employing workers (rank)	145	**Protecting investors** (rank)	57	Cost (% of claim)	18.8
Difficulty of hiring index (0-100)	44	Extent of disclosure index (0-10)	9		
Rigidity of hours index (0-100)	40	Extent of director liability index (0-10)	4	**Closing a business** (rank)	121
Difficulty of redundancy index (0-100)	20	Ease of shareholder suits index (0-10)	4	Time (years)	3.3
Rigidity of employment index (0-100)	35	Strength of investor protection index (0-10)	5.7	Cost (% of estate)	15
Redundancy cost (weeks of salary)	95			Recovery rate (cents on the dollar)	20.2
		Paying taxes (rank)	75		
		Payments (number per year)	15		
		Time (hours per year)	223		
		Total tax rate (% of profit)	44.5		

UGANDA

		Sub-Saharan Africa		GNI per capita (US$)	419
Ease of doing business (rank)	112	Low income		Population (m)	31.7
Starting a business (rank)	129	**Registering property** (rank)	149	✔ **Trading across borders** (rank)	145
Procedures (number)	18	Procedures (number)	13	Documents to export (number)	6
Time (days)	25	Time (days)	77	Time to export (days)	37
Cost (% of income per capita)	84.4	Cost (% of property value)	3.5	Cost to export (US$ per container)	3,190
Minimum capital (% of income per capita)	0.0			Documents to import (number)	7
		Getting credit (rank)	113	Time to import (days)	34
Dealing with construction permits (rank)	84	Strength of legal rights index (0-10)	7	Cost to import (US$ per container)	3,390
Procedures (number)	16	Depth of credit information index (0-6)	0		
Time (days)	143	Public registry coverage (% of adults)	0.0	**Enforcing contracts** (rank)	116
Cost (% of income per capita)	584.0	Private bureau coverage (% of adults)	0.0	Procedures (number)	38
				Time (days)	510
Employing workers (rank)	7	**Protecting investors** (rank)	132	Cost (% of claim)	44.9
Difficulty of hiring index (0-100)	0	Extent of disclosure index (0-10)	2		
Rigidity of hours index (0-100)	0	Extent of director liability index (0-10)	5	**Closing a business** (rank)	53
Difficulty of redundancy index (0-100)	0	Ease of shareholder suits index (0-10)	5	Time (years)	2.2
Rigidity of employment index (0-100)	0	Strength of investor protection index (0-10)	4.0	Cost (% of estate)	30
Redundancy cost (weeks of salary)	13			Recovery rate (cents on the dollar)	41.1
		Paying taxes (rank)	66		
		Payments (number per year)	32		
		Time (hours per year)	161		
		Total tax rate (% of profit)	35.7		

UKRAINE

		Eastern Europe & Central Asia		GNI per capita (US$)	3,213
Ease of doing business (rank)	142	Lower middle income		Population (m)	46.3
Starting a business (rank)	134	**Registering property** (rank)	141	**Trading across borders** (rank)	139
Procedures (number)	10	Procedures (number)	10	Documents to export (number)	6
Time (days)	27	Time (days)	93	Time to export (days)	31
Cost (% of income per capita)	5.8	Cost (% of property value)	2.6	Cost to export (US$ per container)	1,230
Minimum capital (% of income per capita)	153.5			Documents to import (number)	10
		Getting credit (rank)	30	Time to import (days)	36
Dealing with construction permits (rank)	181	Strength of legal rights index (0-10)	9	Cost to import (US$ per container)	1,430
Procedures (number)	30	Depth of credit information index (0-6)	3		
Time (days)	476	Public registry coverage (% of adults)	0.0	**Enforcing contracts** (rank)	43
Cost (% of income per capita)	1,449.3	Private bureau coverage (% of adults)	3.0	Procedures (number)	30
				Time (days)	345
Employing workers (rank)	83	✔ **Protecting investors** (rank)	109	Cost (% of claim)	41.5
Difficulty of hiring index (0-100)	33	Extent of disclosure index (0-10)	5		
Rigidity of hours index (0-100)	20	Extent of director liability index (0-10)	2	**Closing a business** (rank)	145
Difficulty of redundancy index (0-100)	40	Ease of shareholder suits index (0-10)	7	Time (years)	2.9
Rigidity of employment index (0-100)	31	Strength of investor protection index (0-10)	4.7	Cost (% of estate)	42
Redundancy cost (weeks of salary)	13			Recovery rate (cents on the dollar)	9.1
		Paying taxes (rank)	181		
		Payments (number per year)	147		
		Time (hours per year)	736		
		Total tax rate (% of profit)	57.2		

UNITED ARAB EMIRATES

		Middle East & North Africa		GNI per capita (US$)	54,607
Ease of doing business (rank)	33	High income		Population (m)	4.5
✔ **Starting a business** (rank)	44	**Registering property** (rank)	7	✔ **Trading across borders** (rank)	5
Procedures (number)	8	Procedures (number)	1	Documents to export (number)	4
Time (days)	15	Time (days)	2	Time to export (days)	8
Cost (% of income per capita)	6.2	Cost (% of property value)	2.0	Cost to export (US$ per container)	593
Minimum capital (% of income per capita)	0.0			Documents to import (number)	5
		Getting credit (rank)	71	Time to import (days)	9
✔ **Dealing with construction permits** (rank)	27	Strength of legal rights index (0-10)	4	Cost to import (US$ per container)	579
Procedures (number)	17	Depth of credit information index (0-6)	5		
Time (days)	64	Public registry coverage (% of adults)	7.3	**Enforcing contracts** (rank)	134
Cost (% of income per capita)	30.7	Private bureau coverage (% of adults)	12.6	Procedures (number)	49
				Time (days)	537
Employing workers (rank)	50	**Protecting investors** (rank)	119	Cost (% of claim)	26.2
Difficulty of hiring index (0-100)	0	Extent of disclosure index (0-10)	4		
Rigidity of hours index (0-100)	20	Extent of director liability index (0-10)	7	**Closing a business** (rank)	143
Difficulty of redundancy index (0-100)	0	Ease of shareholder suits index (0-10)	2	Time (years)	5.1
Rigidity of employment index (0-100)	7	Strength of investor protection index (0-10)	4.3	Cost (% of estate)	30
Redundancy cost (weeks of salary)	84			Recovery rate (cents on the dollar)	10.2
		Paying taxes (rank)	4		
		Payments (number per year)	14		
		Time (hours per year)	12		
		Total tax rate (% of profit)	14.1		

UNITED KINGDOM

		OECD high income		GNI per capita (US$)	45,394
Ease of doing business (rank)	5	High income		Population (m)	61.4
Starting a business (rank)	16	✔ **Registering property** (rank)	23	**Trading across borders** (rank)	16
Procedures (number)	6	Procedures (number)	2	Documents to export (number)	4
Time (days)	13	Time (days)	8	Time to export (days)	9
Cost (% of income per capita)	0.7	Cost (% of property value)	4.1	Cost to export (US$ per container)	1,030
Minimum capital (% of income per capita)	0.0			Documents to import (number)	4
		Getting credit (rank)	2	Time to import (days)	8
✔ **Dealing with construction permits** (rank)	16	Strength of legal rights index (0-10)	9	Cost to import (US$ per container)	1,160
Procedures (number)	11	Depth of credit information index (0-6)	6		
Time (days)	95	Public registry coverage (% of adults)	0.0	**Enforcing contracts** (rank)	23
Cost (% of income per capita)	69.1	Private bureau coverage (% of adults)	100.0	Procedures (number)	30
				Time (days)	399
Employing workers (rank)	35	**Protecting investors** (rank)	10	Cost (% of claim)	23.4
Difficulty of hiring index (0-100)	11	Extent of disclosure index (0-10)	10		
Rigidity of hours index (0-100)	20	Extent of director liability index (0-10)	7	**Closing a business** (rank)	9
Difficulty of redundancy index (0-100)	0	Ease of shareholder suits index (0-10)	7	Time (years)	1.0
Rigidity of employment index (0-100)	10	Strength of investor protection index (0-10)	8.0	Cost (% of estate)	6
Redundancy cost (weeks of salary)	22			Recovery rate (cents on the dollar)	84.2
		Paying taxes (rank)	16		
		Payments (number per year)	8		
		Time (hours per year)	110		
		Total tax rate (% of profit)	35.9		

UNITED STATES

		OECD high income		GNI per capita (US$)	47,577
Ease of doing business (rank)	4	High income		Population (m)	304.1
Starting a business (rank)	8	**Registering property** (rank)	12	**Trading across borders** (rank)	18
Procedures (number)	6	Procedures (number)	4	Documents to export (number)	4
Time (days)	6	Time (days)	12	Time to export (days)	6
Cost (% of income per capita)	0.7	Cost (% of property value)	0.5	Cost to export (US$ per container)	1,050
Minimum capital (% of income per capita)	0.0			Documents to import (number)	5
		Getting credit (rank)	4	Time to import (days)	5
Dealing with construction permits (rank)	25	Strength of legal rights index (0-10)	8	Cost to import (US$ per container)	1,315
Procedures (number)	19	Depth of credit information index (0-6)	6		
Time (days)	40	Public registry coverage (% of adults)	0.0	**Enforcing contracts** (rank)	8
Cost (% of income per capita)	12.7	Private bureau coverage (% of adults)	100.0	Procedures (number)	32
				Time (days)	300
Employing workers (rank)	1	**Protecting investors** (rank)	5	Cost (% of claim)	14.4
Difficulty of hiring index (0-100)	0	Extent of disclosure index (0-10)	7		
Rigidity of hours index (0-100)	0	Extent of director liability index (0-10)	9	**Closing a business** (rank)	15
Difficulty of redundancy index (0-100)	0	Ease of shareholder suits index (0-10)	9	Time (years)	1.5
Rigidity of employment index (0-100)	0	Strength of investor protection index (0-10)	8.3	Cost (% of estate)	7
Redundancy cost (weeks of salary)	0			Recovery rate (cents on the dollar)	76.7
		Paying taxes (rank)	61		
		Payments (number per year)	10		
		Time (hours per year)	187		
		Total tax rate (% of profit)	46.3		

URUGUAY

		Latin America & Caribbean		GNI per capita (US$)		8,259
Ease of doing business (rank)	114	Upper middle income		Population (m)		3.3
Starting a business (rank)	132	✗ **Registering property** (rank)	165	**Trading across borders** (rank)		131
Procedures (number)	11	Procedures (number)	9	Documents to export (number)		10
Time (days)	65	Time (days)	66	Time to export (days)		19
Cost (% of income per capita)	40.0	Cost (% of property value)	7.1	Cost to export (US$ per container)		1,100
Minimum capital (% of income per capita)	0.0			Documents to import (number)		10
				Time to import (days)		22
Dealing with construction permits (rank)	140	**Getting credit** (rank)	43	Cost to import (US$ per container)		1,330
Procedures (number)	30	Strength of legal rights index (0–10)	5			
Time (days)	234	Depth of credit information index (0–6)	6	**Enforcing contracts** (rank)		96
Cost (% of income per capita)	87.1	Public registry coverage (% of adults)	17.8	Procedures (number)		40
		Private bureau coverage (% of adults)	97.2	Time (days)		720
Employing workers (rank)	64			Cost (% of claim)		19.0
Difficulty of hiring index (0–100)	33	**Protecting investors** (rank)	93			
Rigidity of hours index (0–100)	20	Extent of disclosure index (0–10)	3	✔ **Closing a business** (rank)		46
Difficulty of redundancy index (0–100)	0	Extent of director liability index (0–10)	4	Time (years)		2.1
Rigidity of employment index (0–100)	18	Ease of shareholder suits index (0–10)	8	Cost (% of estate)		7
Redundancy cost (weeks of salary)	31	Strength of investor protection index (0–10)	5.0	Recovery rate (cents on the dollar)		43.0
		Paying taxes (rank)	159			
		Payments (number per year)	53			
		Time (hours per year)	336			
		Total tax rate (% of profit)	46.7			

UZBEKISTAN

		Eastern Europe & Central Asia		GNI per capita (US$)		906
Ease of doing business (rank)	150	Low income		Population (m)		27.3
Starting a business (rank)	92	**Registering property** (rank)	133	**Trading across borders** (rank)		174
Procedures (number)	7	Procedures (number)	12	Documents to export (number)		7
Time (days)	15	Time (days)	78	Time to export (days)		71
Cost (% of income per capita)	11.2	Cost (% of property value)	1.5	Cost to export (US$ per container)		3,100
Minimum capital (% of income per capita)	13.8			Documents to import (number)		11
				Time to import (days)		92
✔ **Dealing with construction permits** (rank)	142	**Getting credit** (rank)	135	Cost to import (US$ per container)		4,600
Procedures (number)	26	Strength of legal rights index (0–10)	2			
Time (days)	260	Depth of credit information index (0–6)	3	**Enforcing contracts** (rank)		44
Cost (% of income per capita)	74.8	Public registry coverage (% of adults)	2.6	Procedures (number)		42
		Private bureau coverage (% of adults)	2.1	Time (days)		195
Employing workers (rank)	95			Cost (% of claim)		22.2
Difficulty of hiring index (0–100)	33	**Protecting investors** (rank)	119			
Rigidity of hours index (0–100)	33	Extent of disclosure index (0–10)	4	**Closing a business** (rank)		125
Difficulty of redundancy index (0–100)	30	Extent of director liability index (0–10)	6	Time (years)		4.0
Rigidity of employment index (0–100)	32	Ease of shareholder suits index (0–10)	3	Cost (% of estate)		10
Redundancy cost (weeks of salary)	22	Strength of investor protection index (0–10)	4.3	Recovery rate (cents on the dollar)		18.7
		✔ **Paying taxes** (rank)	178			
		Payments (number per year)	106			
		Time (hours per year)	356			
		Total tax rate (% of profit)	94.9			

VANUATU

		East Asia & Pacific		GNI per capita (US$)		2,332
Ease of doing business (rank)	59	Lower middle income		Population (m)		0.2
Starting a business (rank)	110	**Registering property** (rank)	104	**Trading across borders** (rank)		141
Procedures (number)	8	Procedures (number)	2	Documents to export (number)		7
Time (days)	39	Time (days)	188	Time to export (days)		26
Cost (% of income per capita)	42.0	Cost (% of property value)	7.0	Cost to export (US$ per container)		1,497
Minimum capital (% of income per capita)	0.0			Documents to import (number)		9
				Time to import (days)		30
Dealing with construction permits (rank)	22	✔ **Getting credit** (rank)	71	Cost to import (US$ per container)		1,392
Procedures (number)	7	Strength of legal rights index (0–10)	9			
Time (days)	51	Depth of credit information index (0–6)	0	**Enforcing contracts** (rank)		73
Cost (% of income per capita)	273.5	Public registry coverage (% of adults)	0.0	Procedures (number)		30
		Private bureau coverage (% of adults)	0.0	Time (days)		430
Employing workers (rank)	75			Cost (% of claim)		74.7
Difficulty of hiring index (0–100)	22	**Protecting investors** (rank)	73			
Rigidity of hours index (0–100)	20	Extent of disclosure index (0–10)	5	**Closing a business** (rank)		52
Difficulty of redundancy index (0–100)	0	Extent of director liability index (0–10)	6	Time (years)		2.6
Rigidity of employment index (0–100)	14	Ease of shareholder suits index (0–10)	5	Cost (% of estate)		38
Redundancy cost (weeks of salary)	56	Strength of investor protection index (0–10)	5.3	Recovery rate (cents on the dollar)		41.2
		Paying taxes (rank)	20			
		Payments (number per year)	31			
		Time (hours per year)	120			
		Total tax rate (% of profit)	8.4			

✔ Reforms making it easier to do business   ✗ Reforms making it more difficult to do business

VENEZUELA, R.B.

		Latin America & Caribbean	GNI per capita (US$)	9,226
Ease of doing business (rank)	177	Upper middle income	Population (m)	27.9
Starting a business (rank)	142	**Registering property** (rank)	97	**Trading across borders** (rank)	166

Ease of doing business (rank) 177
Latin America & Caribbean
Upper middle income
GNI per capita (US$) 9,226
Population (m) 27.9

Starting a business (rank) 142
Procedures (number) 16
Time (days) 141
Cost (% of income per capita) 24.0
Minimum capital (% of income per capita) 0.0

Registering property (rank) 97
Procedures (number) 8
Time (days) 47
Cost (% of property value) 2.2

Trading across borders (rank) 166
Documents to export (number) 8
Time to export (days) 49
Cost to export (US$ per container) 2,590
Documents to import (number) 9
Time to import (days) 71
Cost to import (US$ per container) 2,868

Dealing with construction permits (rank) 94
Procedures (number) 11
Time (days) 395
Cost (% of income per capita) 233.0

Getting credit (rank) 177
Strength of legal rights index (0-10) 2
Depth of credit information index (0-6) 0
Public registry coverage (% of adults) 0.0
Private bureau coverage (% of adults) 0.0

Enforcing contracts (rank) 74
Procedures (number) 29
Time (days) 510
Cost (% of claim) 43.7

Employing workers (rank) 181
Difficulty of hiring index (0-100) 67
Rigidity of hours index (0-100) 40
Difficulty of redundancy index (0-100) 100
Rigidity of employment index (0-100) 69
Redundancy cost (weeks of salary) NOT POSSIBLE

Protecting investors (rank) 178
Extent of disclosure index (0-10) 3
Extent of director liability index (0-10) 2
Ease of shareholder suits index (0-10) 2
Strength of investor protection index (0-10) 2.3

Closing a business (rank) 151
Time (years) 4.0
Cost (% of estate) 38
Recovery rate (cents on the dollar) 6.0

✗ **Paying taxes** (rank) 182
Payments (number per year) 71
Time (hours per year) 864
Total tax rate (% of profit) 61.1

VIETNAM

Ease of doing business (rank) 93
East Asia & Pacific
Low income
GNI per capita (US$) 892
Population (m) 86.3

Starting a business (rank) 116
Procedures (number) 11
Time (days) 50
Cost (% of income per capita) 13.3
Minimum capital (% of income per capita) 0.0

Registering property (rank) 40
Procedures (number) 4
Time (days) 57
Cost (% of property value) 1.1

✔ **Trading across borders** (rank) 74
Documents to export (number) 6
Time to export (days) 22
Cost to export (US$ per container) 756
Documents to import (number) 8
Time to import (days) 21
Cost to import (US$ per container) 940

Dealing with construction permits (rank) 69
Procedures (number) 13
Time (days) 194
Cost (% of income per capita) 248.1

Getting credit (rank) 30
Strength of legal rights index (0-10) 8
Depth of credit information index (0-6) 4
Public registry coverage (% of adults) 19.0
Private bureau coverage (% of adults) 0.0

Enforcing contracts (rank) 32
Procedures (number) 34
Time (days) 295
Cost (% of claim) 28.5

Employing workers (rank) 103
Difficulty of hiring index (0-100) 11
Rigidity of hours index (0-100) 13
Difficulty of redundancy index (0-100) 40
Rigidity of employment index (0-100) 21
Redundancy cost (weeks of salary) 87

Protecting investors (rank) 172
Extent of disclosure index (0-10) 6
Extent of director liability index (0-10) 0
Ease of shareholder suits index (0-10) 2
Strength of investor protection index (0-10) 2.7

Closing a business (rank) 127
Time (years) 5.0
Cost (% of estate) 15
Recovery rate (cents on the dollar) 18.0

✔ **Paying taxes** (rank) 147
Payments (number per year) 32
Time (hours per year) 1,050
Total tax rate (% of profit) 40.1

WEST BANK AND GAZA

Ease of doing business (rank) 139
Middle East & North Africa
Lower middle income
GNI per capita (US$) 1,564
Population (m) 3.8

✗ **Starting a business** (rank) 176
Procedures (number) 11
Time (days) 49
Cost (% of income per capita) 55.0
Minimum capital (% of income per capita) 220.4

✔ **Registering property** (rank) 73
Procedures (number) 7
Time (days) 47
Cost (% of property value) 0.7

Trading across borders (rank) 92
Documents to export (number) 6
Time to export (days) 25
Cost to export (US$ per container) 835
Documents to import (number) 6
Time to import (days) 40
Cost to import (US$ per container) 1,225

Dealing with construction permits (rank) 157
Procedures (number) 21
Time (days) 199
Cost (% of income per capita) 1,110.6

Getting credit (rank) 167
Strength of legal rights index (0-10) 0
Depth of credit information index (0-6) 3
Public registry coverage (% of adults) 6.5
Private bureau coverage (% of adults) 0.0

✔ **Enforcing contracts** (rank) 111
Procedures (number) 44
Time (days) 600
Cost (% of claim) 21.2

Employing workers (rank) 135
Difficulty of hiring index (0-100) 33
Rigidity of hours index (0-100) 40
Difficulty of redundancy index (0-100) 20
Rigidity of employment index (0-100) 31
Redundancy cost (weeks of salary) 91

Protecting investors (rank) 41
Extent of disclosure index (0-10) 6
Extent of director liability index (0-10) 5
Ease of shareholder suits index (0-10) 7
Strength of investor protection index (0-10) 6.0

Closing a business (rank) 183
Time (years) NO PRACTICE
Cost (% of estate) NO PRACTICE
Recovery rate (cents on the dollar) 0.0

Paying taxes (rank) 28
Payments (number per year) 27
Time (hours per year) 154
Total tax rate (% of profit) 16.8

YEMEN, REP.

		Middle East & North Africa		GNI per capita (US$)	950
Ease of doing business (rank)	99	Low income		Population (m)	23.1
✔ **Starting a business** (rank)	53	**Registering property** (rank)	50	✔ **Trading across borders** (rank)	120
Procedures (number)	6	Procedures (number)	6	Documents to export (number)	6
Time (days)	12	Time (days)	19	Time to export (days)	27
Cost (% of income per capita)	83.0	Cost (% of property value)	3.8	Cost to export (US$ per container)	1,129
Minimum capital (% of income per capita)	0.0			Documents to import (number)	9
		✔ **Getting credit** (rank)	150	Time to import (days)	25
Dealing with construction permits (rank)	50	Strength of legal rights index (0-10)	2	Cost to import (US$ per container)	1,475
Procedures (number)	15	Depth of credit information index (0-6)	2		
Time (days)	107	Public registry coverage (% of adults)	0.2	**Enforcing contracts** (rank)	35
Cost (% of income per capita)	144.1	Private bureau coverage (% of adults)	0.0	Procedures (number)	36
				Time (days)	520
Employing workers (rank)	74	**Protecting investors** (rank)	132	Cost (% of claim)	16.5
Difficulty of hiring index (0-100)	22	Extent of disclosure index (0-10)	6		
Rigidity of hours index (0-100)	20	Extent of director liability index (0-10)	4	**Closing a business** (rank)	89
Difficulty of redundancy index (0-100)	30	Ease of shareholder suits index (0-10)	2	Time (years)	3.0
Rigidity of employment index (0-100)	24	Strength of investor protection index (0-10)	4.0	Cost (% of estate)	8
Redundancy cost (weeks of salary)	17			Recovery rate (cents on the dollar)	28.6
		Paying taxes (rank)	148		
		Payments (number per year)	44		
		Time (hours per year)	248		
		Total tax rate (% of profit)	47.8		

ZAMBIA

		Sub-Saharan Africa		GNI per capita (US$)	950
Ease of doing business (rank)	90	Low income		Population (m)	12.6
Starting a business (rank)	94	**Registering property** (rank)	94	**Trading across borders** (rank)	157
Procedures (number)	6	Procedures (number)	6	Documents to export (number)	6
Time (days)	18	Time (days)	39	Time to export (days)	53
Cost (% of income per capita)	28.4	Cost (% of property value)	6.6	Cost to export (US$ per container)	2,664
Minimum capital (% of income per capita)	1.3			Documents to import (number)	9
		✔ **Getting credit** (rank)	30	Time to import (days)	64
Dealing with construction permits (rank)	151	Strength of legal rights index (0-10)	9	Cost to import (US$ per container)	3,335
Procedures (number)	17	Depth of credit information index (0-6)	3		
Time (days)	254	Public registry coverage (% of adults)	0.0	**Enforcing contracts** (rank)	87
Cost (% of income per capita)	912.7	Private bureau coverage (% of adults)	0.4	Procedures (number)	35
				Time (days)	471
Employing workers (rank)	116	**Protecting investors** (rank)	73	Cost (% of claim)	38.7
Difficulty of hiring index (0-100)	11	Extent of disclosure index (0-10)	3		
Rigidity of hours index (0-100)	33	Extent of director liability index (0-10)	6	**Closing a business** (rank)	83
Difficulty of redundancy index (0-100)	20	Ease of shareholder suits index (0-10)	7	Time (years)	2.7
Rigidity of employment index (0-100)	21	Strength of investor protection index (0-10)	5.3	Cost (% of estate)	9
Redundancy cost (weeks of salary)	178			Recovery rate (cents on the dollar)	30.2
		Paying taxes (rank)	36		
		Payments (number per year)	37		
		Time (hours per year)	132		
		Total tax rate (% of profit)	16.1		

ZIMBABWE

		Sub-Saharan Africa		GNI per capita (US$)	237
Ease of doing business (rank)	159	Low income		Population (m)	12.5
Starting a business (rank)	145	✔ **Registering property** (rank)	84	**Trading across borders** (rank)	167
Procedures (number)	10	Procedures (number)	5	Documents to export (number)	7
Time (days)	96	Time (days)	31	Time to export (days)	53
Cost (% of income per capita)	499.5	Cost (% of property value)	10.1	Cost to export (US$ per container)	3,280
Minimum capital (% of income per capita)	0.0			Documents to import (number)	9
		Getting credit (rank)	113	Time to import (days)	73
Dealing with construction permits (rank)	178	Strength of legal rights index (0-10)	7	Cost to import (US$ per container)	5,101
Procedures (number)	19	Depth of credit information index (0-6)	0		
Time (days)	1,426	Public registry coverage (% of adults)	0.0	**Enforcing contracts** (rank)	78
Cost (% of income per capita)	24,468.3	Private bureau coverage (% of adults)	0.0	Procedures (number)	38
				Time (days)	410
Employing workers (rank)	142	**Protecting investors** (rank)	119	Cost (% of claim)	32.0
Difficulty of hiring index (0-100)	0	Extent of disclosure index (0-10)	8		
Rigidity of hours index (0-100)	40	Extent of director liability index (0-10)	1	**Closing a business** (rank)	156
Difficulty of redundancy index (0-100)	60	Ease of shareholder suits index (0-10)	4	Time (years)	3.3
Rigidity of employment index (0-100)	33	Strength of investor protection index (0-10)	4.3	Cost (% of estate)	22
Redundancy cost (weeks of salary)	446			Recovery rate (cents on the dollar)	0.0
		Paying taxes (rank)	130		
		Payments (number per year)	51		
		Time (hours per year)	270		
		Total tax rate (% of profit)	39.4		

Acknowledgments

Contact details for local partners are available on the Doing Business website at http://www.doingbusiness.org

Doing Business 2010 was prepared by a team led by Sylvia Solf, Penelope Brook (through May 2009) and Neil Gregory (from June 2009) under the general direction of Michael Klein (through May 2009) and Penelope Brook (from June 2009). The team comprised Svetlana Bagaudinova, Karim O. Belayachi, Mema Beye, Frederic Bustelo, César Chaparro Yedro, Maya Choueiri, Santiago Croci Downes, Sarah Cuttaree, Marie Delion, Allen Dennis, Jacqueline den Otter, Alejandro Espinosa-Wang, Kjartan Fjeldsted, Carolin Geginat, Cemile Hacibeyoglu, Sabine Hertveldt, Nan Jiang, Palarp Jumpasut, Dahlia Khalifa, Jean Michel Lobet, Oliver Lorenz, Valerie Marechal, Andres Martinez, Alexandra Mincu, Joanna Nasr, C. Njemanze, Dana Omran, Caroline Otonglo, Camille Ramos, Yara Salem, Pilar Salgado-Otónel, Umar Shavurov, Jayashree Srinivasan, Susanne Szymanski, Tea Trumbic, Marina Turlakova, Caroline van Coppenolle and Lior Ziv. Sebastian Fitzgerald and Bryan Welsh assisted in the months prior to publication.

The online service of the *Doing Business* database is managed by Ramin Aliyev, Preeti Endlaw, Felipe Iturralde and Graeme Littler. The *Doing Business 2010* report media and marketing strategy is managed by Nadine Ghannam. The events and road show strategy is managed by Jamile Ramadan. All knowledge management and outreach activities are under the direction and guidance of Suzanne Smith.

We are grateful for valuable comments provided by colleagues across the World Bank Group and for the guidance of World Bank Group Executive Directors.

Oliver Hart and Andrei Shleifer provided academic advice on the project. The paying taxes project was conducted in collaboration with Pricewaterhouse Coopers, led by Robert Morris. The development of the getting electricity indicators was financed by the Norwegian Trust Fund.

Alison Strong copyedited the manuscript. Gerry Quinn designed the report and the graphs, and Alexandra Quinn provided desktopping services.

The report was made possible by the generous contributions of more than 8,000 lawyers, accountants, judges, businesspeople and public officials in 183 economies. Global and regional contributors are firms that have completed multiple surveys in their various offices around the world.

Quotations in this report are from *Doing Business* partners unless otherwise indicated. The names of those wishing to be acknowledged individually are listed below. Contact details are posted on the *Doing Business* website at http://www.doingbusiness.org.

GLOBAL CONTRIBUTORS

ALLEN & OVERY LLP
BAKER & MCKENZIE
CLEARY GOTTLIEB STEEN & HAMILTON LLP
HAWKAMAH - THE INSTITUTE FOR CORPORATE GOVERNANCE
IUS LABORIS, ALLIANCE OF LABOR, EMPLOYMENT, BENEFITS AND PENSIONS LAW FIRMS
KPMG
LAW SOCIETY OF ENGLAND AND WALES
LEX MUNDI, ASSOCIATION OF INDEPENDENT LAW FIRMS
MAYER BROWN LLP
NORONHA ADVOGADOS
PANALPINA
PRICEWATERHOUSECOOPERS
PRICEWATERHOUSECOOPERS LEGAL SERVICES
RUSSELL BEDFORD INTERNATIONAL
SDV INTERNATIONAL LOGISTICS
TOBOC INC.

REGIONAL CONTRIBUTORS

APL LTD
A.P. MOLLER - MAERSK GROUP
BNT
CONSORTIUM OF EUROPEAN BUILDING CONTROL
FEDERACIÓN INTERAMERICANA DE LA INDUSTRIA DE LA CONSTRUCCIÓN
GARCÍA & BODÁN
GLOBALINK TRANSPORTATION & LOGISTICS WORLDWIDE LLP
GRATA LAW FIRM
IKRP ROKAS & PARTNERS
MANICA AFRICA PTY. LTD.
TALAL ABU-GHAZALEH LEGAL (TAG-LEGAL)
THE ADORA GROUP LTD (FREIGHTNET)
THE INTERNATIONAL UNION OF NOTARIES (U.I.N.L)
TRANSUNION INTERNATIONAL
UNIVERSITY OF SOUTH PACIFIC

AFGHANISTAN

Naseem Akbar
AISA

Sayed Javed Andish
KABUL GROUP CONSULTING

Joshua Atkinson
MBC CONSTRUCTION

A. Farid Barakzai
TNT INTERNATIONAL EXPRESS

Abdul Karim Hamid

Muslimul Haq
AFGHANISTAN BANKS ASSOCIATION

Abdul Wassay Haqiqi
HAQIQI LEGAL SERVICES

Saduddin Haziq
AFGHANISTAN INTERNATIONAL BANK

Rashid Ibrahim
A.F. FERGUSON & CO., A MEMBER FIRM OF PRICEWATERHOUSECOOPERS

M. Azam Kargar
AFGHAN TRANSIT COMPANY

Rozbey Kargar
AFGHAN TRANSIT COMPANY

M. Wissal Khan
MANDVIWALLA & ZAFAR

Waseem Ahmed Khan
AARAS SHIPPING & LOGISTICS

Gaurav Lekh Raj Kukreja
AFGHAN CONTAINER TRANSPORT COMPANY

Zahoor Malla
GLOBALINK LOGISTICS GROUP

Tali Mohammed
AFGHANISTAN INVESTMENT SUPPORT AGENCY

Kevin O'Brien
DELOITTE CONSULTING LLP

Gul Pacha
AFGHANISTAN INVESTMENT SUPPORT AGENCY

Rahmatulla Qazizada
AFGHAN TRANSIT COMPANY

Najibullah Rahimi
EXPORT PROMOTION AGENCY OF AFGHANISTAN

Rajab Ali Sanna
AARAS SHIPPING & LOGISTICS

Riaz Ali Sanna
AARAS SHIPPING & LOGISTICS

Said Mubin Shah
AISA

Mirza Taqi Ud-Din Ahmad
PRICEWATERHOUSECOOPERS

Abdul Rahman Watanwal
MBC CONSTRUCTION

ALBANIA

AMERICAN BANK OF ALBANIA

Erjola Aliaj
IKRP ROKAS & PARTNERS

Artur Asllani
TONUCCI & PARTNERS

Sabine Baboci
EME PARTNERS

Ledia Beçi
HOXHA, MEMI & HOXHA

Ilir Bejleri
SON GROUP, ENGINEERING AND CONSTRUCTION

Alban Bello
IKRP ROKAS & PARTNERS

Jona Bica
KALO & ASSOCIATES

Rene Bijvoet
PRICEWATERHOUSECOOPERS

Artan Bozo
TBI LAW FIRM

Dorian Collaku
BANK OF ALBANIA

Dael Dervishi
OPTIMA LEGAL AND FINANCIAL

DISTRIBUTION SYSTEM OPERATOR ALBANIAN POWER CORPORATION

Eniana Dupi
AECO CONSULTING

DYRRAHSPED SH P.K

Eduart Gjokutaj
AL-TAX STUDIO

Valbona Gjonçari
BOGA & ASSOCIATES

MANETCI, TRADING, CONSTRUCTION, INVESTMENT

Emel Haxhillari
KALO & ASSOCIATES

Shpati Hoxha
HOXHA, MEMI & HOXHA

Oltjan Hoxholli
KALO & ASSOCIATES

Erald Ibro
ZIG CONSULTING FIRM

Olsi Ibro
ZIG CONSULTING FIRM

Ilir Johollari
HOXHA, MEMI & HOXHA

Taulant Jorgji
IKRP ROKAS & PARTNERS

Përparim Kalo
KALO & ASSOCIATES

Artur Kociaj
SHEGA GROUP S.A.

Majlinda Kraja
EME PARTNERS

Renata Leka
BOGA & ASSOCIATES

Georgios K. Lemonis
IKRP ROKAS & PARTNERS

Elton Lula
KALO & ASSOCIATES

Nelea Moraru
PRICEWATERHOUSECOOPERS

Loreno Nele
TBI LAW FIRM

Kostanca Papa
TBI LAW FIRM

Loreta Peci
PRICEWATERHOUSECOOPERS

Kristaq Profkola
BOGA & ASSOCIATES

Laura Qorlaze
PRICEWATERHOUSECOOPERS

Artila Rama
BOGA & ASSOCIATES

Miranda Ramajj
BANK OF ALBANIA

Ermira Rapush
TBI LAW FIRM

Anisa Rrumbullaku
KALO & ASSOCIATES

Ardjana Shehi
KALO & ASSOCIATES

Ketrin Topciu
TBI LAW FIRM

Gerhard Velaj
BOGA & ASSOCIATES

Silva Velaj
BOGA & ASSOCIATES

Agim Vërshevci
ALIMENTI NATURALI & PB

BALFIN SH.P.K, BALKAN FINANCE INVESTMENT GROUP

Selena Ymeri
TONUCCI & PARTNERS

Enida Zeneli
TBI LAW FIRM

ALGERIA

Branka Achari-Djokic
BANQUE D'ALGÉRIE

Mohamed Afir
LEFÈVRE PELLETIER & ASSOCIÉS

L. Aimene
MINISTÈRE DE LA JUSTICE

Mohamed Atbi
ETUDE NOTARIALE MOHAMED ATBI

Khodja Bachir
SNC KHODJA & CO.

Hassan Djamel Belloula
CABINET BELLOULA

Tayeb Belloula
CABINET BELLOULA

Mohammed Tahar Benabid
CABINET MOHAMMED TAHAR BENABID

Samir Benslimane
CABINET BENSLIMANE

Adnane Bouchaib
BOUCHAIB LAW FIRM

Fatima-Zohra Bouchemla
LEFÈVRE PELLETIER & ASSOCIÉS

Mohamed Bourouina
CABINET BOUROUINA

Hamid Djamouh
CABINET DJAMOUH

Souhila Djamouh Chaib
CABINET DJAMOUH

Asmaa El Ouazzani
LANDWELL & ASSOCIÉS - PRICEWATERHOUSECOOPERS LEGAL SERVICES

Malik Elkettas
ELKETTAS INTERNATIONAL

Brahim Embouazza
MCDCONSULTING

Mohamed Lehbib Goubi
BANQUE D'ALGÉRIE

Salim Gourine
CABINET DJAMOUH

Nicolas Granier
ALLEANCE ADVISORY MAROC

Mohamed El-Amine Haddad
AVOCAT

Sakina Haddad
CRÉDIT POPULAIRE D'ALGERIE

Farid Hatou
SAR DAR PNEUS

Goussanem Khaled
LAW FIRM GOUSSANEM & ALOUI

Ahmed Khedim
INSPECTION DE L'ENREGISTREMENT ET DU TIMBRE

Arezki Khelout
MINISTÈRE DES FINANCES, DIRECTION GENERALE DU DOMAINE NATIONAL

Nadira Laissaoui
GHELLAL & MEKERBA

Nawel Lammari
MINISTÈRE DE LA JUSTICE

Karine Lasne
LANDWELL & ASSOCIÉS - PRICEWATERHOUSECOOPERS LEGAL SERVICES

Michel Lecerf
ALLEANCE ADVISORY MAROC

Abdelmadjid Mahreche
DIRECTION GENERALE DES DOUANES D'ALGERIE

Tahar Melakhessou
CABINET NOTARIAL MELAKHESSOU

Adnane Merad
ETUDE DE ME KADDOUR MERAD

Mohamed Mokrane
MINISTÈRE DES FINANCES, DIRECTION GENERALE DU DOMAINE NATIONAL

Fares Ouzegdouh
BÉJAIA MEDITERRANEAN TERMINAL

Ahmed Rahou
MINISTÈRE DES FINANCES, DIRECTION GENERALE DU DOMAINE NATIONAL

Dib Said
BANQUE D'ALGÉRIE

Aloui Salima
LAW FIRM GOUSSANEM & ALOUI

SDV LOGISTICS LTD.

Marc Veuillot
ALLEANCE ADVISORY MAROC

ANGOLA

José Rodrigues Alentejo
CÂMARA DE COMÉRCIO E INDÚSTRIA DE ANGOLA

Amorbelo Esanju Amos Martins
EDEL-EP

Fernando Barros
PRICEWATERHOUSECOOPERS

Alain Brachet
SDV AMI INTERNATIONAL LOGISTICS

Pedro Calixto
PRICEWATERHOUSECOOPERS

Maurice Campbell
CROWN AGENTS

Caetano Capitão
*CENTRO DE APOIO
EMPRESARIAL- CAE*

Beatriz Soares Catumbela
*MINISTÉRIO DA JUSTIÇA
REGISTRO PREDIAL DE LUANDA
(1ª SECÇÃO)*

Anacleta Cipriano
*FARIA DE BASTOS, SEBASTIÃO
E LOPES - ADVOGADOS
ASSOCIADOS*

Fátima Freitas
FÁTIMA FREITAS ADVOGADOS

Brian Glazier
EDI ARCHITECTURE INC.

Raul Gomes
ATS LOGISTICS CO.

Helder da Conceição José
*INSTITUTO DE PLANEAMENTO
E GESTÃO URBANA DO
GOVERNO PROVINCIAL DE
LUANDA*

Victor Leonel
ORDEM DOS ARQUIITECTOS

Paulette Lopes
*FARIA DE BASTOS, SEBASTIÃO
E LOPES - ADVOGADOS
ASSOCIADOS*

Teresinha Lopes
*FARIA DE BASTOS, SEBASTIÃO
E LOPES - ADVOGADOS
ASSOCIADOS*

Manuel Malufuene
ORDEM DOS ARQUIITECTOS

Josephine Matambo
KPMG

Rosa Gameiro Mcmahon
KPMG

Julio Gabriel Nunes Monteiro
EDEL-EP

Janota Nzogi
EDEL-EP

Walter Paixão
PRICEWATERHOUSECOOPERS

Alexandre Pegado
*ALEXANDRE PEGADO -
ESCRITÓRIO DE ADVOGADOS*

Douglas Pillinger
*PANALPINA WORLD
TRANSPORT*

Luis Filipe Pizarro
AG & LP

Laurinda Prazeres
*FARIA DE BASTOS, SEBASTIÃO
E LOPES - ADVOGADOS
ASSOCIADOS*

Pedro Manuel Sebastiao
EDEL-EP

N'Gunu Tiny
RCJE ADVOGADOS ASOCIADOS

Isabel Tormenta
GUICHET UNICO DA EMPRESA

Maikel Steve
*CENTER FOR
ENTREPRENEURSHIP IN
CAZENGA*

Van Dunen
*AUGOSTINO NETO LAW
SCHOOL*

António Vicente Marques
AVM ADVOGADOS

ANTIGUA AND BARBUDA

Neil Coates
PRICEWATERHOUSECOOPERS

Brian D'Ornellas
*OBM INTERNATIONAL,
ANTIGUA LTD.*

Vernon Edwards Jr.
*FREIGHT FORWARDING &
DECONSOLIDATING*

Ann Henry
HENRY & BURNETTE

Hugh C. Marshall
MARSHALL & CO.

Septimus A. Rhudd
RHUDD & ASSOCIATES

Patsy Richards
MARSHALL & CO.

Stacy A. Richards-Anjo
RICHARDS & CO.

Cathrona Samuel
*ANTIGUA PUBLIC UTILITIES
AUTHORITY*

Lester Samuel
INVESTMENT AUTHORITY

Patricia Simon-Forde
*CHAMBERS PATRICIA SIMON-
FORDE*

Tish Smith
*S & R ELECTRICAL SALES &
SERVICES*

Arthur Thomas
THOMAS, JOHN & CO.

Charles Walwyn
PRICEWATERHOUSECOOPERS

Hesketh Williams
MINISTRY OF LABOR

ARGENTINA

María Agustina Vítolo
VITOLO ABOGADOS

Dolores Aispuru
PRICEWATERHOUSECOOPERS

Carlos Alfaro
ALFARO ABOGADOS

Lisandro A. Allende
BRONS & SALAS ABOGADOS

María Florencia Angélico
CANOSA ABOGADOS

Ignacio E. Aramburu
*RATTAGAN, MACCHIAVELLO
AROCENA & PEÑA ROBIROSA
ABOGADOS*

Vanesa Balda
*VITALE, MANOFF &
FEILBOGEN*

Gonzalo Carlos Ballester
J.P. O'FARRELL ABOGADOS

Walter Beveraggi de la Serna
*QUATTRINI, LAPRIDA &
ASOCIADOS*

Javier M. Gatto Bicain
*CANDIOTI GATTO BICAIN &
OCANTOS*

Sebastian Bittner
JEBSEN & CO.

Matias Borderes
FORTUNATI

Mariano Bourdieu
*SEVERGNINI ROBIOLA
GRINBERG & LARRECHEA*

Carla Branca
PRICEWATERHOUSECOOPERS

Fernando Campelo
ÁLVAREZ PRADO & ASOCIADOS

Javier Canosa
CANOSA ABOGADOS

Agustina Caratti
PRICEWATERHOUSECOOPERS

Mariano E. Carricart
FORNIELES LAW FIRM

Luis Casares
G. BREUER

Gustavo Casir
*QUATTRINI, LAPRIDA &
ASOCIADOS*

Pablo L. Cavallaro
*ESTUDIO CAVALLARO
ABOGADOS*

Roberto H. Crouzel
ESTUDIO BECCAR VARELA

Hernán Gonzalo Cuenca
Martínez
*PRICEWATERHOUSECOOPERS
LEGAL SERVICES*

Carlos Marcelo D'Alessio
*UNION INTERNACIONAL DEL
NOTARIADO*

Oscar Alberto del Río
*CENTRAL BANK OF
ARGENTINA*

Sabrina Diaz Ibarra
FORTUNATI

Julio C. Durand
CASSAGNE ABOGADOS

Andrés Edelstein
PRICEWATERHOUSECOOPERS

Mercedes Escriña
*QUATTRINI, LAPRIDA &
ASOCIADOS*

Juan M. Espeso
JEBSEN & CO.

Diego Etchepare
PRICEWATERHOUSECOOPERS

Federico Fernández Zavalía
ESTUDIO TREVISÁN

Diego M. Fissore
G. BREUER

Alejandro D. Fiuza
*MARVAL, O'FARRELL &
MAIRAL, MEMBER OF LEX
MUNDI*

Ignacio Funes de Rioja
*FUNES DE RIOJA & ASOCIADOS,
MEMBER OF IUS LABORIS*

Claudia Gizzi
GYPM

Pablo González del Solar
PRICEWATERHOUSECOOPERS

Diego Brian Gosis
*REMAGGI, PICO, JESSEN &
ASOC*

Matías Grinberg
*SEVERGNINI ROBIOLA
GRINBERG & LARRECHEA*

Claudio Guarnieri
*REGISTRO DE LA PROPIEDAD
INMUEBLE DE LA CAPITAL
FEDERAL*

Sandra S. Guillan
*DE DIOS & GOYENA
ABOGADOS CONSULTORES*

Fabián Hilal
*CAMPOS, ETCHEVERRY &
ASOCIADOS*

Daniel Intile
*DANIEL INTILE & ASSOC.
MEMBER OF RUSSELL BEDFORD
INTERNATIONAL*

Martin Jebsen
JEBSEN & CO.

Walter Keiniger
*MARVAL, O'FARRELL &
MAIRAL, MEMBER OF LEX
MUNDI*

Santiago Laclau
*MARVAL, O'FARRELL &
MAIRAL, MEMBER OF LEX
MUNDI*

Francisco Lagger
*SEVERGNINI ROBIOLA
GRINBERG & LARRECHEA*

María Lattanzi
*MARVAL, O'FARRELL &
MAIRAL, MEMBER OF LEX
MUNDI*

María Manuela Lava
*MARVAL, O'FARRELL &
MAIRAL, MEMBER OF LEX
MUNDI*

Dolores Madueño
JEBSEN & CO.

Rodrigo Marchan
GYPM

Pablo Mastromarino
ESTUDIO BECCAR VARELA

Sean McCormick
*SEVERGNINI ROBIOLA
GRINBERG & LARRECHEA*

Julian Melis
*CANDIOTI GATTO BICAIN &
OCANTOS*

José Oscar Mira
*CENTRAL BANK OF
ARGENTINA*

Jorge Miranda
CLIPPERS S.A.

Santiago Montezanti
FORTUNATI

Natalia Muller
*DE DIOS & GOYENA
ABOGADOS CONSULTORES*

Miguel P. Murray
*MURRAY, DÍAZ CORDERO &
SIRITO DE ZAVALÍA*

Isabel Muscolo
*QUATTRINI, LAPRIDA &
ASOCIADOS*

Damián Mauricio Najenson
ESTUDIO SPOTA

Alfredo Miguel O'Farrell
*MARVAL, O'FARRELL &
MAIRAL, MEMBER OF LEX
MUNDI*

Silvina Pandre
*SEVERGNINI ROBIOLA
GRINBERG & LARRECHEA*

Mariano Payaslian
GYPM

María Ximena Pérez Dirrocco
*MARVAL, O'FARRELL &
MAIRAL, MEMBER OF LEX
MUNDI*

Alejandro Poletto
FORTUNATI

Luis Ponsati
J.P. O'FARRELL ABOGADOS

José Puccinelli
ESTUDIO BECCAR VARELA

Julio Pueyrredón
PRICEWATERHOUSECOOPERS

Michael Rattagan
*RATTAGAN, MACCHIAVELLO
AROCENA & PEÑA ROBIROSA
ABOGADOS*

Sebastián Rodrigo
ALFARO ABOGADOS

Ignacio Rodriguez
PRICEWATERHOUSECOOPERS

Galo Rodríguez Vázquez
*QUATTRINI, LAPRIDA &
ASOCIADOS*

Florencia Romero
*QUATTRINI, LAPRIDA &
ASOCIADOS*

Nicolás Rossi Bunge
*MARVAL, O'FARRELL &
MAIRAL, MEMBER OF LEX
MUNDI*

Mariana Sanchez
*QUATTRINI, LAPRIDA &
ASOCIADOS*

Liliana Cecilia Segade
*QUATTRINI, LAPRIDA &
ASOCIADOS*

Adolfo Tombolini
*DANIEL INTILE & ASSOC.
MEMBER OF RUSSELL BEDFORD
INTERNATIONAL*

Pablo Trevisán
ESTUDIO TREVISÁN

Hernan Verly
ALFARO ABOGADOS

Abraham Viera
*PLANOSNET.COM CONSULTORIA
MUNICIPAL*

Federico Villarino
ÁLVAREZ PRADO & ASOCIADOS

Eduardo J. Viñales
*FUNES DE RIOJA & ASOCIADOS,
MEMBER OF IUS LABORIS*

Daniel Roque Vítolo
VITOLO ABOGADOS

Agustin Waisman
FORTUNATI

Joaquín Emilio Zappa
J.P. O'FARRELL ABOGADOS

Octavio Miguel Zenarruza
ÁLVAREZ PRADO & ASOCIADOS

Carlos Zima
PRICEWATERHOUSECOOPERS

Sofia Zuloaga
*RATTAGAN, MACCHIAVELLO
AROCENA & PEÑA ROBIROSA
ABOGADOS*

ARMENIA

Armen L. Alaverdyan
*STATE REVENUE COMMITTEE
OF THE GOVERNMENT*

Sevak Alexanyan
INVESTMENT LAW GROUP LLC

Karen Andreasyan
DEFENSE LTD.

Artak Arzoyan
ACRA CREDIT BUREAU

Sayad S. Badalyan
INVESTMENT LAW GROUP LLC

Vahe Balayan
AMERIA CJSC

Vardan Bezhanyan
Law Faculty, Yerevan State University

Vahe Chibukhchyan
Ministry of Economy

Paul Cooper
PricewaterhouseCoopers

Andrew Coxshall
KPMG

Samvel Danielyan
Yerevan Municipality

Kristina Dudukchyan
KPMG

Electrical Networks of Armenia

Courtney Fowler
PricewaterhouseCoopers

Samvel Gevorgyan
BSC LLC

Shoghik Gharibyan
KPMG

Hayk Ghazazyan
KPMG

Hakob Grigoryan
Hayaudit LLC

Narek Grigoryan
The State Committee of the Real Property Cadastre

Sargis Grigoryan
GPartners

Tigran Grigoryan
Ameria cjsc

Hrayr Gyonjyan
Centre for Socio Economic Research and Analysis

Davit Iskandarian
HSBC Bank

Sargis H. Martirosyan
Trans-Alliance

Armine Hakobyan
Global SPC

Edvard Hambaryan
Hayaudit LLC

Davit Harutyunyan
PricewaterhouseCoopers

Karina Harutyunyan
3R Strategy LLC

Lernik Harutyunyan
Paradigma Armenia' CJSC

Arayilc Hautunyan
The State Committee of the Real Property Cadastre

Elena Kaeva
PricewaterhouseCoopers

Artashes F. Kakoyan
Investment Law Group LLC

Vahe G. Kakoyan
Investment Law Group LLC

Arshak Kamalyan
The State Committee of the Real Property Cadastre

Ishkhan Karapetyan
Small & Medium Entrepreneurship Development National Center

Argam Khachatryan
Hayaudit LLC

Yervand Khoundkaryan
Civil Court of Appeal

Nelly Kirakosyan
Central Bank of Armenia

Vache Kirakosyan
Ministry of Economy

Martin Stepanyan
Hayaudit LLC

Gurgen Migranovich Minasyan
Union of Builders of Amrenia

Armen Mkoyan
"Elite Group" CSJC

Tatevik Mkrtchyan
Trans-Alliance

Tatul Movsisyan
TM Audit

Ashot Mysayan
The State Committee of the Real Property Cadastre

Rajiv Nagri
Globalink Logistics Group

Nerses Nersisyan
PricewaterhouseCoopers

Marianna Nikoghosyan
Global SPC

Artur Nikoyan
Trans-Alliance

Karen Petrosyan
Investment Law Group LLC

Vahe Petrosyan
Logicon Development LLC

Aram Poghosyan
Grant Thornton Amyot

Gagik Sahakyan
Ameria cjsc

David Sargsyan
Ameria cjsc

Artak Shaboyan
State Revenue Committee of the Government

Thomas Samuelian
Arlex International CJSC

Gayane Shimshiryan
Central Bank of Armenia

Tigran Sukiasyan
OSCE

Aleqsey Suqoyan
Court of First Instance

Hakob Tadevosyan
Grant Thornton Amyot

Tigran Yedigaryan
Hayaudit LLC

Artur Tunyan
Judicial Reform Project

Aliya Utegaliyeva
PricewaterhouseCoopers

Araik Vardanyan
Chamber of Commerce and Industry

AUSTRALIA

Paul Agnew
McKay Solicitors

Elizabeth Allen
PricewaterhouseCoopers

Matthew Allison
Veda Advantage

Uma Awasthi
Amerinde Consolidated, Inc.

Lynda Brumm
PricewaterhouseCoopers

David Buda
RBHM Commercial Lawyers

Alicia Castillo
Alicia Castillo Wealthing Group

Gaibrielle Cleary
Gould Ralph Pty Ltd, a member firm of Russell Bedford International

Andrew Coates
McKay Solicitors

Marcus Connor
Chang, Pistilli & Simmons

Tim Cox
PricewaterhouseCoopers

David Cross
Deacons

Michael Daniel
PricewaterhouseCoopers

Jenny Davis
EnergyAustralia

Kathryn Dent
Gadens Lawyers

Anna Dileo
PricewaterhouseCoopers Legal Services

Megan Dyball
PricewaterhouseCoopers

Joan Fitzhenry
Baker & McKenzie

Mark Geniale
Office of State Revenue, NSW Treasury

Mark Grdovich
Blake Dawson

Douglas Hall
Len Hewitt & Company

Eric Herding
Panalpina World Transport Pty Ltd

David Hing
PricewaterhouseCoopers

Michael Hope
Baker & McKenzie

Eva Hucker
Baker & McKenzie

Ian Humphreys
Blake Dawson

Eric Ip
Onward Business Consultants PTY LTD

Doug Jones
Clayton Utz, member of Lex Mundi

Morgan Kelly
Ferrier Hodgson Limited

Sanjay Kinger
Fortune Law Group

Mark Kingston
Tradesafe Australia Pty. Ltd.

John Martin
Thomson Playford

Louise Massey
PricewaterhouseCoopers Legal Services

Mitchell Mathas
Deacons

Nathan Mattock
Marque Lawyers

Mark McGrath
McKay Solicitors

Scott McSwan
McKay Solicitors

Louise Murphy
Marque Lawyers

Enjel Phoon
Marque Lawyers

Mark Pistilli
Chang, Pistilli & Simmons

Michael Quinlan
Allens Arthur Robinson

John Reid
Office of State Revenue, NSW Treasury

Bob Ronai
Import-Export Services Pty. Ltd.

Luke Sayers
PricewaterhouseCoopers

Dean Schiller

Claus Schmidt
Panalpina World Transport Pty Ltd

SDV Logistics Ltd.

Nicholas Sedgwick
Marque Lawyers

Amber Sharp
Marque Lawyers

Damian Sturzaker
Marque Lawyers

Mark Swan
PricewaterhouseCoopers Legal Services

Theo Tavoularis
McKay Solicitors

Roland Taylor
McKay Solicitors

Simon Truskett
Clayton Utz, member of Lex Mundi

David Twigg
EnergyAustralia

Kathleen Ward
PricewaterhouseCoopers

Andrew Wheeler
PricewaterhouseCoopers

Leon Zwier
Arnold Bloch Leibler

AUSTRIA

Franz Althuber
DLA Piper Weiss-Tessbach Rechtsanwälte GmbH

Austrian Regulatory Authority

Clemens Baerenthaler
DLA Piper Weiss-Tessbach Rechtsanwälte GmbH

Georg Brandstetter
Brandstetter Pritz & Partner

Silvia Breyer
PricewaterhouseCoopers

Kraus & Co Warenhandelsgesellschaft mbH

Carina Buerger
PricewaterhouseCoopers

Esther De Raymaeker
Graf & Pitkowitz Rechtsanwälte GMBH

Martin Eckel
e|n|w|c Natlacen Walderdorff Cancola Rechtsanwälte GmbH

Agnes Eigner
Brandstetter Pritz & Partner

Tibor Fabian
Binder Grösswang Rechtsanwälte

Julian Feichtinger
CHSH Cerha Hempel Spiegelfeld Hlawati

Ferdinand Graf
Graf & Pitkowitz Rechtsanwälte GMBH

Patric Grosse
Wolf Theiss

Friederike Hager
e|n|w|c Natlacen Walderdorff Cancola Rechtsanwälte GmbH

Birgit Harasser
DLA Piper Weiss-Tessbach Rechtsanwälte GmbH

Peter Hoffmann
CHSH Cerha Hempel Spiegelfeld Hlawati

Rudolf Kaindl
Koehler, Kaindl, Duerr & Partner, Civil Law Notaries

Susanne Kappel
Kunz Schima Wallentin Rechtsanwälte KEG, member of Ius Laboris

Alexander Klauser
Brauneis Klauser Prändl Rechtsanwälte GmbH

Ulrike Langwallner
Schönherr Rechtsanwälte GmbH / Attorneys-at-Law

Peter Madl
Schönherr Rechtsanwälte GmbH / Attorneys-at-Law

Irene Mandl
Austrian Institute for SME Research

Wolfgang Messeritsch
National Bank of Austria

Nella Nella Hengstler
Austrian Embassy

Alfred Nepf
Ministry of Finance

Thomas Oberholzner
Austrian Institute for SME Research

Ayten Pacariz
KSV 1870

Barbara Pogacar
Law Partners

Friedrich Roedler
PricewaterhouseCoopers

Heidi Scheichenbauer
Austrian Institute for SME Research

Gottfried Schellmann
Brauneis Klauser Prändl Rechtsanwälte GmbH

Georg Schima
Kunz Schima Wallentin Rechtsanwälte KEG, member of Ius Laboris

Stephan Schmalzl
Graf & Pitkowitz Rechtsanwälte GMBH

Ernst Schmidt
Halpern & Prinz

Karin Schöpp
Binder Grösswang Rechtsanwälte

Franz Schwarzinger
Revisionstreuhand, a member firm of Russell Bedford International

Benedikt Spiegelfeld
CHSH Cerha Hempel Spiegelfeld Hlawati

Eva-Maria Springauf
National Bank of Austria

Thomas Trettnak
CHSH Cerha Hempel Spiegelfeld Hlawati

Birgit Vogt-Majarek
Kunz Schima Wallentin Rechtsanwälte KEG, member of Ius Laboris

Peter Voithofer
Austrian Institute for SME Research

Gerhard Wagner
KSV 1870

Irene Welser
CHSH Cerha Hempel Spiegelfeld Hlawati

Gerhard Winkler
National Bank of Austria

Rita Wittmann
DLA Piper Weiss-Tessbach Rechtsanwälte GmbH

Gerold Zeiler
Schönherr Rechtsanwälte GmbH / Attorneys-at-Law

Marcus Zuccato
Ministry of Finance

AZERBAIJAN

Elchin Akberov
PricewaterhouseCoopers

Aliagha Akhundov
Baker & McKenzie

Roman Alloyarov
OMNI Law Firm

Aykhan Asadov
Baker & McKenzie

Natavan Baghirova
BM International LLC.

Sabit A. Bagirov
Entrepreneurship Development Foundation

Bakielektrikshebeke

Samir Balayev
Unibank

Mehriban Efendiyeva
Michael Wilson & Partners Ltd.

Rovshan Farzaliyev
Trans Caspian Alliance Ltd

Zaur Fati-zadeh
Ministry of Taxes

Courtney Fowler
PricewaterhouseCoopers

Rashad Gafarov
Panalpina World Transport

Abbas Guliyev
Baker & McKenzie

Elchin Habibov
National Bank of Azerbaijan

Faiq Haci-Ismaylov
INCE MMC

Adil Hajaliyev
BM International LLC.

Arzu Hajiyeva
Ernst & Young

Nigar Hajiyeva
Baker & McKenzie

Faig Huseynov
Unibank

Jeyhun Huseynzada
PricewaterhouseCoopers

Zumrud Ibrahim
Baker & McKenzie

Afkan Isazade
Deposit Insurance Fund

Delara Israfilova
BM International LLC.

Vagif Karimly
Baker & McKenzie

Gunduz Karimov
Baker & McKenzie

Nuran Kerimov
Deloitte

Abdulfat Maherramov
Ministry of Labor and Social Protection

Nariman Mamedov
Blue Water Shipping Caspian Ltd

Kamal Mamedzade
Salans

Asim Mammadov
Deloitte

Kamil Mammadov
Mammadov & Partners Law Firm

Zaur Mammadov
Ernst & Young

Rena Mammadova
Deloitte

Faiq S. Manafov
Unibank

Daniel Matthews
Baker & McKenzie

Farhad Mirzayev
BM International LLC.

Ruslan Mukhtarov
BM International LLC.

Movlan Pashayev
PricewaterhouseCoopers

Emma Silyayeva
Salans

Murad Yahyayev
Unibank

Mahmud Yusifli
Baker & McKenzie

Ismail Zargarli
OMNI Law Firm

Nazim Ziyadov
OMNI Law Firm

BAHAMAS, THE

Michela Elaine Barnett
Graham, Thompson & Co.

Kevin Basden
Bahamas Electricity Corporation

Rodney W. Braynen
Design Häus

Tara Cooper
Higgs & Johnson

Surinder Deal
Higgs & Johnson

John Delaney
Higgs & Johnson

Chaunece M. Ferguson
Mackay & Moxey Chambers

Amos J. Ferguson jr.
Ferguson Associates & Planners

Anthony Forbes
Bahamas Electricity Corporation

Wendy Forsythe
Import Export Brokers Ltd.

Bethsheba G. Haven
Graham, Thompson & Co.

McKinney, Bancroft & Hughes

Portia Nicholson
Higgs & Johnson

Michael L. Paton
Lennox Paton

Castino D. Sands
Lennox Paton

Rochelle Sealy
PricewaterhouseCoopers

Kevin Seymour
PricewaterhouseCoopers

Everette Sweeting
Bahamas Electricity Corporation

BAHRAIN

Aysha Abdul Malik
Elham Ali Hassan & Associates (EAH Law)

Khaled Hassan Ajaji
Ministry of Justice & Islamic Affairs

Nawaf Bin Ebrahim Al Khalifa
Electricity & Water Authority

Seema Al- Thawadi
Ministry of Municipalities & Agriculture Affairs. Municipal One Stop Shop

Al-Twaijri & Partners Law Firm

Samer Al-Ajjawi
Ernst & Young

Haider Alnoaimi
Mohamed Salahuddin Consulting Engineering Bureau

Shaji Alukkal
Panalpina World Transport

Maaria Ashraf
Hatim S. Zu'bi & Partners

Mohammed Mirza A. Hussain Bin Jaffer
Ministry of Municipalities & Agriculture Affairs. Municipal One Stop Shop

Michael Durgavich
Al Sarraf & Al Ruwayeh

Nicolas Galoppin
Al Sarraf & Al Ruwayeh

Akram Hage
Abu-Ghazaleh Legal - (TAG-Legal)

Abdulwahid A. Janahi
The Benefit Company

Jawad Habib Jawad
BDO Jawad Habib

Lim Ming Huey
PricewaterhouseCoopers

Sara Jawahery
Elham Ali Hassan & Associates

Ebrahim Karolia
PricewaterhouseCoopers

Elie Kassis
Agility Logistics

Mubeen Khadir
Ernst & Young

Abdul-Haq Mohammed
Trowers & Hamlins

Gautam R. Mundkur
Mohamed Salahuddin Consulting Engineering Bureau

Najma A. Redha Hasan
Ministry of Municipalities & Agriculture Affairs. Municipal One Stop Shop

Mohamed Salahuddin
Mohamed Salahuddin Consulting Bureau

Thamer Salahuddin
Mohamed Salahuddin Consulting Engineering Bureau

Ali Sheikh
Al Sarraf & Al Ruwayeh

Esmond Hugh Stokes
Hatim S. Zu'bi & Partners

Robin Watson
The Benefit Company

Adrian Woodcock
Norton Rose

Ivan Zoricic
Ernst & Young

Hatim S. Zu'bi
Hatim S. Zu'bi & Partners

BANGLADESH

Md. Abdul Maleque Mian Abdullah
Credit Information Bureau, Bangladesh Bank

Zainul Abedin
A. Qasem & Co

Ali Akbar
Ruma Leather Industries Ltd.

Tanjib-ul Alam
Dr. Kamal Hossain & Associates

Ashfaq Amin
Integrated Transportation Services Ltd., Agent of Panalpina

Akram Ansari
SAS Corporation

Noorul Azhar
Azhar & Associates

Probir Barua
Knitwear Yarn Dyeing, Ltd.

Md. Halim Bepari
Halim Law Associate

Utpal Bhattacharjee
Infrastructure Investment Facilitation Center

Badrud Doulah
Doulah & Doulah Advocates

Nasirud Doulah
Doulah & Doulah Advocates

Moin Ghani
Dr. Kamal Hossain & Associates

Ummay Habiba Sharmin
Lee, Khan & Partners

K M A Halim
Upright Textile Supports

Md. Nazmul Hasan
Protex International

Kazi Rashed Hassan Ferdous
Proactive

Ajmal Hossain
Hoque Tannery

Kamal Hossain

Md. Sanwar Hossains
Sanwar Hossains Law Firm

Rafique-ul Huq
Huq and Co.

Abdul Hye
Bank of Bangladesh

Amir-Ul Islam
Amir & Amir Law Associates, member of Lex Mundi

Md Aminul Islam
City Apparel-Tex Co.

Shariful Islam

Rabeya Jamali
Huq and Co.

Bahzad Joarder
Huq and Co.

Margub Kabir
Huq and Co.

Sohel Kasem
A. Qasem & Co

Ali Asif Khan
Amir & Amir Law Associates, member of Lex Mundi

Md. Mydul H. Khan
Lee, Khan & Partners

Swapan Mistry
Sukumar & Associates

Md. Abu Nayeem
NAYEEM & ASSOCIATES

Eva Quasem
AMIR & AMIR LAW ASSOCIATES, MEMBER OF LEX MUNDI

Ahmedur Rahim
REGISTRAR, JOINT STOCK COMPANIES & FIRMS

Al Amin Rahman
AL AMIN RAHMAN & ASSOCIATES

Mizanur Rahman
A. QASEM & CO

Shahriar Syeed
V-TEAC FASHION PVT LTD.

Abbas Uddin
HUQ AND CO.

Abdul Wahab
A. WAHAB & CO.

Nurul Wahab
A. WAHAB & CO.

BELARUS

Yevgeny Achinovich
DICSA AUDIT, LAW & CONSULTING

Olga G. Adameyko
THE SUPREME ECONOMIC COURT

Alexey Anischenko
VLASOVA MIKHEL & PARTNERS

Dmitri Antonevich
MUNICIPALITY OF MINSK

Dmitry Arkhipenko
RE VERA GROUP

Olga Baraulya
NATIONAL BANK

Ron J. Barden
PRICEWATERHOUSECOOPERS

Andrey Bartashevich
INSTAR LOGISTICS

Irina A. Belskaya
THE SUPREME ECONOMIC COURT

Vladimir G. Biruk
CAPITAL LTD.

Dmitry Bokhan
BUSINESSCONSULT LAW FIRM

Sergey Borisyuk
STATE CUSTOMS COMMITTEE

Alexander Botian
BOROVTSOV & SALEI LAW OFFICES

Aliaksandr Danilevich
DANILEVICH

Aleksey Daryin
RE VERA GROUP

Madudin Nikolai Dmitrievich
THE SUPREME ECONOMIC COURT

Dmitry Dorofeev
NATIONAL BANK

Sergei Dubovik
NATIONAL BANK

Marina Dymovich
BOROVTSOV & SALEI LAW OFFICES

Andrej Ermolenko
VLASOVA MIKHEL & PARTNERS

Sergey Fedorov
STATE CUSTOMS COMMITTEE

GOMELTRANSNEFT DRUZHBA

Olga Grechko
VLASOVA MIKHEL & PARTNERS

Oleg Grushevich
ERNST & YOUNG

Antonina Ivanova
DICSA AUDIT, LAW & CONSULTING

Aleh Karalevich
DICSA AUDIT, LAW & CONSULTING

Uljana Karpekina
RE VERA GROUP

Alexander Khrapoutsky
VASHKEVICH, SAPEGO & KHRAPOUTSKY

Sergei Klimenko
DSV TRANSPORT (BY) LTD

Nina Knyazeva
BUSINESSCONSULT LAW FIRM

Irina Koikova
DICSA AUDIT, LAW & CONSULTING

Alexander Kononov
ERNST & YOUNG

Oksana Kotel
RE VERA GROUP

Mikhail Kozlov
ASSTRA WEISSRUSSLAND LTD

Anatol A. Kozlovsky
BELSTROYCENTER

Elena Kulchitskaya
ASSTRA WEISSRUSSLAND LTD

Dmitry Labetsky
BUSINESSCONSULT LAW FIRM

Vitaly Lagatsky
INSTAR LOGISTICS

Sergey A. Lazovsky
MINSK CABLE (ELECTRICAL) NETWORK

Oksana Loban
ERNST & YOUNG

Oksana Lyakhova
GLIMSTEDT

Dmitry Matveyev
LAW GROUP ARGUMENT

Konstantin Mikhel
VLASOVA MIKHEL & PARTNERS

Tatiana I. Miller
THE SUPREME ECONOMIC COURT

Valentina Nazaruk
MINISTRY OF ARCHITECTURE AND BUILDING

Anatoly Nichkasov
MINISTRY OF ARCHITECTURE AND BUILDING

Magdalena Patrzyk
PRICEWATERHOUSECOOPERS

Olga Pepenina
GLIMSTEDT

Tatiana Polonskaya
THE SUPREME ECONOMIC COURT

Vassili I. Salei
BOROVTSOV & SALEI LAW OFFICES

Katerina Sereda
LAW GROUP ARGUMENT

Alexander Shevko
NATIONAL BANK

Lubov Slobodchikova
NATIONAL BANK

Paulina Smykovskaya
STEPANOVSKI, PAPAKUL AND PARTNERS LTD.

Natalia Talai
VLASOVA MIKHEL & PARTNERS

Pavel Tzarou
RE VERA GROUP

Svetlana Valueva
STEPANOVSKI, PAPAKUL AND PARTNERS LTD.

Alexander Vasilevsky
VALEX CONSULT

Igor Verkhovodko
BUSINESSCONSULT LAW FIRM

WILO BEL

Maria Yurieva
VLASOVA MIKHEL & PARTNERS

Pavel S. Yurkevich
THE SUPREME ECONOMIC COURT

Ekaterina Zabello
VLASOVA MIKHEL & PARTNERS

Andrey Zhuk
KPMG

Darya Zhuk
GLIMSTEDT

BELGIUM

ALLEN & OVERY LLP

Hubert André-Dumont
MCGUIRE WOODS LLP

Yves Brosens
DLA PIPER LLP

Gilles Carbonez
MCGUIRE WOODS LLP

Pol Cools
MCGUIRE WOODS LLP

Adriaan Dauwe
ALTIUS

Steven de Schrijver
VAN BAEL & BELLIS

Kris de Schutter
LOYENS & LOEFF

Olivier Debray
CLAEYS & ENGELS, MEMBER OF IUS LABORIS

Amaury Della Faille
PRICEWATERHOUSECOOPERS

Jean-Michel Detry
DLA PIPER LLP

Frank Dierckx
PRICEWATERHOUSECOOPERS

David Du Pont
ASHURST

Mario Flamee
DEXIA BANK S.A.

Pierrette Fraisse
SPF FINANCES - AGDP

Ghislaine Goes
DLA PIPER LLP

Sandrine Hirsch
SIMONT BRAUN

Thibaut Hollanders
DLA PIPER LLP

Thomas Hürner
NATIONAL BANK

Stephan Legein
FEDERAL PUBLIC SERVICE FINANCE

Luc Legon
PRICEWATERHOUSECOOPERS

Axel Maeterlinck
SIMONT BRAUN

Philippe Massart
SIBELGA

Dominique Mougenot
COMMERCIAL COURT MONS

Didier Muraille
NATIONAL BANK

Stephan Neetens

Sabrina Otten
PRICEWATERHOUSECOOPERS

Stéphane Robyns
DLA PIPER LLP

Frédéric Souchon
PRICEWATERHOUSECOOPERS

STIBBE

Jan van Celst
DLA PIPER LLP

Ilse van de Mierop
DLA PIPER LLP

MEDICCLEANAIR

Sibylle Vandenberghe
PRICEWATERHOUSECOOPERS

Marie-Noëlle Vanderhoven
PRICEWATERHOUSECOOPERS

Tom Vantroyen
ALTIUS

Reinout Vleugels
SQUIRE, SANDERS & DEMPSEY L.L.P.

Johan Vonckers
MCGUIRE WOODS LLP

Bram Vuylsteke

Christian Willems
LOYENS & LOEFF

Dirk Wouters
WVM-BEDRIJFSREVISOREN BVBA, A MEMBER OF RUSSELL BEDFORD INTERNATIONAL

BELIZE

Emil Arguelles
ARGUELLES & COMPANY LLC

Sherman Ferguson
BELIZE ELECTRICITY LTD.

Gian C. Gandhi
INTERNATIONAL FINANCIAL SERVICES COMMISSION

Rodolfo Gutierrez
BELIZE ELECTRICITY LTD.

Mirna Lara
EUROCARIBE BELIZE SHIPPING SERVICES

Russell Longsworth
CARIBBEAN SHIPPING AGENCIES LTD.

Reynaldo F. Magana
FRONTIER INTERNATIONAL BUSINESS SERVICES LTD.

Tania Moody
BARROW & WILLIAMS

Jose Moreno
BELIZE ELECTRICITY LTD.

Gereld Morris
FRONTIER INTERNATIONAL BUSINESS SERVICES LTD.

Kareem D. Musa
MUSA & BALDERAMOS

Patricia Rodriguez
BELIZE COMPANIES AND CORPORATE AFFAIRS REGISTRY

Dawn Sampson
BELIZE ELECTRICITY LTD.

Janelle Tillett
EUROCARIBE BELIZE SHIPPING SERVICES

Saidi Vaccaro
ARGUELLES & COMPANY LLC

Adelfino Vasquez
MINISTRY OF LABOUR, LOCAL GOVERNMENT AND RURAL DEVELOPMENT

C. Phillip Waight
WAIGHT & ASSOCIATES

Lionel L. R. Welch
SUPREME COURT

Carlton Young
YOUNG'S ENGINEERING CONSULTANCY LTD.

BENIN

Safia Abdoulaye
CABINET D'AVOCATS

Diaby Aboubakar
BCEAO

Irène Adjagba Ichola
ETUDE NOTARIALE ADJAGBA ICHOLA

Saïdou Agbantou
CABINET D'AVOCATS

Paul Agbonihoue
SOCIETE BENINOISE D'ENERGIE ELECTRIQUE (SBEE)

Jean-Paul T. Hervé Ahoyo
SOCIETE BENINOISE D'ENERGIE ELECTRIQUE (SBEE)

Sybel Akuesson
FCA

Rafikou Alabi
CABINET ME ALABI

Moïse Atchade
CABINET DE MAITRE ATCHADE

Innocent Sourou Avognon
TRIBUNAL DE PREMIERE INSTANCE DE COTONOU

CONTINENTAL BANK

Alice Codjia-Sohouenou
CABINET AGBANTOU SAIDOU

Johannès Dagnon
GROUPE HELIOS AFRIQUE

DAE STORES LIMITED

Olivier Dansou
IMOTEPH

Henri Fadonougbo
TRIBUNAL DE PREMIERE INSTANCE DE COTONOU

Guy Médard Agbo Fayemi
ORDRE NATIONAL DES ARCHITECTES ET DES URBANISTES

Sèglan Raymond Cyr Gbessemehlan
CABINET AGBANTOU SAIDOU

Jean-Claude Gnamien
FIDAFRICA / PRICEWATERHOUSECOOPERS

Dominique Lales
ADDAX & ORYX GROUP

Evelyne M'Bassidgé
FIDAFRICA /
PricewaterhouseCoopers

Aline Edwige Odje
Cabinet Agbantou Saidou

Balkissou Osseni Osho
Cabinet d'Avocats

Dakehoun Armand S. Raoul
Ministere des Mines, de
l'Energie et de L'eau

Olagnika Salam
Office Notarial Olagnika

Adegbindin Saliou

Hauvy Seka Mathieu
FIDAFRICA /
PricewaterhouseCoopers

Didier Sterlingot
SDV - SAGA

Dominique Taty
FIDAFRICA /
PricewaterhouseCoopers

Konzo Traore
BCEAO

Jean-Bosco Todjinou
Ordre National des
Architectes et des
Urbanistes

Konate Yacouba
France Transfo

Emmanuel Yehouessi
BCEAO

BHUTAN

Kincho Dorjee
Leko Packers

N.B. Gurung
DHL

Sonam Gyeltshen
Bhutan Power
Corporation Ltd.

Tshering Tobgey
Gyelsa -Tewa Real Estate
Developer (GRED)

Karma Tshering
Lhaki Group

Tshering Wangchuk
Royal Court of Justice

Sonam P. Wangdi
Ministry of Economic
Affairs

Tashi Yezer
Royal Securities Exchange
of Bhutan Ltd.

BOLIVIA

Fernando Aguirre
Bufete Aguirre Soc. Civ.

Carolina Aguirre Urioste
Bufete Aguirre Soc. Civ.

Oswaldo Alvarez Wills
S&V Asociados S.R.L.

Eduardo Aramayo
PricewaterhouseCoopers

Raúl A. Baldivia
Baldivia Unzaga &
Asociados

Adrián Barrenechea
Criales, Urcullo &
Antezana

Hugo Berthin
BDO Berthin Amengual &
Asociados

Alexandra Blanco
Guevara & Gutiérrez S.C.

Walter B. Calla Cardenas
Colegio Departamental de
Arquitectos de La Paz

Mauricio Costa du Rels
Würth Kim Costa du Rels

Carlos Ferreira
C.R. & F. Rojas, member of
Lex Mundi

Nicolas Franulic Casasnovas
Infocred - Servicio de
Informacion Crediticia
BIC s.a.

Jose E. Gamboa T.
Colegio Departamental de
Arquitectos de La Paz

Petronila Gismondi
Consultora "Gismondi" -
Contable Tributario

Primitivo Gutiérrez
Guevara & Gutiérrez S.C.

Carlos Alberto Iacia
PricewaterhouseCoopers

Jorge Luis Inchauste
Guevara & Gutiérrez S.C.

Paola Justiniano Arias
Sanjinés & Asociados Soc.
Civ. Abogados

Mario Kempff
C.R. & F. Rojas, member of
Lex Mundi

César Lora
PricewaterhouseCoopers

Daniel Mariaca
Criales, Urcullo &
Antezana

Gonzalo Mendieta Romero
Estudio de Abogados
Mendieta Romero &
Asociados

Jaime Merida Alvarez
Colegio Departamental de
Arquitectos de La Paz

Ariel Morales Vasquez
C.R. & F. Rojas, member of
Lex Mundi

Daniela Murialdo Lopez
Estudio de Abogados
Mendieta Romero &
Asociados

Pablo Ordonez
Ayoroa & Ordonez

Alejandro Peláez Kay
Indacochea & Asociados

Mariana Pereira Nava
Indacochea & Asociados

Oscar Antonio Plaza Ponte
Entidad De Servicios De
Información Enserbic S.A.

Julio Quintanilla Quiroga
Quintanilla, Soria &
Nishizawa Soc. Civ

Carlos Ramírez
C.R. & F. Rojas, member of
Lex Mundi

Angélica Roca
YPFB Andina S.A

Diego Rojas
C.R. & F. Rojas, member of
Lex Mundi

Fernando Rojas
C.R. & F. Rojas, member of
Lex Mundi

Mariela Rojas
Entidad De Servicios De
Información Enserbic S.A.

Patricio Rojas
C.R. & F. Rojas, member of
Lex Mundi

Pilar Salasar
Bufete Aguirre Soc. Civ.

Sandra Salinas
C.R. & F. Rojas, member of
Lex Mundi

Rodolpho Raul Sanjines
Elizagoyen
Sanjinés & Asociados Soc.
Civ. Abogados

Maria Kim Shin
Würth Kim Costa du Rels

A. Mauricio Torrico Galindo
Quintanilla, Soria &
Nishizawa Soc. Civ

Roberto Viscafé Ureña
PricewaterhouseCoopers

Mauricio Zambrana Cuéllar
Infocred - Servicio de
Informacion Crediticia
BIC s.a.

BOSNIA AND
HERZEGOVINA

Aida Ajanović
IKRP Rokas & Partners

Dunja Arnaut
Law Office Spaho

Feđa Bičakčić
Law Office Spaho

Sead Bijedić
Central Bank

Dario Bišćević
DB Schenker

Mubera Brković
PricewaterhouseCoopers

Sabina Čelik
PricewaterhouseCoopers

Višnja Dizdarević
Branko Marić Law Office

Emir Hadžić
Branko Marić Law Office

Alma Hadžiosmanović
Nedal d.o.o.

Besim Hadžiosmanović
Nedal d.o.o.

Senada Havić Hrenovica
LRC Credit Bureau

Ismeta Huremović
Land Registry Office of
the Sarajevo Municipal
Court

Nusmir Huskić
Branko Marić Law Office

Arela Jusufbasić
Lawyers' Office Bojana
Tkalcic-Djulic & Olodar
Prebanic

Kerim Karabdić
Advokati Salih & Kerim
Karabdić

Almedina Karšić
Law Office of Emir
Kovačević

Muhidin Karšić
Law Office of Emir
Kovačević

Saša Lemez
Central Bank

Anja Margetić
Central Bank

Branko Marić
Branko Marić Law Office

JP Elektroprivreda
BiH Podružnica
"Elektrodistribucija"
Sarajevo

Emir Pasanović
DLA Piper

Edisa Peštek

Đorđe Racković
Central Bank

Alma Ramezić
PricewaterhouseCoopers

Adina Salkanović

Hasib Salkić
Interšped

Nihad Sijerčić
Law Office Spaho

Mehmed Spaho
Law Office Spaho

Anisa Strujić
Branko Marić Law Office

Bojana Tkalčić-Djulić
Lawyers' Office Bojana
Tkalcic-Djulic & Olodar
Prebanic

Belma Zorlak
Branko Marić Law Office

BOTSWANA

John Carr-Hartley
Armstrongs Attorneys

Asamiah Chilume
Chilume & Company

Yvonne K. Chilume
Chilume & Company

Rizwan Desai
Collins Newman & Co.

Diba M. Diba
Minchin & Kelly

Guri Dobo
Dobson and Company,
Certified Public
Accountants

Edward W. Fasholé-Luke II
Luke & Associates

Vincent Galeromeloe
Transunion

M. Gilika
Botswana Unified Revenue
Service (BURS)

Laknath Jayawickrama
PricewaterhouseCoopers

Akheel Jinabhai
Akheel Jinabhai &
Associates

Laurence Khupe
Collins Newman & Co.

Dineo Makati-Mpho
Collins Newman & Co.

Finola McMahon
Osei-Ofei Swabi & Co.

Diniar Minwalla
PricewaterhouseCoopers

Tsemetse Mmolai
Botswana Stock Exchange

Patience Mokgadi
Armstrongs Attorneys,
member of Lex Mundi

Mmatshipi Motsepe
Manica Africa Pty. Ltd.

Jack Allan Mutua
Tectura International
Botswana

Rajesh Narasimhan
Grant Thornton

Kwadwo Osei-Ofci
Osei-Ofei Swabi & Co.

Butler Phirie
PricewaterhouseCoopers

Caroline Polder
Collins Newman & Co.

Claudio Rossi
Sharps Electrical (Pty)
Ltd

Sipho Ziga
Armstrongs Attorneys,
member of Lex Mundi

BRAZIL

Antonio Aires
Demarest e Almeida
Advogados

Diogo Sales Flores Alves
Themag Engenharia e
Gerenciamento S/C Ltda.

Glauco Alves Martins
Fleury Malheiros,
Gasparini, De Cresci e
Nogueira de Lima

Lucia Aragao
Veirano Advogados

Mariana Aranha
Machado, Meyer, Sendacz
e Opice

Pedro Vitor Araujo da Costa
Escritorio de Advocacia
Gouvêa Vieira

Flavia Bailone Marcilio
Barbosa
Veirano Advogados

Flavia Bailoni Marcilio
Barbosa
Veirano Advogados

Priscyla Barbosa
Veirano Advogados

Juliana Bastianello Baldin
Machado, Meyer, Sendacz
e Opice

Guilherme Bertolini
Fernandes dos Santos
Fleury Malheiros,
Gasparini, De Cresci e
Nogueira de Lima

Roberta Bessa
Machado, Meyer, Sendacz
e Opice

Camila Biral
Demarest e Almeida
Advogados

Richard Blanchet
Loeser e Portela
Advogados

Adriano Boni
Noronha Advogados

Adriano Borges
De Vivo, Whitaker, Castro
e Gonçalves Advogados

Altimiro Boscoli
Demarest e Almeida
Advogados

Sergio Bronstein
VEIRANO ADVOGADOS

Clarissa Bruzzi
NORONHA ADVOGADOS

Julio Bueno
PINHEIRO NETO ADVOGADOS

Júlio César Bueno
PINHEIRO NETO ADVOGADOS

Hugo Buser
ELOTRANS TRANSPORTES INTERNACIONAIS LTDA

Paulo Campana
FELSBERG, PEDRETTI, MANNRICH E AIDAR ADVOGADOS E CONSULTORES LEGAIS

Gustavo Carmona
PRICEWATERHOUSECOOPERS

Plinio Cesar Romanini
BANCO CENTRAL DO BRASIL

Renato Chiodaro
DE VIVO, WHITAKER, CASTRO E GONÇALVES ADVOGADOS

Fernanda Cirne Montorfano
ESCRITORIO DE ADVOCACIA GOUVÊA VIEIRA

Flávia Coelho Warde
DEMAREST E ALMEIDA ADVOGADOS

Ana Amélia Corrêa Contro
NORONHA ADVOGADOS

Gilberto Deon Corrêa Junior
VEIRANO ADVOGADOS

Sidinei Corrêa Marques
BANCO CENTRAL DO BRASIL

Mirella da Costa Andreola
NORONHA ADVOGADOS

Gisela da Silva Freire
FLEURY MALHEIROS, GASPARINI, DE CRESCI E NOGUEIRA DE LIMA

Adriana Daiuto
DEMAREST E ALMEIDA ADVOGADOS

Cleber Dal Rovere Peluzo
VISEU CUNHA ORICCHIO ADVOGADOS

Marina Dall´Aglio Pastore Sampaio
NORONHA ADVOGADOS

Bruno Henrique de Aguiar
RAYES, FAGUNDES E OLIVEIRA RAMOS

Sólon de Almeida Cunha
MACHADO, MEYER, SENDACZ E OPICE

Eduardo de Andrade Castro
BANCO CENTRAL DO BRASIL

Aldo de Cresci Neto
FLEURY MALHEIROS, GASPARINI, DE CRESCI E NOGUEIRA DE LIMA

Andréia Laís de Melo Silva Vargas
BANCO CENTRAL DO BRASIL

Edilson De Morais
SERASA S.A.

Luiz Gustavo de Oliveira Ramos
RAYES, FAGUNDES E OLIVEIRA RAMOS

Maria Fernanda de Paulo Antoneli
FLEURY MALHEIROS, GASPARINI, DE CRESCI E NOGUEIRA DE LIMA

Nadia Demoliner Lacerda
MESQUITA BARROS ADVOGADOS, MEMBER OF IUS LABORIS

Felipe Di Marzo Trezza
FLEURY MALHEIROS, GASPARINI, DE CRESCI E NOGUEIRA DE LIMA

Mayna Dias Melo
MACHADO, MEYER, SENDACZ E OPICE

Renato Din Oikawa
FLEURY MALHEIROS, GASPARINI, DE CRESCI E NOGUEIRA DE LIMA

José Ricardo dos Santos Luz Júnior
DUARTE GARCIA, CASELLI GUIMARÃES E TERRA ADVOGADOS

Joao Paulo F.A. Fagundes
RAYES, FAGUNDES E OLIVEIRA RAMOS

Vanessa Felício
VEIRANO ADVOGADOS

Thomas Benes Felsberg
FELSBERG, PEDRETTI, MANNRICH E AIDAR ADVOGADOS E CONSULTORES LEGAIS

Sabrina Fernandes
RAYES, FAGUNDES E OLIVEIRA RAMOS

Mariana Fernandes Conrado
NORONHA ADVOGADOS

Alexsander Fernandes de Andrade
DUARTE GARCIA, CASELLI GUIMARÃES E TERRA ADVOGADOS

Eliana Maria Filippozzi
NORONHA ADVOGADOS

Silvia Fiszman
MACHADO, MEYER, SENDACZ E OPICE

Florencia Ortiz Freuler
MACHADO, MEYER, SENDACZ E OPICE

Rafael Frota Indio do Brasil Ferraz
ESCRITORIO DE ADVOCACIA GOUVÊA VIEIRA

Rafael Gagliardi
DEMAREST E ALMEIDA ADVOGADOS

Pedro Paulo Gasparini
FLEURY MALHEIROS, GASPARINI, DE CRESCI E NOGUEIRA DE LIMA

Thiago Giantomassi
DEMAREST E ALMEIDA ADVOGADOS

Michelle Giraldi Lacerda
PRICEWATERHOUSECOOPERS

Lara Gomes Dias
MACHADO, MEYER, SENDACZ E OPICE

Adriana Grizante de Almeida
PRICEWATERHOUSECOOPERS

Enrique Hadad
LOESER E PORTELA ADVOGADOS

Carlos Alberto Iacia
PRICEWATERHOUSECOOPERS

Marcelo Inglez de Souza
DEMAREST E ALMEIDA ADVOGADOS

Eduardo Takemi Kataoka
CASTRO, BARROS, SOBRAL, GOMES ADVOGADOS

Fernando Koury Lopes

José Paulo Lago Alves Pequeno
NORONHA ADVOGADOS

Fernando Loeser
LOESER E PORTELA ADVOGADOS

Ricardo Loureiro
SERASA S.A.

Marina Maccabelli
DEMAREST E ALMEIDA ADVOGADOS

Viviane Maria Barbosa da Silva
MACHADO, MEYER, SENDACZ E OPICE

Georges Louis Martens Filho
DE VIVO, WHITAKER, CASTRO E GONÇALVES ADVOGADOS

Jose Augusto Martins
BAKER & MCKENZIE

Thiago Martins
ARAÚJO E POLICASTRO ADVOGADOS

Andrea Massei Rossi
MACHADO, MEYER, SENDACZ E OPICE

Laura Massetto Meyer
PINHEIRO GUIMARÃES ADVOGADOS

Rodrigo Matos
MBM TRADING

Eduardo Augusto Mattar
PINHEIRO GUIMARÃES ADVOGADOS

Marianne Mendes Webber
NORONHA ADVOGADOS

Victor Menezes Lopes Gomes
NORONHA ADVOGADOS

Cássio Mesquita Barros
MESQUITA BARROS ADVOGADOS, MEMBER OF IUS LABORIS

Ricardo Messias Sapag
ITATRANS LTDA

Renata Morelli
RAYES, FAGUNDES E OLIVEIRA RAMOS

Anneliese Moritz
FELSBERG, PEDRETTI, MANNRICH E AIDAR ADVOGADOS E CONSULTORES LEGAIS

Paulo Nasser
DEMAREST E ALMEIDA ADVOGADOS

Jorge Nemr
LEITE, TOSTO E BARROS

Walter Abrahão Nimir Junior
DE VIVO, WHITAKER, CASTRO E GONÇALVES ADVOGADOS

João Paulo Nogueira Barros
ESCRITORIO DE ADVOCACIA GOUVÊA VIEIRA

Andrea Oricchio Kirsh
VISEU CUNHA ORICCHIO ADVOGADOS

Adriana Pallis Romano
MACHADO, MEYER, SENDACZ E OPICE

Rafael Passaro
MACHADO, MEYER, SENDACZ E OPICE

Maria Fernanada Pecora
VEIRANO ADVOGADOS

Fabio Luis Pereira Barboza
VISEU CUNHA ORICCHFIO ADVOGADOS

Lilian Pimentel
FLEURY MALHEIROS, GASPARINI, DE CRESCI E NOGUEIRA DE LIMA

Erika Pizardo
NORONHA ADVOGADOS

Durval Portela
LOESER E PORTELA ADVOGADOS

Rodrigo Eduardo Pricoli
RAYES, FAGUNDES E OLIVEIRA RAMOS

Daniela Prieto
MACHADO, MEYER, SENDACZ E OPICE

Maria Fernanda Principe Candotti
FLEURY MALHEIROS, GASPARINI, DE CRESCI E NOGUEIRA DE LIMA

Ronaldo Rayes
RAYES, FAGUNDES E OLIVEIRA RAMOS

Domingos Fernando Refinetti
MACHADO, MEYER, SENDACZ E OPICE

Jose Ribeiro do Pardo Junior
MACHADO, MEYER, SENDACZ E OPICE

Eliane Ribeiro Gago
DUARTE GARCIA, CASELLI GUIMARÃES E TERRA ADVOGADOS

Lia Roston
RAYES, FAGUNDES E OLIVEIRA RAMOS

Marta Saft
VEIRANO ADVOGADOS

José Samurai Saiani
MACHADO, MEYER, SENDACZ E OPICE

Bruno Sanchez Belo
NORONHA ADVOGADOS

Juliano Sarmento Barra
MACHADO, MEYER, SENDACZ E OPICE

Carolina Schreier
KLA-KOURY LOPES ADVOGADOS

Ingrid Schwarz R. de Mendonça
NORONHA ADVOGADOS

Elaine Shimoda
SERASA S.A.

Walter Stuber
WALTER STUBER CONSULTORIA JURIDICA

Enrique Tello Hadad
LOESER E PORTELA ADVOGADOS

Milena Tesser
RAYES, FAGUNDES E OLIVEIRA RAMOS

Marcos Tiraboschi
VEIRANO ADVOGADOS

Carlos Tortelli
CONSULT GROUP (MEMBER OF RUSSELL BEDFORD INTERNATIONAL)

Paulo Trani
NORONHA ADVOGADOS

Juliana Vasconcelos
APEXBRASIL

José Wahle
VEIRANO ADVOGADOS

Eduardo Guimarães Wanderley
VEIRANO ADVOGADOS

Gabriela Weirich Mottin
VEIRANO ADVOGADOS

Marcos Yanaka
MBM TRADING

BRUNEI DARUSSALAM

Aaron Goh
PRICEWATERHOUSECOOPERS

Cyndhia Kong
WIDDOWS KONG & ASSOCIATES

Felicia Kong
B.T. FORWARDING COMPANY

Nancy Lai
LEE CORPORATEHOUSE ASSOCIATES

Kevin Lee
WISMA MANAGEMENT

Kin Chee Lee
LEE CORPORATEHOUSE ASSOCIATES

Lennon Lee
PRICEWATERHOUSECOOPERS

Yew Choh Lee
Y.C. LEE & LEE ADVOCATES & SOLICITORS

Kelvin Lim
K. LIM & CO.

Colin Ong
DR. COLIN ONG LEGAL SERVICES

David Price
ARKITEK IBRAHIM

See Tiat Quek
PRICEWATERHOUSECOOPERS

Shazali Sulaiman
KPMG

BULGARIA

Svetlin Adrianov
PENKOV, MARKOV & PARTNERS

Nikolay Bandakov
KAMBOUROV & PARTNERS

Christo Batchvarov
PRICEWATERHOUSECOOPERS

Kalin Bonev
TSVETKOVA BEBOV & PARTNERS,(LANDWELL BULGARIA)

Nikolai Bozhilov
UNIMASTERS LOGISTICS PLC.

Emil Cholakov
LM LEGAL SERVICES LTD.

Maria Danailova
WOLF THEISS

Borislav Dimitrov
*LANDWELL & ASSOCIÉS -
PRICEWATERHOUSECOOPERS
LEGAL SERVICES*

George Dimitrov
DIMITROV, PETROV & CO.

Kristina Dimitrova
*LANDWELL & ASSOCIÉS -
PRICEWATERHOUSECOOPERS
LEGAL SERVICES*

Vesselin Dinkov
*LANDWELL & ASSOCIÉS -
PRICEWATERHOUSECOOPERS
LEGAL SERVICES*

Lora Docheva
PRICEWATERHOUSECOOPERS

Silvia Dulevska
BULGARIAN NATIONAL BANK

Yanitsa Ganeva
*DJINGOV, GOUGINSKI,
KYUTCHUKOV & VELICHKOV*

Georgy Georgiev
*LANDWELL & ASSOCIÉS -
PRICEWATERHOUSECOOPERS
LEGAL SERVICES*

Plamen Georgiev
*ECONOMOU INTERNATIONAL
SHIPPING AGENCY LIMITED*

Velislava Georgieva
*ECONOMOU INTERNATIONAL
SHIPPING AGENCY LIMITED*

Marieta Getcheva
PRICEWATERHOUSECOOPERS

Ralitsa Gougleva
*DJINGOV, GOUGINSKI,
KYUTCHUKOV & VELICHKOV*

Katerina Gramatikova
*DOBREV, KINKIN &
LYUTSKANOV*

Stella Iossifova
*STOEVA, KUYUMDJIEVA &
VITLIEMOV*

Ginka Iskrova
PRICEWATERHOUSECOOPERS

Stela Ivanova
BNT

Angel Kalaidjiev
*KALAIDJIEV, GEORGIEV &
MINCHEV*

Yavor Kambourov
KAMBOUROV & PARTNERS

Hristina Kirilova
KAMBOUROV & PARTNERS

Lilia Kisseva
*DJINGOV, GOUGINSKI,
KYUTCHUKOV & VELICHKOV*

Donko Kolev
BEDOR EXCEM

Nikolay Kolev
BORISLAV BOYANOV & CO.

Ilya Komarevsky
TSVETKOVA, BEBOV AND CO.

Boika Komsulova
PRICEWATERHOUSECOOPERS

Stephan Kyutchukov
*DJINGOV, GOUGINSKI,
KYUTCHUKOV & VELICHKOV*

Dessislava Lukarova
ARSOV NATCHEV GANEVA

Jordan Manahilov
BULGARIAN NATIONAL BANK

Polina Marinova
*LANDWELL & ASSOCIÉS -
PRICEWATERHOUSECOOPERS
LEGAL SERVICES*

Slavi Mikinski
LEGALEX

Vladimir Natchev
ARSOV NATCHEV GANEVA

Yordan Naydenov
BORISLAV BOYANOV & CO.

Nelii Nedkova
WOLF THEISS

Violeta Nikolova
ARSOV NATCHEV GANEVA

Darina Oresharova
EXPERIAN BULGARIA EAD

Yulia Peeva
*REX CONSULTING LTD, A
MEMBER FIRM OF RUSSELL
BEDFORD INTERNATIONAL*

Vladimir Penkov
PENKOV, MARKOV & PARTNERS

Galina Petkova
ARSOV NATCHEV GANEVA

Irena Petkova
LCONSULT

Borislava Pokrass
*STOEVA, KUYUMDJIEVA &
VITLIEMOV*

Gergana Popova
GEORGIEV, TODOROV & CO.

Nikolay Radev
*DOBREV, KINKIN &
LYUTSKANOV*

Alexander Rangelov
PRICEWATERHOUSECOOPERS

REGISTRY AGENCY

Stela Slavcheva
*ASPOLLY CARRASS
INTERNATIONAL LTD.*

Violeta Slavova
EXPERIAN EAD

Yasser Spassov
TSVETKOVA, BEBOV AND CO.

Martin Stanchev
*DOBREV, KINKIN &
LYUTSKANOV*

Roman Stoyanov
PENKOV, MARKOV & PARTNERS

Margarita Stoyanova
KAMBOUROV & PARTNERS

Yordan Terziev
ARSOV NATCHEV GANEVA

Laura Thomas
LM LEGAL SERVICES LTD.

Anastassia Timanova
EXPERIAN EAD

Kaloyan Todorov
WOLF THEISS

Nikolay Todorov
LCONSULT

Svilen Todorov
*TODOROV & DOYKOVA LAW
FIRM*

Matea Tsenkova
*DJINGOV, GOUGINSKI,
KYUTCHUKOV & VELICHKOV*

Georgi Tsvetkov
*DJINGOV, GOUGINSKI,
KYUTCHUKOV & VELICHKOV*

Irina Tsvetkova
PRICEWATERHOUSECOOPERS

Stefan Tzakov
KAMBOUROV & PARTNERS

Maria Urmanova
*LANDWELL & ASSOCIÉS -
PRICEWATERHOUSECOOPERS
LEGAL SERVICES*

Jasmina Uzova
*DJINGOV, GOUGINSKI,
KYUTCHUKOV & VELICHKOV*

Miroslav Varnaliev
UNIMASTERS LOGISTICS PLC.

Venzi Vassilev
*REX CONSULTING LTD, A
MEMBER FIRM OF RUSSELL
BEDFORD INTERNATIONAL*

BURKINA FASO

Diaby Aboubakar
BCEAO

Seydou Balama
*ETUDE MAÎTRE BALAMA
SEYDOU*

Siaka Barro
AGENCE BARRO

Josephine Bassolet
SONABEL

Babou Bayili
LNBTP

Issaka Belem
SDV

Dolphyne Benny
MAERSK

Fortune Bicaba
*CABINET D'AVOCATS FORTUNÉ
BICABA*

Dieudonne Bonkoungou
*CABINET OUEDRAOGO &
BONKOUNGOU*

Rene Bonou
*SAFTRANS (SOCIETE
D'AFFRETEMENT ET DE
TRANSIT)*

A Theophile Campene
SDV

B. Thierry Compaoré
*INGENIERIE-DESIGN-
ARCHITECTURE*

Bobson Coulibaly
*CABINET D'AVOCATS
BARTHÉLEMY KERE*

Charlotte Coulibaly
*CABINET D'AVOCATS
BARTHÉLEMY KERE*

Denis Dawende
*OFFICE NOTARIAL ME JEAN
CELESTIN ZOURE*

Daouda Diallo
*FISC CONSULTING
INTERNATIONAL*

Ambroise Farama

Sibi Desire Gouba
*OFFICE NOTARIAL ME JEAN
CELESTIN ZOURE*

Fulgence Habiyaremye
*CABINET D'AVOCATS
BARTHÉLEMY KERE*

Oumarou Idani
LAANGANDE TRANSPORTS

Issaka Kargougou
*MAISÓN DE L'ENTREPRISE DU
BURKINA FASO*

Barthélémy Kere
*CABINET D'AVOCATS
BARTHÉLEMY KERE*

Gilbert Kibtonre
CEFAC

Clarisse Kienou
*CENTRE DE FORMALITES DES
ENTREPRISES*

Eddie Komboïgo
KOMBOÏGO & ASSOCIES

Michel Konate
*BANQUE COMMERCIALE DU
BURKINA*

Raphael Kouraogo
SONABEL

Messan Lawson
*SOCIETE NATIONALE DE
TRANSIT DU BURKINA*

Colette Lefebvre
INSPECTION DU TRAVAIL

Zinago Lingani
*DIRECTION GENERALE DES
IMPOTS*

Evelyne M'Bassidgé
*FIDAFRICA /
PRICEWATERHOUSECOOPERS*

Denise Ouedraogo
*ETUDE DE MAÎTRE
OUEDRAOGO*

Martin Ouedraogo
*UNION INTERNATIONALE DE
NOTARIAT LATIN*

N. Henri Ouedraogo
*MINISTERE DES FINANCES ET
DU BUDGET*

Oumarou Ouedraogo
*CABINET OUEDRAOGO &
BONKOUNGOU*

Ousmane Honore Ouedraogo
MAISON DE L'ENTREPRISE

Patrick Herve Ouedraogo
*BANQUE COMMERCIALE DU
BURKINA*

Pascal Ouedraogo
*CABINET D'AVOCATS
BARTHÉLEMY KERE*

Thierry Ismael Ouedraogo
*DIRECTION GÉNÉRALE
DU TRESOR ET DE LA
COMPTABILITÉ PUBLIQUE*

Roger Omer Ouédraogo
*ASSOCIATION
PROFESSIONNELLE
DES TRANSITAIRES &
COMMISSIONNAIRES EN
DOUANE AGRÉES*

Koumbatouressour Palenfo
*CABINET OUEDRAOGO &
BONKOUNGOU*

Aminata Pare
*CABINET YAGUIBOU &
YANOGO*

Sawadogo W. Pulchérie
*TRIBUNAL D'INSTANCE DE
OUAGADOUGOU*

Marie Jeanne Saba
*DIRECTION GENERALE DES
IMPOTS*

Bénéwendé S. Sankara
CABINET MAITRE SANKARA

Hermann Sanon
*OFFICE NOTARIAL ME JEAN
CELESTIN ZOURE*

Adama Saouadogo
ONEA

Boukary Savadogo
*MINISTERE DES FINANCES ET
DU BUDGET*

Moussa Sogodogo

Hyppolite Tapsoba
*TRIBUNAL D'INSTANCE DE
OUAGADOUGOU*

Dominique Taty
*FIDAFRICA /
PRICEWATERHOUSECOOPERS*

Telem
*GUICHET UNIQUE DU
COMMERCE*

Fousséni Traoré
*FIDAFRICA /
PRICEWATERHOUSECOOPERS*

Kassoum Traore
*DIRECTION GENERALE DES
IMPOTS*

Konzo Traore
BCEAO

Moussa Traore
MAISON DE L'ENTREPRISE

Yacouba Traoré
COMMUNE DE OUAGADOUGOU

Laurent Traore Sy
ONEA

Lorcendy L. Traore
*BANQUE COMMERCIALE DU
BURKINA*

Bouba Yaguibou
SCPA YAGUIBOU & YANOGO

Seydou Roger Yamba
CABINET MAITRE SANKARA

Emmanuel Yehouessi
BCEAO

Amado Yoni
*CABINET D'AVOCATS
BARTHÉLEMY KERE*

Francis Zagre
SONABEL

Abdel Mumin Zampalegre
BANK OF AFRICA

Bassinaly Zerbo
*SOCIETE NATIONALE
D'ELECTRICITE*

Rahmatou Zongo
*CABINET YAGUIBOU &
YANOGO*

Rosine Zongo
*CHAMBRE NATIONALE DES
HUISSIERS DE JUSTICE*

Ousmane Prosper Zoungrana
*TRIBUNAL DE GRANDE
INSTANCE DE OUAGADOUGOU*

Jean Celéstin Zoure
*OFFICE NOTARIAL ME JEAN
CELESTIN ZOURE*

Théophane Noël Zoure
*OFFICE NOTARIAL ME JEAN
CELESTIN ZOURE*

BURUNDI

*BANQUE DE CREDIT DE
BUJUMBURA*

Joseph Bahizi
*BANQUE DE LA RÉPUBLIQUE
DU BURUNDI*

Soter Barahirage
*ETUDE NOTARIALE
BARAHIRAJE*

Olivier Binyingo
MKONO & CO. ADVOCATES

Dismas Bucumi
*DIRECTION DE LA PROPRIETE
FONCIERE*

Gervais Gatunange
Faculte de Droit a l'Universite de Burundi

Eddy Karerwa
Deloitte

Nestor Kayobera

Pascal Kirahagazwe
Mkono & Co. Advocates

Dominik Kohlhagen
Chercheur au Laboratoire d'Anthropologie Juridique de Paris

Herve LE Guen
SDV Transami - Groupe Bolloré

Augustin Mabushi
A & JN Mabushi Cabinet d'Avocats

Mathias Manirakiza
Ecobank

Ildephonse Nahimana
Banque de la République du Burundi

Lambert Nigarura
Mkono & Co. Advocates

Bernard Ntahiraja
Cabinet Willy Rubeya

Antoine Ntsigana
SODETRA Ltd.

Happy Ntwari
Mkono & Co. Advocates

Déogratias Nzemba

Prosper Ringuyeneza
Architecture et Construction (A.C.)

Willy Rubeya
Cabinet Willy Rubeya

Benjamin Rufagari
Deloitte

Fabien Segatwa
Etude Me Segatwa

Gabriel Sinarinzi
Cabinet Me Gabriel Sinarinzi

Audace Sunzu
REGIDESO-Burundi

Egide Uwimana
Tribunal du Travail de Bujumbura

Alain George Wakama
Faculte de Droit a l'Universite de Burundi

CAMBODIA

Sar Chesda
Arbitration Council Foundation

Rithy Chey
B.N.G. - Advocates & Solicitors

Oknha Seng Chhay Our
Seng Enterprises Co., Ltd

Sokcheng Chou
Arbitration Council Foundation

Rob Force
DFDL Mekong Law Group

Svay Hay
Acleda Bank Plc.

Tim Holzer
DFDL Mekong Law Group

Visal Iv
Electricite du Cambodge

Song Khun
RAF International Forwarding Inc.

Chhung Kong
DFDL Mekong Law Group

Jean Loi
PricewaterhouseCoopers

Alexander May
DFDL Mekong Law Group

Long Mom
RAF International Forwarding Inc.

Kaing MoniKa
The Garment Manufacturers Association

Vichhra Mouyly
Arbitration Council Foundation

Chong Ngov
PricewaterhouseCoopers

Pin Pisetha
Meng Hong Ing Builder Co., Ltd.

Soleil Della Pong
HR Inc. (Cambodia) Co., Ltd.

Allen Prak
B.N.G. - Advocates & Solicitors

Red Furnesse Co Ltd

Kuntheapini Saing
Arbitration Council Foundation

Muny Samreth
PricewaterhouseCoopers

Marie Seng
Saggara Corporation

Chanthy Sin
Linex

Sorya Sin
SHA Transport Express Co. Ltd.

Billie Jean Slott
Sciaroni & Associates

Lor Sok
Arbitration Council Foundation

Chamnan Som
Cambodian Federation of Employers and Business Associations

Sorphea Sou
Arbitration Council Foundation

Christine Soutif
SDV Ltd.

David Symansky
HR Co., Ltd.

Michael Tan
RAF International Forwarding Inc.

Janvibol Tip
Tip & Partners

Sinath Un
DFDL Mekong Law Group

Seng Vantha
Seng Enterprises Co., Ltd

Potim Yun
DFDL Mekong Law Group

CAMEROON

Roland Abeng
Abeng Law Firm

Mobeh Andre
Maersk S.A.

Gilbert Awah Bongam
Achu and Fon-Ndikum Law Firm

Pierre Bertin Simbafo
BICEC

Hiol Bonheur
Cabinet SFR

Miafo Bonnybonn
Bonnybonn Enterprises

David Boyo
Jing & Partners

Anne Marie Diboundje Njocke
Cabinet Ekobo

Paul Marie Djamen
BICEC

Emmanuel Ekobo
Cabinet Ekobo

Marie Marceline Enganalim
Etude Me Enganalim Marceline

Philippe Fouda Fouda
BEAC

Lucas Florent Essomba
Cabinet Essomba & Associés

Badjeck Esther
Jing & Partners

Atsishi Fon Ndikum
Achu and Fon-Ndikum Law Firm

Caroline Idrissou-Belingar
BEAC

Angoh Angoh Jacob
Legal Power Law Firm

Paul Jing
Jing & Partners

Serge Jokung
Cabinet Maître Marie Andrée NGWE

Alain Serges Mbebi
Cadire

Jean Michel Mbock Biumla
M & N Law Firm, cabinet d'avocats

Augustin Yves Mbock Keked
Cadire

Rosine Mekeu
Nimba Conseil SARL

Valerie Moussombo
Cabinet Maître Marie Andrée NGWE

Henri Moutalen
FIDAFRICA / PricewaterhouseCoopers

Aimé Ndock Len
M & N Law Firm, cabinet d'avocats

Marcelin Ndoum
Etude de notaire Wo'o

Simon Pierre Nemba
Cabinet Maître Marie Andrée NGWE

Julius Ngu Tabe Achu
Achu and Fon-Ndikum Law Firm

Marie-Andrée Ngwe
Cabinet Maître Marie Andrée NGWE

Pierre Njigui
ABB Cameroon

Patrice Guy Njoya
Cabinet Maître Marie Andrée NGWE

Marie Louise Nkoue
Etude Me Nkoue

Jules Blaise Nonga
Nimba Conseil SARL

Lucien Onanga Otando
BEAC

Guy Piam
Nimba Conseil SARL

Julienne Piam
Nimba Conseil SARL

Bolleri Pym
Nimba Conseil SARL

Joseph Mbi Tanyi
Tanyi MBI & Partners

Dominique Taty
FIDAFRICA / PricewaterhouseCoopers

Paul Tchagna
FIDAFRICA / PricewaterhouseCoopers

Nadine Tinen Tchangoum
FIDAFRICA / PricewaterhouseCoopers

Jude Yong Yeh
Cadire

CANADA

David Bish
Goodmans LLP

Cassandra Brown
Blake, Cassels & Graydon, member of Lex Mundi

Colin L. Campbell
Superior Court of Justice of Ontario

Jay A. Carfagnini
Goodmans LLP

Allan Coleman
Osler, Hoskin & Harcourt LLP

Rod Davidge
Osler, Hoskin & Harcourt LLP

Jeremy Fraiberg
Osler, Hoskin & Harcourt LLP

Anne Glover
Blake, Cassels & Graydon, member of Lex Mundi

Steven Golick
Osler, Hoskin & Harcourt LLP

Pamela S. Hughes
Blake, Cassels & Graydon, member of Lex Mundi

Christopher Jovellanos
Borden Ladner Gervais LLP

Matthew Kindree
Baker & McKenzie

Joshua Kochath
Forwarding Unlimited Inc.

Michelle Lee
PricewaterhouseCoopers

Susan Leslie
First Canadian Title

Charles Magerman
Baker & McKenzie

Terry McCann
MLG Enterprises Ltd.

William McCarthy
First Canadian Title

Artem Miakichev
Osler, Hoskin & Harcourt LLP

Michael Nowina
Baker & McKenzie

Thomas O'Brien
PricewaterhouseCoopers

Eric Paton
PricewaterhouseCoopers

John Pirie
Baker & McKenzie

Jonathan Rabinovitch
Heenan Blaikie LLP, member of Ius Laboris

Bruce Reynolds
Borden Ladner Gervais LLP

Damian Rigolo
Osler, Hoskin & Harcourt LLP

Paul Robinson
Corporations Canada

Kelly Russell
PricewaterhouseCoopers

Paul Schabas
Blake, Cassels & Graydon, member of Lex Mundi

Irina Schnitzer
Davis LLP

SDV Logistics Ltd.

Toronto Hydro

Sharon Vogel
Borden Ladner Gervais LLP

CAPE VERDE

Hermínio Afonso
PricewaterhouseCoopers

Mary Braz de Andrade
Firma Braz de Andrade

Susana Caetano
PricewaterhouseCoopers

Ilídio Cruz
Gabinete de Advocacia Consultoria e Procuradoria Juridica

João Dono
João Dono Advogados

Florentino Jorge Fonseca Jesus
Municipality of Praia

Joana Gomes Rosa

Agnaldo Laice
Maersk Line

Jose Manuel Fausto Lima
Electra Praia

Maria de Fatima Lopes Varela
Banco Central de Cabo Verde

Francisco Melo
PricewaterhouseCoopers

João M.A. Mendes
AUDITEC - Auditores & Consultores

Ana Morais
PricewaterhouseCoopers

Milton Paiva
D. Hopffer Almada e Associados

José Manuel Pinto Monteiro
Advogados & Jurisconsultos

Eldetrudes Pires Neves
Araújo, Neves, Santos & Miranda, Advogados Associados

Armando J.F. Rodrigues
PricewaterhouseCoopers

Tito Lívio Santos Oliveira Ramos
Engic

Henrique Semedo Borges

Arnaldo Silva
Arnaldo Silva & Associados

João Carlos Tavares Fidalgo
Banco Central de Cabo Verde

Jorge Lima Teixeira

Lisa Helena Vaz
PricewaterhouseCoopers

Leendert Verschoor
PricewaterhouseCoopers

CENTRAL AFRICAN REPUBLIC

Jean Christophe Bakossa
L'ordre Centrafcain des Architectes

Michel Desprez
SDV

Marie-Edith Douzima-Lawson
Cabinet Douzima & Ministère de la fonction publique

Energie Centrafricaine (ENERCA)

Philippe Fouda Fouda
BEAC

Dolly Gotilogue

Isidore Grothe
Ministère des Finances et du Budget

Groupe Kamach

Gabriel Houndoni
Club OHADA

Caroline Idrissou-Belingar
BEAC

Noel Kelembho
SDV

Serge Médard Missamou
Club OHADA

Yves Namkomokoina
Magistrat, Commerce Tribunal

Jacob Ngaya
Direction Generale des Impots

Lucien Onanga Otando
BEAC

Gina Roosalem
Chambre des Notaires de Centrafrique

François Sabegala
Guichet Unique de Formalités des Entreprises (GUFE)

Bako Sah

Nicolas Tiangaye
Nicolas Tiangaye Law Firm

Bienvenue Clarisse Yackota
Guichet Unique de Formalités des Entreprises (GUFE)

CHAD

Mahamat Hassan Abakar
Cabinet Me Mahamat Hassan Abakar

Abdelkerim Ahmat
SDV Logistics Ltd.

Gabriel Nathé Amady

Oscar D'Estaing Deffosso
FIDAFRICA / PricewaterhouseCoopers

Baba Dina
SAGA/STAT

Thomas Dingamgoto
Cabinet Thomas Dingamgoto

N'Doningar Djimasna
Faculté de Droit, Université de N'Djamena

Philippe Fouda Fouda
BEAC

Caroline Idrissou-Belingar
BEAC

Gérard Leclaire

Béchir Madet
Office Notarial

Narcisse Madjiyore Dongar
Commission Nationale Justice et Paix

Issa Ngarmbassa
Etude Me Issa Ngar mbassa

Lucien Onanga Otando
BEAC

Nissaouabé Passang
Etude Me Passang

Gilles Schwarz
SDV Logistics Ltd.

Nisrine Senoussi
FIDAFRICA / PricewaterhouseCoopers

Kene Soba
Tribunal de Commerce

Dominique Taty
FIDAFRICA / PricewaterhouseCoopers

Nadine Tinen Tchangoum
FIDAFRICA / PricewaterhouseCoopers

Sobdibé Zoua
Cabinet Sobdibe Zoua

CHILE

Daniela Arrese
Bofill Mir & Alvarez Hinzpeter Jana

Carlos Astudillo
Boletin Comercial

Luis Avello
PricewaterhouseCoopers Legal Services

Angeles Barría
Philippi, Yrarrazaval, Pulido & Brunner, Abogados Ltda

Sandra Benedetto
PricewaterhouseCoopers

José Benitez
PricewaterhouseCoopers Legal Services

Enrique Benitez Urrutia
Urrutia & Cía

Jorge Benitez Urrutia
Urrutia & Cía

Mario Bezanilla
Alcaíno, Rodríguez & Sahli Limitada

Miguel Capo Valdes
Besalco S.A.

Héctor Carrasco
Superintendencia de Bancos e Instituciones Financieras

Paola Casorzo
Philippi, Yrarrazaval, Pulido & Brunner, Abogados Ltda

Andrés Chirgwin
Bofill Mir & Alvarez Hinzpeter Jana

Camilo Cortés
Guerrero, Olivos, Novoa y Errázuriz

María Alejandra Corvalán
Yrarrázaval, Ruiz - Tagle Goldenburg, Lagos & Silva

Camila Costagliola
Guerrero, Olivos, Novoa y Errázuriz

Cristián S. Eyzaguirre
Eyzaguirre & Cía.

Rodrigo Galleguillos
Núñez Muñoz y Cia Ltda Abogados

Cristian Garcia-Huidobro
Boletin Comercial

Marcelo Giovanazzi
Alcaíno, Rodríguez & Sahli Limitada

Christian Hermansen Rebolledo
ACTIC Consultores

Javier Hurtado
Cámara Chilena de la Construcción

Fernando Jamarne
Alessandri & Compañía

Daniela Lanel
Bofill Mir & Alvarez Hinzpeter Jana

Didier Lara
PricewaterhouseCoopers

León Larrain
Baker & McKenzie

Cristóbal Leighton
Vial y Palma Abogados

George Lever
Boletin Comercial

Carolina Masihy
Carey y Cía Ltda.

Juan Pablo Matus
Cariola Diez Perez-Copatos & Cia

Enrique Munita
Philippi, Yrarrazaval, Pulido & Brunner, Abogados Ltda

Rodrigo Muñoz
Núñez Muñoz y Cia Ltda Abogados

Cristian Olavarria
Philippi, Yrarrazaval, Pulido & Brunner, Abogados Ltda

Karem Fabiola Opazo Lobos
Universidad de Santiago

Gerardo Ovalle Mahns
Yrarrázaval, Ruiz - Tagle Goldenburg, Lagos & Silva

Juan Eduardo Palma Jr.
Vial y Palma Abogados

Luis Parada Hoyl
Bahamondez, Alvarez & Zegers

Pablo Paredes
Albagli Zaliasnik Abogados

Daniela Peña Fergadiott
Barros & Errázuriz

Fernando Penailillo
Databusiness

Alberto Pulido A.
Philippi, Yrarrazaval, Pulido & Brunner, Abogados Ltda

Beatriz Recart
Baker & McKenzie

Ricardo Riesco
Philippi, Yrarrazaval, Pulido & Brunner, Abogados Ltda

Sebastián Riesco
Eyzaguirre & Cía.

Edmundo Rojas García
Conservador de Bienes Raíces de Santiago

Alvaro Rosenblut
Albagli Zaliasnik Abogados

Pamela Rubio
Núñez Muñoz y Cia Ltda Abogados

Carlos Saavedra
Cruz & Cia. Abogados

Marco Salgado
Alcaíno, Rodríguez & Sahli Limitada

Andrés Sanfuentes
Philippi, Yrarrazaval, Pulido & Brunner, Abogados Ltda

Erich Schnake
Núñez Muñoz y Cia Ltda Abogados

SDV S.A

Francisco Selamé
PricewaterhouseCoopers

Cristián Sepúlveda
Barros & Errázuriz

Marcela Silva
Philippi, Yrarrazaval, Pulido & Brunner, Abogados Ltda

Luis Fernando Silva Ibañez
Yrarrázaval, Ruiz - Tagle Goldenburg, Lagos & Silva

Cristobal Smythe
Bahamondez, Alvarez & Zegers

Elizabeth Soto Provoste
Bofill Mir & Alvarez Hinzpeter Jana

Alan Spencer
Alessandri & Compañía

Sebastián Valdivieso
Yrarrázaval, Ruiz - Tagle Goldenburg, Lagos & Silva

Osvaldo Villagra
PricewaterhouseCoopers

Arturo Yrarrázaval Covarrubias
Yrarrázaval, Ruiz - Tagle Goldenburg, Lagos & Silva

Sebastián Yunge
Guerrero, Olivos, Novoa y Errázuriz

Jean Paul Zalaquett
Chilectra

Matías Zegers
Bahamondez, Alvarez & Zegers

Rony Zimerman M.
Bofill Mir & Alvarez Hinzpeter Jana

CHINA

Allen & Overy LLP

Daniel Chan
DLA Piper

Rex Chan
PricewaterhouseCoopers

Elliott Youchun Chen
Jun Ze Jun Law Offices

Jie Chen
Jun He Law Offices, member of Lex Mundi

Rong Chen
Davis Polk & Wardwell

Xiaojie Chen
Broad & Bright Law Firm

Hugh Dong
Mayer Brown LLP

Grace Fang
Pinsent Masons

Wei Gao
ZY & Partners

Leo Ge
Global Star Logistics Co. Ltd.

Alexander Gong
Baker & McKenzie

Kejun Guo
DeHeng Law Offices

Lawrence Guo
Broad & Bright Law Firm

Hebei Rising Chemical Co., Ltd.

Helen Han
K&L Gates LLP

Kian Heong Hew
Pinsent Masons

Jinquan Hu
King & Wood PRC Lawyers

Hebei Xingshuo Saw Co., Ltd.

Mingyan Jiang
Broad & Bright Law Firm

Yu Jiang
Broad & Bright Law Firm

Kerry EAS Logistics Ltd

John T. Kuzmik
Baker Botts LLP

Meng Lai
Davis Polk & Wardwell

Ian Lewis
Mayer Brown LLP

Clare Li
Noronha Advogados

Sherry Li
Lovells

Deng Liang
Jun He Law Office, member of Lex Mundi

Berry Lin
SDV Logistics Ltd.

Derek Liu
Lovells

Linfei Liu
Jun He Law Office, member of Lex Mundi

Sherry Liu
Noronha Advogados

Yucui Liu
Broad & Bright Law Firm

Zhiqiang Liu
King & Wood PRC Lawyers

Lucy Lu
King & Wood PRC Lawyers

Wei Lu
Broad & Bright Law Firm

Ling Pan
Broad & Bright Law Firm

Gustavo Rabello
Noronha Advogados

Stephen Rynhart
Jones Lang LaSalle

Sichuan Metals & Minerals Import & Export Corp.

Han Shen
Davis Polk & Wardwell

Cathy Shi
Orrick, Herrington & Sutcliffe LLP

Tina Shi
Mayer Brown LLP

Ming Sun
Broad & Bright Law Firm

Emily Tang
Orrick, Herrington & Sutcliffe LLP

Jessie Tang
Global Star Logistics Co. Ltd.

Xin Tong
Samsung Mobile

Terence Tung
Mayer Brown LLP

Venus Holdings HK Co., Ltd.

Celia Wang
PricewaterhouseCoopers

Hongyu Wang
DeHeng Law Offices

Jin Wang
Lovells

Liang Wang
Lovells

William Wang
PricewaterhouseCoopers

Yang Wang
Broad & Bright Law Firm

Cassie Wong
PricewaterhouseCoopers

Kent Woo
Guangda Law Firm

Shanshan Wu
Broad & Bright Law Firm

Tina Xin
Mayer Brown LLP

Frank Yang
Mayer Brown LLP

Sha Yang
Jun He Law Offices, member of Lex Mundi

Natalie Yu
Shu Jin Law Firm

Laura Yuan
King & Wood PRC Lawyers

Xing Yuan
Broad & Bright Law Firm

Shuo Zhan
People's Bank of China

Sarah Zhang
Lovells

Yi Zhang
King & Wood PRC Lawyers

Johnson Zheng
Xiamen All Carbon Corporation

Hao Zhu
Fortune Law Group

Judy Zhu
Mayer Brown LLP

COLOMBIA

Access Global Logistics Ltd

Carlos Alcala
José Lloreda Camacho & Co.

Enrique Alvarez
José Lloreda Camacho & Co.

Asociación Colombiana de Ingenieros Electricistas, Mecánicos, Electrónicos y Afines (ACIEM)

Mauricio Angulo
Computec - DataCrédito

Laurena Arambula
Cárdenas & Cárdenas

Eliana Bernal Castro
PricewaterhouseCoopers

Patricia Arrazola Bustillo
Gómez-Pinzón Zuleta Abogados S.A.

Bernardo Avila
Rodriguez & Cavelier

María Camila Bagés
Brigard & Urrutia, member of Lex Mundi

Luis Alfredo Barragán
Brigard & Urrutia, member of Lex Mundi

Aurora Barroso
Rodriguez & Cavelier

Juan Guillermo Becerra
PricewaterhouseCoopers

Claudia Benavides
Gómez-Pinzón Zuleta Abogados S.A.

Marco Bernal
Posse Herrera & Ruiz

Gloria María Borrero Restrepo
Corporación Excelencia en la Justicia

Leonardo Calderón Perdomo
Colegio de Registradores de Instrumentos Públicos de Colombia

Maria Paula Camacho
CAMACOL

Mario Camargo
HM & Company LTDA

Darío Cárdenas
Cárdenas & Cárdenas

María Catalina Carmona
Cavelier Abogados

Ernesto Cavelier
Rodriguez & Cavelier

Nohora Cortes Cuellar
Curaduria Urbana 4

Felipe Cuberos
Prieto & Carrizosa S.A.

Pablo de la Torre
Rodriguez & Cavelier

María Helena Díaz Méndez
PricewaterhouseCoopers

José Antonio Duran
Excellentia Strategic

EINCE Ltda.

Emilio Ferrero
Cavelier Abogados

Carlos Fradique-Méndez
Brigard & Urrutia, member of Lex Mundi

Luis Hernando Gallo Medina
Gallo Medina Abogados Asociados

Isabella Gandini
Rodriguez & Cavelier

Nathalia García
Posse Herrera & Ruiz

Juan Antonio Gaviria
Rodriguez & Cavelier

GENELEC Ltda.

Ana Giraldo
Prieto & Carrizosa S.A.

Clara Inés Gómez
José Lloreda Camacho & Co.

Santiago Gutiérrez
José Lloreda Camacho & Co.

Catherine Hernández
PricewaterhouseCoopers

Viviana Hernández Grajales
CAMACOL

John Herreno
HM & Company LTDA

Santiago Higuera
CAMACOL

Andres Isaza
Rodriguez & Cavelier

Jorge Lara-Urbaneja
Baker & McKenzie

Alejandro Linares-Cantillo
Gómez-Pinzón Zuleta Abogados S.A.

Cristina Lloreda
Brigard & Urrutia, member of Lex Mundi

José Antonio Lloreda
José Lloreda Camacho & Co.

Ernesto López
Cárdenas & Cárdenas

Natalia López
Posse Herrera & Ruiz

Adriana Lopez Moncayo
Curaduria Urbana 3

Daniel Lucio
Rodriguez & Cavelier

Gabriela Mancero
Cavelier Abogados

Carlos Marchena
Rodriguez & Cavelier

Valentina Marin
Rodriguez & Cavelier

Maria Marquez
Cavelier Abogados

María Nella Marquez
Cavelier Abogados

Ana Maria Navarrete
Posse Herrera & Ruiz

Luis Carlos Neira Mejía
Holguín, Neira & Pombo Abogados

María Neira Tobón
Holguín, Neira & Pombo Abogados

Mónica Pedroza Garcés
Corporación Excelencia en la Justicia

Esteban Pizarro
Gómez-Pinzón Zuleta Abogados S.A.

Carlo Polo
Computec ñ DataCrédito

Carolina Posada
Posse Herrera & Ruiz

Raul Quevedo
José Lloreda Camacho & Co.

Ana María Ramos Serrano
Corporación Excelencia en la Justicia

Daniel Reyes
Curaduria Urbana 3

Irma Rivera
Brigard & Urrutia, member of Lex Mundi

Carlos Rodriguez
PricewaterhouseCoopers

Jaime Rodriguez
Notaria 13 de Bogotá

Sonia Elizabeth Rojas Izaquita
Gallo Medina Abogados Asociados

Cristina Rueda Londoño
Baker & McKenzie

Paula Samper Salazar
Gómez-Pinzón Zuleta Abogados S.A.

SGS Colombia S.A.

Pablo Sierra
Posse Herrera & Ruiz

Paola Spada
Corporación Excelencia en la Justicia

Juan Reinaldo Suarez
Curaduria Urbana 1

José Luis Suárez
Gómez-Pinzón Zuleta Abogados S.A.

Raúl Alberto Suárez Arcila

Jose Alejandro Torres
Posse Herrera & Ruiz

Lina Beatriz Torres
Gómez-Pinzón Zuleta Abogados S.A.

Ricardo Trejos
Baker & McKenzie

Beatriz Uribe Botero
CAMACOL

Verónica Velásquez
Posse Herrera & Ruiz

Carolina Villadiego Burbano
Corporación Excelencia en la Justicia

Maria Carolina Villegas
Rodriguez & Cavelier

Alberto Zuleta
Gómez-Pinzón Zuleta Abogados S.A.

COMOROS

Mohamed Abdallah Halifa
Groupe Hassanati Soilihi - Groupe Hasoil

Aboubakar Abdou
Conseiller Juridique de l'Île Autonome de la Grande Comore

Harimia Ahmed Ali
Cabinet Me Harimia

Hassani Assoumani
C.V.P.-Biocom

Said Ali Said Athouman
Union of the Chamber of Commerce

Remy Grondin
Vitogaz Comores

Ahamada Mahamoudou

Mohamed Maoulida
Audit et Conseil International

Said Ibrahim Mourad

Ibrahim A. Mzimba
Cabinet Mzimba Avocats

Daoud Saidali Toihiri
Ministry of Promotion and Employment

Youssouf Yahaya

CONGO, DEM. REP.

Mukoko Aloni
Université de Kinshasa

Jholy Batupe
Cabinet Jean Bosco Muaka & Associates

Philippe Bihan
Saga Congo - Groupe Bolloré

Jean Adolphe Bitenu
ANAPI

Etienne Blocaille
FIDAFRICA / PricewaterhouseCoopers

Jean-Paul Bokoo
Cabinet d'avocat JCC & A

Patrick Bondonga Lesambo
Cabinet Emery Mukendi Wafwana & Associés

Mathias Buabua wa Kayembe
ANAPI

Armand Ciamala
CIAMALA & PARTNERS

Edmond Cibamba Diata
CABINET EMERY MUKENDI WAFWANA & ASSOCIÉS

Victor Créspel Musafiri
CABINET D'AVOCAT JCC & A

Regis de Oliveira
AGETRAF S.A.R.L. - SDV

Yves Debiesme
AGETRAF S.A.R.L. - SDV

Prosper Djuma Bilali
CABINET MASAMBA

Eugénie Elanga Monkango
CABINET EMERY MUKENDI WAFWANA & ASSOCIÉS

David Guarnieri
PRICEWATERHOUSECOOPERS LEGAL SERVICES

Amisi Herady
ANAPI

José Ilunga Kapanda
CABINET EMERY MUKENDI WAFWANA & ASSOCIÉS

Sandra Kabuya
CABINET JEAN BOSCO MUAKA & ASSOCIATES

Ngalamulume Kalala emmanuel
BARREAU DE KINSHASA/ MATETE

Kafua Katako

Robert Katambu
CABINET JEAN BOSCO MUAKA & ASSOCIATES

Pierre Kazadi Tshibanda
CABINET MASAMBA

Phistian Kubangusu Makiese
CABINET MASAMBA

Pierre-Pépin Kwampuku Latur
CABINET PEPIN KWAMPUKU

G. Le Dourain
AGETRAF S.A.R.L. - SDV

Jean-Délphin Lokonde Mvulukunda
CABINET MASAMBA

Léon Lubamba
CONSERVATION DES TITRES IMMOBILIERS DE LA LUKUNGA

Vital Lwanga Bizanbila
CABINET D'AVOCAT JCC & A

Eugénie Makangha Dunn

Jean Paul Matanga
CABINET JEAN BOSCO MUAKA & ASSOCIATES

Jean Claude Mbaki Siluzaku
CABINET MBAKI ET ASSOCIÉS

Didier Mopiti
MBM CONSEIL

Louman Mpoy
CABINET MPOY - LOUMAN & ASSOCIÉS

Jean Bosco Muaka
CABINET JEAN BOSCO MUAKA & ASSOCIATES

Emery Mukendi Wafwana
CABINET EMERY MUKENDI WAFWANA & ASSOCIÉS

Jacques Munday
CABINET NTOTO & NSWAL

Marius Muzembe Mpungu
CABINET KABASELE - MFUMU & ASSOCIÉS

Joseph Ngalamulume Lukalu
CABINET YOKO ET ASSOCIÉS

Victorine Bibiche Nsimba Kilembe
BARREAU DE KINSHASA/ MATETE

SOCIÉTÉ MINIÈRE DE DÉVELOPPEMENT/RJ TRADERS

SOCIÉTÉ NATIONALE D'ELECTRICITÉ (SNEL)

Christie Madudu Sulubika
CABINET MADUDU SULUBIKA

Dominique Taty
FIDAFRICA / PRICEWATERHOUSECOOPERS

Bénoît Tshibangu Ilunga
CABINET EMERY MUKENDI WAFWANA & ASSOCIÉS

Sylvie Tshilanda Kabongo
CABINET MADUDU SULUBIKA

Toto Wa Kinkela
TOTO & ASSOCIÉS CABINET D'AVOCATS

CONGO, REP.

Roland Bembelly
CABINET D'AVOCATS GOMES

Prosper Bizitou
FIDAFRICA / PRICEWATERHOUSECOOPERS

David Bourion
FIDAFRICA / PRICEWATERHOUSECOOPERS

Claude Coelho
CABINET D'AVOCATS CLAUDE COELHO

Mathias Essereke
CABINET D'AVOCATS CLAUDE COELHO

Philippe Fouda Fouda
BEAC

Henriette Lucie Arlette Galiba
OFFICE NOTARIAL ME GALIBA

Alexis Vincent Gomes
CABINET D'AVOCATS GOMES

Caroline Idrissou-Belingar
BEAC

Sylvert Bérenger Kymbassa Boussi
ETUDE MAITRE BÉATRICE DIANZOLO, HUISSIER DE JUSTICE

François Lavanant
SDV

Emmanuel Le Bras
FIDAFRICA / PRICEWATERHOUSECOOPERS

Parfait Euloge Linvani
CABINET D'AVOCATS GOMES

Salomon Louboula
ETUDE NOTARIALE SENGHOR

Thierry Mamimoue
CABINET D'AVOCATS GOMES

Norbert Diétrich M'Foutou
ETUDE DE MAITRES SÉRAPHIN MCAKOSSO-DOUTA ET NORBERT M'FOUTOU

Lucien Onanga Otando
BEAC

Chimène Prisca Nina Pongui
ETUDE DE ME CHIMÈNE PRISCA NINA PONGUI

Roberto Prota
SDV

Francis Sassa
CABINET D'AVOCATS JEAN PETRO

Yves Simon Tchicamboud
CABINET D'AVOCATS GOMES

COSTA RICA

Aisha Acuña
ANDRÉ TINOCO ABOGADOS

John Aguilar
AGUILAR CASTILLO LOVE

Arnoldo André
ANDRÉ TINOCO ABOGADOS

Luis Fdo. Andrés Jácome
COMPAÑÍA NACIONAL DE FUERZA Y LUZ

Carlos Araya
QUIRÓS & ASOCIADOS CENTRAL LAW

Luis Diego Barahona
PRICEWATERHOUSECOOPERS LEGAL SERVICES

Carlos Barrantes
PRICEWATERHOUSECOOPERS

Alejandro Bettoni Traube
DONINELLI & DONINELLI - ASESORES JURÍDICOS ASOCIADOS

Mauricio Bonilla
OLLER ABOGADOS

Eduardo Calderón-Odio
BLP ABOGADOS

Adriana Calero
PRICEWATERHOUSECOOPERS LEGAL SERVICES

Bernardo Calvo M.
GRUPO MEGA DE COSTA RICA BR, S.A

Gastón Certad
BATALLA & ASOCIADOS

Silvia Chacon
ALFREDO FOURNIER & ASOCIADOS

Daniel Chaves
CINDE

Marybeth Chinchilla
ANDRÉ TINOCO ABOGADOS

COMPAÑÍA NACIONAL DE FUERZA Y LUZ

COLEGIO DE INGENIEROS ELECTRICISTAS, MECÁNICOS E INDUSTRIALES

Melania Dittel
ARIAS & MUÑOZ

Luis Escalante
GRUPO MEGA S.A

Roberto Esquivel
OLLER ABOGADOS

Leticia Garcia
QUIRÓS & ASOCIADOS CENTRAL LAW

Ingrid Jiménez Godoy
PRICEWATERHOUSECOOPERS LEGAL SERVICES

Miguel Golcher Valverde
COLEGIO DE INGENIEROS ELECTRICISTAS, MECÁNICOS E INDUSTRIALES

V. Andrés Gómez
PRICEWATERHOUSECOOPERS

Andrea González
BLP ABOGADOS

Paola Gutiérrez Mora
LEX COUNSEL

Mario Gutiérrez Quintero
LEX COUNSEL

María del Mar Herrera
BLP ABOGADOS

Randall Zamora Hidalgo
COSTA RICA ABC

Yin Ho
TELETEC S.A.

Vicente Lines
ARIAS & MUÑOZ

Ivannia Méndez Rodríguez
OLLER ABOGADOS

Andres Mercado
OLLER ABOGADOS

Gabriela Miranda
OLLER ABOGADOS

Eduardo Montoya Solano
SUPERINTENDENCIA GENERAL DE ENTIDADES FINANCIERAS

Cecilia Naranjo
LEX COUNSEL

Pedro Oller
OLLER ABOGADOS

Ramón Ortega
PRICEWATERHOUSECOOPERS

Laura Perez
CINDE

Sergio Perez
ANDRÉ TINOCO ABOGADOS

Mainor Quesada
TELETEC S.A.

Manrique Rojas
ANDRÉ TINOCO ABOGADOS

Miguel Ruiz Herrera
LEX COUNSEL

Andrea Saenz
AGUILAR CASTILLO LOVE

Sergio Salas
SEYSA CONSULTORÍA Y CONSTRUCCIÓN

Fernando Sánchez
RUSSELL BEDFORD COSTA RICA, MEMBER OF RUSSELL BEDFORD INTERNATIONAL

Luis Sibaja
LEX COUNSEL

Marianela Vargas
PRICEWATERHOUSECOOPERS

Rocio Vega
GRUPO MEGA DE COSTA RICA BR, S.A

Rodrigo Zapata
LEX COUNSEL

Jafet Zúñiga Salas
SUPERINTENDENCIA GENERAL DE ENTIDADES FINANCIERAS

CÔTE D'IVOIRE

ANY RAY & PARTNERS

Diaby Aboubakar
BCEAO

César Asman
CABINET N'GOAN, ASMAN & ASSOCIÉS

Jean-François Chauveau
CABINET JEAN-FRANÇOIS CHAUVEAU

BNETD

COTAM

Dorothée K. Dreesen
ETUDE MAITRE DREESEN

Bertrand Fleury
SDV - SAGA CI

Seyanne Groga
CABINET JEAN-FRANÇOIS CHAUVEAU

Guillaume Koffi
CONSEIL NATIONAL DE L'ORDRE DES ARCHITECTES

Kiyobien Kone
SOCIÉTÉ CIVILE PROFESSIONNELLE D'AVOCATS (SCPA) Le PARACLET

Mahoua Kone
ETUDE DE MAÎTRE KONE MAHOUA

Anne Marie Kouassi
SCPA DOGUÉ-ABBÉ YAO & ASSOCIÉS

Charlotte-Yolande Mangoua
ETUDE DE MAÎTRE MANGOUA

Evelyne M'Bassidgé
FIDAFRICA / PRICEWATERHOUSECOOPERS

Georges N'Goan
CABINET N'GOAN, ASMAN & ASSOCIÉS

Patricia N'guessan
CABINET JEAN-FRANÇOIS CHAUVEAU

Karim Ouattara
SCPA DOGUÉ-ABBÉ YAO & ASSOCIÉS

SABKA

SIMAT

Athanase Raux
CABINET RAUX, AMIEN & ASSOCIÉS

Dominique Taty
FIDAFRICA / PRICEWATERHOUSECOOPERS

Fatoumata Konaté Touré Bebo
CABINET DE NOTAIRE KONATÉ TOURÉ BEBO

Fousséni Traoré
FIDAFRICA / PRICEWATERHOUSECOOPERS

Konzo Traore
BCEAO

Jean Christian Turkson
CIE

Nadia Vanie
CABINET N'GOAN, ASMAN & ASSOCIÉS

Abbé Yao
SCPA DOGUÉ-ABBÉ YAO & ASSOCIÉS

Emmanuel Yehouessi
BCEAO

CROATIA

Andrea August
HITRO.HR

Zoran Avramović
MINISTRY OF JUSTICE

Ivana Bandov
CMS ZAGREB

Zoran Bohaček
CROATIAN BANKING ASSOCIATION

Andrej Bolfek
LEKO & PARTNERS

Marko Borsky
DIVJAK, TOPIĆ & BAHTIJAREVIĆ

Marijana Božić
DIVJAK, TOPIĆ & BAHTIJAREVIĆ

Irena Brezovecki
VIDAN LAW OFFICE

Lana Brlek
PRICEWATERHOUSECOOPERS

Belinda Čačić
ČAČIĆ & PARTNERS

Jasmina Crnalić
CMS ZAGREB

Tamara Crnkić
MAMIĆ REBERSKI & PARTNERS

Ivan Ćuk
VUKMIR LAW OFFICE

Stefanija Čukman
JURIĆ LAW OFFICES

Saša Divjak
DIVJAK, TOPIĆ & BAHTIJAREVIĆ

Anela Dizdarević
ANA SIHTAR ATTORNEYS-AT-LAW

ELEKTRO KROS D.O.O. AND ELEKTRO JURIC D.O.O.

Ivana Dominković
CMS ZAGREB

Daria Dubajić
POROBIJA & POROBIJA LAW FIRM

Gregor Famira
CMS ZAGREB

Tamiko Rochelle Franklin
MATIJEVICH LAW OFFICE

Lino Fučić
MINISTRY OF ENV. PROT., PHISICAL PLANNING AND CONSTRUCTION,

Ivan Gjurgjan
LAW FIRM GJURGJAN & ŠRIBAR RADIĆ

Kresimir Golubić

Tom Hadzija
SIKIRIC HADZIJA ATTORNEY PARTNERSHIP

Lidija Hanžek
HROK

HEP DISTRIBUTION SYSTEM OPERATOR LTD.

Jana Hitrec
ČAČIĆ & PARTNERS

Branimir Iveković
VIDAN LAW OFFICE

Irina Jelčić
HANŽEKOVIĆ, RADAKOVIĆ & PARTNERS, member of LEX MUNDI

Marijana Jelić
LAW OFFICE JELIC

Janos Kelemen
PRICEWATERHOUSECOOPERS

Mirna Kette
PRICEWATERHOUSECOOPERS

Branko Kirin
ČAČIĆ & PARTNERS

Margita Kiš-Kapetanović
POROBIJA & POROBIJA LAW FIRM

KOPGRAD PROJEKT D.O.O.

Marija Krizanec
JURIĆ LAW OFFICES

Anita Krizmanić
MAČEŠIĆ & PARTNERS, ODVJETNICKO DRUSTVO

Dubravka Lacković
CMS ZAGREB

Miroslav Leko
LEKO & PARTNERS

Krešimir Ljubić
LEKO & PARTNERS

Marko Lovirić
DIVJAK, TOPIĆ & BAHTIJAREVIĆ

Mate Lovrić
LAKTIĆ & PARTNERS

Ana Lubura
GARK KONZALTING D.O.O.

Miroljub Mačešić
MAČEŠIĆ & PARTNERS, ODVJETNICKO DRUSTVO

Vladimir Mamić
MAMIĆ REBERSKI & PARTNERS

Josip Marohnić
DIVJAK, TOPIĆ & BAHTIJAREVIĆ

Andrej Matijevich
MATIJEVICH LAW OFFICE

Daša Musulin
MAROVIĆ & PARTNERS

Hrvoje Petrić
PETRIĆ LAW FIRM

Marija Petrović
DIVJAK, TOPIĆ & BAHTIJAREVIĆ

Sanja Porobija
POROBIJA & POROBIJA LAW FIRM

Tihana Posavec
DIVJAK, TOPIĆ & BAHTIJAREVIĆ

Ana Sihtar
ANA SIHTAR ATTORNEYS-AT-LAW

Dragutin Sikirić
SIKIRIC HADZIJA ATTORNEY PARTNERSHIP

Irena Šribar Radić
LAW FIRM GJURGJAN & ŠRIBAR RADIĆ

Mario Štefanić
TRANSADRIA

Goranka Šumonja Laktić
LAKTIĆ & PARTNERS

Ivana Sverak
POROBIJA & POROBIJA TRAST

Vesna Veselin
MINISTRY OF ENV. PROT., PHYSICAL PLANNING AND CONSTRUCTION

Hrvoje Vidan
VIDAN LAW OFFICE

Arn Willems
CB RICHARD ELLIS D.O.O.

Eugen Zadravec
EUGEN ZADRAVEC LAW FIRM

CYPRUS

Alexandros Alexandrou
TORNARITIS LAW LLC

Xeni Anastasiou
INFO CREDIT GROUP

Andreas Andreou
CYPRUS GLOBAL LOGISTICS

Harry S. Charalambous
KPMG

Antonis Christodoulides
PRICEWATERHOUSECOOPERS

Christophoros Christophi
CHRISTOPHI & ASSOCIATES

Kypros Chrysostomides
DRK. CHRYSOSTOMIDES & Co.

Alexis Danos
DANOS & ASSOCIATES

Chrysostomos Danos
DANOS & ASSOCIATES

Achilleas Demetriades
LELLOS P DEMETRIADES LAW OFFICE LLC

Haris Fereos
FEREOS & ASSOCIATES

Angela T. Frangou
CYPRUS STOCK EXCHANGE

Stefani Gabriel
PRICEWATERHOUSECOOPERS

Christina Hadjidemetriou
CHRISTODOULOS G. VASSILIADES & Co LLC

Marios N. Hadjigavriel
ANTIS TRIANTAFYLLIDES & SONS LLC

Spyros Hadjinicolaou
ANTIS TRIANTAFYLLIDES & SONS LLC

Iacovos Hadjivarnavas
CYPRUS GENERAL BONDED AND TRANSIT STORES ASSOCIATION

Samantha G. Hellicar
ANTIS TRIANTAFYLLIDES & SONS LLC

Anthony Indianos
COSTAS INDIANOS & Co

Christina Ioannidou
IOANNIDES DEMETRIOU

Panicos Kaouris
PRICEWATERHOUSECOOPERS

George Karakannas
CH.P. KARAKANNAS ELECTRICAL LTD

Andreas Karmios
FIRST CYPRUS CREDIT BUREAU

Thomas Keane
CHRYSSES DEMETRIADES & Co

Spyros G. Kokkinos
MINISTRY OF COMMERCE, INDUSTRY AND TOURISM

Christina Kotsapa
ANTIS TRIANTAFYLLIDES & SONS LLC

Nicholas Ktenas
ANDREAS NEOCLEOUS & Co. LEGAL CONSULTANTS

Menelaos Kyprianou
MICHAEL KYPRIANOU & Co.

John G. Lefas
ELECTRICITY AUTHORITY OF CYPRUS

George M. Leptos
LEPTOS GROUP

George V. Markides
KPMG

Pieris M. Markou
DELOITTE

Christos Mavrellis
CHRYSSES DEMETRIADES & Co

Neophytos Neophytou
ERNST & YOUNG

Christina Papakyriakou
ANTIS TRIANTAFYLLIDES & SONS LLC

Leandros Papaphilippou
PAPAPHILIPPOU & Co., ADVOCATES AND LEGAL CONSULTANTS

Marios Pelekanos
MESARITIS PELEKANOS ARCHITECTS - ENGINEERS

Lambros Soteriou
MICHAEL KYPRIANOU & Co.

Andreas D. Symeon
GOVERNMENT OF CYPRUS

Citron Tornaritis
TORNARITIS LAW LLC

Stelios Triantafyllides
ANTIS TRIANTAFYLLIDES & SONS LLC

Panikos Tsiailis
PRICEWATERHOUSECOOPERS

Christodoulos Vassiliades
CHRISTODOULOS G. VASSILIADES & Co LLC

CZECH REPUBLIC

ALLEN & OVERY LLP

Viet Anh Nguyen
PETERKA & PARTNERS

Tomas Babacek
AMBRUZ & DARK LAW FIRM

Libor Basl
BAKER & MCKENZIE

Tomáö Běhounek
BNT - PRAVDA & PARTNER, V.O.S.

Martin Bohuslav
AMBRUZ & DARK LAW FIRM

Stephen B. Booth
PRICEWATERHOUSECOOPERS

Alena Brichackova
PETERKA & PARTNERS

Michal Buchta
AMBRUZ & DARK LAW FIRM

Jiří Černý
PETERKA & PARTNERS

Marian Cuprik
DLA PIPER LLP

Matěj Daněk
PRK PARTNERS S.R.O. ADVOKÁTNÍ KANCELÁŘ

Ondřej Dušek
PETERKA & PARTNERS

Tereza Erényi
PRK PARTNERS S.R.O. ADVOKÁTNÍ KANCELÁŘ

Pavel Ficek
PANALPINA S.R.O.

Kristýna Fišerová
PETERKA & PARTNERS

Michal Forytek
LINKLATERS

Jakub Hajek
AMBRUZ & DARK LAW FIRM

Michal Hanko
BUBNIK, MYSLIL & PARTNERS

Jarmila Hanzalova
PRK PARTNERS S.R.O. ADVOKÁTNÍ KANCELÁŘ

Radek Horký
NOTARY CHAMBER

Michal Hrncir
AMBRUZ & DARK LAW FIRM

Katarina Hybenová
SQUIRE, SANDERS & DEMPSEY, V.O.S. ADVOKÁT KANCELÁŘ

Jaroslava Ignacikova
AMBRUZ & DARK LAW FIRM

Pavel Jakab
PETERKA & PARTNERS

Ludvik Juřička
AMBRUZ & DARK LAW FIRM

Alena Klierová
EUROTREND S.R.O, A MEMBER FIRM OF RUSSELL BEDFORD INTERNATIONAL

Veronika Kocova
PETERKA & PARTNERS

Sofia Komrsková
EUROTREND S.R.O, A MEMBER FIRM OF RUSSELL BEDFORD INTERNATIONAL

Adela Krbcová
PETERKA & PARTNERS

Aleš Kubáč
AMBRUZ & DARK LAW FIRM

Petr Kucera
CCB - CZECH BANKING CREDIT BUREAU

Dina Lasova
PRK PARTNERS S.R.O. ADVOKÁTNÍ KANCELÁŘ

Zuzana Luklova
AMBRUZ & DARK LAW FIRM

Ondrej Machala
NOTARY CHAMBER

Jiří Markvart
AMBRUZ & DARK LAW FIRM

Peter Maysenhölder
BNT - PRAVDA & PARTNER, V.O.S.

Petr Mestanek
LINKLATERS

Veronika Mistova
PRK PARTNERS S.R.O. ADVOKÁTNÍ KANCELÁŘ

Lenka Mrazova
PRICEWATERHOUSECOOPERS

David Musil
PRICEWATERHOUSECOOPERS

Jarmila Musilova
CZECH NATIONAL BANK

Robert Nemec
PRK PARTNERS S.R.O. ADVOKÁTNÍ KANCELÁŘ

Petr Novotny
AMBRUZ & DARK LAW FIRM

Jörg Nürnberger
DLA PIPER LLP

Athanassios Pantazopoulos
*IKRP ROKAS & PARTNERS AND
DR. A. PANTAZOPOULOS*

Martina Pavelkova
PANALPINA S.R.O.

Markéta Protivankova
VEJMELKA & WÜNSCH, S.R.O.

Nataša Randlová
*PRK PARTNERS S.R.O.
ADVOKÁTNÍ KANCELÁŘ*

Tomas Richter
*CLIFFORD CHANCE LLP/
INSTITUTE OF ECONOMIC
STUDIES, FACULTY OF
SOCIAL SCIENCES, CHARLES
UNIVERSITY*

Zdenek Rosicky
*SQUIRE, SANDERS & DEMPSEY,
V.O.S. ADVOKÁT KANCELÁŘ*

Leona Ševčíková
PANALPINA S.R.O.

Robert Sgariboldi
PANALPINA S.R.O.

Dana Sládečková
CZECH NATIONAL BANK

Marika Slamova
DLA PIPER LLP

Steven Snaith
PRICEWATERHOUSECOOPERS

Petra Sochorova
*HAVEL & HOLÁSEK S.R.O.,
ADVOKÁTNÍ KANCELÁŘ*

Ondřej Špetla
*EUROTREND S.R.O, A MEMBER
FIRM OF RUSSELL BEDFORD
INTERNATIONAL*

Anna Stankova
*HAVEL & HOLÁSEK S.R.O.,
ADVOKÁTNÍ KANCELÁŘ*

Marie Strachotová
PETERKA & PARTNERS

Růžena Trojánková
LINKLATERS

Klara Valentova
AMBRUZ & DARK LAW FIRM

Jana Večerníková
NOTARY CHAMBER

DENMARK

Elsebeth Aaes-Jørgensen
*NORRBOM VINDING, MEMBER
OF IUS LABORIS*

Peter Bang
*PLESNER SVANE GRØNBORG
ADVOKATFIRMA*

Thomas Bang
LETT LAW FIRM

Mads Bierfreund
*KROMANN REUMERT, MEMBER
OF LEX MUNDI*

Thomas Booker
*ACCURA
ADVOKATAKTIESELSKAB*

Ole Borch
BECH-BRUUN LAW FIRM

Christian Bredtoft Guldmann
*KROMANN REUMERT, MEMBER
OF LEX MUNDI*

Peter Burhøj
*KROMANN REUMERT, MEMBER
OF LEX MUNDI*

Jeppe Buskov
*KROMANN REUMERT, MEMBER
OF LEX MUNDI*

CARGO WORLD A/S

Frants Dalgaard-Knudsen
PLESNER

Mogens Ebeling
JONAS BRUUN

Eivind Einersen
PHILIP & PARTNERE

Lars Fogh
*ACCURA
ADVOKATAKTIESELSKAB*

Lita Misozi Hansen
PRICEWATERHOUSECOOPERS

Jens Hjortskov
PHILIP & PARTNERE

Heidi Hoelgaard
EXPERIAN NORTHERN EUROPE

Peter Honoré
*KROMANN REUMERT, MEMBER
OF LEX MUNDI*

Jens Steen Jensen
*KROMANN REUMERT, MEMBER
OF LEX MUNDI*

Camilla Jørgensen
PHILIP & PARTNERE

Jeppe Jørgensen
BECH-BRUUN LAW FIRM

William Kanta
*KROMANN REUMERT, MEMBER
OF LEX MUNDI*

Dorte Kjærgaard
*ACCURA
ADVOKATAKTIESELSKAB*

Aage Krogh
MAGNUSSON

Christine Larsen
*PLESNER SVANE GRØNBORG
ADVOKATFIRMA*

Jakob Hüttel Larsen
PHILIP & PARTNERE

Susanne Schjølin Larsen
*KROMANN REUMERT, MEMBER
OF LEX MUNDI*

Lars Lindencrone
BECH-BRUUN LAW FIRM

Alexander M. P. Johannessen
*KROMANN REUMERT, MEMBER
OF LEX MUNDI*

Helle Næsager
LETT LAW FIRM

Andreas Nielsen
JONAS BRUUN

Susanne Nørgaard
PRICEWATERHOUSECOOPERS

Jim Øksnebjerg
*ADVOKATAKTIESELSKABET
HORTEN*

Niels Bang Sørensen
*GORRISSEN FEDERSPIEL
KIERKEGAARD*

Kim Trenskow
*KROMANN REUMERT, MEMBER
OF LEX MUNDI*

DJIBOUTI

Rahma Abdi Abdillahi
*BANQUE CENTRALE DE
DJIBOUTI*

Abdillahi Aidid Farah

Wabat Daoud

Jean Phillipe Delarue
*SOCIÉTÉ MARITIME L. SAVON
& RIES*

Luc Deruyer
*SOCIÉTÉ MARITIME L. SAVON
& RIES*

Ali Dini

ELECTRICITÉ DE DJIBOUTI

Félix Emok N'Dolo
CHD GROUP

Mourad Farah

Ibrahim Hamadou Hassan
*BANQUE POUR LE COMMERCE
ET L'INDUSTRIE*

Fatouma Mahamoud Hassan
CABINET MAHAMOUD

Mayank Metha
MAERSK SEALAND LINE

Ibrahim Mohamed Omar
CABINET CECA

Oubah Mohamed Omar
*SOCIÉTÉ MARITIME L. SAVON
& RIES*

Jerome Passicos
*SOCIÉTÉ MARITIME L. SAVON
& RIES*

Lantosoa Hurfin Ralaiarinosy
*GROUPEMENT COSMEZZ
DJIBOUTI S.A.*

Aicha Youssouf Abdi
CABINET CECA

DOMINICA

Kirtiste Augustus
*WATERFRONT AND ALIED
WORKERS UNION*

Joffrey C.G. Harris
HARRIS & HARRIS

Marvlyn Estrado
*KPB CHARTERED
ACCOUNTANTS*

F. Adler Hamlet
REALCO COMPANY LIMITED

Stephen K.M. Isidore
*EMANUEL & ISIDORE
CHAMBERS*

Foued Issa
ISSA TRADING LTD.

Alick C. Lawrence
*LAWRENCE ALICK C.
CHAMBERS*

Severin McKenzie
*MCKENZIE ARCHITECTURAL &
CONSTRUCTION SERVICES INC.*

Richard Peterkin
PRICEWATERHOUSECOOPERS

Joan K.R. Prevost
PREVOST & ROBERTS

J. Gildon Richards
*J. GILDON RICHARDS
CHAMBERS*

Mark Riddle
DOMLEC

Eugene G. Royer
*EUGENE G. ROYER CHARTERED
ARCHITECT*

Jason Timothy
DOMLEC

Laurina Vidal
*LAWRENCE ALICK C.
CHAMBERS*

DOMINICAN
REPUBLIC

Carla Alsina
BIAGGI & MESSINA

Lissette Balbuena
*STEWART TITLE DOMINICANA,
S.A.*

Caroline Bono
PRICEWATERHOUSECOOPERS

Ana Isabel Caceres
TRONCOSO Y CACERES

Juan Manuel Caceres
TRONCOSO Y CACERES

Giselle Castillo
*SUPERINTENDENCIA DE
BANCOS*

Rodolfo Colon
ESTRELLA & TUPETE

Laureana Corral
ESTRELLA & TUPETE

Leandro Corral
ESTRELLA & TUPETE

Mariano Corral
ESTRELLA & TUPETE

José Cruz Campillo
JIMÉNEZ CRUZ PEÑA

Marcos de Leon
*SUPERINTENDENCIA DE
BANCOS*

Sarah de León
*HEADRICK RIZIK ALVAREZ &
FERNÁNDEZ*

Juan Carlos De Moya
GONZÁLEZ & COISCOU

Romeo Del Valle
GONZÁLEZ & COISCOU

Rosa Díaz
JIMÉNEZ CRUZ PEÑA

Rafael Dickson Morales
*MG&A MEDINA GARNES &
ASOCIADOS ABOGADOS*

Joaquín Guillermo Estrella
Ramia
ESTRELLA & TUPETE

Alejandro Fernández de
Castro
PRICEWATERHOUSECOOPERS

Mary Fernández Rodríguez
*HEADRICK RIZIK ALVAREZ &
FERNÁNDEZ*

Jose Ernesto Garcia A.
TRANSGLOBAL LOGISTIC

Gloria Gasso
*HEADRICK RIZIK ALVAREZ &
FERNÁNDEZ*

Jetti Gomez
BIAGGI & MESSINA

Pablo Gonzalez Tapia
GONZÁLEZ & COISCOU

Ralvin Gross
*HEADRICK RIZIK ALVAREZ &
FERNÁNDEZ*

Fabio Guzmán-Ariza
GUZMÁN-ARIZA

José Antonio Logroño Morales
ADAMS GUZMAN & LOGROÑO

José Ramón Logroño Morales
ADAMS GUZMAN & LOGROÑO

Annie Luna
*PELLERANO & HERRERA,
MEMBER OF LEX MUNDI*

Xavier Marra Martínez
DHIMES & MARRA

Fernando Marranzini
*HEADRICK RIZIK ALVAREZ &
FERNÁNDEZ*

Carlos Marte
*AGENCIA DE COMERCIO
EXTERIOR CM*

Melina Martinez
GONZÁLEZ & COISCOU

Fabiola Medina
MEDINA & RIZEK, ABOGADOS

Elizabeth Mena
*PELLERANO & HERRERA,
MEMBER OF LEX MUNDI*

Natia Núñez
*HEADRICK RIZIK ALVAREZ &
FERNÁNDEZ*

Ana Ortega Terrero
*AGENCIA DE COMERCIO
EXTERIOR CM*

Ramón Ortega
PRICEWATERHOUSECOOPERS

Luis R. Pellerano
*PELLERANO & HERRERA,
MEMBER OF LEX MUNDI*

Edward Piña Fernandez
BIAGGI & MESSINA

Julio Pinedo
PRICEWATERHOUSECOOPERS

Maria Portes
CASTILLO Y CASTILLO

Alejandro Miguel Ramirez
Suzaña
RIZIK Y ASOC

TRANSUNION

Carolina Silié
*HEADRICK RIZIK ALVAREZ &
FERNÁNDEZ*

Maricell Silvestre Rodriguez
JIMÉNEZ CRUZ PEÑA

Juan Tejeda
PRICEWATERHOUSECOOPERS

Urbano Tupete
ESTRELLA & TUPETE

Guiraldis Velásquez Ramos
DHIMES & MARRA

Vilma Verras Terrero
JIMÉNEZ CRUZ PEÑA

Chery Zacarias
MEDINA & RIZEK, ABOGADOS

ECUADOR

Gerardo Aguirre
VIVANCO & VIVANCO

Pablo Aguirre
PRICEWATERHOUSECOOPERS

Diego Cabezas-Klaere
CABEZAS & CABEZAS-KLAERE

Xavier Andrade Cadena
*ANDRADE VELOZ &
ASOCIADOS*

Lucía Cordero Ledergerber
FALCONI PUIG ABOGADOS

Renato Coronel
*PINTO & GARCES ASOC. CIA
LTDA, MEMBER OF RUSSELL
BEDFORD INTERNATIONAL*

Fernando Del Pozo Contreras
*GALLEGOS, VALAREZO &
NEIRA*

Juan Carlos Gallegos Happle
*GALLEGOS, VALAREZO &
NIERA*

Leopoldo González R.
PAZ HOROWITZ

Vanessa Izquierdo D.
*IZQUIERDO ABOGADOS/API
ECUADOR*

Rodrigo Jijón
*PÉREZ, BUSTAMANTE Y PONCE,
MEMBER OF LEX MUNDI*

Francisco Javier Naranjo
Grijalva
PAZ HOROWITZ

*MZ SISTEMAS ELECTRICOS Y
ELECTRONICOS*

María Dolores Orbe
VIVANCO & VIVANCO

Esteban Ortiz
*PÉREZ, BUSTAMANTE Y PONCE,
MEMBER OF LEX MUNDI*

Pablo Padilla Muirragui
ECUADOR CARGO SYSTEM

Daniel Pino Arroba
CORONEL Y PÉREZ

Ramiro Pinto
*PINTO & GARCES ASOC. CIA
LTDA, MEMBER OF RUSSELL
BEDFORD INTERNATIONAL*

Patricia Ponce Arteta
BUSTAMANTE Y BUSTAMANTE

Martin Portilla
VIVANCO & VIVANCO

Diego Ramírez Meseo
*FABARA & COMPAÑIA
ABOGADOS*

Sandra Reed
*PÉREZ, BUSTAMANTE Y PONCE,
MEMBER OF LEX MUNDI*

Veronica Sofia Ruales Díaz
BUSTAMANTE & BUSTAMANTE

German Saona
PRICEWATERHOUSECOOPERS

César Vélez Calderón
COVELCAL

EGYPT, ARAB REP.

Abdel Aal Aly
AFIFI WORLD TRANSPORT

Naguib Abadir
NACITA CORPORATION

Mohamed Abd El-Sadek
*ABU-GHAZALEH LEGAL -
(TAG-LEGAL)*

Girgis Abd El-Shahid
SARWAT A. SHAHID LAW FIRM

Sara Abdel Gabbar
TROWERS & HAMLINS

Ibrahim Mustafa Ibrahim
Abdel Khalek
*GENERAL AUTHORITY FOR
INVESTMENT GAFI*

Ahmed Abdel Warith
AAW CONSULTING ENGINEERS

Mohamed Abdelaal
*IBRACHY & DERMARKAR LAW
FIRM*

Ramez Mounir Abdel-Nour
KARIM ADEL LAW OFFICE

Ahmed Abou Ali
HASSOUNA & ABOU ALI

Sameh Abu Zeid
CAPITAL MARKET AUTHORITY

Nermin Abulata
*MINISTRY OF TRADE &
INDUSTRY*

Ghada Adel
PRICEWATERHOUSECOOPERS

Ahmed Adel Kamel
KARIM ADEL LAW OFFICE

Hazem Ahmed Fathi
HASSOUNA & ABOU ALI

Rana Al Nahal
SARWAT A. SHAHID LAW FIRM

Yousef AlAmly
*ABU-GHAZALEH LEGAL -
(TAG-LEGAL)*

Yasmin Al-Gharbawie
*SHALAKANY LAW OFFICE,
MEMBER OF LEX MUNDI*

Abd El Wahab Aly Ibrahim
ABD EL WAHAB SONS

Tim Armsby
TROWERS & HAMLINS

Amr Mohamed Mahmoud
Atta
KARIM ADEL LAW OFFICE

Abdelhamid Attalla
KPMG

Khaled Balbaa
KPMG

Louis Bishara
*BISHARA TEXTILE & GARMENT
MANUFACTURING CO*

Karim Dabbous
*SHERIF DABBOUS, AUDITORS
& FINANCIAL CONSULTANCIES,
A MEMBER FIRM OF RUSSELL
BEDFORD INTERNATIONAL*

Sherif Dabbous
*SHERIF DABBOUS, AUDITORS
& FINANCIAL CONSULTANCIES,
A MEMBER FIRM OF RUSSELL
BEDFORD INTERNATIONAL*

Sameh Dahroug
*IBRACHY & DERMARKAR LAW
FIRM*

Ibrahim Hassan Daker
KARIM ADEL LAW OFFICE

Said Diab
*SHERIF DABBOUS, AUDITORS
& FINANCIAL CONSULTANCIES,
A MEMBER FIRM OF RUSSELL
BEDFORD INTERNATIONAL*

Abdallah El Adly
PRICEWATERHOUSECOOPERS

Mahmoud El Gharabawy
*NADOURY & NAHAS LAW
OFFICES*

Mohamed El Gharably
*NADOURY & NAHAS LAW
OFFICES*

Mohamed EL Gindy
*WAAD TRADE &
DEVELOPMENT CO.*

Mohamed Refaat El Houshy
*THE EGYPTIAN CREDIT
BUREAU I-SCORE*

Hassan El Maraashly
AAW CONSULTING ENGINEERS

Amr El Monayer
MINISTRY OF FINANCE

Mohamed El Sayed
*NADOURY & NAHAS LAW
OFFICES*

Hasan El Shafiey
*NADOURY & NAHAS LAW
OFFICES*

Karim Elhelaly
AL-AHL FIRM

Ashraf Elibrachy
IBRACHY LAW FIRM

Mohamed El-Labboudy
*NADOURY & NAHAS LAW
OFFICES*

Rana El-Nahal
SARWAT A. SHAHID LAW FIRM

Mustafa Elshafei
IBRACHY LAW FIRM

Sherihan Elshal
*ABU-GHAZALEH LEGAL -
(TAG-LEGAL)*

Hassan Fahmy
MINISTRY OF INVESTMENT

Tarek Gadallah
IBRACHY LAW FIRM

Tareq Gadallah
IBRACHY LAW FIRM

Ashraf Gamal El-Din
*EGYPTIAN INSTITUTE OF
DIRECTORS*

Ahmed Gawish
MINISTRY OF TRANSPORT

Karim Adel Kamel Ghobrial
KARIM ADEL LAW OFFICE

Zeinab Saieed Gohar
CENTRAL BANK OF EGYPT

Maha Hassan
AFIFI WORLD TRANSPORT

Omneia Helmy
*EGYPTIAN CENTER FOR
ECONOMIC STUDIES*

Lobna Mohamed Hilal
CENTRAL BANK OF EGYPT

Mohamed Hussein
*ABU-GHAZALEH LEGAL -
(TAG-LEGAL)*

Ashraf Ihab
*SHALAKANY LAW OFFICE,
MEMBER OF LEX MUNDI*

Mohamed Kamel
AL KAMEL LAW OFFICE

Ghada Kaptan
*SHALAKANY LAW OFFICE,
MEMBER OF LEX MUNDI*

Mohanna Khaled
BDO, KHALED & CO

Taha Khaled
BDO, KHALED & CO

Sally Kotb
*NADOURY & NAHAS LAW
OFFICES*

Mustafa Makram
BDO, KHALED & CO

Sherif Mansour
PRICEWATERHOUSECOOPERS

Diaa Mohamed
*ABU-GHAZALEH LEGAL -
(TAG-LEGAL)*

Mostafa Mostafa
AL KAMEL LAW OFFICE

Ashraf Nadoury
*NADOURY & NAHAS LAW
OFFICES*

Ragia Omran
*SHALAKANY LAW OFFICE,
MEMBER OF LEX MUNDI*

Tarek Fouad Riad
KOSHERI, RASHED & RIAD

Mohamed Serry
SERRY LAW OFFICE

Safwat Sobhy
PRICEWATERHOUSECOOPERS

*SOUTH CAIRO ELECTRICITY
DISTRIBUTION COMPANY*

Randa Tharwat
NACITA CORPORATION

Greiss Youssef
AFIFI WORLD TRANSPORT

Eman Zakaria
*MINISTRY OF MANPOWER &
MIGRATION*

Mona Zobaa
MINISTRY OF INVESTMENT

Mona Zulficar
*SHALAKANY LAW OFFICE,
MEMBER OF LEX MUNDI*

EL SALVADOR

Carlos Roberto Alfaro
PRICEWATERHOUSECOOPERS

Miguel Angel
ALE CARGO S.A. DE C.V.

Ana Margoth Arévalo
*SUPERINTENDENCIA DEL
SISTEMA FINANCIERO*

Ernesto Argueta
*BDO FIGUEROA JIMÉNEZ
& CO.*

Francisco Armando Arias
Rivera
ARIAS & MUÑOZ

Irene Arrieta de Díaz Nuila
ARRIETA BUSTAMANTE

Francisco José Barrientos
AGUILAR CASTILLO LOVE

Andrew Bennett
*BDO FIGUEROA JIMÉNEZ
& CO.*

Carlos Castillo
*ROMERO PINEDA &
ASOCIADOS, MEMBER OF LEX
MUNDI*

Diana Castro
LEXINCORP

Ricardo Cevallos
*CONSORTIUM CENTRO
AMÉRICA ABOGADOS*

Walter Chávez Velasco
GOLD SERVICE / MSI

Geraldo Cruz
GARCÍA & BODÁN

Laura de Jimenez
*ASOCIACIÓN PROTECTORA DE
CRÉDITOS DE EL SALVADOR
(PROCREDITO)*

Mayra de Morán
*PRESIDENTIAL PROGRAM EL
SALVADOR EFICIENTE*

Maria Marta Delgado
ARIAS & MUÑOZ

Roberta Gallardo de
Cromeyer
ARIAS & MUÑOZ

Erwin Alexander Haas
Quinteros
*RUSCONI, VALDEZ, MEDINA &
ASOCIADOS*

Carlos Henriquez
GOLD SERVICE / MSI

America Hernandez
ALE CARGO S.A. DE C.V.

Gloria Lizama de Funes
*ORGANO JUDICIAL DE EL
SALVADOR*

Thelma Dinora Lizama de
Osorio
*SUPERINTENDENCIA DEL
SISTEMA FINANCIERO*

Jerson Lopez
GOLD SERVICE / MSI

Fidel Márquez
ARIAS & MUÑOZ

Daniel Martinez
GARCÍA & BODÁN

Diego Martin-Menjivar
*CONSORTIUM CENTRO
AMÉRICA ABOGADOS*

Luis Alonso Medina Lopez
*RUSCONI, VALDEZ, MEDINA &
ASOCIADOS*

Astrud María Meléndez
*ASOCIACIÓN PROTECTORA DE
CRÉDITOS DE EL SALVADOR
(PROCREDITO)*

José Walter Meléndez
CUSTOMS

Jorge Mendez
*ROMERO PINEDA &
ASOCIADOS, MEMBER OF LEX
MUNDI*

Antonio R. Mendez Llort
*ROMERO PINEDA &
ASOCIADOS, MEMBER OF LEX
MUNDI*

Edgar Mendoza
PRICEWATERHOUSECOOPERS

Pedro Alejandro Mendoza
*ESPINO NIETO & ASOCIADOS,
MEMBER OF IUS LABORIS*

Miriam Eleana Mixco Reyna
GOLD SERVICE / MSI

Jocelyn Mónico
AGUILAR CASTILLO LOVE

Ramón Ortega
PRICEWATERHOUSECOOPERS

Susana Palacios
ARIAS & MUÑOZ

Carlos Pastrana
*COLEGIO DE ARQUITECTOS DE
EL SALVADOR*

Jessica Pineda Machuca
ACZALAW

Mónica Guadalupe Pineda
Machuca
ACZALAW

Francisco Eduardo Portillo
CEPA

Ana Patricia Portillo Reyes
*GUANDIQUE SEGOVIA
QUINTANILLA*

Hector Rios
*CONSORTIUM CENTRO
AMÉRICA ABOGADOS*

Roxana Romero
*ROMERO PINEDA &
ASOCIADOS, MEMBER OF LEX
MUNDI*

Adonay Rosales
PRICEWATERHOUSECOOPERS

Manuel Telles Suvillaga
LEXINCORP

Carlos Torres
ACZALAW

María Alejandra Tulipano
Consortium Centro
América Abogados

Mauricio Antonio Urrutia
Superintendencia del
Sistema Financiero

Julio Valdés
Arias & Muñoz

Luis Mario Villalta
Consortium Centro
América Abogados

EQUATORIAL
GUINEA

Gabriel Amugu
Interactivos GE

Leoncio-Mitogo Edjang Avoro

Philippe Fouda Fouda
BEAC

Caroline Idrissou-Belingar
BEAC

Mariam Laine
Airfreight

Sébastien Lechêne
PricewaterhouseCoopers /
Fidafrica

Paulino Mbo Obama
Oficina de estudieos -
ATEG

François Münzer
PricewaterhouseCoopers /
Fidafrica

Honorio Ndong Obama

Jenaro Obuno Ela
Ministerio de Hacienda y
Presupuesto

Lucien Onanga Otando
BEAC

Dominique Taty
FIDAFRICA /
PricewaterhouseCoopers

ERITREA

Biniam Fesehatzion
Berhane Gila-Michael
Law Firm

Berhane Gila-Michael
Berhane Gila-Michael
Law Firm

Kebreab Habte Michael
Kebreab Habte Michael
Legal Consulting

Tekeste Mesghenna
MTD Enterprises PLC

ESTONIA

Angela Agur
MAQS Law Firm

Katrin Altmets
Sorainen

Aet Bergmann
Law Office Luiga Mody
Hääl Borenius

Mark Butzmann
BNT Legal & Tax

Jane Eespõld
Sorainen

Indrek Ergma
Sorainen

Valters Gencs
Gencs Valters Law Firm

Daniel Haab
Paul Varul Attorneys-
at-Law

Pirkko-Liis Harkmaa
Lepik & Luhaäär LAWIN

Marget Henriksen
MAQS Law Firm

Triinu Hiob
Lepik & Luhaäär LAWIN

Risto Hübner
Law Office Tark & Co.

Andres Juss
Estonian Land Board

Peep Kalamae
PricewaterhouseCoopers

Aidi Kallavus
KPMG

Ants Karu
Lextal Law Office

Gerli Kilusk
Lepik & Luhaäär LAWIN

Ermo Kosk
Lepik & Luhaäär LAWIN

Igor Kostjuk
Hough, Hübner, Hütt &
Partners

Villu Kõve
Estonian Supreme Court

Tanja Kriisa
PricewaterhouseCoopers

Kaia Läänemets
Law Office Tark & Co.

Priit Lepasepp
Sorainen

Indrek Link
Hough, Hübner, Hütt &
Partners

Liina Linsi
Lepik & Luhaäär LAWIN

Karin Madisson
Sorainen

Siiri Malmberg
Hansa Law Offices

Olger Marjak
Law Office Tark & Co.

Johan Maunsbach
MAQS Law Firm

Marko Mehilane
Lepik & Luhaäär LAWIN

Veiko Meos
Krediidiinfo A.S.

Jaanus Mody
Luiga Mody Hääl Borenius

Margus Mugu
Luiga Mody Hääl Borenius

Kaspar Noor
MAQS Law Firm

Arne Ots
Raidla Lejins & Norcous

Karl J. Paadam
Sorainen

Raino Paron
Raidla Lejins & Norcous

Kirsti Pent
Law Office Tark & Co.

Kaitti Persidski
Estonian Chamber of
Notaries

Tarmo Peterson
Paul Varul Attorneys-
at-Law

Leho Pihkva
Sorainen

Kristiina Puuste
KPMG

Ants Ratas
CF&S AS

Dmitri Rosenblat
Lepik & Luhaäär LAWIN

Piret Saartee
Ministry of Justice

Martin Simovart
Lepik & Luhaäär LAWIN

Monika Tamm
Lepik & Luhaäär LAWIN

Marjaa Teder
Luiga Mody Hääl Borenius

Villi Töntson
PricewaterhouseCoopers

Veikko Toomere
MAQS Law Firm

Maris Tudre
Centre of Registers &
Information Systems

Kristi Uibo
Ministry of Justice

Urmas Ustav
Lextal Law Office

Neve Uudelt
Raidla Lejins & Norcous

Paul Varul
Paul Varul Attorneys-
at-Law

Urmas Veinberg
MAQS Law Firm

Vahur Verte
Luiga Mody Hääl Borenius

Peeter Viirsalu
Paul Varul Attorneys-
at-Law

Mirjam Vili
BNT Legal & Tax

Andres Vinkel
Hansa Law Offices

Joel Zernask
KPMG

ETHIOPIA

Teodros Abraham
SDV Transami Ltd.

Adem Ahmed
Express Transit Service
Enterprise PLC.

Yoseph Alemu
Ministry of Trade &
Industry

Befukado Assefa
Lewa PLC

Bekure Assefa
Bekure Assefa Law Office

Yonas Ayalew
SUR Construction PLC

Berhanu Yegezu Beyene
GAD construction PLC

Teshome Gabre-Mariam
Bokan
Teshome Gabre-Mariam
Law Firm

Wossen Teshome Bokan
Teshome Gabre-Mariam
Law Firm

Teferra Demiss
Legal and Insurance
Consultant and Attorney

Shimelise Eshete
MIDROC Construction PLC

Nega Getahun
City Administration of
Addis Ababa

Jennifer Gohlke
GE Foundation

Yosef Kebede
Dashen Bank S.C.

Berhe Kinfe
EEPCo

Getachew Kitaw Yitateku
Ethiopian Bar Association

Taddesse Lencho
Addis Ababa University

Yared Lencho
SUR Construction PLC

Yirga Tadesse Matewos
The Federal Ministry
of Justice, Documents
Authentication and
Registration Office

Molla Mengistu
Addis Ababa University

Belachew Moges
EEPCo

Getahun Nana
National Bank of Ethiopia

Hailye Sahle Seifu

Sintayehu Tefera Mekonnen
The Federal Ministry
of Justice, Documents
Authentication and
Registration Office

Eyasu Tequame
Jehoiachin Techno Pvt.
Ltd. Co.

Tibebu Tesfaye Haile
Tibebu Tesfaye Haile Legal
Consultant

Seyoum Yonhannes Tesfy
Addis Ababa University

Mesfin Tilahun
Main City Administration
of Addis Ababa

Wolde Tsadik Someno
Ministry of Trade &
Industry

Amsale Tsehaye
Amsale Tsehaye &
Associates Law Office

Aklilu Woldemariam
Ethiopian Investment
Agency

Marcos Wolde-Sanbet Lobicka
Law Firm Marcos Wolde-
Sanbet Lobicka

Tameru Wondmagegnehu
Tameru Wondmagegnehu
Law Offices

FIJI

David Aidney
Williams & Gosling Ltd.

Caroll Sela Ali
Cromptons Solicitors

Eddielin Almonte
PricewaterhouseCoopers

John Apted
Munro Leys Notaries
Public

Nehla Basawaiya
Munro Leys Notaries
Public

Mahendra Chand
Munro Leys Notaries
Public

Jamnadas Dilip
Jamnadas and Associates

Aca Domolailai
Colonial Bank

Delores Elliott

Florence Fenton
Munro Leys Notaries
Public

Anita Jowitt
University of the South
Pacific

Paul McDonnell
Cromptons Solicitors

Litiana Morris
Howards Lawyers

Richard Naidu
Munro Leys Notaries
Public

Vandnha Narayan
Colonial Bank

Nalin Patel
PKF Fiji

Pradeep Patel
PKF Fiji

Ana Rasovo
Howards Lawyers

Varun Shandil
Munro Leys Notaries
Public

Om Dutt Sharma
Fiji Electricity Authority

Dudley Simpson
Cromptons Solicitors

Shelvin Singh
Parshotam & Co.

Narotam Solanki
PricewaterhouseCoopers

Moto Solvalu
Williams & Gosling Ltd.

Chirk Yam
PricewaterhouseCoopers

Eddie Yuen
Williams & Gosling Ltd.

FINLAND

Sakari Aalto
Roschier Attorneys Ltd.,
member of Ius Laboris &
Lex Mundi

Miia Aho
Roschier Attorneys Ltd.,
member of Ius Laboris &
Lex Mundi

Manne Airaksinen
Roschier Attorneys Ltd.,
member of Ius Laboris &
Lex Mundi

Kasper Björkstén
Helen Sähköverkko Oy

Claudio Busi
Castrén & Snellman
Attorneys Ltd.

Cargoworld Ab/Oy

Mikko Eerola
Waselius & Wist

Marja Eskola
PricewaterhouseCoopers

Tuukka Fabritius
Roschier Attorneys Ltd.,
member of Ius Laboris &
Lex Mundi

Esa Halmari
Hedman Partners

Johanna Haltia-Tapio
Hannes Snellman
Attorneys at Law Ltd.

Tuija Hartikainen
PricewaterhouseCoopers

Risto Hietanen
National Board of Patents
& Registration

Jani Hovila
Hannes Snellman
Attorneys at Law Ltd.

Mia Hukkinen
Roschier Attorneys Ltd.,
member of Ius Laboris &
Lex Mundi

Lauri Jääskeläinen
Building Control
Department of the City of
Helsinki

Juuso Jokela
Suomen Asiakastieto Oy -
Finska

Sakari Kauppinen
National Board of Patents
& Registration

Gisela Knuts
Roschier Attorneys Ltd.,
member of Ius Laboris &
Lex Mundi

Olli Koikkalainen
National Board of Patents
& Registration

Elina Kumpulainen
PricewaterhouseCoopers
Legal Services

Kirsi Lahtinen
National Board of Patents
& Registration

Mina Lang
Castrén & Snellman
Attorneys Ltd.

Patrik Lindfors
P. Lindfors & Co,
Attorneys-at-Law Ltd.

Tomas Lindholm
Roschier Attorneys Ltd.,
member of Ius Laboris &
Lex Mundi

Risto Löf
PricewaterhouseCoopers

Tuomas Lukkarinen
National Land Survey

Vuori Marko
Krogerus Attorneys Ltd

Ilona Paakkala
PricewaterhouseCoopers

Mikko Peltoniemi
Waselius & Wist

Ilkka Pesonen
Wabuco Oy

Jyrki Prusila
Roschier Attorneys Ltd.,
member of Ius Laboris &
Lex Mundi

Marja Ramm-Schmidt
Krogerus Attorneys Ltd

Mikko Reinikainen
PricewaterhouseCoopers

Petri Seppälä
PricewaterhouseCoopers

Tatu Simula
Roschier Attorneys Ltd.,
member of Ius Laboris &
Lex Mundi

Sini Soini
Roschier Attorneys Ltd.,
member of Ius Laboris &
Lex Mundi

Suomen Asiakastieto Oy -
Finska

Helena Viita
Roschier Attorneys Ltd.,
member of Ius Laboris &
Lex Mundi

Anna Vuori
Hedman Partners

Gunnar Westerlund
Roschier Attorneys Ltd.,
member of Ius Laboris &
Lex Mundi

Kai Wist
PricewaterhouseCoopers

FRANCE

Allen & Overy LLP

Kempton Bedell-Harper
Russell Bedford
International

Franck Buffaud
Delsol & Associés

Arnaud Chastel
Landwell & Associés -
PricewaterhouseCoopers
Legal Services

Frédérique Chifflot Bourgeois

Christian Courivaud
SCP Courivaud - Morange
- Volniac

Ann Creelman
Vatier & Associés

Raphaëlle de Ruffi de Pontevès
Landwell & Associés -
PricewaterhouseCoopers
Legal Services

Isabelle Didier
Cabinet Isabelle Didier &
Associés

Jean-Philippe Dom
Landwell & Associés -
PricewaterhouseCoopers
Legal Services

Electricité de France

Benoit Fauvelet
Banque de France

Sylvie Ghesquiere
Banque de France

Guillaume Glon
Landwell & Associés -
PricewaterhouseCoopers

Florence Grillier
Cabinet TAJ

Kevin Grossmann
Mayer Brown

Philipe Guibert
FIEEC

Sabrina Henocq
Delsol & Associés

Marc Jobert
Jobert & Associés

Daniel Arthur Laprès
Cabinet d'Avocats

Nicolas Mordaunt-Crook
Landwell & Associés -
PricewaterhouseCoopers
Legal Services

Nathalie Morel
Mayer Brown

Anne-Marie Moulin
Banque de France

Agathe Penning-Reef
Confédération
Française du Commerce
Interentreprises

Jacques Pourciel
Paris Notaire

Arnaud Raynouard
University Paris IX
Dauphine

Bernard Reynis
Etude Notariale

Frédéric Roussel
Fontaine, Roussel &
Associés

Hugues Roux
Banque de France

Isabelle Smith Monnerville
Vaughan Avocats

Caroline Stéphane
Delsol & Associés

Salli A. Swartz
Phillips Giraud Naud et
Swartz

Samia Tighilt
Landwell & Associés -
PricewaterhouseCoopers

Sandra Tripathi
Gide Loyrette Nouel.

Philippe Xavier-Bender
Gide Loyrette Nouel

Claire Zuliani
Transparence, a member
of Russel Bedford
International

GABON

Charles Adenet
FIDAFRICA /
PricewaterhouseCoopers

Y.A. Adetona
Cabinet Fidexce

Marcellin Massila
Akendengue
SEEG, Societe d'Energie et
d'Eau du Gabon

Gianni Ardizzone
Panalpina World
Transport

Marie Carmel Ketty
Ayimambenwe
Banque Internationale
pour le Commerce et
l'Industrie du Gabon

Claude Barone
GETMA

Henri Bernhardt
GETMA

François Coron
Panalpina S.A.

Jean Delahaye
Bolloré

Léopold Effah
Etude Mekam'Ne & Effah
Avocats Associés

Augustin Fang

Philippe Fouda Fouda
BEAC

Anne Gey Bekale

Caroline Idrissou-Belingar
BEAC

Jacques Lebama
Ministere de la Justice,
Garde des Sceaux

Pélagie Massamba Mouckocko
FIDAFRICA /
PricewaterhouseCoopers

Jean Mbagou
Banque Internationale
pour le Commerce et
l'Industrie du Gabon

Abel Mouloungui

Celestin Ndelia
Etude Maitre Ndelia
Célestin

Ruben Mindonga Ndongo
Cabinet Me Anguiler

Thierry Ngomo
ArchiPro International

Lubin Ntoutoume

Josette Cadie Olendo
Cabinet Olendo

Lucien Onanga Otando
BEAC

Marie-Jose Ongo Mendou
FFA Juridique & Fiscal

Carine Peron
Union Gabonaise de banque

Laurent Pommera
FIDAFRICA /
PricewaterhouseCoopers

Christophe A. Relongoué
FIDAFRICA /
PricewaterhouseCoopers

Dominique Taty
FIDAFRICA /
PricewaterhouseCoopers

GAMBIA, THE

Victoria Andrews
Amie Bensouda & Co.

Alpha Amadou Barry
Deloitte

Abdul Aziz Bensouda
Amie Bensouda & Co.

Amie N.D. Bensouda
Amie Bensouda & Co.

Lamin B.S. Camara
Dandimayo Cambers

Sulayman B. Chune
TAF Construction

A.N.M Ousainu Darboe
Basangsang Chambers

Abeku Gyan-Quansah
PricewaterhouseCoopers

Birgitta Hardmark
Maersk Line

Alhaji Jallow
National Water &
Electricity Company Ltd.

Cherno Alieu Jallow
Deloitte

Lamin S. Jatta
Deloitte

Zainab Jawara-Alami
Gambia Revenue Authority

Sulayman M. Joof
S.M. Joof Agency

Nani Juwara
National Water and
Electricity Company Ltd.

Abdou Rahman Mboob

Thomas Nielsen
Gambia Shipping Agencies

Omar Njie
Law Firm Omar Njie

Mary Abdoulie Samba-
Christensen
Legal Practitioner

Mama Fatima Singhateh
GT Bank

Hawa Sisay-Sabally

Darcy White
PricewaterhouseCoopers

GEORGIA

Natalia Babakishvili
Mgaloblishvili, Kipiani,
Dzidziguri (MKD) Law Firm

Merab Barbakadze

Giorgi Begiashvili
Begiashvili & Co. Limited
Law Offices

Ketevan Beradze
BGI Legal

Sandro Bibilashvili
BGI Legal

Zaza Bibilashvili
BGI Legal

Vladimer Chkhaidze
National Agency of Public
Registry

Paul Cooper
PricewaterhouseCoopers

Aaron Crouch
Deloitte

Tsotne Ebralidze
ARCI Architecture &
Development

ENERGO PRO Georgia

Courtney Fowler
PricewaterhouseCoopers

Unana Gogokhia
BGI Legal

Mamuka Gordeziani
GTS Trans Logistics

Levan Gotua
Georgian Financial
Supervisory Agency

Batu Gvasalia
National Agency of Public
Registry

Irakli Gvilia
Credit Info Georgia

David Kakabadze
Georgian Legal
Partnership

Maka Khutsishvili
CaucasTransExpress

Anastasia Kipiani
PricewaterhouseCoopers

Sergi Kobakhidze
PricewaterhouseCoopers

Aieti Kukava
Alliance Group Holding

Kakhaber Nariashvil
Georgian Legal Partnership

Vakhtang Paresishvili
DLA Piper Gvinadze & Partners LP

Irakli Pipia
DLA Piper Gvinadze & Partners LP

Joseph Salukvadze
Tbilisi State University

Manzoor Shah
Globalink Logistics Group

Rusa Sreseli
PricewaterhouseCoopers

Avto Svadnize
DLA Piper Gvinadze & Partners LP

Anna Tabidze
Mgaloblishvili, Kipiani, Dzidziguri (MKD) Law Firm

Giorgi Tavartkiladze
Deloitte

GERMANY

Allen & Overy LLP

Gabriele Apfelbacher
Cleary Gottlieb Steen & Hamilton LLP

Sven Bäumler
Vattenfall Europe Distribution Hamburg GmbH

Henning Berger
White & Case

Astrid Berle
Schufa Holding AG

Jennifer Bierly
Avocado rechtsanwälte

Michael Brems
Cleary Gottlieb Steen & Hamilton LLP

Manon Brindöpke
Linklaters Oppenhoff & Rädler

Thomas Büssow
PricewaterhouseCoopers

Thomas Buhl
Cleary Gottlieb Steen & Hamilton LLP

Curtis Mallet - Prevost, Colt & Mosle LLP

Helge Dammann
PricewaterhouseCoopers Legal AG

Andreas Eckhardt
PricewaterhouseCoopers Legal Services

Dieter Endres
PricewaterhouseCoopers

Markus J. Goetzmann
C·B·H Rechtsanwälte

Bjoern Grund
Cleary Gottlieb Steen & Hamilton LLP

Andrea Gruss
Ashurst

Klaus Günther
Linklaters Oppenhoff & Rädler

Robert Gutte
Cleary Gottlieb Steen & Hamilton LLP

Rüdiger Harms
Cleary Gottlieb Steen & Hamilton LLP

Ilka Heinemeyer
SJ Berwin LLP

Manfred Heinrich
Deutsche Bundesbank

Stefan Heinrich
Cleary Gottlieb Steen & Hamilton LLP

Silvanne Helle
Linklaters Oppenhoff & Rädler

Götz-Sebastian Hök
Dr. Hök Stieglmeier & Partner

Markus Jakoby
Jakoby Rechtsanwälte

Christof Kautzsch
Salans

Henrik Kirchhoff
Latham & Watkins LLP

Jörg Kraffel
White & Case

Peter Limmer
Notare Dr. Limmer & Dr. Friederich

Christoph Lindenau
PricewaterhouseCoopers Legal AG Rechtsanwaltsgesellschaft

Frank Lohrmann
Cleary Gottlieb Steen & Hamilton LLP

Cornelia Marquardt
Norton Rose

Susanne Mattern
PricewaterhouseCoopers

Jan Geert Meents
DLA Piper LLP

Werner Meier
Cleary Gottlieb Steen & Hamilton LLP

Thomas Miller
Krohn Rechtsanwälte

Eike Najork
C·B·H Rechtsanwälte

Wolfgang Nardi
Kirkland & Ellis LLP Germany Munich

Isaschar Nicolaysen
DLA Piper LLP

Dirk Otto
Norton Rose

Daniel Panajotow
Cleary Gottlieb Steen & Hamilton LLP

Jan Christoph Pfeffer
Cleary Gottlieb Steen & Hamilton LLP

Peter Polke
Cleary Gottlieb Steen & Hamilton LLP

Sebastian Prügel
White & Case

Christopher Schauenburg
Cleary Gottlieb Steen & Hamilton LLP

Ralf M. Schnaittacher
Mayer Brown LLP

Friedrich Tobias Schoene
Hogan & Hartson LLP

Marc Schuett
Latham & Watkins LLP

Thomas Schulz
Nörr Stiefenhofer Lutz, member of Lex Mundi

Ingrid Seitz
Deutsche Bundesbank

Bernd Siebers
DLA Piper LLP

Hanno Sperlich
Cleary Gottlieb Steen & Hamilton LLP

Dirk Stiller
PricewaterhouseCoopers Legal AG Rechtsanwaltsgesellschaft

Tobias Taetzner
PricewaterhouseCoopers

Holger Thomas
SJ Berwin LLP

Valentin Todorow
Hogan & Hartson LLP

Christoph Torwegge
PricewaterhouseCoopers Legal AG Rechtsanwaltsgesellschaft

Heiko Vogt
Panalpina Welttransport GmbH

Katharina von Rosenstiel
Orrick Hölters & Elsing

Raimund E. Walch
Wendler Tremml Rechtsanwälte

Lena Wallenhorst
Cleary Gottlieb Steen & Hamilton LLP

Torsten Wehrhahn
Latham & Watkins LLP

Annekatren Werthmann-Feldhues
PricewaterhouseCoopers Legal AG Rechtsanwaltsgesellschaft

Senatsverwaltung für Stadtentwicklung Berlin

Stefan Wirsch
Latham & Watkins LLP

Gerlind Wisskirchen
CMS Hasche Sigle

GHANA

Seth Adom-Asomaning
Peasah-Boadu & Co.

Kwame Agati
Law Offices of Kwame Agati

Benjamin Agbotse
H & G Architects and Consultants

Nene Amegatcher
Sam Okudzeto & Associates

Wilfred Kwabena Anim-Odame
Land Valuation Board

Adwoa S. Asamoah Addo
Fugar & Co.

Adam Imoru Ayarna
Maersk Logistics Ltd.

Ellen Bannerman
Bruce-Lyle Bannerman & Thompson

Kojo Bentsi-Enchill
Bentsi-Enchill & Letsa, member of Lex Mundi

Stella Bentsi-Enchill
Lexconsult and Company

Sarah Adei Brown
DS Global Logistics

Jeremiah Coleman
Clearfreight Shipping Agencies Ltd.

Kwasi Darkwah
Ghana Investment Promotion Centre

William Edem Fugar
Fugar & Co.

John Robert Jenkins
Golden Jubilee Terminal

George Kwatia
PricewaterhouseCoopers

Kenneth D. Laryea
Laryea, Laryea & Co. P.C.

Lackson Agbeko Legah
Logistics @ Legacy Ltd.

Sam Okudzeto
Sam Okudzeto & Associates

Kingsford Otoo
Golden Jubilee Terminal

Kingsley Owusu-Ewli
PricewaterhouseCoopers

Jacob Saah
Saah & Co.

Lois Tankam

Darcy White
PricewaterhouseCoopers

Adwoa Yarney
Saah & Co.

Smart Yeboah
Electricity Company of Ghana

GREECE

Ioanna Argyraki
Kyriakides Georgopoulos & Daniolos Issaias

Nektaria Berikou
Ministry of Development

Alkistis - Marina Christofilou
IKRP Rokas & Partners

Vassilis Chryssomalis
Sarantitis Law Firm

Sotiris Constantinou
Grant Thornton

Theodora D. Karagiorgou
Law Office T. J. Koutalidis

Eleni Dikonimaki
Teiresias S.A. Interbanking Information Systems

Anastasia Dritsa
Kyriakides Georgopoulos & Daniolos Issaias

Alexandra Economou
Drakopoulos Law Firm

Margarita Flerianou
Economou International Shipping Agencies

Leonidas Georgopoulos
Kyriakides Georgopoulos & Daniolos Issaias

Sotiris Gioussios
Grant Thornton

Periklis Kakkavas
John M. Tripidakis and Associates

Elina Kanataki
Drakopoulos Law Firm

Constantinos Kapitsinos
Spyridakis Tsoukala Law Firm (ST LAW FIRM)

Evangelos Karaindros
Evangelos Karaindros Law Firm

Fotini D. Katrakaza
Law Office T. J. Koutalidis

Anna Kazantzidou
Panagopoulos, Vainanidis, Schina, Economou

Yannis Kelemenis
Kelemenis & Co.

Evita Kirykopoulou
Kremalis Law Firm, member of Ius Laboris

Constantinos Klissouras
Anagnostopoulos Bazinas

Paul Knoll
George A. Callitsis Succsrs S.A.

Alexandra Kondyli
Karatzas & Partners

Nicholas Kontizas
Zepos & Yannopoulos, member of Lex Mundi

Panos Koromantzos
Bahas, Gramatidis & Partners

Dimitrios Kremalis
Professor K. Kremalis & Partners, member of Ius Laboris

Tom Kyriakopoulos
Kelemenis & Co.

Vassiliki G. Lazarakou
Zepos & Yannopoulos, member of Lex Mundi

Konstantinos Logaras
Zepos & Yannopoulos, member of Lex Mundi

Charis Loizou
Elias Paraskevas Attorneys 1933

Viktoria - Maria Louri
Spyridakis Tsoukala Law Firm (ST LAW FIRM)

Evangelia Martinovits
IKRP Rokas & Partners

John Mazarakos
Elias Paraskevas Attorneys 1933

Effie G. Mitsopoulou
Kyriakides Georgopoulos & Daniolos Issaias

Athanassia Papantoniou
Kelemenis & Co.

Dimitris E. Paraskevas
Elias Paraskevas Attorneys 1933

Konstantinos Pistiolis
ELIAS PARASKEVAS ATTORNEYS 1933

Katerina Politi
KYRIAKIDES GEORGOPOULOS & DANIOLOS ISSAIAS

Mary Psylla
PRICEWATERHOUSECOOPERS

Alexandros Sakipis
PRICEWATERHOUSECOOPERS

Vasiliki Salaka
KARATZAS & PARTNERS

Constantine Sarantis
ZEPOS & YANNOPOULOS, MEMBER OF LEX MUNDI

Katerina Sefteli
VIVARTIA S.A

Harris Skordakis
PRICEWATERHOUSECOOPERS LEGAL SERVICES

Eleftherios Stavropoulos
MINISTRY OF DEVELOPMENT

Alexia Stratou
KREMALIS LAW FIRM, MEMBER OF IUS LABORIS

John Tripidakis
JOHN M. TRIPIDAKIS AND ASSOCIATES

Antonios Tsavdaridis
IKRP ROKAS & PARTNERS

Eleni Tsoukala
SPYRIDAKIS TSOUKALA LAW FIRM (ST LAW FIRM)

Mania Tsoumita
KELEMENIS & CO.

Vicky Xourafa
KYRIAKIDES GEORGOPOULOS & DANIOLOS ISSAIAS

Fredy Yatracou
PRICEWATERHOUSECOOPERS

GRENADA

Raymond Anthony
RAYMOND ANTHONY & CO.

Evelyn Cenac
CUSTOMS

GRENADA ELECTRICITY SERVICES LTD.

Leroy Flavigny
CUSTOMS

Cyrus Griffith
LABOUR DEPARTMENT

Claudette Joseph
AMICUS ATTORNEYS

Henry Joseph
PANNELL KERR FORSTER

Niel Noel
HENRY HUDSON - PHILLIPS & CO.

David Sinclair
SINCLAIR ENTERPRISES LIMITED

Trevor St. Bernard
LEWIS & RENWICK

Phinsley St. Louis
ST. LOUIS SERVICE

SUPREME COURT REGISTRY

Roselyn Wilkinson
WILKINSON, WILKINSON & WILKINSON

GUATEMALA

Gabriella Aguirre
RODRIGUEZ, CASTELLANOS, SOLARES & AGUILAR, S.C. -CONSORTIUM LEGAL

Rodolfo Alegria Toruno
CARRILLO & ASOCIADOS

Ana Rosa Alfaro
MAYORA & MAYORA, S.C.

Joaquin Alvarado
CARRILLO & ASOCIADOS

Norka Aragón
MAYORA & MAYORA, S.C.

Pedro Aragón
ARAGÓN & ARAGÓN

Elias Arriaza
RODRIGUEZ, CASTELLANOS, SOLARES & AGUILAR, S.C. -CONSORTIUM LEGAL

Ruby María Asturias Castillo
ACZALAW

Amaury Barrera
DHV CONSULTANTS

Cecilia Bonilla
AGUILAR CASTILLO LOVE

Maria del Pilar Bonilla
BONILLA, MONTANO, TORIELLO & BARRIOS

Eva Cacacho González
QUIÑONES, IBARGÜEN & LUJÁN

Rodrigo Callejas Aquino
CARRILLO & ASOCIADOS

Jose Alfredo Candido
SUPERINTENDENCIA DE BANCOS

Juan Pablo Carrasco de Groote
DÍAZ-DURÁN & ASOCIADOS CENTRAL LAW

Alfonso Carrillo
CARRILLO & ASOCIADOS

Juan Carlos Castillo Chacón
AGUILAR CASTILLO LOVE

José Cerezo
PRICEWATERHOUSECOOPERS LEGAL SERVICES

Luis Manuel Contreras Ramírez
DÍAZ-DURÁN & ASOCIADOS CENTRAL LAW

Paola van der Beek de Andrino
CÁMARA GUATEMALTECA DE LA CONSTRUCCIÓN

Karla de Mata
CPS LOGISTICS

Rolando De Paz Barrientos
TransUNION GUATEMALA

Samuel Elías
PRICEWATERHOUSECOOPERS

Lopez Enio
TransUNION GUATEMALA

Rodolfo Fuentes
PROTECTORA DE CRÈDITO COMERCIAL

Jorge Gálvez
BAC / CREDOMATIC

Rafael Garavito
BUFETE GARAVITO

GAUSS, NACIONAL DE INSTALADORES, S.A.

Oscar Ernesto Garcia Sierra
RUSSELL BEDFORD GUATEMALA GARCÍA SIERRA Y ASOCIADOS, S.C., MEMBER OF RUSSELL BEDFORD INTERNATIONAL

Veronika Sofia Gonzalez Bran
DÍAZ-DURÁN & ASOCIADOS CENTRAL LAW

Juan Jegerlehner
SARAVIA & MUÑOZ

Rossana Lopez
PALACIOS & ASOCIADOS

Guillermo Lopez-Davis
BUFETE LOPEZ CORDERO

María Isabel Luján Zilbermann
QUIÑONES, IBARGÜEN & LUJÁN

Estuardo Mata Palmieri
QUIÑONES, IBARGÜEN & LUJÁN

Eduardo Mayora Alvarado
MAYORA & MAYORA, S.C.

Edgar Mendoza
PRICEWATERHOUSECOOPERS

Hugo Menes
MAYORA & MAYORA, S.C.

Jorge Meoño
DÍAZ-DURÁN & ASOCIADOS CENTRAL LAW

Pablo Mogollon
TransUNION GUATEMALA

Amarilis Ondina Navas Portillo
BELTRANENA, DE LA CERDA Y CHAVEZ

Jose Orive
ARIAS & MUÑOZ

Roberto Ozaeta
PRICEWATERHOUSECOOPERS LEGAL SERVICES

Marco Antonio Palacios
PALACIOS & ASOCIADOS

Luis Rene Pellecer Lopez
CARRILLO & ASOCIADOS

Jose Enrique Pensabene
PALACIOS & ASOCIADOS

Melida Pineda
CARRILLO & ASOCIADOS

Evelyn Rebuli
QUIÑONES, IBARGÜEN & LUJÁN

Marco Tulio Reyna
CÁMARA GUATEMALTECA DE LA CONSTRUCCIÓN

Alfredo Rodríguez Mahuad
RODRIGUEZ, CASTELLANOS, SOLARES & AGUILAR, S.C. -CONSORTIUM LEGAL

Rodrigo Salguero
PRICEWATERHOUSECOOPERS

Salvador A. Saravia Castillo
SARAVIA & MUÑOZ

José Augusto Toledo Cruz
ARIAS & MUÑOZ

Arelis Torres de Alfaro
SUPERINTENDENCIA DE BANCOS

Elmer Vargas
ACZALAW

Raquel Villeda
MAYORA & MAYORA, S.C.

Ernesto Viteri Arriola
VITERI & VITERI

GUINEA

Aminatou Bah
NIMBA CONSEIL SARL

Aminata Bah Tall
NIMBA CONSEIL SARL

Alpha Bakar Barry
CABINET ALPHA BAKAR BARRY

Boubacar Barry
SCP D'AVOCATS JURIFIS CONSULT GUINEE

CABINET OUSMANE CAMARA

Mohamed Camara
SOCOPAO - SDV

Pierre-Stéphane Chabert
SOCOPAO- SDV

Oumar Dabo
ARCHI

Aïssata Diakite
NIMBA CONSEIL SARL

Ahmadou Diallo
CHAMBRES DES NOTAIRES

Abdel Aziz Kaba
NIMBA CONSEIL SARL

Lansana Kaba
CARIG

Lahlou Mohamed
FIDAFRICA / PRICEWATERHOUSECOOPERS

Guy Piam
NIMBA CONSEIL SARL

Raffi Raja
CABINET KOÛMY

Kalissa Safiatou
FIDAFRICA / PRICEWATERHOUSECOOPERS

Yansane Soumah
MANQUEPAS

Ibrahima Sory Sow
BANQUE CENTRALE DE GUINEE

Dominique Taty
FIDAFRICA / PRICEWATERHOUSECOOPERS

Aboubacar Salimatou Toure
NIMBA CONSEIL SARL

GUINEA-BISSAU

Diaby Aboubakar
BCEAO

Duarte Adolfo
BANCO DA ÁFRICA OCIDENTAL, S.A.

José Alves Té
MINISTÉRIO DA JUSTIÇA

Emílio Ano Mendes
OCTÁVIO LOPES ADVOGADOS - MIRANDA ALLIANCE

Marceano Barbosa
REGISTRAR

Felicidade Brito Abelha
BCEAO

Jose Carlos Casimiro
PRDSP

Jaimentino Có
MINISTÉRIO DO COMÉRCIO

Francisco Correa Jr.
PORTLINE

Rui Paulo Coutinho de Mascarenhas Ataíde

Adelaida Mesa D'Almeida

Agostinho Joaquim Gomes
MUNICIPALITY OF BISSAU

Djamila Mary Pereira Gomes

Josue Gomes de Almeida
PROJECTO DE REABILITACAO E DESENVOLVIMENTO DO SECTOR PRIVADO

José Henriques Duarte
PORTLINE

Mamadú Saliu Jaló Pires
CONSELHO JUDICIAL DA MAGISTRADURA, REPÚBLICA DA GUINÉ - BISSAU

Octávio Lopes
OCTÁVIO LOPES ADVOGADOS - MIRANDA ALLIANCE

Suzette Maria Lopes da Costa Graça
MINISTÉRIO DA JUSTIÇA

Emilfreda M. de Oliveira
ECOBANK

Armando Mango
ORDEM DOS ADVOGADOS DA GUINÉ-BISSAU

Miguel Mango
AUDI - CONTA LDA

Ismael Mendes de Medina
OCTÁVIO LOPES ADVOGADOS - MIRANDA ALLIANCE

Julio Albino Nhaga
TRIBUNAL DE SECTOR BISSAU

Osiris Francisco Pina Ferreira
CONSELHO JUDICIAL DA MAGISTRADURA, REPÚBLICA DA GUINÉ - BISSAU

Augusto Regala

Rogério Reis
ROGÉRIO REIS DESPACHANTE

Alpha Ousman Camara Ribeiro

A. Carlos Ricardo
PORTLINE

Carlitos Rutt
SERVIÇO - BAO

Amine M. Saad
AMINE SAAD & ADVOGADOS

Alex Bassucko Santos Lopes

A. Ussumane So
LOSSER LDA BUSINESS DEVELOPMENT CONSULTANTS

Konzo Traore
BCEAO

Djunco Suleiman Ture
MUNICIPALITY OF BISSAU

Carlos Vamain
GOMES & VAMAIN ASSOCIADOS

Jan van Maanen
MAVEGRO

João Daniel Vaz Jr.
TRANSVAZ, LDA

Emmanuel Yehouessi
BCEAO

GUYANA

Geoffrey Da Silva
GUYANA OFFICE FOR INVESTMENT

DEMERARA BANK

Lucia Loretta Desir
D & J Shipping Services

C. A. Nigel Hughes
Hughes, Fields & Stoby

Rakesh Latchana
Ram & McRae

R.N. Poonai
Poonai & Poonai

Christopher Ram
Ram & McRae

Vishwamint Ramnarine
PFK Barcellos, Narine & Co

Republic Bank

William Sampson
Lincoln Chambers & Associates

Gidel Thomside
National Shipping Corporation Ltd.

Josephine Whitehead
Cameron & Shepherd

HAITI

Lionel Allen

Marc Kinson Antoine
A.I. Shipping International

Jean Baptiste Brown
Brown Legal Group

Martin Camille Cangé
Electricité d'Haïti

Djacaman Charles
Cabinet Gassant

Philippe-Victor Chatelain
Chatelain Cargo Services

Jean Gerard Eveillard
Cabinet Eveillard

Lucien Fresnel
Cabinet Gassant

Enerlio Gassant
Cabinet Gassant

Gilbert Giordani
Etude Brisson Cassagnol

Marc Hebert Ignace
Banque de la République d'Haïti

Wilhelm E. Lemke, Jr
Enmarcolda (D'adesky)

Kathia Magloire
Cabinet Gassant

Alexandrine Nelson
Chatelain Cargo Services

Leon Saint -Louis

Jean Frederic Sales
Cabinet Sales

Paul Emile Simon

Salim Succar
Cabinet Lissade

Antoine Turnier
Firme Turnier - Comptable Professionnels Agréés Conseils de Direction

HONDURAS

José Antonio Abate
Consultores Ascodidos

Juan José Alcerro Milla
Aguilar Castillo Love

José Simón Azcona
IABSA

Tatiana Zelaya Bustamante
TransUnion

César Cabrera
TransUnion

Jorge Omar Casco
Bufete Casco & Asociados

Tania Vanessa Casco
Bufete Casco & Asociados

Janeth Castañeda de Aquino
Grupo Cropa Panalpina

Carmen Chevez
CNBS - Comision Nacional de Bancos y Seguros

Jaime Colindres Rosales
DYCELES S de R.L.

Ramón Discua
Batres, Discua, Martinez Abogados

Lillizeth Garay
CNBS - Comision Nacional de Bancos y Seguros

Jennifer Gonzalez Garcia
García & Bodán

Jessica Handal
Arias & Muñoz

Camilo Janania
Aguilar Castillo Love

Juan Diego Lacayo
Aguilar Castillo Love

Marcela López Carrillo
PricewaterhouseCoopers

Heidi Luna
García & Bodán

Doris A. Madrid-Lezama
Cámara de Comercio e Industria de Tegucigalpa

Dennis Matamoros Batson
Arias & Muñoz

Iván Alfredo Vigíl Molina

Ramón Ortega
PricewaterhouseCoopers

Vanessa Oquelí
García & Bodán

Dino Rietti
Arquitecnic

José Rafael Rivera Ferrari
Consortium - J.R. Paz & Asociados

Enrique Rodriguez Burchard
Aguilar Castillo Love

Fanny Rodríguez del Cid
Arias & Muñoz

Martha R Saenz
Zacarías & Asociados

Armando Sarmiento
Revenue Executive Directorate Honduras

René Serrano
Arias & Muñoz

Godofredo Siercke
García & Bodán

Edgardo H. Sosa
Empresa Nacional de Energía Eléctrica

Marco Valladares

Roberto Manuel Zacarías Urrutia
Zacarías & Asociados

Mario Rubén Zelaya
Energía Integral S. de R.L. de C.V.

HONG KONG, CHINA

Allen & Overy LLP

Christine Au
Economic & Trade Office

Brian Barron
Baker & McKenzie

Albert P.C. Chan
The Hong Kong Polytechnic University

Allan Chan
The Land Registry

Nicholas Chan
Squire, Sanders & Dempsey

Vashi Chandi
Excellence International

Deborah Y. Cheng
Squire, Sanders & Dempsey L.L.P.

William Chong
SDV Logistics Ltd.

Andrew Dale
Coudert Brothers in association with Orrick, Herrington & Sutcliffe

Thomas Duplan
SDV Logistics Ltd.

Patrick Fontaine
Linklaters

Bertrand Gruez
SDV Logistics Ltd.

Andrew Halkyard
University of Hong Kong

Keith Man Kei Ho
Wilkinson & Grist

Rod Houng-Lee
PricewaterhouseCoopers

Tam Yuen Hung
Guangdong and Hong Kong Feeder Association Ltd

Simon Kai
SDV Logistics Ltd.

Howard Lam
Linklaters

Kwok Ho Lam
CLP Power Limited

Damon Law
DLA Piper

Phila Law
Economic Analysis and Business Facilitation Unit,

Ian Lee
Russell Bedford Hong Kong Limited, a member firm of Russell Bedford International

Cecil Leung
Linklaters

Angie Lim
Hong Kong Association of Freight Forwarding & Logistics

Justin Ma
Linklaters

MAERSK Ltd.

Cliff Mok
Coudert Brothers in association with Orrick, Herrington & Sutcliffe

Matthew Mui
Financial Secretaryís Office

James Ngai
Russell Bedford Hong Kong Limited, a member firm of Russell Bedford International

Andrea Pellicani
Overseas Asia

Martinal Quan
Metopro Associates Limited

Jude Ryan
Orrick, Herrington & Sutcliffe LLP

Sara Tong
Temple Chambers

Anita Tsang
PricewaterhouseCoopers

Laurence Tsong
TransUnion

Tak Kei Wan
CLP Power Limited

Billy Wong
Coudert Brothers in association with Orrick, Herrington & Sutcliffe

Fergus Wong
PricewaterhouseCoopers

Jackson Wong
Hong Kong Economic & Trade Office

Ricky Yiu
Baker & McKenzie

HUNGARY

Mark Balastyai
Futureal Group

Béla Balogh
Balogh és Tarsai Ltd., member of Russell Bedford International

Péter Bárdos
Dr. Bárdos Attorney-at-Law

Sándor Békési
Partos & Noblet Lovells

Judit Bókai
Dr Bókai Notary Office

Hedi Bozsonyik
Szecskay Attorneys-at-Law

Jan Burmeister
Law Firm "bnt Szabó Tom Burmeister Ügyvédi Iroda"

Hellmann Worldwide Logistics Kft

Gabriella Erdos
PricewaterhouseCoopers

György Fehér
PRK Bellák & Partners Law Office, member of Ius Laboris

Anna Gáspár
Build-Econ Ltd.

Csaba Attila Hajdu
Law Firm "bnt Szabó Tom Burmeister Ügyvédi Iroda"

Dóra Horváth
Réti, Antall & Madl Landwell Law Firm

Norbert Izer
PricewaterhouseCoopers

IFS Ltd.

Zsuzsanna Károlyi
PRK Bellák & Partners Law Office, member of Ius Laboris

Daniel Kelemen
Réti, Antall & Madl Landwell Law Firm

Gyula Kőrösy
bpv | Legal Jádi Németh

Zoltan Krausz
Build-Econ Ltd.

László Mohai
Morley Allen & Overy Iroda

Judit Nagy
PRK Bellák & Partners Law Office, member of Ius Laboris

Robert Nagy
BISZ

Sándor Németh
Szecskay Attorneys-at-Law

Tamás Pásztor
Nagy és Trócsányi Law Office, member of Lex Mundi

Tamás Saád
Build-Econ Ltd.

István Sándor
Kelemen, Meszaros, Sandor & Partners

Andrea Soós
PRK Bellák & Partners Law Office, member of Ius Laboris

Boglárka Szánthó
Nagy és Trócsányi Law Office, member of Lex Mundi

András Szecskay
Szecskay Attorneys-at-Law

Ágnes Szent-Ivány
Sándor Szegedi Szent-Ivány Komáromi Eversheds

Viktória Szilágyi
Nagy és Trócsányi Law Office, member of Lex Mundi

Adrienn Tar
Szecskay Attorneys-at-Law

Ádám Tóth
Dr. Tóth & Dr. Gáspár Közjegyzői Iroda

Gábor Varga
BISZ

Virág Vass
PricewaterhouseCoopers

ICELAND

Halla Ýr Albertsdóttir
PricewaterhouseCoopers

Kristján Ásgeirsson
Arkitektastofan OG

Guðrún Bergsteinsdóttir
BBA Legal

Eymundur Einarsson
Endurskoðun og ráðgjöf ehf, member of Russell Bedford International

Ólafur Eiríksson
LOGOS, member of Lex Mundi

Erlendur Gíslason
LOGOS, MEMBER OF LEX MUNDI

Guðrún Guðmundsdóttir
JÓNAR TRANSPORT

Hjördís Gulla Gylfadóttir
BBA LEGAL

Bryndís Gunnlaugsdóttir
PRICEWATERHOUSECOOPERS

Reynir Haraldsson
JÓNAR TRANSPORT

Jón Ingi Ingibergsson
PRICEWATERHOUSECOOPERS

Hrafnhildur Kristinsdóttir
LOGOS, MEMBER OF LEX MUNDI

Ásta Kristjánsdóttir
PRICEWATERHOUSECOOPERS LEGAL SERVICES

Jóhann Magnús Jóhannsson
LOGOS, MEMBER OF LEX MUNDI

Benedetto Nardini
BBA LEGAL

Kristján Pálsson
JÓNAR TRANSPORT

Gunnar Sturluson
LOGOS, MEMBER OF LEX MUNDI

Rúnar Svavar Svavarsson
ORKUVEITA REYKJAVÍKUR, DISTRIBUTION-ELECTRICAL SYSTEM

Bergþór Þormóðsson
ISTAK

Omar Torfason
CREDITINFO ICELAND

INDIA

Dulal Acharyya
PARASNATH TECH GARMENTS PVT., LTD.

Amit Agarwal
PRICEWATERHOUSECOOPERS

Bhavuk Agarwal
SINGHANIA & CO. LLP

Vinod Agarwal
UNIVERSAL ADVISORY SERVICES

AJIT BHUTA AND ASSOCIATES

Tushar Ajinkya
DSK LEGAL

Palanikumar Arumugam
VARIETY FASHIONS

AUM ARCHITECTS

Ameet Awasthi
FORTUNE LAW GROUP

Gauri Bajaj
KNM & PARTNERS, LAW OFFICES

Manik Bakshi
KNM & PARTNERS, LAW OFFICES

P. V. Balasubramaniam
BFS LEGAL

Vikas Bansal
PRICEWATERHOUSECOOPERS

M.L Bhakta
KANGA & CO.

BHASIN INTERNATIONAL

Pranav Bhaskar
FOX MANDAL

Varghese Binu
BINLEES

Ugen Bhutia
FOX MANDAL

CANAR EXPORTS

Rajarshi Chakrabarti
KOCHHAR & CO.

Aman Chanda
PRICEWATERHOUSECOOPERS

Harshala Chandorkar
CREDIT INFORMATION BUREAU LTD.

Jyoti Chaudhari
LEGASIS SERVICES PVT. LTD.

Prashant Chauhan

Daizy Chawla
SINGH & ASSOCIATES ADVOCATES AND SOLICITORS

Harminder Chawla
CHAWLA & CO.

Manjula Chawla
PHOENIX LEGAL

Amanpreet Singh Chhina

Sachin Chugh
SINGHI CHUGH & KUMAR, CHARTERED ACCOUNTANTS

Mridul Das

Vishwang Desai
DESAI & DIWANJI

Prashant Dharia
ANANT INDUSTRIES

Rahul Dhawan
FOX MANDAL

Darshana Dubhashi
G.D. SMABHARE AND CO.

Thambi Durai
T. DURAI & CO.

EMERALD INTERNATIONAL

Shrikant Gajjar
GAJJAR & ASSOCIATES

Rahul Garg
PRICEWATERHOUSECOOPERS

Vijay Goel
SINGHANIA & CO. LLP

Chandrika Gogia
PRICEWATERHOUSECOOPERS

Neha Goyal
TRILEGAL

Anil Gupta
HITECH GROUP

Chander Gupta
MR TOBACCO PVT., LTD.

Nikhil Gupta
PRICEWATERHOUSECOOPERS

Radhika Iyer
NISHITH DESAI ASSOCIATES

Ashok Jain
SURAJ OVERSEAS

Sarul Jain
AVINASH KUMAR

Sarul Jain
AMARCHAND & MANGALDAS & SURESH A. SHROFF & CO.

Dharmendra Johari
STONEX INC.

Rajat Joneja
KNM & PARTNERS, LAW OFFICES

Sumeet Kachwaha
KACHWAHA & PARTNERS

Swaminathan Kalyanaraman
DAKSHIN KREATIONS PRIVATE LIMITED

Dinesh Kanabar
PRICEWATERHOUSECOOPERS

Kandallan
MUNICIPAL CORPORATION OF GREATER MUMBAI

A.V. Kane
THE BRIHAN MUMBAI ELECTRIC SUPPLY & TRANSPORT UNDERTAKING

Vaishal Kapadia
SHIDIMO INTERAUX PVT. LTD.

Rajas Kasbekar
LITTLE & CO.

Anuj Kaul
LEGASIS SERVICES PVT. LTD.

Jagdeep Kaur
INTERNATIONAL LAW AFFILIATES

Ramandeep Kaur

Rajesh Khandelwal
SUMAN ENTERPRISES

Ajay Khatlawala
FOX MANDAL

Rajnish Khattar
AMERINDÉ CONSOLIDATED

Vinod Khotari
VINOD KOTHARI & CO., COMPANY SECRETARIES

Jawahar Kothari
USINDIATAX LLP

Vilas R. Koyanne
MUNICIPAL CORPORATION OF GREATER MUMBAI

Abhishek Kumar
SINGHANIA & PARTNERS, SOLICITORS & ADVOCATES

Avinash Kumar
AVINASH KUMAR

Dalip Kumar
SINGHANIA & CO. LLP

Harsh Kumar
SINGHI CHUGH & KUMAR, CHARTERED ACCOUNTANTS

Mukesh Kumar
KNM & PARTNERS, LAW OFFICES

Parveen Kumar
HARNANDI SHIPPING & LOGISTICS

Ravindra Kumar
SINGHANIA & CO. LLP

Sailesh Kumar
DRAGON EXPRESS MARITIME PVT LTD.

Saji Kumar
DRAGON EXPRESS FREIGHT PVT. LTD.

Suraj Kumar
AMARCHAND & MANGALDAS & SURESH A. SHROFF & CO.

Dilip kumar Niranjan
SINGH & ASSOCIATES ADVOCATES AND SOLICITORS

Manoj Kumar Singh
SINGH & ASSOCIATES ADVOCATES AND SOLICITORS

Vijay Kumar Singh
SINGH & ASSOCIATES ADVOCATES AND SOLICITORS

Dinesh Kunal
INFOSOL INFORMATION SOLUTION WORD

Shreedhar Kunte
SHARP AND TANNAN - MEMBER OF RUSSELL BEDFORD

LEO CIRCUIT BOARDS PVT. LTD.

Manish Madhukar
INFINI JURIDIQUE

Som Mandal
FOX MANDAL

Vipender Mann
KNM & PARTNERS, LAW OFFICES

Vaishali Manubarwala
DESAI & DIWANJI

Tushar A. Mavani
MULLA & MULLA & CRAIGIE BLUNT & CAROE

Dara Mehta
LITTLE & CO.

Jitesh Mehta
SOURCE INDIA

Preeti G. Mehta
KANGA & CO.

Sharad Mishra
NEO MULTIMEDIAN

Saurabh Misra
PARAS KUHAD & ASSOCIATES, ADVOCATES (PKA)

Sourish Mitra
FOX MANDAL

Vishwajeet Mohite
SINGHANIA & PARTNERS, SOLICITORS & ADVOCATES

M/s GLOBE EXPORTS

R. Muralidharan
PRICEWATERHOUSECOOPERS

Satish Murti
MURTI & MURTI INTERNATIONAL LAW PRACTICE

EXCEL ENTERPRISES

Vijay Nair
KNM & PARTNERS, LAW OFFICES

NINE INTERNATIONAL

Anand Nivas
DRAGON EXPRESS FREIGHT PVT. LTD.

Gunita Pahwa
SINGH & ASSOCIATES ADVOCATES AND SOLICITORS

G. Pal
LITTLE & CO.

Tejas R. Parekh
NISHITH DESAI ASSOCIATES

Amir Z. Singh Pasrich
INTERNATIONAL LAW AFFILIATES

Shreyas Patel
FOX MANDAL

Sanjay Patil
BDH INDUSTRIES LTD.

Ashish Patole
ACCENT TRENDZ

Niti Paul
AMARCHAND & MANGALDAS & SURESH A. SHROFF & CO.

PORTOWORLD

Anand Prasad
TRILEGAL

PRAKASHDEEP ENTERPRISES

Anil Raj
PHOENIX LEGAL

Raj
BRAHMA SHIPPING & LOGISTICS

Vasanth Rajasekaran
KACHWAHA & PARTNERS

Mohan Rajasekharan
PHOENIX LEGAL

Mohan Ramakrishnan
SATHYA AUTO PRIVATE LIMITED

Ashok Ramgir
HARSH IMPEX

Ami Ranjan
SINGHANIA & PARTNERS, SOLICITORS & ADVOCATES

Dipak Rao
SINGHANIA & PARTNERS, SOLICITORS & ADVOCATES

Rahul Renavikar
PRICEWATERHOUSECOOPERS

ROOPA TEXTILES AND TRIMMINGS

Kehsav Saini
KNM & PARTNERS, LAW OFFICES

Abhishek Saket
INFINI JURIDIQUE

Sudhir Saksena
ICFAI SCHOOL OF FINANCIAL STUDIES

Aditi Sambhar
KNM & PARTNERS, LAW OFFICES

Richie Sancheti
NISHITH DESAI ASSOCIATES

Radhika Sankaran
FOX MANDAL

V. Siva Sankaran
T.S. CLASSIQUE

Ramani Seshadri
DPAS GROUPS

Mrugank Shah
DESAI & DIWANJI

Parag Shah
PARAG G SHAH AND ASSOCIATES

Parag Shah
FOX MANDAL

Anand Sharma
R.K. INDUSTRIES

Anuradha Sharma
KACHWAHA & PARTNERS

Aparna Sharma
INFINI JURIDIQUE

Manoranjan Sharma
KNM & PARTNERS, LAW OFFICES

Vina Sharma
INFINI JURIDIQUE

Vikram Shroff
NISHITH DESAI ASSOCIATES

Dilip Sidhpura
D.L.SIDHPURA ASSOCIATES

Harsimran Singh
*SINGH & ASSOCIATES
ADVOCATES AND SOLICITORS*

Praveen Singh
FOX MANDAL

Ravinder Singh
INTERNATIONAL TOOLS CO.

Ravinder Singhania
*SINGHANIA & PARTNERS,
SOLICITORS & ADVOCATES*

Arvind Sinha
BUSINESS ADVISORS GROUP

Lalan Sinha
*KNM & PARTNERS, LAW
OFFICES*

Sumit Sinha
TRILEGAL

Shipra Sukhija
FORTUNE LAW GROUP

Prajakta Telang
LEGASIS SERVICES PVT. LTD.

Thacker
*MUNICIPAL CORPORATION OF
GREATER MUMBAI*

Chetan Thakkar
KANGA & CO.

Smita Thakur
DESAI & DIWANJI

Praveen Tiwary
FOX MANDAL

Kannan Venkatasamy
PERIPHERALCONNEXIONS

Saji Vijayadas
*DRAGON EXPRESS FREIGHT
PVT. LTD.*

Saral Kumar Yadav
*INFOSOL INFORMATION
SOLUTION WORD*

ZEDD TRADE

INDONESIA

Nafis Adwani
*ALI BUDIARDJO, NUGROHO,
REKSODIPUTRO, MEMBER OF
LEX MUNDI*

Bambang Agus Setiadi
*LOCAL OFFICE OF
BUILDING SUPERVISION AND
ADMINISTRATION FOR THE
PROVINCE OF DKI JAKARTA*

Almer Apon
*PT BUANA MAS CITRA
LESTARI*

Adi Ariantara
*JAKARTA INVESTMENT AND
PROMOTION BOARD*

Feri Astuti
MARIAM DARUS & PARTNERS

Hamud M. Balfas
*ALI BUDIARDJO, NUGROHO,
REKSODIPUTRO, MEMBER OF
LEX MUNDI*

Rukman Basit
MINISTRY OF TRADE

Fabian Buddy Pascoal
*HANAFIAH PONGGAWA &
PARTNERS*

Tony Budidjaja
*BUDIDJAJA & ASSOCIATES LAW
OFFICES*

S.H Juni Dani
*BUDIDJAJA & ASSOCIATES LAW
OFFICES*

Mariam Darus
MARIAM DARUS & PARTNERS

Kemala Dewi
MARIAM DARUS & PARTNERS

Utari Dyah Kusuma
*BRIGITTA I. RAHAYOE &
PARTNERS*

Ira A. Eddymurthy
*SOEWITO SUHARDIMAN
EDDYMURTHY KARDONO*

Sani Eka Duta
BANK INDONESIA

Dedet Hardiansyah
BUDIMAN AND PARTNERS

Ray Headifen
*PT PRIMA WAHANA CARAKA /
PRICEWATERHOUSECOOPERS*

Erwandi Hendarta
*HADIPUTRANTO, HADINOTO &
PARTNERS*

Rahayu N. Hoed
MAKARIM & TAIRA S.

Sri Nurhayati Ibrahim
MARIAM DARUS & PARTNERS

Brigitta Imam Rahayoe
*BRIGITTA I. RAHAYOE &
PARTNERS*

Mohammad Kamal
FURNITURE FIKAMAR

Iswahjudi A. Karim
KARIMSYAH LAW FIRM

Mirza Karim
KARIMSYAH LAW FIRM

S.H. Diasha Kashatri
*BUDIDJAJA & ASSOCIATES LAW
OFFICES*

H. Kirno
*MUNICIPAL OFFICE OF
BUILDING LICENSING SERVICE*

Herry N. Kurniawan
*ALI BUDIARDJO, NUGROHO,
REKSODIPUTRO, MEMBER OF
LEX MUNDI*

Rudy Kusmanto
MAKARIM & TAIRA S.

Winita E. Kusnandar
KUSNANDAR & CO.

Erma Kusumawati
BANK INDONESIA

Luh Lely Ariestianti
*LOCAL OFFICE OF
BUILDIING SUPERVISION AND
ADMINISTRATION FOR THE
PROVINCE OF DKI JAKARTA*

Ferry P. Madian
*ALI BUDIARDJO, NUGROHO,
REKSODIPUTRO, MEMBER OF
LEX MUNDI*

Eric Mancini
PT SDV LOGISTICS

Ella Melany
*HANAFIAH PONGGAWA &
PARTNERS*

Karen Mills
KARIMSYAH LAW FIRM

Serafina Muryanti
*ALI BUDIARDJO, NUGROHO,
REKSODIPUTRO, MEMBER OF
LEX MUNDI*

Norma Mutalib
MAKARIM & TAIRA S.

Feria Ningsih
MAKARIM & TAIRA S.

Yusuf Pramono
MARIAM DARUS & PARTNERS

Ilman Rakhmat
KARIMSYAH LAW FIRM

Muhammad Razikun
*MUC CONSULTING GROUP,
A MEMBER FIRM OF RUSSELL
BEDFORD INTERNATIONAL*

Diah Retnosari
MARIAM DARUS & PARTNERS

Arno F. Rizaldi
KUSNANDAR & CO.

Choriana Saragih
*CENTRAL JAKARTA DISTRICT
COURT*

Mahardikha K. Sardjana
*HADIPUTRANTO, HADINOTO &
PARTNERS*

Nur Asyura Anggini Sari
BANK INDONESIA

Marinza Savanthy
WIDYAWAN & PARTNERS

Yanty Selviany Damanik
MARIAM DARUS & PARTNERS

Indra Setiawan
*ALI BUDIARDJO, NUGROHO,
REKSODIPUTRO, MEMBER OF
LEX MUNDI*

Kevin Omar Sidharta
*ALI BUDIARDJO, NUGROHO,
REKSODIPUTRO, MEMBER OF
LEX MUNDI*

Ronny Silitonga
PT SUCOFINDO - DENPASAR

Ricardo Simanjuntak
*RICARDO SIMANJUNTAK &
PARTNERS*

Manhore Singh
*M & N MANAGEMENT
CONSULTANTS*

Sukhbir Singh
*M & N MANAGEMENT
CONSULTANTS*

Bambang Soelaksono
*THE SMERU RESEARCH
INSTITUTE*

Galinar R. Kartakusuma
Summitmas
MAKARIM & TAIRA S.

Darwin Syam Siregar
*CITY ZONING OFFICE FOR
NORTH JAKARTA*

Ernst G. Tehuteru
*ALI BUDIARDJO, NUGROHO,
REKSODIPUTRO, MEMBER OF
LEX MUNDI*

Rudy Tjandra
*PT PRIMA WAHANA CARAKA /
PRICEWATERHOUSECOOPERS*

Gatot Triprasetio
WIDYAWAN & PARTNERS

Adhie Wicaksono
BANK INDONESIA

Aditya Kesha Wijayanto
WIDYAWAN & PARTNERS

Robertus Winarto
*PT PRIMA WAHANA CARAKA /
PRICEWATERHOUSECOOPERS*

IRAN, ISLAMIC REP.

Mostafa Agah
AGAH LAW FIRM

Najad Akbari

Mohsen Bahrami Arz Aghdas
*CHASHM ANDAZE JAHAN
TRADING CO.*

Behrooz Akhlaghi
*INTERNATIONAL LAW OFFICE
OF DR. BEHROOZ AKHLAGHI &
ASSOCIATES*

Hossein Ali Amiri

Mostafa Arafati
GHODS NIROO ENGINEERS

Ebrahim Asadi
*ELECTRICAL INDUSTRY
DEVELOPMENT (EID
CONSULTANT CO.)*

Reza Askari
*FOREIGN LEGAL AFFAIRS
GROUP*

Saeideh Atefvahid
CENTRAL BANK OF IRAN

Maryam Babayee
FARJAM LAW OFFICE

Malihe Dafnouk
BANK TEJARAT OF IRAN

Gholamhossein Davani
*DAYARAYAN AUDITING &
FINANCIAL SERVICES*

Hamid Derakhshani
*CHASHM ANDAZE JAHAN
TRADING CO.*

Morteza Dezfoulian

Mahmoud Ebadi Tabrizi
*M. EBADI TABRIZI &
ASSOCIATES*

Pejman Eshtehardi
IRAN COUNSELORS

Shirzad Eslami

Mostafa Farmahini Farahani
GHODS NIROO ENGINEERS

Ali Ghaemi
TEHRAN MUNICIPALITY

Mohammad Reza Hajian
CENTRAL BANK OF IRAN

Rouzbeh Hazrati
IRAN COUNSELORS

Mehdi Heidarzadeh
*ALVAND SAYAN
INTERNATIONAL TRADING
Co, LTD.*

Maryam Hosseini
ATIEH ASSOCIATES

Asadollah Jalalabadi
BANK TEJARAT OF IRAN

Abdolhossein Jalili Namini

Kiumars Kermanshahi
*IRAN TRADE PROMOTION
ORGANIZATION*

Hossein Lotfi
H. LOTFI & ASSOCIATES

Majid Mahallati
*MAHALLATI & CO.
CHARTERED ACCOUNTANTS*

Shahrzad Majdameli
*INTERNATIONAL LAW OFFICE
OF DR. BEHROOZ AKHLAGHI &
ASSOCIATES*

Malakootian
BANK TEJARAT OF IRAN

M. R. Matine
PARS ASSOCIATES

Mansour Missaghian
GHODS NIROO ENGINEERS

Ali Baheshi Moqadam

Mozaffar Mohammadian
*TEEMA BAR INTERNATIONAL
TRANSPORT*

Mehrdad Mostaghimi
GHODS NIROO ENGINEERS

Homayoon Naddaf Shargh
*PORT AND MARITIME
ORGANIZATION EXPERT*

Sedigheh Naimian

Babak Namazi
ATIEH ASSOCIATES

Nazari
BANK TEJARAT OF IRAN

Farmand Pourkarim
TEHRAN MUNICIPALITY

Saeid Rasaei
BANK TEJARAT OF IRAN

Yehya Rayegani
FARJAM LAW OFFICE

Behrooz Rezazadeh
PSDC GROUP

Ghalamreza Saffarpour
GHODS NIROO ENGINEERS

Jamal Seifi
*DR. JAMAL SEIFI &
ASSOCIATES*

Encyeh Seyed Sadr
*INTERNATIONAL LAW OFFICE
OF DR. BEHROOZ AKHLAGHI &
ASSOCIATES*

Mariam Sahrabin
KHADEM GROUP

Mir Shahbiz Shafe'e
*DR. JAMAL SEIFI &
ASSOCIATES*

Cyrus Shafizadeh
TAVAKOLI & SHAHABI

Javad Bahar Shanjani
FARJAM LAW OFFICE

Farzan Shirranbeigi
TEHRAN MUNICIPALITY

Ebrahim Tavakoli
TAVAKOLI & SHAHABI

Vrej Torossian
*TOROSSIAN, AVANESSIAN &
ASSOCIATE*

Nasrin Zandi

Mahmoud Zirak
BANK TEJARAT OF IRAN

IRAQ

Hadeel Salih Abboud
Al-Janabi
*MENA ASSOCIATES,
MEMBER OF AMERELLER
RECHTSANWÄLTE*

Nisreen Abdul Hadi Al
Hamirie
*NEW IRAQ FOR LEGAL
PRACTICE AND CONSULTANCY*

Salman Al Doushan
Abu-Ghazaleh Legal - (TAG-Legal)

Mohammad Al Jabouri
Abu-Ghazaleh Legal - (TAG-Legal)

Aziz Al Jaff
New Iraq for Legal Practice and Consultancy

Hadeel Al Janabi
Mena Associates, member of Amereller Rechtsanwälte

Ahmad Al Jannabi
Mena Associates, member of Amereller Rechtsanwälte

Farquad Al-Salman
F.H. Al-Salman & Co.

Mustafa Alshawi
Iraq Center for Economic Reform

Florian Amereller
Amereller Rechtsanwälte

Husam Addin Hatim
Gezairi Transport Iraqi Company Ltd.

Stephan Jäger
Amereller Rechtsanwälte

Imad Makki
Al Qarya Group Co.

Raed Raghib
New Iraq for Legal Practice and Consultancy

Ahmed Salih Al-Janabi
Mena Associates, member of Amereller Rechtsanwälte

IRELAND

Margaret Austin
Eugene F. Collins Solicitors

Alan Browning
LK Shields Solicitors, member of Ius Laboris

Susan Connolly
LK Shields Solicitors, member of Ius Laboris

Eoin Cunneen
LK Shields Solicitors, member of Ius Laboris

Richard Curran
LK Shields Solicitors, member of Ius Laboris

Gavin Doherty
Eugene F. Collins Solicitors

ESB Networks

Paul Glenfield
Matheson Ormsby Prentice

Micheál Grace
Mason Hayes & Curran

Thomas Jhonson
Irish Building Control Institute

William Johnston
Arthur Cox, member of Lex Mundi

Bruneau Joseph
LK Shields Solicitors, member of Ius Laboris

Margaret Masterson
PricewaterhouseCoopers

Niamh Murray
LK Shields Solicitors, member of Ius Laboris

Gavan Neary
PricewaterhouseCoopers

Regan O' Driscoll
Matheson Ormsby Prentice

Richard O'Sullivan
P.J. O'Driscolls

Judith Riordan
Mason Hayes & Curran

Brendan Sharkey
Reddy Charlton McKnight

Gavin Simons
BCM Hanby Wallace

Michael Treacy
Property Registration Authority

Colm Walsh
Irish International Freight Association

Maeve Walsh
Reddy Charlton McKnight

ISRAEL

Paul Baris
Yigal Arnon & Co.

Ofer Bar-On
Shavit Bar-On Gal-On Tzin Nov Yagur, Law Offices

Jeremy Benjamin
Goldfarb Levy Eran Meiri Tzafrir & Co.

Dina Brown
Elchanan Landau Law Offices

Yitzchak Chikorel
Deloitte

Koby Cohen
PricewaterhouseCoopers

Lior Crystal
PricewaterhouseCoopers

Danny Dilbary
Goldfarb Levy Eran Meiri Tzafrir & Co.

Ido Gonen
Goldfarb Levy Eran Meiri Tzafrir & Co.

Roee Hecht
Shavit Bar-On Gal-On Tzin Nov Yagur, Law Offices

Aaron Jaffe
Yigal Arnon & Co.

Zeev Katz
PricewaterhouseCoopers

Vered Kirshner
PricewaterhouseCoopers

Adam Klein
Goldfarb Levy Eran Meiri Tzafrir & Co.

Gideon Koren
Gideon Koren & Co. Law Offices

Orna Kornreich-Cohen
Shavit Bar-On Gal-On Tzin Nov Yagur, Law Offices

Gil Lazar
Strauss Lazer & Co, CPA's

Shlomit Lev- Ran
Gideon Fisher & Co.

Benjamin Leventhal
Gideon Fisher & Co.

Nicole Levin
Nicole Levin Law Offices

Michelle Liberman
S. Horowitz & Co., member of Lex Mundi

Chaim Nortman
Gideon Fisher & Co.

Hanit Nov
Shavit Bar-On Gal-On Tzin Nov Yagur, Law Offices

David Rosen
Idility Consulting

Matt Rosenbaum
Hacohen & Wolf Law Offices

Gerry Seligman
PricewaterhouseCoopers

Yifat Shkedi-Shatz
S. Horowitz & Co., member of Lex Mundi

Daniel Singerman
Business Data Israel + Personal Check

The Israel Electric Corporation Ltd.- Dan district

Daphna Tsarfaty
Goldfarb Levy Eran Meiri Tzafrir & Co.

Eylam Weiss
Weiss- Porat & Co.

Dave Wolf
Hacohen & Wolf Law Offices

ITALY

Allen & Overy LLP

Marianna Abbaticchio
Ristuccia & Tufarelli

Fabrizio Acerbis
PricewaterhouseCoopers

Alberto Angeloni
Studio Legale Tributario Associato

APL

Roberto Argeri
Cleary Gottlieb Steen & Hamilton LLP

Gaetano Arnò
TLS / PricewaterhouseCoopers Legal Services

Maria Pia Ascenzo
Bank of Italy

Romina Ballanca
PricewaterhouseCoopers

Paola Barazzetta
TLS / PricewaterhouseCoopers Legal Services

Gianluigi Baroni
TLS / PricewaterhouseCoopers Legal Services

Matteo Bascelli
Orrick, Herrington & Sutcliffe LLP

Susanna Beltramo
Studio Legale Beltramo

Stefano Biagioli
TLS / PricewaterhouseCoopers Legal Services

Guido Boni
European University Institute

Gianluca Borghetto
Nunziante Magrone

Carlo Bruno
Ashurst

Sergio Calderara
Almaviva S.p.A. / G.Matica S.r.l.

Alessandro Cardia
Grieco e Associati

Cecilia Carrara
Legance

Stefano Cesati
Pirola Pennuto Zei Associati

Giorgio Cherubini
Pirola Pennuto Zei Associati

Domenico Colella
Portolano Colella Cavallo Studio Legale

Fabrizio Colonna
CBA Studio Legale e Tributario

Mattia Colonnelli de Gasperis
Lombardi Molinari e Associati Studio Legale

Barbara Corsetti
Portolano Colella Cavallo

Filippo Corsini
Chiomenti Studio Legale

CRIF S. P. A.

Salvatore Cuzzocrea
PricewaterhouseCoopers

Elena Davanzo
Studio Legale Tributario Associato

Antonio de Martinis
Spasaro De Martinis Law Firm

Claudio Di Falco
Cleary Gottlieb Steen & Hamilton LLP

Massimo Diterlizzi
Pirola Pennuto Zei Associati

Carlo Falcetto
Nunziante Magrone

Pier Andrea Fré Torelli Massini
Carabba & Partners

Leonardo Giani
Norton Rose Studio Legale

Vincenzo Giannantonio
Ashurst

Vincenzo Fabrizio Giglio
Studio Legale Giglio

Antonio Grieco
Grieco e Associati

Paolo Grondona
Norton Rose

Valentino Guarini
TLS / PricewaterhouseCoopers Legal Services

Federico Guasti
Studio Legale Guasti

Goffredo Guerra
Studio Legale Tributario Associato

Christian Iannacccone
Studio Legale Tributario Associato

Francesco Iodice
Cleary Gottlieb Steen & Hamilton LLP

Giovanni Izzo
Abbatescianni Studio Legale e Tributario

Maurizio Lauri
MUC Consulting Group, a member firm of Russell Bedford International

Paolo Lucarini
PricewaterhouseCoopers

Stefano Macchi di Cellere
Jones Day

Barbara Magni
CBA Studio Legale e Tributario

Cristiano Martinez
Orrick, Herrington & Sutcliffe LLP

Patrizia Masselli
Cleary Gottlieb Steen & Hamilton LLP

Gennaro Mazzuoccolo
Norton Rose

Riccardo Micheli
Ristuccia & Tufarelli

Elena Morini
TLS / PricewaterhouseCoopers Legal Services

Francesco Nuzzolo
PricewaterhouseCoopers

Anna Oneto
Norton Rose

Luciano Panzani
Supreme Court

Paolo Pasqualis

Giovanni Patti
Abbatescianni Studio Legale e Tributario

Cristina Pellegrino
Studio Legale Macchi di Cellere Gangemi

Federica Peres
Portolano Colella Cavallo

Michael Poole
Norton Rose Studio Legale

Laura Prosperetti
Cleary Gottlieb Steen & Hamilton LLP

Giuseppe Antonio Recchia
University of Bari

Marianna Ristuccia
Ristuccia & Tufarelli

Tommaso Edoardo Romolotti
CBA Studio Legale e Tributario

Carlo Umberto Rossi
Rossi Budelli Law Firm

Giovanni B. Sandicchi
Cleary Gottlieb Steen & Hamilton LLP

Lamberto Schiona
Studio Legale Schiona

SDV Logistics Ltd.

Massimiliano Silvetti
Nunziante Magrone

Jessica Smith
CLEARY GOTTLIEB STEEN &
HAMILTON LLP

Piervincenzo Spasaro
SPASARO DE MARTINIS LAW
FIRM

Maria Antonietta Tanico
STUDIO LEGALE TANICO

TEDIOLI LAW FIRM

Francesca Tironi
TLS /
PRICEWATERHOUSECOOPERS
LEGAL SERVICES

Franco Toffoletto
TOFFOLETTO E SOCI LAW
FIRM, MEMBER OF IUS LABORIS

Luca Trovato
CURTIS MALLET - PREVOST,
COLT & MOSLE LLP

Luca Tufarelli
RISTUCCIA & TUFARELLI

Luca Valdameri
PIROLA PENNUTO ZEI
ASSOCIATI

Mario Valentini
PIROLA PENNUTO ZEI
ASSOCIATI

Matilde Vergallo
ORRICK, HERRINGTON &
SUTCLIFFE LLP

Vito Vittore
NUNZIANTE MAGRONE

Angelo Zambelli
DEWEY & LEBOEUF

Filippo Zucchinelli
TLS /
PRICEWATERHOUSECOOPERS
LEGAL SERVICES

JAMAICA

Christopher Bovell
DUNNCOX

Theresa Bowen
LEX CARIBBEAN

Robert Colliy
MYERS, FLETCHER & GORDON,
MEMBER OF LEX MUNDI

Natalie Farrell-Ross
MYERS, FLETCHER & GORDON,
MEMBER OF LEX MUNDI

Nicole Foga
FOGA DALEY

Dave García
MYERS, FLETCHER & GORDON,
MEMBER OF LEX MUNDI

Stephanie Gordon
LEX CARIBBEAN

Herbert Winston Grant
GRANT, STEWART, PHILLIPS
& CO.

Errol Greene
KINGSTON AND ST. ANDREW
CORPORATION

Corrine N. Henry
MYERS, FLETCHER & GORDON,
MEMBER OF LEX MUNDI

S. Hudson
JAMAICA TRADE AND INVEST

Alicia P. Hussey
MYERS, FLETCHER & GORDON,
MEMBER OF LEX MUNDI

Anthony Jenkinson
NUNES, SCHOLEFIELD DELEON
& CO.

Grace Lindo
MYERS, FLETCHER & GORDON,
MEMBER OF LEX MUNDI

Noelle Llewellyn Heron
TAX ADMINISTRATION
SERVICES DEPARTMENT

Andrine McLaren
KINGSTON AND ST. ANDREW
CORPORATION

Natalie Messado
CLAYTON MORGAN AND
COMPANY

Sandra Minott-Phillips
MYERS, FLETCHER & GORDON,
MEMBER OF LEX MUNDI

Janet Morgan
DUNNCOX

Gina Phillipps-Black
MYERS, FLETCHER & GORDON,
MEMBER OF LEX MUNDI

Hilary Reid
MYERS, FLETCHER & GORDON,
MEMBER OF LEX MUNDI

Anneke Rousseau
JAMAICA CUSTOMS
DEPARTMENT

Heather Rowe
JAMAICA PUBLIC SERVICE
COMPANY LIMITED

Lisa N. Russell
MYERS, FLETCHER & GORDON,
MEMBER OF LEX MUNDI

Arturo Stewart
GRANT, STEWART, PHILLIPS
& CO.

Paul Tai
NUNES, SCHOLEFIELD DELEON
& CO.

Humprey Taylor
TAYLOR CONSTRUCTION LTD.

Sophia Williams
NATIONAL LAND AGENCY

Maliaca Wong
MYERS, FLETCHER & GORDON,
MEMBER OF LEX MUNDI

JAPAN

ALLEN & OVERY GAIKOKUHO
KYODO

APL

Miho Arimura
HATASAWA & WAKAI LAW
FIRM

CREDIT INFORMATION CENTER
CORP.

Toyoki Emoto
ATSUMI & PARTNERS

Mijo Fujita
ADACHI, HENDERSON,
MIYATAKE & FUJITA

Tastuya Fukui
ATSUMI & PARTNERS

Shigeru Hasegawa
ZEIRISHI-HOJIN
PRICEWATERHOUSECOOPERS

Tamotsu Hatasawa
HATASAWA & WAKAI LAW
FIRM

Akiko Hiraoka
ATSUMI & PARTNERS

Taro Honda
ATSUMI & PARTNERS

Rie Imai
O'MELVENY & MYERS LLP

Yuko Inui
ORRICK, HERRINGTON &
SUTCLIFFE LLP

Michiya Iwasaki
ATSUMI & PARTNERS

Hideki Thurgood Kano
ANDERSON MORI &
TOMOTSUNE

Susumi Kawaguchi
OBAYASHI CORPORATION

Kotaku Kimu
ZEIRISHI-HOJIN
PRICEWATERHOUSECOOPERS

Yukie Kurosawa
O'MELVENY & MYERS LLP

Yoji Maeda
O'MELVENY & MYERS LLP

Nobuaki Matsuoka
OSAKA INTERNATIONAL LAW
OFFICES

Toshio Miyatake
ADACHI, HENDERSON,
MIYATAKE & FUJITA

Michihiro Mori
NISHIMURA & ASAHI

Takafumi Nihei
NISHIMURA & ASAHI

Kazutoshi Nishijima
ADACHI, HENDERSON,
MIYATAKE & FUJITA

Takuji Nozaka
ATSUMI & PARTNERS

Naoko Sato
ANDERSON MORI &
TOMOTSUNE

Takefumi Sato
ANDERSON MORI &
TOMOTSUNE

Tetsuro Sato
BAKER & MCKENZIE

Yoshihito Shibata
BINGHAM MCCUTCHEN
MURASE, SAKAI & MIMURA
FOREIGN LAW JOINT
ENTERPRISE

Sachiko Sugawara
ATSUMI & PARTNERS

Eri Sugihara
NISHIMURA & ASAHI

Hidetaka Sumomogi
NISHIMURA & ASAHI

Hiroyuki Suzuki
ZEIRISHI-HOJIN
PRICEWATERHOUSECOOPERS

Yuri Suzuki
ATSUMI & PARTNERS

Hiroaki Takahashi
ATSUMI & PARTNERS

Chikako Tamakoshi
ATSUMI & PARTNERS

Junichi Tobimatsu
MORI HAMADA &
MATSUMOTO

Yoshiki Tsurumaki
ATSUMI & PARTNERS

Masatoshi Ujimori
ATSUMI & PARTNERS

Jun Yamada
ANDERSON MORI &
TOMOTSUNE

Michi Yamagami
ANDERSON MORI &
TOMOTSUNE

Akio Yamamoto
KAJIMA CORPORATION

Kazuhiro Yanagida
NISHIMURA & ASAHI

Ishizuka Yoichi
GRANT THORNTON LLP

JORDAN

Anas Abunameh
LAW & ARBITRATION CENTRE

Maha Al Abdallat
CENTRAL BANK OF JORDAN

Eman M. Al-Dabbas
INTERNATIONAL BUSINESS
LEGAL ASSOCIATES

Arafat Alfayoumi
CENTRAL BANK OF JORDAN

Omar Aljazy
ALJAZY & CO.ADVOCATES &
LEGAL CONSULTANTS

Sabri S. Al-Khassib
AMMAN CHAMBER OF
COMMERCE

Micheal T. Dabit
MICHAEL T. DABIT &
ASSOCIATES

Anwar Elliyan
THE JORDANIAN ELECTRIC
POWER CO. LTD. (JEPCO)

GREATER AMMAN
MUNICIPALITY

Tariq Hammouri
HAMMOURI & PARTNERS

George Hazboun

Ra'ied Hiassat
LAND AND SURVEY
DIRECTORATE

Tayseer Ismail
EAST ECHO CO.

Zeina Jaradat
PRICEWATERHOUSECOOPERS

Basel Karwa
KAWAR TRANSPORT AND
TRANSIT- KARGO

Enad Khirfan
ALI SHARIF ZU'BI, ADVOCATES
& LEGAL CONSULTANTS,
MEMBER OF LEX MUNDI

Rasha Laswi
ZALLOUM & LASWI LAW FIRM

Husam Jamil Madanat
LAND AND SURVEY
DIRECTORATE

Firas Malhas
INTERNATIONAL BUSINESS
LEGAL ASSOCIATES

Amer Mofleh
INTERNATIONAL BUSINESS
LEGAL ASSOCIATES

Amer Nabulsi
DLA PIPER

Mustfa Nasserddin
ABU-GHAZALEH LEGAL -
(TAG-LEGAL)

Mutasem Nsair
KHALIFEH & PARTNERS

Osama Y. Sabbagh
THE JORDANIAN ELECTRIC
POWER CO. LTD. (JEPCO)

Mohammad Sawafeen
LAND AND SURVEY
DIRECTORATE

Mazen Shotar
DEPARTMENT OF LANDS AND
SURVEY

Stephan Stephan
PRICEWATERHOUSECOOPERS

Abu Mariam Tarek
ABU-GHAZALEH LEGAL -
(TAG-LEGAL)

Azzam Zalloum
ZALLOUM & LASWI LAW FIRM

Kareem Zureikat
ALI SHARIF ZU'BI, ADVOCATES
& LEGAL CONSULTANTS,
MEMBER OF LEX MUNDI

KAZAKHSTAN

Timur Abdreimov
FEDEX

Askar Abubakirov
AEQUITAS LAW FIRM

Kirill Afanasyev
KAZAKHSTAN CONSULTING

Zulfiya Akchurina
GRATA LAW FIRM

Anvar Akhmedov
FIRST CREDIT BUREAU

Sabina Barayeva
JS VENTURE INVESTMENT
FUND JSC

Ildus Bariev
GLOBALINK LOGISTICS GROUP

Jypar Beishenalieva
MICHAEL WILSON & PARTNERS
LTD.

Assel Bekturganova
GRATA LAW FIRM

Irina Chen
M&M LOGISTICS

Almaz Dosserbekov

Ardak Dyussembayeva
AEQUITAS LAW FIRM

Kim Tatyana Feliksovna
MARKA AUDIT ACF LLP

Courtney Fowler
PRICEWATERHOUSECOOPERS

Vladimir P. Furman
MCGUIRE WOODS LLP

Assel Gilmanova
GRATA LAW FIRM

Oleg Gnoevykh
M&M LOGISTICS

Natalya Grinkevich
RBS

Semion Issyk
AEQUITAS LAW FIRM

Dinara M. Jarmukhanova
MCGUIRE WOODS LLP

Thomas Johnson
DENTON WILDE SAPTE

Mariyash Kabikenova
REHABILITATION MANAGER

Pasha Karim
GLOBALINK LOGISTICS GROUP

Assel Kazbekova
MICHAEL WILSON & PARTNERS
LTD.

Alexander Kurganov
M&M LOGISTICS

Vsevolod Markov
MCGUIRE WOODS LLP

Bolat Miyatov
Grata Law Firm

Assel Musina
Denton Wilde Sapte

Esenbaer Karabi Nuriuly
Urban Planning and Architecture Department of City of Almaty

Yuliya Penzova
Aequitas Law Firm

Saniya Perzadayeva
Macleod Dixon

Yuliya V. Petrenko
McGuire Woods LLP

Aliya Prenova
Michael Wilson & Partners Ltd.

Elvis Robert
M&M Logistics

Asem Shaidildinova
PricewaterhouseCoopers Tax and Advisory LLP

Timur M. Suleimenov
Ministry of Economy and Budget Planning

Tatyana Suleyeva
Aequitas Law Firm

Zhaniya Ussen
Assistance, LLC Law Firm

Yekaterina V. Kim
Michael Wilson & Partners Ltd.

Michael Wilson
Michael Wilson & Partners Ltd.

Mario Wolosz
Kazakhstan Consulting

Dubek Zhabykenov
BA Services International LLC

Danat Zhakenov
Zhakenov & Partners in association with Grundberg Mocatta Rakison

Valerie A. Zhakenov
Zhakenov & Partners in association with Grundberg Mocatta Rakison

KENYA

Abdulwahid Aboo
Abdulwahid Aboo & Company, a member firm of Russell Bedford International

George Arego
Siginon Freight Ltd

Anil Madhavan Changwony
Siginon Freight Ltd

Oliver Fowler
Kaplan & Stratton

Peter Gachuhi
Kaplan & Stratton

Wahu Gathuita
Muriu Mungai & Co Advocates

Francis Gichuhi
Prism Designs Africa

Edmond Gichuru
Post Bank

William Ikutha Maema
Iseme, Kamau & Maema Advocates

Shellomith Irungu
Anjarwalla & Khanna Advocates

Nigel Jeremy
Daly & Figgis Advocates

James Kamau
Iseme, Kamau & Maema Advocates

Patrick Karara
PricewaterhouseCoopers

Judith Kavuki
SCI Koimburi Tucker & Co.

Hamish Keith
Daly & Figgis Advocates

Luke Kenei
Siginon Freight Ltd

Peter Kiara
Peter Kiara- Individual Architect

Morris Kimuli
B.M. Musau & Co. Advocates

Francis Kinyua
Muriu Mungai & Co Advocates

Felix Kioko
B.M. Musau & Co. Advocates

Meshack T. Kipturgo
Siginon Freight Ltd

Owen Koimburi
SCI Koimburi Tucker & Co.

Alexandra Kontos
Walker Kontos Advocates

Georgina Kurutu
SCI Koimburi Tucker & Co.

Gilbert Langat
Kenya Shippers Council

Anthony Maina
Ameritrans Freight International

Georges Maina
Ameritrans Freight International

Victor Majani
Osoro and Co, Certified Public Accountants

Nicholas Malonza
B.M. Musau & Co. Advocates

Rosemary Mburu
Institute of Trade Development

Evelyn Mukhebi
PricewaterhouseCoopers

Peter Mungai
Siginon Freight Ltd

Murigu Murithi
ARCS Africa

Benjamin Musyimi
Alexandria Freight Forwarders Ltd.

Washington Muthamia
Alexandria Freight Forwarders Ltd.

Anthony Mwangi
Ameritrans Freight International

Wachira Ndege
Credit Reference Bureau Africa Ltd.

Christina Ndiho
Kaplan & Stratton

James Ngomeli
The Kenya Power and Lighting Company Ltd.

Beatrice Nyabira
Iseme, Kamau & Maema Advocates

Julia Nyaga
Kaplan & Stratton

Bosire Nyamori
Iseme, Kamau & Maema Advocates

Stephen Okello
PricewaterhouseCoopers

Metropol East Africa Ltd.

Moses Osano Osoro
Muriu Mungai & Co Advocates

Cephas Osoro
Osoro and Co, Certified Public Accountants

Don Priestman
The Kenya Power and Lighting Company Ltd.

Dominic Rebelo
Daly & Figgis Advocates

Ruman shipcontractors Limited

Sonal Sejpal
Anjarwalla & Khanna Advocates

Rodgers Abwire Sekwe
Muriu Mungai & Co Advocates

Deepen Shah
Walker Kontos Advocates

John Syekei Nyandieka
Muriu Mungai & Co Advocates

David Tanki
Lan-X Africa Ltd.

Joseph Taracha
Central Bank of Kenya

Adrian Topoti
B.M. Musau & Co. Advocates

Samuel Wainaina
Kaplan & Stratton

KIRIBATI

Kenneth Barden

Rawbeta Beniata
Office of the People's Lawyer

William Wylie Clarke

Anita Jowitt
University of the South Pacific

Lawrence Muller
Betio City Council

Ports Authority

Matereta Raiman
Ministry of Finance & Economic Development

Batira Tekanito
Development Bank of Kiribati

KOREA, REP.

Dong-Ook Byun
Korea Customs Service

Min-Sook Chae
Korea Credit Bureau

Hyeong-Tae Cho
Samil PricewaterhouseCoopers

Sun Joo Cho
YEJIN

Han-Jun Chon
Samil PricewaterhouseCoopers

Eui Jong Chung
Bae, Kim & Lee LLC

Sean C. Hayes
Ahnse Law Offices

Joong Hoon Kwak
Lee & Ko

Ju Myung Hwang
Hwang Mok Park P.C., member of Lex Mundi

C.W. Hyun
Kim & Chang

James I.S. Jeon
Sojong Partners

Bo-Sup Kim
Korea Credit Bureau

Gee-Hong Kim
Jisung Horizon

Hye-Jin Kim
Korea Credit Bureau

Jung-In Kim
Korea Credit Bureau

Keunyeop Kim
Panalpina IAF Ltd.

Kum-Sun Kim
Sojong Partners

Kyu-Dong Kim
Samil PricewaterhouseCoopers

S.E. Stephan Kim
Sojong Partners

Wonhyung Kim
Yoon Yang Kim Shin & Yu

Ki Hyun Kwon
Cheon Ji Accounting Corporation, a member firm of Russell Bedford International

Hye Jeong Lee
Ahnse Law Offices

Jin-Young Lee
Samil PricewaterhouseCoopers

Jung Myung Lee
Hwang Mok Park P.C., member of Lex Mundi

Kyu Wha Lee
Lee & Ko

Sung Whan Lee
Ahnse Law Offices

Sun-Kyoo Lee
Samil PricewaterhouseCoopers

Ji Woong Lim
Yulchon

Byung-Hun Nam
NamSun Industries Co.

Yon-Kyun Oh
Kim & Chang

Jung-Taek Park
Kim & Chang

Sang Il Park
Hwang Mok Park P.C., member of Lex Mundi

Soo-Hwan Park
Samil PricewaterhouseCoopers

Ae-Ryun Rho
Kim & Chang

Jeong Seo
Kim & Chang

Yoo Soon Shim
Cheon Ji Accounting Corporation, a member firm of Russell Bedford International

Yong-Sock
PANKO Corporation

Won-Il Sohn
Yulchon

Jin-Ho Song
Kim & Chang

Ki Won Suh
Cheon Ji Accounting Corporation, a member firm of Russell Bedford International

Dong-Suk Wang
Korea Credit Bureau

Dong Soo Yang
Hwang Mok Park P.C., member of Lex Mundi

Jee Yeon Yu
Kim & Chang

KOSOVO

Adem Ajvazi
Commercial Court

Allied Pickfords

Erion Bejko
KPMG

Agron E. Beka
Immobilia

Xhevdet Beqiri
KPMG

Imer Berisha
Koslex

Shyqiri Bttyqi
Boga & Associates

John Burns
KPMG

Customs Administration

Sokol Elmazaj
Boga & Associates

Maliq Gjyshinca
Intereuropa

Musa Gashi
Customs

Mustafa Hasani
Kosovo Investment Promotion Agency

Ahmet Hasolli
Kalo & Associates

Menagjer Rarhim Hoxha
ISARS

Virtyt Ibrahimaga
Dr. Krieg & Kollegen

Albert Islami
Albert Islami & Partners

Ali Ismajli
Customs

Bejtush Isufi
LEKA COMPANY J.S.C

Besarta Kllokoqi
BOGA & ASSOCIATES

Arben Mustafa
INTEREUROPA

Gazmend Pallaska
PALLASKA & ASSOCIATES

Naim Sahiti
*KOSOVO ENERGY
CORPORATION J.S.C.*

Agron Selimaj
SELIMAJ LAW OFFICE

Iliriana Osmani Serreqi
AVOKATURA OSMANI

Jeton Vokshi
INTEREUROPA

Shaha Zylfiu
*CENTRAL BANK OF THE
REPUBLIC OF KOSOVO*

KUWAIT

Labeed Abdal
*THE LAW FIRM OF LABEED
ABDAL*

Amal Abdallah
AL-SALEH & PARTNERS

Mahmoud Abdulfattah
*THE LAW OFFICES OF MISHARI
AL-GHAZALI*

Waleed Abdulrahim
*ABDULLAH KH. AL-AYOUB &
ASSOCIATES, MEMBER OF LEX
MUNDI*

Lina A.K. Adlouni
*ABDULLAH AL-AYOUB
ABDULLAH KH. AL-AYOUB &
ASSOCIATES, MEMBER OF LEX
MUNDI*

Mishari M. Al-Ghazali
*THE LAW OFFICES OF MISHARI
AL-GHAZALI*

*AL-TWAIJRI & PARTNERS LAW
FIRM (TLF)*

Firas Al-Saifi
*ABU-GHAZALEH LEGAL -
(TAG-LEGAL)*

Abdullah Bin Ali
*PACKAGING AND PLASTIC
INDUSTRIES CO. (KSC)*

Paul Day
AL SARRAF & AL RUWAYEH

Nazih Abdul Hameed
AL-SALEH & PARTNERS

Sunil Jose
*ABU-GHAZALEH LEGAL -
(TAG-LEGAL)*

Mazen A. Khoursheed
*PACKAGING AND PLASTIC
INDUSTRIES CO. (KSC)*

Chirine Krayem Moujaes
*THE LAW OFFICES OF MISHARI
AL-GHAZALI*

Dany Labaky
*THE LAW OFFICES OF MISHARI
AL-GHAZALI*

Medhat M. Mubarak
AL-SALEH & PARTNERS

Anupama Nair
*ABDULLAH KH. AL-AYOUB &
ASSOCIATES, MEMBER OF LEX
MUNDI*

KYRGYZ REPUBLIC

Kunduz Abdaldieva
JDN CO

Kadyr Kubanovich Abykeev
*CONSTRUCTION COMPANY
'AVANGARD STYLE' LTD*

Gulnara Ahmatova
*INTERNATIONAL BUSINESS
COUNCIL*

Jannat Aidazalieva
GLOBALINK LOGISTICS GROUP

Niyazbek Aldashev
LORENZ LAW FIRM

Natalia Alenkina
CONSULTANT HOLDING

Bakyt Asanov
TEXTONIC CJSC

Zharkymbai Muktarovich
Baiganchuk
*CONSTRUCTION COMPANY
'KEP-STROI" LTD*

Turar Bekbolotov
LAW FIRM ÌPARTNERÎ

Bekbolot Bekiev

Andrei Georgievich Dogadin
*ENTREPRENEURS' UNION OF
KYRGYZSTAN*

Natalia Dolinskaya
*INTERNATIONAL BUSINESS
COUNCIL*

Akjoltoi Elebesova
*CREDIT INFORMATION BUREAU
ISHENIM*

Courtney Fowler
PRICEWATERHOUSECOOPERS

Valeria Getman
*UNION OF ACCOUNTANTS AND
AUDITORS*

Dmitriy Gorachek
BUSINESS KLERK

Anatoliy Inishenko
*NOGARO LTD., CARGO
EXPEDITION*

Jarkynai Isaeva
LAW FIRM PARTNER

Nurilya Isaeva
LORENZ LAW FIRM

Saltanat Ismailova
PRICEWATERHOUSECOOPERS

Nurbek Ismankulov
*M&M TRANSPORT LOGISTIC
SERVICES*

Ruslan Kagirov
ASIA UNIVERSAL BANK

Gulnara Kalikova
*KALIKOVA & ASSOCIATES LAW
FIRM*

Liudmila Kasyanova

Bella Kazakbaeva
LAW FIRM LEX

Vitaliy Khabarov
LAW FIRM PARTNER

Diana Kim
"PARTNER" REAL ESTATE FIRM

Tatyana Kim
*CHAMBER OF TAX
CONSULTANTS*

Galina Kucheryavaya
*DEMIR KYRGYZ
INTERNATIONAL BANK*

Anna Litvinova
BUREAU OF TAX CONSULTANTS

Barno Marazykova
LAW FIRM ÌPARTNERÎ

Tatyana Marchenko
LORENZ LAW FIRM

Anara Mukasheva
SWEDESURVEY

Almas Nakipov
PRICEWATERHOUSECOOPERS

Karlygash Ospankulova
*KALIKOVA & ASSOCIATES LAW
FIRM*

Ekaterina Rumyantseva
CONSULTANT HOLDING

Nurbek Sabirov
*KALIKOVA & ASSOCIATES LAW
FIRM*

Aida Satylganova
*KALIKOVA & ASSOCIATES LAW
FIRM*

Anastasia Shloeva
GLOBALINK LOGISTICS GROUP

Maksim Smirnov
*KALIKOVA & ASSOCIATES LAW
FIRM*

Alina Stamova
*KYRGYZ INVESTMENT CREDIT
BANK*

Aibek Tolubaev
KYRGYZ STOCK EXCHANGE

Ermek Umankulov
ASIA UNIVERSAL BANK

Gulnara Uskenbaeva
ALPHA SHEERSFIELD

Azim Usmanov
GRATA LAW FIRM

Raisa Usupova
*CHAMBER OF TAX
CONSULTANTS*

Alexander Alexandrovich
Vachtel
SENTYABR STROI LTD

Bakai Zhunushov
iCAP INVESTMENT

LAO PDR

Chan Chan
DEXTRATRANSPORT

Lasonexay Chanthavong
DFDL MEKONG LAW GROUP

Sounthorn Chanthavong
DFDL MEKONG LAW GROUP

Erin Dann
LAO BAR ASSOCIATION

Aristotle David
DFDL MEKONG LAW GROUP

Daodeuane Duangdara
PRICEWATERHOUSECOOPERS

Grant Follett
DFDL MEKONG LAW GROUP

Walter Heiser
DFDL MEKONG LAW GROUP

Trasane Inpeng
KPMG LAO CO. LTD

Richard Irwin
PRICEWATERHOUSECOOPERS

Ganesan Kolandevelu
KPMG LAO CO. LTD

Darika Kriengsuntikul
PRICEWATERHOUSECOOPERS

Somphone Lakenchanh
LAO BAR ASSOCIATION

Chris Manley
DFDL MEKONG LAW GROUP

Ketsana Phommachanh
*MINISTRY OF JUSTICE,
LAW RESEARCH AND
INTERNATIONAL COOPERATION
INSTITUTE*

Thavorn Rujivanarom
PRICEWATERHOUSECOOPERS

Vichit Sadettan
*LAO FREIGHT FORWARDER
CO. LTD.*

Siri Sayavong
LAO LAW & CONSULTANCY

Sivath Sengdouangchanh

Senesakoune Sihanouvong
DFDL MEKONG LAW GROUP

Khamphone Sipaseuth
MINISTRY OF JUSTICE

Khamphui Sisomphone
*LEGAL AID CLINIC, LAO BAR
ASSOCIATION*

Vilasay Songvilay
*LEGAL AID CLINIC, LAO BAR
ASSOCIATION*

Danyel Thomson
DFDL MEKONG LAW GROUP

Kerrod Thomas
*ANZ VIENTIANE COMMERCIAL
BANK LTD*

Sengdara Tiamtisack
*LAO FREIGHT FORWARDER
CO. LTD.*

Andrea Wilson
DFDL MEKONG LAW GROUP

LATVIA

Ilze Abika
*SKUDRA & UDRIS LAW
OFFICES*

Martins Aljens
RAIDLA LEJINS & NORCOUS

Laura Ausekle
LATVIJAS BANKA

Elina Bedanova
RAIDLA LEJINS & NORCOUS

Iveta Berzina
*SKUDRA & UDRIS LAW
OFFICES*

Zana Bule
KLAVINS & SLAIDINS LAWIN

Andis Burkevics
SORAINEN

Andis Čonka
LATVIJAS BANKA

Ainis Dabols
*LATVIAN ASSOCIATION OF TAX
ADVISERS*

Artis Dobrovolskis
KLAVINS & SLAIDINS LAWIN

Dace Drice
KLAVINS & SLAIDINS LAWIN

Zane Džule
LIEPA, SKOPIŅA/ BORENIUS

Elina Eihentale
*LATVIAN ASSOCIATION OF TAX
ADVISERS*

Zlata Elksnina-Zascirinska
PRICEWATERHOUSECOOPERS

Valters Gencs
GENCS VALTERS LAW FIRM

Aigars Gozitis
RAIDLA LEJINS & NORCOUS

Andris Ignatenko
ESTMA LTD

Janis Irbe
LATVENERGO AS

Aija Klavinska
PRICEWATERHOUSECOOPERS

Dainis Leons
SADALES TĪKLS AS

Indrikis Liepa
LIEPA, SKOPIŅA/ BORENIUS

Zane Paeglite
SORAINEN

Ivars Pommers
*LAW FIRM OF GLIMSTEDT AND
PARTNERS*

Sergejs Rudans
LIEPA, SKOPIŅA/ BORENIUS

Dace Silava-Tomsone
RAIDLA LEJINS & NORCOUS

Marcis Skadmanis
*LAW OFFICE "BLUEGER AND
PLAUDE"*

Sarmis Spilbergs
KLAVINS & SLAIDINS LAWIN

Zane Štālberga – Markvarte
*MARKVARTE LEXCHANGE LAW
OFFICE*

Marite Straume-Cerbule
RE & RE LTD.

Brigita Terauda
SORAINEN

Ziedonis Udris
*SKUDRA & UDRIS LAW
OFFICES*

Maris Vainovskis
*EVERSHEDS BITĀNS -
ATTORNEYS-AT-LAW*

Vilmars Vanags
RE & RE LTD.

Maija Volkova
RAIDLA LEJINS & NORCOUS

Daiga Zivtina
KLAVINS & SLAIDINS LAWIN

LEBANON

Wadih Abou Nasr
PRICEWATERHOUSECOOPERS

Soha Al Masri
*ABU-GHAZALEH LEGAL -
(TAG-LEGAL)*

Manal Assir
UNDP

Maya Atieh
ADIB & HOUALLA LAW OFFICE

Antoine Baaklini
BAB INTERNATIONAL

Tarek Baz
HYAM G. MALLAT LAW FIRM

Katia Bou Assi
*MOGHAIZEL LAW FIRM,
MEMBER OF LEX MUNDI*

Rita Bou Habib
*AUDIT DEPARTMENT - VAT
DIRECTORATE*

Najib Choucair
CENTRAL BANK OF LEBANON

Sanaa Daakour
THE LEVANT LAWYERS

Bassam Darwich
P & G Levant

Michel Doueihy
Badri and Salim El Meouchi Law Firm, member of Interleges

Electricité du Liban

Eddy El-Maghariki
Attayyar Law Firm in association with Alem & Associates

Chadia El Meouchi
Badri and Salim El Meouchi Law Firm, member of Interleges

Tarek Farran
Farran Law Firm

Dania George
PricewaterhouseCoopers

Samer Ghalayini
The Levant Lawyers

Abdallah Hayek
Hayek Group

Walid Honein
Badri and Salim El Meouchi Law Firm, member of Interleges

Maher Hoteit
The Levant Lawyers

Chawkat Houalla
Adib & Houalla Law Office

Dany Issa
Moghaizel Law Firm, member of Lex Mundi

Marie-Anne Jabbour
Badri and Salim El Meouchi Law Firm, member of Interleges

Fady Jamaleddine
The Levant Lawyers

Elie Kachouh
ELC Transport Services SAL

Georges Kadige
Kadige & Kadige Law Firm

Michel Kadige
Kadige & Kadige Law Firm

Najib Khattar
Khattar Associates

Georges Mallat
Hyam G. Mallat Law Firm

Nabil Mallat
Hyam G. Mallat Law Firm

Rachad Medawar
Obeid & Medawar Law Firm

Joseph Merhy
Central Bank of Lebanon

Fadi Moghaizel
Moghaizel Law Firm, member of Lex Mundi

Mario Mohanna
Patrimoine Conseil SARL

Mirvat Mostafa
The Levant Lawyers

Rania Mrad
Khattar Associates

Toufic Nehme
Law Office of Albert Laham

Mireille Richa
Tyan & Zgheib Law Firm

Jihane Rizk Khattar
Khattar Associates

Jihad Rizkallah
Badri and Salim El Meouchi Law Firm, member of Interleges

Rached Sarkis
Rached Sarkis Office

Camille C. Sifri
PricewaterhouseCoopers

Nady Tyan
Tyan & Zgheib Law Firm

Patricia Yammine
PricewaterhouseCoopers

Rania Yazbeck
Tyan & Zgheib Law Firm

LESOTHO

Harley & Morris

Lebereko Lethobane
Labour Court

Qhalehang Letsika
Mei & Mei Attorneys Inc.

Bokang Makhaketso
Mofolo, Tau - Thabane and Co.

Tseliso Daniel Makhaphela
Ministry of Local Government

Thakane Makume
Lesotho Electricity Company (Pty) Ltd

Maseru Electro Services Pty Ltd

Mathias Matshe
Sheeran & Associates

Denis Molyneaux
Webber Newdigate

Kuena Mophethe
K. Mophethe Law Chambers

Theodore Ntlatlapa
DNT Architects

Jerry Padi

A.R.Thabiso Ramokoena
NedBank Lesotho Ltd.

Duduzile Seamatha
Sheeran & Associates

Lindiwe Sephomolo
Association of Lesotho Employers and Business

Phoka Thene
Sello-Mafatle Attorneys

LIBERIA

Kelvin Abdallah
PricewaterhouseCoopers

Christian Allison
Central Bank of Liberia

Amos P. Andrews
EcoBank

Landry Bedell
Safeway Cargo Handling SVG

Amos Z. Benjamin
Investors Choice International

Betty Lamin Blamol
Sherman & Sherman

Joseph N. Blidi
J. Nagbe Blidi Law firm & Consultancy, Inc.

Josephys Burgess, Sr.
Ministry of Lands, Mines & Energy

F. Augustus Caesar, Jr.
Caesar Architects, Inc.

Nelson Chineh
Magisterial Court of Monrovia

Henry Reed Cooper
Cooper & Togbah Law Firm

Sandei Cooper Jr.
Ecobank

Roland Dakagboi
Safeway Cargo Handling SVG

Frank Musah Dean
Dean & Associates

Daniel D. Doe
Liberia Water and Sewage Corporation

S. Peter Doe-Kpar
Monthly and Probate Court

Peter Doe-Sumah
Gbehzon Holdings (Liberia) Inc.

Francis S. Dopoh, II
Ministry of Finance,

Patrick S. Fallah
EcoBank

James T. Folleh
Ministry of Finance,

Christine Sonpon Freeman
Cooper & Togbah Law Firm

Deweh Gray
Female Lawyers Association of Liberia

Paul Greene
Ministry of Finance

John C. Harris
City Corporation of Monrovia

Winleta Henries Reeves
Dean & Associates

Anthony Henry
Cuttington University Graduate School

Emmanuel M. Horton
National Port Authority

David A.B. Jallah
David A.B. Jallah Law Firm

Cyril Jones
Jones & Jones

Ernest B. Jones
Ministry of Lands, Mines & Energy

Abu Kamara
Ministry of Commerce & Industry

Mussah Kamara
Central Bank of Liberia

Elijah Karnley
Ministry of Public Works

Krubo B. Kollie
Ministry of Foreign Affairs

Anthony Kumeh
Verdier and Associates

Martha Lackay
Liberia Electricity Corporation

Henry Lewis Sr.
Liberia Electricity Corporation

Jonathan Massaquoi Sr.
National Port Authority

Marie Norman
City Corporation of Monrovia

Jerome G.N. Nyenka
Environmental Protection Agency

Chan-Chan A. Paegar
Sherman & Sherman

G. Moses Paegar
Sherman & Sherman

Patrick W. Paye
City Corporation of Monrovia

Vincent Sackeyfio
Voscon, Certified Public Accountants

Bloh Sayeh
Center for National Documents & Records / National Archives

Eugene Shannon
Ministry of Lands, Mines & Energy

E. Murana Sheriff
Ministry of Lands, Mines & Energy

Joseph N. Siaway
Maersk Ltd.

Amos Siebo
Liberia Reconstruction and Development Committee

Abraham T. Swen
Ministry of Foreign Affairs

Wilson Tarpeh
University of Liberia

Sampson Toe
City Corporation of Monrovia

Nyenati Tuan
Tuan Wreh Law Firm

G. Lahaison Waritay
Ministry of Public Works

Francis Weah
Magisterial Court of Monrovia

Darcy White
PricewaterhouseCoopers

Ben Wolo
Liberia Telecommunications Corporation

Melvin Yates
Compass Inc., Clearing and Forwarding

Harvy T. Yuan, Sr.
Liberia Electricity Corporation

LITHUANIA

Petras Baltusevicius
DSV Transport UAB

Kim Bartholdy
DSV Transport UAB

Kristina Bartuseviciene
PricewaterhouseCoopers

Egidijus Bernotas
Bernotas & Dominas Glimstedt

Arturas Blotnys
Vilnius City Municipality

Andrius Bogdanovicius
JSC "Creditinfo Lietuva"

Sergej Butov
Law Firm Lideika, Petrauskas, Valiūnas ir partneriai LAWIN, member of Lex Mundi

Robertas Ciocys
Law Firm Lideika, Petrauskas, Valiūnas ir partneriai LAWIN, member of Lex Mundi

Radville Ciricaite
Foigt & Partners / Regija Borenius

Giedre Dailidenaite
BNT Attorneys APB

Vita Dauksaite
Law Firm Lideika, Petrauskas, Valiūnas ir partneriai LAWIN, member of Lex Mundi

Giedre Domkute
AAA Baltic Service Company -Law firm

Ieva Dosinaite
Raidla Lejins & Norcous

Vilma Dovidauskiene
Competent Amerinde Consolidated

Kornelija Francuzeviciute
Bank of Lithuania

Dalia Geciene
Amerinde Consolidated, Inc

Valters Gencs

Gencs Valters Law FirmNeringa Grazinyte
Sutkiene, Pilkauskas & Partners

Simas Gudynas
Law Firm Lideika, Petrauskas, Valiūnas ir partneriai LAWIN, member of Lex Mundi

Frank Heemann
BNT Attorneys APB

Egle Ivanauskaite
Law Firm Lideika, Petrauskas, Valiūnas ir partneriai LAWIN, member of Lex Mundi

Eglė Jankauskaitė
Bernotas & Dominas Glimstedt

Agne Jonaitytė
Sorainen

Julija Julija
Fortune Law Group

Povilas Junevicius
Law Firm Lideika, Petrauskas, Valiūnas ir partneriai LAWIN, member of Lex Mundi

Viktorija Kapustinskaja
Sorainen

Agne Kazlauskiene
Businesslt

Jonas Kiauleikis
Foigt & Partners / Regija Borenius

Jurate Kraujalyte
AMERINDE CONSOLIDATED, INC

Reda Kruope
LAW FIRM LIDEIKA, PETRAUSKAS, VALIŪNAS IR PARTNERIAI LAWIN, MEMBER OF LEX MUNDI

Egidijus Kundelis
PRICEWATERHOUSECOOPERS

Egle Kundrotaite
AMERINDE CONSOLIDATED, INC

Žilvinas Kvietkus
RAIDLA LEJINS & NORCOUS

Gytis Malinauskas
SORAINEN

Linas Margevicius
LEGAL BUREAU OF LINAS MARGEVICIUS

Sergej Markevic
DSV TRANSPORT UAB

Tomas Mieliauskas
LAW FIRM FORESTA

Ieva Navickaitė
LAW FIRM ZABIELA, ZABIELAITE & PARTNERS

Simona Oliškevičiūtė-Cicėnienė
LAW FIRM LIDEIKA, PETRAUSKAS, VALIŪNAS IR PARTNERIAI LAWIN, MEMBER OF LEX MUNDI

Žygimantas Pacevičius
FOIGT & PARTNERS / REGIJA BORENIUS

Rytis Paukste
LAW FIRM LIDEIKA, PETRAUSKAS, VALIŪNAS IR PARTNERIAI LAWIN, MEMBER OF LEX MUNDI

Algirdas Pekšys
SORAINEN

Laura Remeikaite
FORTUNE LAW GROUP

Gediminas Sagatys
RAIDLA LEJINS & NORCOUS

Jolita Salciunaite
AMERINDE CONSOLIDATED, INC

Rimantas Simaitis
RAIDLA LEJINS & NORCOUS

Julija Solovjova
PRICEWATERHOUSECOOPERS

Darius Ulvydas
BERNOTAS & DOMINAS GLIMSTEDT

Jurgita Valinciute
FORTUNE LAW GROUP

Rolandas Valiunas
LAW FIRM LIDEIKA, PETRAUSKAS, VALIŪNAS IR PARTNERIAI LAWIN, MEMBER OF LEX MUNDI

Agne Vilutiene
LAW FIRM FORESTA

Darius Zabiela
LAW FIRM ZABIELA, ZABIELAITE & PARTNERS

Giedre Zalpyte
BNT ATTORNEYS APB

Audrius Žvybas
BERNOTAS & DOMINAS GLIMSTEDT

LUXEMBOURG

ALLEN & OVERY LLP

Jalila Bakkali
PRICEWATERHOUSECOOPERS

Karine Bellony
PRICEWATERHOUSECOOPERS

Eleonora Broman
LOYENS & LOEFF

Guy Castegnaro
CASTEGNARO CABINET D'AVOCATS, MEMBER OF IUS LABORIS

Paula Crymble
OOSTVOGELS PFISTER FEYTEN

Christophe Domingos
CASTEGNARO CABINET D'AVOCATS, MEMBER OF IUS LABORIS

Christel Dumont
OOSTVOGELS PFISTER FEYTEN

Thomas Ecker
VILLE DE LUXEMBOURG - SERVICE DE L'ÉLECTRICITÉ

Gérard Eischen
CHAMBER OF COMMERCE

Martine Gerber Lemaire
OOSTVOGELS PFISTER FEYTEN

Anabela Fernandes Gonçalves
PRICEWATERHOUSECOOPERS

GROUPE AOH S.A.

Anthony Husianycia
PRICEWATERHOUSECOOPERS

Audrey Jarreton
LOYENS & LOEFF

François Kremer
ARENDT & MEDERNACH

Roxanne Le Ligeour
LOYENS & LOEFF

Michael Lockman
PRICEWATERHOUSECOOPERS

Nuria Martin
LOYENS & LOEFF

Séverine Moca
PRICEWATERHOUSECOOPERS

Peter Moons
LOYENS & LOEFF

Anne Murrath
PRICEWATERHOUSECOOPERS

Elisabeth Omes
BONN SCHMITT STEICHEN, MEMBER OF LEX MUNDI

Simon Paul
LOYENS & LOEFF

Wim Piot
PRICEWATERHOUSECOOPERS

Judith Raijmakers
LOYENS & LOEFF

Jean-Luc Schaus
LOYENS & LOEFF

PAUL WURTH S.A. ENGINEERING & PROJECT MANAGEMENT

Alex Schmitt
BONN SCHMITT STEICHEN, MEMBER OF LEX MUNDI

Dara Sychareun
LOYENS & LOEFF

MACEDONIA, FYR

Artan Abazi
NATIONAL BANK OF THE REPUBLIC OF MACEDONIA

Natasa Andreeva
NATIONAL BANK OF THE REPUBLIC OF MACEDONIA

Svetlana Andreovska
MONEVSKI LAW FIRM

Zlatko Antevski
LAWYERS ANTEVSKI

Aleksandra Arsoska
IKRP ROKAS & PARTNERS

Rubin Atanasoski
TIMELPROJECT ENGINEERING

Dragan Blažev
TIMELPROJECT ENGINEERING

Vladimir Bocevski
MENS LEGIS CAKMAKOVA ADVOCATES

Slavica Bogoeva
NATIONAL BANK OF THE REPUBLIC OF MACEDONIA

Violeta Bogojeska
CENTRAL REGISTER

Goran Bonevski
PUBLIC REVENUE OFFICE

Jela Boskovic
IKRP ROKAS & PARTNERS

Biljana Briskoska-Boskovski
MINISTRY OF JUSTICE

Biljana Čakmakova
MENS LEGIS CAKMAKOVA ADVOCATES

Katerina Carceva-Todorova
PRICEWATERHOUSECOOPERS

Tanja Cenova-Mitrovska
KATASTAR

Aco Damcevski
STRUMICA

Aspasija Desovska
EMO

Aleksandar Dimić
POLENAK LAW FIRM

Aleksandar Dimitrievski
LAW OFFICE NIKOLOVSKI

Dimitar Dimovski
MINISTRY OF TRANSPORT AND COMMUNICATIONS

Dragi Dimovski
STRUMICA

Aleksandra Donevska
LAWYERS ANTEVSKI

Jakup Fetai
KATASTAR

Daniel Georgievski
NATIONAL BANK OF THE REPUBLIC OF MACEDONIA

Ljupco Georgievski
KATASTAR

Angelina Gogusevska
STRUMICA

Pavlinka Golejski
MENS LEGIS CAKMAKOVA ADVOCATES

Goce Gruevski
KATASTAR

Ana Hadzieva
POLENAK LAW FIRM

Verica Hadzi-Vasileva Markovska
AGG

Slobodan Hristovski
POLENAK LAW FIRM

Natasha Hroneska

Biljana Ickovska
LAW OFFICE NIKOLOVSKI

Aleksandar Ickovski
PRICEWATERHOUSECOOPERS

Dragan Ivanovski
CUSTOMS ADMINISTRATION

Ilija Janoski
CUSTOMS ADMINISTRATION

Branuo Jilgougui
MINISTRY OF TRANSPORT AND COMMUNICATIONS

Katerina Jordanova
LAWYERS ANTEVSKI

Aneta Jovanoska - Trajanovska
LAWYERS ANTEVSKI

KOMERCIJALNA BANKA AD SKOPJE

Katerina Jovanovska
STOPANSKA BANKA AD

Lence Karpuzovska
EVN

Dejan Knezović
LAW OFFICE KNEZOVIC & ASSOCIATES

Zlatko T. Kolevski
KOLEVSKI LAW OFFICE

Antonio Kostanov
ENFORCEMENT AGENT REPUBLIC OF MACEDONIA

Lidija Krstevska
EU HARMONIZATION UNIT

Marija Leova-Dimeska
MINISTRY OF FINANCE PUBLIC REVENUE OFFICE

Irena Mitkovska
LAWYERS ANTEVSKI

Biljana Mladenovska
LAWYERS ANTEVSKI

Valerjan Monevski
MONEVSKI LAW FIRM

Gorgi Naumovski
CUSTOMS ADMINISTRATION

Vladimir Naumovski
CENTRAL REGISTER

Goran Nikolovski
LAW OFFICE NIKOLOVSKI

Kirl Papazoski
MONEVSKI LAW FIRM

Vesna Paunkoska
DIRECTORATE FOR PERSONAL DATA PROTECTION

Teodor Pecov
TIR - INTERNATIONAL FREIGHT FORWARDERS

Vasko Pejkov
SECURITIES AND EXCHANGE COMMISSION

Valentin Pepeljugoski
LAW OFFICE PEPELJUGOSKI

Sonja Peshevska
LAW OFFICE PEPELJUGOSKI

Aco Petrov
STRUMICA

Ilija Petrovski
MINISTRY OF JUSTICE,

Nesa Petrusevska
KATASTAR

Kristijan Polenak
POLENAK LAW FIRM

Tatjana Popovski Buloski
POLENAK LAW FIRM

Gligor Ralev
KATASTAR

Spiro Ristovski
MINISTRY FOR LABOR AND SOCIAL POLICY

Ljubica Ruben
MENS LEGIS LAW FIRM

Lidija Sarafimova Danevska
NATIONAL BANK OF THE REPUBLIC OF MACEDONIA

Valentina Saurek
MINISTRY OF JUSTICE

Bob Savic
PRICEWATERHOUSECOOPERS

Charapich Sinisha
TIR - INTERNATIONAL FREIGHT FORWARDERS

Tatjana Siskovska
POLENAK LAW FIRM

Jasna Smileva
SECURITIES AND EXCHANGE COMMISSION

Ivica Smilevski
STRUMICA

Aljosa Sopar

Pavlovic Srdjan
LUMEN COMPANY

Dejan Stojanoski
LAW OFFICE PEPELJUGOSKI

Aleksandar Stojanov
KATASTAR

Lujza Tomovska
SECURITIES AND EXCHANGE COMMISSION

Magdalena Tondeva Pavlovska
PRICEWATERHOUSECOOPERS

Stojam Trajanov
MINISTRY FOR LABOR AND SOCIAL POLICY

Slavica Trckova
LAW OFFICE TRCKOVA

Tina Tutevska
LAW OFFICE NIKOLOVSKI

Vladimir Vasilevski
BETASPED INTERNATIONAL FREIGHT FORWARDING

Sanja Veljanovska
MENS LEGIS LAW FIRM

Metodija Velkov
POLENAK LAW FIRM

Goce Videvski
EMO

Depru Vostovski

MADAGASCAR

Tsiry Andriamisamanana
MADAGASCAR CONSEIL INTERNATIONAL

Harimahefa Andriamitantsoa
TRIBUNAL DE PREMIÈRE INSTANCE

Josoa Lucien Andrianelinjaka
BANQUE CENTRALE DE MADAGASCAR

Andriamanalina Andrianjaka
Office Notarial de Tamatave

Pascal Bezençon
GasyNet S.A

Yves Duchateau
SDV

Guy Escarfail
Bureau de Liaison SGS

Raphaël Jakoba
Madagascar Conseil International

Hanna Keyserlingk
Cabinet HK Jurifisc.

Pascaline R. Rasamoeliarisoa
Deloitte

Sahondra Rabenarivo
Madagascar Law Offices

Anthony Rabibisoa
Maersk Logistics S.A.

Pierrette Rajaonarisoa
SDV

Heritianna Rakotosalama
Madagascar Law Offices

Lanto Tiana Ralison
FIDAFRICA / PricewaterhouseCoopers

Laingoniaina Ramarimbahoaka
Madagascar Conseil International

Michel Ramboa
Madagascar Law Offices

Giannie Ranaivo
Madagascar Law Offices

Seheno Ranaivoson
Banque Centrale de Madagascar

André Randranto
Randranto

Iloniaina Randranto
Randranto

William Randrianarivelo
FIDAFRICA / PricewaterhouseCoopers

Sahondra Rasoarisoa
Deloitte

Andrianirina R. Rasolonjatovo
SDV

Michel Ratrimo
Madagascar International Container Terminal Services Ltd

Théodore Raveloarison
JARY - Bureau d'Etudes Architecture Ingenierie

Andriamisa Ravelomanana
FIDAFRICA / PricewaterhouseCoopers

Jean Marcel Razafimahenina
Deloitte

Njiva Razanatsoa
Banque Centrale de Madagascar

Louis Sagot
Cabinet d'Avocat Louis Sagot

Ida Soamiliarimana
Madagascar Conseil International

Dominique Taty
FIDAFRICA / PricewaterhouseCoopers

MALAWI

Sylvia Ali
Knight Frank

Johann Boshoff
PricewaterhouseCoopers

Kevin M. Carpenter
PricewaterhouseCoopers

Richard Chakana
2PS Cargo Co.

Marshal Chilenga
TF & Partners

Alan Chinula

Aamir Rashid Jakhura
Fargo Group of Companies

Kalekeni Kaphale
Kalekeni Kaphale

Enoch Kasumbara
Kas Freight

Alfred Majamanda
Mbendera & Nkhono Associates

Alison Matthews
Watt Consultancies

Modecai Msisha
Nyirenda & Msisha Law Offices

Misheck Msiska
PricewaterhouseCoopers

Godwin Mwale
2PS Cargo Co.

Bernard Ndau

Grant C. Nyirongo
Elemech Designs

Davis Njobvu
Savjani & Co.

Dinker A. Raval
Wilson & Morgan

Duncan Singano
Savjani & Co.

Samuel Tembenu
Tembenu, Masumbu & Co.

Don Whayo
Knight Frank

Angela Deborah Zakeyu
PricewaterhouseCoopers

MALAYSIA

Nor Azimah Abdul Aziz
Companies Commission of Malaysia

Sonia Abraham
Azman, Davidson & Co.

Siti Haswanida Ahmad Jais
Azmi & Associates

Maseru Electro Services Pty Ltd

Michel Barbesier
SDV Sdn Bhd

Tan Kee Beng
SDV Sdn Bhd

Azryain Borhan
Companies Commission of Malaysia

Hong Yun Chang
Tay & Partners

Boon Hong Chen
Skrine & Co., member of Lex Mundi

Yuan Yuan Cheng
Skrine & Co., member of Lex Mundi

Tze Keong Chung
CTOS Sdn Bhd

Elaine Ho
Skrine & Co., member of Lex Mundi

Ghazali Ismail
Companies Commission of Malaysia

Mohammed Zanyuin Ismail
Companies Commission of Malaysia

Ismail Kamat
Azmi & Associates

Kumar Kanagasabai
Skrine & Co., member of Lex Mundi

Geeta Kaur
SDV Sdn Bhd

Chuan Keat Khoo
PricewaterhouseCoopers

Christopher Lee
Wong & Partners

Koon Huan Lim
Skrine & Co., member of Lex Mundi

Theresa Lim
PricewaterhouseCoopers

Kok Leong Loh
Russell Bedford LC & Company - member of Russell Bedford International

Caesar Loong
Raslan - Loong

Joanne Low
Zain & Co.

Len Toong Low
North Port

Suhara Mohamad Sidik
Azmi & Associates

Azmi Mohd Ali
Azmi & Associates

Zuhaidi Mohd Shahari
Azmi & Associates

Rajendra Navaratnam
Azman, Davidson & Co.

Hjh Rokiah Mhd Noor
Companies Commission of Malaysia

Shahri Omar
North Port

Gayathiry Ramalingam
Zain & Co.

S Parameswaran Shanmughanathan
Tenaga Nasional Berhad

Lay Sim
Russell Bedford LC & Company - member of Russell Bedford International

Hsian Siong
Wong & Partners

Ahmed Soffian
Ministry of International Trade and Industry

Francis Tan
Azman, Davidson & Co.

Heng Choon Wan
PricewaterhouseCoopers

Peter Wee
PricewaterhouseCoopers

Keat Ching Wong
Zul Rafique & Partners, Advocate & Solicitors

Chong Wah Wong
Skrine & Co., member of Lex Mundi

Ahmad Syahir Yahya
Azmi & Associates

Felicia Yap Peck Yee
Russell Bedford LC & Company - member of Russell Bedford International

Kim Hoe Yeo
North Port

Melina Yong
Raslan - Loong

MALDIVES

Jatindra Bhattray
PricewaterhouseCoopers

Asma Chan-Rahim
Shah, Hussain & Co. Barristers & Attorneys

Carlos Frias
PricewaterhouseCoopers

Mohamed Hameed
Antrac Pvt. Ltd.

Nadiya Hassan
Bank of Maldives Plc.

Dheena Hussain
Shah, Hussain & Co. Barristers & Attorneys

Rashfa Jaufa
Bank of Maldives Plc.

Laila Manik
Shah, Hussain & Co. Barristers & Attorneys

Fathimath Manike
Bank of Maldives Plc.

Aishath Samah
Bank of Maldives Plc.

Shuaib M. Shah
Shah, Hussain & Co. Barristers & Attorneys

Ahmed Shibau

Mariyam Sunaina
Bank of Maldives Plc.

Abdul Mallik Thoufeeg
STELCO

MALI

Imirane Abdoulaye
Direction Nationale de l'Urbanisme et de l'Habitat

Diaby Aboubakar
BCEAO

Traore Baba
TMS - Transit Manutention Services SARL

Oumar Bane
Jurifis Consult

Bouare
LABOGEC

Amadou Camara
SCP Camara Traoré

Céline Camara Sib
Etude Me Celine Camara Sib

Mahamane I. Cisse
Cabinet Lexis Conseils

Boubacar Coulibaly
Matrans Mali sarl

Mamadou Dante
Cabinet Dante

Famakan Dembele
Ministere de la Justice, Garde des Sceaux

Sekou Dembele
Etude de Maître Sekou Dembele

Mady Diakite
Direction Nationale du Commerce et de la Concurrence

Diakite
Direction Nationale de l'Urbanisme et de l'Habitat

Abou Diallo
API Mali

Ahmadou Diallo
Office Notarial Ahmadou Toure, Notaire a Bamako

Yacouba Diarra
Matrans Mali sarl

Boubacar S. Diarrah
Ministere de la Justice, Garde des Sceaux

Mohamed Abdoulaye Diop
SDV

Mahamane Djiteye
Jurifis Consult

Diafara Doucouré
Ministere des Finances

Ecobank

Kouma Fatoumata Fofana
Etude Kouma Fofana

Mansour Haidara
API Mali

Gaoussou Haïdara
Etude Gaoussou Haidara

Seydou Ibrahim Maiga
Cabinet d'Avocats Seydou Ibrahim Maiga

Modibo Keita
Direction générale des Impôts

Yacouba Massama Keïta

Mamadou Ismaïla Konate
Jurifis Consult

Mathias Konate
Direction générale des Impôts

Gaoussou A. G. Konaté
Cabinet d'Architecture - Etudes Techniques

Amadou Maiga
Direction Nationale de l'Urbanisme et de l'Habitat

Maiga Mamadou
Kafo Jiginew

Adeline Messou
FIDAFRICA / PricewaterhouseCoopers

Bérenger Y. Meuke
Jurifis Consult

Ministère de l'Economie de l'Industrie et du Commerce

Keita Zeïnabou Sacko
API

Sanogo
*DIRECTION DE L'INSPECTION
DU TRAVAIL*

Nohoum Sidibe
*DIRECTION NATIONALE DE
L'URBANISME ET DE L'HABITAT*

Moussa Saïba Sissoko
*DIRECTION NATIONALE DES
DOMAINES ET DU CADASTRE*

Baboucar Sow
*CABINET SOW &
COLLABORATEURS*

Malick Badara Sow
*ATELIER D'ARCHITECTURE ET
D'URBANISME*

Perignama Sylla
ARCHITECT DE/AU

Dominique Taty
*FIDAFRICA /
PRICEWATERHOUSECOOPERS*

Fatoma Théra
*MINISTERE DE LA JUSTICE,
GARDE DES SCEAUX*

Boubacar Thiam

Ahmadou Toure
*OFFICE NOTARIAL AHMADOU
TOURE, NOTAIRE A BAMAKO*

Konzo Traore
BCEAO

Mahamadou Traore

Emmanuel Yehouessi
BCEAO

MARSHALL ISLANDS

Kenneth Barden

Ave R. Gimao Jr.
*MARSHALL ISLANDS SOCIAL
SECURITY ADMINISTRATION*

Anita Jowitt
*UNIVERSITY OF THE SOUTH
PACIFIC*

Jerry Kramer
PACIFIC INTERNATIONAL, INC.

Philip A. Okney
*LAND REGISTRATION
ADMINISTRATION AUTHORITY*

Dennis Reeder
RMI RECEIVERSHIPS

Scott H. Stege
LAW OFFICES OF SCOTT STEGE

David M. Strauss
*MAJURO CHAMBER OF
COMMERCE*

Philip Welch
*MICRONESIAN SHIPPING
AGENCIES INC.*

MAURITANIA

Ishagh Ahmed Miske
CABINET ISHAGH MISKE

Tidiane Bal
BSD & ASSOCIÉS

Youssoupha Diallo
BSD & ASSOCIÉS

Fatoumata Diarra
BSD & ASSOCIÉS

Mohamed Lemine Bouchraya
Lam
BSD & ASSOCIÉS

Wedou Mohamed
MAURIHANDLING

Mine Ould Abdoullah

Brahim Ould Daddah
CABINET DADDAH CONSEILS

Brahim Ould Ebetty

Aliou Sall
ASSURIM CONSULTING

Ndeye Khar Sarr
BSD & ASSOCIÉS

Dominique Taty
*FIDAFRICA /
PRICEWATERHOUSECOOPERS*

MAURITIUS

Bruno Beche
*KROSS BORDER TRUST
SERVICES LTD, A MEMBER
FIRM OF RUSSELL BEDFORD
INTERNATIONAL*

André Bonieux
PRICEWATERHOUSECOOPERS

Urmila Boolell
*BANYMANDHUB BOOLELL
CHAMBERS*

Nicolas Carcasse
*DAGON INGENIEUR CONSEIL
LTÉE*

Jean Phillipe Chan See
MAERSK LTD.

D.P. Chinien
*REGISTRAR OF COMPANIES
AND BUSINESSES, OFFICE
OF THE REGISTRAR OF
COMPANIES*

Sootam Chutoori
*DAGON INGENIEUR CONSEIL
LTÉE*

Roland Constantin
CHAMBERS OF NOTARIES

Bert C. Cunningham
*CUSTOMS AND EXCISE
DEPARTMENT*

Rajendra Dassyne
CHAMBERS OF NOTARIES

Kalyanee Dayal
*BANYMANDHUB BOOLELL
CHAMBERS*

Martine de Fleuriot de la
Colinière
DE COMARMOND & KOENIG

Robert Ferrat
LEGIS & PARTNERS

Yannick Fok
GLOVER & GLOVER CHAMBERS

Gavin Glover
GLOVER & GLOVER CHAMBERS

Yandraduth Googoolye
BANK OF MAURITIUS

Darmalingum Goorriah
CHAMBERS OF NOTARIES

Arvin Halkhoree
CITILAW

Edouard Gregory Hart de
Keating
CHAMBERS OF NOTARIES

Mikash Hassamal
GLOVER & GLOVER CHAMBERS

Nitish Hurnaum
GLOVER & GLOVER CHAMBERS

Nirmala Jeetah
BOARD OF INVESTMENT

Jaye C Jingree
*KROSS BORDER TRUST
SERVICES LTD, A MEMBER*

*FIRM OF RUSSELL BEDFORD
INTERNATIONAL*

Marie Louis Jérome Koenig
CABINET NOTARIAL KOENIG

Thierry Koenig
DE COMARMOND & KOENIG

Anthony Leung Shing
PRICEWATERHOUSECOOPERS

Loganayagan Munian
ARTISCO INTERNATIONAL

Cristelle Parsooramen
*BANYMANDHUB BOOLELL
CHAMBERS*

André Robert

Anjali Roy
ETUDE GUY RIVALLAND

Wenda Sawmynaden
*CABINET DE NOTAIRE
SAWMYNADEN*

Deviantee Sobarun
*MINISTRY OF FINANCE &
ECONOMIC DEVELOPMENT*

Reza Subratty
MAERSK LTD.

Vikash Takoor
BANK OF MAURITIUS

Parikshat Teeluck
MAERSK LTD.

PRIMECOM LTD.

Dhanun Ujoodha
*KROSS BORDER TRUST
SERVICES LTD, A MEMBER
FIRM OF RUSSELL BEDFORD
INTERNATIONAL*

Muhammad R.C. Uteem
UTEEM CHAMBERS

Rosemary Yeung Sin Hing

MEXICO

Gabriel I. Aguilar Bustamente
PRICEWATERHOUSECOOPERS

Isis Anaya
SEDECO

Francisco Samuel Arias
González
NOTARY PUBLIC 28

Alberto Balderas
*JÁUREGUI, NAVARRETE Y
NADER, S.C.*

Rafael Barragan Mendoza
COMAD, S. C.

Emmanuel Cardenas Rojas
*BARRERA, SIQUEIROS Y TORRES
LANDA*

María Casas López
BAKER & MCKENZIE

Rodrigo Conesa
RITCH MUELLER, S. C.

Santiago Corcuera
*CURTIS MALLET - PREVOST,
COLT & MOSLE LLP*

Eduardo Corzo Ramos
*HOLLAND & KNIGHT-
GALLÁSTEGUI Y LOZANO, S.C.*

Jose Covarrubias-Azuela
*SOLORZANO, CARVAJAL,
GONZALEZ Y PEREZ-CORREA,
S.C.*

Raul de la Sierra Scauley
*BARRERA, SIQUEIROS Y TORRES
LANDA*

Oscar de La Vega
*BASHAM, RINGE Y CORREA,
MEMBER OF IUS LABORIS*

Olea De Noriega
*BARRERA, SIQUEIROS Y TORRES
LANDA*

Guillermo Escamilla
*MEXICO CITY NOTARIES
COLLEGE*

Luis Esparza
PRICEWATERHOUSECOOPERS

César Fernández Gómez
*BARRERA, SIQUEIROS Y TORRES
LANDA*

Julio Flores Luna
*GOODRICH, RIQUELME Y
ASOCIADOS*

Manuel Galicia
GALICIA Y ROBLES, S.C.

Celina Cossette Garcia
*PRICEWATERHOUSECOOPERS
LEGAL SERVICES*

Alexander Christian Gardea
PRICEWATERHOUSECOOPERS

Gerardo Garreto-Chavez
*BARRERA, SIQUEIROS Y TORRES
LANDA*

Hans Goebel
*JÁUREGUI, NAVARRETE Y
NADER, S.C.*

Daniel Gómez Alba
CAAAREM

Teresa de Lourdes Gómez
Neri
*GOODRICH, RIQUELME Y
ASOCIADOS*

Alvaro Gonzalez-Schiaffino
PRICEWATERHOUSECOOPERS

Carlos Grimm
BAKER & MCKENZIE

Benito Guerrero
CAAAREM

Yves Hayaux-du-Tilly
*JÁUREGUI, NAVARRETE Y
NADER, S.C.*

Jorge Jiménez
*RUSSELL BEDFORD MEXICO,
MEMBER OF RUSSELL BEDFORD
INTERNATIONAL*

Jorge León-Orantes
*GOODRICH, RIQUELME Y
ASOCIADOS*

Ricardo León-Santacruz
*SANCHEZ DEVANNY ESEVERRI,
S.C.*

Adriana Lopez
*PRICEWATERHOUSECOOPERS
LEGAL SERVICES*

Gerardo Lozano Alarcón
*HOLLAND & KNIGHT-
GALLÁSTEGUI Y LOZANO, S.C.*

Lucia Manzo
GALICIA Y ROBLES, S.C.

José Antonio Marquez
González
NOTARY PUBLIC 28

A. Martinez
SKYNET

Carla Mendoza
BAKER & MCKENZIE

Alonso Martin Montes
*PRICEWATERHOUSECOOPERS
LEGAL SERVICES*

Rocío Montes
PRICEWATERHOUSECOOPERS

Humberto Morales- Barron
*SANCHEZ DEVANNY ESEVERRI,
S.C.*

Michelle Muciño
PMC ASOCIADOS

Julio Nunez
VANGUARDIA

Arturo Perdomo
GALICIA Y ROBLES, S.C.

Juan Manuel Perez
*PRICEWATERHOUSECOOPERS
LEGAL SERVICES*

Erika Pérez
SKYNET

Gabriela Pérez Castro Ponce
de León
MIRANDA & ESTAVILLO, S.C.

Fernando Perez-Correa
*SOLORZANO, CARVAJAL,
GONZALEZ Y PEREZ-CORREA,
S.C.*

Guillermo Piecarchic
PMC ASOCIADOS

José Piecarchic
PMC ASOCIADOS

Gerardo Prado-Hernandez
*SANCHEZ DEVANNY ESEVERRI,
S.C.*

David Puente-Tostado
*SANCHEZ DEVANNY ESEVERRI,
S.C.*

Cecilia Rojas
GALICIA Y ROBLES, S.C.

Carlos Sánchez-Mejorada y
Velasco
*SÁNCHEZ-MEJORADA Y
ASOCIADOS*

Cristina Sánchez-Urtiz
MIRANDA & ESTAVILLO, S.C.

Fernando Santamaria-Linares
*PRICEWATERHOUSECOOPERS
LEGAL SERVICES*

Monica Schiaffino Pérez
*BASHAM, RINGE Y CORREA,
MEMBER OF IUS LABORIS*

*SECRETARÍA DE HACIENDA Y
CRÉDITO PÚBLICO*

Daniel Sosa
SKYNET

Mario Tellez
SKYNET

Juan Francisco Torres Landa
Ruffo
*BARRERA, SIQUEIROS Y TORRES
LANDA*

Maribel Trigo Aja
*GOODRICH, RIQUELME Y
ASOCIADOS*

Layla Vargas Muga
*GOODRICH, RIQUELME Y
ASOCIADOS*

Carlos Vela
PRICEWATERHOUSECOOPERS

Rafael Villamar-Ramos
*SANCHEZ DEVANNY ESEVERRI,
S.C.*

MICRONESIA, FED. STS.

Kenneth Barden

Wayne Bricknell
E - CAD Project Management

Sarah Dorsett
Pohnpei State Government

Stephen V. Finnen
Stephen Finnen's Law Corporation

Anita Jowitt
University of the South Pacific

Patrick Mackenzie
Bank of FSM

Silberio S. Mathias
FSM Social Security Administration

Kevin Pelep
Office of the Registrar of Corporations

MOLDOVA

Eduard Boian
PricewaterhouseCoopers

Victor Burac
Victor Burac Law Firm

Andrei Caciurenco
ACI Partners

Georghu Calugharu
Union of Employers in Building and Construction Materials Industry

Andrian Candu
PricewaterhouseCoopers Legal Services

Octavian Cazac
Turcan & Turcan

Svetlana Ceban
PricewaterhouseCoopers

Marin Chicu
Turcan & Turcan

Vitalie Ciofu
Gladei & Partners

Bogdan Ciubotaru
Turcan & Turcan

Alla Cotos
PricewaterhouseCoopers

Sergiu Dumitrasco
PricewaterhouseCoopers

Roger Gladei
Gladei & Partners

Roman Gutu
Activ Broker

Oxana Guțu
Mobiasbanca Groupe Societe Generale

Catalina Levcenco
PricewaterhouseCoopers

Union Fenosa International

Cristina Martin
ACI Partners

Georgeta Mincu
IOM

Marin Moraru
PricewaterhouseCoopers

Alexandru Munteanu
PricewaterhouseCoopers

Alexandr Muravschi
Dartax Consulting SRL

National Energy Regulatory Agency of the Republic of Moldova

Igor Odobescu
ACI Partners

Aelita Orhei
Gladei & Partners

Ilona Panurco
PricewaterhouseCoopers

Ruslan Pirnevu
Quehenberger-Hellmann SRL

Maria Popescu
PricewaterhouseCoopers

Mariana Stratan
Turcan & Turcan

Serghei Toncu
PricewaterhouseCoopers

Irina Verhovetchi
ACI Partners

Carolina Vieru
IM PAA SRL

MONGOLIA

Tomas Balco
PricewaterhouseCoopers

Badarch Bayarmaa
Lynch & Mahoney

Batzaya Bodikhuu
Anand & Batzaya Advocates Law Firm

Volodya Bolormaa
Anand & Batzaya Advocates Law Firm

Richard Bregonje
PricewaterhouseCoopers

David Buxbaum
Anderson & Anderson

Batbayar Byambaa
GTs Advocates LLC

Ralph Cerveny
Anderson & Anderson

Khatanbat Dashdarjaa
Arlex Consulting Services

Byambatseren Dorjpurev
Arlex Consulting Services

Courtney Fowler
PricewaterhouseCoopers

Tuvshin Javkhlant
GTs Advocates LLC

Jeroen Kerbusch
PricewaterhouseCoopers

Odmaa Khurelbold
Anderson & Anderson

Daniel Mahoney
Lynch & Mahoney

Sebastian Merriman
PricewaterhouseCoopers

Leylim Mizamkhan
PricewaterhouseCoopers

Odonhuu Muuzee
Tsets Law Firm

Enkhriimaa N.
Tuushin Company Ltd.

Zorigt N.
Tuushin Company Ltd.

Sarantsatsral Ochirpurev
Urkh Company

Baatarsuren Sukhbaatar
The Bank of Mongolia

Tsogt Tsend
Administrative Court of Capital City

Arslaa Urjin
Ulaanbaatar Electricity Distribution Network Company

MONTENEGRO

Bojana Andrić
Čelebić

Veselin Anđušić
Čelebić

Bojana Bošković
Ministry of Finance

Vasilije Bošković
Law Firm Bošković

Peter Burnie
PricewaterhouseCoopers

Vladimir Dasić
PricewaterhouseCoopers Bojović & Dašić

Milena Drakić
Crnogorska Komercijalna Banka AD Podgorica

Vuk Drašković
Bojovic Dasic Kojovic Attorneys at Law

Darko Globarević
Zetatrans

Rina Ivančević
Municipality of Podgorica

Ana Ivanović
Ministry of Finance

Marko Ivković
KN Karanović & Nikolić

Maja Jokanović
Ministry for Economic Development

Nada Jovanović
Central Bank of Montenegro

Rade Jovanović
Jovanović Law Firm

Lidija Klikovac
Deputy Registrar

Drenka Knežević
Ministry of Labor and Social Welfare

Jovan Kostić
Employment Registrar

Đorđe Krivokapić
KN Karanović & Nikolić

Ana Krsmanović

Sefko Kurpejović
Ministry of Finance

Amela Lekić
Crnogorska Komercijalna Banka AD Podgorica

Mirjana Ljumović
Real Estate Administration

Milan Martinović
Customs Administration

Borislav Mijović
Mercedes-Benz - Ljetopis Automotive d.o.o.

Željko Mijović
Zetatrans

Momir Miličković
Tax Authority

Aleksandar Miljković
PricewaterhouseCoopers

Montenegro Business Alliance

Montenegrin Commercial Bank AD Podgorica

Stojanka Milošević
Customs Administration

Mirjana Mladenović
Bojovic Dasic Kojovic Attorneys at Law

Dragoslav Nikolić
Customs Administration

Goran Nikolić
Ministry for Economic Development

Veljko Pavičević
Opportunity Bank

Aleksander Perović
Tax Authority

Nikola Perović
Plantaže

Zorica Peshic-Bajceta
Law Office Vujačić

Novica Pešić
Law Office Vujačić

Snežana Pešić
PricewaterhouseCoopers

Tijana Prelević
Ministry of Labor and Social Welfare

Dragana Radević
Center for Enterpreneurship and Economic Development

Ana Radivojević
PricewaterhouseCoopers

Vladimir Radovanić
Ministry of Labor and Social Welfare

Novo Radović
Tax Authority

Radmila Radunović
Government of the Republic of Montenegro

Dragan Rakočević
Commercial Court

Slobodan Raščanin

Danijela Saban
Čelebić

Biljana Šćekić
PC Krusevac

Slaven Šćepanović

Lidija Šećković
Tax Authority

Slavko Simović
Real Estate Administration

Velimir Strugar
EPCG AD Nikšić

Sasha Vujačić
Law Office Vujačić

Mileva Vujadinović
Crnogorska Komercijalna Banka AD Podgorica

Jelena Vujisić
Law Office Vujačić

Irena Vujović
Deputy Registrar

Predrag Vujović
Zetatrans

Veselin Vuković
Central Bank

MOROCCO

Benali Abdelmajid
Exp Services

Aziz Abouelouafa
Globex Maritime Co.

Najat Aboulfadl
Cabinet Notarial Houcine Sefrioui

Agence Med s.a.r.l.

Samir Agoumi
Dar Alkhibra

My Hicham Alaoui
Globex Maritime Co.

Meredith Allen-Belghiti
Kettani Law Firm

Younes Anibar
Cabinet Younes Anibar

Bank Al-Maghrib

Khaled Battash
Abu-Ghazaleh Legal - (TAG-Legal)

Maria Belafia
Cabinet Notarial Belafia

Linda Oumama Benali

Aicha Benghanem
Cabinet Notarial Houcine Sefrioui

Myriam Emmanuelle Bennani
Amin Hajji & Associés Association d'Avocats

Richard Cantin
Juristructures - Project Management & Legal Advisory Services LLP

Zineb Chigar
Cabinet Notarial Houcine Sefrioui

Fatima Zohra Gouttaya
Cabinet Notarial Houcine Sefrioui

Amin Hajji
Amin Hajji & Associés Association d'Avocats

Zohra Hasnaoui
Hasnaoui Law Firm

Bahya Ibn Khaldoun
Université Mohamed V

Naoual Jellouli
Ministère de l'économie et des finances

Mehdi Kettani
Kettani Law Office

Nadia Kettani
Kettani Law Firm

Bouchaib Labkiri
Globex Maritime Co.

Karine Lasne
Landwell & Associés - PricewaterhouseCoopers Legal Services

Wilfried Le Bihan
CMS Bureau Francis Lefebvre

Lapirama Group International

Lydec

Anis Mahfoud
*ABOUAKIL & BENJELLOUN
AVOCATS - AB AVOCATS*

Mohamed Maliki
ETUDE MAITRE MALIKI

Del Monsieur Marc
*LANDWELL & ASSOCIÉS -
PRICEWATERHOUSECOOPERS
LEGAL SERVICES*

Azdine Nekmouche
*ORDRE DES ARCHITECTES DE
CASABLANCA*

Hicham Oughza
DAR ALKHIBRA

Réda Oulamine
OULAMINE LAW GROUP

Jamal Rahal
EXP SERVICES

Hassane Rahmoun
*ETUDE NOTARIALE HASSANE
RAHMOUN*

Nesrine Roudane
NERO BOUTIQUE LAW FIRM

Morgane Saint-Jalmes
KETTANI LAW FIRM

Aurelie Santos
*LANDWELL & ASSOCIÉS -
PRICEWATERHOUSECOOPERS
LEGAL SERVICES*

Houcine Sefrioui
*CABINET NOTARIAL HOUCINE
SEFRIOUI*

MOZAMBIQUE

Faizal Antonio
SDV AMI

Carolina Balate
PRICEWATERHOUSECOOPERS

António Baltazar Bungallah
*SAL & CALDEIRA -
ADVOGADOS E CONSULTORES,
LDA*

José Manuel Caldeira
*SAL & CALDEIRA -
ADVOGADOS E CONSULTORES,
LDA*

Eduardo Calú
*SAL & CALDEIRA -
ADVOGADOS E CONSULTORES,
LDA*

Paulo Centeio
*MGA ADVOGADOS &
CONSULTORES*

Anastácia Chamusse
BANCO DE MOÇAMBIQUE

Dipak Chandulal
*MGA ADVOGADOS &
CONSULTORES*

Ahmad Chothia
*MANICA FREIGHT SERVICES
S.A.R.L*

Pedro Couto
*H. GAMITO, COUTO,
GONÇALVES PEREIRA
E CASTELO BRANCO &
ASSOCIADOS*

Avelar Da Silva
INTERTEK INTERNATIONAL LTD

Carlos de Sousa e Brito
*CARLOS DE SOUSA & BRITO &
ASSOCIADOS*

Fulgêncio Dimande
*MANICA FREIGHT SERVICES
S.A.R.L*

Jose Forjaz
JOSE FORJAZ ARQUITECTOS

Rita Furtado
*H. GAMITO, COUTO,
GONÇALVES PEREIRA
E CASTELO BRANCO &
ASSOCIADOS*

Martins Garrine
*MANICA FREIGHT SERVICES
S.A.R.L*

Jennifer Garvey

Jorge Graça
*MGA ADVOGADOS &
CONSULTORES*

Ássma Omar Nordine Jeque
*SAL & CALDEIRA -
ADVOGADOS E CONSULTORES,
LDA*

Esmè Joaquim
*SAL & CALDEIRA -
ADVOGADOS E CONSULTORES,
LDA*

Rufino Lucas
*TEC TÉNICOS CONSTRUTORES,
LDA*

Eugénio Luis
BANCO DE MOÇAMBIQUE

Jaime Magumbe
*SAL & CALDEIRA -
ADVOGADOS E CONSULTORES,
LDA*

Fatima Marques
*CARLOS DE SOUSA & BRITO &
ASSOCIADOS*

Carlos Martins
AFRILEGIS, LDA

Joao Martins
PRICEWATERHOUSECOOPERS

Genaro Moura
*MANICA FREIGHT SERVICES
S.A.R.L*

Lara Narcy
*H. GAMITO, COUTO,
GONÇALVES PEREIRA
E CASTELO BRANCO &
ASSOCIADOS*

Auxílio Eugénio Nhabanga
*FBLP - R.FURTADO, N.
BHIKHA, R.LOFORTE, M.
POPAT & ASSOCIADOS,
ADVOGADOS, LDA*

Paulo Pimenta
*PIMENTA, DIONÍSIO E
ASSOCIADOS*

Alvaro Pinto Basto
*MGA ADVOGADOS &
CONSULTORES*

José Augusto Tomo Psico
BANCO DE MOÇAMBIQUE

Malaika Ribeiro
PRICEWATERHOUSECOOPERS

Luís Filipe Rodrigues
*SAL & CALDEIRA -
ADVOGADOS E CONSULTORES,
LDA*

Firza Sadek
*PIMENTA, DIONÍSIO E
ASSOCIADOS*

Sérgio Sumbana
*PIMENTA DIONÍSIO &
ASSOCIADOS*

Élio Teixeira
AFRILEGIS, LDA

António Veloso
*PIMENTA, DIONÍSIO E
ASSOCIADOS*

NAMIBIA

Joos Agenbach
KOEP & PARTNERS

Benita Blume
H.D. BOSSAU & CO.

Jaco Boltman
*G.F. KÖPPLINGER LEGAL
PRACTITIONERS*

Hanno D. Bossau
H.D. BOSSAU & CO.

Albe Botha
PRICEWATERHOUSECOOPERS

Lorna Celliers
BDO SPENCER STEWARD

Dirk Hendrik Conradie
CONRADIE & DAMASEB

Ferdinand Diener
*CITY OF WINDHOEK
ELECTRICITY DEPARTMENT*

Hennie Fourie
PRICEWATERHOUSECOOPERS

Jana Gous
PRICEWATERHOUSECOOPERS

Chantell Husselmann
PRICEWATERHOUSECOOPERS

Denis Hyman
PRICEWATERHOUSECOOPERS

Sakaria Kadhila Amoomo
PEREIRA FISHING (PTY) LTD

Herman Charl Kinghorn
*HC KINGHORN LEGAL
PRACTITIONER*

Peter Frank Koep
KOEP & PARTNERS

Patrick Kohlspaedt
MANICA AFRICA PTY. LTD.

Frank Köpplinger
*G.F. KÖPPLINGER LEGAL
PRACTITIONERS*

Jackie Kotzke
PRICEWATERHOUSECOOPERS

John D. Mandy
NAMIBIAN STOCK EXCHANGE

Richard Traugott Diethelm
Mueller
KOEP & PARTNERS

Carina Oberholzer
PRICEWATERHOUSECOOPERS

Ndapewa Shipopyeni
H.D. BOSSAU & CO.

Apie Small
*G.F. KÖPPLINGER LEGAL
PRACTITIONERS*

Axel Stritter
*ENGLING, STRITTER &
PARTNERS*

Marius van Breda
TRANSUNION NAMIBIA

Renate Williamson
KOEP & PARTNERS

NEPAL

Mahesh P. Acharya
*NEPAL ELECTRICITY
AUTHORITY*

Anil Chandra Adhikari
*CREDIT INFORMATION BUREAU
OF NEPAL*

Lalit Aryal
*LA & ASSOCIATES CHARTERED
ACCOUNTANTS*

Janak Bhandari
GLOBAL LAW ASSOCIATES

Tulasi Bhatta
*UNITY LAW FIRM &
CONSULTANCY*

Narayan Chaulagain
PIONEER LAW ASSOCIATES

Ajay Ghimire
APEX LAW CHAMBER

Komal Prakash Ghimire

Jagat B. Khadka
*SHANGRI-LA FREIGHT PVT.
LTD.*

Gourish K. Kharel
KTO INC.

Nirmal Koirala
*ALFA FURNITURES AND
INTERIORS PVT. LTD*

Mahesh Kumar Thap
SINHA - VERMA LAW CONCERN

Namgyal Lama
*NEPAL FREIGHT FORWARDERS
ASSOCIATION*

LD Mahat
*CSC & CO. /
PRICEWATERHOUSECOOPERS*

Ashok Man Kapali
*SHANGRI-LA FREIGHT PVT.
LTD.*

Matrika Niraula
*NIRAULA LAW CHAMBER &
CO.*

Rajan Niraula
*NIRAULA LAW CHAMBER &
CO.*

Saroj Niraula
AYURVEDA HERBALS PVT. LTD.

Dev Raj Paudyal
*MINISTRY OF LAND REFORM
AND MANAGEMENT*

Devendra Pradhan
PRADHAN & ASSOCIATES

Purnachitra Pradhan
*KARJA SUCHANA KENDRA
LTD(CIB)*

Anup Raj Upreti
PIONEER LAW ASSOCIATES

Krishna Prasad Sapkota
*MINISTRY OF LAND REFORM
AND MANAGEMENT*

Purna Man Shakya
RELIANCE LAW FIRM

Madan Krishna Sharma
*CSC & CO. /
PRICEWATERHOUSECOOPERS*

Bigyan P. Shreshtha

Ramji Shrestha
PRADHAN & ASSOCIATES

Sudheer Shrestha
KUSUM LAW FIRM

Anil Kumar Sinha
SINHA - VERMA LAW CONCERN

Nab Raj Subedi
*MINISTRY OF LAND REFORM
AND MANAGEMENT*

Ram Chandra Subedi
APEX LAW CHAMBER

NETHERLANDS

Joos Achterberg
KENNEDY VAN DER LAAN

Richard Bakker
*OCEAN - TRANS
INTERNATIONAL B.V.*

Dirk-Jan Berkenbosch
PRICEWATERHOUSECOOPERS

BERKMAN FORWARDING B.V.

Jan Bezem
PRICEWATERHOUSECOOPERS

Karin W.M. Bodewes
BAKER & MCKENZIE

Mark Bodt
PRICEWATERHOUSECOOPERS

Roland Brandsma
PRICEWATERHOUSECOOPERS

Huub Brinkman
BAKER & MCKENZIE

Margriet de Boer
*DE BRAUW BLACKSTONE
WESTBROEK*

Sijmen de Ranitz
*DE BRAUW BLACKSTONE
WESTBROEK*

Rolef de Weijs
HOUTHOFF BURUMA N.V.

Myrna Dop
*ROYAL NETHERLANDS
NOTARIAL ORGANIZATION*

Fons Hoogeveen
PRICEWATERHOUSECOOPERS

Ruud Horak
*ELEKTROTECHNIEK BOERMANS
B.V.*

Elsa Jonker-Grootenhuis
PRICEWATERHOUSECOOPERS

Alexander Kaarls
HOUTHOFF BURUMA N.V.

Marcel Kettenis
PRICEWATERHOUSECOOPERS

Stefan Leening
PRICEWATERHOUSECOOPERS

Hans Noordermeer
*BDO CAMPSOBERS
ACCOUNTANTS &
BELASTINGADVISEURS B.V.*

Hugo Oppelaar
HOUTHOFF BURUMA N.V.

Femke Pos
*ROYAL NETHERLANDS
NOTARIAL ORGANIZATION*

Hugo Reumkens
VAN DOORNE N.V.

Piet Schroeder
BAKER & MCKENZIE

SDV B.V.

Salima Seamari
*DE BRAUW BLACKSTONE
WESTBROEK*

Hans Londonck Sluijk
HOUTHOFF BURUMA N.V.

Birgit Snijder-Kuipers
*ROYAL NETHERLANDS
NOTARIAL ORGANIZATION*

Fedor Tanke
BAKER & MCKENZIE

Maarten Tinnemans
*DE BRAUW BLACKSTONE
WESTBROEK*

Helene van Bommel
PRICEWATERHOUSECOOPERS

Annekarien van de Velde
BAKER & MCKENZIE

Liane van de Vrugt
VéDéVé Legal B.V.

Robert van der Laan
PricewaterhouseCoopers

Femke van der Zeijden
PricewaterhouseCoopers

Gert-Jan van Gijs
VAT Logistics (Ocean Freight) B.V.

Jan van Oorschot
Liander

Petra van Raad
PricewaterhouseCoopers

Frederic Verhoeven
Houthoff Buruma N.V.

Michiel Wesseling
Houthoff Buruma N.V.

Hylda Wiarda
Bronsgeest Deur Advocaten, member of Ius Laboris

Marcel Willems
Kennedy Van der Laan

Christiaan Zijderveld
Houthoff Buruma N.V.

NEW ZEALAND

Douglas Alderslade
Chapman Tripp

Matthew Allison
Veda Advantage

Kevin Best
PricewaterhouseCoopers

Geoff Bevan
Chapman Tripp

Kara Bonnevie
New Zealand Companies Office

Toni Brown
Bell Gully

Liz Caughley
Bell Gully

Shelley Cave
Simpson Grierson, member of Lex Mundi

John Cuthbertson
PricewaterhouseCoopers

Vince Duffin
Vector Electricity

Wendy Duggan
Bell Gully

Koustabh Gadgil
Investment New Zealand

Chris Gordon
Bell Gully

Don Grant
Land Information New Zealand

Emma Harding
Chapman Tripp

David Harte
Insolvency and Trustee Services

Kate Lane
Minter Ellison Rudd Watts

John Lawrence
Auckland City Council

Thomas Leslie
Bell Gully

Aaron Lloyd
Minter Ellison Rudd Watts

Andrew Minturn
Department of Housing and Building

Robert Muir
Land Information New Zealand

Catherine Otten
New Zealand Companies Office

Ian Page
BRANZ

Mihai Pascariu
Minter Ellison Rudd Watts

John Powell
Russell McVeagh

Jim Roberts
Hesketh Henry Lawyers

Catherine Rowe
PricewaterhouseCoopers

Mark Russell
Simpson Grierson, member of Lex Mundi

SDV Logistics Ltd.

Neill Sullivan
Land Information New Zealand

Murray Tingey
Bell Gully

Rob Towner
Bell Gully

NICARAGUA

Diana Aguilar
ACZALAW

Aguilar Castillo Love

Guillermo Alemán Gómez
ACZALAW

Bertha Argüello de Rizo
F.A. Arias & Muñoz

Roberto Argüello Villavicencio
Arias & Muñoz

Minerva Adriana Bellorín Rodríguez
ACZALAW

María José Bendaña Guerrero
Bendaña & Bendaña

Christopher Blandino
Carrión, Somarriba & Asociados

Carlos Alberto Bonilla López
Superintendencia de Bancos

Humberto Carrión
Carrión, Somarriba & Asociados

Ramón Castro
Arias & Muñoz

Juan Carlos Cortes Espinoza
PricewaterhouseCoopers

Disnorte-Dissur (Union Fenosa)

Maricarmen Espinosa de Molina
Molina & Asociados Central Law

G.E. Electromecánica & Cia Ltda.

Mario José Gutiérrez Avendaño
ACZALAW

Eduardo Jose Gutierrez Rueda
Consortium Taboada y Asociados

Mauricio Herdocia
García & Bodán

Gerardo Hernandez
Consortium Taboada y Asociados

Ruth Huete
PricewaterhouseCoopers

Rodrigo Ibarra
Arias & Muñoz

María Fernanda Jarquín
Arias & Muñoz

Mariela Jiménez
ACZALAW

Javiera Latino
Aseguradora Mundial

Alvaro Molina
Molina & Asociados Central Law

Yalí Molina Palacios
Molina & Asociados Central Law

Haroldo Montealegre
Arias & Muñoz

Roberto Montes
Arias & Muñoz

Soraya Montoya Herrera
Molina & Asociados Central Law

Francisco Ortega
Francisco Ortega & Asociados

Silvio G. Otero Q.
GlobalTrans Internacional

Ramón Ortega
PricewaterhouseCoopers

Jaime Rivera
Carrión, Somarriba & Asociados

Ana Teresa Rizo Briseño
Arias & Muñoz

Multiconsult, S.A.

Felipe Sánchez
ACZALAW

Alfonso José Sandino Granera
Consortium Taboada y Asociados

Julio E. Sequeira
Evenor Valdivia P. & Asociados

Arnulfo Somarriba
TransUnion

Rodrigo Taboada
Consortium Taboada y Asociados

Manuel Ignacio Tefel
PricewaterhouseCoopers

Carlos Tellez
García & Bodán

NIGER

Diaby Aboubakar
BCEAO

Mamoudou Aoula
Projet de Développement des Infrastructures Locales-PDIL-Bureau National de Coor

Mahamane Baba
SDV

Alain Blambert
SDV

Aïssa Degbey
Ecobank

Aïssatou Djibo
Etude de Me Djibo Aïssatou

Sani Halilou
Maersk S.A.

Dodo Dan Gado Haoua
Etude de Maître Dodo Dan Gado Haoua

Ali Idrissa Sounna
Toutelec Niger SA

Issoufou Issa
Ministère de l'Economie et des Finances

Bernar-Oliver Kouaovi
Cabinet Kouaovi

Lambert Lainé
Etude de Maître Achimi Riliwanou

Diallo Rayanatou Loutou
Cabinet Loutou - Architectes

Laouali Madougou
Etude d'Avocats Marc Le Bihan & Collaborateurs

Boubacar Nouhou Maiga
E.N.G.E.

Saadou Maiguizo
Bureau d'Etudes Techniques d'Assistance et de Suirveillance en Construction Civile

Yayé Mounkaïla
Cabinet d'Avocats Mounkaila-Niandou

Ibrahim Mounouni
Bureau d'Etudes Bala & Himo

Laurent Puerta
SDV

Achimi M. Riliwanou
Etude de Maître Achimi Riliwanou

Boubacar Salaou
Etude de Maître Boubacar Salaou

Abdou Moussa Sanoussi
E.N.G.E.

Ousmane Sidibé
Audit & Conseil Sidibé & Conseil (A.C.S.A.)

Dominique Taty
FIDAFRICA / PricewaterhouseCoopers

Idrissa Tchernaka
Etude d'Avocats Marc Le Bihan & Collaborateurs

Konzo Traore
BCEAO

Ramatou Wankoye
Office Notarial Wankoye

Hamadou Yacouba
Etude de Maître Djibo Aïssatou

Hamado Yahaya
Societe Civile Professionnelle d'Avocats Yankori et associés

Emmanuel Yehouessi
BCEAO

NIGERIA

Oluseyi Abiodun Akinwunmi
Akinwunmi & Busari, Legal Practioners (A & B)

Olaleye Adebiyi
WTS Adebiyi & Associates

Kunle Adegbite
Adegbite - Stevens & Co

Temitayo Adegoke
Aluko & Oyebode

Adeola Adeiye
Udo Udoma & Belo-Osagie

Olufunke Adekoya
AELEX, Legal Practitioners & Arbitrators

Folaranmi Adetunji Adegbite
F.A. Adegbite & Associates

Francis Adewale
Vista Bridge Global Resources Limited

Duro Adeyele
Bayo Ojo & Co.

Olusola Adun
Nouveau Associates

Adesegun Agbebiyi
Aluko & Oyebode

Olufunke Agbedana
Olaniwun Ajayi LP

Emuesiri Agbeyi
PricewaterhouseCoopers

Daniel Agbor
Udo Udoma & Belo-Osagie

Uche Ajaegbu
Nigeria Employers' Consultative Assembly

Ayo Ajayi
The Propertarium

Konyin Ajayi
Olaniwun Ajayi LP

Olukoyinsola Ajayi
Olaniwun Ajayi LP

O.C. Akamnonu
PHCN, Eko Zone

Tolulola Akintimehin
Nouveau Associates

Owolabi Animashaun
Scotech Universal Resources Limited

Linda Arifayan
WTS Adebiyi & Associates

Esther Atoyebi
Okonjo, Odiawa & Ebie

Ajibola Basiru
M.A.B. & Associates

Chinwe Chiwete
Punuka Attorneys & Solicitors

Peter Crabb
Nnenna Ejekam Associates

Silas Damson
Aluko & Oyebode

Oluwayemisi Diya
Olaniwun Ajayi LP

Kofo Dosekun
Aluko & Oyebode

Russell Eastaugh
PricewaterhouseCoopers

Nnenna Ejekam
Nnenna Ejekam Associates

Olusoji Elias
OLUSOJI ELIAS AND COMPANY

Anse Agu Ezetah
CHIEF LAW AGU EZETAH
& CO.

Lawrence Ezetah
CHIEF LAW AGU EZETAH
& CO.

R. Finco
ETCO NIGERIA LTD

Bimbola Fowler-Ekar
JACKSON, ETTI & EDU

Inegogo Fubara
UDO UDOMA & BELO-OSAGIE

Okorie Kalu
PUNUKA ATTORNEYS &
SOLICITORS

Tomisin Lagundoye
UDO UDOMA & BELO-OSAGIE

Ibrahim Eddy Mark

Jjeamaka Nwizu
BEAUFORT CHAMBERS

Victor Obaro
LIBRA LAW OFFICE

Oghor Ogboi
UDO UDOMA & BELO-OSAGIE

Godson Ogheneochuko
UDO UDOMA & BELO-OSAGIE

Ozofu Ogiemudia
UDO UDOMA & BELO-OSAGIE

Alayo Ogunbiyi
ABDULAI, TAIWO & CO.

Ayodeji Ojo
JACKSON, ETTI & EDU

Mathias Okojie
PUNUKA ATTORNEYS &
SOLICITORS

Patrick Okonjo
OKONJO, ODIAWA & EBIE

Osita Okoro

Chioma Okwudiafor
PUNUKA ATTORNEYS &
SOLICITORS

Dozie Okwuosah
CENTRAL BANK OF NIGERIA

Stephen Ola Jagun
JAGUN ASSOCIATES

Titilola Olateju
OKONJO, ODIAWA & EBIE

Ayodeji Olomojobi
ALUKO & OYEBODE

Chris Erhi Omoru
CHANCERY SOLICITORS

Fred Onuobia
G. ELIAS & CO. SOLICITORS
AND ADVOCATES

Tochukwu Onyiuke
PUNUKA ATTORNEYS &
SOLICITORS

Nestor Orji
NNENNA EJEKAM ASSOCIATES

Christian Oronsaye
ALUKO & OYEBODE

Theo Chike Osanakpo
DR. T. C. OSANAKPO & CO.

Kola Osholeye
ELEKTRINT (NIGERIA) LIMITED

Olufemi Ososanya
HLB Z.O. OSOSANYA & CO.

Gbenga Oyebode
ALUKO & OYEBODE

Taiwo Oyedele
PRICEWATERHOUSECOOPERS

Oyindamola Oyedutan
ALUKO & OYEBODE

Afolabi Samuel
PHCN, ISLANDS DISTRICT

Yewande Senbore
OLANIWUN AJAYI LP

Serifat Solebo
LAND SERVICES DIRECTORATE

Adeola Sunmola
UDO UDOMA & BELO-OSAGIE

Ladi Taiwo
ABDULAI, TAIWO & CO.

Chima Polly Ubechu
CENOUXS LOGISTICS LTD

Reginald Udom
ALUKO & OYEBODE

Aniekan Ukpanah
UDO UDOMA & BELO-OSAGIE

Maxwell Ukpebor
WTS ADEBIYI & ASSOCIATES

Adamu M. Usman
F.O. AKINRELE & CO.

Tokunbo Wahab
ALUKO & OYEBODE

NORWAY

Anders Aasland Kittelsen
ADVOKATFIRMAET SCHJØDT
DA

Kristian Berentsen
ADVOKATFIRMA DLA PIPER
NORWAY DA

Stig Berge
THOMMESSEN KREFTING
GREVE LUND AS, MEMBER OF
LEX MUNDI

Rune Birkeland
GRIEG LOGISTICS AS

Eirik Brønner
KVALE & CO. ADVOKATFIRMA
ANS

Carl Arthur Christiansen
RAEDER ADVOKATFIRMA

Lars Ekeland
ADVOKATFIRMAET HJORT DA,
MEMBER OF IUS LABORIS

Knut Ekern
PRICEWATERHOUSECOOPERS

Simen Aasen Engebretsen
DELOITTE

Yngvil Erichsen
ADVOKATFIRMA DLA PIPER
NORWAY DA

Stein Fagerhaug
DALAN ADVOKATFIRMA DA

Claus R. Flinder
SIMONSEN ADVOKATFIRMA DA

Amund Fougner
ADVOKATFIRMAET HJORT DA,
MEMBER OF IUS LABORIS

Geir Frøholm
ADVOKATFIRMAET SCHJØDT
DA

Mads Fuglesang
ADVOKATFIRMAET SELMER DA

Line Granhol
ADVOKATFIRMA DLA PIPER
NORWAY DA

Andreas Hanssen
ADVOKATFIRMA DLA PIPER
NORWAY DA

Therese Høyer Grimstad
ADVOKATFIRMAET HJORT DA,
MEMBER OF IUS LABORIS

Odd Hylland
PRICEWATERHOUSECOOPERS

Hanne Karlsen
RAEDER ADVOKATFIRMA

Niels R. Kiaer
RIME ADVOKATFIRMA DA

Bjørn H. Kise
ADVOKATFIRMA VOGT &
WIIG AS

Baard Koppang
ADVOKATFIRMAET
PRICEWATERHOUSECOOPERS
AS

Knut Martinsen
THOMMESSEN KREFTING
GREVE LUND AS, MEMBER OF
LEX MUNDI

Ole Fredrik Melleby
RAEDER ADVOKATFIRMA

Karl Erik Nedregotten
PRICEWATERHOUSECOOPERS

Thomas Nordgård
VOGT & WIIG AS

Ole Kristian Olsby
HOMBLE OLSBY
ADVOKATFIRMA AS

Johan Ratvik
ADVOKATFIRMA DLA PIPER
NORWAY DA

Ståle Skutle Arneson
ADVOKATFIRMA VOGT &
WIIG AS

Simen Smeby Lium
WIKBORG, REIN & CO.

Christel Spannow
PRICEWATERHOUSECOOPERS

Liv Stølen
SIMONSEN ADVOKATFIRMA DA

Knut Storheim
GRIEG LOGISTICS AS

Stine Sverdrup
PRICEWATERHOUSECOOPERS

Ingvill Tollman Fosse
ADVOKATFIRMAET SELMER DA

Espen Trædal
PRICEWATERHOUSECOOPERS

Ole Andreas Uttberg
ADVOKATFIRMA HJORT DA,
MEMBER OF IUS LABORIS

OMAN

Jehanzeb Afridi
AL BUSAIDY, MANSOOR JAMAL
& CO.

Syed Nasir Ahmed
MAERSK LINE

Hamad Al Abri
MUSCAT ELECTRICITY
DISTRIBUTION COMPANY

Zubaida Fakir Mohamed Al
Balushi
CENTRAL BANK OF OMAN

Fahmy Al Hinai
POLY PRODUCTS L.L.C

Salem Ben Nasser Al Ismaily
THE OMANI CENTER FOR
INVESTMENT PROMOTION

& EXPORT DEVELOPMENT
(OCIPED)

Mauwiya Ali Suleiman
AL BUSAIDY, MANSOOR JAMAL
& CO.

Mohammed Alshahri
MOHAMMED AISHAHRI &
ASSOCIATES

Hamad M. Al-Sharji
HAMAD AL-SHARJI, PETER
MANSOUR & CO.

Pradhnesh Bhonsale
MAERSK LINE

Mehdi Bin Ali Bin Juma
THE OMANI CENTER FOR
INVESTMENT PROMOTION
& EXPORT DEVELOPMENT
(OCIPED)

Archie Campbell
DENTON WILDE SAPTE

Mehreen B. Elahi
AL BUSAIDY, MANSOOR JAMAL
& CO.

Candida Fernandez
AL BUSAIDY, MANSOOR JAMAL
& CO.

Zareen George
AL BUSAIDY, MANSOOR JAMAL
& CO.

Alessandro Gugolz
SAID AL SHAHRY LAW OFFICE

Justine Harding
DENTON WILDE SAPTE

Sarah Hestad
CURTIS MALLET - PREVOST,
COLT & MOSLE LLP

Hussein
MUSCAT ELECTRICITY
DISTRIBUTION COMPANY

Diana Jarrar
ABU-GHAZALEH LEGAL -
(TAG-LEGAL)

Saqib Jillani
AL BUSAIDY, MANSOOR JAMAL
& CO.

Sunil Joseph
MAERSK LINE

JOTUN PAINTS LLC

Mehdi Ali Juma
GULF AGENCY COMPANY LLC

Ziad Khattab
ABU-GHAZALEH LEGAL -
(TAG-LEGAL)

P.E. Lalachen MJ

KHIMJI RAMDAS

Pushpa Malani
PRICEWATERHOUSECOOPERS

Mansoor Jamal Malik
AL BUSAIDY, MANSOOR JAMAL
& CO.

Kapil Mehta
MAERSK LINE

Subha Mohan
CURTIS MALLET - PREVOST,
COLT & MOSLE LLP

Natarajan Narayana Swami
POLY PRODUCTS L.L.C

Bruce Palmer
CURTIS MALLET - PREVOST,
COLT & MOSLE LLP

Dali Rahmattala Habboub
DENTON WILDE SAPTE

Antonia Robinson
DENTON WILDE SAPTE

Muntasir Said Al Sawafi
MAERSK LINE

Mark Schmidt
DENTON WILDE SAPTE

Charles Schofield
TROWERS & HAMLINS

Paul Sheridan
DENTON WILDE SAPTE

Balaji Srinivasan
TOWELL AL ZAWRA
ENGINEERING SERVICES
COMPANY

Paul Suddaby
PRICEWATERHOUSECOOPERS

Ahsan Syed Anwar
POLY PRODUCTS L.L.C

Naji Taha
ABU-GHAZALEH LEGAL -
(TAG-LEGAL)

THE LIGHTHOUSE

Jeff Todd
PRICEWATERHOUSECOOPERS

Simon Ward
AL BUSAIDY, MANSOOR JAMAL
& CO.

Norman Williams
MAJAN ENGINEERING
CONSULTANTS

Sarah Wright
DENTON WILDE SAPTE

PAKISTAN

Ghulam Abbas
KHURSHEED KHAN &
ASSOCIATES

Sh. Farooq Abdullah
ABRAHAM & SARWANA

Ali Jafar Abidi
STATE BANK OF PAKISTAN

Jawad Ahmed
MUHAMMAD FAROOQ & CO.
CHARTERED ACCOUNTANTS

Kamran Ahmed
MANDVIWALLA & ZAFAR

Ahmad Syed Akhter
PYRAMID TRANSPORTATION
GROUP

AMIR SONS

Hyder Hussain Baig, Mirza
HAIDER SHAMSI & CO.,
CHARTERED ACCOUNTANTS

Major Javed Bashir
GREENFIELDS INTERNATIONAL

Kashif Butt
ZEESHAN ENTERPRISES

Zeeshan Butt
ZEESHAN ENTERPRISES

Fouad Rashid Dar
TARGET LOGISTICS INTL.
PRIVATE LTD.

Faisal Daudpota
KHALID DAUDPOTA & CO.

Junaid Daudpota
KHALID DAUDPOTA & CO.

Khalid Habibullah
ABRAHAM & SARWANA

Syed Ahmad Hassan Shah
HASSAN KAUNAIN NAFEES

Aman Ullah Iqbal
Crown Trading Company

Fiza Islam
Legis Inn (Attorneys & Corporate Consultants)

Muzaffar Islam
Legis Inn (Attorneys & Corporate Consultants)

Masooma Jaffer
Abraham & Sarwana

Faisal Jamil
Feroze Textile Industries

Farooq uz-Zaman Khan
Association of Builders and Developers of Pakistan

Zulfiqar Khan
Khursheed Khan & Associates

Asim Khan Hameed
Ivon Trading Company Pvt. Ltd.

Muhammad Maki
Abraham & Sarwana

Rashid Mehmood

Nasir Mehmood Ahmed
Bunker Logistics

Rashid Rahman Mir
Rahman Sarfaraz Rahim Iqbal Rafiq Chartered Accountants, member of Russell Bedford International

T. Ud-Din A. Mirza
A.F. Ferguson & Co, a member firm of PricewaterhouseCoopers

Saqib Munir
Zafar & Associates LLP

Javed Naushahi
ECRC

Faiza Rafique
Legis Inn

Abdul Rahman
Qamar Abbas & Co.

Zaki Rahman
Ebrahim Hosain, Advocates and Corporate Counsel

Muhammad Saleem Rana
State Bank of Pakistan

Abdur Razzaq
Qamar Abbas & Co.

Khalid Rehman
Surridge & Beecheno

Abdu Salam
Legis Inn

Beenish Saleem
Securities and Exchange Commission

Hamza Saleem
Mandviwalla & Zafar

Jawad A. Sarwana
Abraham & Sarwana

Shahid Sattar
Apex Power Solutions (Pvt.) Ltd.

Adil Shafi
Mandviwalla & Zafar

Huma Shah
M/s Sheikh Shah Rana & Ijaz

Nazir Shaheen
Securities and Exchange Commission

Ghulam Haider Shamsi
Haider Shamsi & Co., Chartered Accountants

Muhammad Siddique
Securities and Exchange Commission

Muhammad Yousuf
Haider Shamsi & Co., Chartered Accountants

Ilyas Zafar
Zafar & Associates LLP

Akhtar Zaidi
Karachi Electricity Supply Company

PALAU

Kenneth Barden

Ricardo Bausoch
Bureau of Revenue, Customs and Taxation

Cristina Castro
Western Caroline Trading Co.

Yukiwo P. Dengokl

Anita Jowitt
University of the South Pacific

Lolita Gibbons-Decheny
Koror Planning and Zoning Office

William L. Ridpath

David Shadel
The Law Office of Kirk and Shadel

Peter C. Tsao
Western Caroline Trading Co.

PANAMA

Alejandro Alemán
Alfaro, Ferrer & Ramírez

Renan Arjona
CAPAC (Cámara Panameña de la Construcción)

Gilberto Arosemena
Arosemena Noriega & Contreras, member of Ius Laboris and Lex Mundi

Khatiya Asvat
Patton, Moreno & Asvat

Francisco A. Barrios G.
PricewaterhouseCoopers

Klaus Bieberach
PricewaterhouseCoopers

Jose Ignacio Bravo
COCOLPLAN

Panamá Soluciones Logísticas Int. - PSLI

Luis Chalhoub
Icaza, Gonzalez-Ruiz & Aleman

Julio Cesar Contreras III
Arosemena Noriega & Contreras, member of Ius Laboris and Lex Mundi

Rigoberto Coronado
Mossack Fonseca & Co.

Guadalupe de Coparropa
CEVA Logistics

Amanda de Wong
PricewaterhouseCoopers

Jeanina Diaz
PricewaterhouseCoopers

Marisol Ellis
Icaza, Gonzalez-Ruiz & Aleman

Michael Fernandez
CAPAC (Cámara Panameña de la Construcción)

Enna Ferrer
Alfaro, Ferrer & Ramírez

Jorge R. González Byrne
Arias, Alemán & Mora

Jetzabel Luque
Arosemena Noriega & Contreras, member of Ius Laboris and Lex Mundi

Ricardo Madrid
PricewaterhouseCoopers

Ana Lucia Márquez
Arosemena Noriega & Contreras, member of Ius Laboris and Lex Mundi

Ivette Elisa Martínez Saenz
Patton, Moreno & Asvat

José Miguel Navarrete
Arosemena Noriega & Contreras, member of Ius Laboris and Lex Mundi

Ramón Ortega
PricewaterhouseCoopers

Sebastian Perez
Union Fenosa - EDEMET - EDECHI

Jorge Quijano
Arosemena Noriega & Contreras, member of Ius Laboris and Lex Mundi

Alfredo Ramírez Jr.
Alfaro, Ferrer & Ramírez

Manuel E. Rodriguez
Union Fenosa - EDEMET - EDECHI

Luz María Salamina
Asociación Panameña de Crédito

Valentín Ureña III
Arosemena Noriega & Contreras, member of Ius Laboris and Lex Mundi

Luis Vásquez
FTC - Financial, Tax & Consulting Group, S.A., correspondent of Russell Bedford International

Raúl Zuñiga Brid
Aleman, Cordero, Galindo & Lee

PAPUA NEW GUINEA

David Caradus
PricewaterhouseCoopers

Loani R. Henao
Henaos Lawyers

Anita Jowitt
University of the South Pacific

Michael Kambao
Steeles Lawyers

John Leahy
Peter Allan Lowing Lawyers

Leah Minimbi
PricewaterhouseCoopers

Peter Murton
Steamships Shipping Agency

Steven O'Brien
O'Briens

Kapu Rageau
Rageau, Manua & Kikira Lawyers

Benjamin Samson
Registrar Titles Office

Thomas Taberia
Peter Allan Lowing Lawyers

PARAGUAY

Perla Alderete
Vouga & Olmedo Abogados

Eduardo Alfaro
Peroni, Sosa, Tellechea, Burt & Narvaja, member of Lex Mundi

Florinda Benitez
Notary public

Hugo T. Berkemeyer
Berkemeyer, Attorneys & Counselors

Luis Alberto Breuer
Berkemeyer, Attorneys & Counselors

Esteban Burt
Peroni, Sosa, Tellechea, Burt & Narvaja, member of Lex Mundi

Ramón Antonio Castillo Saenz
Informconf S. A.

María Debattisti
Servimex SACI

Lorena Dolsa
Berkemeyer, Attorneys & Counselors

Estefanía Elicetche
Peroni, Sosa, Tellechea, Burt & Narvaja, member of Lex Mundi

Natalia Enciso Benitez
Notary public

Jorge Figueredo
Vouga & Olmedo Abogados

Ana Franco
BDO Rubinsztein & Guillén

Néstor Gamarra
Servimex SACI

Guillermo Gomez
PricewaterhouseCoopers

Nadia Gorostiaga
PricewaterhouseCoopers

Diego Guillen
BDO Rubinsztein & Guillén

Oscar Guillen
BDO Rubinsztein & Guillén

Carl Thomas Gwynn
Gwynn & Gwynn - Attorneys, Consultants and Translators

María Antonia Gwynn
Berkemeyer, Attorneys & Counselors

Norman Gwynn
Gwynn & Gwynn - Attorneys, Consultants and Translators

Carlos R. Gwynn S.
Gwynn & Gwynn - Attorneys, Consultants and Translators

Administración Nacional de Electricidad

Jorge Jimenez Rey
Banco Central del Paraguay

Nestor Loizaga
Ferrere Attorneys

Roberto Moreno Rodríguez Alcalá
Moreno Ruffinelli & Asociados

Rocío Penayo
Moreno Ruffinelli & Asociados

Yolanda Pereira
Berkemeyer, Attorneys & Counselors

Juan Pablo Pesce
Vivion S.A.

Beatriz Pisano
Ferrere Attorneys

Armindo Riquelme
Fiorio, Cardozo & Alvarado

Natalio Rubinsztein
BDO Rubinsztein & Guillén

Carlos Ruffinelli
Moreno Ruffinelli & Asociados

Angela Schaerer de Sosa
Escribana Pública

Ruben Taboada
PricewaterhouseCoopers

Maria Gloria Triguis Gonzalez
Berkemeyer, Attorneys & Counselors

PERU

Walter Aguirre
PricewaterhouseCoopers

Marco Antonio Alarcón Piana
Estudio Echecopar

Humberto Allemant
PricewaterhouseCoopers

Ana Maria Amésquita
Barzola & Asociados s.c., a member firm of Russell Bedford International

Jimy Atunga Rios
M.A.V. Logistica y Transporte S.A.

Guilhermo Auler
Forsyth & Arbe Abogados

Sergio Barboza
Pizarro, Botto & Escobar Abogados

Milagros A. Barrera
Barrios Fuentes Gallo Abogados

German Barrios
Barrios Fuentes Gallo Abogados

Raul Barrios
Barrios Fuentes Gallo Abogados

Maritza Barzola
Barzola & Asociados s.c., a member firm of Russell Bedford International

Vanessa Barzola
PricewaterhouseCoopers Legal Services

Marianell Bonomini
PricewaterhouseCoopers Legal Services

Ursula Caro
Estudio Rubio, Leguía, Normand y Asociados

Luis Enrique Malpartida Cárpena
Peru Compite

José Ignacio Castro
Estudio Rubio, Leguía, Normand y Asociados

Fernando Castro Kahn
Muñiz, Ramírez, Peréz-Taiman & Luna Victoria Attorneys at Law

Cecilia Catacora
Estudio Olaechea, member of Lex Mundi

Sandro Cogorno
Forsyth & Arbe Abogados

Javier de la Vega
PricewaterhouseCoopers

Alfonso De Los Heros Pérez Albela
Estudio Echecopar

Paula Devescovi
Barrios Fuentes Gallo Abogados

Juan Carlos Durand Grahammer
Durand Abogados

Arturo Ferrari
Muñiz, Ramírez, Peréz-Taiman & Luna Victoria Attorneys at Law

Jorge Fuentes
Estudio Rubio, Leguía, Normand y Asociados

Luis Fuentes
Barrios Fuentes Gallo Abogados

Juan García Montúfar
Estudio Rubio, Leguía, Normand y Asociados

Cecilia Guzman-Barron
Barrios Fuentes Gallo Abogados

Alfonso Higueras Suarez
Equifax Peru S.A.

Jose A. Honda
Estudio Olaechea, member of Lex Mundi

Diego Huertas del Pino
Barrios Fuentes Gallo Abogados

Kuno Kafka Prado
Estudio Rubio, Leguía, Normand y Asociados

Lima Chamber of Commerce

Adolfo Lopez
PricewaterhouseCoopers

German Lora
Payet, Rey, Cauvi Abogados

Ursula Luna
Estudio Rubio, Leguía, Normand y Asociados

Milagros Maravi
Estudio Rubio, Leguía, Normand y Asociados

Carlos Martinez Ebell
Estudio Rubio, Leguía, Normand y Asociados

Jesús Matos
Estudio Olaechea, member of Lex Mundi

Milagros Mendoza
Estudio Rubio, Leguía, Normand y Asociados

Jorge Mogrovejo
Superintendentency of Banking

Marlene Molero
Estudio Rubio, Leguía, Normand y Asociados

Leonardo Muñante Carpio
Municipalidad Metropolitana de Lima

Miguel Mur
PricewaterhouseCoopers

Franco Muschi Loayza
Payet, Rey, Cauvi Abogados

Gabriel Musso Canepa
Estudio Rubio, Leguía, Normand y Asociados

Notary Office of Donato Hernan Carpio Velez

Rafael Ordoñez
Barzola & Asociados s.c., a member firm of Russell Bedford International

Cristina Oviedo
Barrios Fuentes Gallo Abogados

Carmen Padrón
Estudio Rubio, Leguía, Normand y Asociados

Panalpina Transportes Mundiales S.A.

Claudia Pareja
Estudio Rubio, Leguía, Normand y Asociados

César Yaipén Passalacqua
CEDETEC

Adolfo J. Pinillos
Durand Abogados

Lucianna Polar
Estudio Olaechea, member of Lex Mundi

Bruno Marchese Quintana
Estudio Rubio, Leguía, Normand y Asociados

Carlos Javier Rabanal Sobrino
Durand Abogados

Fernando M. Ramos
Barrios Fuentes Gallo Abogados

Sonia L. Rengifo
Barrios Fuentes Gallo Abogados

Alonso Rey Bustamante
Payet, Rey, Cauvi Abogados

Guillermo Acuña Roeder
Estudio Rubio, Leguía, Normand y Asociados

Renzo Rufasto Lira
Payet, Rey, Cauvi Abogados

Emil Ruppert
Estudio Rubio, Leguía, Normand y Asociados

Carolina Sáenz Llanos
Estudio Rubio, Leguía, Normand y Asociados

Adolfo Sanabria Mercado
Muñiz, Ramírez, Peréz-Taiman & Luna Victoria Attorneys at Law

Diego Sanchez
PricewaterhouseCoopers

José Alfredo Paino Scarpati
CEDETEC

Martin Serkovic
Estudio Olaechea, member of Lex Mundi

Claudia Sevillano
Pizarro, Botto & Escobar Abogados

Hugo Silva
Rodrigo, Elías, Medrano Abogados

Peggy Sztuden
Peru Compite

Agnes Franco Temple
National Competitiveness Council

Carlos Gallardo Torres
General Agency of Foreign Economic Matters, Competition and Private Investment

Liliana Tsuboyama
Estudio Echecopar

Manuel A. Ugarte
Delmar Ugarte Abogados

Jack Vainstein
Vainstein & Ingenieros S.A.

José Antonio Valdez
Estudio Olaechea, member of Lex Mundi

Manuel Villa-García
Estudio Olaechea, member of Lex Mundi

Ursula Villanueva
Estudio Rubio, Leguía, Normand y Asociados

Agustín Yrigoyen
Estudio Aurelio García Sayán- Abogados

Eulogio Zapata Gamarra
Municipalidad Metropolitana de Lima

Hector Zegarra
Payet, Rey, Cauvi Abogados

PHILIPPINES

Emilio Amaranto
Puyat Jacinto Santos Law Office

Myla Gloria Amboy
Jimenez Gonzales Bello Valdez Caluya & Fernandez

Manuel Batallones
BAP Credit Bureau

Anna Bianca Torres
PJS Law

Antonio T. Bote
International Consolidator Philippines, Inc.

Alexander B. Cabrera
PricewaterhouseCoopers / Isla Lipana & Co.

Christopher R. Cadano
Globe Link Cargo Logistics Inc.

Jean Caillard
Bansard International

Ernesto Caluya Jr
Jimenez Gonzales Bello Valdez Caluya & Fernandez

Cecile M.E. Caro
SyCip Salazar Hernandez & Gatmaitan

Joseph Omar A. Castillo
Puyat Jacinto Santos Law Office

Kenneth Chua
Quisumbing Torres, member firm of Baker and McKenzie

Barbara Jil Clara
SyCip Salazar Hernandez & Gatmaitan

Barbra Jill Clara
SyCip Salazar Hernandez & Gatmaitan

Emerico O. de Guzman
Angara Abello Concepcion Regala & Cruz Law Offices (ACCRALAW)

Dante Desierto
Romulo, Mabanta, Buenaventura, Sayoc & de los Angeles, member of Lex Mundi

Benedicta Du-Baladad
Punongbayan & Araullo

Fast-Tract Freight, Inc.

Anthony Fernandes
First Balfour, Inc

Rachel Follosco
Follosco Morallos & Herce

Catherine Franco
Quisumbing Torres, member firm of Baker and McKenzie

Gilberto Gallos
Angara Abello Concepcion Regala & Cruz Law Offices (ACCRALAW)

Geraldine S. Garcia
Follosco Morallos & Herce

Andres Gatmaitan
SyCip Salazar Hernandez & Gatmaitan

Gwen Grecia-de Vera
PJS Law

Tadeo F. Hilado
Angara Abello Concepcion Regala & Cruz Law Offices (ACCRALAW)

Clifton James Sawit
Quasha Ancheta Pena & Nolasco

Karen Jimeno
Baker & McKenzie

Rafael Khan
Siguion Reyna Montecillo & Ongsiako

Jennifer Laygo
Jimenez Gonzales Bello Valdez Caluya & Fernandez

Jennifer I Lim
SyCip Salazar Hernandez & Gatmaitan

Victoria Limkico
Jimenez Gonzales Bello Valdez Caluya & Fernandez

Erich H. Lingad
International Consolidator Philippines, Inc.

Anna Manalaysay
Jimenez Gonzales Bello Valdez Caluya & Fernandez

Recio Marichelle
Angara Abello Concepcion Regala & Cruz Law Offices (ACCRALAW)

Lory Anne McMullin
Jimenez Gonzales Bello Valdez Caluya & Fernandez

Yolanda Mendoza-Eleazar
Castillo Laman Tan Pantaleon & San Jose

Elmer R. Mitra, Jr
PricewaterhouseCoopers / Isla Lipana & Co.

Cheryll Grace Montealegre
PricewaterhouseCoopers / Isla Lipana & Co.

Jesusito G. Morallos
Follosco Morallos & Herce

Freddie Naagas
OOCL Logistics

Alan Ortiz
Follosco Morallos & Herce

Carla Ortiz
Romulo, Mabanta, Buenaventura, Sayoc & de los Angeles, member of Lex Mundi

Emmanuel C. Paras
SyCip Salazar Hernandez & Gatmaitan

Zayber B. Protacio
PricewaterhouseCoopers / Isla Lipana & Co.

Kristine Quimpo
Jimenez Gonzales Bello Valdez Caluya & Fernandez

Senen Quizon
Punongbayan & Araullo

Grace Rallos

Janice Kae Ramirez
Quasha Ancheta Pena & Nolasco

Judy Alice Repol
Angara Abello Concepcion Regala & Cruz Law Offices (ACCRALAW)

Roderick Reyes
Jimenez Gonzales Bello Valdez Caluya & Fernandez

Ricardo J. Romulo
Romulo, Mabanta, Buenaventura, Sayoc & de los Angeles, member of Lex Mundi

Celia Cristina Rosario Cabrera
SyCip Salazar Hernandez & Gatmaitan

Jose Manuel Santos
MERALCO

Felix Sy
Baker & McKenzie

Sheryl Tanquilut
Romulo, Mabanta, Buenaventura, Sayoc & de los Angeles, member of Lex Mundi

Angelo Tapales
Quisumbing Torres, member firm of Baker and McKenzie

Ma. Melva Valdez
Jimenez Gonzales Bello Valdez Caluya & Fernandez

Enrique W. Galang
Castillo Laman Tan Pantaleon & San Jose

Redentor C. Zapata
Quasha Ancheta Pena & Nolasco

Gil Roberto Zerrudo
Quisumbing Torres, member firm of Baker and McKenzie

POLAND

Allen & Overy, A. Pędzich sp. k.

Michal Barłowski
Wardyński & Partners, member of Lex Mundi

Aleksander Borowicz
Biuro Informacji Kredytowej S.A.

Agnieszka Chamera
PKF Tax Sp. z o.o

Krzysztof Cichocki
Sołtysiński Kawecki & Szlęzak

Krzysztof Ciepliński
Gide Loyrette Nouel, member of Lex Mundi

Bożena Ciosek
Wierzbowski Eversheds, member of Eversheds International Ltd.

Jaroslaw Czech
Wardyński & Partners, member of Lex Mundi

Monika Czekałowska
Salans

Karolina Doruchowska
DLA Piper Wiater sp.k

Tomasz Duchniak
Sołtysiński Kawecki & Szlęzak

Rafal Dziedzic
Gide Loyrette Nouel, member of Lex Mundi

Lech Giliciński
White & Case W. Daniłowicz, W. Jurcewicz i Wspólnicy sp. k.

Paweł Grześkowiak
Gide Loyrette Nouel, member of Lex Mundi

Piotr Kaim
PricewaterhouseCoopers

Iwona Karasek
Jagiellonian University Krakow

Edyta Kolkowska
Squire Sanders Święcicki Krześniak sp. k.

Szymon Kolodziej

Tomasz Korczyński
Wierzbowski Eversheds, member of Eversheds International Ltd.

Ewa Lachowska - Brol
Wierzbowski Eversheds, member of Eversheds International Ltd.

Mazars & Guerars Audyt sp. z o.o.

Agata Mierzwa
Wierzbowski Eversheds, member of Eversheds International Ltd.

Ministry of Economy

Barbara Misterska-Dragan
Misters Audytor Sp. z o.o., member of Russell Bedford International

Michal Niemirowicz-Szczytt
bnt Neupert Zamorska & Partnerzy s.c.

Dariusz Okolski
Okolski Law Office

Macie Owczarewicz
Gide Loyrette Nouel, member of Lex Mundi

Krzysztof Pawlak
Sołtysiński Kawecki & Szlęzak

Bożena Pawłowska-Krawczyk
Misters Audytor Sp. z o.o., member of Russell Bedford International

Weronika Pelc
Wardyński & Partners, member of Lex Mundi

Michal Piotrowski
PKF Tax Sp. z o.o.

Anna Maria Pukszto
Salans

Bartłomiej Raczkowski
Bartłomiej Raczkowski Kancelaria Prawa Pracy

Anna Ratajczyk
Gide Loyrette Nouel, member of Lex Mundi

Katarzyna Sarek
Bartłomiej Raczkowski Kancelaria Prawa Pracy

Karolina Schiffter
Sołtysiński Kawecki & Szlęzak

Zbigniew Skórczyński
Chadbourne & Parke LLP

Dorota Slizawska
PKF Tax Sp. z o.o.

Dariusz Smiechowski
Union of Polish Architects

Iwona Smith
PricewaterhouseCoopers

Ewelina Stobiecka
e/n/w/c Rechtsanwalte E.Stobiecka Kancelaria prawna sp.k.

Łukasz Szegda
Wardyński & Partners, member of Lex Mundi

Dariusz Tokarczuk
Gide Loyrette Nouel, member of Lex Mundi

Dominika Wagrodzka
bnt Neupert Zamorska & Partnerzy s.c.

Dariusz Wasylkowski
Wardyński & Partners, member of Lex Mundi

Radoslaw Waszkiewicz
Sołtysiński Kawecki & Szlęzak

Anna Wietrzyńska
DLA Piper Wiater sp.k

Tomasz Zabost

Andrzej Zacharzewski
Nikiel i Zacharzewski Adwokaci i Radcowie prawni

Malgorzata Zamorska
bnt Neupert Zamorska & Partnerzy s.c.

Sylwester Zydowicz
Gide Loyrette Nouel, member of Lex Mundi

PORTUGAL

Victor Abrantes
Victor Abrantes - International Sales Agent

Paula Alegria Martins
Mouteira Guerreiro, Rosa Amaral & Associados - Sociedade de Advogados R.L.

Bruno Andrade Alves
PricewaterhouseCoopers

Miguel Azevedo
J & A Garrigues, S.L.

Barbara Berckmoes
PricewaterhouseCoopers

Marco Bicó da Costa
Credinformações/ Equifax

José Pedro Briosa e Gala
Barrocas Sarmento Neves

Marcio Carreira Nobre
Abreu Advogados

Tiago Castanheira Marques
Abreu Advogados

Inês Castelo Branco
CGM Gonçalo Capitão, Gali Macedo e associados

Gabriel Cordeiro
Direcção Municipal de Gestão Urbanística

Pedro de Almeida Cabral
Ministry of Justice

Duarte de Athayde
Abreu Advogados

João Cadete de Matos
Banco de Portugal

Ana Duarte
PricewaterhouseCoopers

John Duggan
PricewaterhouseCoopers

Eduardo Fernandes
Portugal Order of Notaries

Bruno Ferreira
J & A Garrigues, S.L.

Pedro Gil Pereira
JMSROC, lda, member of Russell Bedford International

João Gonçalves Assunção
Abreu Advogados

Melanie Guerra
Noronha Advogados

Paulo Henriques
University of Coimbra

Miguel Inácio Castro
Mouteira Guerreiro, Rosa Amaral & Associados - Sociedade de Advogados R.L.

Maria João Ricou
Gonçalves Pereira, Castelo Branco & Associados

Martim Krupenski
Barrocas Sarmento Neves

Patric Lamarca
Noronha Advogados

Maria Manuel Leitão Marques
Secretary of State for Administrative Modernisation

Diogo Léonidas Rocha
J & A Garrigues, S.L.

Antonio Lopes
PricewaterhouseCoopers

Tiago Gali Macedo
CGM Gonçalo Capitão, Gali Macedo e associados

Ana Margarida Maia
Miranda Correia Amendoeira & Associados

Nuno Mansilha
Miranda Correia Amendoeira & Associados

Miguel Marques dos Santos
J & A Garrigues, S.L.

Isabel Martínez de Salas
J & A Garrigues, S.L.

Susana Melo
Grant Thornton Consultores, Lda.

Joaquim Luis Mendes
Grant Thornton Consultores, Lda.

José Monteiro
JMSROC, lda, member of Russell Bedford International

António Mouteira Guerreiro
Mouteira Guerreiro, Rosa Amaral & Associados - Sociedade de Advogados R.L.

Rita Nogueira Neto
J & A Garrigues, S.L.

Catarina Nunes
PricewaterhouseCoopers

Ema Palma
JMSROC, lda, member of Russell Bedford International

Rui Peixoto Duarte
Abreu Advogados

Tiago Pereira
Barrocas Sarmento Neves

Pedro Pereira Coutinho
J & A Garrigues, S.L.

Acácio Pita Negrão
PLEN - Sociedade de Advogados, RL

Carla Ramos
Barros, Sobral, G. Gomes & Associados

Ana Rita Reis
Neville de Rougemont & Associados

Cristina Reis
PricewaterhouseCoopers

César Sá Esteves
Simmons & Simmons

David Salgado Areias
Areias Advogados

Francisco Salgueiro
Neville de Rougemont & Associados

Maria Santiago
Noronha Advogados

Pedro Santos
Grant Thornton Consultores, Lda.

Fillipe Santos Barata
Gonçalves Pereira, Castelo Branco & Associados

Claudia Santos Cruz
Barrocas Sarmento Neves

Eliana Silva Pereira
CGM Gonçalo Capitão, Gali Macedo e associados

Manuel Silveira Botelho
António Frutuoso de Melo e Associados - Sociedade de Advogados, R.L.

Isa Simones de Carvalho
Noronha Advogados

Carla Soares
Portugal Order of Notaries

Ricardo Soares Domingos
Noronha Advogados

Carmo Sousa Machado
Abreu Advogados

João Paulo Teixeira de Matos
J & A Garrigues, S.L.

Nuno Telleria
Barros, Sobral, G. Gomes & Associados

Maria Valente
Simmons & Simmons

Gonçalo Xavier
Barros, Sobral, G. Gomes & Associados

PUERTO RICO

Viviana Aguilu
PricewaterhouseCoopers

Ignacio Alvarez
Pietrantoni Méndez & Alvarez LLP

Alfredo Alvarez-Ibañez
O'Neill & Borges

Juan Aquino
O'Neill & Borges

James A. Arroyo
TransUnion De Puerto Rico

Hermann Bauer
O'Neill & Borges

Nikos Buxeda Ferrer
Adsuar Muñiz Goyco Seda & Pérez-Ochoa, P.S.C

Mildred Caban
Goldman Antonetti & Córdova P.S.C

Jorge Capó Matos
O'Neill & Borges

Walter F. Chow
O'Neill & Borges

Miguel A. Cordero
PUERTO RICO ELECTRIC POWER AUTHORITY

Alberto G. Estrella
WILLIAM ESTRELLA LAW OFFICES

Carla Garcia
O'NEILL & BORGES

Virginia Gomez
PUERTO RICO ELECTRIC POWER AUTHORITY

Carlos Hernandez
REICHARD & ESCALERA

Gerardo Hernandez
WILLIAM ESTRELLA LAW OFFICES

Francisco Hernández-Ruiz
REICHARD & ESCALERA

Donald E. Hull
PIETRANTONI MÉNDEZ & ALVAREZ LLP

Ana Lago
O'NEILL & BORGES

Luis Marini
O'NEILL & BORGES

Rubén M. Medina-Lugo
CANCIO, NADAL, RIVERA & DÍAZ

Oscar O Meléndez - Sauri
COTO MALLEY & TAMARGO, LLP

Juan Carlos Méndez
MCCONNELL VALDÉS LLC

Luis Mongil-Casasnovas
MARTINEZ ODELL & CALABRIA

Joaquin M Nieves
SUN AIR EXPEDITE SERVICE

Jorge Peirats
PIETRANTONI MÉNDEZ & ALVAREZ LLP

Rafael Pérez-Villarini
FPV & GALINDEZ CPAs, PSC, MEMBER OF RUSSELL BEDFORD INTERNATIONAL

Edwin Quiñones
QUIÑONES & SÁNCHEZ, PSC

Victor Rodriguez
MULTITRANSPORT & MARINE Co.

Victor Rodriguez
PRICEWATERHOUSECOOPERS

Frank Rodríguez
PUERTO RICO ELECTRICAL CONTRACTORS ASSOCIATION

Patricia Salichs
O'NEILL & BORGES

Anthonio Santos
PIETRANTONI MÉNDEZ & ALVAREZ LLP

Jose Torres
PUERTO RICO ELECTRICAL CONTRACTORS ASSOCIATION

Yasmin Umpierre-Chaar
O'NEILL & BORGES

Carlos Valldejuly
O'NEILL & BORGES

Fernando Van Derdys
REICHARD & ESCALERA

Travis Wheatley
O'NEILL & BORGES

QATAR

Naveed Abdulla
GULF STAR GROUP

Abdelmoniem Abutiffa
QATAR INTERNATIONAL LAW FIRM

A. Rahman Mohamed Al-Jufairi

Khalil Al-Mulla
CUSTOMS AND PORTS GENERAL AUTHORITY

Ian Clay
PRICEWATERHOUSECOOPERS

Richard Dib
ABU-GHAZALEH LEGAL - (TAG-LEGAL)

Daoud Adel Issa
QATAR PETROLEUM

Sajid Khan
PRICEWATERHOUSECOOPERS

Abdul Muttalib
GULF STAR GROUP

Terence G.C. Witzmann
HSBC

ROMANIA

Daniel Aghel
PRICEWATERHOUSECOOPERS

Adriana Almasan
STOICA & ASOCIATII ATTORNEYS-AT-LAW

Suzana Alsamadi
SOVA & PARTNERS

Marcela Anghel
D & B DAVID SI BAIAS S.C.A.

Andrei Badiu
3B EXPERT AUDIT, MEMBER OF RUSSELL BEDFORD INTERNATIONAL

Emanuel Bancila
D&B DAVID SI BAIAS SCA

Irina Bănică
MUŞAT & ASOCIAŢII

Irina Barbu
D & B DAVID SI BAIAS S.C.A.

Cristian Bichi
NATIONAL BANK OF ROMANIA

Monica Biciusca
ANGHEL STABB & PARTNERS

Roxana Bolea
D & B DAVID SI BAIAS S.C.A.

Cosmin Bonea
SALANS

Alin Buftea
MARIAN DINU LAW OFFICE

Radu Cernov
SOVA & PARTNERS

Chirica Cezara
D&B DAVID SI BAIAS SCA

Victor Ciocîltan
OANCEA CIOCÎLTAN & ASOCIATII

Dorin Coza
BABIUC SULICA PROTOPOPESCU VONICA

Tiberiu Csaki
SALANS

Anca Danilescu
ZAMFIRESCU RACOŢI PREDOIU LAW PARTNERSHIP

Cristina Dascalu
SOVA & PARTNERS

Peter De Ruiter
PRICEWATERHOUSECOOPERS

Luminita Dima
NESTOR NESTOR DICULESCU KINGSTON PETERSEN

Alexandru Dobrescu
LINA & GUIA S.C.A

Ion Dragulin
NATIONAL BANK OF ROMANIA

Laura Adina Duca
NESTOR NESTOR DICULESCU KINGSTON PETERSEN

Cristina Ene
PRICEWATERHOUSECOOPERS

Serban Epure
BIROUL DE CREDIT

Iulia Feraru
GEBRUEDER WEISS SRL

Adriana Gaspar
NESTOR NESTOR DICULESCU KINGSTON PETERSEN

Monica Georgiadis
MARIAN DINU LAW OFFICE

Gina Gheorghe
TANASESCU, LEAUA, CADAR & ASOCIATII

Georgiana Ghitu
MARIAN DINU LAW OFFICE

Sergiu Gidei
D & B DAVID SI BAIAS S.C.A.

Andra Gogulescu
MARIAN DINU LAW OFFICE

Alexandru Gosa
D & B DAVID SI BAIAS S.C.A.

Mihai Guia
LINA & GUIA S.C.A

HERCULE IMPEX

Oana Ionascu
SALANS

Vasile Iulian
CONELECTRO

Mihaela Ivan
SALANS

Crenguta Leaua
TANASESCU, LEAUA, CADAR & ASOCIATII

Cristian Lina
LINA & GUIA S.C.A

George Manciu
ZAMFIRESCU RACOŢI PREDOIU LAW PARTNERSHIP

Simona Manea
PRICEWATERHOUSECOOPERS

Dumitru Viorel Manescu
NATIONAL UNION OF CIVIL LAW NOTARIES OF ROMANIA

Oana Manuceanu
PRICEWATERHOUSECOOPERS

Gelu Titus Maravela
MUŞAT & ASOCIAŢII

Carmen Medar
D & B DAVID SI BAIAS S.C.A.

Anca Mihailescu
MARIAN DINU LAW OFFICE

Irina Mihalache
PRICEWATERHOUSECOOPERS

Mihaela Mitroi
PRICEWATERHOUSECOOPERS

Rodica Miu
PRICEWATERHOUSECOOPERS

Dominic Morega
MUŞAT & ASOCIAŢII

Adriana Neagoe
NATIONAL BANK OF ROMANIA

Manuela Marina Nestor
NESTOR NESTOR DICULESCU KINGSTON PETERSEN

Madalin Niculeasa
NESTOR NESTOR DICULESCU KINGSTON PETERSEN

Tudor Oancea
OANCEA CIOCÎLTAN & ASOCIATII

Delia Paceagiu
NESTOR NESTOR DICULESCU KINGSTON PETERSEN

Marius Pătrăşcanu
MUŞAT & ASOCIAŢII

Alina Popescu
MUŞAT & ASOCIAŢII

Cristina Popescu
LINA & GUIA S.C.A

Mariana Popescu
NATIONAL BANK OF ROMANIA

Diana Emanuela Precup
NESTOR NESTOR DICULESCU KINGSTON PETERSEN

Cristian Predan
GEBRUEDER WEISS SRL

Irina Preoteasa
PRICEWATERHOUSECOOPERS

Alina Proteasa
LINA & GUIA S.C.A

Radu Protopopescu
BABIUC SULICA PROTOPOPESCU VONICA

Adriana Puscas
BABIUC SULICA PROTOPOPESCU VONICA

Laura Radu
STOICA & ASOCIATII ATTORNEYS-AT-LAW

Raluca Radu
SALANS

RADU TĂRĂCILĂ PĂDURARI RETEVOESCU SCA IN ASSOCIATION WITH ALLEN & OVERY LLP

Alina Rafaila
PRICEWATERHOUSECOOPERS

Diana Ristici
MARIAN DINU LAW OFFICE

Anda Rojanschi
D & B DAVID SI BAIAS S.C.A.

Alex Rosca

Angela Rosca

Andrei Săvescu
SĂVESCU SI ASOCIATII

Romana Schuster
PRICEWATERHOUSECOOPERS

Alexandru Slujitoru
D&B DAVID SI BAIAS SCA

Irina Sokolova
LEGALEX

Ileana Sovaila
MUŞAT & ASOCIAŢII

Oana Sovian
SALANS

David Stabb
ANGHEL STABB & PARTNERS

Marta Stefan
ANGHEL STABB & PARTNERS

Cristiana Stoica
STOICA & ASOCIATII ATTORNEYS-AT-LAW

Sorin Corneliu Stratula
STRATULA MOCANU & ASOCIATII

Potyesz Tiberu
BITRANS LTD., MEMBER OF WORLD MEDIATRANS GROUP

Anca Vatasoiu
SALANS

Mihai Vintu
PRICEWATERHOUSECOOPERS

Catalin Alexandru Vlasceanu
SALANS

RUSSIAN FEDERATION

ALLEN & OVERY LLP

Marat Agabalyan
HERBERT SMITH CIS LLP

Fedor Bogatyrev
LAW FIRM ALRUD

Yuri Boyarshinov
BAKER & MCKENZIE

Ilya Bulgakov
DLA PIPER RUS LIMITED

Maria Bykovskaya
GIDE LOYRETTE NOUEL VOSTOK

Andrey Dukhin
GIDE LOYRETTE NOUEL VOSTOK

Ilya Fainberg
GIDE LOYRETTE NOUEL VOSTOK

Valery Fedoreev
BAKER & MCKENZIE

Olga Fonotova
MACLEOD DIXON

Roman Golovatsky
DLA PIPER RUS LIMITED

Maria Gorban
GIDE LOYRETTE NOUEL VOSTOK

Igor Gorchakov
BAKER & MCKENZIE

Dina Gracheva
LAW FIRM ALRUD

Vitaly Grekhov
RUSSIA CONSULTING

Elena Kataeva
PRICEWATERHOUSECOOPERS

Alia Khalikova
LINIYA PRAVA

Alexander Khretinin
HERBERT SMITH CIS LLP

Anastasia Konovalova
MACLEOD DIXON

Maria Kosova
ORRICK, HERRINGTON & SUTCLIFFE LLP

Alyona Kozyreva
MACLEOD DIXON

Dmitry Kurochkin
HERBERT SMITH CIS LLP

Ekatarina Kvaskova
RUSSIA CONSULTING

David Lasfargue
GIDE LOYRETTE NOUEL VOSTOK

Michael Likonge
CONTINENTAL ALLIANCE

Konstantin Litvinenko
MACLEOD DIXON

Svetlana London

Dmitry Lyakhov
RUSSIN & VECCHI, LLC.

Tatiana Menshenina
MGAP ATTORNEYS AT LAW

Elena Nikulina
GIDE LOYRETTE NOUEL VOSTOK

Maria Priezzheva
ORRICK, HERRINGTON & SUTCLIFFE LLP

Elvira Sagetdinova
CONSULTING GROUP MIKHAILOV & PARTNERS, member of RUSSELL BEDFORD INTERNATIONAL

Ulf Schneider
RUSSIA CONSULTING

Olga Sirodoeva
ORRICK, HERRINGTON & SUTCLIFFE LLP

Steven Snaith
PRICEWATERHOUSECOOPERS

Pavel Solovyev
MAGNUSSON

Denis Sosedkin
DLA PIPER RUS LIMITED

Rainer Stawinoga
RUSSIA CONSULTING

Maria Tiftikidis
CMS INTERNATIONAL BV

Pavel Timofeev
HANNES SNELLMAN ATTORNEYS AT LAW LTD.

Natalia Vygovskaya
DLA PIPER RUS LIMITED

RWANDA

BANCOR, ACCESS BANK

Alberto Basomingera
CABINET D'AVOCATS MHAYIMANA

Pierre Célestin Bumbakare
RWANDA REVENUE AUTHORITY

Annie Kairaba-Kyambadde
RWANDA INITIATIVE FOR SUSTAINABLE DEVELOPMENT / LANDNET

Marcellin Kamanzi

Angélique Kantengwa
NATIONAL BANK OF RWANDA

Theophile Kazaneza
KIGALI BAR ASSOCIATION

Isaïe Mhayimana
CABINET D'AVOCATS MHAYIMANA

Donatien Mucyo
MUCYO & ASSOCIÉS

Alexandre Mugenzangabo
MUCYO & ASSOCIÉS

Richard Mugisha
TRUST LAW CHAMBERS

Elonie Mukandoli
NATIONAL BANK OF RWANDA

Léopold Munderere

Pothin Muvara
OFFICE OF THE REGISTRAR OF LAND TITLES

Radedonge Nimenya
NATIONAL BANK OF RWANDA

Eric Nsengimana
WORLD FREIGHT S.A.R.L.

Abel Nsengiyumva
CABINET ABEL NSENGIYUMVA

Anjaleedevi Ramdin
COMMERCIAL COURT OF NYARUGENGE

Jean Marie Vianney Ruzagiriza
MUCYO & ASSOCIÉS

Frank Twegire
RWANDA DEVELOPMENT BOARD

André Verbruggen

Stephen Zawadi
RWANDA REVENUE AUTHORITY

SAMOA

Mike Betham
TRANSAM LTD.

Denis Brady
LAND REGISTRATION ADVISER

Murray Drake
DRAKE & CO.

Ruby Drake
DRAKE & CO.

Karanita L. Enari
KRUSE, ENARI & BARLOW

Graham Hogarth
TRANSAM LTD.

Anita Jowitt
UNIVERSITY OF THE SOUTH PACIFIC

Herman Kruse
KRUSE, ENARI & BARLOW

George Latu
LATU EY & CLARKE LAWYERS

Maiava Peteru
LAW FIRM MAIAVA V.R. PETERU

John Ryan
TRANSAM LTD.

Patea Malo Setefano
MINISTRY OF NATURAL RESOURCES & ENVIRONMENT

Toleafoa RS Toailoa
TO'AILOA LAW OFFICE

Shan Shiraz Ali Usman
TRADEPAC MARKETING LTD.

SÃO TOMÉ AND PRINCIPE

António de Barros A. Aguiar
SOCOGESTA

Amaro
METALURGICA SANTO AMARO

André Aureliano Aragão
ANDRÉ AURELIANO ARAGÃO JURISCONSULTA & ADVOGADO

Abreu Conceição
SOARES DA COSTA

Frederico da Glória
TRIBUNAL DE 1A INSTÂNCIA (3O JUÍZO)

EMAE

Luisélio Pinto
UNITED INVESTMENTS

Deodato Gomes Rodrigues
ENAPORT

Maria do Céu Silveira
DIRECÇÃO DE OBRAS PÚBLICAS E URBANISMO

Carlos Stock
DIRECÇÃO DOS REGISTROS E NOTARIADO

SAUDI ARABIA

Emad Fareed Abdul Jawad
GLOBE MARINE SERVICES CO.

Ali Abedi
THE ALLAINCE OF ABBAS F. GHAZZAWI & CO. AND HAMMAD, AL-MEHDAR & CO.

Asad Abedi
THE ALLAINCE OF ABBAS F. GHAZZAWI & CO. AND HAMMAD, AL-MEHDAR & CO.

Danya Abulola
BAFAKIH & NASSIEF

Anas Akel
BAFAKIH & NASSIEF

Naïm Al Chami
ABU-GHAZALEH LEGAL - (TAG-LEGAL)

Sheikh Yousef Al Farraj
MINISTRY OF JUSTICE

Omar Al Saab
LAW OFFICE OF MOHANNED BIN SAUD AL-RASHEED IN ASSOCIATION WITH BAKER BOTTS LLP

Abdullah Fawaz Al Tamimi
AL TAMIMI & COMPANY ADVOCATES & LEGAL CONSULTANTS

Mashuor M. Al Tubaishi
RIYADH MUNICIPALITY

Nasser H. AlAamry
NATIONAL WATER COMPANY

Ibrahim Mohamed Al-But'hie
RIYADH MUNICIPALITY

Fayez Aldebs
AL JURAID & COMPANY / PRICEWATERHOUSECOOPERS

Ali. R. Al-Edrees
AL-BASSAM

Mohammed Al-Ghamdi
FULBRIGHT & JAWORSKI LLP

Abdullah Al-Hashim
AL-JADAAN & PARTNERS LAW FIRM

Hussam Salah Al-Hejailan
THE LAW FIRM OF SALAH AL-HEJAILANY

Hesham Al-Homoud
THE LAW FIRM OF DR. HESHAM AL-HOMOUD

Mohammed Al-Jaddan
AL-JADAAN & PARTNERS LAW FIRM

Fahad Almalki
AL TAMIMI & COMPANY ADVOCATES & LEGAL CONSULTANTS

Nabil Abdullah Al-Mubarak
SAUDI CREDIT BUREAU - SIMAH

Fayez Al-Nemer
TALAL BIN NAIF AL-HARBI LAW FIRM

Saad Al-Owain
UNIFIED REGISTRY- MINISTRY OF COMMERECE & INDUSTRY

Mohammed Al-Soaib
AL-SOAIB LAW FIRM

Wicki Andersen
BAKER BOTTS LLP

Abdul Moeen Arnous
LAW OFFICE OF HASSAN MAHASSNI

Joseph Castelluccio
FULBRIGHT & JAWORSKI LLP

Salah Deeb
AL TAMIMI & COMPANY ADVOCATES & LEGAL CONSULTANTS

Nicholas Diacos
AL TAMIMI & COMPANY ADVOCATES & LEGAL CONSULTANTS

Mothanna El Gasseer
AL TAMIMI & COMPANY ADVOCATES & LEGAL CONSULTANTS

Adel El Said
PANALPINA WORLD TRANSPORT

Nasser A. Elhaidib
RIYADH MUNICIPALITY

Mahmoud Yahya Fallatah
NATIONAL WATER COMPANY

Imad El-Dine Ghazi
LAW OFFICE OF HASSAN MAHASSNI

Andreas Haberbeck
THE ALLAINCE OF ABBAS F. GHAZZAWI & CO. AND HAMMAD, AL-MEHDAR & CO.

Alan Hall
AL TAMIMI & COMPANY ADVOCATES & LEGAL CONSULTANTS

Shadi Haroon
LAW OFFICE OF MOHANNED BIN SAUD AL-RASHEED IN ASSOCIATION WITH BAKER BOTTS LLP

Jochen Hundt
AL-SOAIB LAW FIRM

Ziad Jibril
ABU-GHAZALEH LEGAL - (TAG-LEGAL)

Marcus Latta
THE LAW FIRM OF SALAH AL-HEJAILANY

Glenn Lovell
AL TAMIMI & COMPANY ADVOCATES & LEGAL CONSULTANTS

Zaid Mahayni
LAW OFFICE OF HASSAN MAHASSNI

Ahmed Makkaw
BAFAKIH & NASSIEF

Ahmed Mekkawi
BAFAKIH & NASSIEF

Maher Melhem
ABU-GHAZALEH LEGAL - (TAG-LEGAL)

Muntasir Osman
LAW OFFICE OF HASSAN MAHASSNI

K. Joseph Rajan
GLOBE MARINE SERVICES CO.

Prabagaran Ramasamy
PANALPINA WORLD TRANSPORT

Murtaza Rao
AL-WALLAN LOGISTICS

SAMTCO

SAUDI CREDIT BUREAU - SIMAH

Mohammad Arif Saeed
AL TAMIMI & COMPANY ADVOCATES & LEGAL CONSULTANTS

Mustafa Saleh
EMAD ARRIYADH TRADING

Abdul Shakoor
GLOBE MARINE SERVICES CO.

Rehana Shukkur
THE ALLAINCE OF ABBAS F. GHAZZAWI & CO. AND HAMMAD, AL-MEHDAR & CO.

Peter Stansfield
AL-JADAAN & PARTNERS LAW FIRM

Sameh M. Toban
TOBAN LAW FIRM

Juergen Villmer
AL-SOAIB LAW FIRM

Michael Webb
NATIONAL WATER COMPANY

Natasha Zahid
BAKER BOTTS LLP

Abdul Aziz Zaibag
ALZAIBAG CONSULTANTS

Soudki Zawaydeh
AL JURAID & COMPANY / PRICEWATERHOUSECOOPERS

SENEGAL

Diaby Aboubakar
BCEAO

Khaled Abou El Houda
CABINET KANJO KOITA

Magatte Dabo
TRANSFRET DAKAR

Ibrahima Diagne
GAINDE 2000

Fallou Diéye
APIX -AGENCE CHARGÉE DE LA PROMOTION DE L'INVESTISSEMENT ET DES GRANDS TRAVAUX

Issa Dione
SENELEC

Alassane Diop
DP WORLD

Amadou Diop
GAINDE 2000

Babacar Biram Diop
CABINET BABACAR BIRAM DIOP

Fodé Diop
ART INGEIERIE AFRIQUE

Amadou Drame
CABINET D'AVOCAT

Cheikh Fall
CABINET D'AVOCAT

Mame Adama Gueye
Mame Adama Gueye &
Associes

Matthias Hubert
FIDAFRICA /
PricewaterhouseCoopers

Steven Jansen
Maersk Logistics

Edgar Julienne
Maersk Logistics

Papa Ismaél Ka
Etude Notariale Ka

Oumy Kalsoum Gaye
Chambre de Commerce
d'Industrie et
d'Agriculture de Dakar

Abdou Dialy Kane
S.C.P. D'avocats

Seydina Kane
Senelec

Sidy Kanoute

Ousseynou Lagnane
BDS

Patricia Lake Diop
Etude Me Patricia Lake
Diop

Moussa Mbacke
Etude notariale Moussa
Mbacke

Dame Mbaye
Transfret Dakar

Mamadou Mbaye
SCP Mame Adama Gueye &
Associés

Amadou Ndiaye
Port Autonome de Dakar

François Ndiaye
Port Autonome de Dakar

Cheikh Tidiane Ndiaye
Secom-Afrique

Magatte Ndoye
Ministere du Commerce

Moustapha Ndoye

Madior Niang
Transcontinental Transit

Bara Sady
Port Autonome de Dakar

SDV Logistics Ltd.

Djibril Sy
Secom-Afrique

Thierno Baila Talla
Port Autonome de Dakar

Dominique Taty
FIDAFRICA /
PricewaterhouseCoopers

Ousmane Thiam
Maersk Logistics

Simon Pierre Thiaw
Douanes du Senegal

Ibra Thiombane
SCP Mame Adama Gueye &
Associés

Adama Traore
SCP Mame Adama Gueye &
Associés

Baba Traore
Transfret

Konzo Traore
BCEAO

Emmanuel Yehouessi
BCEAO

SERBIA

Bojana Babić
Bojović Dašić Kojović

Rade Bačkovic
Association of Serbian
Banks

Marija Bojović
Bojović Dašić Kojović

Christophe Boyer
Gide Loyrette Nouel,
member of Lex Mundi

Vuk Božović
Gide Loyrette Nouel,
member of Lex Mundi

Milan Brković
Association of Serbian
Banks

Ana Čalić
Prica & Partners Law
Office

Ivana Čalić
Law Office Kosić

Marina Cvijanović
Gide Loyrette Nouel,
member of Lex Mundi

Vladimir Dabić
The International Center
for Financial Market
Development

Danica Dajović
Regulatory Review Unit

Predrag Dejanović
Ninković Law Office

François d'Ornano
Gide Loyrette Nouel,
member of Lex Mundi

Dragan Draca
PricewaterhouseCoopers

Jelena Edelman
Prica & Partners Law
Office

Zorana Gajić
Regulatory Review Unit

Ivan Grac
Panalpina World
Transport

Olga Serb Gretić
Ninković Law Office

Harrison Solicitors

Slavica Janojlić
ElektroDistribucija
Beograd (EDB)

Dejan Jeremić
Republic Geodetic
Authority

Andrija Jerinić
Regulatory Review Unit

Martina Jović
PricewaterhouseCoopers
Bojović & Dašić

Dubravka Kosić
Law Office Kosić

Ivan Krsikapa
Ninković Law Office

Zach Kuvizić
Kuvizić Law Office

Marc Lassman
Booz Allen Hamilton

Law Office Baklaja Igric
Mujezinovic in association
with Clyde & Co LLP

Marijana Malidzan
Regulatory Review Unit

Aleksandar Mančev
Prica & Partners Law
Office

Milena Manojlović
Gide Loyrette Nouel,
member of Lex Mundi

Andreja Marušić

Dragana Miletić
Municipality of Surcin

Vladimir Milić
PricewaterhouseCoopers

Nenad Mraković
Elektroprivreda Srbije

Ana Nesić
Law Office Kosić

Dimitrije Nikolić
Cargo T. Weiss d.o.o.

Djurdje Ninković
Ninković Law Office

Bojan Obradović
Omega Electro

Zvonko Obradović
Serbian Business Registers
Agency

Darija Ognjenović
Prica & Partners Law
Office

Igor Oljačić
Law Office Kosić

Tamara Ostojić
Prica & Partners Law
Office

Vladimir Perić
Prica & Partners Law
Office

Snežana Petrović
Panalpina World
Transport

Mihajlo Prica
Prica & Partners Law
Office

Branko Radulović
Regulatory Review Unit

Carol Santoni
Gide Loyrette Nouel,
member of Lex Mundi

Nebojsa Savičević
Trimo inzenjering d.o.o.

Sladjana Sredojević
Association of Serbian
Banks

Ana Stanković
Moravčevic, Vojnović
& Zdravković o.a.d. u
saradnji sa Schönherr

Nenad Stanković
JSP

Dragana Stanojević
Booz Allen Hamilton

Milan Stefanović
Regulatory Review Unit

Milo Stevanovich
Booz Allen Hamilton

Petar Stojanović
Joksovic, Stojanovic and
Partners

Aleksandar Tasić
Kuvizić Law Office

Jovana Tomić
Živković & Samardžić Law
Office

Mile Tomić
Municipality of Surcin

Snežana Tosić
Serbian Business Registers
Agency

Biljana Trencev
The International Center
for Financial Market
Development

Tanja Vukotić Marinković
Serbian Business Registers
Agency

Miloš Vulić
Prica & Partners Law
Office

Miloš Živković
Živković & Samardžić Law
Office

SEYCHELLES

Gerry Adam
Mahe Shipping Co. Ltd.

Laura. A. Alcindor Valabhji
Sterling Offshore Limited

Leslie Boniface
Ministry of Employment
and Human Resource
Development

France Gonzalves Bonte

Bobby Brantley Jr.
Sterling Offshore Limited

L. Charlette
Stamp Duty Commission

Andre D. Ciseau
Seychelles Ports
Authority

Daniel Houareau
Seychelles Ports
Authority

Melanie Kemp
Sterling Offshore Limited

Conrad Lablache
Pardiwalla Twomey
Lablache

MEJ Electrical

Joe Morin
Mahe Shipping Co. Ltd.

Margaret Nourrice
Stamp Duty Commission

Pesi Pardiwalla
Pardiwalla Twomey
Lablache

Bernard L. Pool
Pool & Patel

Public Utilities
Corporation

Unice Romain
Seychelles Ports
Authority

Kieran B. Shah

SIERRA LEONE

Abdul Bai Kanu
Sonnie Davies Electrical

Desmond D. Beckley
Dalttech / DESMI
Enterprises

A.Y Brewah
Brewah & Co.

H.C. Bright
Rokel Commercial Bank

Nicholas Colin Browne-Marke
Court of Appeals

Charles Campbell
Charles Campbell & Co.

Emile Carr
Leone Consultants

H.E.C. Carter
Rokel Commercial Bank

John Carter
KPMG

Roy Chalkley
Shipping Agencies Ltd.

Leslie Theophilus Clarkson
Ahmry Services

Victor Keith Cole
Rokel Commercial Bank

Michael A. Collier
Rokel Commercial Bank

Mabinty Daramy
Ministry of Trade &
Industry

Fraser Davies
Ministry of Employment &
Social Security

Vidal Decker
KPMG

Festina Douganson
SIERRATEL

Mariama Dumbuya
Renner Thomas & Co.,
Adele Chambers

William L. Farmer
Ministry of Lands,
Country Planning and the
Environment

Dzidzedze Fiadjoe
PricewaterhouseCoopers

Eke Ahmed Halloway
Halloway & Partners

Millicent Hamilton-Hazeley
Clas Legal

James M. Heyburn
Safmarine Container Lines
(Maersk Ltd.)

Michael A.O. Johnson
City Alliance

Augustin Kai Banya
Ministry of Lands,
Country Planning and the
Environment

Mariama Kallay
Government of Sierra
Leone

Ibrahim Sorie Kamara
National Revenue
Authority

Jusifu Anthony Kamara
Guma Valley Water
Company

M.B. Kargbo
Ministry of Finance

Hassan Kavqsa
SIERRATEL

Shiaka Kawa
Edra Consultancy

Alieyah Keita

Arthur William Lewis
Freetown City Council

Centus Macauley Esq.
Macauley, Bangura & Co.

Sullay A. Mannah
Bank of Sierra Leone

Ibrahim Mansaray

Noah Mansaray
Sierra Leone Ports Authority

Corneleius Adeyemi Max-Williams I
Shipping Agencies Ltd.

E.V. Morgan J.P.
Institute of Architects Sierra Leone

Augustine Musa, Esq.
Brewah & Co.

Alfred Navo
Ministry of Employment & Social Security

Easmon Ngakui
Brewah & Co.

Oliver Nylander
Adele Chambers

Rev. Dan Oalmer
National Power Authority

Christopher J. Peacock
Serpico Trading Enterprises

H.O. Peacock-Sawyer
Ministry of Lands, Country Planning and the Environment

Ade Renner-Thomas
Renner Thomas & Co., Adele Chambers

Roger Rogers
International Construction Co. Ltd.

Mohamed Salisu
Ministry of Finance, Revenue & Tax Policy Division

Julia Sarkodie-Mensah

Sahid Mohammed Sesay
Serry Kamal & Co

Shipping Agencies Ltd.

Susan Sisay
Sisay & Associate

Eddinia Swallow
Wright & Co.

Lornard Taylor
Macauley, Bangura & Co.

Rodney O. Temple
EROD Construction & Engineering Services

Alhanji Timbo
National Power Authority

Mohamed Ahmad Tunis
Ahmry Services

Darcy White
PricewaterhouseCoopers

Claudius Williams-Tucker
KPMG

Solomon Wilson
Sierra Leone Investment Information Portal (SLIIP)

Amy Wright
Ecobank

Rowland Wright
Wright & Co.

SINGAPORE

Malcolm BH Tan
Insolvency & Public Trustee's Office

Ronald Cai
Ministry of Manpower

Hooi Yen Chin
Gateway Law Corporation

Paerin Choa
TSMP Law Corporation

Kit Min Chye
Tan Peng Chin LLC

Seema Dadlani

Paula Eastwood
PricewaterhouseCoopers

Energy Market Authority

Soo Geok Keen
Steven Tan PAC, member of Russell Bedford International

Global Trade Well Singapore

Aaron Goh
PricewaterhouseCoopers

Haryad Hadi
Donaldson & Burkinshaw

May Ching Ida Han
Donaldson & Burkinshaw

Yvonne Hill
Yeo-Leong & Peh

Sheau Peng Hoo
Subordinate Courts

Ashok Kumar
Allen & Gledhill LLP

Nanda Kumar
Rajah & Tann

Shirene Li
Credit Bureau Pte Ltd.

Yik Wee Liew
WongPartnership LLP

William Lim
Credit Bureau Pte Ltd.

Mei Xin Loh
Wong Tan & Molly Lim LLC

Hwei Min Ng

Sheikh Babu Nooruddin
Al Noor International Pte. Ltd.

Beng Hong Ong
Wong Tan & Molly Lim LLC

See Tiat Quek
PricewaterhouseCoopers

Shook Lin & Bok (in joint venture with Allen & Overy)

Douglas Tan
Steven Tan PAC, member of Russell Bedford International

Winston Tay
Customs Authority

Siu Ing Teng
Land Authority

Paul Wong
Rodyk & Davidson LLP

Daniel Yap

Jennifer Yeo
Yeo-Leong & Peh

Stefanie Yuen Thio
TSMP Law Corporation

SLOVAK REPUBLIC

Martina Behuliaková
Geodesy, Cartography and Cadastre Authority

Radmila Benkova
PricewaterhouseCoopers

Genc Boga
Boga & Associates

Jana Borská
Čechová & Partners, member of Lex Mundi

Todd Bradshaw
PricewaterhouseCoopers

Miroslava Budínska
Dedák & Partners

Ján Budinský
Slovak Credit Bureau, s.r.o.

Kristina Cermakova
Peterka & Partners

Elena Chorvátová
Peterka & Partners

Miroslava Greštiaková
PricewaterhouseCoopers

Michaela Jurková
Čechová & Partners, member of Lex Mundi

Tomáš Kamenec
Dedák & Partners

Roman Konrad
Profinam, s.r.o.

Miloslav Kovac
General Counciller of the UINL

Sona Krockova
PricewaterhouseCoopers

Štefan Kutenič
Chamber of Notaries

Katarina Leitmannová
Geodesy, Cartography and Cadastre Authority

Lubomir Lesko
Peterka & Partners

Přemysl Marek
Peterka & Partners

Tomáš Maretta
Čechová & Partners, member of Lex Mundi

Peter Mateja
PricewaterhouseCoopers Legal Services

Clare Moger
PricewaterhouseCoopers

Panalpina Welttransport GmbH

Jakub Ondrejka
Čechová & Partners, member of Lex Mundi

Ladislav Pompura
Monarex audit consulting

Zora Puškáčová
Zukalová - Advokátska kancelária s.r.o.

Zuzana Satkova
PricewaterhouseCoopers

Martin Senkovic
BNT - Sovova Chudackova & Partner, s.r.o.

Jaroslav Škubal
PRK Partners s.r.o. advokátní kancelář

Lucia Slezakova
PricewaterhouseCoopers

Lubica Suhajova
PricewaterhouseCoopers

Maria Svidroňová
Monarex audit consulting

Michal Toman
PricewaterhouseCoopers

Roman Turok-Hetes
National Bank of Slovakia

Peter Varga
PRK Partners s.r.o. advokátní kancelář

Zuzana Wallova
National Bank of Slovakia

Michal Zeman
Čechová & Partners, member of Lex Mundi

Dagmar Zukalová
Zukalová - Advokátska kancelária s.r.o.

SLOVENIA

Tina Ajster
PricewaterhouseCoopers

Andrej Andrić
Rojs, Peljhan, Prelesnik & partnerji, o.p., d.o.o.

Barbara Balantič
Odvetniki Šelih & Partnerji

Nataša Božović
Bank of Slovenia

Eva Budja
Law Office Jadek & Pensa d.o.o.

Vid Čibej
PricewaterhouseCoopers

Thomas Dane
PricewaterhouseCoopers

Elektro Ljubljana d.d.

Energy Agency of the Republic of Slovenia

Aleksander Ferk
PricewaterhouseCoopers

Ana Filipov
Filipov, Petrovič, Jeraj in partnerji o.p., d.o.o. in cooperation with Schönherr

Ana Grabnar
Rojs, Peljhan, Prelesnik & partnerji, o.p., d.o.o.

Boštjan Grešak
Odvetniška pisarna Avbreht, Zajc in partnerji

Damjana Iglič
Bank of Slovenia

Andrej Jarkovič
Janežič & Jarkovič Attorneys-at-Law & Patent Attorneys

Saša Jemc
Law Office Jadek & Pensa d.o.o.

Jernej Jeraj
Filipov, Petrovič, Jeraj in partnerji o.p., d.o.o. in cooperation with Schönherr

Urška Jereb
Avbreht, Zajc & partners

Mia Kalas
Odvetniki Šelih & Partnerji

Danijel Kerševan
Panalpina Welttransport GmbH

Tina Klemenc
PricewaterhouseCoopers

Barbara Knez
Avbreht, Zajc & partners

Vid Kobe
Filipov, Petrovič, Jeraj in partnerji o.p., d.o.o. in cooperation with Schönherr

Karl-Heinz Krois
Panalpina Welttransport GmbH

Ana Lešnik
Avbreht, Zajc & partners

Iztok Milac
Miro Senica in Odvetniki

Siniša Nišavić
Data d.o.o

Matic Novak
Rojs, Peljhan, Prelesnik & partnerji, o.p., d.o.o.

Sonja Omerza
PricewaterhouseCoopers

Pavle Pensa
Law Office Jadek & Pensa d.o.o.

Bostjan Petauer
BDO EOS Svetovanje d.o.o.

Tomaž Petrovič
Schönherr Rechtsanwälte GmbH / Attorneys-at-Law

Natasa Pipan Nahtigal
Odvetniki Šelih & Partnerji

Jure Planinšek
Odvetniki Šelih & Partnerji

Petra Plevnik
Miro Senica in Odvetniki

Bojan Podgoröek

Andrej Poglajen
Chamber of Craft and Small Busines

Marjana Ristevski
PricewaterhouseCoopers

Maöa Rozman
PricewaterhouseCoopers

Tomo Sbrizaj
Agency for public legal records and related services

Bostjan Sedmak
Schönherr Rechtsanwälte GmbH / Attorneys-at-Law

Tamara äerdoner
PricewaterhouseCoopers

Branka Španič
Law Office Jadek & Pensa d.o.o.

Renata Šterbenc Štrus
Law Office Jadek & Pensa d.o.o.

Anja Strojin Štampar
Miro Senica in Odvetniki

Melita Trop
Miro Senica in Odvetniki

Nives Uljan
*PANALPINA WELTTRANSPORT
GMBH*

Nevenka Vratanar
*AGENCY OF THE REPUBLIC
OF SLOVENIA FOR PUBLIC
LEGAL RECORDS AND RELATED
SERVICES*

Katja Wostner
BDO EOS SVETOVANJE D.O.O.

Aleš Zevnik
DATA D.O.O

Katja Šegedin Zevnik
DATA D.O.O

Brigita Žunič
DELOITTE

Tina Žvanut Mioč
*LAW OFFICE JADEK & PENSA
D.O.O.*

SOLOMON ISLANDS

James Apaniai
JAMES APANIAI LAWYERS

Don Boykin
PACIFIC ARCHITECTS LTD

Julie Haro
AJ&G BLUM LTD

Anita Jowitt
*UNIVERSITY OF THE SOUTH
PACIFIC*

John Katahanas
SOL - LAW

Haelo Pelu
DEPUTY REGISTRAR GENERAL

Ramon Jun Quitales
*QUITALES MANAGEMENT
SERVICES*

Roselle R. Rosales
PACIFIC ARCHITECTS LTD

Gregory Joseph Sojnocki
*MORRIS & SOJNOCKI
CHARTERED ACCOUNTANTS*

John Sullivan
SOL - LAW

SOUTH AFRICA

Theo Adendorff
KCSA

Ross Alcock
*EDWARD NATHAN
SONNENBERGS INC.*

Mark Badenhorst
PRICEWATERHOUSECOOPERS

Jacque Bagg
*FORDHAM & OSHRY INC. -
MEMBER OF RUSSELL BEDFORD
INTERNATIONAL*

Kobus Blignaut
*EDWARD NATHAN
SONNENBERGS INC.*

Boitumelo Bogatsu
GARLICKE & BOUSFIELD INC

Anthony Brislin
*BDO SPENCER STEWARD
SOUTHERN AFRICAN
CO-ORDINATION (PTY)
LIMITED*

Beric Croome
*EDWARD NATHAN
SONNENBERGS INC.*

Gabriel Davel
NATIONAL CREDIT REGULATOR

Gretchen de Smit
*EDWARD NATHAN
SONNENBERGS INC.*

Hiren Desai
BUSINESS ADVISORS GROUP

Rudolph Du Plessis
*BOWMAN GILFILLAN, MEMBER
OF LEX MUNDI*

Justin Ducie
PRICEWATERHOUSECOOPERS

Flip Dwinger
*CIPRO (COMPANIES & IPR
REGISTRATION OFFICE)*

ESKOM

Miranda Feinstein
*EDWARD NATHAN
SONNENBERGS INC.*

Darryl Fordham
*FORDHAM & OSHRY INC. -
MEMBER OF RUSSELL BEDFORD
INTERNATIONAL*

Daniel Francois Fyfer
CLIFFE DEKKER HOFMEYR INC.

Sean Gilmour
PRICEWATERHOUSECOOPERS

GO FREIGHT BROKERS

Tim Gordon-Grant
*BOWMAN GILFILLAN, MEMBER
OF LEX MUNDI*

Kim Goss
*BOWMAN GILFILLAN, MEMBER
OF LEX MUNDI*

Roelof Grové
ADAMS & ADAMS

Jenna Hopwood
TWB

Simone Immelman
CLIFFE DEKKER HOFMEYR INC.

Mark Klinkert
*FORDHAM & OSHRY INC. -
MEMBER OF RUSSELL BEDFORD
INTERNATIONAL*

Anli Koen
TWB

Unathi Kondile
*BOWMAN GILFILLAN, MEMBER
OF LEX MUNDI*

Paul Lategan
*EDWARD NATHAN
SONNENBERGS INC.*

Irvin Lawrence
GARLICKE & BOUSFIELD INC

Veema Makan
*EDWARD NATHAN
SONNENBERGS INC.*

Joey Mathekga
*CIPRO (COMPANIES & IPR
REGISTRATION OFFICE)*

Brian Mbatha
*OFFICE OF THE CHIEF
REGISTRAR OF DEEDS*

Gabriel Meyer
*DENEYS REITZ / AFRICA
LEGAL*

Glory Moumakwe
*CIPRO (COMPANIES & IPR
REGISTRATION OFFICE)*

Sizwe Msimang
*BOWMAN GILFILLAN, MEMBER
OF LEX MUNDI*

Kemp Munnik
*BDO SPENCER STEWARD
SOUTHERN AFRICAN*

*CO-ORDINATION (PTY)
LIMITED*

Gasant Orrie
CLIFFE DEKKER HOFMEYR INC.

Dave Oshry
*FORDHAM & OSHRY INC. -
MEMBER OF RUSSELL BEDFORD
INTERNATIONAL*

Eamonn Quinn
*EAMONN DAVID QUINN
ATTORNEY*

Andres Sepp
*OFFICE OF THE CHIEF
REGISTRAR OF DEEDS*

Richard Shein
*BOWMAN GILFILLAN, MEMBER
OF LEX MUNDI*

Rob Smorfitt
*CHAMBER OF COMMERCE &
INDUSTRIES*

TRANSUNION

Llewellyn van Wyk
CSIR

Claire van Zuylen
*BOWMAN GILFILLAN, MEMBER
OF LEX MUNDI*

Ralph Zulman
SUPREME COURT OF APPEAL

SPAIN

ALLEN & OVERY LLP

ALTIUS S.A.

Ana Armijo
ASHURST

Cristina Ayo Ferrándiz
*URÍA & MENÉNDEZ, MEMBER
OF LEX MUNDI*

Jacobo Baltar
BAKER & MCKENZIE

Juan Bolás Alfonso
NOTARIADO

Agustín Bou
JAUSAS

Héctor Bouzo Cortejosa
SOLCAISUR S.L.

Cristina Calvo
ASHURST

Teresa Camacho Artacho
*URÍA & MENÉNDEZ, MEMBER
OF LEX MUNDI*

Laura Camarero
BAKER & MCKENZIE

Ariadna Cambronero Ginés
*URÍA & MENÉNDEZ, MEMBER
OF LEX MUNDI*

Nazaret Clemente
CLIFFORD CHANCE

Francisco Conde Viñuelas
GONÇALVES PEREIRA

Jaume Cornudella Marquès
*LANDWELL, ABOGADOS Y
ASESORES FISCALES*

Fernando de la Puente Alfaro
*COLEGIO DE REGISTRADORES
DE LA PROPIEDAD Y
MERCANTILES DE ESPAÑA*

Agustín Del Río Galeote
*GÓMEZ-ACEBO & POMBO
ABOGADOS*

Iván Delgado González
PÉREZ - LLORCA

Anselmo Diaz Fernández
BANK OF SPAIN

Rossanna D'Onza
BAKER & MCKENZIE

Antonio Fernández
J & A GARRIGUES, S.L.

Valentín García González
GONÇALVES PEREIRA

Borja García-Alamán
J & A GARRIGUES, S.L.

Cristina Gomendio
J & A GARRIGUES, S.L.

Juan Ignacio Gomeza Villa
NOTARIO DE BILBAO

Jorge Hernandez
EQUIFAX IBERICA

Luiz Jimenez Lopez
*COLEGIO OFICIAL
DE APAREJADORES Y
ARQUITECTOS TECNICOS DE
MADRID*

Igor Kokorev
PÉREZ - LLORCA

Joaquin Macias
ASHURST

Daniel Marín
*GÓMEZ-ACEBO & POMBO
ABOGADOS*

Jorge Martín - Fernández
CLIFFORD CHANCE

Gabriel Martínez
*MARTINEZ, OJEDA Y
ASOCIADOS, MEMBER
OF RUSSELL BEDFORD
INTERNATIONAL*

José Manuel Mateo
J & A GARRIGUES, S.L.

Nicolás Nogueroles Peiró
*ARBO (ASOCIACION DE
REGISTRADORES BIENVENIDO
OLIVER)*

Ana Novoa
BAKER & MCKENZIE

Alberto Núñez-Lagos
Burguera
*URÍA & MENÉNDEZ, MEMBER
OF LEX MUNDI*

Daniel Parejo Ballesteros
J & A GARRIGUES, S.L.

Jose Luis Perales
NOTARIADO

Pedro Pérez-Llorca Zamora
PÉREZ - LLORCA

Roser Ràfols
JAUSAS

Juan Ramon-Ramos
*LANDWELL, ABOGADOS Y
ASESORES FISCALES*

Carlos Rico
CLIFFORD CHANCE

Enrique Rodriguez
ALTIUS S.A.

Déborah Rodríguez
CLIFFORD CHANCE

Eduardo Rodríguez-Rovira
*URÍA & MENÉNDEZ, MEMBER
OF LEX MUNDI*

Iñigo Sagardoy
*SAGARDOY ABOGADOS,
MEMBER OF IUS LABORIS*

L. Salvado
EQUIFAX IBERICA

Eduardo Santamaría Moral
J & A GARRIGUES, S.L.

Ramón Santillán
BANK OF SPAIN

Catalina Santos
J & A GARRIGUES, S.L.

Pablo Santos
*GÓMEZ-ACEBO & POMBO
ABOGADOS*

Luis Siles
*DAVIES ARNOLD COOPER
SPAIN*

Cristina Soler
*GÓMEZ-ACEBO & POMBO
ABOGADOS*

Raimon Tagliavini
*URÍA & MENÉNDEZ, MEMBER
OF LEX MUNDI*

Francisco Téllez
J & A GARRIGUES, S.L.

Adrián Thery
J & A GARRIGUES, S.L.

Alejandro Valls
BAKER & MCKENZIE

Juan Verdugo
J & A GARRIGUES, S.L.

SRI LANKA

Shanaka Amarasinghe
JULIUS & CREASY

Chiranga Amirthiah
*F.J. & G. DE SARAM, MEMBER
OF LEX MUNDI*

APL

Savantha De Saram
D.L. & F. DE SARAM

Chamari de Silva
*F.J. & G. DE SARAM, MEMBER
OF LEX MUNDI*

Sharmela de Silva
TIRUCHELVAM ASSOCIATES

Sadhini Edirisinghe
*F.J. & G. DE SARAM, MEMBER
OF LEX MUNDI*

Chamindi Ekanayake
NITHYA PARTNERS

Amila Fernando
JULIUS & CREASY

Champika Fernando
TIRUCHELVAM ASSOCIATES

*FREIGHT LINKS
INTERNATIONAL (PTE) LTD*

Jivan Goonetilleke
D.L. & F. DE SARAM

Naomal Goonewardena
NITHYA PARTNERS

Sunil Hapuarachchi
*STATE ENGINEERING
CORPORATION*

Sonali Jayasuriya
D.L. & F. DE SARAM

Tudor Jayasuriya
*F.J. & G. DE SARAM, MEMBER
OF LEX MUNDI*

Inoka Jayawardhana
*F.J. & G. DE SARAM, MEMBER
OF LEX MUNDI*

Vishwamithra Kadurugamuwa
*F.J. & G. DE SARAM, MEMBER
OF LEX MUNDI*

Yudhishtran Kanagasabai
PRICEWATERHOUSECOOPERS

Janaka Lakmal
Credit Information Bureau Ltd.

LAN Management Development Service

Fathima Amra Mohamed
Sudath Perera Associates

Dian Nanayakkara
Tiruchelvam Associates

Jagath Perera
MIT Cargo (Pvt) Ltd.

Santushi Perera
Julius & Creasy

Sudath Perera
Sudath Perera Associates

Sudesh Peter
F.J. & G. De Saram, member of Lex Mundi

Progressive Design Associates

Hiranthi Ratnayake
PricewaterhouseCoopers

Paul Ratnayeke
Paul Ratnayeke Associates

Perera Sanjeevani
Nithya Partners

Sanath Senaratne
Ceylon Electricity Board

Shifana Sharifuddin
John Wilson Partners

Shane Silva
Julius & Creasy

Priya Sivagananathan
Julius & Creasy

Mathy Tharmaratnam
Tiruchelvam Associates

Harini Udugampola
F.J. & G. De Saram, member of Lex Mundi

Charmalie Weerasekera
Sudath Perera Associates

Shashi Weththasinghe
Julius & Creasy

Nihal Wicramasooriya
Ceylon Electricity Board

John Wilson Jr.
John Wilson Partners

ST. KITTS AND NEVIS

Michella Adrien
Michella Adrien Law Office

Nicholas Brisbane
N. Brisbane & Associates

Scott Caines
Frank B. Armstrong Ltd.

Neil Coates
PricewaterhouseCoopers

Dollrita Jack-Cato
Webster Dyrud Mitchell

Dahlia Joseph
Daniel Brantley & Associates

Randy Prentice
Frank B. Armstrong Ltd.

Anastacia Saunders
Frank B. Armstrong Ltd.

St. Kitts Electricity Department

Warren Thompson
Constsvcs

Charles Walwyn
PricewaterhouseCoopers

ST. LUCIA

Gilland Adjodha
Cotton Bay Resorts

Thea Alexander
Francis & Antoine

Thaddeus M. Antoine
Francis & Antoine

Gerard Bergasse
Tropical Shipping

Desma F. Charles
Registry of Companies and Intellectual Property

Willibald Charles
Baron Shipping & Brokerage Inc.

Peter I. Foster
Peter I. Foster & Associates

Peterson D. Francis
Peterson D. Francis Worldwide Shipping & Customs Services Ltd.

Annick Gajadhar
Tropical Shipping

Carol J. Gedeon
Chancery Chambers

Simon Jeffers
Tropical Shipping

Lucelec

Duane C. Marquis
NLBA Architects

Marguerite Nicholas
Gordon & Gordon Co.

Eldris Pierre-Mauricette
Tropical Shipping

The Bank of Nova Scotia

Leandra Gabrielle Verneuil
Gordon & Gordon Co.

Andie A. Wilkie
Gordon & Gordon Co.

Brenda M. Williams
Chase, Skeete & Boland

ST. VINCENT AND THE GRENADINES

Kay R.A. Bacchus-Browne
Kay Bacchus - Browne Chambers

Bernadine Dublin
Labour Department

First Caribbean Bank

Tamara Gibson-Marks
High Court Registrary

Sean Joachim
CaribTrans

Serge L'Africain
Scotiabank

Moulton Mayers
Moulton Mayers Architects

Marcelle Myers
Caribbean International Law Firm

Floyd A. Patterson
Pannell Kerr Forster

Richard Peterkin
PricewaterhouseCoopers

St. Vincent Customs Authority

St. Vincent Electricity Services Ltd.

Nicole O.M. Sylvester
Caribbean International Law Firm

L.A. Douglas Williams
Law Firm of Phillips & Williams

Andrea Young-Lewis
Commerce & Intellectual Property Office (CIPO)

SUDAN

Abdullah Abozaid
Law Office of Abdullah A. Abozaid

Mohamed Ibrahim Adam
Dr. Adam & Associates

Jamal Ibrahim Ahmed

Eihab Babiker
Eihab Babiker & Associates - Advocates

Mojtaba Banaga
Elkarib and Medani

Elmugtaba Bannaga
Elkarib and Medani

Amani Ejami
El Karib & Medani Advocates

Ashraf A.H. El Neil
Mahmoud Elsheikh Omer & Associates Advocates

Tariq Mohmoud Elsheikh Omer
Mahmoud Elsheikh Omer & Associates Advocates

Eshraga Fadlalla
Eshraga Fadlalla Law Office

William E. Kosar
IRIS Center

Ahmed Mahdi
Mahmoud Elsheikh Omer & Associates Advocates

Amin Mekki Medani
El Karib & Medani Advocates

Osman Mekki Abdurrahman
HLCS

Abdalla Mohamed
A. Mohamed & Associates

Tarig Monim

Mohamed Alaa Eldin Mohamed
Darka for Trading & Services Co. Ltd.

Alaa Eldin Mohamed Osman
Darka for Trading & Services Co. Ltd.

R. Parekh
MTS Cargo Services

Mohamed Samir
Tristar

Amel M. Sharif
Mahmoud Elsheikh Omer & Associates Advocates

Abdel Gadir Warsama
Dr. Abdel Gadir Warsama Ghalib & Associates Legal Firm

SURINAME

G. Clide Cambridge
Paramaribo Custom Broker & Packer

Marcel K. Eyndhoven
N.V. Energiebedrijven Suriname

Johan Kastelein
KDV Architects

R.J.S. Kensenhuis
NBM Groep

Stanley Marica
Advokatenkantoor Marica Law Firm

Anouschka Nabibaks
BDO Abrahams Raijmann & Partners

Rita Ramdat
Chamber of Commerce & Industry

Angèle J. Ramsaransing-Karg
BDO Abrahams Raijmann & Partners

Adiel Sakoer
N.V. Global Expedition

Inder Sardjoe
N.V. Easy Electric

Albert D. Soedamah
Lawfirm Soedamah & Associates

Radjen A. Soerdjbalie
Notariaat R.A. Soerdjbalie

Jennifer van Dijk-Silos
Law Firm Van Dijk-Silos

Rene van Essen
Vereniging Surinaams Bedrijfsleven, Suriname Trade & Industry Association

Dayenne Wielingen-Verwey
Vereniging Surinaams Bedrijfsleven, Suriname Trade & Industry Association

Perry D. Wolfram
BroCad N.V.

SWAZILAND

Vincent Galeromeloe
TransUnion ITC

Phumlile Tina Khoza
Municipal Council of Manzini

Paul Lewis
PricewaterhouseCoopers

Andrew Linsey
PricewaterhouseCoopers

C.J. Littler
C.J. Littler & Co.

Welile Mabuza
Mabuza Attorneys

Service Magagula

Shadrack Mnisi
Sharp Freight SWD Pty. Ltd.

Bongani Mtshali
Federation of Swaziland Employers and Chamber of Commerce

Jerome Ndzimandze
Speed Limit Construction

Knox Nxumalo
Robinson Bertram

José Rodrigues
Rodrigues & Associates

Moira Rose
PKF International

Bradford Mark Walker
Brad Walker Architects

SWEDEN

Magnus Andersson
Gärde Wesslau Advokatbyrå

Martin Bergander
Gärde Wesslau Advokatbyrå

Mats Berter
MAQS Law Firm

Annica Börjesson
MAQS Law Firm

Alexander Broch
Brochs Redovisningsbyraa KB

Linda Broström-Cabrera
PricewaterhouseCoopers

Jenny Dangre
Advokatfirman Vinge KB, member of Lex Mundi

Henric Diefke
Mannheimer Swartling Advokatbyrå

Lina Fransson
Elmzell Advokatbyrå AB, member of Ius Laboris

Roger Gavelin
PricewaterhouseCoopers

Loreta Greivyte
Fortune Law Group

Lars Hartzell
Elmzell Advokatbyrå AB, member of Ius Laboris

Linda Hasselblad
MAQS Law Firm

Emil Hedberg
Advokatfirman Vinge KB, member of Lex Mundi

Bengt Kjellson
Lantmäteriet

Niklas Körling
Setterwalls Advokatbyrå

Tommy Larsson
Ministry of Employment

Johan Lindberg
Advokatfirman Lindahl

Christoffer Monell
Mannheimer Swartling Advokatbyrå

Dain Nevonen
Advokatfirman Vinge KB, member of Lex Mundi

Michael Nyman
Advokatfirman Lindahl

Karl-Arne Olsson
Gärde Wesslau Advokatbyrå

Ola Lo Olsson
Elmzell Advokatbyrå AB, member of Ius Laboris

Mattias Örnulf
Hökerberg & Söderqvist Advokatbyrå KB

Carl Östring
Magnusson

Panalpina AB

Linn Samuelsson
MAQS LAW FIRM

Jesper Schönbeck
ADVOKATFIRMAN VINGE KB,
MEMBER OF LEX MUNDI

Odd Swarting
SETTERWALLS ADVOKATBYRÅ

UC AB

Caroline Vartia
GÄRDE WESSLAU
ADVOKATBYRÅ

SWITZERLAND

Amr Abdel Aziz
CMS VON ERLACH HENRICI
AG

Peter R. Altenburger
ALTENBURGER

Beat M. Barthold
FRORIEP RENGGLI

Marc Bernheim
STAIGER SCHWALD & PARTNER

Sébastien Bettschart
TAVERNIER TSCHANZ

Jacques Bonvin
TAVERNIER TSCHANZ

Bernhard G. Burkard
NOTARIAT BERNHARD
BURKARD

Andrea Cesare Canonica
SWISS CUSTOMS

COMMERCIAL REGISTER OF
THE CANTON ZURICH

Mauro Cavadini
BRUNONI MOLINO MOTTIS
ADAMI

Damien Conus
TAVERNIER TSCHANZ

Philippe de Salis
STONEHAGE S.A.

Robert P. Desax
PRICEWATERHOUSECOOPERS

Suzanne Eckert
WENGER PLATTNER

Erwin Griesshammer
VISCHER ATTORNEYS AT LAW

Mark Hippenmeyer
ALTENBURGER

David Hürlimann
CMS VON ERLACH HENRICI
AG

Hanspeter Klaey
PRICEWATERHOUSECOOPERS

Urs Klöti
PESTALOZZI LACHENAL PATRY,
MEMBER OF LEX MUNDI

Armin Marti
PRICEWATERHOUSECOOPERS

Michel Merlotti
NOTARY & CONSULTANT

MIGROS-GENOSSENSCHAFTS-
BUND

Andrea Molino
BRUNONI MOLINO MOTTIS
ADAMI

Georg Naegeli
HOMBURGER

Pierre Natural
PIERRE NATURAL, NOTAIRE

Sebastian Neufang
PRICEWATERHOUSECOOPERS

Roland Niklaus
NOTARIAT BERNHARD
BURKARD

Gema Olivar
PRICEWATERHOUSECOOPERS

Gion Pagnoncini
PESTALOZZI LACHENAL PATRY,
MEMBER OF LEX MUNDI

Sara Rousselle-Ruffieux
TAVERNIER TSCHANZ

Daniel Schmitz
PRICEWATERHOUSECOOPERS

Daniel Steudler
SWISSTOPO, DIRECTORATE FOR
CADASTRAL SURVEYING

Barbara Stöckli Klaus
FRORIEP RENGGLI

Edmond Tavernier
TAVERNIER TSCHANZ

Brigitte Umbach-Spahn
WENGER PLATTNER

Stephane Valat
ORRICK, HERRINGTON &
SUTCLIFFE LLP

Beatrice Vetsch
PRICEWATERHOUSECOOPERS

Andrin Waldburger
PRICEWATERHOUSECOOPERS

Patrick Weber
EKZ ELEKTRIZITÄTSWERKE
DES KANTONS ZÜRICH

Roman Werder
PRICEWATERHOUSECOOPERS

ZEK SWITZERLAND

SYRIAN ARAB REPUBLIC

Muhamed Agha
UNDP

Sulafah Akili
MINISTRY OF ECONOMY &
TRADE

Mouazza Al Ashhab
AUDITING CONSULTING
ACCOUNTING CENTER

Rawaa Al Midani
MINISTRY OF TRADE &
ECONOMY

Nabih Alhafez
SFS (SPEED FORWARD
SHIPPING)

Ziad Al-Sairafi
ABU-GHAZALEH LEGAL -
(TAG-LEGAL)

Abdul Raouf Hamwi
CIVIL ENGINEERING OFFICE

Yaser Hmedan
YASER HMEDAN LAW OFFICE

Antoun Joubran
SYRIAN ARAB CONSULTANTS
LAW OFFICE

Mazen N. Khaddour
INTERNATIONAL LEGAL
BUREAU

AUDITING CONSULTING
ACCOUNTING CENTER

Gabriel Oussi
SYRIAN ARAB CONSULTANTS
LAW OFFICE

Yazan Quandour
ABU-GHAZALEH LEGAL -
(TAG-LEGAL)

Housam Safadi
SAFADI BUREAU

Samer Sultan
SULTANS LAW

TAIWAN, CHINA

Jersey Chang
PUHUA & ASSOCIATES

Vera Chang
LCS & PARTNERS

Victor Chang
LCS & PARTNERS

John Chen
FORMOSA TRANSNATIONAL

Nicholas V. Chen
PAMIR LAW GROUP

Tina Chen
WINKLER PARTNERS

Wei-cheng Chen
MINISTRY OF THE INTERIOR

Abraham Cheng
LEXCEL PARTNERS

Chun-Yih Cheng
FORMOSA TRANSNATIONAL

Yu-Chung Chiu
MINISTRY OF THE INTERIOR

Julie C. Chu
JONES DAY

Steven Go
PRICEWATERHOUSECOOPERS

Barbara Hsu
SDV LOGISTICS LTD.

Robert Hsu
SDV LOGISTICS LTD.

Tony Hsu
PAMIR LAW GROUP

Yuling Hsu
FORMOSA TRANSNATIONAL

Margaret Huang
LCS & PARTNERS

T.C. Huang
HUANG & PARTNERS

Jui-Lung Hung
PUHUA & ASSOCIATES

Charles Hwang
YANGMING PARTNERS

Joan Jing
PUHUA & ASSOCIATES

Wen-Horng Kao
PRICEWATERHOUSECOOPERS

Chih-Shan Lee
WINKLER PARTNERS

HUANG & PARTNERS

Kate Li
YANGMING PARTNERS

Yu-Hsun Li
PUHUA & ASSOCIATES

Justin Liang
BAKER & MCKENZIE

Emily Lin
PAMIR LAW GROUP

Frank Lin
REXMED INDUSTRIES CO., LTD.

Jennifer C. Lin
TSAR & TSAI LAW FIRM,
MEMBER OF LEX MUNDI

Ming-Yen Lin
DEEP & FAR, ATTORNEYS-
AT-LAW

Rich Lin
LCS & PARTNERS

Yishian Lin
PRICEWATERHOUSECOOPERS

Catherine Liu
SDV LOGISTICS LTD.

Julia Liu
SDV LOGISTICS LTD.

Kang-Shen Liu
LEXCEL PARTNERS

Jennifer Lo
PRICEWATERHOUSECOOPERS

Mike Lu
LEXCEL PARTNERS

Joseph Ni
GOOD EARTH CPA

Lawrence S. Ong
PUHUA & ASSOCIATES

Lloyd G. Roberts III
WINKLER PARTNERS

Michael Schreiber
YANGMING PARTNERS

Tanya Y. Teng
HUANG & PARTNERS

Bee Leay Teo
BAKER & MCKENZIE

C.F. Tsai
DEEP & FAR, ATTORNEYS-
AT-LAW

Eric Tsai
PUHUA & ASSOCIATES

Rita Tsai
APL

YEONG UONG ENTERPRISE CO.

Chao-Yu Wang
YANGMING PARTNERS

Chien-jui Wang
CEPD

Richard Watanabe
PRICEWATERHOUSECOOPERS

Pei-Yu Wu
BAKER & MCKENZIE

Shin Mei Wu
JOINT CREDIT INFORMATION
CENTER

Shih-Ming You
MINISTRY OF THE INTERIOR

TAJIKISTAN

Bakhtiyor Abdulhamidov
AKHMEDOV, AZIZOV &
ABDULHAMIDOV ATTORNEYS

Rasul Abdullaev
REPRESENTATIVE OF
ZARUBEZGNEFTEGAZ

Bakhtiyor Abdulloev
ABM TRANS SERVICE LLC

Zarrina Adham
HUMO

Shavkat Akhmedov
AKHMEDOV, AZIZOV &
ABDULHAMIDOV ATTORNEYS

Tolib Alimatov

Ruslan Amanbaev
SOZIDANIE LLC

ARCHITECTURE DEPARTMENT
TAJIKISTAN

Najib Ashraf
KN IBRAKOM FZCO.

Nazira Avazova
MINISTRY OF LABOR & SOCIAL
PROTECTION

Farhad Azizov
AKHMEDOV, AZIZOV &
ABDULHAMIDOV ATTORNEYS

Abdulbori Baybayev
LAW FIRM LEX

Shamsibonu Djurayeva

Rakhmatzoda Hshurali
CENTRE FOR
ENTREPRENURSHIP
DEVELOPMENT SUPPORT IN
DUSHANBE

Ashraf Sharifovich Ikromov
LLC "MOVAROUNNAHR"

Azim Ishmatov
AB GROUP

Mirali Kadyrov
CENTRE FOR
ENTREPRENURSHIP
DEVELOPMENT SUPPORT IN
DUSHANBE

Munir Kalemulloev
TAJIKISTAN UNIVERSITY

Mynir Kalemyloev
ASSOCIATION OF ANTI CRISIS
MANAGERS TAJIKISTAN

Assel Khamzina
PRICEWATERHOUSECOOPERS

Nigina Mahmudova
GENDER VA TARAKKIET

MASHVARAT LIMITED
LIABILITY COMPANY

Dilovar Mavlonov
ASSOCIATION OF ANTI CRISIS
MANAGERS TAJIKISTAN

Karimova Muhabbat
CENTRAL NOTARY'S OFFICE

Takhir Nabiev
AITEN CONSULTING GROUP

Mizrobiddin Nugmanov
GLOBALINK LOGISTICS GROUP

Jurabek Toshtemurovich
Okhonov
LLC "MOVAROUNNAHR"

Emin Sauginov
MINISTRY OF LABOR & SOCIAL
PROTECTION

Tahmina Qodiri
AITEN CONSULTING GROUP

Jamshed Rahmonberdiev
SOMON CAPITAL JSC

Ravshan Rashidov
LAW FIRM LEX

Zimfera Rizvanova
REPUBLIC COMMITTEE OF
LABOR UNION

Firdavs Sadikov
SOMON CAPITAL JSC

Yuri Samolyov
LAW FIRM LEX

Takdir Sharifov
ASSOCIATION OF ANTI CRISIS
MANAGERS TAJIKISTAN

Shuhrat Shorakhmonov
ASSOCIATION FOR
MICROFINANCE
ORGANIZATIONS OF TAJIKISTAN

Elena Simonova
KONSULTANT AUDIT

Maltuba Ujdjabaeva
NATIONAL ASSOCIATION OF
BUSINESS

Saidali Valiev
AGROINVESTBANK

Tohir Zubaidov
AITEN CONSULTING GROUP

TANZANIA

Patrick Ache
MKONO & CO. ASSOCIATE

Steven de Backer

Theresia Dominic
UNIVERSITY OF DAR ES
SALAAM

Santosh Gajjar
SUMAR VARMA ASSOCIATES

Farija Ghikas
REX ATTORNEYS

Nasra Hassan
MKONO & CO. ASSOCIATE

Johnson Jasson
JOHNSON JASSON &
ASSOCIATES ADVOCATES

Leopold Thomas Kalunga
KALUNGA & CO. ADVOCATES

Wilbert B. Kapinga
MKONO & CO. ASSOCIATE

Rehema Khalid-Saria
MKONO & CO. ASSOCIATE

Ngwaru Maghembe
MKONO & CO. ASSOCIATE

Lotus Menezes
MKONO & CO. ASSOCIATE

Nimrod Mkono
MKONO & CO. ASSOCIATE

Arafa Mohamed
REX ATTORNEYS

Chris Msuya
HORWARTH TANZANIA

Exaud Mushi
NORPLAN TANZANIA LIMITED

Shabani Mwatawala
PSM ARCHITECTS CO. LTD.

Alex Thomas Nguluma
REX ATTORNEYS

Eric Rwelamira
RINGO & ASSOCIATES,
MEMBER OF THE AFRICA
LEGAL NETWORK

Emmy Salewi
NORPLAN TANZANIA LIMITED

Rishit Shah
PRICEWATERHOUSECOOPERS

Eve Hawa Sinare
REX ATTORNEYS

Mohamed H. Sumar
SUMAR VARMA ASSOCIATES

David Tarimo
PRICEWATERHOUSECOOPERS

Mustafa Tharoo
RINGO & ASSOCIATES,
MEMBER OF THE AFRICA
LEGAL NETWORK

Sinare Zaharan
REX ATTORNEYS

THAILAND

ALLEN & OVERY LLP

Janist Aphornratana
PRICEWATERHOUSECOOPERS

APL

Chalee Chantanayingyong
SECURITIES AND EXCHANGE
COMMISSION

Phadet Charoensivakorn
NATIONAL CREDIT BUREAU
CO. LTD.

Thunyaporn Chartisathian
ALLENS ARTHUR ROBINSON /
SIAM PREMIER INTERNATIONAL
LAW OFFICE LIMITED

Chinnavat Chinsangaram
WEERAWONG, CHINNAVAT &
PEANGPANOR LTD

Sasirusm Chunhakasikarn
TILLEKE & GIBBINS
INTERNATIONAL LTD., MEMBER
OF LEX MUNDI

John Fotiadis
TILLEKE & GIBBINS
INTERNATIONAL LTD., MEMBER
OF LEX MUNDI

Seetha Gopalakrishnan
PRICEWATERHOUSECOOPERS

Vira Kammee
SIAM CITY LAW OFFICES LTD.

Yingyong Karnchanapayap
TILLEKE & GIBBINS
INTERNATIONAL LTD., MEMBER
OF LEX MUNDI

Sakares Khamwalee
BAKER & MCKENZIE

Komkrit Kietduriyakul
BAKER & MCKENZIE

LAWPLUS LTD.

Chanida Leelanuntakul
SIAM CITY LAW OFFICES LTD.

William Lehane
ALLENS ARTHUR ROBINSON /
SIAM PREMIER INTERNATIONAL
LAW OFFICE LIMITED

Sakchai Limsiripothong
WEERAWONG, CHINNAVAT &
PEANGPANOR LTD

Pratchayapa Mahamontree
SIAM CITY LAW OFFICES LTD.

Pauline A. Manzano
PRICEWATERHOUSECOOPERS

Steven Miller
MAYER BROWN LLP

Sally Mouhim
TILLEKE & GIBBINS
INTERNATIONAL LTD., MEMBER
OF LEX MUNDI

Surapol Opasatien
NATIONAL CREDIT BUREAU
CO. LTD.

Viroj Piyawattanametha
BAKER & MCKENZIE

Cynthia M. Pornavalai
TILLEKE & GIBBINS
INTERNATIONAL LTD., MEMBER
OF LEX MUNDI

Supan Poshyananda
SECURITIES AND EXCHANGE
COMMISSION

Chanet Precharonaset
APL LOGISTICS SERVICES LTD.

Sudthana Puntheeranurak
NATIONAL CREDIT BUREAU
CO. LTD.

Piyanuj Ratprasatporn
TILLEKE & GIBBINS
INTERNATIONAL LTD., MEMBER
OF LEX MUNDI

Dussadee Rattanopas
TILLEKE & GIBBINS
INTERNATIONAL LTD., MEMBER
OF LEX MUNDI

Suraphon Rittipongchusit
DLA PIPER LIMITED

Maythawee Sarathai
MAYER BROWN LLP

Patsamon Sirigoonpattanasarn
SIAM CITY LAW OFFICES LTD.

Ekkachat Sirivichai
DLA PIPER LIMITED

Jeffrey Sok
ALLENS ARTHUR ROBINSON /
SIAM PREMIER INTERNATIONAL
LAW OFFICE LIMITED

Kowit Somwaiya
LAWPLUS LTD.

Picharn Sukparangsee
SIAM CITY LAW OFFICES LTD.

Hunt Talmage
CHANDLER & THONG-EK

Paralee Techajongjintana
BAKER & MCKENZIE

Paisan Tulapornpipat
BLUE OCEAN LOGISTICS CO.,
LTD.

Pattara Vasinwatanapong
VICKERY & WORACHAI LTD.

Chinachart Vatanasuchart
TILLEKE & GIBBINS
INTERNATIONAL LTD., MEMBER
OF LEX MUNDI

Harold K. Vickery Jr.
VICKERY & WORACHAI LTD.

Pimvimol Vipamaneerut
TILLEKE & GIBBINS
INTERNATIONAL LTD., MEMBER
OF LEX MUNDI

Vorawan Wachirakajorn
PRICEWATERHOUSECOOPERS

Supamorm Yaowakron
DLA PIPER LIMITED

TIMOR-LESTE

Maria Jose Amaral
SERVIÇO DO IMPOSTO DE
TIMOR LESTE

Julio Araujo da Silva
SERVIÇO DO IMPOSTO DE
TIMOR LESTE

Jumar Balonkita
UNIDO

Jose Pedro Camoes
LBH-TL

Miguel Carreira Martins
CRA TIMOR

EDTL

LAW OFFICE BAKLAJA IGRIC
MUJEZINOVIC IN ASSOCIATION
WITH CLYDE & CO LLP

Eusebio Guterres
UNIDO BUSINESS
REGULATORY CONSULTANT

Alzira Lay
SDV LOGISTICS LTD.

Simon McKenna
PT PRIMA WAHANA CARAKA /
PRICEWATERHOUSECOOPERS

Rafael Ribeiro
SDV LOGISTICS LTD.

Tjia Soh Siang
TJIA & TCHAI ASSOCIATES

Francisco Soares
SERVIÇO DO IMPOSTO DE
TIMOR LESTE

TOGO

Diaby Aboubakar
BCEAO

Jean-Marie Adenka
CABINET ADENKA

Kokou Gadémon Agbessi
CABINET LUCREATIF

Martial Akakpo
SCP MARTIAL AKAKPO

Adzewoda Ametsiagbe
DIRECTION GÉNÉRALE
DE LÍURBANISME ET DE
LÍHABITAT

Coffi Alexis Aquereburu
AQUEREBURU AND PARTNERS
CABINET D'AVOCATS

Cecile Assogbavi
ETUDE NOTARIALE SENGHOR

Philippe Attoh
SCP MARTIAL AKAKPO

Sylvanus Dodzi Awutey
CABINET LUCREATIF

BOLLORÉ

Jonathan Darboux
BCEAO

Koffi Joseph Dogbevi
CABINET LUCREATIF

Jean Claude Gnamien
FIDAFRICA /
PRICEWATERHOUSECOOPERS

Kodjo John Kokou
CABINET D'AVOCATS JOHN
KOKOU

Atchroe Leonard Johnson
SCP AQUEREBURU &
PARTNERS

Akpénè Amito Kpégba
SCP MARTIAL AKAKPO

Seka Hauvy Mathieu
FIDAFRICA /
PRICEWATERHOUSECOOPERS

Félix Mawuglo Agbobli
KEKAR TOGO

Comlan Eli-Eli N'soukpoé
SCP MARTIAL AKAKPO

Olivier Pedanou
CABINET LUCREATIF

Galolo Soedjede

Dominique Taty
FIDAFRICA /
PRICEWATERHOUSECOOPERS

Inès Mazalo Tekpa
CABINET LUCREATIF

Fousséni Traoré
FIDAFRICA /
PRICEWATERHOUSECOOPERS

Konzo Traore
BCEAO

Edem Zotchi
SCP MARTIAL AKAKPO

Emmanuel Yehouessi
BCEAO

TONGA

Inoke Afu
DATELINE SHIPPING & TRAVEL
LTD.

Ramsey Dalgety
ELECTRICITY COMMISSION

William Clive Edwards
LAW OFFICE

Anthony Ford
SUPREME COURT

INLAND REVENUE

Anita Jowitt
UNIVERSITY OF THE SOUTH
PACIFIC

Ashleigh Matheson
WESTPAC BANK OF TONGA

Ian Skelton
SHORELINE DISTRIBUTION LTD

Dana Stephenson
LAW OFFICE

Tohi
DATELINE SHIPPING & TRAVEL
LTD.

Christine Uta'atu
UTA'ATU & ASSOCIATES

Jone Vuli
WESTPAC BANK OF TONGA

TRINIDAD AND
TOBAGO

Andre Bass
THE FAST FREIGHT GROUP

Steve Beckles
DELOITTE

Ronald Bhagan
M. HAMEL-SMITH & CO.,
MEMBER OF LEX MUNDI

Cecil Camacho
LEX CARIBBEAN

Terry Curtis
TRANSUNION

Stacy Lee Daniell
M. HAMEL-SMITH & CO.,
MEMBER OF LEX MUNDI

Rehanna de la Borde
PRICEWATERHOUSECOOPERS

Nicole Ferreira-Aaron
M. HAMEL-SMITH & CO.,
MEMBER OF LEX MUNDI

Nadia Henriques
M. HAMEL-SMITH & CO.,
MEMBER OF LEX MUNDI

Peter Inglefield
PRICEWATERHOUSECOOPERS

Colin Laird
COLIN LAIRD ASSOCIATES

Marcia Leonard
THE FAST FREIGHT GROUP

Keomi Lourenco
M. HAMEL-SMITH & CO.,
MEMBER OF LEX MUNDI

Ramesh Lutchman
TRANSUNION

Susan Morgan
PRICEWATERHOUSECOOPERS

Sonji Pierre Chase
LEX CARIBBEAN

Fanta Punch
M. HAMEL-SMITH & CO.,
MEMBER OF LEX MUNDI

Ramdath Dave Rampersad
R.D. Rampersad & Co.

Danzel Reid
Trinidad & Tobago
Electricity Commission

Stephen A. Singh
Lex Caribbean

Jonathan Walker
M. Hamel-Smith & Co.,
member of Lex Mundi

Allyson West
PricewaterhouseCoopers

TUNISIA

Rachid Aguirr
Ben Said et Associés

Mokhtar Amor
Société Tunisienne de
l'Electricité et du Gaz

Mohamed Moncef Barouni
ACR

Belgacem Barrah
Tribunal de 1ère Instance
de Tunis

Anis Bejaoui
Chafter Raouadi &
Associés

Adly Bellagha
Adly Bellagha &
Associates

Hend Ben Achour
Adly Bellagha &
Associates

Rafika Ben Aissa Bouslama
Ministère de la Justice

Othman Ben Arfa
Société Tunisienne de
l'Elecricite et du Gaz

Ismail Ben Farhat
Adly Bellagha &
Associates

Elyès Ben Mansour
Avocats Conseils Associés

Miriam Ben Rejeb
PricewaterhouseCoopers
Legal Services

Anis Ben Said
Global Auditing &
Advising

Kamel Ben Salah
Gide Loyrette Nouel,
member of Lex Mundi

Salah Ben Youssef
République Tunisienne
Centre Informatique du
Ministere des Finances

Abdelfattah Benahji
Ferchiou & Associés
Meziou Knani

Peter Bismuth
Tunisie Electro Technique

Manel Bondi
PricewaterhouseCoopers

Mustafa Bouafif
Ministry of State Property
and Land Affairs

Institut d'Economie
Quantitative

Elyes Chafter
Chafter Raouadi &
Associés

Zine el abidine Chafter
Chafter Raouadi &
Associés

Faouzi Cheikh
Banque Centrale de
Tunisie

Abdelmalek Dahmani
Dahmani Transit
International

Mohamed Lotfi El Ajeri
Avocat a la Cour et
mediateur agree par le
B.B.MC

Mourad El Aroui
Amen Bank

Yassine El Hafi
Adly Bellagha &
Associates

Faïza Feki
Banque Centrale de
Tunisie

Ali Fekih
Chafter Raouadi &
Associés

Abderrahmen Fendri
PricewaterhouseCoopers

Yessine Ferah
CE&P Law Firm

Amel Ferchichi
Gide Loyrette Nouel,
member of Lex Mundi

Noureddine Ferchiou
Ferchiou & Associés
Meziou Knani

Lamia Harguem
Gide Loyrette Nouel,
member of Lex Mundi

Badis Jedidi
Gide Loyrette Nouel,
member of Lex Mundi

Najla Jezi
ACR

Amina Larbi
Gide Loyrette Nouel,
member of Lex Mundi

Mouelhi Lotfi
Maersk Logistics

Mabrouk Maalaoui
PricewaterhouseCoopers

Khaled Marzouk
République Tunisienne
Centre Informatique du
Ministere des Finances

Mohamed Ali Masmoudi
PricewaterhouseCoopers
Legal Services

Sarah Mebezaa
Comete Engineering

Radhi Meddeb
Comete Engineering

Faouzi Mili
Mili and Associates

Ben Afia Mohamed Salah
Orga Audit, a member
firm of Russell Bedford
International

Mohamed Taieb Mrabet
Banque Centrale de
Tunisie

Atf Nasri
Ferchiou & Associés
Meziou Knani

Imen Nouira
Conservation Foncière
Tunisia

Habiba Raouadi
Chafter Raouadi &
Associés

Lotfi Rebai
Cabinet Rebai

Sakoudi Ridha
A. T. I. S.

Imed Tanazefti
Gide Loyrette Nouel,
member of Lex Mundi

Faiza Telissi
Adly Bellagha &
Associates

Rachid Tmar
PricewaterhouseCoopers
Legal Services

Wassim Turki
AWT Audit & Conseil

Anis Wahabi
AWT Audit & Conseil

TURKEY

Burcu Acartürk Yıldız
Karataş Yıldız Borovali

Sezin Akoğlu
Pekin & Pekin

Ceren Aktaş
PricewaterhouseCoopers

Murat Akturk
Union of Chambers and
Commodity Exchanges

Duygu Alkan
Alkan Deniz Mavioğlu
Dilmen Law Office

Mustafa Alper
YASED - International
Investors Association

Arda Alposkay
Devres Law office

Melsa Ararat
Corporate Governance
Forum of Turkey, Sabanci
University

Abdulla Atalay
Boğaziçi Elektik Dağıtim
A.Ş. (Bedaş)

Selen Atlı
Gürcan Law Offices

Pınar Aybek
Bener Law Office, member
of Ius Laboris

Levent Aydaş
Aydaş Liman Kurman
Attorneys at Law

Yasemin Aydoğmuş
Mehmet Gün & Partners

Elvan Aziz Bikmen
Paksoy Law Firm

Derya Baksı Pekyalçın
Tarlan & Pekyalçın Law
Office

Naz Bandik
Çakmak Avukatlik Bürosu

Arzu Basmacı
Mehmet Gün & Partners

Sinan Borovalı
Karataş Yıldız Borovali

Ebru Boz
SDV - Horoz Logistics

Murat Bozkurt
PricewaterhouseCoopers

Idil Cagal
PricewaterhouseCoopers

Burcu Çakallı
KPMG

Esin Çamlıbel
Turunç Law Office

Maria Lianides Çelebi
Bener Law Office, member
of Ius Laboris

M. Fadlullah Cerrahoğlu
Cerrahoğlu Law Firm

Fikret Çetinkaya
KPMG

Orçun Çetinkaya
Mehmet Gün & Partners

Niyazi Çömez
Deloitte

Gulnisa Coşkun
Pekin & Pekin

Yavuz Dayıoğlu
PricewaterhouseCoopers

Kürşat Demirezen
ICT International Trading

Eda Denize
Alkan Deniz Mavioğlu
Dilmen Law Office

Rüçhan Derici
3E Danışmanlik Ltd. Şti.

Kazım Derman
Kredit Kayit Bureau

Emine Devres
Devres Law office

Başak Diclehan
KPMG

Tarık Dilek
Bolero Socks

Aykut Dincer
PricewaterhouseCoopers

Murat Volkan Dülger
Dülger Law Firm

Dilara Duman
Sariibrahimoğlu Law
Office

Çisil Durgun
Cerrahoğlu Law Firm

Murat Emirhanoğlu
KPMG

Sedat Eratalar
Deloitte

Gökben Erdem Dirican
Pekin & Pekin

Esin Erkal
PricewaterhouseCoopers

Esin Ertek
PricewaterhouseCoopers

Luc Fourcade
SDV - Horoz Logistics

Umurcan Gago
PricewaterhouseCoopers

Arman Gezer
Deloitte

Caglar Gezer
PricewaterhouseCoopers

Yağız Gökmen
Orhaner Law Office

Osman Nuri Gönenç
Central Bank of the
Republic of Turkey

Sait Gözüm
Deloitte

Onur Gülsaran
Cerrahoğlu Law Firm

Rıfat Günay
Central Bank of the
Republic of Turkey

Sezin Güner
Pekin & Pekin

Berna Güngenci
Çakmak Avukatlik Bürosu

A. Feridun Güngör
Ernst & Young

Cüneyd Gürcan
Gürcan Law Offices

Ayşegül Gürsoy
Cerrahoğlu Law Firm

Senem Gürsoy
Bircanoğlu Law Firm

Salih Zeki Haklı
TOBB

Gül Incesulu
Çakmak Avukatlik Bürosu

Şebnem Işık
Mehmet Gün & Partners

Ibrahim Kara
Kredit Kayit Bureau

Egemen Karaduman
Ernst & Young

Ramazan Karakurt
Istanbul Land Registry and
Cadastre

Selahaddin Karataş

Elif Kavuşturan
Bener Law Office, member
of Ius Laboris

Aslan Kaya
DMF System International
Independent Auditing,
Consulting & Certified
Public Accounting Co.,
member of Russell Bedford
International

Gözde Kayacık
Pekin & Bayar Law Firm

Betül Kencebay
YASED - International
Investors Association

Özlem Kızıl
Çakmak Avukatlik Bürosu

Sertak Kokenek
Bener Law Office, member
of Ius Laboris

Nergis Kundakçıoğlu
Cerrahoğlu Law Firm

Kürşat Kunter
Central Bank of the
Republic of Turkey

Oğuz Kupeli
SDV - Horoz Logistics

Sait Kurşuncu
Cerrahoğlu Law Firm

Zeki Kurtçu
Deloitte

Alpaslan Hamdi Kuzucuoğlu
Istanbul Metropolitan
Municipality

Altan Liman
Aydaş Liman Kurman
Attorneys at Law

Orhan Yavuz Mavioğlu
ADMD Law Firm

Rana Mazlum Yılmaz
Yilmaz Law Offices

Özlem Özgür Meriç
ABU-GHAZALEH LEGAL -
(TAG-LEGAL)

Banu Mert
CERRAHOĞLU LAW FIRM

MINISTRY OF INDUSTRY &
TRADE

Sıla Muratoğlu
BAYIRLI & MURATOĞLU LAW
FIRM

Diğdem Muslu
BAŞARAN NAS YMM A.S.

Lerzan Nalbantoğlu
TURUNÇ LAW OFFICE

Yılmaz Nalçakar
MED SHIPPING LOGISTICS
TRANSPORT & TRADE LTD.
CORPORATION

Adnan Nas
PRICEWATERHOUSECOOPERS

Zeynephan Oğuz
CERRAHOĞLU LAW FIRM

Sezin Okkan
PEKIN & PEKIN

Şebnem Önder
ÇAKMAK AVUKATLIK BÜROSU

Mert Oner
KPMG

Çağlayan Orhaner Dündar
ORHANER LAW OFFICE

Gamze Ovacık
ÇAKMAK AVUKATLIK BÜROSU

Saban Ozdemir
SABAN OZDEMIR TRADING
CONSULTANCY

Ekin Kavukçuoğlu Özgülsen
DELOITTE

Tuba Özsezen
YASED - INTERNATIONAL
INVESTORS ASSOCIATION

Ferhat Pekin
PEKIN & BAYAR LAW FIRM

Suzet Rodikli
PRICEWATERHOUSECOOPERS

Çağıl Şahin Biber
PRICEWATERHOUSECOOPERS

Batuhan Sahmay
PEKIN & PEKIN

Bilge Saltan
DÜLGER LAW FIRM

Tamer Saracık
ISTANBUL LAND REGISTRY AND
CADASTRE

Hasan Sarıçiçek
KPMG

Selim Sarıibrahimoğlu
SARIIBRAHIMOĞLU LAW
OFFICE

Duygu Şeftalici
CERRAHOĞLU LAW FIRM

Ayşe Sert
ÇAKMAK AVUKATLIK BÜROSU

Ömer Kayhan Seyhun
CENTRAL BANK OF THE
REPUBLIC OF TURKEY

Sinan
DMF SYSTEM INTERNATIONAL
INDEPENDENT AUDITING,
CONSULTING & CERTIFIED
PUBLIC ACCOUNTING CO.,
MEMBER OF RUSSELL BEDFORD
INTERNATIONAL

Defne Zeynep Sirakaya
CERRAHOĞLU LAW FIRM

Ufuk Soğütlüoğlu
DELOITTE

SUMERMAN INTERNATIONAL

Sezai Sur
BENER LAW OFFICE, MEMBER
OF IUS LABORIS

Naz Tamer
MEHMET GÜN & PARTNERS

Aylin Tarlan Tüzemen
TARLAN & PEKYALÇIN LAW
OFFICE

Ferya Taş
TURUNÇ LAW OFFICE

Elif Tezcan Bayırlı
BAYIRLI & MURATOĞLU LAW
FIRM

Pelin Tırtıl
BENER LAW OFFICE, MEMBER
OF IUS LABORIS

Güzel Toker
PRICEWATERHOUSECOOPERS

TURKISH INDUSTRIALISTS' AND
BUSINESSMEN'S ASSOCIATION
(TUSIAD)

Noyan Turunç
TURUNÇ LAW OFFICE

Ibrahim Tutar
PENETRA CONSULTING AND
AUDITING

Ebru Tuygun
DELOITTE

Gökçe Ucuzal
BENER LAW OFFICE, MEMBER
OF IUS LABORIS

Furkan Ünal
PGLOBAL GLOBAL ADVISORY
SERVICES LTD.

Hilal Ünal
GOKSER MACHINE LTD

Beste Üner
BENER LAW OFFICE, MEMBER
OF IUS LABORIS

Yegan Üreyen
MEHMET GÜN & PARTNERS

METROPOLITAN
MUNICIPALITY OF ISTANBUL

H.Barış Yalçın
PRICEWATERHOUSECOOPERS

Selcen Yalçın
MEHMET GÜN & PARTNERS

Ayşegül Yalçınmani Merler
CERRAHOĞLU LAW FIRM

Sadık Yamaç
MINISTRY OF PUBLIC WORKS
& SETTLEMENT

Begüm Yavuzdoğan
MEHMET GÜN & PARTNERS

Banu Yılmaz
UNION OF CHAMBERS AND
COMMODITY EXCHANGES

Cağatay Yılmaz
YILMAZ LAW OFFICES

Hülya Yılmaz
DELOITTE

Aylin Yontar
CERRAHOĞLU LAW FIRM

Filiz Yüksel
CERRAHOĞLU LAW FIRM

Murat Yülek
PGLOBAL GLOBAL ADVISORY
SERVICES LTD.

Çağlar Yurttürk
ADMD LAW FIRM

Serap Zuvin
SERAP ZUVIN LAW OFFICES

UGANDA

Bernard Baingana
PRICEWATERHOUSECOOPERS

Joseph Baliddawa
PRICEWATERHOUSECOOPERS

Bernard Bamwine
KWESIGABO, BAMWINE &
WALUBIRI ADVOCATES

Augus Jonah Bwiragura
MINISTRY OF LANDS, HOUSING
& URBAN DEVELOPMENT

Clare de Wet
SDV TRANSAMI LTD.

Nicholas Ecimu
SEBALU & LULE ADVOCATES
AND LEGAL CONSULTANTS

Matuvo Emmy
MARMA TECHNICAL SERVICES

EXPOLANKA FREIGHT LIMITED

Sarfaraz Jiwani
SEYANI BROS. & CO.

Busingye Kabumba
MMAKS ADVOCATES

Charles Kalu Kalumiya
KAMPALA ASSOCIATED
ADVOCATES

Richard Kamajugo
REVENUE AUTHORITY

Oscar Kambona
KAMPALA ASSOCIATED
ADVOCATES

Francis Kamulegeya
PRICEWATERHOUSECOOPERS

KARGO INTERNATIONAL LTD

Phillip Karugaba
MMAKS ADVOCATES

David Katende
ENVIROKAD

Didymus Byenkya Kato
ATACO FREIGHT SERVICES LTD

Eeshi Katugugu
PRICEWATERHOUSECOOPERS

Sophie Kayemba
PRICEWATERHOUSECOOPERS

Andrew Kibaya
SHONUBI, MUSOKE & CO.
ADVOCATES

Robert Kiggundu
ARCH FORUM LTD.

Kiryowa Kiwanuka
KIWANUKA & KARUGIRE
ADVOCATES

Allan Kokeyo
KAMPALA ASSOCIATED
ADVOCATES

Robert Komakec
ARCH FORUM LTD.

Maliza Kwera
MMAKS ADVOCATES

James Kyazze
SHONUBI, MUSOKE & CO.
ADVOCATES

Timothy Kyepa
SHONUBI, MUSOKE & CO.
ADVOCATES

Brenda Kyokwijuka
SEBALU & LULE ADVOCATES
AND LEGAL CONSULTANTS

Nicolas Legal
SDV TRANSAMI LTD.

Joseph Luswata
SEBALU & LULE ADVOCATES
AND LEGAL CONSULTANTS

Robinah Lutaaya
PRICEWATERHOUSECOOPERS

Ben Luwum
BVL & CO.

Charles Maina
SDV TRANSAMI LTD.

Peter Malinga
REVENUE AUTHORITY

Paul Mare
UMEME LIMITED

David F.K. Mpanga
A.F. MPANGA ADVOCATES

James Mukasa
SEBALU & LULE ADVOCATES
AND LEGAL CONSULTANTS

Cornelius Mukiibi
C.MUKIIBI.SENTAMU & CO.
ADVOCATES

Andrew Munaunra Kamuteera
SEBALU & LULE ADVOCATES
AND LEGAL CONSULTANTS

Peters Musoke
SHONUBI, MUSOKE & CO.
ADVOCATES

Rachel Mwanje Musoke
MMAKS ADVOCATES

Charles Mwebembezi
SDV TRANSAMI LTD.

Noah Mwesigwa
SHONUBI, MUSOKE & CO.
ADVOCATES

Fatuma Nabulime
SDV TRANSAMI LTD.

Eddie Nsamba-Gayiya
CONSULTANT SURVEYORS AND
PLANNERS

Charles Odere
LEX UGANDA ADVOCATES &
SOLICITORS

Julius Ojok
SEBALU & LULE ADVOCATES
AND LEGAL CONSULTANTS

Silver Adowa Owaraga
MAGEZI, IBALE & CO.
ADVOCATES

Alex Rezida
NANGWALA, REZIDA & CO.
ADVOCATES

Kenneth Rutaremwa
KATEERA & KAGUMIRE
ADVOCATES

Ruth Sebatindira
LIGOMARC ADVOCATES

Ali Sengendo
MWEBE, SEBAGGALA & CO.

Alan Shonubi
SHONUBI, MUSOKE & CO.
ADVOCATES

Manish Siyani
SEYANI BROTHERS & CO. (U)
LTD

Parbat Siyani
SEYANI BROTHERS & CO. (U)
LTD

Godfrey Songa
ARCH FORUM LTD.

Sebadduka Swaibu
SHABA MOTORS LTD.

Christopher Walugembe
MMAKS ADVOCATES

UKRAINE

Oleg Y. Alyoshin
VASYL KISIL & PARTNERS

Andrey Astapov
ASTAPOV LAWYERS
INTERNATIONAL LAW GROUP

Olga Balytska
DLA PIPER LLC

Olena Basanska
CMS CAMERON MCKENNA

Olena Bilozor
DLA PIPER LLC

Eugene Blinov
ASTAPOV LAWYERS
INTERNATIONAL LAW GROUP

Timur Bondaryev
ARZINGER & PARTNERS
INTERNATIONAL LAW FIRM

Maksym Borodchuk
CHADBOURNE & PARKE LLP

Olena Brodovska
CMS CAMERON MCKENNA

Tetyana Buchko
ASTERS

Taras Burhan
CMS CAMERON MCKENNA

Olga Burlyuk
CMS CAMERON MCKENNA

Andriy Buzhor
CMS CAMERON MCKENNA

Serhiy Chorny
BAKER & MCKENZIE

Diana Gladka
DLA PIPER LLC

Sergiy Gryshko
CMS CAMERON MCKENNA

Ivanna Honina
GRISCHENKO & PARTNERS

Victoria Kaplan
CMS CAMERON MCKENNA

Natalya Kim
CHADBOURNE & PARKE LLP

Andriy Kirmach
CHADBOURNE & PARKE LLP

Maksym Kopeychykov
ILYASHEV & PARTNERS

Evgeniy Kornievskiy
KONNOV & SOZANOVSKY

Natalia Kozyar
THE UKRAINIAN JOURNAL OF
BUSINESS LAW

Svitlana Kulish
CMS CAMERON MCKENNA

Tatyana Kuzmenko
ASTAPOV LAWYERS
INTERNATIONAL LAW GROUP

Oleksiy Levenets
CMS CAMERON MCKENNA

Mykola Likhachov
CMS CAMERON MCKENNA

Borys Lobovyk
Konnov & Sozanovsky

Yulia Logunova
DLA Piper LLC

Olga Mikheieva
CMS Cameron McKenna

Vadim Mizyakov
Asters

Robert Morris
PricewaterhouseCoopers

Nataliya Nakonechna
CMS Cameron McKenna

Yuliya Nogovitsyna
KPMG

Dmytro Orendarets
Arzinger & Partners International Law Firm

Yaroslav Petrov
CMS Cameron McKenna

Sava P. Poliakov
Grischenko & Partners

Sergiy Portnoy
DLA Piper Ukraine LLC

Vitaliy Pravdyuk
Konnov & Sozanovsky

Maria Prysyazhnyuk
PricewaterhouseCoopers

Yuliana Revyuk
KPMG

Oleksandr Rudenko
Astapov Lawyers International Law Group

Olga Serbul
Law Firm IP & C. Consult, LLC

Mykhailo Shchitka
Vasyl Kisil & Partners

Hanna Shtepa
Baker & McKenzie

Igor Svechkar
Asters

Olga Usenko
The Ukrainian Journal of Business Law

Penny Vaughn
PricewaterhouseCoopers

Elina Vavryshchuk
DLA Piper LLC

Zeeshan Wani
Globalink Transportation & Logistics Worldwide LLP

Olexiy Yanov
Law Firm IP & C. Consult, LLC

Yulia Yashenkova
Astapov Lawyers International Law Group

Kateryna Zabara
DLA Piper LLC

Tatiana Zamorska
KPMG

UNITED ARAB EMIRATES

Karim Abaza
Shalakany Law Office, member of Lex Mundi

Rami Abdellatif
Abu-Ghazaleh Legal - (TAG-Legal)

Dawoud Abdel Rahman Al-Hajri
Dubai Municipality

Qurashi AlSheikh AbdulGhani
Dubai Municipality

Moutaz Abdullah
Abu-Ghazaleh Legal - (TAG-Legal)

Ahmad Subhu Ahmad
Herbert Smith LLP

Mariam S.A. Al Afridi
Dubai World

Basil T. Al Kilani
Dubai World

Rasha Al Saeed
Baker Botts LLP

Marwan Al Sharkah
Galadari and Associates

Essam Al Tamimi
Al Tamimi & Company Advocates & Legal Consultants

Shouqi Al Yousuf
Dubai Electricity and Water Authority

Mahmood Albastaki
Dubai World

Saeed Al-Hamiz
Central Bank of the UAE

Maryam Ahmed Al-Hammadi
Dubai Municipality

Ashraf Ali
Golden Building Materials Trading

Sagar Ali
Business Advisors Group

Hadif Alowais
Alowais & Manfield Lawyers

Moustapha Al-Sharkawi
Dubai Courts

Blaise Amikat
Trium Logistics LLC

Wicki Andersen
Baker Botts LLP

Lisa W Anderson
PricewaterhouseCoopers

Rasha Arayqat
Dubai Electricity and Water Authority

Nakul Asthana
Afridi & Angell, member of Lex Mundi

Ali Awais
Baker Botts LLP

T Sureh Babu
Landmark group

Gitanjali Baja
DLA Piper Middle East LLP

Akhila Basith
Afridi & Angell, member of Lex Mundi

Prakash Bhanushali
Al Sahm Al Saree Transport & Clearing

Hiten Bhatia
Silver Line Shipping

Jennifer Bibbings
Trowers & Hamlins

James Bowden
Afridi & Angell, member of Lex Mundi

R Chandran
Sea Bridge Shipping

Dalmook Dalmook
Dalmook Mohd. Dalmook Attorney and Legal Consultants

Mohammad A. El-Ghul
Habib Al Mulla & Co.

Anthea Fernandes
Shalakany Law Office, member of Lex Mundi

Laetitia Fernandez
Helene Mathieu Legal Consultants

Nazia Hameed
Afridi & Angell, member of Lex Mundi

Samer Hamzeh
Trowers & Hamlins

Omar Hegazy
Shalakany Law Office, member of Lex Mundi

Sydene Helwick
Al Tamimi & Company Advocates & Legal Consultants

Fadi Hourani
Hourani & Associates

Sameer Huda
Hadef & Partners

Narmin Issa
DLA Piper Middle East LLP

Samir Ja'afar
Ja'afar Alwan Al Jaziri & Associates

Talib Abdul-Kareem Julfar
Dubai Municipality

Zaid Kamhawi
Emcredit

Mohammad Z. Kawasmi
Al Tamimi & Company Advocates & Legal Consultants

Vipul Kothari
Kothari Auditors & Accountants

K Senthil Kumar
G.L.G Shipping & Logistics

Ravi Kumar
Dubai Trade

Suneer Kumar
Al Suwaidi & Co.

Nathan Landis
DLA Piper Middle East LLP

Jacqueline Latham
DLA Piper Middle East LLP

Charles S. Laubach
Afridi & Angell, member of Lex Mundi

Valeria Lysenko

Mohamed Mahmoud Mashroom
Dubai Municipality

Gagan Malhotra
Dubai Trade

Helene Mathieu
Helene Mathieu Legal Consultants

Omar Momany
Freshfields Bruckhause Deringer

Yasser Omar
Shalakany Law Office, member of Lex Mundi

Vijendra Vikram Singh Paul
Abu-Ghazaleh Legal - (TAG-Legal)

Prakash
Al Tajir Glass

Samer Qudah
Al Tamimi & Company Advocates & Legal Consultants

Dean Rolfe
PricewaterhouseCoopers

Shoeb Saher
Habib Al Mulla & Co.

Luke Sajan
Damco

Khalid Mohamed Saleh
Dubai Municipality

Moahmmed Ahmed Saleh
Dubai Municipality

Herbert Schroder
Emcredit

Ruth Sharry
PricewaterhouseCoopers

Douglas Smith
Habib Al Mulla & Co.

Khalid A. Wahab
Al Midfa & Associates

Stan Wright
Dubai Customs

Rania Yousseph
Habib Al Mulla & Co.

Natasha Zahid
Baker Botts LLP

UNITED KINGDOM

Allen & Overy LLP

Kwame Asamoah
HW Chartered Accountants

Anna Austin
The Stokes Partnership

Guy Bailey
CBI - The Confederation of British Industry

Bank of Baroda

Paul Barker
Cleary Gottlieb Steen & Hamilton LLP

Robin Baron
Robin Baron Commercial Lawyers

Graham Bartlett
SITPRO Ltd

Hannah Belton
Lowless Commercial Solicitors

Nick Benwell
Simmons & Simmons

Georgie Blyth
PricewaterhouseCoopers Legal Services

Dan Bongiorono
Cleary Gottlieb Steen & Hamilton LLP

Harender Branch
Dawsons LLP

David Breakell
DLA Piper LLP

Paul Brehony
PricewaterhouseCoopers Legal Services

Penny Bruce
PricewaterhouseCoopers Legal Services

Peter Caplehorn
Scott Brownrigg

Fran Claes
DLA Piper LLP

Richard Clark
Slaughter and May

Philip Clarke
Simmons & Simmons

Roger Collier
DLA Piper LLP

Richard Collier-Keywood
PricewaterhouseCoopers

Companies House

Simon Cookson
Ashurst

Lyn Crawford
Davies Arnold Cooper LLP

Annalie Croney
PricewaterhouseCoopers Legal Services

Rob Cummings
CBI - The Confederation of British Industry

Shreya Damodaran
Cleary Gottlieb Steen & Hamilton LLP

Vera Dantas Innes
Noronha Advogados

Paul de Bernier
Mayer Brown LLP

Gordon Deane
Shepherd & Wedderburn

Ben Digby
CBI - The Confederation of British Industry

Rob Don
CBI - The Confederation of British Industry

Kate Douglas-Hamilton
Slaughter and May

EDF Energy Networks Ltd

Victoria Egan
DLA Piper LLP

Nick Francis
PricewaterhouseCoopers

Paul Gilbert

Ghislaine Goes
DLA Piper LLP

Helen Hall
DLA Piper LLP

Brenda Harris
Shepherd & Wedderburn

Rebecca Hildred
DLA Piper LLP

Gary Hodkinson
Citizens Advice

Neville Howlett
PricewaterhouseCoopers

HSBC

Stephen Hubner
Shepherd & Wedderburn

Simon Jay
Cleary Gottlieb Steen & Hamilton LLP

Nistha Jeram-Dave
PricewaterhouseCoopers Legal Services

Gillian Key-Vice
Experian Ltd.

Shinoj Koshy
Cleary Gottlieb Steen & Hamilton LLP

Tim Lake
DLA Piper LLP

Piers Larbey
Dawsons LLP

Catherine Ledger
Dawsons LLP

Kristi Lehtis
Simmons & Simmons

Chris Lister
DLA Piper LLP

Gemma Lodge
DLA Piper LLP

Mushtak Macci
Lubbock Fine, member of Russell Bedford International

James Macdonald
Noronha Advogados

Andrew Maple
Approved Inspector Services Limited

Charles Mayo
Simmons & Simmons

Julia McCabe
DLA Piper LLP

Kate McGough
DLA Piper LLP

Neil Morgan
DLA Piper LLP

Sandra Morrison
George Davies Solicitors LLP

Alison Murrin
Ashurst

Poonam Rai Nagi

Bagyasree Nambron
Mayer Brown LLP

Ofgem

Gabriel Olearnik
Mayer Brown LLP

Eng-Lye Ong
Cleary Gottlieb Steen & Hamilton LLP

Rachel Orton
DLA Piper UK LLP

Helen Paramor
Simmons & Simmons

Amy Perry
Shepherd & Wedderburn

Stewart Perry
DLA Piper LLP

David Pickstone
PricewaterhouseCoopers Legal Services

Anna Portsmouth
DLA Piper LLP

Rachel Power
DLA Piper LLP

Richard Pull
Dawsons LLP

Eleanor Richardson
Davies Arnold Cooper LLP

Jocelyn Roberts
Cleary Gottlieb Steen & Hamilton LLP

Susan Roye
Aerona (Air & Sea) Customs Clearing Agents Ltd.

Jack Seddon
Mayer Brown LLP

Shulmans Solicitors

Andrew Shutter
Cleary Gottlieb Steen & Hamilton LLP

Paul Speirs
Experian Ltd.

Clare Stammers
Shepherd & Wedderburn

Alice Steward
Simmons & Simmons

Paul Timmins
Approved Inspector Services Limited

David Toube
Cleary Gottlieb Steen & Hamilton LLP

Nicola Walker
CBI - The Confederation of British Industry

Geoffrey Wilkinson
MLM Building Control

Sally Willcock
Weil, Gotshal & Manges LLP

Helen Willmot
DLA Piper LLP

Andrew Wilson
Andrew Wilson & Co

Dermot Winters
Freeth Cartwright LLP

UNITED STATES

APL

Stephen Anderson
PricewaterhouseCoopers

Asheet Awasthi
Fortune Law Group

Birute Awasthi
Amerinde Consolidated Inc.

Rasa Baranauskaite
Amerinde Consolidated Inc.

Luke A. Barefoot
Cleary Gottlieb Steen & Hamilton LLP

Berkman Forwarding LLC

LaShante Boyd
Amerinde Consolidated Inc.

Courtney Brown
Cleary Gottlieb Steen & Hamilton LLP

Vaiva Cepukaiciuke
Fortune Law Group

Carmine Chiappetta
RBSM LLP, member of Russell Bedford International

Victor Chiu
Cleary Gottlieb Steen & Hamilton LLP

Richard Conza, Esq.
Cleary Gottlieb Steen & Hamilton LLP

Margaret Cowan
Cleary Gottlieb Steen & Hamilton LLP

James Denn
New York State Public Service Commission

Joshua L. Ditelberg
Seyfarth Shaw LLP

Lindsay Dunn
Cleary Gottlieb Steen & Hamilton LLP

Elisabeth Frost
Cleary Gottlieb Steen & Hamilton LLP

Patrick Fuller Fuller, Esq.
Cleary Gottlieb Steen & Hamilton LLP

Julija Gecaite
Amerinde Consolidated Inc.

Benjamin E. Gehrt
Seyfarth Shaw LLP

Lindsee P. Granfield
Cleary Gottlieb Steen & Hamilton LLP

Boris Grosman
L & B electrical international

Rehana Gubin
Cleary Gottlieb Steen & Hamilton LLP

Yevgeniy Gutsalo
Corporate Suites Business Centers

Adam Heintz
Morrison and Foerster

Steven Horowitz
Cleary Gottlieb Steen & Hamilton LLP

Jolanta Kalitkevic
Fortune Law Group

Charles L. Kerr
Morrison and Foerster

Arthur Kohn
Cleary Gottlieb Steen & Hamilton LLP

Michael Lazerwitz, Esq.
Cleary Gottlieb Steen & Hamilton LLP

Bradford L. Livingston
Seyfarth Shaw LLP

Paul Marquardt
Cleary Gottlieb Steen & Hamilton LLP

Kelly J. Murray
PricewaterhouseCoopers

Philippe A. Naudin
SDV Logistics Ltd.

Samuel Nolen
Richards, Layton & Finger, P.A., member of Lex Mundi

Sean O'Neal
Cleary Gottlieb Steen & Hamilton LLP

Jeffrey Penn
Cleary Gottlieb Steen & Hamilton LLP

Stephen Raslavich
United States Bankruptcy Court

Jonathan Reinstein
Cleary Gottlieb Steen & Hamilton LLP

Sandra Rocks
Cleary Gottlieb Steen & Hamilton LLP

Hanno Schop
Global Trade & Transport Consultancy Ltd.

David Snyder
Snyder & Snyder, LLP

Nathaniel Stankard
Cleary Gottlieb Steen & Hamilton LLP

Peter Stefanou
RBSM LLP, member of Russell Bedford International

TransUnion

Rima Trofimovaite
Fortune Law Group

Frederick Turner
Snyder & Snyder, LLP

Juta Vecerskyte
Fortune Law Group

URUGUAY

Fernando Bado
Estudio Dr. Mezzera

Alicia Barral
PricewaterhouseCoopers

Jonás Bergstein
Estudio Bergstein

Carlos Brandes
Guyer & Regules, member of Lex Mundi

Stephanie Brown
Navarro Abogados

Matías Campomar
Jimenez de Aréchaga Viana & Brause

Leonardo Couto
Jose Maria Facal & Co.

Jorge De Vita
Jorge de Vita Studio

Guillermo Duarte
Estudio Dr. Mezzera

María Durán
Hughes & Hughes

Noelia Eiras
Hughes & Hughes

Gabriel Ejgenberg
Estudio Bergstein

María Sofía Estellano
Guyer & Regules, member of Lex Mundi

Agustín Etcheverry Reyes
Estudio Blanco & Etcheverry

Marcelo Femenías Vidal
Bado, Kuster, Zerbino & Rachetti

Agustina Fernádez Giambruno
Guyer & Regules, member of Lex Mundi

Javier Fernández Zerbino
Bado, Kuster, Zerbino & Rachetti

Juan Federico Fischer
LVM Attorneys at Law

Federico Florin
Guyer & Regules, member of Lex Mundi

Federico Formento
LVM Attorneys at Law

Sergio Franco
PricewaterhouseCoopers

Diego Galante
Galante & Martins

Daniel Garcia
PricewaterhouseCoopers

Karina Goday
Navarro Abogados

Gabriela Gutierrez
Estudio Bergstein

Andres Hessdorfer Rozen
Olivera & Delpiazzo

Ariel Imken
Superintendencia de Instituciones de Intermediación Financiera - Banco Central del Uruguay

Alfredo Inciarte Blanco
Estudio Pérez del Castillo, Inciarte, Gari Abogados

Francisco Etcheverry Iruleguy
Estudio Dr. Mezzera

Alma Kubachek
Estudio Juridico Notarial de Alma Kubachek

Ricardo Mezzera
Estudio Dr. Mezzera

Matilde Milicevic Santana
Clearing de Informes

Alfredo H. Navarro
Navarro Abogados

Alfredo Navarro Castex
Navarro Abogados

Juan Martín Olivera
Olivera & Delpiazzo

María Concepción Olivera
Olivera & Delpiazzo

Ricardo Olivera-García
Olivera & Delpiazzo

María Cecilia Orlando
Guyer & Regules, member of Lex Mundi

Martin Pérez Tomeo
Galante & Martins

Ismael Pignatta Sánchez
Guyer & Regules, member of Lex Mundi

Agustín Rachetti
Bado, Kuster, Zerbino & Rachetti

María Noel Riotorto
Guyer & Regules, member of Lex Mundi

Fabian Rivero
Guyer & Regules, member of Lex Mundi

Lucia Salaverry
Guyer & Regules, member of Lex Mundi

Eliana Sartori
PricewaterhouseCoopers

Betania Silvera
Guyer & Regules, member of Lex Mundi

Carina Soffer
JULIO SOFFER LAWS

Julio Soffer
JULIO SOFFER LAWS

Romina Soria
NAVARRO ABOGADOS

Alvaro Tarabal
GUYER & REGULES, MEMBER OF LEX MUNDI

Diego Tognazzolo
PRICEWATERHOUSECOOPERS

Juan Troccoli
LVM ATTORNEYS AT LAW

Horacio Viana
JIMENEZ DE ARÉCHAGA VIANA & BRAUSE

María Noel Vidal
PRICEWATERHOUSECOOPERS

Gerardo Viñoles
VIÑOLES ARQUITECT STUDIO

Martin Vivo
LVM ATTORNEYS AT LAW

Alexandra Weisz

UZBEKISTAN

Jakhongir Abdurazaqov
AVENT ADVOCAT

Ravshan Adilov
DENTON WILDE SAPTE

Mels Akhmedov
BAS

Natalya Apukhtina
DENTON WILDE SAPTE

Umid Aripdjanov
GRATA LAW FIRM

Khalid Farooq
GLOBALINK LOGISTICS GROUP

Courtney Fowler
PRICEWATERHOUSECOOPERS

Babur Karimov
GRATA LAW FIRM

Sayora Khakimova
GRATA LAW FIRM

Nurali Eshibaevich Khalmuratov
NATIONAL INSTITUTE OF CREDIT INFORMATION

Sergney Maiorov
SIMAY KOM

Abdulkhamid Muminov
PRICEWATERHOUSECOOPERS

Malika Norova
GRATA LAW FIRM

Laziza Rakhimova
GRATA LAW FIRM

Ravshan Rakhmanov
GRATA LAW FIRM

Akmal Rustamov
PRICEWATERHOUSECOOPERS

Petros Tsakanyan
AZIZOV & PARTNERS

Alisher Zufarov
PRICEWATERHOUSECOOPERS

VANUATU

Garry Blake
RIDGEWAY BLAKE PARTNERS

Christopher Dawson
DAWSON BUILDERS

FR8 LOGISTICS LTD

Anita Jowitt
UNIVERSITY OF THE SOUTH PACIFIC

John Malcolm

Mark Stafford
BDO BARRETT & PARTNERS

SOUTH SEA SHIPPING LTD

VENEZUELA, R.B.

Jorge Acedo-Prato
HOET PELAEZ CASTILLO & DUQUE, MEMBER OF LEX MUNDI

Yanet Aguiar
MACLEOD DIXON

Juan Enrique Aigster
HOET PELAEZ CASTILLO & DUQUE, MEMBER OF LEX MUNDI

Servio T. Altuve Jr.
SERVIO T. ALTUVE R. & ASOCIADOS

Ramon Alvins
MACLEOD DIXON

Mercedes Briceño
CONAPRI

Diego Castagnino
HOET PELAEZ CASTILLO & DUQUE, MEMBER OF LEX MUNDI

María Paola D´Onghia
HOET PELAEZ CASTILLO & DUQUE, MEMBER OF LEX MUNDI

Carlos Domínguez Hernández
HOET PELAEZ CASTILLO & DUQUE, MEMBER OF LEX MUNDI

Jose Fereira
RODRIGUEZ & MENDOZA

Alejandro Giolito
PRICEWATERHOUSECOOPERS

Jose Giral
BAKER & MCKENZIE

Alfredo Hurtado
HURTADO ESTEBAN & ASOCIADOS, MEMBER OF RUSSELL BEDFORD INTERNATIONAL

Maigualida Ifill
PRICEWATERHOUSECOOPERS

Enrique Itriago
RODRIGUEZ & MENDOZA

Daniela Londoño
PRICEWATERHOUSECOOPERS

Maritza Meszaros
BAKER & MCKENZIE

Fernando Miranda
PRICEWATERHOUSECOOPERS

Bruno Paredes
LOGISTIKA TSM

Fernando Pelaez-Pier
HOET PELAEZ CASTILLO & DUQUE, MEMBER OF LEX MUNDI

Bernardo Pisani
RODRIGUEZ & MENDOZA

Eduardo Porcarelli
CONAPRI

Juan Carlos Pró-Rísquez
MACLEOD DIXON

Melissa Puga Santaella
CONAPRI

Pedro Saghy
MACLEOD DIXON

Laura Silva Aparicio
HOET PELAEZ CASTILLO & DUQUE, MEMBER OF LEX MUNDI

Victorino Tejeras
MACLEOD DIXON

Oscar Ignacio Torres
TRAVIESO EVANS ARRIA RENGEL & PAZ

John Tucker
HOET PELAEZ CASTILLO & DUQUE, MEMBER OF LEX MUNDI

VIETNAM

Daniel Chernov
DFDL MEKONG

Giles Thomas Cooper
DUANE MORRIS LLC

Anne Delerable
GIDE LOYRETTE NOUEL.

François d'Hautefeuille
GIDE LOYRETTE NOUEL.

Dang The Duc
INDOCHINE COUNSEL

Tran Duc Hoai
VIETBID LAW FIRM

Minh Duong
ALLENS ARTHUR ROBINSON

Thanh Long Duong
PBC PARTNERS

John Farmer
ORRICK, HERRINGTON & SUTCLIFFE LLP

David Fitzgerald
PRICEWATERHOUSECOOPERS

Albert Franceskinj
DS AVOCATS

Quynh Uyen Ha
PBC PARTNERS

Giang Ha Thi Phuong
PRICEWATERHOUSECOOPERS

Nguyen Hoang Kim Oanh
BAKER & MCKENZIE

Le Hong Phong
BIZCONSULT LAW FIRM

Lê Thj Hônh Hai
HOA BINH CHINH PHUC DINH CAO

Tuong Long Huynh
GIDE LOYRETTE NOUEL

Etienne Laumonier
GIDE LOYRETTE NOUEL

Thuy Le Nguyen Huy
INDOCHINE COUNSEL

Thuy Anh Le Phan
VILAF - HONG DUC LAW FIRM

Kevin Lê Viêt Há
CITY OCEAN LOGISTICS CO., LTD.

Nguyen Phan Manh Long
HUNG & PARTNERS

Ho Phuong Luan
INDOCHINE COUNSEL

Hoang Minh Duc
DUANE MORRIS LLC

Dao Nguyen
MAYER BROWN LLP

Huong Nguyen
MAYER BROWN LLP

Linh D. Nguyen
VILAF - HONG DUC LAW FIRM

Minh Tuan Nguyen
HABUBANK

Ngoc Tuong Ngan Nguyen
BAKER & MCKENZIE

Tat Thuong Nguyen
PBC PARTNERS

Tran Van Quynh Nguyen
BAKER & MCKENZIE

Van Anh Nguyen
VIETBID LAW FIRM

Xuan Quy Nguyen
PBC PARTNERS

Tram Nguyen - Huyen
GIDE LOYRETTE NOUEL

Mark Oakley
DUANE MORRIS LLC

Vu Anh Phan
INDOCHINE COUNSEL

Dinh Thi Quynh Van
PRICEWATERHOUSECOOPERS

Thi Thanh Hao Tran
BAKER & MCKENZIE

Pham Thi Thanh Huyen
INDOCHINE COUNSEL

Nguyen Thi Thu Hong
GIDE LOYRETTE NOUEL

Nguyen Thi Thu Huyen
GIDE LOYRETTE NOUEL

Nhung Thieu Hong
PRICEWATERHOUSECOOPERS

Ngo Quang Thuy
DUANE MORRIS LLC

Lan Tran
ORRICK, HERRINGTON & SUTCLIFFE LLP

V.N. Trinh
PANALPINA WORLD TRANSPORT

Nam Hoai Truong
INDOCHINE COUNSEL

Dzung Vu
YKVN LAWYERS

Trang Vu
CREDIT INFORMATION CENTRE - STATE BANK OF VIETNAM

WEST BANK AND GAZA

Hani Abdel Jaldeh
JERUSALEM DISTRICT ELECTRICITY COMPANY (JDECo)

Riyad Mustafa Abu Shehadeh
PALESTINIAN MONETARY AUTHORITY

Ata Al Biary
JERUSALEM DISTRICT ELECTRICITY COMPANY (JDECo)

Ma'ali Al Shawish
NETHAM, DPK CONSULTING, A DIVISION OF ARD

Haytham L. Al-Zu'bi
AL-ZU'BI LAW OFFICE, ADVOCATES & LEGAL CONSULTANTS

Mohammed Amarneh
THE DEMOCRACY AND WORKERS RIGHTS CENTER

Moyad Amouri
PRICEWATERHOUSECOOPERS

Khalil Ansara
CATHOLIC RELIEF SERVICES

Maha Assali
PRICEWATERHOUSECOOPERS

Susan Coleman
NETHAM, DPK CONSULTING, A DIVISION OF ARD

Ali Faroun
PALESTINIAN MONETARY AUTHORITY

Nader Hamadneh
NETHAM, DPK CONSULTING, A DIVISION OF ARD

Ali Hamoudeh
JERUSALEM DISTRICT ELECTRICITY CO. LTD.

Samir Huleileh
PADICO

Hiba Husseini
HUSSEINI & HUSSEINI

Nabil Isifan
NETHAM, DPK CONSULTING, A DIVISION OF ARD

Mohamed Khader
LAUSANNE TRADING CONSULTANTS

MUHAMMAD NASSAR STONE

Wael Saadi
PRICEWATERHOUSECOOPERS

Andrea Sahlieh
CATHOLIC RELIEF SERVICES

Husein Sholi
NETHAM, DPK CONSULTING, A DIVISION OF ARD

Maysa Sirhan
PALESTINIAN MONETARY AUTHORITY

Samer Tammam
TAMMAM TRADE

Kosty Ziadeh
ZIADEH LAW OFFICE

Maurice Ziadeh
ZIADEH LAW OFFICE

YEMEN, REP.

Tariq Abdullah
LAW OFFICES OF SHEIKH TARIQ ABDULLAH

Khaled Al Buraihi
KHALED AL BURAIHI FOR ADVOCACY & LEGAL SERVICES

Yaser Al-Adimi
ABDUL GABAR A. AL-ADIMI FOR CONSTRUCTION & TRADE

Rashad Khalid Al-Howaidi
CENTRAL BANK OF YEMEN

Abdalla Al-Meqbeli
ABDALLA AL-MEQBELI & ASSOCIATES

Ismail Ahmed Alwazir
ALWAZIR CONSULTANTS, ADVOCATES & LEGAL RESEARCH

Arshad Ali Bajwa
FIVE STAR LOGISTICS CO LTD

Randall Cameron
KPMG

Fadel Mohamed Karhash
Public Electricity Corporation

Moh'd Ali Lajam
Middle East Shipping Co. Ltd.

Abdulla Farouk Luqman
Yemen Legal Advocates & Legal Consultants

Nowar M. Mejanni
KPMG

Sanjay Prajapapi
Ratco for Trading & Services

Zuhair Abdul Rasheed
Law Offices of Sheikh Tariq Abdullah

Aref Al Selwi Rufaid
Five Star Logistics Co Ltd

Khaled Mohammed Salem Ali
Yemen Legal Advocates & Legal Consultants

ZAMBIA

Sudhir Balsure
Swift Freight International

Chewe K. Bwalya
D.H. Kemp & Co.

Bonaventure Chibamba Mutale
Ellis & Co.

Mwelwa Chibesakunda
Chibesakunda & Company (part of DLA Piper Group)

Darlington Chiiko
Lumwana Mining Company

Emmanuel Chulu
PricewaterhouseCoopers

Eddie Musonga Chunga
Ministry of Land

David Doyle
Manica Zambia Ltd

Robin Durairajah
Chibesakunda & Company (part of DLA Piper Group)

Grant Henderson
Chibesakunda & Company (part of DLA Piper Group)

Andrew Howard
Sharpe Howard & Mwenye

Annalise Jolly
Chibesakunda & Company (part of DLA Piper Group)

Chance Kaonga
National Council for Construction

Mutale Kasonde
Chibesakunda & Company (part of DLA Piper Group)

Kirstie Krige
Chibesakunda & Company (part of DLA Piper Group)

Anila Kuntawala
Celtic Freight

Alexander Lwatula
Stanbic Bank Zambia Limited

Mumba Makumba
PACRO

Bonaventure Mbewe
Barclays Bank

Jyoti Mistry
PricewaterhouseCoopers

Namwene Mkadawire
Sikaulu Lungu Mupeso Legal Practitioners

Paul Frobisher Mugambwa
PricewaterhouseCoopers

Bubile Mupeso
Sikaulu Lungu Mupeso Legal Practitioners

Henry Musonda
Kiran & Musonda Associates

Teddie Mwale
ZESCO Ltd

Francis Mwape
National Council for Construction

Robby Ngalashi
Lumwana Mining Company

Kanti Patel
Christopher, Russell Cook & Co.

Solly Patel
Christopher, Russell Cook & Co.

Mabvuto Sakala
Corpus Globe Advocates

Valerie Sesia
Customized Clearing And Forwarding Ltd.

Kim Shelsby
Zambia Threshold Project

Nelson Williams
Swift Freight International

Anderson Zikonda
High Court Judge

ZIMBABWE

Gulshen Afridi
SDV

Richard Beattie
The Stone/ Beattie Studio

Peter Cawood
PricewaterhouseCoopers

Innocent Chagonda
Atherstone & Cook

Beloved Dhlakama
Byron Venturas & Partners

Canaan Dube
Dube, Manikai and Hwacha Legal Practitioners

Paul Fraser
Lofty & Fraser

P. Gomes
Interfreight Ltd.

Obert Chaurura Gutu
Gutu & Chikowero

Reri Gwasera
Anlink Freight (Pvt) Ltd

Peter Lloyd
Gill, Godlonton & Gerrans

Manuel Lopes
PricewaterhouseCoopers

Jackson Joe Makani
Zimbabwe Revenue Authority

Trust Salpisio Manjegwah
Wintertons Law Firm

Gloria Mawarire
Mawere & Sibanda Legal Practitioners

Jim McComish
Pearce McComish Architects

Lloyd Mhishi
Dube, Manikai and Hwacha Legal Practitioners

Piniel Mkushi
Sawyer & Mkushi

Sternford Moyo
Scanlen & Holderness

B.J. Mukandi
Freight World

Canicious Mushavi
CNMIG

Ostern Mutero
Sawyer & Mkushi

Duduzile Ndawana
Gill, Godlonton & Gerrans

Maxwell Ngorima
BDO Kudenga & Company

Felix Nyaruwanga
Freight World

C.M. Ruzengwe
HLB Ruzengwe & Company

Unity Sakhe
Kantor & Immerman